Contents

Trade Policy Review – United States 2018

The Trade Policy Review of the United States took place on 17 and 19 December 2018.

Introduction

The Trade Policy Review Mechanism (TPRM) was first established on a trial basis by the GATT contracting parties in April 1989. The Mechanism became a permanent feature of the World Trade Organization under the Marrakesh Agreement which established the WTO in January 1995.

The objectives of the TPRM are to contribute to improved adherence by all WTO Members to rules, disciplines and commitments made under the Multilateral Trade Agreements and, where applicable, the Plurilateral Trade Agreements, and hence to the smoother functioning of the multilateral trading system, by achieving greater transparency in, and understanding of, the trade policies and practices of Members. Accordingly, the review mechanism enables the regular collective appreciation and evaluation of the full range of individual Members' trade policies and practices and their impact on the functioning of the multilateral trading system. It is not intended to serve as a basis for the enforcement of specific obligations under the Agreements or for dispute settlement procedures, or to impose new policy commitments on Members.

The assessment carried out under the TPRM takes place, to the extent relevant, against the background of the wider economic and developmental needs, policies and objectives of the Member concerned, as well as its external environment. However, the function of the review mechanism is to examine the impact of a Member's trade policies and practices on the multilateral trading system.

Under the TPRM, the trade policies of all Members are subject to periodic review. The four largest trading entities in terms of world market share, counting the European Union as one, are reviewed every two years, the 16 next largest trading entities every four years, and other Members every six years; a longer period may be fixed for least-developed countries.

The reviews are conducted by the Trade Policy Review Body (TPRB) on the basis of two documents: a policy statement by the Member under review and a comprehensive report drawn up by the WTO Secretariat on its own responsibility.

Key trade policy facts

Average applied MFN tariff rates, by HS section, 2016 and 2018

■ MFN 2018
■ MFN 2016

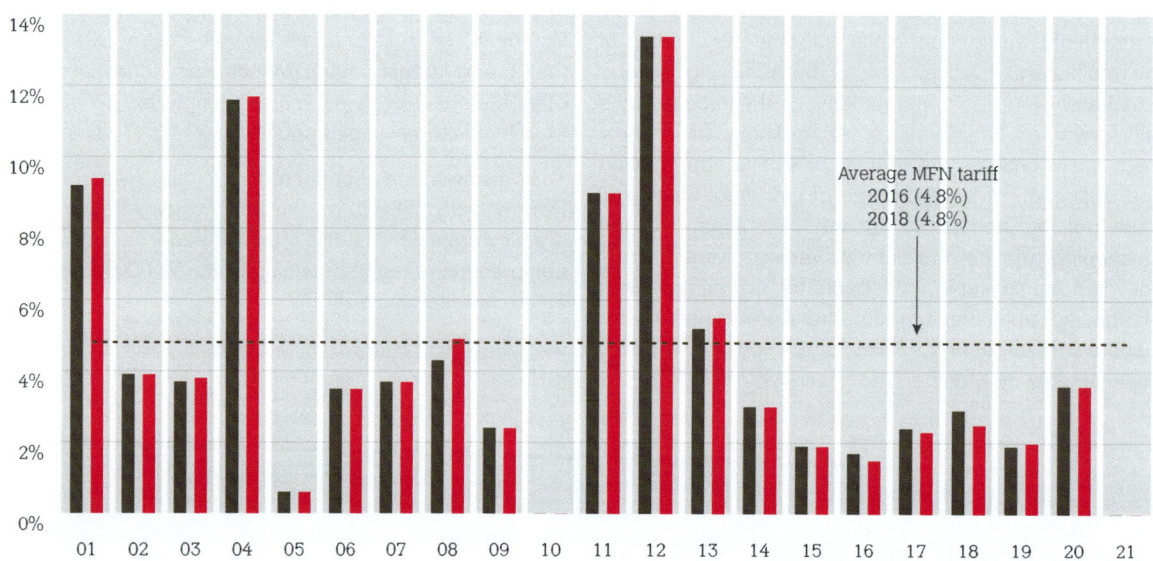

Average MFN tariff
2016 (4.8%)
2018 (4.8%)

01 Live animals & products	08 Hides & skins	15 Base metals & products
02 Vegetable products	09 Wood & articles	16 Machinery
03 Fats & oils	10 Pulp, paper, etc.	17 Transport equipment
04 Prepared food, etc.	11 Textile & articles	18 Precision instruments
05 Mineral products	12 Footwear, headgear	19 Arms & ammunition
06 Chemical & products	13 Articles of stone	20 Miscellaneous manufacturing
07 Plastics & rubber	14 Precious stones, etc.	21 Works of art, etc.

Note: the 2016 tariff is in the HS12 nomenclature, and the 2018 tariff in the HS17 nomenclature. The tariffs are excluding in-quota rates and including ad valorem equivalents provided by the U.S. authorities.

Highlights

Since the last Review in 2016, the focus of U.S. trade policy has shifted to adopting policies that are intended to support its national security and strengthen its economy. These priorities are reflected in the President's 2018 Trade Policy Agenda, which also calls for negotiating better trade deals, enforcing U.S. trade laws and U.S. rights under existing trade agreements, and reforming the multilateral trading system.

The U.S. economy is in its ninth consecutive year of expansion. In 2017, real GDP growth averaged 2.2%, up from 1.6% in 2016. In the first quarter of 2018, real GDP rose at an annual rate of 2.2%, before accelerating in the second quarter to 4.1%.

Exports of goods totalled US$1.55 trillion in 2017, while imports reached US$2.35 trillion. The merchandise trade deficit reached US$807.5 billion (4.2% of GDP) in 2017. On the other hand, the services and primary income balances showed important surpluses in 2017.

The largest export category is machinery and mechanical appliances, accounting for nearly a quarter of merchandise exports, followed by vehicles and chemicals; their share of total exports did not vary substantially during the review period.

The EU-28, China, Japan, Canada and Mexico are the United States' main trading partners. The United States continues to be the world's main recipient of foreign direct investment (FDI). The main FDI sources are: the EU-28 (59% of the FDI stock in the United States in 2017), Japan (12%), Canada (11%), and Switzerland (8%).

The United States submitted numerous notifications during the period under review, covering areas such as agriculture, anti-dumping, subsidies and countervailing measures, SPS, TBT, and import licensing, among others. During the review period, the United States was involved in 21 dispute settlement cases as a respondent and 13 as a complainant.

In February 2018, the U.S. Customs and Border Protection (CBP) announced that its Automated Commercial Environment (ACE) had been completed. Importers and exporters may use the electronic portal to declare goods, obtain permits, and access transaction and trade data.

At 4.8% overall, the simple average tariff remains virtually unchanged. Duty-free entry is provided for 37.5% of all tariff lines, and a further 30.4% of the lines' items face import duty of 5% or less. The highest tariffs, sometimes exceeding 100%, are applied on certain agricultural items (e.g., tobacco and peanuts).

The United States continues to be an active user of anti-dumping (AD) duties. Between 2015 and 2017, the number of AD investigation initiations increased, totalling 133. There were 340 AD orders in place as of end-July 2018, compared with 269 on 30 June 2016. The trading partners most affected by the measures were China, Chinese Taipei, the European Union, India, Japan and the Republic of Korea.

In August 2017, an investigation under Section 301 of the Trade Act of 1974 was initiated into China's acts, policies, and practices related to technology transfer, intellectual property, and innovation. On 15 June 2018, USTR issued a list of products covering 1,102 separate tariff lines, valued at approximately US$50 billion, which would be subject to an additional ad valorem tariff of 25%. The measure entered into effect on 6 July for 818 lines, covering approximately US$34 billion worth of imports from China.

The United States remains one of the main producers and exporters of goods and services that embody intellectual property (IP). IP is present in some 60% of U.S. goods exports, and IP-intensive industries account for over one third of U.S. GDP.

The 2014 Farm Bill was amended in early 2018, through the passage of the Bipartisan Budget Act of 2018, to provide support for seed cotton, to make the Margin Protection Programme more attractive for small and medium-sized dairy farms, and to make additional disaster relief available.

U.S. production of crude oil reached 11 million barrels per day in July 2018, for the first time in history, and the United States is now a net exporter of petroleum products and natural gas.

The United States does not have a national target for renewable energy or an explicit federal support mechanism. However, 29 states and the District of Columbia have adopted "renewable portfolio standards".

A new regulatory order on telecommunications was issued in December 2017, which removed the prior requirements that providers of broadband Internet access services be subject to some of the same rules that apply to common carriers, and returned to the lighter-touch framework that had been in place before.

The construction industry has few economic barriers to entry, and there are no restrictions on the repatriation of capital or profits. Market access conditions vary somewhat, depending on whether the project is public or private. Private construction activities are open to foreigners with few limitations, while public construction activities are subject to Buy American provisions and to the provisions of the GPA and FTAs.

Part A

Concluding remarks by the Chairperson of the Trade Policy Review Body, Ms. Sunanta Kangvalkulkij of Thailand at the Trade Policy Review of the United States, 17 and 19 December 2018.

Concluding Remarks by the Chairperson

This fourteenth Trade Policy Review of the United States has, once again, allowed Members to take a close look at the economic, trade, and investment policies of the world's single largest trader, and a key Member of the WTO. I would like to thank H.E. Ambassador Dennis C. Shea and his dedicated team for their forthright and active engagement. My gratitude also goes to our discussant, Ambassador Frances Lisson, for her thoughtful comments and remarks and last, but not least, to the 66 delegations that took the floor during these two days.

Members noted that the United States economy had performed well since the last review. The economy was in its ninth consecutive year of expansion, more recently also stimulated by a procyclical fiscal policy. The unemployment rate was at its lowest level in 50 years, consumer and business confidence were high, while inflation remained subdued. Strong economic growth had been accompanied by a widening current account deficit. The United States remained a net exporter of services, and the leading exporter of goods and services that embody intellectual property. The United States was both a top source and destination for foreign direct investment.

Members were of the view that the trade and investment regime of the United States remained overall open and liberal. The United States had bound all its tariffs, except for two tariff lines, and the simple average applied tariff rate was 4.8% with little or no tariff escalation. Taking account of trade preferences, nearly 70% of all imports entered duty free. The United States had taken measures to further facilitate trade, by completing the deployment of core capabilities in its Automated Commercial Environment. It strongly backed the entry into force of the WTO Agreement on Trade Facilitation, and was supporting other WTO Members in implementing the Agreement. Several Members appreciated the renewal of trade preferences granted under the Generalized System of Preferences (GSP) and the African Growth and Opportunity Act (AGOA).

Several Members stressed the increasingly active recourse to anti-dumping and countervailing measures by the United States, as well as their long duration, and expressed their reservations with respect to certain methodologies used in investigations. It was also noted that, in the period under review, the United States had applied global safeguard measures on solar cell products and large residential washing machines. In addition, the

United States had taken action under Section 232 of the Trade Expansion Act of 1962, related to U.S. national security, in the form of additional tariffs on imports of steel and aluminium products. The United States had also taken action as a result of an investigation under section 301 of the Trade Act of 1974.

Members also raised concerns with respect to the introduction of new "Buy American" provisions with respect to government procurement legislation. The low uptake of international standards in the United States, which may result in unnecessary trade barriers, was noted, as well as the level of protection of geographical indications, that some Members considered insufficient. The need to reform outdated maritime and cabotage legislation was stressed. Some Members questioned the effect on third parties of the introduction of new rules of origin in the automotive sector resulting from the renegotiation of regional trade agreements.

While noting the United States' efforts to reform global agricultural trade, some Members reiterated their longstanding concerns regarding aspects of U.S. agricultural policy, particularly the limited market access for sugar, dairy and cotton, high tariffs, and the continued use of trade distorting support. The launch of a USD 12 billion aid package for agricultural producers hurt by market disruption and retaliatory tariffs was a subject of wide interest. In services, it was noted that the U.S. economy is open to foreign service providers with limited exceptions, and that regulatory processes are transparent, accessible and open to public input.

The United States was complimented for being among the main architects of a rules-based international trading system that had underpinned decades of economic growth and prosperity at home and abroad. Nonetheless, it was noted that a shift had occurred in U.S. trade policy in the period under review, with a distinct new emphasis

on national security considerations in the pursuit of free, fair and reciprocal trade relations. In the course of this review, the five pillars of the present U.S. Trade Policy Agenda were repeatedly highlighted: the adoption of trade policies supporting the national security policy, building a stronger U.S. economy, the negotiation of better trade deals, vigorous enforcement of domestic trade laws and rights under existing trade agreements, and reform of the multilateral trading system.

Members highlighted the traditional leadership role of the United States in the GATT and the WTO, and expressed their commitment to engage with the United States on constructive proposals to improve the functioning of the rules-based multilateral trading system. It was noted that the WTO was facing unprecedented challenges, and that positive initiatives to deal with them could include steps to strengthen the notification and transparency functions of the WTO, enhance compliance, and end the impasse regarding the dispute settlement mechanism. On the negotiating front, appreciation was expressed regarding the productive engagement of the United States on services domestic regulation disciplines, its determination to establish WTO rules prohibiting harmful fisheries subsidies, and its active role in the Joint Statement Initiative on Electronic Commerce. Building on work in the G20 and APEC, the reform of fossil fuel subsidies could also be brought onto the WTO agenda.

In the view of the Members, although the short term economic outlook for the United States remained positive, mounting public debt, higher interest rates, and increasing trade tensions were clouds gathering on the horizon. It was in this context that the continued support and commitment of the United States to a predictable, rules based multilateral trading system took on a critical dimension, not only for its trading partners near and far, but also for the long-term economic wellbeing of the United States itself.

The United States received more than 1,700 written questions prior to this Trade Policy Review, and it has already responded to most of them. In a month's time, Members should receive replies to late submissions and follow-up questions that are still outstanding, which will then mark the successful conclusion of this TPR.

Part A
Concluding remarks

Part B

Report by the WTO Secretariat

This report was drafted by Mr. Angelo Silvy, Mr. Cato Adrian, Mr. Pierre Latrille, Mr. Usman Ali Khilji, and Ms Fatima Chaudhri.

Willy Alfaro
Director
Trade Policies Review Division

Part B
Report by the WTO Secretariat

Summary

This is the 14th Trade Policy Review of the United States. Since the last Review in 2016, the focus of U.S. trade policy has shifted to adopting policies that are intended to support its national security and strengthen its economy. These priorities are reflected in the President's 2018 Trade Policy Agenda, which also calls for negotiating better trade deals, enforcing U.S. trade laws and U.S. rights under existing trade agreements, and reforming the multilateral trading system.

The U.S. economy is in its ninth consecutive year of expansion. In 2017, real GDP growth averaged 2.2%, up from 1.6% in 2016. In the first quarter of 2018, real GDP rose at an annual rate of 2.2%, before accelerating in the second quarter to 4.1%.

Fiscal policy turned pro-cyclical in 2018, with the enactment of the Tax Cuts and Jobs Act of 2017, the Bipartisan Budget Act of 2018 and the Consolidated Appropriations Act of 2018. Tax rates were lowered for businesses and individuals: the top corporate tax rate was reduced from 35% to 21%, and the tax system was changed from global to territorial. Federal budget deficits are projected to continue increasing, from 4.2% of GDP in 2018 to 5.1% in 2022.

The Federal Reserve tightened the monetary stance during the review period. A sustained increase in economic activity, the continued strengthening of the labour market and firming inflation have resulted in moderate rises in the federal funds rate since 2015. In the first half of 2018, the rate was increased twice, bringing it to a range of 1.75-2.0%. Inflation, as measured by the 12month percentage change in the personal consumption expenditures (PCE) index, has remained at or around the 2% target throughout the review period.

The U.S. current account deficit has been increasing since 2013, and reached US$469.1 billion in 2017 (2.4% of GDP), mirroring a widening of the gap between gross national savings and gross investment. Exports of goods totalled US$1.55 trillion in 2017, while imports reached US$2.35 trillion. The merchandise trade deficit reached US$807.5 billion (4.2% of GDP) in 2017. On the other hand, the services and primary income balances showed important surpluses in 2017.

The United States is one of the world's largest exporters and it has a diversified export base. The largest export category is machinery and mechanical appliances, accounting for nearly a quarter of merchandise exports, followed by vehicles and chemicals; their share of total exports did not vary substantially during the review period. The share of mineral products experienced a sharp decline between 2014 and 2016, before rising again in 2017. This behaviour can be ascribed to the fall in oil prices and their subsequent recovery in 2017. The United States is also one of the world's main importers. U.S. imports are diversified: the largest categories are machinery and mechanical appliances, vehicles, mineral products, and chemicals. Reflecting sustained GDP growth, the shares of machinery and mechanical appliances, vehicles, and chemicals in total imports have risen. In contrast, the share of mineral products has declined. The EU-28, China, Japan, Canada and Mexico are the United States' main trading partners. The United States continues to be the world's main recipient of foreign direct investment (FDI). The main FDI sources are: the EU-28 (59% of the FDI stock in the United States in 2017), Japan (12%), Canada (11%), and Switzerland (8%).

The U.S. Congress has legislative and oversight authority over trade issues; Congress works together with the Executive Branch, which negotiates and implements trade agreements. The main executive agency responsible for trade policy formulation continues to be the Office of the United States Trade Representative (USTR), which is part of the Executive Office of the President.

As mentioned above, the thrust of trade policy changed during the review period. The President's 2018 Trade Policy Agenda is driven to achieve "free, fair, and reciprocal" trade relations, considered critical to the U.S. national security policy. It also focuses on renegotiating and revising trade deals. In terms of reforming the multilateral trading system, the Agenda advocates for "sensible and fair reforms to the WTO". It notes that the United States remains committed to working with all WTO Members who share the United States' goal of fair and reciprocal trade deals.

The United States is an original Member of the WTO. It is a party to the Agreement on Government Procurement (GPA), a participant in the expanded Information Technology Agreement (ITA), and a signatory to the Agreement on Trade in Civil Aircraft. The United States deposited its instrument of acceptance of the Trade Facilitation Agreement (TFA) to the WTO in January 2015. The United States submitted numerous notifications during the period under review, covering areas such as agriculture, anti-dumping, subsidies and countervailing measures, SPS, TBT, and import licensing, among others. During the review period, the United States was involved in 21 dispute settlement cases as a respondent and 13 as a complainant.

The United States has 14 FTAs in force with 20 countries, as was the case at the time of the previous Review. Most of them cover both goods and services, except the FTA with Israel (goods only). The United States has notified all its FTAs to the WTO. At the time of completion of this report, the United States was renegotiating NAFTA, with the aims of modernizing the Agreement, and reducing the U.S. trade deficit with NAFTA partners. In August 2018, the United States and Mexico reached an agreement in principle to amend NAFTA. In October, an agreement with Canada was announced. The United States-Korea Free Trade Agreement (KORUS) has also been renegotiated, and the revised Agreement was signed on 24 September 2018. The United States withdrew from the proposed Trans-Pacific Partnership (TPP) in 2017. Negotiations with the European Union on the proposed Trans-Atlantic Trade and Investment Partnership (T-TIP) agreement were paused at the end of 2016. Currently, the United States has four main unilateral preference programmes: the African Growth and Opportunity Act (AGOA), the GSP, the Caribbean Basin Initiative (CBI)/Caribbean Basin Trade Partnership Act (CBTPA), and the Nepal Trade Preference Program (NTPP).

The U.S. foreign investment regime remained unchanged during the review period. The investment regime is generally open, with a few sector-specific limitations, and review procedures on foreign investment in a few industries, including the airline and nuclear energy industries. Additionally, the United States has a national security review process, applicable to foreign investment that might affect national security interests. International investment agreements and investment chapters in FTAs are used by the United States to foster foreign investment.

The Committee on Foreign Investment in the United States (CFIUS) continues to oversee the national security implications of foreign investment. CFIUS reviews transactions based on voluntary notifications filed by the parties, or on its own initiative if it believes the transaction is a covered transaction and may raise national security concerns. Each transaction is reviewed on a case-by-case basis, based on individual facts and circumstances. If national security concerns are identified during the review, CFIUS may impose conditions, or CFIUS and the transacting parties may negotiate a mitigation agreement to resolve any national security concerns. If CFIUS determines that the national security concerns cannot be resolved and the parties do not withdraw and abandon the transaction, the Committee will recommend that the President prohibit the transaction.

Having formally accepted the WTO TFA in January 2015, the United States provided its notification on transparency, the operation of its single window, measures on the use of customs brokers, and the TFA contact point in June 2017. In February 2018, the U.S. Customs and Border Protection (CBP) announced that its Automated Commercial Environment (ACE) had been completed. Importers and exporters may use the electronic portal to declare goods, obtain permits, and access transaction and trade data. Within CBP, ten Centers of Excellence have been established to specialize in all aspects of customs processing in several areas.

The United States operates several programmes to facilitate trade, while also addressing national security concerns as a joint public-private partnership. Among these programmes, the Customs-Trade Partnership Against Terrorism (C-TPAT) encompasses the entire supply chain, involving enhanced security measures and best practices, the Importer Self-Assessment Program

(ISA) builds on C-TPAT to achieve an even higher level of compliance, and the Free and Secure Trade (FAST) Program speeds the clearance of low-risk shipments arriving from Canada or Mexico. Maritime cargo destined for the United States is pre-screened at foreign ports under the Container Security Initiative (CSI). CBP has security-based arrangements in force with 11 other customs administrations, and has signed joint work plans towards mutual recognition with six countries.

The MFN tariff regime is generally characterized by stable and, for the most part, low or no tariffs. At 4.8% overall, the simple average tariff remains virtually unchanged. Duty-free entry is provided for 37.5% of all tariff lines, and a further 30.4% of the lines' items face import duty of 5% or less. The highest tariffs, sometimes exceeding 100%, are applied on certain agricultural items (e.g., tobacco and peanuts). Outside of agriculture, above-average applied rates are mainly found in textiles, clothing and footwear.

The United States continues to be an active user of anti-dumping (AD) duties. Between 2015 and 2017, the number of AD investigation initiations increased, totalling 133. There were 340 AD orders in place as of end-July 2018, compared with 269 on 30 June 2016. The trading partners most affected by the measures were China, Chinese Taipei, the European Union, India, Japan and the Republic of Korea. The investigations initiated during the period were mainly concentrated in the steel industry. Of the 109 countervailing duty (CVD) measures in place as of end-July 2018, some 50.5% were also applied on iron and steel products. There were 123 sunset review initiations of AD orders during the period from 1 January 2016 to end-June 2018. During the same period, there were eight revocations, while 104 orders were continued. There were 52 sunset review initiations of CVD orders during the period from 1 January 2016 to end-April 2018. During the same period, 27 sunset reviews of CVD orders were concluded; there were six revocations, while the remaining orders were continued.

Between 2016 and 2018, two new safeguard investigations (on Crystalline Silicon Photovoltaic Cells; and Large Residential Washers) were conducted by the United States under Sections 201-204 of the Trade Act of 1974. Both investigations were notified to the WTO. The USITC made affirmative serious injury determinations in both cases, and the President applied a safeguard measure in each one.

The Enforce and Protect Act of 2015 (EAPA), which entered into force in 2016 and aimed at preventing evasion of contingency measures, created a new framework for CBP to investigate allegations of evasion of AD/CVD orders. Between August 2016 and 1 July 2018, 19 investigations stemming from allegations of evasion of duties were initiated. In all but one of these investigations, interim measures were applied. As of July 2018, a final determination had been made for 12 investigations. Remedies generally involve suspending the liquidation for any entry after a certain date, and requiring that the importer post a cash deposit prior to the entry's release.

During the review period, the United States reverted to conducting Section 232 investigations to determine the effects of imports of any article on national security, and to recommend the application of countermeasures, including an increase in tariffs, to the President. The Department of Commerce has conducted 18 Section 232 investigations since 1980, of which 14 were concluded before or in 2001. In 2018, four new investigations were initiated on: steel, aluminium, auto imports, and uranium imports. Up to September 2018, import surcharges were announced on the first two investigations. This announcement was followed by countermeasures by trading partners.

In August 2017, an investigation under Section 301 of the Trade Act of 1974 was initiated into China's acts, policies, and practices related to technology transfer, intellectual property, and innovation. On 15 June 2018, USTR issued a list of products covering 1,102 separate tariff lines, valued at approximately US$50 billion, which would be subject to an additional *ad valorem* tariff of 25%. The measure entered into effect on 6 July for 818 lines, covering approximately US$34 billion worth of imports from China; public comment was sought on the application of the duty on 284 tariff lines, covering some US$16 billion worth of imports. China responded to the initial action by imposing increased duties on goods imported from the United States. In response, USTR proposed to take further action in the form of an additional 10% *ad valorem* duty on Chinese products covered in 6,031 tariff subheadings, with an annual trade value of approximately US$200 billion. Under the new Section 306(c) of the 1974 Trade Act, the USTR may reinstate, upon written request from the industry, a previously terminated Section 301 action in order to exercise a WTO authorization to suspend trade concessions. One such case emerged in December 2016 concerning a 1999 beef dispute with the European Union; as of mid-2018 no action had been taken.

The Office of Foreign Assets Control (OFAC) of the U.S. Department of the Treasury administers nearly 30 programmes involving economic and trade sanctions. In general, the measures are designed to counter terrorism, transnational criminal organizations, cyber-related crimes, drugs trafficking, human rights abuses, corruption, trade in rough diamonds, and the proliferation of weapons of mass destruction. Many of the measures target individuals or entities rather than jurisdictions. Country-specific sanctions have been tightened against the Democratic People's Republic of Korea, Iran and Cuba during the period under review, while programmes related to Myanmar and Côte d'Ivoire were terminated in 2016.

The framework for export promotion and export finance has remained broadly unchanged during the period under review. The United States has no overarching legal framework governing assistance to sectors or industries at the federal or sub-federal level. Traditionally,

federal assistance programmes have been in the form of grants, tax concessions, loan guarantees, and direct payments; they are listed in the Catalog of Federal Domestic Assistance (CFDA), and are mostly related to public health and safety, the environment, education, infrastructure, community assistance, and research and development.

The basic legal framework for the preparation and adoption of standards and technical regulations has not changed during the review period. Federal law specifically prohibits any government agency from engaging in any standards-related activity that creates unnecessary obstacles to the foreign commerce of the United States, and federal agencies are obliged to ensure that imported goods are treated no less favourably than like domestic products in the application of standards-related activities.

In the area of sanitary and phytosanitary measures, work has continued on certain trade-related aspects of the implementation of the 2011 Food Safety Modernization Act, including risk-based supplier identification, the certification of food-producing entities in foreign countries, and the launch of the Voluntary Qualified Imports Program (VQIP), an expedited review and entry programme for food. No applications for admittance into the VQIP were received before this year's deadline, as the process to issue accreditations to third-party auditors was still ongoing.

U.S. federal antitrust laws are applied on domestic and foreign conduct that has a substantial and intended effect in the United States. Government institutions, including those engaging in commercial activity, are exempted from federal antitrust legislation unless a statute clearly provides otherwise. Limited immunity also applies to specific aspects of agriculture, fisheries, shipping, and insurance. During the review period, the U.S. authorities have devoted substantial resources to prosecutions and sentencings in criminal antitrust proceedings; as a result, some US$400 million in criminal fines and penalties were obtained by the U.S. Department of Justice, mainly with respect to auto parts, real estate, and foreign currency exchange. The number of mergers reviewed increased during the review period: in FY2017, 2,052 transactions were reviewed, representing a 12.0% increase from FY2016.

The United States is a party to the WTO GPA. The Protocol amending the GPA entered into force for the United States in April 2014. No major institutional or legal changes with respect to government procurement have taken place since the last Review in 2016. Procurement at the federal level is decentralized, and is carried out through the procurement systems of the various executive agencies. Procurement at the state level is also decentralized. U.S. government procurement policy encourages the participation of small businesses, including veteran-owned, women-owned, and disadvantaged small businesses. To this end, it carries out a policy of fixing set-asides when market research concludes that small businesses are available and able to perform the work or provide the products being procured by the Government. The Buy American Act (BAA) and the Trade Agreements Act (TAA) remain the main laws regarding government procurement. The BAA requires the Federal Government to purchase domestic goods, while the TAA provides authority for the President to waive purchasing requirements, such as those contained in the BAA. These requirements are waived for GPA participants, trading partners with which the United States has an FTA that covers procurement, and beneficiaries of preferences.

The United States remains one of the main producers and exporters of goods and services that embody intellectual property (IP). IP is present in some 60% of U.S. goods exports, and IP-intensive industries account for over one third of U.S. GDP. No major changes with respect to IP legislation have taken place since the last Review in 2016. The protection and enforcement of IP rights (IPRs) has remained a top trade policy priority for the U.S. Administration, as IP is considered critical for economic growth. The objectives are to reduce counterfeit and infringing goods in domestic and international supply chains and identify unjustified impediments to effective enforcement action against the financing, production, trafficking, or sale of counterfeit or infringing goods.

Among IPR enforcement tools, USTR conducts annual reviews of the state of IPR protection and enforcement in U.S. trading partners around the world under "Special 301" provisions. As a result of these reviews, USTR identifies trading partners found to deny adequate and effective IPR protection, or deny fair and equitable market access to U.S. persons that rely upon IPR protection. In its 2018 Special 301 report, released on 30 April 2018, 36 trading partners were identified as failing to provide adequate and effective IPR protection. Under Section 337 of the Tariff Act of 1930, investigations into allegations of infringement of certain statutory IPRs and other forms of unfair competition in import trade are conducted. Between early January 2016 and late May 2018, 137 Section 337 investigations were initiated. Most of them dealt with patent infringement; the remainder dealt with copyright, trade secrets and trademarks or with several IPRs combined. Investigations covered products from 37 trading partners and from the United States.

Support to agriculture is primarily authorized by "farm bills", i.e. multi-year omnibus legislation covering a wide array of agricultural and food programmes. While some of the programmes have permanent authorization (e.g. crop insurance), others are authorized only for the life of the farm bill. Authorization for most programmes under the Agricultural Act of 2014 was to expire on 30 September 2018. Based on expected and actual outlays, the 2014 Farm Bill has been dominated by the Supplemental Nutrition Assistance Program (SNAP), providing food assistance to low-income households, which has accounted for nearly 80% of the projected

expenditure. The 2014 Farm Bill was amended in early 2018, through the passage of the Bipartisan Budget Act of 2018, to provide support for seed cotton, to make the Margin Protection Programme more attractive for small and medium-sized dairy farms, and to make additional disaster relief available. A programme to support the cost of cotton ginning was re-introduced as a temporary measure in March 2018. The legislative process for the 2018 Farm Bill is ongoing.

The United States is a major producer and consumer of primary energy resources, and technological breakthroughs in the domestic production of shale oil and gas have had a profound effect on global energy markets over the last ten years. U.S. production of crude oil reached 11 million barrels per day in July 2018, for the first time in history, and the United States is now a net exporter of petroleum products and natural gas. On the demand side, U.S. primary energy consumption has levelled off, as the economy has become ever more energy efficient. Natural gas has replaced coal as the principal resource in electricity generation, but coal-fired power plants still deliver 30% of the electricity produced. About 17% of the electricity generated in the United States in 2017 was made from renewable energy resources. The United States does not have a national target for renewable energy or an explicit federal support mechanism. However, 29 states and the District of Columbia have adopted "renewable portfolio standards" or similar binding targets, and a further 8 states (and one territory) have set non-binding targets. States apply numerous measures to promote the development and use of renewable energy resources.

The Economic Growth, Regulatory Relief and Consumer Protection Act, enacted in May 2018, introduced several amendments to the regulation of financial services, including with respect to regulatory relief, consumer access to mortgage credit, and regulations for bank holding companies. The most noteworthy changes include: allowing banks with between US$50 billion and US$250 billion in assets to be run with less regulatory oversight; exempting banks with less than US$10 billion from the Volcker Rule (banning banks from engaging in proprietary trading); requiring the Federal Reserve to tailor regulations with respect to bank size rather than "one size fits all"; and enabling large foreign banks to avoid regulations by allowing them to tally their U.S. assets in certain ways that keeps them below the US$250 billion threshold.

A new regulatory order on telecommunications was issued in December 2017, which removed the prior requirements that providers of broadband Internet access services be subject to some of the same rules that apply to common carriers, including a prohibition on unjust or unreasonable practices or unreasonable discrimination. The 2017 Restoring Internet Freedom Order reversed the policy applied in the sector, and returned to the lighter-touch framework that had been in place before. The Order, among other things, ended utility-style regulation of the Internet in favour of market-based policies, restored broadband Internet access service to the information service classification, eliminated certain reporting requirements, and restored the authority of the Federal Trade Commission (FTC) to police the privacy practices of Internet service providers (ISPs).

Postal and courier services are open to competition, with the exception of services reserved for the United States Postal Service (USPS), the designated operator for universal service. Private carriers may accept and deliver any item which does not fall within the reserved category, including items not considered as letters, such as merchandise, newspapers, and periodicals. However, under "the mailbox rule", delivery must be made by means that do not involve access to mailboxes or post office boxes in USPS retail units, unless postage is affixed to the privately carried matter. USPS rates and fees are established by its Board of Governors, and are subject to a review process by the Postal Regulatory Commission, which regulates the USPS but not the postal services activities of the private sector.

With the exception of some sub-federal and local non-discriminatory limitations on the sales of alcohol and firearms, the applied regime for distribution services does not contain any market access or national treatment limitations. There is no federal law governing franchising; however, there are both federal regulations and state laws regulating it. State laws vary from state to state. Franchising is regulated by the FTC and by various state agencies.

Construction is not regulated at the federal level, but safety issues are. Safety regulations concerning the construction industry are enforced by the Occupational Safety and Health Administration at the federal level, or by equivalent state agencies. All states require contractors to have workers' compensation insurance. There are also a number of environment-related laws, including those related to asbestos, lead, and industrial waste. The construction industry has few economic barriers to entry, and there are no restrictions on the repatriation of capital or profits. Market access conditions vary somewhat, depending on whether the project is public or private. Private construction activities are open to foreigners with few limitations, while public construction activities are subject to Buy American provisions and to the provisions of the GPA and FTAs.

The regulatory framework of maritime transport and air transport services has not changed during the period under review and restrictions to cabotage remain. Regarding maritime transport, preferences are accorded to U.S.-flag vessels to encourage a privately-owned and operated U.S.-flag merchant marine. The United States maintains two maritime transport programmes related to national defense: the Maritime Security Program (MSP) and the Voluntary Intermodal Sealift Agreement (VISA) Program. No domestic preferential treatment is granted with respect to the use of port and harbour facilities. An MFN exemption is maintained, covering restrictions on performance of longshore work by crews of foreign vessels owned and flagged in countries that similarly restrict U.S. crews on U.S.-flag vessels from longshore work.

Only U.S.-built ships qualify for domestic service; the United States was granted an exemption from GATT rules for measures prohibiting the use, sale, or lease of foreign-built or foreignreconstructed vessels in commercial applications between points in national waters or the waters of an exclusive economic zone. There are no restrictions on foreign investment in U.S. shipyards or ship-repair facilities, but floating dry-docks are eligible for loan guarantees under the Federal Ship Financing Program only if owned by U.S. citizens.

The tourism services regime is open; the United States undertook full market access GATS commitments for modes 1, 2 and 3, and full national treatment commitments for all four modes for all four sectors. The National Travel and Tourism Office (NTTO), part of the U.S. Department of Commerce, coordinates travel and tourism policies and programmes across federal agencies through the Tourism Policy Council, and works to enhance the international competitiveness of the travel and tourism industry and increase its exports.

The United States does not have a general e-commerce law; however, e-commerce is subject to a number of federal and state measures that address various aspects of it. Two federal agencies oversee different aspects of e-commerce: the Federal Trade Commission (FTC) and the Federal Communications Commission (FCC). The FTC has authority over unfair and deceptive practices in commerce on various aspects of e-commerce, and it may bring enforcement actions for such practices. The FCC regulates the communications aspect of e-commerce. Electronic contracts are governed by the Electronic Signatures in Global and National Commerce Act of 2000 (ESIGN Act), as well as by state laws that meet the requirements in the ESIGN Act.

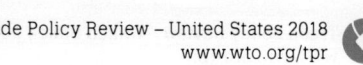

Economic environment

MAIN FEATURES OF THE ECONOMY

The United States is the largest economy in the world, and is highly integrated into the global economy. Any changes in it have far-reaching consequences for the world at large, as was evidenced by the financial crisis of 2008, the impact of which reverberated around the world. The United States continues to be the largest recipient of international capital flows, which has resulted in a strengthening of the U.S. dollar. An appreciating U.S. dollar has implications for competitiveness, and thus trade. As such, coupled with weaker international demand, the share of total trade in goods and services (imports and exports) on a balance-of-payments (BOP) basis has declined from 29.8% of Gross Domestic Product (GDP) in 2014 to 27% of GDP in 2017.

The U.S. economy is dominated by the services sector (including government services), whose share in GDP has risen since 2015; services now account for over 80% of GDP, while the share of manufacturing has fallen below 12% (11.6% in 2017) and agriculture's contribution was less than 1% in 2017 (Chart 1.1).

ECONOMIC DEVELOPMENTS

The U.S. economy is in its ninth consecutive year of expansion, buoyed by rising incomes, wealth gains, high levels of consumer confidence, business sector confidence, supportive financial conditions, and a favorable external environment, and in the later stages, buoyed by the strong labour market. In 2017, real GDP growth averaged 2.2%, up from 1.6% in 2016 (Table 1.1). In the first quarter of 2018, real GDP rose at an annual rate of 2.2%, before accelerating in the second quarter to 4.2%.

Accounting for some 68% of GDP, growth in personal consumption expenditures is essential to overall growth. In fact, in 2017, real GDP growth was driven by consumer spending, which grew at 2.5% and accounted for 78.6% (1.73 percentage points) of the growth. Consumption of goods represented 35% of total consumption, while consumption of services accounted for 65%. They contributed 0.95 and 0.78 percentage points to GDP growth, respectively. Consumption of non-durable goods represented 64.3% of consumption of goods and 22.5% of total consumption, while consumption of durable goods accounted for 35.9% and 12.6%, contributing 0.48 and 0.30 percentage points to annual GDP growth, respectively. Consumption growth was spread over a number of different categories: housing and utilities, and health care accounted for the largest share of consumer expenditures, with approximately 17% of the total each. Other important items included food and beverages (7.5% of total spending), financial services and insurance (6.8%), motor vehicles and parts (4.0%), recreational goods and vehicles (3.8%), clothing and footwear (3.1%), and furnishings and household equipment (2.9%).[1]

Gross private domestic investment contributed 22% to growth. Government consumption and gross investment have been slightly positive, and net exports have made a negative contribution of 3% to real GDP growth on an accounting basis (Chart 1.2). Non-residential fixed investment grew by 6.3% in 2017, compared with 0.7% in 2016. Equipment spending went up by 8.8%, spending on structures rose by 3.7%, while spending on intellectual property products increased 4.8%.

Chart 1.1 Value added by industry, 2017

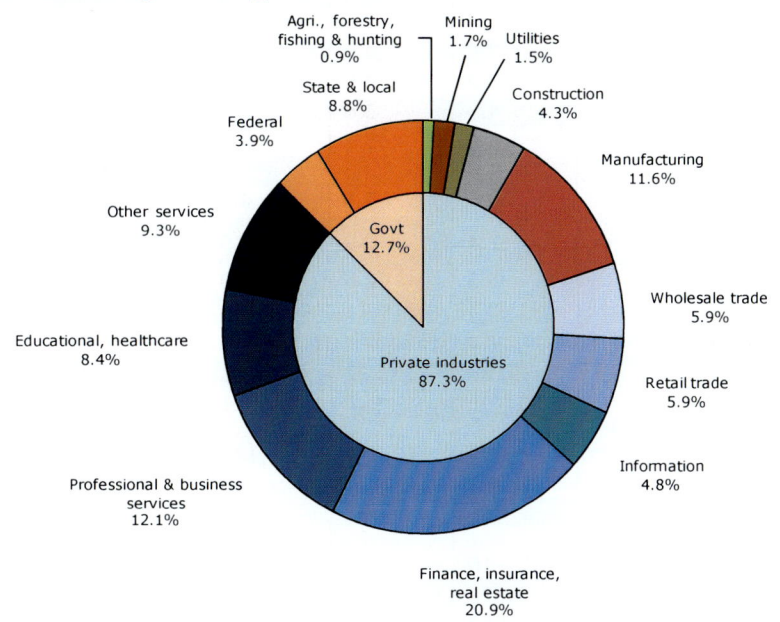

Agri., forestry, fishing & hunting 0.9%
Mining 1.7%
Utilities 1.5%
State & local 8.8%
Construction 4.3%
Federal 3.9%
Manufacturing 11.6%
Other services 9.3%
Govt 12.7%
Wholesale trade 5.9%
Educational, healthcare 8.4%
Private industries 87.3%
Retail trade 5.9%
Information 4.8%
Professional & business services 12.1%
Finance, insurance, real estate 20.9%

Gross domestic product: US$19,391 billion

Source: WTO Secretariat, based on Bureau of Economic Analysis (BEA) online information.

Part B
Report by the WTO Secretariat

Table 1.1 Main economic indicators, 2013-18Q2

	2013	2014	2015	2016	2017	2018Q2
GDP (current US$ billion)	16,785	17,522	18,219	18,707	19,485	20,412
Real GDP (chained 2012 US$ billion)	16,495	16,900	17,387	17,659	18,051	18,515
Real GDP growth (%)	1.8	2.5	2.9	1.6	2.2	4.2
GDP per capita (current US$)	53,016	54,935	56,701	57,797	59,774	..
GDP by expenditure (as a % share of current GDP)						
Personal consumption expenditures	67.4	67.5	67.5	68.2	68.4	68.0
Goods	22.2	22.0	21.5	21.4	21.3	21.2
Durable goods	7.1	7.1	7.2	7.2	7.2	7.1
Non-durable goods	15.1	14.9	14.3	14.2	14.1	14.1
Services	45.2	45.4	46.0	46.9	47.0	46.8
Gross private domestic investment	16.8	17.3	17.6	16.9	17.3	17.6
Fixed investment	16.2	16.9	16.9	16.8	17.2	17.6
Non-residential	13.2	13.7	13.4	13.1	13.3	13.7
Residential	3.0	3.2	3.5	3.7	3.9	3.9
Change in private inventories	0.6	0.5	0.7	0.2	0.1	0.0
Net exports of goods and services	-2.9	-2.9	-2.9	-2.8	-3.0	-2.7
Exports	13.5	13.5	12.4	11.9	12.1	12.6
Goods	9.3	9.2	8.2	7.7	7.9	8.4
Services	4.3	4.3	4.2	4.1	4.2	4.2
Imports	16.5	16.4	15.3	14.6	15.0	15.3
Goods	13.7	13.6	12.6	11.9	12.2	12.4
Services	2.8	2.8	2.7	2.8	2.8	2.9
Government consumption expenditures and gross investment	18.7	18.1	17.8	17.6	17.3	17.2
Federal	7.3	6.9	6.7	6.6	6.5	6.4
State and local	11.4	11.1	11.1	11.0	10.8	10.7
GDP by expenditure (real growth rates)						
Personal consumption expenditures	1.5	2.9	3.7	2.7	2.5	3.8
Goods	3.1	4.0	4.7	3.6	3.7	5.4
Durable goods	6.1	7.2	7.6	5.5	6.8	8.6
Non-durable goods	1.8	2.6	3.4	2.7	2.1	3.7
Services	0.6	2.4	3.2	2.3	2.0	3.1
Gross private domestic investment	6.9	5.4	4.8	-1.3	4.8	0.4
Fixed investment	5.6	6.3	3.4	1.7	4.8	6.2
Non-residential	4.1	6.9	1.8	0.5	5.3	8.5
Residential	12.4	3.9	10.1	6.5	3.3	-1.6
Change in private inventories	..	..	..	..	..	..
Net exports of goods and services	..	..	..	..	..	..
Exports	3.6	4.3	0.6	-0.1	3.0	9.1
Goods	3.2	4.6	-0.3	0.3	3.3	13.3
Services	4.5	3.6	2.4	-0.9	2.5	1.6
Imports	1.5	5.1	5.5	1.9	4.6	-0.4
Goods	1.8	5.6	5.8	1.4	4.6	-0.3
Services	0.5	2.6	4.0	4.2	4.4	-0.8
Government consumption expenditures and gross investment	-2.4	-0.9	1.9	1.4	-0.1	2.3
Federal	-5.5	-2.6	0.0	0.4	0.7	3.7
State and local	-0.3	0.1	3.0	2.0	-0.5	1.6
Federal government revenue and expenditure (US$ billion)						
Current receipts	3,138	3,292	3,446	3,476	3,559	3,469
Current tax receipts	1,745	1,900	2,021	2,035	2,055	1,945
Contributions for government social insurance	1,092	1,140	1,191	1,225	1,283	1,341
Income receipts on assets	243	172	160	138	135	113
Current transfer receipts	69	87	78	80	87	80
Current surplus of government enterprises	-10	-7	-4	-2	-2	-9
Current expenditures	3,777	3,894	4,015	4,141	4,254	4,454
Consumption expenditures	957	950	956	968	987	1,028

	2013	2014	2015	2016	2017	2018Q2
Current transfer payments	2,344	2,447	2,573	2,657	2,725	2,829
Interest payments	416	439	429	455	481	538
Subsidies	59	58	57	61	61	59
Net federal government saving	-638	-602	-569	-665	-695	-985
Social insurance funds	-289	-286	-309	-330	-333	-350
Other	-349	-316	-260	-336	-362	-635
Addenda:						
Total receipts	3,160	3,311	3,467	3,496	3,832	3,492
Total expenditures	3,857	3,962	4,050	4,200	4,348	4,529
Net lending or net borrowing (-)	-697	-651	-584	-704	-516	-1,037
As share of current GDP (%)	-4.2	-37	-3.2	-3.8	-2.6	-5.1
Public debt (US$ billion)[a]	11,983	12,780	13,117	14,168	14,666	..
As share of current GDP (%, fiscal year)	73.1	76.1	75.8	80.4	82.3	..
Prices						
Consumer price index (annual average, % change)	1.5	1.6	0.1	1.3	2.1	2.2
Interest rates						
Federal funds rate, effective (%, annual average)	0.11	0.09	0.13	0.39	1.00	..
Treasury note (%, annual average)	2.35	2.54	2.14	1.84	2.33	..
Employment						
Total employment[b] ('000)	141,186	143,878	146,631	148,658	..	..
Employment in manufacturing[c] ('000)	12,023	12,190	12,332	12,343	..	..
as share of total employment (%)	8.5	8.5	8.4	8	..	..
Unemployment rate (%)	7.4	6.2	5.3	4.9	4.4	..
Memorandum						
Goods trade to GDP ratio	23.2	23.0	20.8	19.6	20.1	..

.. Not available.

a Fiscal year.

b Full-time and part-time employees.

c Estimates are based on the 2002 North American Industry Classification System (NAICS).

Source: WTO Secretariat, based on Bureau of Economic Analysis online information. Viewed at: http://www.bea.gov/; Board of Governors of the Federal Reserve System online information. Viewed at: http://www.federalreserve.gov/econresdata/default.htm; and Bureau of Labor Statistics online information. Viewed at: http://www.bls.gov/.

Growth in overall private fixed investment (residential and non-residential) was 5.4% in 2017, compared with virtually zero growth in 2016, and 2.4% the year before.

The acceleration of growth in the second quarter of 2018 to an annual rate of 4.2% was caused by strong consumption expenditures and a sharp increase in exports, in particular exports of goods. The BEA GDP Advanced Estimate shows that consumption rose at an annual rate of 4% and contributed 2.7 percentage points to GDP growth, while net exports of goods expanded at an annual rate of 13.3% and contributed 1.1 percentage points to growth.[2] The contribution of fixed capital formation was slightly negative (0.1%), while government spending contributed 0.4 percentage points to GDP growth.[3]

Despite solid economic growth, productivity growth has been weak and below the rates recorded during previous expansions. In the current expansion, labour productivity growth has averaged only 1.2%, well below the 2.6% observed in the previous expansion (1994-2007) and the long run average of 2.1% during the post-World War II period from 1947 to 2016. According to the OECD,

contributing factors to slowing productivity include the slow pace of non-residential investment, weak rates of business entry and exit, tighter regulations, and the lack of knowledge spillovers among firms.[4] According to the Office of Management and Budget's (OMB), the Administration has already adopted policies to deal with the issue of low productivity. These include the passage of the Tax Cuts and Jobs Act in December 2017, and the elimination of unnecessary regulations under Executive Orders 13771 and 13777. In addition, the OMB notes that the Administration is pursuing policies to encourage domestic energy development and investments in infrastructure, reform welfare programmes, negotiate more attractive trade agreements, and reduce federal budget deficits; all actions together should encourage investment by U.S. firms and stimulate productivity growth.[5]

Based on the assumption that all the policy proposals mentioned in the President's fiscal year 2019 budget proposal would be implemented, the U.S. authorities estimate that the economy would expand by 3.1% in 2018 and increase slightly to 3.2% in 2019 before edging down to 2.8% in the long run.[6]

Chart 1.2 Contributions to percentage change in real GDP, 2010-18Q2

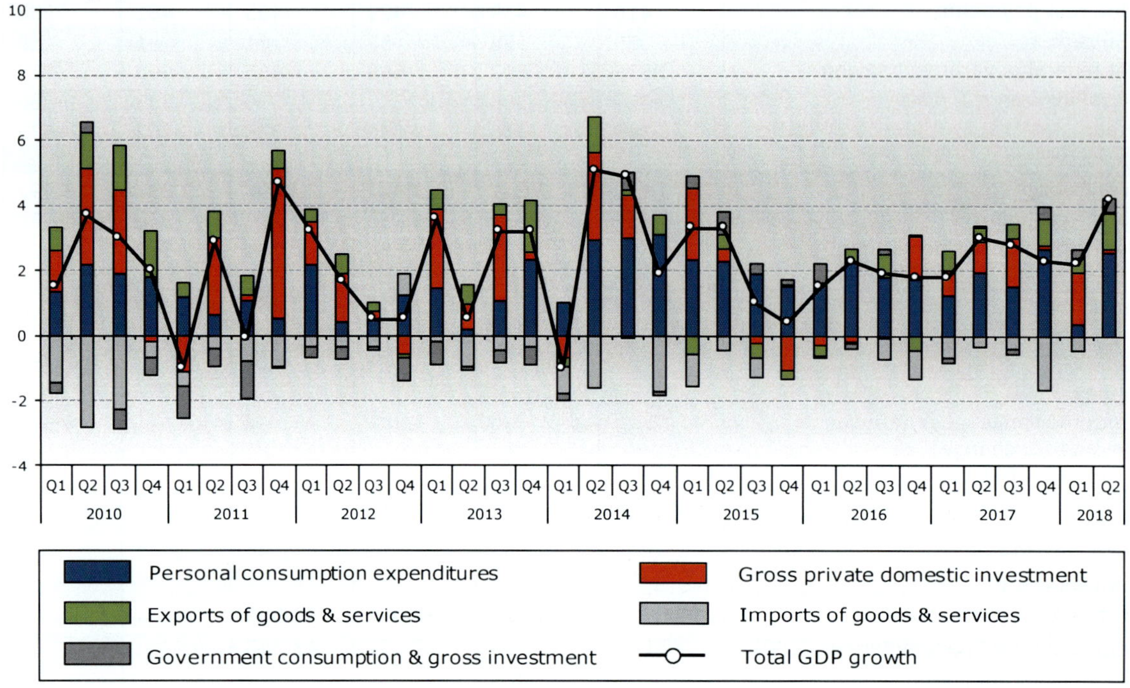

Percentage points

Legend:
- Personal consumption expenditures
- Gross private domestic investment
- Exports of goods & services
- Imports of goods & services
- Government consumption & gross investment
- Total GDP growth

Source: WTO Secretariat, based on BEA online information. Viewed at: http://www.bea.gov.

In the last United States Article IV consultation, the IMF noted that the near-term outlook for the economy is one of strong growth and job creation, aided by a fiscal stimulus, a recovery of private investment, and supportive financial conditions. These positive outturns have supported, and been reinforced by a favourable external environment. However, despite good near-term prospects, a number of vulnerabilities are being built up, and the IMF estimates that potential GDP growth could decline to 1.8% over the medium term. The higher federal deficit could trigger a faster-than-expected rise in inflation, prompting a more rapid rise in interest rates that could increase market volatility both in the United States and abroad. There is also a risk of a reversal of capital flows. The IMF also considers that the net effect of budget and tax policy choices will result in an increase in public debt, and leave few budget resources available to invest in needed supply-side reforms, including infrastructure spending. Recent trade tensions have added to these risks.[7]

The U.S. Administration regards the IMF's forecasts as pessimistic, particularly concerning the prospects for long-term growth; it noted that the Administration's framework is based on average growth of 3% over 2018–28. This higher growth, relative to IMF staff forecasts, incorporates longrun growth effects arising from a US$1.5 trillion investment in infrastructure, the impact of the overhaul of the tax system, higher labour force participation, and a continuing process of deregulation that has already eliminated 22 existing regulations for each new one that was created. With

respect to trade, the U.S. Administration notes that its trade policy agenda seeks to address serious, long-term challenges that have been facing the multilateral trading system.[8]

Fiscal policy

In recent years, a number of deficit-reducing measures were put in place, including both tax increases (rates on top earners, termination of the temporary payroll tax holiday) under the Tax Relief, Unemployment Reauthorization, and Job Creation Act of 2010, and spending cuts under the Budget Control Act of 2011. Additionally, the Bipartisan Budget Act of 2015 suspended the debt ceiling until March 2017, and avoided the risk of government shutdown by locking in appropriations for 2016. This Act also raised the caps on discretionary funding by US$50 billion in 2016, and by US$30 billion in 2017. The fiscal deficit came in at 2.6% of GDP in 2017. Public debt as a share of GDP, however, continued to rise (Table 1.1).

There was a policy shift in 2018, when fiscal policy turned pro-cyclical, with the enactment of the Tax Cuts and Jobs Act of 2017 (TCJA) (Box 1.1), the Bipartisan Budget Act of 2018 and the Consolidated Appropriations Act of 2018. The TCJA substantially altered the taxation of personal and business income. The Bipartisan Budget Act of 2018 increased the caps on discretionary funding in 2018 and 2019, and provided substantial funding for emergency disaster assistance. The Consolidated Appropriations Act, 2018, provided appropriations for 2018.

Box 1.1 The Tax Cuts and Jobs Act of 2017 (TCJA)

The President signed into law the Tax Cuts and Jobs Act (TCJA) of 2017 on 22 December 2017. The Act introduced a number of tax reforms aimed at: making the U.S. business tax competitive; providing tax relief to lower- and middle-income Americans; lowering statutory rates and broadening tax bases; and simplifying the tax system for some taxpayers.

The Act:
(i) Lowers tax rates for businesses and individuals;
(ii) Simplifies personal taxes by increasing the standard deduction and child and family tax credits;
(iii) Eliminates personal exemptions and makes it less beneficial to itemize deductions;
(iv) Limits deductions for state and local taxes, property taxes and mortgage interest; and
(v) Eliminates the alternative minimum tax for corporations and raises the threshold for individuals. The TCJA also reduces the number of estates impacted by the estate tax, and repeals the individual mandate of the Affordable Care Act.

Most of the changes to personal income tax are temporary and will expire at the end of 2025, after which the tax system will revert to that which was operational in 2017. However, changes affecting corporations are permanent.

The main changes with respect to personal income tax include:
(i) Although the number of income tax bands with regard to personal income tax remains unchanged, at seven, the income range for most bands has changed, and each band has a lower rate, but a change in the indexation methodology of the tax bands to reflect inflation more accurately will result in people moving to higher tax bands quicker;
(ii) The estate tax threshold was doubled to US$11.2 million per decedent;
(iii) Personal exemptions were eliminated, while state and local tax deductions were capped at US$10,000;
(iv) Deductions in lieu of mortgage interest were capped at US$750,000 worth of loans, a decline with respect to the previous US$1 million cap;
(v) Deductions for education and medical expenses were also reduced; and
(vi) The TCJA allows for a temporary 20% deduction on qualified business income received from pass-through businesses; this is significant as many businesses are unincorporated entities, such as sole proprietorships, partnerships and S-Corporations, whereby owners pay taxes at individual rates.

The main changes in corporate taxation include:
(i) A reduction in the top corporate tax rate from 35% to 21%, probably the most significant change in the TCJA, as well as a change from a global towards a territorial tax system with base erosion protections for corporate income tax. The implication of this is that a foreign subsidiary can generally distribute earnings to corporate U.S. shareholders free of additional U.S. tax. However, the foreign subsidiary may be subject to tax in the United States on its excess returns, to the extent such returns are not subject to at least a 13.125% effective foreign tax rate. In other words, under this system, the corporation could save the difference between the generally higher U.S. tax rate and the lower tax rate of the country in which the subsidiary is established, if the subsidiary is subject to tax at a rate of at least 13.125%; and (ii) The TCJA allows for a one-time tax on un-repatriated foreign earnings. The tax will be levied at a rate of 8% for illiquid assets and 15.5% on cash. The purpose of this measure is to avoid providing a windfall for U.S. MNEs with an accumulated stock of previously untaxed unrepatriated earnings, which are estimated at nearly US$3 trillion.

The authorities expect the new tax law to result in higher levels of investment, employment and GDP. They consider that a lower corporate income tax rate and temporary expensing should serve as an incentive for increased investment, while lower personal income tax rates should be a motivating factor for increased participation in the labour force. According to the Congressional Budget Office (CBO), the heightened economic activity is projected to increase GDP by 0.7% on average annually, between 2018 and 2028. On the other hand, the CBO also expects the total budget deficit to increase by about US$1 trillion over a 10-year period. Furthermore, the stronger output growth would also result in slightly higher inflation and an appreciation of the U.S. dollar. The CBO also expects that the strengthening of the labour market and higher inflation may lead the Federal Reserve to raise interest rates.

Source: CBO: The Budget and Economic Outlook: 2018 to 2028 April 2018. Viewed at: https://www.cbo.gov/system/files?file=115th-congress-2017-2018/reports/53651-outlook.pdf.

The implementation of the three previously-mentioned Acts would result in reduced revenues and increased outlays. According to CBO estimates, revenues are expected to remain at the 2018 level of 16.6% of GDP for the next few years, before increasing steadily to 17.5% of GDP by 2025. At the end of that year, many provisions of the 2017 TCJA expire, causing receipts to rise sharply, to a projected 18.1% of GDP in 2026, and 18.5% in 2027 and 2028. The CBO projects that outlays for the next three years will remain near 21% of

GDP, after which they will grow more quickly than the economy, reaching 23.3% of GDP by 2028. Against a background of an ageing population, an increase in expenditure is expected on account of significant growth in mandatory spending due to rising health care costs per beneficiary and increased spending for Social Security and Medicare, among other programmes. The increase in expenditure also reflects growth in interest costs, which are projected to grow more quickly than any other major component of the budget; this will be as a result

Part B
Report by the WTO Secretariat

of rising interest rates and mounting debt. By 2028, net outlays for interest are projected to be roughly triple what they are this year in nominal terms, and roughly double when measured as a percentage of GDP. In contrast, discretionary spending in the projections declines in relation to the size of the economy.[9]

Consequently, the CBO projects budget deficits to continue increasing after 2018, from 4.2% of GDP in 2018 to 5.1% in 2022. Deficits are expected to remain at 5.1% of GDP between 2022 and 2025, before declining at the end of the period, mainly on account of the expiration of the tax provisions previously mentioned, which is expected to lead to an increase in revenues. The projected annual average budget deficit over the 2021–28 period is 4.9% of GDP.[10] As a result of rising deficits, the CBO estimates that public debt will rise from 78% of GDP (or US$16 trillion) at the end of 2018 to 96% of GDP (or US$29 trillion) by 2028. According to the CBO, the rising debt could have negative consequences for the budget and the economy.[11]

The IMF staff considers that the combination of revenue losses from the TCJA and the approved increase in spending will lead to an increase in the fiscal deficit in the next few years; it is estimated that the deficit will be 4.5% of GDP in 2019. In the IMF staff's view, the increase in the federal deficit will exacerbate the upward dynamic in the public debt-to-GDP ratio. Even with the planned fiscal consolidation scheduled to start in 2020, the federal debt will continue to climb, exceeding 90% of annual GDP by 2024. The IMF staff deems that the expansion in the deficit leaves few budget resources available to invest in a range of needed supply-side reforms that could boost medium-term growth and raise living standards.[12]

The U.S. Administration has a differing view with respect to the effect of the tax reforms, as noted in its budget proposal.[13] It noted that the stronger growth path envisaged under the new legislation will reduce the fiscal deficit by an average of around 0.25% of GDP each year over the next 10 years. Additionally, it recalled that the Administration plans to reduce federal non-defense expenditures while providing an additional US$200 billion to finance infrastructure spending. The Administration noted that half of these expenditure savings would come from a reorganization of the Federal Government. The remainder would accrue mostly from the repeal of the Affordable Care Act, reforms to the welfare system and student loans, reductions in Medicare spending, and a phase-down of defense spending currently being undertaken through Overseas Contingency Operations funding. According to the Administration's budget, over the 10-year budget horizon, these envisaged spending cuts would result in a 44% real reduction in discretionary, non-defense spending. However, mandatory spending would increase to 78% of non-interest federal spending.[14] As a result of these measures, and faster growth, the authorities expect the fiscal deficit to fall to 1.1% of GDP by 2028,

and public debt to peak at 82% of GDP in 2022, declining afterwards. The authorities consider that no negative growth effects are anticipated from the various reductions in federal programmes, and that this policy is fully consistent with an expansionary growth outlook, as jobs are expected to be created in the private sector at a pace that more than offsets the economic drag from reductions in inefficient federal spending.[15]

Monetary policy

The Federal Reserve conducts monetary policy in the United States. Legislation specifies that, in conducting monetary policy, the Federal Reserve System and the Federal Open Market Committee (FOMC) should seek "to promote effectively the goals of maximum employment, stable prices, and moderate long-term interest rates".[16] The Federal Reserve adjusts the key tools of monetary policy — open market operations, the discount rate, reserve requirements, and interest on reserves — to influence demand and supply conditions in the federal funds market, and keep the federal funds rate within the target range established by the FOMC. The FOMC specifies a longerrun goal for inflation, rather than a target. The goal is currently 2%, and is for the price index for personal consumption expenditures rather than for consumer price inflation.[17]

In the aftermath of the 2008 financial crisis, the Federal Reserve pursued an accommodative monetary policy, so as to support employment and growth, and stem disinflationary pressures. The nominal federal funds rate was held near zero for seven years. As unemployment dropped and inflation started to edge towards the Federal Reserve's goal of 2%, the FOMC raised the target range for the federal funds rate by 25 basis points at the end of 2015. A sustained increase in economic activity, the continued strengthening of the labour market and firming inflation have resulted in moderate rate rises since 2015. In the first half of 2018, the FOMC raised the federal funds rate twice, to bring it to its current range of 1.75-2.0%. According to the Federal Reserve, "the decisions to increase the target range for the federal funds rate reflected the economy's continued progress toward the Committee's objectives of maximum employment and price stability. Even with these policy rate increases, the stance of monetary policy remains accommodative, thereby supporting strong labour market conditions and a sustained return to 2% inflation".[18]

After remaining at below, or close to, the FOMC's objective of 2% between 2013 and 2017, the 12-month percentage change in the personal consumption expenditures (PCE) index exceeded this goal in the first half of 2018. The 12-month change in the PCE index in June 2018 was 2.2%, boosted by a sizable increase in consumer energy prices. With inflation near its objective, and continued strong labour market conditions, the FOMC has indicated that, based on its economic outlook, further gradual increases in the federal funds rate are likely to be appropriate.

 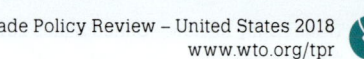

Balance of payments

The U.S. current account deficit has been increasing since 2013, and reached US$449.1 billion in 2017 (2.4% of GDP), as the gap between gross national savings and gross investment widened (Table 1.2).

Exports of goods declined from US$1.63 trillion in 2014 to US$1.46 trillion in 2016, but subsequently increased to US$1.55 trillion in 2017. The decline was due to lower exports of food, animal feeds, and beverages, industrial supplies and materials; and capital goods except automotive products. In 2015 and 2016, the real exchange of the dollar appreciated, prices for many commodity exports fell, and trade growth outside the United States was weak. In 2017, the dollar depreciated, commodity prices rose, and trade growth outside the United States was stronger. Goods imports also declined from US$2.38 trillion in 2014 to US$2.21 trillion in 2016, before increasing to US$2.36 trillion in 2017. All categories of goods showed an increase in imports, except industrial supplies and materials. Consequently, the balance on goods deteriorated from US$749.9 billion (4.3% of GDP) in 2014 to US$807.5 billion (4.2% of GDP) in 2017 (Chart 1.3).

There has been a significant shift within the goods balance. The U.S. petroleum deficit has fallen to its lowest level in decades, due to lower international prices and higher domestic production. In contrast, the non-oil goods deficit is nearing its historic peak (Chart 1.4). The increasing non-oil goods deficit is due to strong import growth and very sluggish export growth, which is manifested in the relatively stronger domestic demand in the United States compared to its trading partners, as well as the strengthening of the U.S. dollar.[19] Furthermore, the strong demand and the trade-in-goods deficit is also reflected in the U.S. savings pattern. Since the mid-1970s, the United States has seen a secular decline in the household savings rate. This downward trend was temporarily reversed after the financial crisis but has, more recently, resumed. The evidence instead points to the 2008–13 increase in the personal savings rate as being mainly the result of the path for lower disposable income, higher unemployment and the significant fall in wealth that was experienced during this period and that led people to save more for the future. The IMF predicts that the household savings rate will continue falling, and will eventually revert to the downward trend that was in place before 2007. Additionally, disposable income growth and household wealth gains will lead to a further decline in the savings rate, resulting in an increase in the U.S. current account deficit.[20] On the other hand, a recent comprehensive National Income and Products Accounts revision by the BEA shows significant upwards revisions for the personal savings rate over the past five years.[21]

The United States is the world's largest exporter and importer of services (15% and 10% of global trade in 2016, respectively), and has been running a surplus on the services account for many years (Chart 1.3). However, between 2014 and 2016, the surplus was on a declining trend, before increasing in 2017, when it totaled US$255.2 billion (1.4% of GDP). It was up 4.4% for the first six months of 2018 on a BOP basis.

The main services export categories are travel, other business services, charges for use of intellectual property, financial services, and transport. Exports of other business services and travel have shown a marked increase since 2014, while exports of transport services and use of intellectual property have declined. With regard to services imports, the largest categories are travel, other business services, transport, insurance, and charges for the use of intellectual property. Since 2014, imports of transport services, travel services, other business services, and charges for the use of intellectual property have risen, while those of insurance services have declined. The latter declined in 2015 by over 6%, to US$47,822 million from US$51,011 million, but slightly increased in 2016 to US$48,077 million. In this period, imports of auxiliary insurance services rose, but a decline in imports of direct insurance and reinsurance appears to account for the decrease.

Europe accounted for the majority of U.S. total trade in services. The United Kingdom accounted for 9% of U.S. services exports and 10% of services imports in 2016, 28% of U.S. exports of services went to other European destinations, and 32% of U.S. imports of services came from there. Canada accounted for 7% of U.S. services exports and was the source of 6% of U.S. services imports; China's shares were 7% and 3%, respectively, while other Asian and Pacific countries accounted for 23% and 24%, respectively. Japan's consumption of U.S. services was similar to that of China, but it accounted for approximately double the amount of U.S. services imports.

The United States also runs a significant surplus on the primary income account, which rose to US$221.7 billion in 2017 (1.1% of GDP). Primary income receipts rose mainly on the back of reinvested earnings and dividends on equity other than investment fund shares, while the increase on primary income payments was due mainly to reinvested earnings and interest on debt securities. The surpluses realized on the services and primary income account partially offset the trade deficit.

According to the BEA, at the end of 2017, the U.S. net international investment position stood at a deficit of US$7.8 trillion (40.5% of GDP), an improvement of more than US$470 billion compared to end-2016. The value of U.S.-owned foreign assets was US$27.6 trillion, while the value of foreignowned U.S. assets stood at US$35.5 trillion. Recent improvement in the net position has been supported by valuation effects that increased the dollar value of U.S. assets held abroad, as well as by the strong relative performance of foreign equity markets in 2017, which also boosted the value of U.S. assets held abroad.[22]

Part B
Report by the WTO Secretariat

Table 1.2 U.S. international transactions, 2013-18Q2

(US$ million)

	2013	2014	2015	2016	2017	2018 Q2
Current account						
Exports of goods and services, and income receipts (credits)	3,212,991	3,341,768	3,207,288	3,183,783	3,433,239	1,838,572
Exports of goods and services	2,294,199	2,376,657	2,266,691	2,215,844	2,351,072	1,255,827
Goods	1,593,708	1,635,563	1,511,381	1,456,957	1,553,383	840,680
Services	700,491	741,094	755,310	758,888	797,690	415,146
Primary income receipts	792,819	824,543	810,073	830,174	928,118	515,959
Investment income	786,206	818,040	803,494	823,709	921,816	512,760
Compensation of employees	6,613	6,503	6,578	6,466	6,302	3,199
Secondary income (current transfer) receipts	125,973	140,567	130,525	137,764	154,049	66,787
Imports of goods and services, and income payments (debits)	3,561,792	3,706,967	3,615,053	3,616,656	3,882,380	2,061,742
Imports of goods and services	2,755,334	2,866,241	2,765,216	2,717,846	2,903,349	1,543,628
Goods	2,294,247	2,385,480	2,273,249	2,208,008	2,360,878	1,264,640
Services	461,087	480,761	491,966	509,838	542,471	278,988
Primary income payments	586,842	606,152	606,464	637,151	706,386	393,939
Investment income	570,816	589,093	588,809	618,013	686,699	383,967
Compensation of employees	16,026	17,059	17,656	19,139	19,687	9,972
Secondary income (current transfer) payments						124,175
Capital account						
Capital transfer receipts and other credits	0	0	0	0	24,788	0
Capital transfer payments and other debits	412	45	42	59	42	2
Financial account						
Net U.S. acquisition of financial assets excluding financial derivatives (net increase in assets/financial outflow (+))	649,587	866,523	202,208	348,625	1,182,749	76,014
Direct investment assets	392,796	387,528	307,058	312,975	379,222	-168,298
Portfolio investment assets	481,298	582,676	160,410	36,283	586,695	280,357
Other investment assets	-221,408	-100,099	-258,968	-2,723	218,522	-39,106
Reserve assets	-3,099	-3,583	-6,292	2,090	-1,690	3,061
Net U.S. incurrence of liabilities excluding financial derivatives (net increase in liabilities/financial inflow (+))	1,052,068	1,109,443	501,121	741,529	1,537,683	383,337
Direct investment liabilities	288,131	251,857	509,087	494,455	354,829	82,514
Portfolio investment liabilities	511,987	697,607	213,910	231,349	799,182	311,574
Other investment liabilities	251,949	159,979	-221,876	15,725	383,671	-10,751
Financial derivatives other than reserves, net transactions	2,222	-54,335	-27,035	7,827	23,074	12,055
Statistical discrepancy	-51,046	67,989	81,859	47,855	92,536	-72,095
Balances						
Balance on current account	-348,801	-365,199	-407,764	-432,873	-449,142	-223,170
Balance on goods and services	-461,135	-489,584	-498,525	-502,001	-552,277	-287,801
Balance on goods	-700,539	-749,917	-761,868	-751,051	-807,495	-423,960
Balance on services	239,404	260,333	263,343	249,050	255,219	136,158
Balance on primary income	205,977	218,391	203,608	193,023	221,731	122,020
Balance on secondary income	-93,643	-94,006	-112,848	-123,895	-118,597	-57,389

	2013	2014	2015	2016	2017	2018 Q2
Balance on capital account	-412	-45	-42	-59	24,746	-2
Net lending (+) or net borrowing (-) from current- and capital-account transactions	-349,213	-365,244	-407,807	-432,932	-424,395	-223,172
Net lending (+) or net borrowing (-) from financial-account transactions	-400,259	-297,255	-325,948	-385,078	-331,860	-295,267

Source: Bureau of Economic Analysis.

Chart 1.3 U.S. Current account and net financial flows, 2006-17

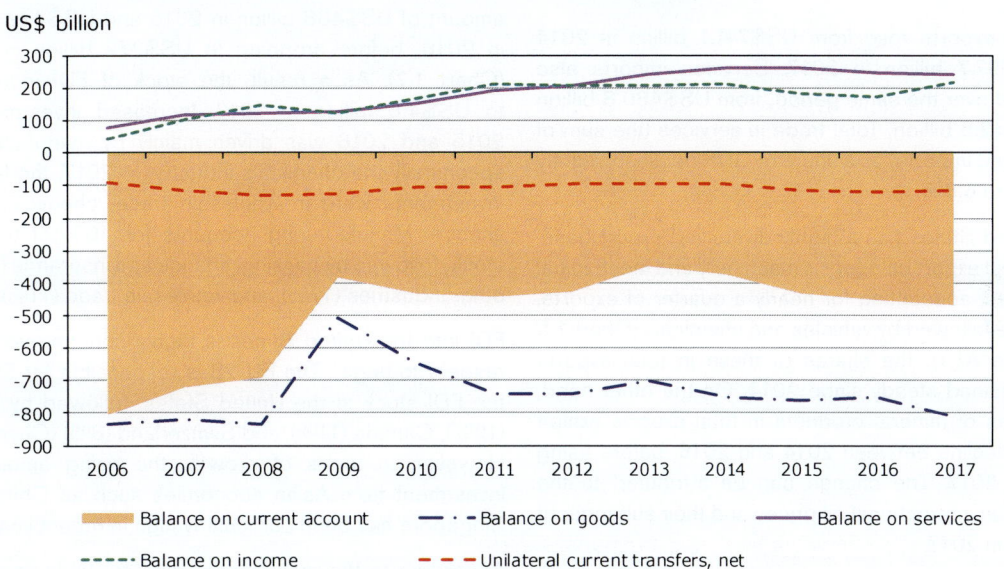

Source: Bureau of Economic Analysis. Viewed at: http://www.bea.gov.

Chart 1.4 U.S. Current account and oil products trade, 2010Q1-18Q2

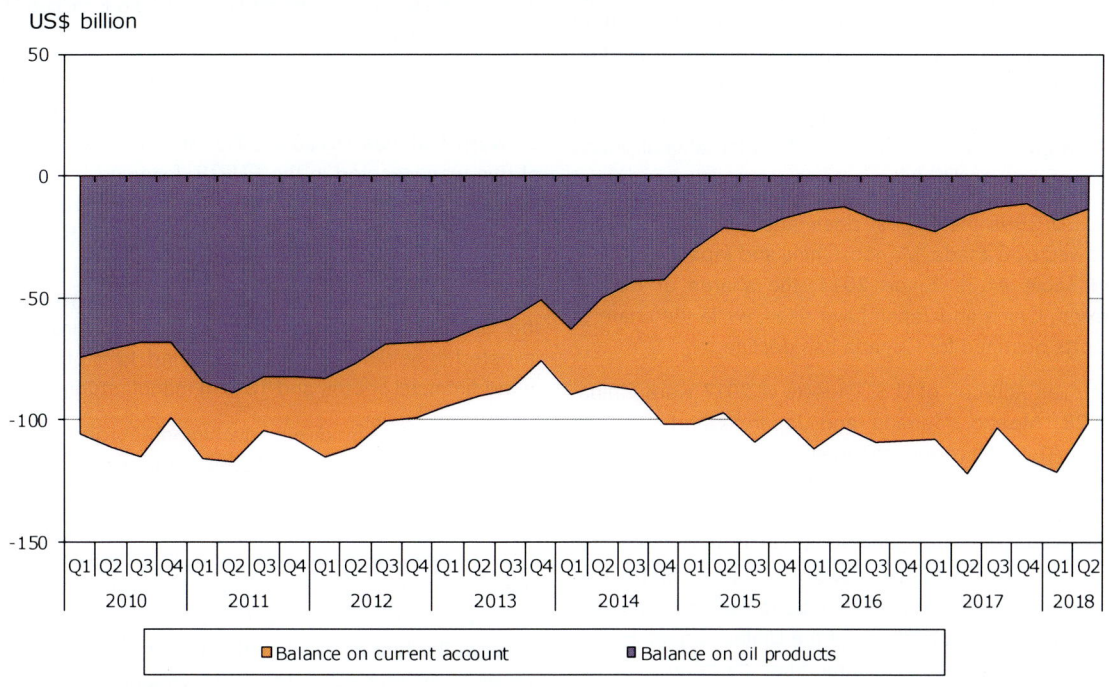

Source: Bureau of Economic Analysis. Viewed at: http://www.bea.gov.

Part B
Report by the WTO Secretariat

DEVELOPMENTS IN TRADE AND INVESTMENT

Trends and patterns in merchandise and services trade

After peaking at US$1.62 trillion in 2014, merchandise exports declined to US$1.46 trillion in 2016, before rising to US$1.55 trillion in 2017. Over the same period, merchandise imports also declined, albeit negligibly. As per balance of payments data, total merchandise trade (the sum of exports and imports) declined from the equivalent of 23.1% of GDP in 2014 to 20.4% of GDP in 2017.

Services exports rose from US$741.1 billion in 2014 to US$797.7 billion in 2017. Services imports also increased over the same period, from US$480.8 billion to US$542.5 billion. Total trade in services (the sum of exports and imports) as a share of GDP declined slightly from 7% to 6.8%.

The United States has a highly diversified export base. The largest export category is machinery and mechanical appliances, accounting for nearly a quarter of exports. These are followed by vehicles and chemicals (Chart 1.5 and Table A1.1); the shares of these in total exports have remained steady since 2014. On the other hand, the shares of mineral products in total exports exhibit a sharp decline between 2014 and 2016, before rising again in 2017. The change can be attributed to the sharp fall in international oil prices and their subsequent recovery in 2017.

Imports are equally diversified. The largest import categories are machinery and mechanical appliances, vehicles, mineral products, and chemicals (Chart 1.5 and Table A1.2). Since 2014, the shares of machinery and mechanical appliances, vehicles, and chemicals in total imports have risen. This reflects the sustained growth of the economy and a strengthening of the labour market. In contrast, the share of mineral products has declined, mainly on account of increased domestic production of oil and gas, as well as the fall in the international prices of those commodities.

The EU-28 is the largest destination for U.S. exports, followed by Canada, Mexico, China and Japan (Chart 1.6 and Table A1.3). Since 2014, the shares of EU-28, Mexico, China and Japan have risen, while the share of exports destined for Canada has declined.

The main sources of U.S. imports in 2017 were China, EU-28, Mexico, Canada and Japan (Chart 1.6 and Table A1.4). Mirroring changes in export destinations, the shares of China, the EU28, Mexico and Japan as sources of imports have risen, while the share of Canada has declined since 2014. The United States and Canada have a substantial two-way trade in petroleum and natural gas products that does not exist with the other large trading partners of the United States. Falling world prices for those commodities therefore had the greatest effect, both for imports and exports, on U.S. trade with Canada.

Trends and patterns in Foreign Direct Investment (FDI)

The United States continues to be the world's foremost destination for Foreign Direct Investment (FDI) because of its open markets, liberal investment regime, large consumer base, higher education system, skilled and productive workforce, a business environment that encourages innovation, legal protections, and the world's largest venture capital and private equity market. FDI inflows on a historic cost basis reached a record amount of US$468 billion in 2015 and US$472 billion in 2016, before dropping to US$277 billion in 2017 (Chart 1.7). As a result, the stock of FDI increased to US$4.0 trillion in 2017. Increased investment in 2015 and 2016 was driven mainly by manufacturing, specifically the chemicals industry. In 2017, the largest investments were in wholesale trade, chemicals, and finance. Manufacturing accounts for 40% of the FDI stock, followed by banking, finance and insurance (18%); other industries (17%); and wholesale trade (11%).

FDI into the United States is highly concentrated with respect to origin. The EU-28 is responsible for 59% of the FDI stock in the United States, followed by Japan (12%), Canada (11%), and Switzerland (8%) (Chart 1.8). However, in terms of growth, the rising amount of investment from Asian economies such as China and Singapore has been particularly high in recent years.

According to the most recent data available, majority-owned U.S. affiliates of foreign entities exported nearly US$353 billion in goods in 2015, accounting for over 23% of total merchandise exports. Such entities were also responsible for nearly 16% of R&D spending in 2015 in the United States and employed 6.8 million U.S. workers in 2015.[23]

The United States continues to be the largest foreign investor abroad. On a historical cost basis, the stock of outward FDI was US$5.3 trillion in 2016. Nearly 54% of this was invested in the EU-28, followed by Canada (7%), Bermuda (6%), British Caribbean islands (6%), and Singapore (5%). Furthermore, 96% of this outward FDI stock comprised of reinvested earnings, 10% of equity capital and -5.8% of intercompany debt (payments to the United States). More than half of outward FDI is invested in holding companies; around 12% of the total in the financial sector, and 13% in manufacturing.[24]

The effect of U.S. direct investment abroad on U.S. workers and wages was addressed in a recent report to Congress. The report shows that 74% of the accumulated U.S. FDI abroad is concentrated in high-income developed countries, and, in recent years, the share of investment going to developing countries has fallen. Evidence also shows that U.S. firms invest abroad to serve the foreign local market rather than to produce goods to export back to the United States.[25]

The Administration expects that the recent tax measures (Box 1.1) may result in increased investment in the United States and will encourage U.S. firms to increase repatriated earnings that can be invested in the United States.

Chart 1.5 Merchandise trade by main HS sections, 2014 and 2017

(a) Exports

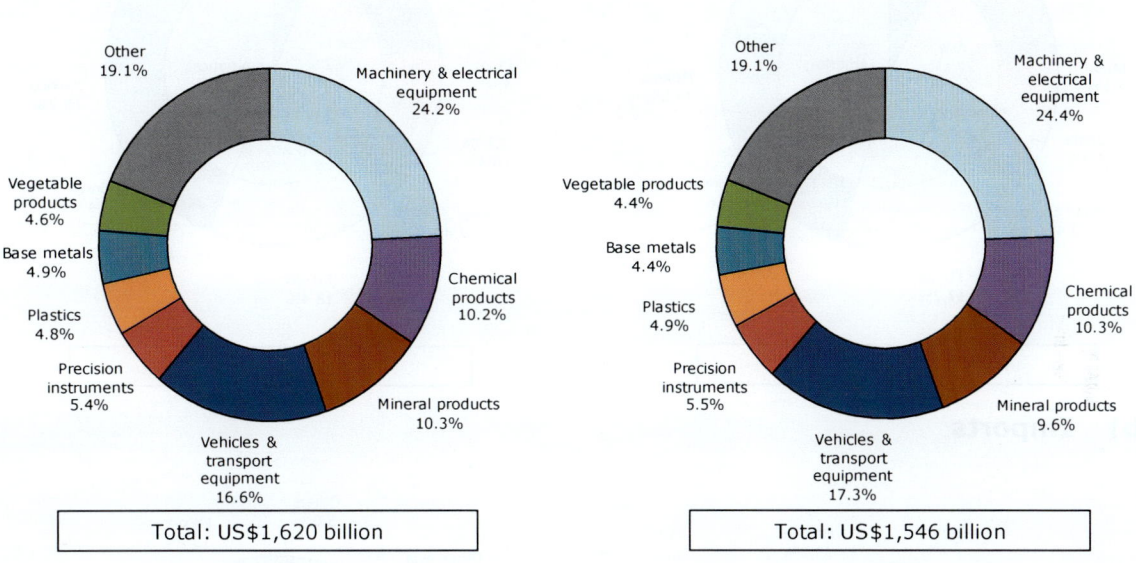

2014

Other 19.1%
Machinery & electrical equipment 24.2%
Vegetable products 4.6%
Base metals 4.9%
Plastics 4.8%
Precision instruments 5.4%
Chemical products 10.2%
Mineral products 10.3%
Vehicles & transport equipment 16.6%

Total: US$1,620 billion

2017

Other 19.1%
Machinery & electrical equipment 24.4%
Vegetable products 4.4%
Base metals 4.4%
Plastics 4.9%
Precision instruments 5.5%
Chemical products 10.3%
Mineral products 9.6%
Vehicles & transport equipment 17.3%

Total: US$1,546 billion

(b) Imports

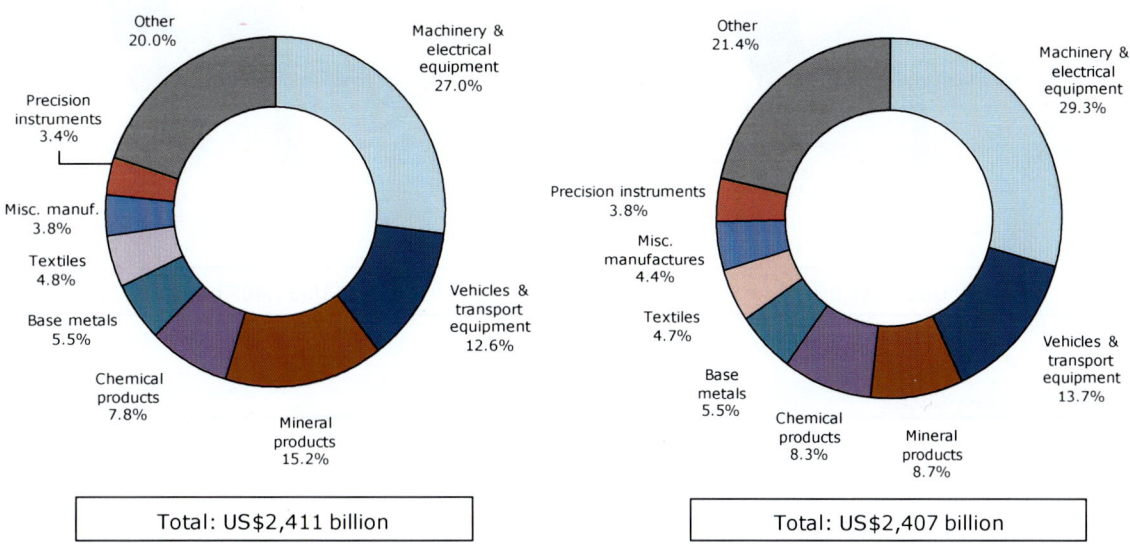

2014

Other 20.0%
Machinery & electrical equipment 27.0%
Precision instruments 3.4%
Misc. manuf. 3.8%
Textiles 4.8%
Base metals 5.5%
Chemical products 7.8%
Mineral products 15.2%
Vehicles & transport equipment 12.6%

Total: US$2,411 billion

2017

Other 21.4%
Machinery & electrical equipment 29.3%
Precision instruments 3.8%
Misc. manufactures 4.4%
Textiles 4.7%
Base metals 5.5%
Chemical products 8.3%
Mineral products 8.7%
Vehicles & transport equipment 13.7%

Total: US$2,407 billion

Source: UNSD, Comtrade database.

Part B
Report by the WTO Secretariat

Chart 1.6 Merchandise trade by main origin and destination, 2014 and 2017

| 2014 | 2017 |

(a) Exports

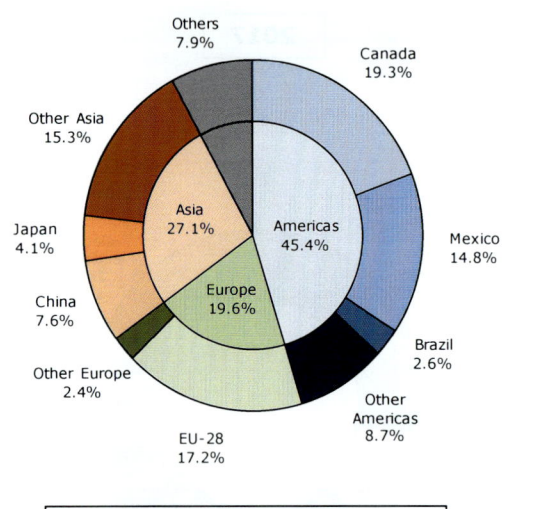

Total: US$1,620 billion

Total: US$1,546 billion

(b) Imports

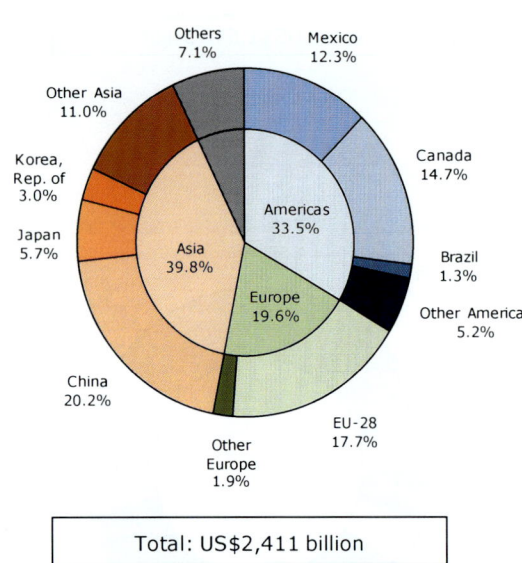 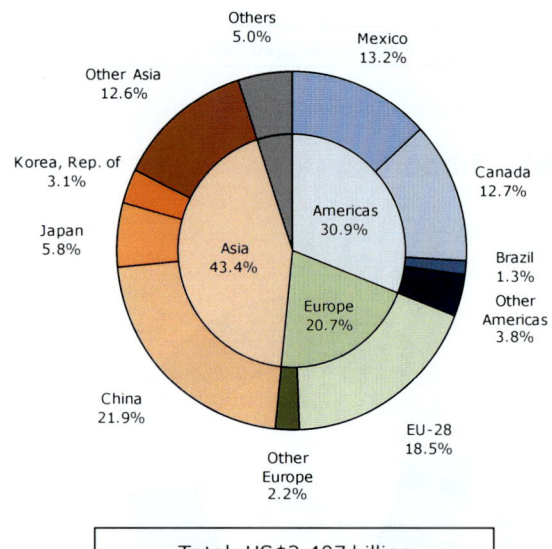

Total: US$2,411 billion

Total: US$2,407 billion

Source: UNSD Comtrade database.

Chart 1.7 Foreign Direct Investment into the United States, 2008-17

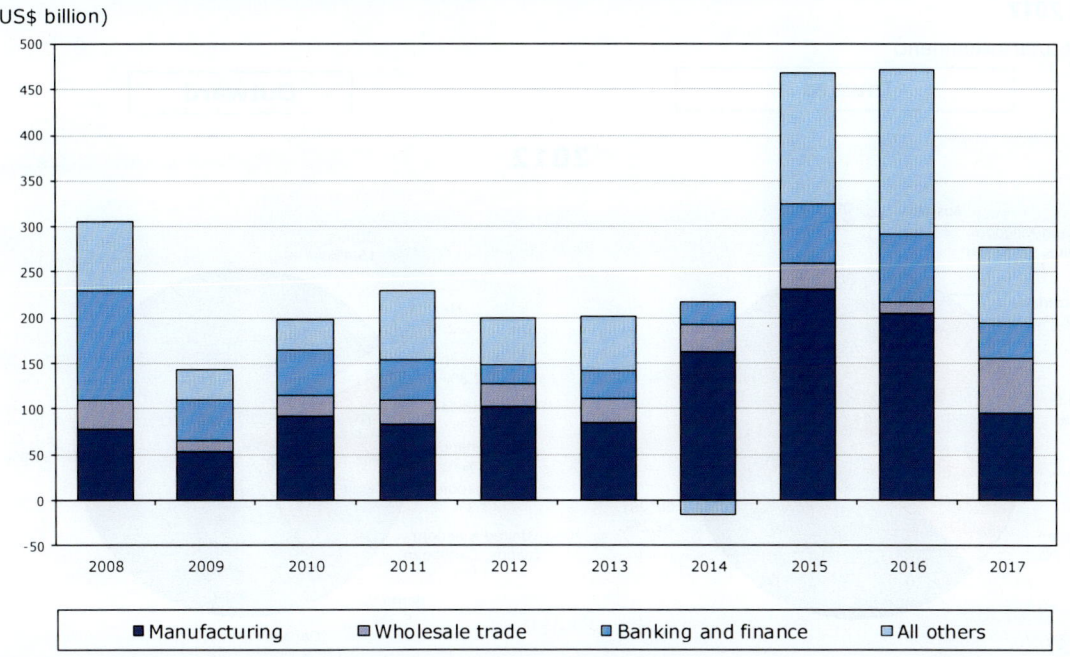

Source: Bureau of Economic Analysis online information. Viewed at: http://www.bea.gov.

Chart 1.8 Direct investment position on a historical-cost basis, by selected partners, 2012 and 2017

(% of total investment)

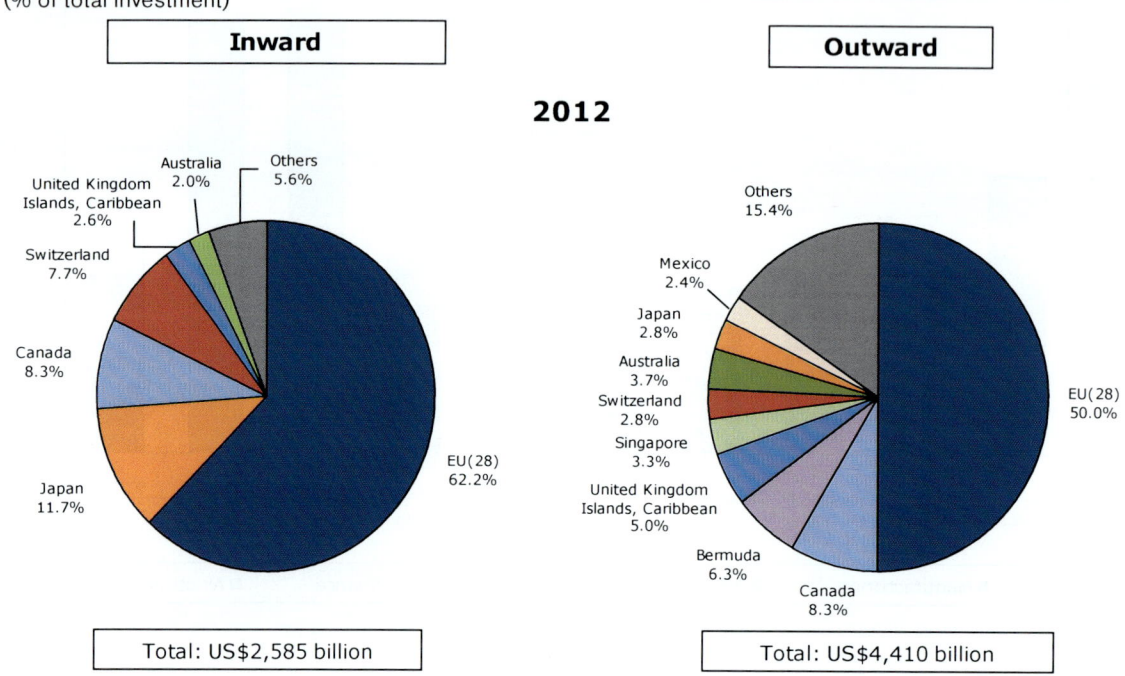

2012

Inward

- Others 5.6%
- Australia 2.0%
- United Kingdom Islands, Caribbean 2.6%
- Switzerland 7.7%
- Canada 8.3%
- Japan 11.7%
- EU(28) 62.2%

Total: US$2,585 billion

Outward

- Others 15.4%
- Mexico 2.4%
- Japan 2.8%
- Australia 3.7%
- Switzerland 2.8%
- Singapore 3.3%
- United Kingdom Islands, Caribbean 5.0%
- Bermuda 6.3%
- Canada 8.3%
- EU(28) 50.0%

Total: US$4,410 billion

2017

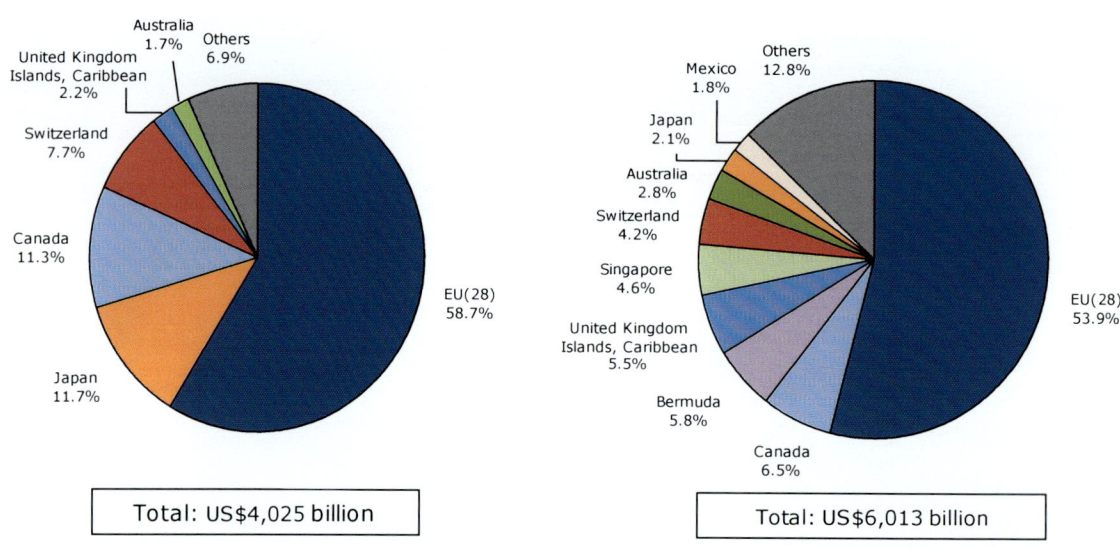

Inward

- Australia 1.7%
- Others 6.9%
- United Kingdom Islands, Caribbean 2.2%
- Switzerland 7.7%
- Canada 11.3%
- Japan 11.7%
- EU(28) 58.7%

Total: US$4,025 billion

Outward

- Others 12.8%
- Mexico 1.8%
- Japan 2.1%
- Australia 2.8%
- Switzerland 4.2%
- Singapore 4.6%
- United Kingdom Islands, Caribbean 5.5%
- Bermuda 5.8%
- Canada 6.5%
- EU(28) 53.9%

Total: US$6,013 billion

Source: WTO Secretariat, based on Bureau of Economic Analysis online information. Viewed at: http://www.bea.gov.

Endnotes

1 Based on chained (2012) dollars data. BEA online information. Viewed at: https://www.bea.gov/iTable/iTable.cfm?reqid=19&step=2#reqid=19&step=3&isuri=1&1910=x&0=-9&1921=survey&1903=36&1904=2016&1905=2018&1906=a&1911=0.

2 BEA online information. Viewed at: https://www.bea.gov/news/2018/gross-domestic-product-2nd-quarter-2018-advance-estimate-and-comprehensive-update.

3 BEA online information. Viewed at: https://www.bea.gov/iTable/iTable.cfm?reqid=19&step=2#reqid=19&step=3&isuri=1&1921=survey&1903=2.

4 OECD (2018), OECD Economic Surveys, United States, Sustaining Growth and Raising Employment, June 2018. The Overview may be viewed at: http://www.oecd.org/eco/surveys/Overview-United-States-2018-OECD.pdf.

5 OMB (2018), *An American Budget Mid-Session Review*. Viewed at: https://www.whitehouse.gov/wp-content/uploads/2018/07/19msr.pdf.

6 OMB (2018), *Economic Assumptions and Interactions with the [Administration's Fiscal Year 2019] Budget*. Viewed at: https://www.whitehouse.gov/wp-content/uploads/2018/02/ap_2_assumptions-fy2019.pdf.

7 IMF (2018), United States: 2018 Article IV Consultation – Press Release; Staff Report and Statement by the Executive Director for United States. Viewed at: https://www.imf.org/en/Publications/CR/Issues/2018/07/03/United-States-2018-Article-IV-Consultation-Press-Release-Staff-Report-and-Statement-by-the-46048; and OMB (2018), *Economic Assumptions and Interactions with the [Administration's Fiscal Year 2019] Budget*. Viewed at: https://www.whitehouse.gov/wp-content/uploads/2018/02/ap_2_assumptions-fy2019.pdf.

8 IMF (2018), United States: 2018 Article IV Consultation – Press Release; Staff Report and Statement by the Executive Director for United States. Viewed at: https://www.imf.org/en/Publications/CR/Issues/2018/07/03/United-States-2018-Article-IV-Consultation-Press-Release-Staff-Report-and-Statement-by-the-46048.

9 CBO: The Budget and Economic Outlook: 2018 to 2028, April 2018. Viewed at: https://www.cbo.gov/system/files?file=115th-congress-2017-2018/reports/53651-outlook.pdf.

10 CBO: The Budget and Economic Outlook: 2018 to 2028, April 2018. Viewed at: https://www.cbo.gov/system/files?file=115th-congress-2017-2018/reports/53651-outlook.pdf.

11 CBO: The Budget and Economic Outlook: 2018 to 2028, April 2018. Viewed at: https://www.cbo.gov/system/files?file=115th-congress-2017-2018/reports/53651-outlook.pdf.

12 IMF (2018), United States: 2018 Article IV Consultation – Press Release; Staff Report and Statement by the Executive Director for United States. Viewed at: https://www.imf.org/en/Publications/CR/Issues/2018/07/03/United-States-2018-Article-IV-Consultation-Press-Release-Staff-Report-and-Statement-by-the-46048.

13 OMB (2018), *Economic Assumptions and Interactions with the [Administration's Fiscal Year 2019] Budget*. Viewed at: https://www.whitehouse.gov/wp-content/uploads/2018/02/ap_2_assumptions-fy2019.pdf.

14 CBO: The Budget and Economic Outlook: 2018 to 2028, April. Viewed at: https://www.cbo.gov/publication/53651; and OMB (2018), *Economic Assumptions and Interactions with the [Administration's Fiscal Year 2019] Budget*. Viewed at: https://www.whitehouse.gov/wp-content/uploads/2018/02/ap_2_assumptions-fy2019.pdf.

15 IMF (2018), United States: 2018 Article IV Consultation – Press Release; Staff Report and Statement by the Executive Director for United States. Viewed at: https://www.imf.org/en/Publications/CR/Issues/2018/07/03/United-States-2018-Article-IV-Consultation-Press-Release-Staff-Report-and-Statement-by-the-46048.

16 Federal Reserve Board, *Purposes and Functions*. Viewed at: http://www.federalreserve.gov/pf/pf.htm.

17 Federal Reserve Board online information, *Statement on Longer-Run Goals and Monetary Policy Strategy. Adopted effective January 24, 2012; as amended effective January 26, 2016*. Viewed at: https://www.federalreserve.gov/monetarypolicy/files/FOMC_LongerRunGoals_20160126.pdf.

18 Federal Reserve (2018), *Monetary Policy Report - July 2018*. Viewed at: https://www.federalreserve.gov/monetarypolicy/2018-07-mpr-summary.htm.

19 Department of the Treasury, *Macroeconomic and Foreign Exchange Policies of Major Trading Partners of the United States*, April 2018. Viewed at: https://home.treasury.gov/sites/default/files/2018-04/2018-04-13-Spring-2018-FX-Report-FINAL.pdf.

20 IMF (2018), United States: 2018 Article IV Consultation – Press Release; Staff Report and Statement by the Executive Director for United States. Viewed at: https://www.imf.org/en/Publications/CR/Issues/2018/07/03/United-States-2018-Article-IV-Consultation-Press-Release-Staff-Report-and-Statement-by-the-46048.

21 BEA online information. Viewed at: https://www.bea.gov/news/2018/personal-income-and-outlays-june-2018.

22 Department of the Treasury (2018), *Macroeconomic and Foreign Exchange Policies of Major Trading Partners of the United States*, April. Viewed at: https://home.treasury.gov/sites/default/files/2018-04/2018-04-13-Spring-2018-FX-Report-FINAL.pdf; and BEA online information. Viewed at: https://www.bea.gov/data/intl-trade-investment/international-investment-position.

23 BEA online information. Viewed at: http://www.bea.gov.

24 Congressional Research Service (2017), U.S. Direct Investment Abroad: Trends and Current Issues, 29 June 2017. Viewed at: https://fas.org/sgp/crs/misc/RS21118.pdf.

25 Congressional Research Service (2017), U.S. Direct Investment Abroad: Trends and Current Issues, 29 June 2017. Viewed at: https://fas.org/sgp/crs/misc/RS21118.pdf.

Trade and investment regimes

GENERAL FRAMEWORK

The United States Constitution assigns authority over the regulation of foreign trade to Congress. Article I, Section 8, gives Congress the power to "regulate Commerce with foreign Nations…" and to "…lay and collect Taxes, Duties, Imposts, and Excises…".[1] Congress has legislative and oversight authority over trade policy, and works with the Executive Branch to shape and implement trade agreements. Trade legislation is enacted in the same manner as other laws, through passage by both houses of Congress and approval by the President. Generally, multiple Executive Branch agencies are involved in developing and implementing trade policy, therefore interagency coordination is an important part of the process.

Under Article II of the Constitution, the President of the United States has authority to negotiate treaties and international agreements, and exercises broad authority over the conduct of the nation's foreign affairs.[2] If any such agreement requires changes in statutory law, however, it can be implemented only through legislation enacted by Congress.

U.S. law and policy regarding international trade in goods is largely the responsibility of the Federal Government. The U.S. legal regime for services, investment and intellectual property is a combination of federal and state law, with state regulation predominant in certain areas, such as insurance, professional services, and franchising (p. 121). Intellectual property rights issues are covered by federal legislation in the case of patents and copyright, while trademarks are protected by both federal and state laws.

Over time, Congress has delegated to the President the administration of certain trade policy functions. For instance, since the 1930s, Congress has recurrently given the President authority to implement tariff cuts and reductions in other barriers to trade in exchange for trade concessions from other countries.[3] Beginning with the Trade Act of 1974, the Congress has passed several acts providing for trade authorities procedures to be known as the "fast track", and more recently the Trade Promotion Authority (TPA), that provide for the expedited ratification of trade agreements on the condition that the administration fulfil the trade policy priorities and negotiating objectives set by Congress.[4] The current trade authorities procedures are contained in the Bipartisan Congressional Trade Priorities and Accountability Act of 2015 (Title I of Public Law (P.L.) 114–26) (TPA 2015), enacted on 29 June 2015. The procedures were designed to preserve Congress' constitutional role in the regulation of foreign commerce, while offering the President and U.S. trading partners the assurance of an up or down vote within a specific time frame when an agreement is brought before Congress. Without this process, such legislation would follow the general rules of procedure, which would allow Congress to introduce amendments to the implementing legislation of the agreement, which could risk the reopening of negotiations. The TPA also establishes a Congressional requirement for the Executive Branch to notify and consult with Congress, with trade advisory committees, and with the public, when conducting trade agreement negotiations.

In order to be eligible for this fast-track procedure, a trade agreement must be negotiated during the limited time period in which the TPA is in effect. The current Act granting TPA applies with respect to any trade agreement entered into by the United States before 1 July 2018. The TPA timeframe was extended to 1 July 2021 as a result of the President requesting such extension on 20 March 2018, and neither House of Congress adopting an extension disapproval resolution before 1 July 2018.

TRADE POLICY FORMULATION AND OBJECTIVES

Trade policy objectives

The President's 2018 Trade Policy Agenda is driven "to open foreign markets, obtain more efficient global markets and fairer treatment for American workers".[5] The trade policy focuses on five major priorities:

- Adopting trade policies that support U.S. national security policy;

- Strengthening the U.S. economy;

- Negotiating better trade deals that work for all Americans;

- Enforcing U.S. trade laws and U.S. rights under existing trade agreements; and

- Reforming the multilateral trading system.

The Agenda notes that free, fair, and reciprocal trade relations are critical to the U.S. national security policy. It also focuses on strengthening the U.S. economy, and renegotiating and revising trade deals. In terms of reforming the multilateral trading system, the Agenda advocates "for sensible and fair reforms to the WTO, promoting rules for efficient markets, expanded trade, and greater wealth for all nations".[6] The Agenda notes that the United States remains committed to working with all WTO Members who share in the United States' goal of fair and reciprocal trade deals. The Agenda also points to its current negotiations to improve the North American Free Trade Agreement (NAFTA) and the U.S.-Korea Free Trade Agreement (KORUS), as well as its plans for negotiating a trade agreement with the United Kingdom after it leaves the European Union.

Congress outlines the trade negotiating objectives in TPA legislation. For an agreement to qualify for trade

 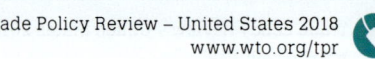

authorities' procedures, it must make progress in achieving the applicable purposes, policies, priorities, and objectives of the TPA. The trade negotiating objectives of the United States are set out in the Bipartisan Congressional Trade Priorities and Accountability Act of 2015; some objectives were added in the Trade Facilitation and Trade Enforcement Act of 2015 (TFTEA). The trade objectives are divided into three categories: overall objectives (broad goals and the general direction trade negotiations are expected to take); principal objectives (considered more specific and politically critical); and capacity building and other priorities (include the provision of technical assistance to trading partners).

The overall trade objectives state the goals of U.S. trade negotiations, including: to obtain more open, equitable, and reciprocal market access; to obtain reductions in barriers to trade and investment which decrease U.S. market opportunities; to strengthen the system of international trade and investment disciplines, including dispute settlement; to foster economic growth and rising living standards, enhanced competitiveness and full employment in the United States, and to enhance the global economy; to ensure trade and environmental policies are mutually supportive; to promote respect for workers' rights; to seek provisions in trade agreements ensuring that they do not weaken or reduce the protections afforded in domestic environmental and labour laws; to ensure equal access to trade opportunities to small and medium-sized enterprises (SMEs); to promote the universal ratification of the International Labour Organization (ILO) Convention concerning the prohibition of child labour; to ensure that trade agreements reflect the interrelatedness and multi-sectoral nature of trade and investment; to recognize the growing significance of the digital economy; to take into account legitimate domestic objectives, such as protection of health, safety, security, and consumer interests, and the laws and regulations pertaining thereto; to take account of the religious freedom of any party negotiating a trade agreement with the United States; to ensure trade agreements do not require changes to immigration laws or obligate the United States to grant access or expand access to visas; and to ensure that trade agreements do not establish obligations regarding greenhouse gas emissions.[7]

In TPA 2015, Congress updated its principal negotiating objectives, including addressing barriers to innovation and digital trade, state-owned enterprises and localization policies. The principal negotiating objectives on services were also expanded by considering the utilization of global chains in the goal of trade liberalization, and calling for liberalized trade in services including through plurilateral trade agreements. In terms of agriculture trade, TPA 2015 added three new negotiating objectives: more detail included on trade rules on sanitary and phytosanitary (SPS) measures; ensuring transparency in tariff-rate quota administration; and seeking to prevent improper use of geographical indications.

Trade policy formulation

The procedure to formulate trade policy in the United States remains the same since the last Review. Trade policy is developed and administered through: Congress; the Executive Branch; independent agencies; and the private and public sectors. Congress also sets trade negotiating objectives and the scope of notifications and consultation requirements for proposed negotiations through the TPA.

In Congress, the House Ways and Means Committee and the Senate Finance Committee have primary responsibility for trade matters, due to the revenue implications in most trade agreements and trade policy changes. Other committees may be involved when they have jurisdiction over a specific legislation that could be affected by a trade agreement. TPA 2015 replaced the Congressional Oversight Group (COG), which had been established by the Trade Act of 2002, with the Congressional Advisory Groups on Negotiations (CAGs). CAGs are established for a House Advisory Group on Negotiations (HAG), presided by the chair of the Ways and Means Committee, and a Senate Advisory Group on Negotiations (SAG), led by the chair of the Finance Committee.

Through its legislative and oversight authority, Congress works together with the Executive Branch, which negotiates and implements trade agreements.

The principal trade advisor to, and negotiator and spokesperson on trade policy for the President is the United States Trade Representative (the USTR). The USTR is also responsible for developing and coordinating United States international trade, commodity, and direct investment policy, and overseeing negotiations with other countries.[8] The USTR reports annually on the President's trade policy agenda and on foreign trade barriers. The main agency responsible for trade policy formulation is the Office of the USTR, which is part of the Executive Office of the President and is headed by the USTR.

USTR deals with all WTO matters, and with trade, commodity, and direct investment issues in the OECD and UNCTAD. It works in consultation with Congress, particularly with the House Ways and Means Committee, the Senate Finance Committee, the five Members from each House who are appointed as official Congressional advisors on trade policy, and other Senators or Representatives who have been appointed as advisors on particular issues or negotiations. It reports annually to Congress, on behalf of the President, on the U.S. trade agreements program and its implementation, including WTO activities. USTR is also in charge of monitoring foreign countries' compliance with trade agreements, representing the United States in dispute settlement procedures in the WTO and under free trade agreements (FTAs), and applying and enforcing certain trade laws. It also administers the Generalized System of Preferences (GSP).

Under the Trade Expansion Act of 1962, Congress established an interagency trade policy mechanism

Part B
Report by the WTO Secretariat

to advise the USTR on trade policy. The mechanism has three tiers: the Trade Policy Committee (Cabinet level), the sub-cabinet-level Trade Policy Review Group (TPRG), and the stafflevel Trade Policy Staff Committee (TPSC). USTR consults with other government agencies on trade policy matters through the TPRG and the TPSC, both composed of 20 federal agencies and offices. Both the TPSC and TPRG are chaired by the USTR, and they consist of staff- and sub-cabinet-level officials, respectively, of the Departments of Treasury, Commerce, State, Agriculture, Labour, Defense, Energy, Health and Human Services, Homeland Security, Interior, Justice, and Transportation; the Environmental Protection Agency; the U.S. Agency for International Development; the Small Business Administration; the Office of Management and Budget; the Council on Environmental Quality; the Council of Economic Advisors; the National Economic Council; and the National Security Council.[9]

The TPSC is the primary operating group, with representation at the senior civil service level. Supporting the TPSC are more than 90 subcommittees responsible for specialized areas, and several task forces that work on particular issues. If agreement is not reached in the TPSC, then issues may be brought to the TPRG or to Cabinet Principals.[10]

The private and public sector also have a role in the formulation of U.S. trade policy through the trade advisory committee system, established by Congress in the Trade Act of 1974. Congress enhanced the role of this system most recently in the Trade Act of 2002. The system was created to ensure that trade policy and trade negotiating objectives adequately reflect public and private sector interests. It also ensures that USTR senior officials receive input from a wide range of public interests. It consists of 26 advisory committees, with up to 1,000 advisors, administered by the USTR's Office of Intergovernmental Affairs and Public Engagement (IAPE) in collaboration with the U.S. Departments of Agriculture, Commerce, and Labor. The system includes: the President's Advisory Committee for Trade Policy and Negotiations (ACTPN)[11]; five general policy advisory committees dealing with environment, labour, agriculture, Africa, and intergovernmental issues; and 20 technical advisory committees in the areas of industry and agriculture.[12] The committees provide information and advice on U.S. negotiating objectives and positions for trade agreement negotiations and other matters arising in connection with the development, implementation, and administration of U.S. trade policy. They are required to prepare a report on proposed trade agreements subject to trade authorities' procedures for the Administration and Congress, which are made public on USTR's website.[13]

TRADE AGREEMENTS AND ARRANGEMENTS

WTO

The United States is an original Member of the WTO. It is a party to the Agreement on Government Procurement

(GPA), a participant in the Information Technology Agreement (ITA) and the expanded Information Technology Agreement (ITAE), and a signatory to the Agreement on Trade in Civil Aircraft. The United States deposited its instrument of acceptance of the Trade Facilitation Agreement (TFA) to the WTO in January 2015.

According to the 2018 Trade Policy Agenda, the WTO is viewed as an important institution, and the United States has a "strong track record of building coalitions of like-minded Members to use the WTO committee system, in particular, to pressure non-complying economies to bring measures into conformity with WTO rules, to advance transparency and predictability in global trade rules, and to avert the need to resort to dispute settlement".[14] Furthermore, the United States views that the WTO has achieved positive results and has the potential to achieve even more in the future. At the same time, the Trade Policy Agenda notes that the United States has long been concerned that the WTO is not operating as the contracting parties envisioned. In addition, the Agenda emphasizes that, if the WTO is to be a vibrant negotiating and implementing forum, Members must take advantage of every opportunity to advance work and seize results as they present themselves.[15]

The Trade Policy Agenda also notes that Members agreed on several important outcomes at the WTO's Eleventh Ministerial Conference in Buenos Aires in December 2017. These outcomes included: the Ministerial decision on fisheries subsidies; a work programme on electronic commerce, including an extension of the moratorium on customs duties on electronic transmissions; and the creation of a working party on accession for South Sudan, among others.[16] Going forward, the United States seeks to work with other WTO Members before the twelfth Ministerial Conference "to begin the process of identifying opportunities to achieve accomplishments, even if incremental ones, and avoid buying into the predictable, and often risky, formula of leaving everything to a package of results for Ministerial action".

The last U.S. TPR took place in 2016, and U.S. trade policies have been reviewed 13 times. The United States submitted numerous notifications during the period under review, covering areas such as agriculture, anti-dumping, subsidies and countervailing measures, SPS, TBT, and import licensing, among others (Table A2.1). The United States also submitted several counter-notifications during the period under review, including one on India's market price support for wheat and rice, its fourth one on China's subsidies, its second one on China's state-trading enterprises (STEs), and one on Viet Nam's STEs.[17]

During the review period, the United States was involved in 13 dispute settlement cases as a complainant (Table A2.2) and 21 cases as a respondent (Table A2.3). During the period under review, the United States has continued to raise concerns with respect to the functioning of the WTO dispute settlement system.[18]

Regional and preferential agreements

Reciprocal agreements

The United States has 14 free trade agreements (FTAs) in force with 20 countries: Australia; Bahrain; Chile; Colombia; Israel; Jordan; Korea, Rep. of; Morocco; Oman; Panama; Peru; Singapore; DR-CAFTA (Costa Rica, Dominican Republic, El Salvador, Guatemala, Honduras, and Nicaragua); and NAFTA (Canada and Mexico). These include 12 bilateral agreements and 2 plurilateral agreements (NAFTA and CAFTA-DR). Most of the agreements cover both goods and services, except the FTA with Israel (goods only). The United States has notified all of its FTAs to the WTO Committee on Regional Trade Agreements.

The United States is renegotiating NAFTA, which came into force on 1 January 1994, with the aim of improving market access for agriculture, expanding investment and intellectual property protections, enhancing regulatory transparency, and including chapters on competition and SMEs, among other things.[19] Through the renegotiation, the Administration has two principal objectives: (a) to modernize the Agreement, including through improved provisions to protect intellectual property and facilitate efficient cross-border trade, among other updates, and through new provisions on digital trade; and (b) to rebalance NAFTA with a view to reducing the U.S. trade deficit with the NAFTA countries.[20] The U.S. Administration's proposals include correcting policies that have encouraged outsourcing, and ensuring strong, enforceable provisions on labour and the environment that will help level the playing field for U.S. workers.[21] In August 2018, the United States and Mexico reached an agreement in principle to modernize NAFTA. The agreement in principle makes amendments to existing provisions on different areas and covers some new issues.[22]

The United States-Korea Free Trade Agreement (KORUS), which came into force on 15 March 2012, is also being renegotiated. The United States and the Republic of Korea reached an agreement in principle in March 2018, which includes outcomes related to truck tariffs, trade in automobiles, and investment. In addition, outcomes to address implementation concerns related to pharmaceuticals and customs were also secured.[23]

The United States withdrew from the proposed Trans-Pacific Partnership (TPP) in 2017.[24] In 2013, the United States and the European Union launched negotiations on the proposed TransAtlantic Trade and Investment Partnership (T-TIP) agreement. At the end of 2016, the negotiations were paused.

Unilateral preferences

Since the Trade Act of 1974, which established the Generalized System of Preferences (GSP), the United States trade preference programmes have provided special duty-free privileges to goods from developing countries which meet certain eligibility criteria. These preference programmes aim to support domestic reforms and economic growth through trade. Currently, the United States has four main programmes: the African Growth and Opportunity Act (AGOA), the GSP, the Caribbean Basin Initiative (CBI)/Caribbean Basin Trade Partnership Act (CBTPA), and the Nepal Trade Preference Program (NTPP). In 2017, each programme's share of total U.S. preferential (non-reciprocal) imports was: GSP, 61.8% (US$21.3 billion); AGOA (excluding GSP), 35.4% (US$12.2 billion); CBI/CBTPA, 2.8% (US$960 million); and NTPP, 0.01% (US$2.4 million). Also, in 2017, imports benefiting from preferential access under these programmes amounted to US$34.5 billion, an 18.7% increase from 2016.[25]

Generalized System of Preferences (GSP)

The GSP is a preference programme designed to promote economic growth in developing and least-developed countries (LDCs) by providing preferential duty-free entry. To qualify for GSP, a beneficiary country must meet mandatory GSP eligibility criteria established by Congress, including respecting arbitral awards, combating child labour, respecting internationally-recognized worker rights, providing adequate and effective intellectual property protection, and providing the United States with equitable and reasonable market access. The programme has effective dates, specified in relevant legislation, and requires periodical reauthorization in order to remain in effect. The GSP expired on 31 December 2017; legislation to renew it (the Consolidated Appropriations Act, 2018, P.L. 115-141) was enacted on 23 March 2018, and extended the programme from 1 January 2018 to 31 December 2020.[26]

The GSP programme currently provides duty-free treatment for over 3,500 products (based on eight-digit U.S. Harmonized Tariff Schedule tariff lines (HTSUS)) from 121 developing countries and an additional 1,500 products from 44 LDCs. GSP rules of origin require that a good must be either obtained or sufficiently manufactured in a GSP beneficiary country, and at least 35% of the appraised value of the product must have been added in the beneficiary country. Products eligible for duty-free entry are presented in the HTSUS, published by the United States International Trade Commission (USITC). Under the programme, eligible products include: selected manufactured and semi-manufactured goods; certain agricultural and fishery products; and several types of chemicals, minerals, and building materials. The programme does not grant duty-free entry to certain sensitive imports, such as textiles and apparel, watches, most footwear, certain glassware, and some gloves and leather products.

GSP country and product eligibility are subject to an annual review conducted by the GSP Subcommittee of the TPSC, which receives and considers requests seeking to add or remove products from the duty-free list under the GSP. Any person may petition the GSP Subcommittee to request modifications to the list of

Part B
Report by the WTO Secretariat

countries eligible for GSP treatment, and modifications are made following the annual review, and are implemented by Presidential Proclamation.

The 2018 Trade Policy Agenda placed new emphasis on enforcement of the GSP eligibility criteria, to ensure that all countries receiving GSP benefits are meeting the criteria established by Congress. This new effort includes a triennial assessment by the USTR and other relevant agencies of each GSP beneficiary country's compliance with the statutory eligibility criteria.[27] This interagency process complements the current petition and public input process for country practice reviews, which will remain unchanged.

During the period under review, Argentina was reinstated as a beneficiary developing country on 1 January 2018, and Seychelles, Uruguay, and the Bolivarian Republic of Venezuela were officially graduated from GSP status on 1 January 2017. In addition, Ukraine's GSP status was partially suspended; this became effective 120 days after the Presidential Proclamation issued on 22 December 2017; the transition period granted to provide Ukraine the opportunity to improve its protection of intellectual property rights. Cases for GSP eligibility are open for: Indonesia and Uzbekistan (intellectual property rights); the Plurinational State of Bolivia, Georgia, Iraq, Kazakhstan, Thailand and Uzbekistan (worker rights and/or child labour concerns); India, Indonesia, and Thailand (market access); and Ecuador (arbitral awards). An application for new GSP benefits for Laos is pending.[28]

In 2017, the top GSP products (by value) imported into the United States were: motor vehicle parts (US$1.3 billion); ferroalloys (US$769 million); precious metal jewellery (US$756 million); monumental or building stone (US$557 million); and rubber tyres (US$480 million). The leading developing country exporters (by value) to the United States under the GSP programme in 2017 were India, Thailand, Brazil, Indonesia, and Turkey. In addition, LDC exporters were led by Cambodia, Myanmar, Democratic Republic of Congo, Nepal, and Mozambique.

The African Growth and Opportunity Act (AGOA)
The AGOA was enacted on 18 May 2000 (P.L. 106-200).[29] It provides eligible sub-Saharan African countries with duty-free market access for more than 5,000 product tariff lines, by opening 1,800 product tariff lines beyond those already eligible for duty-free treatment under the GSP. Therefore, the AGOA provides tariff benefits well beyond those available under the GSP. The additional products under the AGOA include apparel and footwear, wine, certain motor vehicle components, a variety of agricultural products, chemicals, and certain steel products, among other products. The AGOA expires in 2025. In 2017, the leading AGOA exporters were Nigeria, Angola, South Africa, Chad, and Kenya. Mineral fuels, motor vehicles and parts, woven apparel, ferroalloys, and knit apparel were the top U.S. imports under the AGOA programme.[30] Total U.S. goods

imported from sub-Saharan Africa were US$24.9 billion in 2017, up 23.7% from 2016. Total imports under the AGOA were US$6.2 billion in 2017, a 58% year-on-year increase from 2016. In the same year, GSP imports from Africa increased 11.2%. In 2018, 40 sub-Saharan African countries are eligible for AGOA benefits.[31]

The AGOA requires the U.S. President to determine annually the eligibility of a sub-Saharan African beneficiary country, based on criteria established by Congress. These criteria require, among other things, a country to have established, or make continual progress toward establishing: (i) political pluralism, the rule of law, and a market-based economy; (ii) elimination of barriers to U.S. trade and investment; (iii) protection of internationally recognized worker rights; (iv) a system to combat corruption and bribery; and (v) economic policies to reduce poverty. AGOA criteria also require that countries not engage in gross violations of internationally recognized human rights. On 22 December 2017, the U.S. President reinstated The Gambia and Eswatini (formerly Swaziland) as AGOA beneficiaries, effective 1 January 2018.

The legislation that extended the AGOA through 2025 established a petition process to allow an interested party to petition the Government regarding whether an AGOA beneficiary is meeting eligibility requirements. On 20 June 2017, an out-of-cycle review of Rwanda, Tanzania, and Uganda's AGOA eligibility was initiated in response to a petition. As a result of the actions undertaken by Tanzania and Uganda to address the concerns raised in the petition, the U.S. President determined that both countries meet the AGOA's eligibility requirements. On 30 July 2018, the President determined that Rwanda was out of compliance with the AGOA's eligibility requirements, and issued a proclamation suspending the application of duty-free treatment for all AGOA-eligible apparel products from Rwanda, effective 31 July 2018.

Caribbean Basin Initiative (CBI)
The CBI provides beneficiary countries with duty-free access to the U.S. market for many goods. Initially launched in 1983 by the Caribbean Basin Economic Recovery Act (CBERA) and substantially expanded in 2000 with the U.S.-Caribbean Basin Trade Partnership Act (CBTPA), the CBI was further expanded in the Trade Act of 2002. In 1990, the CBERA was made permanent. The CBTPA is scheduled to expire on 30 September 2020.[32] There are 17 CBERA beneficiary countries, 8 of whom are also beneficiaries under the CBTPA. U.S imports from CBI beneficiary countries in 2017 totalled US$5.9 billion, while U.S. exports were US$12.2 billion in the same year.

The United States provides additional apparel and textile benefits to Haiti through the Haitian Hemispheric Opportunity through Partnership Encouragement Act of 2006 ("HOPE Act"), the Haitian Hemispheric Opportunity through Partnership Encouragement Act of

2008 ("HOPE II"), and the Haiti Economic Lift Program Act of 2010 ("HELP Act"). These preferences are scheduled to expire on 30 September 2025.

In December 2017, the USTR submitted its twelfth biannual report to Congress on the operation of CBERA.[33] On an annual basis, the USTR is required to submit a report to Congress regarding the implementation of HOPE II.[34]

The Nepal Trade Preference Program (NTPP)

The Nepal Trade Preference Program (NTPP) provides duty-free entry to the United States for certain products imported from Nepal. Under Section 915 of the Trade Facilitation and Trade Enforcement Act (TFTEA) of 2015, passed by Congress in February 2016, the United States may grant duty-free access for 66 eight-digit HTSUS tariff lines from Nepal. The programme was implemented by Presidential Proclamation on 15 December 2016, and provides non-reciprocal preferential trade benefits to Nepal until 31 December 2025. These preferences were provided to assist Nepal in its recovery from the April 2015 earthquake and subsequent aftershocks. Due to changes in the U.S. Harmonized Tariff System, the number of eight-digit tariff lines for which Nepal is exempt from customs duties increased in July 2016 to 77. Of these, 31 are also duty free under the GSP scheme. The remainder were not GSP-eligible at the time. In 2017, the first full year the NTPP had been in place, total imports under the programme were US$2 million, and accounted for 2.5% of total imports from Nepal; the largest import products included hats and headgear (US$778,000) and shawls and scarves (US$453,000).[35]

INVESTMENT REGIME

During the review period, the U.S. foreign investment regime remained unchanged. Despite the investment regime being open, there are some sector-specific limitations, with review procedures on foreign investment in a few industries, including the airline and nuclear energy industries. Additionally, the United States has a national security review process applicable to foreign investment that might affect national security interests.

International investment agreements are used in the United States to foster foreign investment. These agreements include trade and investment framework agreements (TIFAs), bilateral investment treaties (BITs), and FTAs that contain investment provisions. TIFAs provide frameworks for dialogue on trade and investment issues between the United States and the other parties to the TIFA, and are generally the first step in establishing stronger trade and investment links. The objective of these agreements is to develop opportunities for the United States and partner countries to enhance opportunities for trade and investment. Topics for cooperation usually include: market access issues; labour; environmental protection; and the enforcement of intellectual property rights.[36]

BITs are at the core of promoting a rules-based system for international investment. These treaties may contain provisions on non-discriminatory treatment of investments by the host country, limits on expropriation of investments, and access to impartial binding procedures to settle investment-related disputes with host governments, among other things. BITs, as international treaties, only require Senate ratification, unlike FTAs which require a vote in Congress on implementing legislation. FTA investment chapters generally contain provisions identical or similar to those in BITs. Of the 14 FTAs signed by the United States, 12 contain investment provisions.

SelectUSA, established in 2011[37], is a government programme led by the Department of Commerce to promote inward investment in the United States.[38] The programme has two main stakeholders: foreign-owned firms considering investing in the United States, and U.S. economic development organizations (EDOs) seeking to attract high-impact FDI. The services it provides include information, counselling, and advisory services; ombudsman assistance; investment advocacy; and marketing and promotion through global events.

For analytical and statistical purposes, the International Investment and Trade in Services Survey Act requires that U.S. businesses report all foreign direct investment to relevant authorities if a foreign person (or foreign entity) owns 10% or more of the voting interest in a U.S. entity.[39] The Bureau of Economic Analysis, in the Department of Commerce, collects information on FDI to compile statistics on the scale of foreign-owned business activities in the United States and the effects these activities have on the U.S. economy.

The Committee on Foreign Investment in the United States (CFIUS) continues to oversee the national security implications of foreign investment. CFIUS is an inter-agency committee authorized to review transactions that could result in control of a U.S. business by a foreign person ("covered transaction"), in order to determine the effect of such transactions on the national security of the United States.[40] CFIUS was established by Executive Order 11858 in 1975, with the primary responsibility of monitoring the impact of foreign investment in the United States. In 1988, Congress passed the "Exon Florio" amendment, which gives CFIUS the authority to review and approve, or approve with conditions, covered transactions and gives the President the authority to prohibit or suspend covered transactions that threaten national security.[41] The Foreign Investment and National Security Act of 2007 (P.L. 110-49) strengthened Exon-Florio and enhanced the CFIUS process, in order to enable greater oversight by Congress and increase transparency and reporting by the Committee on its decisions. In addition, the Act broadened the factors considered in determining whether a transaction poses a national security risk[42], and required greater scrutiny by CFIUS of certain types of FDI.[43]

CFIUS reviews transactions based on voluntary notifications filed by the parties, or on its own initiative in the absence of a voluntary notification if it believes the transaction is a covered transaction and may raise national security concerns. Each transaction is reviewed on a case-by-case basis based on individual facts and circumstances. Once a formal notification is submitted, CFIUS conducts an initial review. If during the initial review period CFIUS cannot make a final determination, the case will proceed to an investigation phase. If national security concerns are identified during the review and investigation phase, CFIUS may impose conditions, or CFIUS and the transacting parties may negotiate a mitigation agreement to resolve any national security concerns. If CFIUS determines that the national security concerns cannot be resolved and the parties do not withdraw and abandon the transaction, the Committee will recommend that the President prohibit the transaction.

In 2015, 143 notices were filed with CFIUS and 66 transactions were subject to investigation (Table 2.1). The number of notices decreased slightly from 2014, although the number of investigations increased.

In the period 2013-15 (latest data available), the manufacturing sector accounted for the largest number of industry reviews by CFIUS (172 out of a total 387). Within the manufacturing sector, 43% of all the investment transactions notified to CFIUS between 2013 and 2015 were in the computer and electronic products sectors. This was followed by the machinery; transportation equipment; and electrical equipment, appliance, and component manufacturing sectors. There were 112 reviews regarding finance, information, and services industries; 66 reviews with respect to mining, utilities, and construction; and 37 of wholesale trade and retail trade transactions. According to data based on notices provided to CFIUS by foreign investors, Chinese investors were the most active in the number of filings during the 2013-15 period, followed by Canada, the United Kingdom, Japan and France. With respect to China, investment notifications were concentrated in the following sectors: manufacturing; finance, information, and services; and mining, utilities, and construction. Investment notifications from Canada were focused on the mining, utilities, and construction sector, and the United Kingdom had its largest number of filings in manufacturing.

Table 2.1 Foreign investment "covered transactions" reviewed by CFIUS, 2013-15

Year	Number of notices	Notices withdrawn during review	Number of investigations	Notices withdrawn during investigation	Presidential decisions
2013	97	3	48	5	0
2014	147	3	51	9	0
2015	143	3	66	10	0
Total	387	9	165	24	0

Source: Annual Report to Congress, Report Period CY 2015, Committee on Foreign Investment in the United States, September 2017.

Table 2.2 Origin of foreign investor and industry reviewed by CFIUS, 2013-15

Partner	Manufacturing	Finance, information, and services	Mining, utilities, and construction	Wholesale trade and retail trade	Total
China	39	15	13	7	74
Canada	9	9	19	12	49
United Kingdom	25	15	3	4	47
Japan	20	12	5	4	41
France	8	9	1	3	21
Germany	9	5	0	0	14
Netherlands	4	8	2	0	14
Switzerland	10	2	0	0	12
Singapore	3	5	3	1	12
Hong Kong, China	6	3	0	0	9
Israel	7	2	0	0	9
Australia	1	2	4	1	8
South Korea	2	3	2	1	8
Other	31	22	14	4	71
Total	172	112	66	37	387

Source: Annual Report to Congress, Report Period CY 2015, Committee on Foreign Investment in the United States, September 2017.

Endnotes

1   The Constitution of the United States, Article I, Section 8.

2   The Constitution of the United States, Article II, Section 2.

3   Under the Reciprocal Trade Agreements Act of 1934, Congress delegated authority to the President to modify or reduce tariffs up to 50%, in exchange for reciprocal concessions negotiated with U.S. trading partners. The renewal of this authority was the base for U.S. participation in the early GATT rounds of tariff negotiations. The Act was extended 11 times. When negotiations in the GATT advanced to include non-tariff measures, Congress extended the President's tariff proclamation authority, and also put in place fast-track procedures, first enacted in the Trade Act of 1974. Under these procedures, Congress agreed to expedited consideration and vote, without amendment, on trade legislation submitted by the President to implement trade agreements, provided that the President notified and consulted with Congress over the course of the negotiation according to prescribed rules.

4   United States Trade Representative (USTR) online information. Viewed at: https://ustr.gov/trade-topics/trade-promotion-authority, and the Bipartisan Congressional Trade Priorities and Accountability Act of 2015, Senate Report, 12 May 2015, p. 4. Viewed at: https://www.finance.senate.gov/imo/media/doc/TPA%20Report%20as%20filed.pdf.

5   USTR (2018), *2018 Trade Policy Agenda and 2017 Annual Report of the President of the United States on the Trade Agreements Program*. Viewed at: https://ustr.gov/sites/default/files/files/Press/Reports/2018/AR/2018%20Annual%20Report%20FINAL.PDF.

6   USTR online information, *2018 Trade Policy Agenda and 2017 Annual Report of the President of the United States on the Trade Agreements Program*. Viewed at: https://ustr.gov/sites/default/files/files/Press/Reports/2018/AR/2018%20Annual%20Report%20FINAL.PDF.

7   Bipartisan Congressional Trade Priorities and Accountability Act of 2015 (Title I of Public Law (P.L.) 114–26). Viewed at: https://www.congress.gov/114/plaws/publ26/PLAW-114publ26.pdf.

8   USTR online information, "Mission of the USTR". Viewed at: https://ustr.gov/about-us/about-ustr.

9   USTR online information, "Mission of the USTR". Viewed at: https://ustr.gov/about-us/about-ustr.

10   USTR online information, "Mission of the USTR". Viewed at: https://ustr.gov/about-us/about-ustr.

11   The President appoints up to 45 ACTPN members administered by the USTR for two-year terms. The 1974 Trade Act requires that membership broadly represent key economic sectors affected by trade.

12   USTR online information, "Advisory Committees". Viewed at: https://ustr.gov/about-us/advisory-committees; and "Mission of the USTR". Viewed at: https://ustr.gov/about-us/about-ustr.

13   USTR online information, "Mission of the USTR". Viewed at: https://ustr.gov/about-us/about-ustr.

14   USTR (2018), *2018 Trade Policy Agenda and 2017 Annual Report of the President of the United States on the Trade Agreements Program*. Viewed at: https://ustr.gov/about-us/policy-offices/press-office/reports-and-publications/2018/2018-trade-policy-agenda-and-2017.

15   USTR (2018), 2018 Trade Policy Agenda and 2017 Annual Report of the President of the United States on the Trade Agreements Program. Viewed at: https://ustr.gov/about-us/policy-offices/press-office/reports-and-publications/2018/2018-trade-policy-agenda-and-2017.

16   USTR (2018), *2018 Trade Policy Agenda and 2017 Annual Report of the President of the United States on the Trade Agreements Program*. Viewed at: https://ustr.gov/about-us/policy-offices/press-office/reports-and-publications/2018/2018-trade-policy-agenda-and-2017.

17   WTO documents G/AG/W/174, 9 May 2018; G/SCM/Q2/CHN/71, 19 April 2017; G/C/W/749 and G/STR/Q1/CHN/9, 13 December 2017; and G/C/W/750 and G/STR/Q1/VNM/4, 11 January 2018, respectively.

18   See for example, WTO documents WT/DSB/M/409, 6 June 2018; WT/DSB/M/412, 1 August 2018; and WT/DSB/M/413, 31 August 2018.

19   USTR online information. Viewed at: https://ustr.gov/about-us/policy-offices/press-office/press-releases/2017/november/ustr-releases-updated-nafta.

20   USTR (2018), *2018 Trade Policy Agenda and 2017 Annual Report of the President of the United States on the Trade Agreements Program*. Viewed at: https://ustr.gov/sites/default/files/files/Press/Reports/2018/AR/2018%20Annual%20Report%20FINAL.PDF.

21   USTR (2018), *The President's Trade Agenda and Annual Report*, Fact Sheet. Viewed at: https://ustr.gov/sites/default/files/uploads/factsheets/USTR%20-%20POTUS%20Trade%20Agenda%20-%20Fact%20Sheet%20-%20FINAL.pdf.

22   USTR (2018), *United States–Mexico Trade Fact Sheet Modernizing NAFTA into a 21ˢᵗ Century Trade Agreement.* Viewed at: https://ustr.gov/about-us/policy-offices/press-office/fact-sheets/2018/august/united-states%E2%80%93mexico-trade-fact-sheet-1; *United States–Mexico Trade Fact Sheet Strengthening North American Trade in Agriculture*. Viewed at: https://ustr.gov/about-us/policy-offices/press-office/fact-sheets/2018/august/united-states%E2%80%93mexico-trade-fact-sheet-0; and *United States–Mexico Trade Fact Sheet Rebalancing Trade To Support Manufacturing*. Viewed at: https://ustr.gov/about-us/policy-offices/press-office/fact-sheets/2018/august/united-states%E2%80%93mexico-trade-fact-sheet.

23   USTR online information. Viewed at: https://ustr.gov/about-us/policy-offices/press-office/press-releases/2018/march/joint-statement-united-states-trade.

24   USTR (2018), *2018 Trade Policy Agenda and 2017 Annual Report of the President of the United States on the Trade Agreements Program*. Viewed at: https://ustr.gov/sites/default/files/files/Press/Reports/2018/AR/2018%20Annual%20Report%20FINAL.PDF.

25   USITC DataWeb. Viewed at: https://dataweb.usitc.gov/ [7 August 2018].

26   The Consolidated Appropriations Act, effective 22 April 2018, provided for the retroactive extension of GSP benefits for eligible goods having entered during the period 1 January 2018 through 21 April 2018. Viewed at: https://www.cbp.gov/trade/priority-issues/trade-agreements/special-trade-legislation/generalized-system-preferences.

27   USTR online information. Viewed at: https://ustr.gov/about-us/policy-offices/press-office/press-releases/2017/october/ustr-announces-new-enforcement.

28 USTR online information. Viewed at: https://ustr.gov/issue-areas/trade-development/preference-programs/generalized-system-preference-gsp/current-review-0.

29 P.L. 106–200. Viewed at: https://agoa.info/images/documents/2/AGOA_legal_text.pdf.

30 USTR (2018), *2018 Biennial Report on the Implementation of the African Growth and Opportunity Act*. Viewed at: https://ustr.gov/sites/default/files/2018%20AGOA%20Implementation.pdf.

31 USTR online information. *Fact Sheet: African Growth and Opportunity Act: 2018 Biennial Report*. Viewed at: https://ustr.gov/about-us/policy-offices/press-office/fact-sheets/2018/june/fact-sheet-african-growth-and-opportunity.

32 USTR online information. Viewed at: https://ustr.gov/issue-areas/trade-development/preference-programs/caribbean-basin-initiative-cbi.

33 USTR (2017), *Twelfth Report to Congress on the Operation of the Caribbean Basin Economic Recovery Act*. Viewed at: https://ustr.gov/sites/default/files/assets/reports/2017%20CBI%20Report.pdf.

34 The latest HOPE II Report is available at: https://ustr.gov/sites/default/files/2018%20USTR%20Report%20Haiti%20HOPE%20II.PDF.

35 USTR (2018), *2018 Trade Policy Agenda and 2017 Annual Report of the President of the United States on the Trade Agreements Program*. Viewed at: https://ustr.gov/sites/default/files/files/Press/Reports/2018/AR/2018%20Annual%20Report%20FINAL.PDF.

36 USTR online information. "Trade and Investment Framework Agreements". Viewed at: https://ustr.gov/trade-agreements/trade-investment-framework-agreements.

37 Established in 2011 by Executive Order. Viewed at: https://obamawhitehouse.archives.gov/the-press-office/2011/06/15/executive-order-13577-selectusa-initiative.

38 About SelectUSA. Viewed at: https://www.selectusa.gov/about-selectusa.

39 P.L. 94-472. Viewed at: https://www.gpo.gov/fdsys/pkg/USCODE-2011-title22/html/USCODE-2011-title22-chap46.htm.

40 Treasury online information. Viewed at: https://www.treasury.gov/resource-center/international/foreign-investment/Documents/CFIUS-Final-Regulations-new.pdf.

41 The Exon-Florio Provision was implemented in 1988 and is covered under Section 721 of the Defence Production Act of 1950.

42 The term national security includes issues relating to homeland security, including its application to critical infrastructure. The term critical infrastructure includes "systems and assets, whether physical or virtual, so vital to the United States that the incapacity or destruction of such systems or assets would have a debilitating impact on national security". Viewed at: https://www.congress.gov/110/plaws/publ49/PLAW-110publ49.pdf.

43 On 13 August 2018, the Foreign Investment Risk Review Modernization Act of 2018 (FIRRMA) was enacted, modernizing and strengthening the CFIUS process.

Trade policies and practices by measure

MEASURES DIRECTLY AFFECTING IMPORTS

Customs procedures, valuation, and requirements

Introduction

Since the passage of the Customs Modernization Act (P.L. 103-182) in 1993, compliance with customs rules has been regarded as a joint responsibility between the Government and traders, and measures have been put in place gradually to facilitate this partnership. The Department of Homeland Security (DHS) was created in 2002 among efforts to safeguard the United States against terrorism; its new border security agency, the U.S. Customs and Border Protection (CBP), was formed in 2003 by merging the legacy organizations of the U.S. Customs Service with other services overseeing the cross-border movement of goods and persons. Nonetheless, some 30 federal agencies continue to be involved in trade enforcement activities on the Government's side.

Provisions to constitute a body of the trade community were included in the Omnibus Budget Reconciliation Act of 1987, and the current Commercial Customs Operations Advisory Committee (COAC) is mandated by the Trade Facilitation and Trade Enforcement Act of 2015 (P.L. 114-125). The role of the 20-member COAC is to provide advice on any aspect of the commercial operations of CBP and related Treasury and DHS functions. It meets periodically with CBP officials to discuss the balance of security and trade facilitation measures. The present COAC has held quarterly meetings open to the public since April 2015. The COAC has formed six subcommittees covering the following topics: One U.S. Government at the Border; safe and expedited movement of cargo through the Global Supply Chain; Exports (procedures, enforcement, and facilitation issues); input for the Trusted Trader Program of CBP; Trade Modernization; and Trade Enforcement and Revenue Collection. Moreover, the subcommittees have established working groups to examine specific issues in further detail, including emerging technologies and e-commerce.

The United States formally accepted the WTO Agreement on Trade Facilitation (TFA) on 23 January 2015. Since the entry into force of the TFA on 22 February 2017, the United States has, as a developed country Member, been bound by all the commitments contained in the Agreement. It provided its notification on transparency, the operation of its single window, measures on the use of customs brokers, and TFA contact point in June 2017.[1] The Office of the United States Trade Representative (USTR) leads an interagency National Trade Facilitation Committee that organizes coordination and implementation of the TFA as part of its responsibilities to develop, coordinate, and implement trade policy. This is the national committee on trade facilitation for Article 23.2 of the TFA.[2] More than 20 federal agencies participate in the national committee, including the Departments of Agriculture, Commerce, Defense, Energy, Health and Human Services, Homeland Security (including CBP), Interior, Justice, Labor, State, Transportation, and Treasury; the Environmental Protection Agency, the Small Business Administration, and the U.S. Agency for International Development (USAID). Input from the private sector is mainly sought through the Industry Trade Advisory Committee (ITAC) on Customs Matters and Trade Facilitation. For agricultural trade issues, the national committee is aided by an Agricultural Policy Advisory Committee as well as six technical advisory committees.

Single window

The planning of an Automated Commercial Environment (ACE) to ensure proper assessment and collection of duties and taxes was initiated in 1994. It was initially foreseen to be deployed gradually between 1998 through 2005. The Security and Accountability for Every Port Act of 2006 (P.L. 109-347) subsequently called for the establishment of a "single portal" International Trade Data System (ITDS) to, among other things, enhance the enforcement of laws and regulations related to trade, and eliminate redundant information requirements. After several unsuccessful efforts to complete ACE as a single window application, including a complete standstill of work in 2010, CBP switched its focus to the development and launch of "core capabilities" in ACE in small consecutive stages from 2013. Consistent with an Executive Order issued in February 2014, the end of 2016 was set as the new deadline for the completion of the single window for import and export processing.[3] The Executive Order also mandated the creation of a Border Interagency Executive Council (BIEC) to enhance coordination between the border management authorities. The Trade Facilitation and Trade Enforcement Act of 2015 reinforced the deadline, as it called for all core trade processing capabilities to be included in ACE by 30 September 2016.

The mandatory filing of all electronic manifests in ACE took effect on 1 May 2015, and the obligatory filing of other data was introduced gradually during 2016. At the same time CBP began to phase out its legacy Automated Commercial System (ACS) to support the new system. However, it became apparent that the deadline for the completion of ACE would slip during summer 2016. After further delays, CBP announced in June 2017 that the remaining sets of core capabilities would be launched in three stages, the final stage ending in February 2018. The deployment of core capabilities was finalized on 24 February 2018 with the inclusion in ACE of post-release functions covering reconciliation, liquidation, and drawback.[4]

The Lacey Act (16 U.S.C. §§ 3371–3378) is a conservation law that combats trafficking in wildlife, fish, and plants, and Lacey Act declarations (PPQ Form 505) are required for the importation of certain plants and plant products. CBP encourages such declarations to be filed electronically, and more than 90% of them are currently filed in ACE. In the event that declarations are filed in hard copy, CBP will not forward the paper forms to the U.S Department of Agriculture's (USDA) Animal and Plant Health Inspection Service (APHIS) but will return them to the importer (or his agent) for onward submission. Areas still requiring paper forms include Kimberley Certificates for conflict diamonds, and ATF Form 6 for imports of firearms.

According to CBP, the elimination of paper-based procedures through ACE has automated 269 forms used by CBP and its 47 partner government agencies, including the 22 partner agencies that require documentation to verify and release cargo for import or export.[5] Among the many positive effects, ACE is credited with having speeded up the processing of bond applications by around 68 times, and having cut the waiting time for the processing of trucks at land ports of entry by 44%. The estimated savings from CBP investments in automated and streamlined systems, including ACE, is said to have reduced importation costs by 1.42% on average, or US$6.5 billion in total, in FY2016.[6] As for the costs of deploying ACE, CBP expenditures totalled US$3.81 billion through FY2017, and a further US$890 million is estimated to be needed for maintenance and further development until 2026, i.e. through the anticipated life cycle of ACE.[7]

The United States Government Accountability Office (GAO) released a report to the Congressional Committees on ACE in March 2018.[8] Regarding the organization of future work on ACE, the GAO noted some differences of opinion between CBP and other users of ACE as to whether certain functions not included in ACE at present could be considered core capabilities and, in the absence of a cost-sharing strategy, would need to be funded by CBP. Moreover, it noted that a process for the establishment of priorities in the further improvement of ACE had not been established. In response to the report, CBP agreed to work with the BIEC to develop a cost-sharing plan for the operation, maintenance, and further development of ACE, including a mechanism to prioritize all ACE/Single Window enhancements. The plan for the interagency approach to the post-core management of ACE, which utilizes a pay as you go model, should be finalized by 31 October 2018.

Other trade facilitation measures

Customs-Trade Partnership Against Terrorism (C-TPAT) was launched in November 2001 as a voluntary public private partnership programme (PPP) to strengthen international supply chains and to improve security along U.S. borders. C-TPAT was codified in 2006 through the Security and Accountability for Every Port Act of 2006.

It spans the entire community engaged in cross-border trade including U.S. importers and exporters, foreign manufacturers (Mexico and Canada), licensed customs brokers, transporters and carriers (air, rail, highway, and sea), and transportation intermediaries. The application to join C-TPAT, performed online at: https://ctpat.cbp. dhs.gov/trade-web/registerUser.html, is as such free of charge. However, by joining it, the applicant agrees to protect the supply chain, identify potential security gaps, and implement specific security measures and best practices.

On the basis of the Company Profile and Security Profile submitted by the applicant, CBP will determine the company's ability to fulfil the minimum security requirements set by C-TPAT, and arrange for an on-site inspection of the company's security practices. Enterprises found to satisfy the C-TPAT requirements upon inspection are validated as Tier II companies and eligible for the full benefits of the programme. A higher level (Tier III) is reserved for companies that employ security measures above and beyond the minimum requirements of C-TPAT.

Participation in C-TPAT does not pre-empt security examinations of cargo at the border, but Tier II and III companies are considered to be of low risk and may therefore be exempt from stratified exams, their merchandise is inspected with much less frequency, and priority access and expedited procedures apply at the border. C-TPAT members may be eligible to participate in pilot programmes of CBP partner agencies such as the Secure Supply Chain Program of the U.S. Food and Drug Administration.

Participation in the Free and Secure Trade (FAST) programme, a commercial clearance programme for low-risk shipments entering the United States from Canada or Mexico, requires all elements of the supply chain (i.e. manufacturers, carriers, drivers, and importers) to be enrolled in C-TPAT. CBP inspects and validates the supply-chain security measures of the foreign C-TPAT members on a regular basis. Truck drivers who are U.S., Canadian or Mexican citizens may enrol in FAST and use the streamlined procedures of dedicated FAST lanes at 34 land border crossings. More than 78,000 commercial drivers have joined the programme. The processing fee for a five-year membership in FAST is US$50/Can$50. The fee applies only to drivers.

Importers that are C-TPAT members, reside in the United States or Canada, and have a minimum of two years import experience, may also submit a memorandum of understanding (MoU) to CBP to join the Importer Self-Assessment Program (ISA). By signing the MoU and completing an ISA questionnaire, the importer, *inter alia,* agrees to comply with all applicable customs law and regulations; establish, document, and implement internal controls; conduct regular risk-based tests of the internal systems and make appropriate adjustments (as necessary); and confirm, once a year, that all ISA requirements continue to be met. In return, the importer is exempted from all comprehensive compliance audits, has access to a dedicated customs team (account manager, auditor, and trade analyst), and receives various other benefits including expedited cargo release and enhanced prior disclosure. CBP has established Centers of Excellence and Expertise at 10 points of entry across the United States, and the Centers serve as single points of processing with priority access for enterprises that participate in C-TPAT and the ISA.

CBP began the development of its Centers of Excellence and Expertise as a test programme in 2012. At the end of 2016, CBP decided to make the Centers a permanent organizational component with effect from 19 January 2017.[9] The Centers specialize in all aspects of the customs processing of a particular industry. The centralization of the decision-making authority implies, for example, that the Los Angeles office handles imports and exports for the electronics industry, while the Miami office deals with the agricultural sector. In general, importers are assigned to their respective centres based on the predominant (HS four-digit) classification of the types of goods that they are importing.

Participation in the C-TPAT of the United States also provides recognition as a trusted trade partner by foreign customs administrations that have signed mutual recognition agreements (MRAs) with the United States. Consistent with the SAFE Framework of Standards to Secure and Facilitate Global Trade of the World Customs Organization, CBP has security-based arrangements in force with 11 other customs administrations. The last such MRA was signed with the Dominican Republic on 7 December 2015. Joint work plans towards mutual recognition have been signed with China, Peru, Uruguay, Brazil, India, and Australia. As of July 2018, the number of C-TPAT operators totalled 11,549, including 4,112 importers, 352 exporters, and 1,695 foreign manufacturers.[10]

Upon request, CBP issues binding advance rulings on how it will treat a prospective import or carrier transaction. Advance rulings are not provided on hypothetical issues or on matters subject to ongoing litigation. The ruling control number should be indicated (or a copy of the ruling provided) with the filing of the entry documents at the time of importation. Advance rulings must be requested by letter for decisions concerning valuation or carriers, whereas requests pertaining to tariff classification or certain marking, country of origin, NAFTA, AGOA, and other trade programme rulings may be submitted online to the National Commodity Specialist Division (NCSD) of Regulations and Rulings (in New York). The NCSD confirms receipt of properly filed requests within one business day and generally aims at issuing its eRulings within 30 calendar days of receipt. Requests that require referral to Regulations and Rulings headquarters are issued by mail, normally within 90 days of receipt. CBP issued more than 4,500 rulings in 2017. The CBP inventory of advance rulings and other binding decisions may be consulted at its Customs Rulings On-line Search

(CROSS) facility (http://rulings.cbp.gov/).[11] Rulings are also published in the weekly Customs Bulletin and Decisions (http://www.cbp.gov/trade/ rulings/bulletin-decisions), or in some cases through pertinent notices in the Federal Register.

For goods shipped to the United States by ocean vessel, certain advance cargo information must be submitted electronically in the form of an Importer Security Filing (ISF - commonly known as "10+2").[12] The requirement applies to goods destined for the customs territory of the United States or to a Foreign Trade Zone (FTZ) located in the United States. Information regarding the seller, buyer, importer of record number (or FTZ applicant identification number), and consignee number must be provided no later than 24 hours before the cargo is laden aboard the vessel in the foreign port. Information pertaining to the manufacturer (or supplier), country of origin, HS tariff line number, and ship to party must be indicated prior to departure, and the ISF may be updated to include precise data on these elements no later than 24 hours prior to the arrival of the cargo in the United States. Information regarding the container stuffing location and the consolidator must also have been provided by that time. The purpose of the filing requirement is to allow CBP to identify in advance high-risk shipments prone to smuggling or giving rise to other potential safety and security issues.

About 80% of all maritime cargo destined to the United States is pre-screened at foreign ports under the Container Security Initiative (CSI). Launched in 2002, the CSI is authorized under the 2006 SAFE Port Act (PL 109-347). It is operational at 61 ports world-wide. All containerized cargo deemed high-risk is inspected manually by using large scale non-intrusive imaging (NII) and radiological detection equipment. Further to Section 232 of the Act, the Secure Freight Initiative (SFI) was launched, in an effort to test the feasibility of 100% scanning of cargo awaiting shipment to the United States at selected ports. However, all pilot ports, with the exception of Qasim (Pakistan), were reverted to targeting for high-risk cargo after an evaluation of the costs versus potential benefits and various other concerns.

Foreign Trade Zones (FTZs)

FTZs have been established in every U.S. State, although some of the designated FTZs may be without activity at any given moment. FTZs are located at, or close to, U.S. ports of entry, in industrial parks, or at terminal warehouse facilities, but FTZ subzones or "usage driven sites" may be created in any designated area, including on the private facility of a user. Goods may be brought into the zones for processing, or held for storage and exhibition purposes. In 2016, active operations were carried out in 195 out of 263 approved FTZs, and the 3,300 firms that used FTZ facilities employed more than 420,000 workers.[13]

FTZs are proposed, sponsored, and managed by agencies at the regional and local level. However, decisions to establish or modify FTZs are taken centrally by the Foreign-Trade Zones Board in accordance with the Foreign Trade Zones Act (19 U.S.C. 81a-81u) of 18 June 1934. Proposed sites for FTZ activation must be approved by CBP prior to the Board's decision, and activities carried out in the zones remain under close CBP supervision. FTZs are legally outside the customs territory of the United States. Thus, formal customs entries are not filed for foreign goods, no customs duties are levied, and U.S. excises and other taxes may be deferred. Domestic goods brought into the zones are considered exported, and excise tax rebates and duty drawback may be claimed for such goods. For foreign goods subject to processing in FTZs before entry into the customs territory of the United States, the owner may choose between payment of import duty on the finished product or on the original foreign materials. Apart from customs matters, FTZs are geographically part of the United States, and federal and local laws apply within them. FTZ activities are governed by regulations issued by the Foreign-Trade Zones Board and CBP (15 CFR Part 400 and 19 CFR Part 146). Since January 2009, expanding general-purpose FTZs have had the option to reorganize their zones under the Alternative Site Framework, offering a more flexible link between the designated FTZ space and the space activated with CBP.

Retail trade is prohibited in FTZs, and manufacturing or processing must be specifically authorized by the Foreign-Trade Zones Board. The processing activities typically combine significant amounts of domestically-produced goods with foreign inputs. In 2016, the value of domestic status merchandise constituted 63% of the total value goods brought into the zones (US$610 billion), and the ratio was markedly higher for production (72%) than for warehousing and distribution activities (48%).[14] Oil refining, motor vehicle parts, electronics, and pharmaceuticals constitute the main industrial output of FTZs. Based on the value of the entering merchandise, the most important FTZs are located in Texas, Louisiana, and California. Net direct exports from FTZs amounted to US$75.7 billion in 2016, a decline of nearly US$25 billion since the peak year 2014.[15] Falling oil prices, which also affect the value of refined products, was the main factor behind this decline.

Bonded warehouses

About 1,500 bonded warehouses exist across the United States. As set forth in Title 19 U.S.C. Section 1555, customs bonded warehouses are buildings or other secured areas where imported merchandise may be stored, manipulated, or undergo manufacturing operations without payment of import duty, but are subject to a warehouse bond covering the customs liability when goods enter a warehouse.[16] Import duty is not collected until the goods are withdrawn for consumption in the United States, which must occur within five years from the date of importation unless extended upon request. Alternatively, the merchandise

may be exported, withdrawn for supply to a vessel or aircraft, or destroyed under CBP supervision.

Applications to establish a bonded warehouse are addressed to the local CBP port director. Applications should indicate the general nature of the goods to be kept in storage and include an estimate of the maximum duties and taxes due on the stored goods at any time. CBP does not charge application or supervisory fees for bonded warehouses, but the warehouse operator is responsible for the safekeeping of goods held in custody, and the facilities must be available for CBP inspection at any time. Imported merchandise and goods for export may be stored simultaneously at a bonded facility, but must be separated physically in accordance with security measures approved by the port director.

Customs valuation

Title II of the Trade Agreements Act of 1979 (45 FR 45135) subjects goods imported into the United States to a uniform system of valuation, stipulating the transaction value as the principal and preferred method of appraisement. The hierarchy of alternative valuation methods is presented in sequential order as laid down in the WTO Customs Valuation Agreement. Customs value excludes transportation and landed costs.

The Trade Agreements Act of 1979 implemented the Customs Valuation Agreement negotiated in the Tokyo Round. In 1996, the United States notified the WTO that the legislation it had notified to the GATT had not been changed and thus remained valid under the WTO Customs Valuation Agreement.[17] No changes have been made to the customs valuation regulations during the period under review.

Marking requirements

In accordance with longstanding laws and regulations, the United States requires every article of foreign origin to be legibly marked to indicate the English name of the country of origin to an ultimate purchaser in the United States.[18] These rules are distinct and separate from eligibility determinations for customs purposes. Additional labelling requirements apply to specific products, e.g. clothing (fabric content and washing instructions), tobacco (Warning Statement of the Surgeon General), food, pharmaceuticals, and motor vehicles.

Rules of origin

Non-preferential

U.S. non-preferential rules of origin distinguish between "wholly obtained" products, i.e. those entirely grown, produced or manufactured in a particular country, and goods that have been subject to "substantial transformation", i.e. a change in name, character or use, in the country of origin. The substantial transformation criterion is applied case-by-case. For certain transactions, CBP may also use value added or change in nature or essential character of a product to determine the country of origin. The United States notified its non-preferential rules of origin to the WTO in 1995 and administrative rulings of the U.S. Customs Service in 1996.[19]

Preferential

Each FTA concluded by the United States has its own set of origin criteria. The variety of methods applied reflects the outcome of the negotiations, including industry preferences for particular methods, notably in textiles. NAFTA and other FTAs concluded by the United States have incorporated a change in tariff classification ("tariff shift") method to determine the eligibility for FTA benefits. However, it also uses other methods, e.g. local/regional value content or technical criteria, to determine origin beyond the "wholly obtained" criterion. Importers claiming preferential tariff treatment must certify the origin of the good and present certificates of origin or other supporting documents when requested by CBP. NAFTA prescribes a specific format for the certificates of origin, but most other FTAs or preferential agreements do not.

The United States notified preferential rules of origin to the WTO in 1995, and again in 2013.[20] Minor changes to the preferential rules of origin may be introduced from time to time.

Tariffs

The Harmonized Tariff Schedule of the United States (HTSUS) is published and maintained by the U.S. International Trade Commission (USITC). The tariff schedule is updated regularly to reflect changes in applied tariff rates and other provisions, including preferential rules of origin. Goods are classified according to the Harmonized System nomenclature of the World Customs Organization (WCO) in Chapters 1 through 97, and Chapters 98 and 99 are added to specify special duty treatment (with or without quantitative limits) pertaining to certain goods, such as imports by non-profit institutions, commitments under FTAs and the AGOA, and temporary tariff remissions. Importers claiming special treatment must identify the tariff line number (within HS Chapters 1 to 97), as well as the functional number within Chapters 98 and 99.

The United States implemented the 2017 edition of the nomenclature established under the International Convention on the Harmonized Commodity Description and Coding System effective 1 January 2017. The revised U.S. nomenclature was consistent with the Recommendation of 27 June 2014 of the WCO. As for the corrections and complementary amendments to HS Chapter 44, contained in a WCO Recommendation of 11 June 2015, the United States obtained a WTO waiver to implement these changes until 31 December 2017.[21] It implemented these changes in Presidential Proclamation 9771 of 30 July 2018, effective on 1 October 2018.[22]

Schedule XX contains the WTO tariff commitments of the United States. The last modifications to Schedule XX were undertaken in 2016 to incorporate the formal adherence of the United States to the Declaration on the Expansion of Trade in Information Technology Products.[23] The United States remains under waiver to implement changes stemming from HS2012.[24] Over the years, various changes to the HTSUS have not been notified to the WTO as changes to Schedule XX, including Chapter Notes, the Article XXVIII renegotiation (tobacco), and the third and fourth revisions to the pharmaceutical coverage.

In Schedule XX, the United States has bound all its tariffs (except for two tariff lines) and all "other duties and charges" (ODCs) within the meaning of Article II.1(b) of the GATT. Left unbound for reasons of national security, the two tariff lines concern crude petroleum (HS 2709.00.10 and 2709.00.20).[25] Except for seven tariff lines, all ODCs are bound at zero.

Applied rates

The current HTSUS, in effect since 1 January 2018, has 10,878 tariff lines at the eight-digit level. The three-column tariff distinguishes between imports from trading partners that are subject to either: (i) the general rate (i.e. MFN treatment), (ii) "special" duty (i.e. preferential treatment) stemming from unilateral or reciprocal agreements and arrangements[26], or (iii) other (i.e. higher) import duty.[27] The MFN rates are mostly *ad valorem,* but specific and compound duty rates are applied for approximately 11% of the tariff lines (predominantly agriculture, fish, fuels, textiles, and footwear items). The MFN rates are generally identical to their bound levels and have remained virtually unchanged for 10 years or more.

The MFN tariff regime is generally characterized by stable and, for the most part, low or no tariffs. At 4.8% overall, the simple average tariff remains virtually unchanged year by year (Table 3.1).[28] Duty-free entry is provided for 37.5% of all tariff lines, and a further 30.4% of the line items face import duty of 5% or less (Chart 3.1).[29] The highest tariffs (i.e. above 100% *ad valorem* or estimated *ad valorem* equivalent (AVE)) affect certain agricultural items, in particular dairy products, peanuts, and tobacco. Outside of agriculture, above-average applied rates are mainly found in textiles, clothing and footwear (Tables 3.1 and A3.1). Overall, the U.S. tariff structure shows little or no tariff escalation.

The United States has not been granting temporary tariff suspensions for several years, as the enabling legislation for such relief on several hundred products of interest to U.S. manufacturers expired at the end of 2012.[30] The American Manufacturing Competitiveness Act of 2016 (H.R. 4923) introduced a new procedure for the consideration of temporary tariff suspensions and reductions. Petitions for relief are addressed to the USITC, which examines them and invites comments from the public. Key criteria to be evaluated with respect to petitions include (i) whether the petition is enforceable by CBP; (ii) whether the estimated revenue loss associated with the petition would exceed US$500,000; and (iii) whether there is domestic production and objections

Table 3.1 Structure of the tariff schedules, selected years[a]

(%)

		2009	2012	2014	2016[b]	2018[c]
1.	Total number of tariff lines	10,253	10,511	10,514	10,516	10,878
2.	Non-*ad valorem* tariffs (% of all tariff lines)	10.7	10.9	10.9	10.9	10.6
3.	Non-*ad valorem* with no AVEs (% of all tariff lines)	0.0	0.0	0.0	0.0	0.0
4.	Lines subject to tariff quotas (% of all tariff lines)	1.9	1.9	1.9	1.9	1.9
5.	Duty free tariff lines (% of all tariff lines)	36.3	37.0	36.8	36.8	37.5
6.	Dutiable lines tariff average rate (%)	7.6	7.5	7.6	7.6	7.8
7.	Simple average tariff (%)	4.8	4.7	4.8	4.8	4.8
8.	WTO agriculture	8.9	8.5	9.0	9.1	9.4
9.	WTO non-agriculture (incl. petroleum)	4.0	4.0	4.0	4.0	4.0
10.	Agriculture, hunting, forestry and fishing (ISIC 1)	5.7	5.6	6.7	6.5	5.8
11.	Mining and quarrying (ISIC 2)	0.4	0.4	0.4	0.4	0.4
12.	Manufacturing (ISIC 3)	4.8	4.7	4.8	4.8	4.8
13.	First stage of processing	3.7	3.7	4.3	4.3	3.9
14.	Semi-processed products	4.2	4.2	4.2	4.2	4.2
15.	Fully processed products	5.3	5.2	5.3	5.3	5.4
16.	Domestic tariff "peaks" (% of all tariff lines)[d]	6.7	6.7	6.7	6.7	6.7
17.	International tariff "peaks" (% of all tariff lines)[e]	5.3	5.0	5.1	5.1	5.1
18.	Overall standard deviation	11.8	11.9	13.7	14.0	13.6
19.	Applied rates greater than 0% but inferior or equal to 2%. (% of tariff lines)	7.2	7.7	7.8	7.8	7.7
20.	Bound tariff lines (% of all tariff lines)[f]	100.0	100.0	100.0	100.0	100.0

a   The tariff is provided at the 8-digit level. Averages exclude in-quota rates and lines. Calculations include AVEs for non-*ad valorem* duties that were calculated by the authorities using import price data.

b   As of January 2016.

c   As of February 2018.

d   Domestic tariff peaks are defined as whose exceeding three times the overall average applied rate.

e   International tariff peaks are defined as those exceeding 15%.

f   Two lines applying to crude petroleum are not bound.

Source: WTO Secretariat calculations, based on data provided by the authorities and notifications.

have been raised by a domestic supplier or other party. Based on more than 2,500 petitions filed between 15 October and 12 December 2016, the USITC prepared a preliminary report in June 2017 and a final report for Congressional consideration in August 2017.[31] The USITC recommended that duty suspensions be accorded to more than 1,600 products, mostly chemicals. The House of Representatives approved the Miscellaneous Tariff Bill Act of 2018 (H.R. 4318) in January 2018. The Miscellaneous Tariff Bill Act of 2018 was approved with amendments by the Senate in July 2018 (S.Amend. 3664). After reconciliation, the Miscellaneous Tariff Bill Act was submitted to the President, who signed it on 13 September 2018. The tariff suspensions are valid until the end of 2020.

Tariff rate quotas

The 54 tariff-rate quotas (TRQs) maintained by the United States cover approximately 1.9% of the tariff lines in the HTSUS (Table 3.1). Among them, 19 TRQs concern the dairy sector (dried milk, butter, butter oil, cream, cheeses, ice cream, etc.), and 6 cover cotton. Other imports subject to TRQs include beef, peanuts and peanut butter, sugar, chocolate, cocoa, olives, mandarin oranges (satsumas), animal feed, and tobacco. Fill rates may vary significantly between the TRQs and over time as a result of differing market conditions. Quotas with low fill rates are generally administered on a first come, first served basis.[32]

Other charges affecting imports

Customs user fees

The principal customs user fee is the Merchandise Processing Fee (MPF), equal to 0.34674% of the customs value (not including duty, freight, or insurance charges) of formally declared commercial imports.[33] Although the fee is *ad valorem* and its rate has remained unchanged in the period under review, the prescribed minimum and maximum levels of the MPF were adjusted upwards on 1 January 2018 to US$25.67 and US$497.99, respectively. For informal entries, e.g. personal imports and commercial imports valued at less than US$2,500, the MPF is not applied *ad valorem,* but at flat rates depending on whether the customs entries are (i) entirely automated (US$2.05); (ii) prepared manually, but not by CBP staff (US$6.16); or (iii) requiring preparation by CBP officials (US$9.24). The MPF is not levied on express and postal shipments, e.g. the receipt of online orders from abroad, below the *de minimis* threshold of US$800.[34] Instead, a fee capped at US$1.03 (minimum US$0.36) is charged for each waybill or bill of lading. Some of the preferential trade programmes of the United States and many of its FTAs include provisions that exempt such imports from the MPF.[35]

The Consolidated Omnibus Reconciliation Act of 1985 (PL 99-272) (COBRA) - introduced a number of customs user fees, including fees for processing and inspection services. The Fixing America's Surface Transportation

Chart 3.1 Frequency distribution of MFN tariff rates, 2018

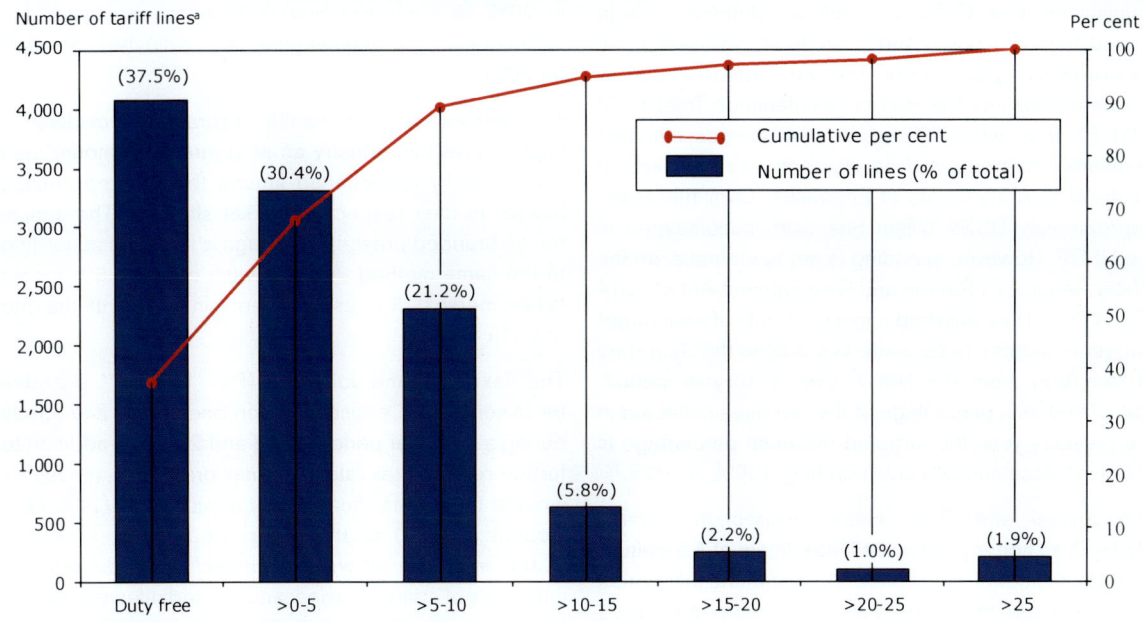

a   The total number of lines is 10,878.

Source: WTO Secretariat calculations based on data provided by the authorities.

Table 3.2 COBRA fees, applicable from 1 January 2018

Fee	Reference	Fee rate/annual decal/cap/ user fee	Note
Commercial vessel	19 CFR 24.22(b)(1)	US$448.70/US$6,114.46 (cap)	
Commercial vehicle	19 CFR 24.22(c)	US$5.65/US$102.68 (annual cap)	
Rail cars	19 CFR 24.22(d)	US$8.47/US$102.68 (prepay)	
Private aircraft/vessel	19 CFR 24.22(e)	US$28.24 (annual decal)	
Air/sea passenger	19 CFR 24.22(g)	US$5.65 (per arrival)	Exemption for Canada, Mexico, and U.S. territories, possessions or adjacent islands
Cruise vessel and ferry passenger travel from Canada, Mexico, and U.S. territories, possessions or adjacent islands	19 CFR 24.22(g)(ii)	US$1.98 (per arrival)	
Dutiable mail	19 CFR 24.22(f)	US$5.65 (per dutiable package)	
Customs broker permit	19 CFR 24.22(c)	US$141.70 (annual fee)	
Barge/bulk carriers from Canada and Mexico	19 CFR 24.22(b)(2)(i)	US$112.95/US$1,540.17 (cap)	

Source: WTO (2016), updated according to the relevant announcement in the Federal Register (82 FR 50659).

Act of 2015 (PL 114-94) (FAST Act) - subsequently amended COBRA by requiring the user fees to be adjusted periodically to account for inflation, taking 2014 as the base year. CBP accordingly determined that these fees should be increased by 2.677% for fiscal year 2018 with effect from 1 January 2018. COBRA fees are collected for services such as the issuance of annual customs broker permits, the treatment of dutiable mail, and the processing of private vessels, commercial trucks, and passengers and cargo arriving by air, sea or rail. The fees vary according to the mode of transport and

may be collected for each passage or on a yearly basis with the use of decals or transponders (Table 3.2).[36]

The Water Resources Development Act of 1986 (P.L. 99-662) established a harbour maintenance fee, thereby requiring users (i.e. importers, exporters, and passengers) to contribute to the upkeep of U.S. ports and harbours. The collection of the tax on exports was discontinued in 1998, as the Supreme Court ruled that such practice was unconstitutional. Currently, the tax, collected by CBP on loading or unloading from commercial cargo or passenger cruise vessels, amounts to 0.125% of the value of waterborne commercial cargo, i.e. imports, admissions into FTZs, as well as domestic cargo moved between ports, and 0.125% of the ticket price for cruise ship passengers. The proceeds from the tax are deposited into the Harbor Maintenance Trust Fund (HMTF), from which Congress appropriates amounts to maintain harbours and development work carried out by the U.S. Army Corps of Engineers. Over the years, approximately US$9 billion has been accumulated in the HMTF. However, spending is set to increase, as the Water Resources Reform and Development Act of 2014 (P.L. 113-121) established minimum levels of total target budget resources to be made available to the Secretary of the Army from the HMTF over a 10-year period. Calculated as a percentage of the revenues collected in the previous year, the targeted minimum percentage is set to increase annually until reaching 100% in 2025.[37]

The Animal and Plant Health Inspection Service (APHIS), an agency within the Department of Agriculture (USDA), collects Agriculture and Quarantine Inspection (AQI) fees and shares them with CBP under an agreed allocation. The fees were amended in late 2015, in response to a 2013 report from the GAO, to improve the alignment of fee revenues with programme costs.[38] The alignment led to significantly lower fees for some services (railway cargo and international air passengers) but markedly higher charges for aircraft clearance, commercial vessels, and trucking fees. A new fee for the treatment of pests of quarantine significance prescribed by APHIS is being phased in over a five-year period. The fee, US$142 in 2018, is set to rise to US$237 as from 28 December 2019.[39] Fees are also collected for veterinary and laboratory services (Table 3.3).

Excise taxes

Excise taxes may be levied at the federal, state, local, or municipal level, and some products are taxed at more than one level. More than 100 excise taxes are maintained at the federal level (Table 3.4). The revenue from these taxes are either dedicated to specific purposes (trust funds) or held for general expenditure (general funds). Goods taxed at state or local level include fuels, cigarettes and other tobacco products, and alcoholic beverages. Rates vary widely from state to state. Excise taxes are applied equally to imported and domestically produced goods and services.

Excise taxes have been accounting for a steadily declining share of Federal Government revenue, and their current share is somewhat less than 3%.[40] The most important revenue-raising taxes, each contributing more than US$10 billion annually, are the excise taxes on motor fuels, domestic air tickets, tobacco, and alcoholic beverages, and the yearly fee on health insurance providers.[41] Many excise taxes have a permanent legal basis, while others would expire at regular intervals unless renewed. For example, the excise tax on crude oil for the Oil Spill Liability Trust Fund, which had expired at the end of 2017, was reinstated effective 1 March 2018

until the end of the year at the same rate as that applied in 2017 (9 cents per barrel). Taxes on domestic and international air passengers are adjusted annually for inflation.

The annual fee for health insurance providers is imposed on the industry as an aggregate amount, and subsequently apportioned among the covered entities based on their respective market shares.[42] The annual fee on branded prescription drugs is imposed according to the same method. A moratorium on the 2.3% excise tax on medical devices is currently in force until the end of 2019.[43]

The Tax Cuts and Jobs Act (P.L. 115-97)[44] provides for lower federal excise taxes on beer, wine, and spirits during a two-year period (2018 and 2019). In addition to further reduced tax rates for small producers, measures include the reclassification of certain wines (14%-16% alcohol content) to the lower tax bracket; extension of tax credits to all wineries, including producers and importers of sparkling wine; and relaxed rules on tax-free transfers of production between manufacturers.

Import prohibitions, restrictions, and licensing

Prohibitions and restrictions

CBP enforces laws that may prohibit or restrict the importation of certain goods on behalf of over 40 federal agencies. Importation may be: (i) prohibited outright; (ii) allowed under certain conditions; or (iii) subject to special requirements such as designated ports of entry or routing restrictions (Table A3.2).

The National Oceanic and Atmospheric Administration's National Marine Fisheries Service (NOAA Fisheries) issued its final rule regarding the establishment of a Seafood Import Monitoring Program (SIMP) in December 2016.[45] The Program is set up pursuant to the Magnuson-Stevens Fishery Conservation and Management Reauthorization Act (MSRA) of 2006 to cover imported fish and fish products at particular risk of illegal, unreported, and unregulated (IUU) fishing and seafood fraud. It requires the importers of record to obtain an annual International Fisheries Trade Permit (IFTP), report data on the harvest of fish and fish products, retain additional supply chain data, and retain the records supporting their import filings for a period of two years. The harvest and landing documentation for U.S. imports (and exports) is filed electronically through the Automated Commercial Environment of the U.S. International Trade Data System (ITDS). SIMP may eventually cover additional seafood products.[46] However, the Program has been introduced for 13 "priority species" identified as particularly vulnerable to IUU fishing or seafood fraud, including tunas (albacore, bigeye, skipjack, yellowfin, and bluefin), swordfish, sharks, Atlantic and Pacific cod, grouper, red snapper, and sea cucumber. Although SIMP is only applicable to imported seafood, similar reporting requirements also apply to domestic capture fisheries

Table 3.3 Agricultural fees, applicable since 28 December 2015

Fee	Legal reference	Reason	Amount of fee
AQI Aircraft Clearance	Food, Agriculture and Conservation Act of 1990; also MOU	Agricultural quarantine and inspection services	US$225.00 per arrival
AQI Commercial Cargo Vessel	Food, Agriculture and Conservation Act of 1990; also MOU	Agricultural quarantine and inspection services	US$825.00 per arrival
AQI Commercial Truck	Food, Agriculture and Conservation Act of 1990; also MOU	Agricultural quarantine and inspection services	US$7.55 per arrival
AQI Commercial Truck with transponder (one annual payment)	Food, Agriculture and Conservation Act of 1990; also MOU	Agricultural quarantine and inspection services	US$301.67
AQI Commercial Vessel (Cruise) Passenger	Food, Agriculture and Conservation Act of 1990; also MOU	Agricultural quarantine and inspection services	US$1.75 per arrival
AQI International Air Passenger	Food, Agriculture and Conservation Act of 1990; also MOU	Agricultural quarantine and inspection services	US$3.96 per arrival
AQI Loaded Rail Car	Food, Agriculture and Conservation Act of 1990; also MOU	Agricultural quarantine and inspection services	US$2.00 per arrival
AQI Treatment	Food, Agriculture and Conservation Act of 1990; also MOU	Agricultural quarantine and inspection services	First year: US$47.00 Second year: US$95.00 Third year: US$142.00 Fourth year: US$190.00 Fifth year: US$237.00
Avocado Import Assessment	7 CFR 1219.54	Avocado research, promotion, consumer information	US$0.025 per pound
Beef Import Assessment	7 CFR Part 1260	Beef research, promotion, consumer information	Varies according to the product and HTS code
Blueberry Import Assessment	7 CFR 1218.52	Blueberry research, promotion, consumer information	US$0.01984 per kg
Christmas Tree Import Assessment	7 CFR 1214.52	Christmas tree research, promotion, consumer information	US$0.15 per Christmas tree
Cotton Import Assessment	Cotton Research and Promotion Act of 1989 7 CFR 1205	Cotton research, promotion, consumer information	Varies according to the product and HTS number
Dairy Import Assessment	7 CFR Part 1150	Dairy research, promotion, consumer information	US$0.01327 per kg of milk solids
Honey Import Assessment	7 CFR 1212.52	Honey research, promotion, consumer information	Varies according to the product and HTS number
Mango Import Assessment	7 CFR 1206.42	Mango research, promotion, consumer information	US$0.0075 per pound
Mushroom Import Assessment	Food, Agriculture and Conservation Act of 1990 7 CFR 1209	Mushroom research, promotion, consumer information	Varies according to the product and HTS number
Paper and Packaging Import Assessment	7 CFR 1222.52	Paper and packaging research, promotion, consumer information	US$0.00000386 per kg
Pork Import Assessment	7 CFR Part 1230	Pork research, promotion, consumer information	Varies according to the product and HTS number
Potato Import Assessment	Food, Agriculture and Conservation Act of 1990 7 CFR 1207	Potato research, promotion, consumer information	Varies according to the product and HTS number
Raspberry Import Assessment	7 CFR 1208.52	Raspberry research, promotion, consumer information	Varies according to the product and HTS number
Softwood Lumber Import Assessment	7 CFR 1217.52	Softwood lumber research, promotion, consumer information	US$0.1483 per cubic metre
Veterinary Diagnostic User Fees	9 CFR 130.14 through 130.19	Costs for tests from the national Veterinary Services Laboratories	Varies depending on the type of test
Veterinary Services User Fees	9 CFR 130.2 through 130.30	Costs for veterinary services	Varies by type of service
Watermelon Import Assessment	Watermelon Research and Promotion Act 7 CFR 1210	Watermelon research, promotion, consumer information	Varies according to the product and HTS number

Source: CBP online information. Viewed at: http://www.cbp.gov/sites/default/files/documents/userfee0407_3.pdf and https://www.aphis.usda.gov/aphis/ourfocus/business-services/user_fees/aqi_user_fees; and information provided by the authorities.

Part B
Report by the WTO Secretariat

Table 3.4 Federal excise taxes

Fund/subject	Products
Trust funds	
Highway Trust Fund	Petrol, diesel, and alcohol fuels; ethanol, liquid fuel, ethanol, methanol, bio-diesel, CNG, LPG, LNG, other special fuels, highway tractors, heavy trucks, trailers, tyres for heavy vehicles, highway use by heavy vehicles
Airport and Airway Trust Fund	Domestic and international air passengers transportation, air cargo, aviation fuels[a]
Inland Waterways Trust Fund	Diesel fuel and other liquid fuels
HMTF	Commercial cargo
Leaking Underground Storage Tank Trust Fund Excise Tax	Certain fuels; methanol and ethanol fuels produced from coal
Oil Spill Liability Trust Fund	Crude oil and imported petroleum products
Sport Fish Restoration and Boating Trust Fund	Fishing rods, reels, and other fishing equipment, motorboat fuel, small-engine fuel
Land and Water Conservation Fund	Bows and arrows, regular firearms and ammunition, motorboat fuel
Black Lung Disability Trust Fund	Coal
Vaccine Injury Compensation Trust Fund	Certain taxable vaccines
Patient-Centered Outcomes Research Trust Fund	Specified health insurance policy; self-insured plans
Medicare Part B Trust Fund	Annual fee on branded prescription pharmaceutical manufacturers and importers
General funds	
Distilled spirits, wine, and beer	Distilled spirits, wine (including champagne and hard apple cider), and beer
Tobacco	Tobacco products, cigarette papers and tubes
Communications	Local telephone service, local teletypewriter service, and telephone cards (local-only service)
Gas guzzlers	Automobiles (tax is related to vehicle fuel economy rating)
Water transportation passengers	Per passenger per covered voyage on commercial vessels
Ozone-depleting chemicals	Certain CFC and related chemicals
Foreign procurement	Specified federal procurement payments
Health care	Indoor tanning services; certain medical devices; and health insurance providers
Non-regular firearms	Machine guns, destructive devices, sawed off shotguns, etc.
Wagering	Tax on the amount of wager and on persons engaged or employed in business of accepting wagers
Domestic private foundation net investment income	Tax on tax-exempt and taxable foundations
Foreign private foundation net investment income	Tax on gross investment income from sources within the United States
Insurance policies issued by foreign insurers	Insurance (tax on premium paid)

a   26 U.S.C. 4221 provides for an exemption, based on reciprocity, from U.S. excise taxes on fuel for civil aircraft engaged in foreign trade with the United States and any of its possessions, where the Department of Commerce has made a finding that a foreign country allows, or will allow, substantially reciprocal privileges in respect of aircraft registered in the United States.

Note: Excise taxes related to certain private foundations, excess lobbying expenses, real estate investment, "golden parachutes", or miscellaneous regulatory excise taxes are not included as they are not trade related.

Source: Joint Committee on Taxation (2015), *Present Law and Background Information on Federal Excise Taxes*, 13 July. Viewed at: https://www.jct.gov/publications.html?func=showdown&id=4798.

and aquaculture. SIMP entered into force for 11 of the 13 species on 1 January 2018.[47] As for the two remaining priority species (abalone and shrimp), the effective date has been delayed for one year, as the enforcement of SIMP for these two species is linked to the establishment of appropriate reporting and/or record-keeping disciplines for the domestic aquaculture production of abalone and shrimp.

Section 607 of the High Seas Driftnet Fishing Moratorium Protection Act (PL 104-43) requires the Secretary of Commerce to provide a biennial report to Congress identifying countries whose fishing vessels are engaged in IUU fishing, or whose fishing activities result in bycatch of certain protected living marine resources, or whose vessels are engaged in shark fishing on the high seas under certain practices. NOAA Fisheries then engages with countries thus identified to seek improvement in their fisheries management and enforcement practices. Following a two-year consultative process, the countries receive either a positive or negative certification that the fishing activities for which they were identified have been adequately addressed. The consequences of a negative certification include U.S. port restrictions and potential import restrictions on certain fish and fish products from the country concerned.[48]

Import licensing

The United States has provided two notifications covering its import licensing regime in the period under review.[49] The system, applied in accordance with various statutes and for various purposes, has remained stable (Table A3.3). Seven agencies enforce import licensing: the Departments of Agriculture, Commerce (steel), Energy (natural gas), Interior (fish and wildlife), and Justice (firearms, explosives, and drugs), the Treasury (alcohol and tobacco), and the Nuclear Regulatory Commission. Licences are either automatic or non-automatic. The Steel Import Monitoring and Analysis System (SIMA), a programme operated under the authority of the International Trade Administration (ITA) of the Department of Commerce, is designed to provide statistical data seven weeks in advance of when it would normally become available. Dating back to 2002, the original programme has been extended at regular intervals. SIMA was prolonged until 21 March 2017 further to a decision taken in 2013[50], and a further extension – until 21 March 2022 – was announced on 5 January 2017.[51] No additional changes have been made in the monitoring programme other than its extension.

Controls, special procedures, or diplomatic measures

The Office of Foreign Assets Control (OFAC) of the U.S. Department of the Treasury administers nearly 30 programmes that involve economic and trade sanctions directed against specific countries or measures generally designed to counter terrorism, transnational criminal organizations, cyber-related crimes, drugs trafficking, human rights abuses, corruption, trade in rough diamonds, or the proliferation of weapons of mass destruction. Due to the many sanctions programmes that target individuals and entities (rather than jurisdictions), OFAC maintains a current Specially Designated Nationals and Blocked Persons (SDNs) list on its website that identifies the individuals and entities whose assets are frozen under its authorities. The SDN list currently contains around 6,400 individuals and entities that U.S. persons are precluded from dealing with regardless of location. Beyond the main SDN list, OFAC also maintains some other lists identifying individuals or entities subject to sanctions other than asset freezes.[52] Countries with the broadest set of sanctions levied against their business include the Democratic People's Republic of Korea (DPRK), Iran, Syria, Sudan, and Cuba. Programmes related to Myanmar and Côte d'Ivoire were terminated in 2016.

The current sanctions programmes targeting the DPRK, introduced in 2008, have been tightened in successive steps. On 21 September 2017, the President issued Executive Order 13810, which, *inter alia,* contained new prohibitions related to aircraft and vessels and provided additional broad designation authority, including authority to target foreign financial institutions. The Countering America's Adversaries Through Sanctions Act (CAATSA), signed into law on 2 August 2017 (P.L. 115-44), included measures that, *inter alia,* prohibit the importation of goods produced with DPRK labour. CAATSA also tightened sanctions applicable to Iran, directed against its military capability and as a response to human rights issues. The United States lifted nuclear-related sanctions on Iran in early 2016 as part of a Joint Comprehensive Plan of Action (JCPOA) agreed between Iran and the United States and its partners on 14 July 2015.[53] The President announced on 8 May 2018 the end of U.S. participation in the JCPOA.

Although an easing of certain policies, including sanctions, against Cuba took place during 2015 and 2016, the embargo essentially remained in place. As a result of the National Security Presidential Memorandum on Strengthening the Policy of the United States Toward Cuba of 16 June 2017, the Cuban Assets Control Regulations (CACR) have been amended with effect from 9 November 2017. The changes seek to, among others: "end economic practices that disproportionately benefit the Cuban Government or its military, intelligence, or security agencies or personnel at the expense of the Cuban people; ensure adherence to the statutory ban on tourism to Cuba; support the economic embargo of Cuba; amplify efforts to support the Cuban people through the expansion of Internet services, free press enterprise and association, and lawful travel; advancing Cuban human rights; and encouraging the growth of a Cuban private sector independent of government control."[54]

Title IV of the Trade Act of 1974 (known as the Jackson-Vanik amendment) is still applied with respect to Azerbaijan, Belarus, Cuba, Kazakhstan, People's Democratic Republic of Korea, Tajikistan, Turkmenistan, and Uzbekistan. Following the accessions of Tajikistan and Kazakhstan to the WTO, Congress needs to pass legislation to allow the United States to grant permanent normal trade relations (PNTR) to these two countries.

Anti-dumping, countervailing, and safeguard measures

Anti-dumping and countervailing measures

Legal and administrative framework

Main laws and regulations

Title VII of the Tariff Act of 1930, as amended by the Trade Agreements Act of 1979 contains the main U.S legislation with respect to anti-dumping (AD) and countervailing duties (CVD). The Trade and Tariff Act of 1984, the Omnibus Trade and Competitiveness Act of 1988, and the Uruguay Round Agreements Act of 1994 (URAA) introduced further modifications to AD and CVD legislation. The main regulations governing AD and CVD investigations (including reviews) are included in Title 19 of the Code of Federal Regulations, Parts 201, 207, and 351. The most recent substantive changes to AD and CVD legislation were included in the Trade Preferences Extension Act (TPEA) of 2015, P.L. 114-27, and in the Trade Facilitation and Trade Enforcement Act of 2015,

Part B
Report by the WTO Secretariat

P.L. 114-125. The main amendments to regulations since early 2016 include the Modifications of Regulations Regarding Price Adjustments in Anti-dumping Duty Proceedings, 81 Fed. Reg. 15641 (24 March 2016), and the procedures for the Investigation of Claims of Evasion of Anti-dumping and Countervailing Duties, 81 Fed. Reg. 56477 (22 August 2016).[55]

Title V of the TPEA[56], Improvements to Anti-dumping and Countervailing Duty Laws, also known as the American Trade Enforcement Effectiveness Act, introduced five amendments to U.S. AD and CVD laws: (i) Section 502 amends Section 776 of the Tariff Act of 1930, to modify the provisions addressing the selection and corroboration of certain information that may be used as facts otherwise available with an adverse inference in an AD or CVD proceeding; (ii) Section 503 amends Section 771(7) of the Tariff Act of 1930 in certain respects, pertaining to determinations of "material injury" or "threat of material injury" in AD and CVD proceedings; (iii) Section 504 amends Sections 771(15) and 773 of the Tariff Act of 1930, to modify the definition of "ordinary course of trade" and the provisions governing the treatment of a "particular market situation (PMS)" in AD proceedings; (iv) Section 505 amends Section 773(b)(2) of the Tariff Act of 1930, to modify the treatment of distorted prices or costs in AD proceedings; and (v) Section 506 amends Section 782(a) of the Tariff Act of 1930, to modify the provision regarding accepting voluntary respondents in AD and CVD proceedings. The Department of Commerce (USDOC) issued a notice stating that all sections of the Act, except Section 503, would be applied to determinations made on or after 6 August 2015.[57] The USITC has applied the amendments in Section 503 of the TPEA to its AD and CVD determinations since September 2015.[58]

In addition, the Trade Facilitation and Trade Enforcement Act of 2015 amended the Tariff Act of 1930. Title IV of the Act, Prevention of Evasion of Anti-dumping and Countervailing Duty Orders, known also as the Enforce and Protect Act of 2015 (EAPA), contains provisions to strengthen enforcement to prevent the evasion of the payment of duties. The EAPA, notified to the WTO in 2016[59], is aimed at preventing evasion of contingency measures. To strengthen enforcement of these measures, the Act created the Trade Remedy Law Enforcement Division (TRLED) within U.S. Customs and Border Protection (CBP) in the U.S. Department of Homeland Security, to: (a) develop and administer policies to prevent and counter evasion, including procedures for investigating claims of evasion of AD and CVD orders; (b) direct enforcement and compliance assessment activities concerning evasion; (c) develop and conduct commercial risk assessment targeting, with respect to cargo destined for the United States; (d) issue trade alerts; and (e) develop policies for the application of single entry and continuous bonds for entries of covered merchandise to sufficiently protect the collection of AD and CV duties commensurate with the level of risk of non-collection.

The EAPA created a new framework for CBP to investigate allegations of evasion of AD/CVD orders, under the newly created Section 517 (Procedures for Investigating Claims of Evasion of Antidumping and Countervailing Duty Orders). Section 421 of the EAPA requires the CBP Commissioner to initiate an investigation within 15 business days of the receipt of a properly filed allegation from an interested party or referral from another Federal agency that reasonably suggests that merchandise covered by an AD/CVD order has entered the customs territory of the United States through evasion. EAPA allegations may be filed via the EAPA option on the e-Allegations web portal or through other means.[60] The party submitting the allegation may provide information to CBP during the proceeding, and will receive notification of interim measures and the final determination from CBP; small businesses may receive technical assistance.[61]

The EAPA provides for an interim measures mechanism to ensure that duties can be collected on entries of covered merchandise made during the pendency of an investigation. Under this mechanism, CBP will determine within 90 calendar days of initiation of an EAPA investigation whether there exists reasonable suspicion that covered merchandise subject to an allegation was entered through evasion. If CBP determines that such reasonable suspicion exists, it will suspend the liquidation of unliquidated entries of the covered merchandise entered after the date of initiation, and extend the period for liquidating the unliquidated entries that entered before the initiation of the investigation. It will also take any additional measures necessary to protect the ability to collect appropriate duties, which may include requiring a single transaction bond or posting cash deposits.

The EAPA also requires CBP to determine, not later than 300 calendar days (or 360 calendar days in extraordinarily complicated cases) after the date of initiation of an EAPA investigation, whether there is substantial evidence that merchandise covered by an AD/CVD order was entered into the customs territory of the United States through evasion. The EAPA further requires CBP, no later than five business days after making a determination, to communicate the determination to the interested party who made an allegation that initiated the evasion investigation. CBP posts its decisions as to interim measures and final determination of evasion on its website.[62]

If CBP makes an affirmative evasion determination, it will suspend the liquidation of unliquidated entries of the covered merchandise, and extend the period for liquidating the unliquidated entries that entered before the initiation of the investigation. It will also, when necessary, notify the USDOC of the determination, and request that it determine the appropriate duty rates for such covered merchandise, and require importers of covered merchandise to post cash deposits and assess duties on the covered merchandise. Additionally, if a

violation of the Customs Act is identified as part of an affirmative determination, CBP may impose penalties under Section 1592 of the Tariff Act of 1930, or use any of its other enforcement authorities.[63] In August 2016, the United States introduced interim regulations for the application of the EAPA, and notified them to the WTO (see below).[64]

The EAPA also calls for cooperation with foreign countries on preventing evasion of trade remedy laws, by seeking to negotiate and enter into bilateral agreements with their customs authorities or other appropriate authorities. These bilateral agreements should allow for the provision of production, trade, and transit documents and other information necessary to determine whether exports from the exporting country are subject to the importing country's trade remedy laws; they should also allow the importing country to participate in verification in the exporting country, including through a site visit. Interim regulations on CBP Investigations of Claims of Evasion of Anti-dumping and Countervailing Duties became effective in August 2016.[65]

A Presidential Executive Order on Establishing Enhanced Collection and Enforcement of Anti-dumping and Countervailing Duties and Violations of Trade and Customs Laws was issued on 31 March 2017. The Order establishes that it is the policy of the United States to impose appropriate bonding requirements, based on risk assessments, on entries of articles subject to AD and CV duties, when necessary to protect the revenue of the United States in cases where importers unlawfully evade AD and CV duties, and mandates the development of an Implementation Plan within 90 days of the date of the Order.[66]

In 2016, some changes in practice related to AD and CVD investigation procedures were introduced. The USDOC modified its regulation concerning the extension of time limits for submissions in AD and CVD proceedings.[67] The USDOC also modified its regulations pertaining to price adjustments in AD duty proceedings, to clarify that it does not intend to accept a price adjustment made after the time of sale unless the interested party demonstrates its entitlement to such an adjustment.[68]

In the WTO Committee on Anti-Dumping Practices, Members have expressed concerns with respect to some issues linked to AD investigations procedures or rules.[69]

Administrative procedures

Responsibility for the administration of laws and agreements with respect to AD and CVD measures in the United States lies jointly with the U.S. Department of Commerce's (USDOC) International Trade Administration (ITA) and with the United States International Trade Commission (USITC). The ITA's Enforcement and Compliance Unit (E&C) is responsible for the enforcement of AD and CVD laws. The ITA is in charge of the determination of the existence and amount of dumping and subsidy in AD and CVD investigations. The Customs Unit within E&C serves as the liaison with U.S. Customs and Border Protection (CBP) on matters pertaining to the collection of AD/CVD duties, and on issues of potential fraud associated with AD/CVD proceedings.[70] The USITC determines whether an industry, or the establishment of an industry, is materially retarded by reason of dumped or subsidized imports.[71] The TRLED, within the Office of Trade at CBP, is entrusted with the development and administration of policies to prevent and counter evasion, and is responsible for directing enforcement and compliance assessment activities concerning evasion, as well as for conducting commercial risk assessment targeting, with respect to cargo destined for the United States; and for the development of policies for the assessment of risk of importers, to better determine the application of single entry and continuous bonds for entries of covered merchandise, to sufficiently protect the collection of AD and CV duties.

AD and CVD investigations may be initiated at the request of petitioners, or may be self-initiated by the USDOC, although this has seldom been the case. There was one such case during the period under review: on 28 November 2017, the USDOC announced the self-initiation of AD and CVD investigations of imports of common alloy aluminium sheet from China. Prior to 2017, there had been three such self-initiations by the USDOC since 1980, most recently in 1991. Investigation petitions must be filed simultaneously with the USDOC's ITA and the USITC. A U.S. industry petitioning for the initiation of an AD or CVD investigation must provide a reasonable basis to believe or suspect that dumping and/or subsidization of a particular product is occurring, that there is material injury or threat thereof to the domestic industry, and that there is a causal link between them. Before initiating an investigation, the ITA must determine whether the petition contains information reasonably available to the petitioner supporting the allegations. This includes determining that a petition is filed by an interested party and has industry support, for which it must meet two criteria: (a) domestic producers or workers who support the petition must account for at least 25% of the total production of the domestic like product; and (b) the domestic producers or workers who support the petition must account for more than 50% of the production of the domestic like product produced by that portion of the industry expressing support for, or opposition to, the petition. The petition must also clearly identify and define the domestic like product as well as all its producers, and must provide information relating to the degree of industry support for the petition, including the total volume and value of U.S. production of the domestic like product, and the volume and value of U.S. production of the domestic like product produced by the petitioner(s) and each domestic producer identified.

In general, a determination on whether or not to initiate an investigation is made within 20 days after the date of filing of the petition, as specified in Section 732(c) of the Act and 19 CFR 351.203. However, the ITA has the authority to postpone the initiation of an investigation by up to 20 days to "poll the industry", or otherwise determine support for the petition. The USITC has 45 days from the filing of the petition or self-initiation by the USDOC or, if the time has been extended to poll the industry, 25 days after USDOC informs it of the initiation of the investigation, to make a preliminary determination of whether there is a reasonable indication of material injury or threat thereof. If the USITC's injury determination is negative, the investigation is terminated; if it is affirmative, the investigation continues. After a determination of injury has been made by the USITC, the ITA has 115 days to issue a preliminary AD determination, or 85 days to issue a preliminary CVD determination.[72] Whether the preliminary determination is affirmative or negative, the investigation continues, even if no margin of dumping or subsidization is found, or the margin found is below the *de minimis* threshold.[73] The ITA has an additional 75 days to determine the final margin of dumping. For the determination of the margin of dumping, the ITA compares prices in the United States to a Normal Value (NV), the calculation of which varies according to the circumstances. For example, the NV may be based on the company's actual costs and prices in the comparison market, which can be either the respondent's home country or some other suitable third country or, if the ITA does not find a suitable comparison market, it may base the NV on the Constructed Value (CV) which is a cost-based build-up of a surrogate price.

If a "reasonable indication" of material injury is found by the USITC, and the ITA makes an affirmative preliminary determination, preliminary AD or CVD measures, generally the posting of a cash deposit in an amount equivalent to the estimated margin of dumping or preliminary subsidy rate, may be applied for a period of six months. If the ITA makes a preliminary determination of critical circumstances, preliminary measures may be applied retroactively to subject imports entered up to 90 days before the determination was published in the Federal Register.[74] If the ITA's final determination finds a margin of dumping or a subsidy rate above the *de minimis* level, the investigation goes back to the USITC, which has 45 days to issue a final determination of injury. A final decision must then be taken within 280 days from the filing of the petition for AD investigations or 205 days for CVD investigation, or 260 (185) days after the beginning of the investigation. If the USITC's final determination is affirmative, the ITA issues an order imposing AD or CVD duties; if it is negative, the investigation is terminated, no order is issued, provisional measures are lifted, and any cash deposits are returned, with interest.[75] The imposition of an order in the case of an affirmative determination, or of the termination of the application of provisional measures and return of the bond, in case of a negative determination, takes place within the 287th day (212th for CVDs) and is published in the Federal Register.

Affirmative determinations are subject to administrative reviews at the request of an interested party, and to sunset reviews after five years (see below).

Suspension agreements

AD and CVD investigations may be suspended under some circumstances, based on an agreement to cease exports, or to eliminate the injurious effect (suspension agreements). These agreements are generally voluntary limits on exports or price undertakings, or involve the elimination of subsidies by the investigated countries.[76] In the case of AD investigations, under suspension agreements, exporters may agree to accept price undertakings or to cease exports. AD suspension agreements reached with non-market economies (NMEs) may combine price undertakings and additional elements, in order to prevent price suppression or undercutting. In CVD cases, a suspension agreement may be reached if the Government alleged to be providing the subsidy agrees to eliminate the subsidy, to completely offset the net subsidy, or to cease or limit exports to the United States. Suspension agreements entered into with a WTO Member considered a market economy may involve only price undertakings in the case of AD investigations. Agreements with respect to CVD investigations may also involve quantitative restrictions.

Administrative reviews

Administrative reviews of CVD and AD orders in effect each year may be requested by interested parties during the anniversary month of the publication of the order.[77] The list of orders eligible for review is published in the Federal Register. An interested party must specify the individual producers or exporters covered by the order or suspension agreement for which they are requesting a review, and the basis for the request.[78] In a review of a suspension agreement, the USDOC reviews the current status of, and compliance with, the agreement. In administrative reviews of AD/CVD orders, the USDOC examines a particular company's entries, exports, or sales made 12 months immediately preceding the anniversary month in which the review was requested (review period). The review determines the actual weighted-average amount of dumping/subsidy and duty assessments for that period, and the future cash deposit rate. If no review is requested for a particular 12-month period, final duties are assessed in the amount deposited for that period. Requests for duty absorption rulings may also be made in administrative reviews, but only for those initiated two or four years after publication of the AD order. The results of the reviews are normally issued within 12 months from the date of initiation.

Sunset reviews

Sunset reviews of AD and CVD orders are provided for under Section 751(c) of the Tariff Act of 1930, as amended by the URAA. The USDOC and the USITC initiate sunset reviews no later than 30 days before the fifth anniversary of publication in the Federal Register of an AD or CVD order or suspension agreement, with the aim of determining whether the revocation of the order would be likely to lead to continuation or recurrence of dumping or countervailable subsidies (USDOC) and of material injury to the domestic industry (USITC).

 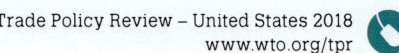

Initiations of the reviews are automatic. USDOC policy is to provide a one-month advance notification of sunset reviews in the Federal Register.

Sunset reviews are order-specific (country- and product-specific) but may be grouped in an investigation; suspension agreements are also subject to sunset review. In its determination of whether revocation of an order or termination of a suspended investigation would likely lead to continuation or recurrence of dumping, the USDOC considers the rates established in the investigation and/or reviews conducted during the sunset review period, as well as the volume of imports for the periods before and after issuance of the order or acceptance of the suspension agreement. There are no sunset reviews for AD orders on products from non-WTO Members.

Anti-dumping measures

Between 2015 and 2017, the number of AD investigation initiations totalled 133. Although the number of initiations decreased from 42 in 2015 to 37 in 2016, it increased to 54 in 2017 (Table 3.5). Of the 37 investigations initiated in 2016, 34 resulted in the imposition of definitive measures by end April 2018; in one case, no final duty was applied. In all the 2016 investigations, provisional duties were applied. As of 30 June 2018, 22 of the investigations initiated in 2017 had resulted in the imposition of definitive measures, and 8 had been terminated due to a no-injury finding. Between 1995 and 2017, the United States initiated 659 AD investigations.[79]

The number of AD measures in force increased during the period under review. As of 31 December 2017,

Table 3.5 Anti-dumping investigations, 2015-June 2018

	2015	2016	2017	2018 (June)
Investigation initiations	42	37	54	22
Provisional measures applied	10	53	38	26
Duty orders imposed	15	35	32	24
Suspension agreements	0	0	0	0
Sunset review initiations	36	50	46	19
Continuation of orders	31	23	25	21
Revocations	5	6	1	1

Source: WTO Secretariat based on data received from the USDOC; the USITC; and notifications.

Table 3.6 AD measures in force, by trading partner (including suspension agreements), 2015 to 17 July 2018

	2015	2016	2017	17 July 2018
Trading partner/region	265	293	321	340
Argentina	1	1	1	2
Australia	2	2	2	2
Belarus	1	1	1	2
Brazil	7	11	11	12
Canada	2	2	3	3
Chile	1	1	1	1
China	97	102	110	116
Chinese Taipei	21	22	22	23
EU (28)	20	22	30	32
India	15	19	21	21
Indonesia	8	9	9	10
Iran	1	1	1	1
Japan	15	17	19	19
Kazakhstan	1	1	1	1
Korea, Rep. of	15	18	23	24
Malaysia	4	4	4	4
Mexico	11	12	13	13
Republic of Moldova	2	2	2	2
Oman	1	3	3	2
Pakistan	0	1	1	1
Philippines	1	1	1	1
Russian Federation	6	4	4	5
South Africa	3	3	3	5
Switzerland	0	0	0	1
Thailand	7	7	7	7
Turkey	5	7	8	9
Trinidad and Tobago	1	1	1	1
Ukraine	7	6	6	5
United Arab Emirates	2	3	3	4
Venezuela, Bolivarian Rep. of	1	1	1	1
Viet Nam	9	9	9	10

Source: G/ADP/N/308/USA, 21 March 2018; G/ADP/N/294/USA, 9 March 2017; and G/ADP/N/280/USA, 11 March 2016; information received from the USDOC; and USITC online information. Viewed at: http://www.usitc.gov/trade_remedy/documents/orders.xls.

Part B
Report by the WTO Secretariat

excluding suspension agreements, 321 definitive AD measures were in force. At that date, 314 AD duty orders and seven suspension agreements were in effect, compared with 293 in December 2016, and 265 in December 2015. In accordance with information from the USDOC and the USITC, 340 AD orders were in place as of 17 July 2018 (Table 3.6).[80]

The trading partners subject to the largest amount of AD orders as of July 2018 were China (116); the European Union (32); Korea, the Republic of (24); Chinese Taipei (23); and India (21). Of the 340 AD measures in place as of 17 July 2018, 179 (52.6% of the total) were applied on iron and steel products, 55 (16.2%) on miscellaneous manufactured products, 40 (11.8%) on chemicals and pharmaceuticals, 25 (7.4%) on metals and minerals, 21 (6.2%) on agricultural products, 14 (4.1%) on plastics and rubber, 3 (0.9%) on textiles and apparel, and 2 (0.6%) on machinery and equipment.[81]

Of the 333 AD measures in place (excluding suspension agreements) at 17 July 2018, 215 had been renewed after a sunset review, that is, they had been in place for over five years. The average duration of an AD measure in place at the end of 2017 was some 11 years. At the end of 2017, 61 AD and 5 CVD measures had been in place for more than 20 years; and 159 AD and 14 CVD measures had been in place for over 10 years. The longest-lasting AD measure in place dates from 1977, and is applied on pressure sensitive plastic tape from Italy; a measure on pre-stressed concrete steel wire strand from Japan dates from 1978.

Duties applied during the period under review varied significantly. The level of AD definitive duties applied during 1 January 2016–31 December 2017 range from 0.00% to 493.46%; provisional duties applied over the same period also range from 0.00% to 493.46%.

At the end of 2017, seven suspension agreements were in place, with Argentina (1), Mexico (2), Russian Federation (2), and Ukraine (2), relating to lemon juice, fresh tomatoes, sugar, carbon steel plate, uranium, and oil country tubular goods, respectively. Four of the agreements involve price undertakings, one involves export limits, and the other involves export limits combined with a price undertaking.

According to information provided by the U.S. Department of Homeland Security, in FY2016, US$14 billion of imported goods were subject to AD/CVD, and CBP collected US$1.5 billion in AD/CVD cash deposits. CBP's collection of AD/CVD cash deposits increased by over 25% since FY2015, and by almost 200% since FY2014.[82] As of the end of FY2017, US$3.1 billion of AD/CVD duties were owed to the U.S. Government for imports going back to 2001.

There were 123 sunset review initiations of AD orders during the period from 1 January 2016 to end-June 2018 (50 in 2016, 46 in 2017 and 21 in 2018). During the same period, there were eight revocations (six in 2016, one in 2017, and one in 2018), while 104 orders were continued.[83] The revocations during that period included iron and steel products as well as chemicals and food; they covered five trading partners.[84] There were 104 administrative reviews of AD orders initiated in 2016, and 119 administrative reviews initiated in 2017.

During the review period, some aspects of U.S. AD investigation procedures and findings were the subject of WTO disputes (Table A2.3).

Countervailing measures

Between 2015 and 2017, the number of CVD investigation initiations totalled 63, of which 23 in 2015, 16 in 2016, and 24 in 2017 (Table 3.7). There were also 17 initiations in the first six months of 2018. Of the investigations initiated in 2017, 21 had resulted in the imposition of definitive measures by April 2018, and 2 had been terminated without duties being applied due to a negative injury determination by the USITC. As of 30 April 2018, eight of the investigations initiated in 2017 had resulted in the imposition of definitive duties. Twenty-four investigations initiated in 2017 were subject to provisional measures.[85]

Overall, there were 109 CVD orders in place and one suspension agreement with Mexico regarding sugar as at 17 July 2018, involving 17 trading partners, where China was the most affected.[86] Of these 109 CVD measures, 55 (50.5% of the total) were applied on iron and steel products, 18 (16.5%) on miscellaneous manufactured products, 13 (11.9%) on chemicals and pharmaceuticals, 9 (8.3%) on plastics and rubber, 7 (6.4%) on agricultural products, 2 (1.9%) on metals and minerals, 2 (1.8%) on textiles and apparel, and 1 (1%) on machinery and equipment.

There were 52 sunset review initiations of CVD orders during the period from 1 January 2016 to end-April 2018 (43 in 2016, 4 in 2017 and 5 in 2018). During the same period, 27 sunset reviews of CVD orders were concluded; there were six terminations revocations (all in 2016), while the remaining orders were continued.

Table 3.7 CVD investigations and measures imposed, 2015-June 18

	2015	2016	2017	June 2018
Investigation initiations	23	16	24	17
Provisional measures applied	14	53	20	13
Duty orders imposed	10	16	11	13
Suspension agreements	0	0	0	0

Note: Figures refer to the year in which the investigation was initiated. Some provisional or definitive duties may have been applied the following year.

Source: WTO, based on information from the USDOC, the USITC, and notifications.

EAPA investigations

As previously described, the EAPA created a new framework for CBP to investigate allegations of evasion of AD/CVD orders, under the newly created Section 517 (Procedures for Investigating Claims of Evasion of Anti-dumping and Countervailing Duty Orders). EAPA allegations must be filed via the EAPA option on the e-Allegations web portal.[87] The Trade Remedy Law Enforcement Directorate (TRLED) within CBP is responsible for conducting EAPA investigations.

Since the EAPA came into effect in August 2016, and until July 2018, the TRLED initiated 19 investigations from allegations of evasion of duties. After consolidation of some of those investigations, the TRLED issued 10 notices of initiation and one notice of non-initiation during that period. In all but one of these initiated investigations, interim measures were applied.[88] Interim measures have generally consisted of: extension of suspension of the liquidation of entries; a "live entry" requirement for all future imports, meaning that all entry documents and duties are required before cargo is released by CBP into the U.S. commerce; rejecting previously filed entries that are within the entry reject period and requiring them to be refiled with applicable AD/CVD cash deposits; and collection of a bond equivalent to the application or adjustment of AD/CVD duties to imports previously subject to no or lower AD/CVD duties due to their being identified as having entered the United States through evasion. As of July 2018, the TRLED had made a final determination in five cases, one of them involving eight investigations (Table 3.8).

Safeguards

Global safeguards

Main laws and regulations

In the period under review, the United States initiated its first safeguard investigation since 2001. Safeguard action is authorized under U.S. law in Sections 201-204 of the Trade Act of 1974, as amended. Sections 201-204 provide the legal framework through which the President may provide import relief. This authority relates to the rights of a WTO Member under Article XIX of the GATT 1994 to take emergency action by suspending obligations it has incurred. Under Section 201, domestic industries alleging that they are seriously injured, or threatened with serious injury, by increased imports may petition the USITC for import relief.[89] An investigation may also start with a request from the President or the USTR, or with a resolution of the House Committee on Ways and Means or the Senate Committee on Finance. The USITC may also self-initiate an investigation. A petitioner may submit to the USITC an adjustment plan, detailing steps it envisions will facilitate positive adjustment to import competition. An adjustment plan may be submitted either at the time the petition is filed or within 120 days of the filing of the petition.[90]

Upon receipt of a petition, request, or resolution as described above, the USITC is required, under Section 202(b)(1), to make an investigation to determine whether an article is being imported into the United States in such increased quantities as to be a substantial cause of serious injury, or the threat thereof, to the domestic industry producing an article like, or directly competitive with, the imported article. If the USITC makes an affirmative determination, or is equally divided in its determination, it must recommend to the President the action that would address the serious injury, or threat thereof, to the domestic industry, and be most effective in facilitating the efforts of the domestic industry to make a positive adjustment to import competition (Section 202(e)). The types of actions the USITC may recommend, and limitations on the actions, are set out in Section 202(e)(2)-(5). The USITC is authorized to recommend an increase in, or the imposition of, any duty on the imported article; a tariff rate quota; a modification or imposition of any quantitative restriction on the importation of the article; one or more appropriate adjustment measures, including the provision of trade adjustment assistance; or any combination of the actions previously described. In addition, the USITC may also recommend that the President initiate international negotiations to address the underlying cause of the increase in imports of the article, or otherwise to alleviate the injury or threat; implement any other action authorized under law. In general, the USITC is required to make its determination under Section 202(b) within 120 days of the filing of the petition, receipt of the request or resolution, or adoption of the motion, and to transmit its report, including its findings and any recommendations, and an explanation of the basis therefore, within 180 days of the filing of the petition, receipt of the request or resolution, or adoption of the motion. These periods are extended if a request for provisional relief is included with the petition. If the President decides to apply a safeguard measure, the USITC must monitor developments in the industry and submit a report on the results of its monitoring during the period of application of the measure (relief period). At the termination of any relief period, the USITC is required to report to the President and Congress on the effectiveness of the safeguard measure in facilitating the positive adjustment of the domestic industry to import competition.[91]

No amendments were made to regulations pertaining safeguards during the period under review. The most recent amendments date from 2015, as notified by the United States to the WTO, and relate to provisions of the USITC's Rules of Practice and Procedure concerning safeguard actions. The amendments are part of the USITC's retrospective analysis of its Rules that attempt to determine whether rules should be modified, streamlined, expanded, or repealed so as to make the agency's regulatory programme more effective or less burdensome in achieving regulatory objectives.

Safeguard investigations 2016-18

Between 2016 and 2018, two new safeguard investigations were conducted by the United States under Sections 201-204 of the Trade Act of 1974.

Table 3.8 EAPA investigations (eligible for public disclosure), 2016-July 2018

Investigation/date of initiation	Interim measures	Final determination
Eastern Trading NY Inc.: Evasion of the AD duty order on steel wire garment hangers from China (circumvention through Thailand)/11 October 2016	Yes. Entries under this investigation that entered the United States as not subject to AD duties were rate-adjusted to reflect that they were subject to the AD duty order on steel wire garment hangers from China, and cash deposits were owed. Additionally, "live entry" is required for all future imports for Eastern Trading, before cargo is released by CBP into the U.S. commerce. CBP suspended the liquidation for any entry that had entered on or after 11 October 2016; and extended the period for liquidation for all unliquidated entries that entered before that date.	Affirmative Determination of Evasion. CBP will continue to suspend the liquidation for any entry that has entered on or after 11 October 2016; and will continue to extend the period for liquidation for all unliquidated entries that entered before that date. CBP will continue to request that Eastern Trading post cash deposits of 187.25% on its entries of steel wire hangers, and for any future imports of covered hangers, CBP will require live entry, which requires Eastern Trading to post cash deposits in the amount of 187.25% prior to their release. Eastern Trading's continuous bond will remain at the increased level and will be reviewed in accordance with CBP's policies.
Diamond Tools Technology LLC: Suspicion of evasion of the AD duty order on Diamond Sawblades from China/22 March 2017	Yes. On-site verification: measures applied after walk-through of production floor. Entries under this investigation that entered the United States as not subject to AD duties, to be rate-adjusted to reflect that they are subject to the AD duty order on diamond sawblades from China; cash deposits are owed. Additionally, "live entry" is required for all future imports for Diamond Tools Technology.	Pending a determination on a scope referral to the USDOC.
Aspects Furniture International, Inc.: Evasion of the AD duty order on Wooden Bedroom Furniture from China/9 May 2017	Yes. Entries of subject merchandise under this investigation that entered the United States as not subject to AD duties were rate-adjusted, and cash deposits were owed. Additionally, "live entry" was required for all future imports for Aspects. CBP to further suspend the liquidation for any entry that entered on or after 9 May 2017, and extend the period for liquidation for all unliquidated entries that entered before that date.	Pending a determination on a scope referral to the USDOC.
Certain importers of wire hangers from Malaysia: Evasion of the AD duty order on Wire Garment Hangers from China (eight investigations consolidated into one)/12 May 2017	Yes. Entries under this investigation for Brooklyn Knights, Garment Cover, Casa USA, Nice Guy, GL Paper, Newtown Supply, Subcos Percha, and Masterpiece Supply that entered the United States as not subject to AD duties, were rate-adjusted to reflect that they are subject to the AD order on steel wire garment hangers from China, and cash deposits were owed. In addition, "live entry" was required for all future imports of each of the named importers. CBP suspended the liquidation for any entry that had entered on or after 12 May 2017, and extended the period for liquidation for all unliquidated entries that entered before that date. CBP would reliquidate any entries liquidated and for which CBP's reliquidation authority had not yet lapsed. CBP would also evaluate the continuous bonds for each of the named importers to determine their sufficiency.	Affirmative Determination of Evasion. In light of CBP's determination, CBP will continue to suspend the liquidation for any entry that has entered on or after 12 May 2017. CBP will also continue to extend the period for liquidation for all unliquidated entries that entered before that date. CBP will continue to require live entry, which requires that the importer post the applicable cash deposit prior to the entry's release. Finally, CBP will evaluate the continuous bonds of these companies in accordance with CBP's policies.
Power Tek Tool, Inc. and Lyke Industrial Tool, LLC: Evasion of the AD duty order on Diamond Sawblades from China/18 July 2017	Yes. Unliquidated entries not subject to AD duties were rate-adjusted, and cash deposits owed. "Live entry" was required for all future imports for Power Tek and Lyke. CBP to further suspend the liquidation for any entry entered on or after 18 July 2017, and extend the period for liquidation for all unliquidated entries that entered before that date.	Affirmative Determination of Evasion. In light of CBP's determination, CBP will continue to suspend the liquidation for any entry that has entered on or after 18 July 2017. CBP will also continue to extend the period for liquidation for all unliquidated entries that entered before that date. CBP will continue to require live entry, which requires that the importer post the applicable cash deposit prior to the entry's release. Finally, CBP will evaluate the continuous bonds

Investigation/date of initiation	Interim measures	Final determination
		of these companies in accordance with CBP's policies.
American Pacific Rubber, Inc.: Evasion of the AD duty order on Oil Country Tubular Goods from Viet Nam/18 July 2017	Yes. All unliquidated entries of subject merchandise that entered the United States as not subject to AD duties to be rate-adjusted, and cash deposits owed. "Live entry" required for all future imports. CBP to suspend the liquidation for any entry entered on or after 18 July, and extend the period for liquidation for all unliquidated entries entered before that date.	Affirmative Determination of Evasion. In light of CBP's determination, CBP will continue to suspend the liquidation for any entry that has entered on or after 18 July 2017. CBP will also continue to extend the period for liquidation for all unliquidated entries that entered before that date. CBP will continue to require live entry, which requires that the importer post the applicable cash deposit prior to the entry's release. Finally, CBP will evaluate the continuous bonds of these companies in accordance with CBP's policies.
Ceka Nutrition Inc.: Evasion of the AD duty order on Glycine from China/28 August 2017	Yes. Entries under this investigation that entered the United States as not subject to AD duties to be rate-adjusted, and cash deposits owed. "Live entry" required for all future imports for Ceka Nutrition. CBP to suspend the liquidation for any entry that has entered on or after 28 August 2017, and extend the period for liquidation for all unliquidated entries entered before that date.	Affirmative Determination of Evasion. In light of CBP's determination, CBP will continue to suspend the liquidation for any entry that has entered on or after 28 August 2017. CBP will also continue to extend the period for liquidation for all unliquidated entries that entered before that date. CBP will continue to require live entry, which requires that the importer post the applicable cash deposit prior to the entry's release. Finally, CBP will evaluate the continuous bonds of these companies in accordance with CBP's policies.
Choice Refrigerants: Evasion of the AD duty order on Hydrofluorocarbon Blends from China/5 September 2017	Pending. CBP was unable to determine whether the merchandise imported by LM Supply is subject to the AD order. Accordingly, pursuant to the EAPA, it referred this matter to the USDOC for a determination as to whether the merchandise at issue is within the scope of the AD order.	Pending a determination on a scope referral to the USDOC.
Sun Bright International, Corp. and Fair Importing Corp.: Evasion of the AD and CVD duty orders on Aluminium Extrusions from China/5 February 2018	Yes. Entries under this investigation that entered the United States as not subject to AD and CVD duties to be rate-adjusted, and cash deposits owed. "Live entry" required for all future imports for Sun Bright and Fair Importing. CBP to suspend the liquidation for any entry that has entered on or after 5 February 2018, and extend the period for liquidation for all unliquidated entries entered before that date.	Pending. Final determination to be issued not later than 3 December 2018.
Columbia Aluminium Products, LLC: Evasion of the AD and CVD duty orders on Aluminium Extrusions from China/9 February 2018	Yes. Entries under this investigation that entered the United States as not subject to AD and CVD duties to be rate-adjusted, and cash deposits owed. "Live entry" required for all future imports for Columbia Aluminium. CBP to suspend the liquidation for any entry that has entered on or after 9 February 2018, and extend the period for liquidation for all unliquidated entries entered before that date.	Pending. Final determination to be issued not later than 6 December 2018.
Royal Brush Manufacturing, Inc.: Evasion of the AD duty order on Cased Pencils from China/27 March 2018	Yes. Entries under this investigation that entered the United States as not subject to AD duties to be rate-adjusted, and cash deposits owed. "Live entry" required for all future imports for Royal Brush. CBP to suspend the liquidation for any entry that has entered on or after 27 March 2018, and extend the period for liquidation for all unliquidated entries entered before that date.	Pending. Final determination to be issued not later than 21 January 2019.

Source: WTO Secretariat based on CBP online information. Viewed at: https://www.cbp.gov/trade/trade-enforcement/tftea/enforce-and-protect-act-eapa.

Part B
Report by the WTO Secretariat

Both investigations were notified to the WTO. The USITC made affirmative serious injury determinations in both cases, and the President applied a safeguard measure in each (see below).

Crystalline Silicon Photovoltaic Cells

The first safeguard investigation notified to the WTO during the period under review involved Crystalline Silicon Photovoltaic Cells (Whether or Not Partially or Fully Assembled into Other Products). On 25 May 2017, pursuant to Article 12.1(a) of the WTO Agreement on Safeguards, the United States notified that the USITC had initiated, on 17 May 2017, a safeguard investigation with respect to certain crystalline silicon photovoltaic (CSPV) cells, whether or not partially or fully assembled into other products, including, but not limited to, modules, laminates, panels, and building-integrated materials. The investigation was initiated following receipt of a petition filed by Suniva, Inc., a producer of CSPV cells and CSPV modules in the United States. The investigation covered CSPV cells of a thickness equal to or greater than 20 micrometers (HTSUS subheading 8541.40.60), whether or not the cell had undergone other processing.[92] Excluded from the investigation were CSPV cells manufactured in the United States, whether or not partially or fully assembled into other products.[93] The petition alleged that the quantity of imports had risen by 51.6% between 2012 and 2016, while the value of imports had risen by 62.8%, from US$5.1 billion in 2012 to US$8.3 billion in 2016; domestic market share had fallen from 21.0% in 2012 to 11.0% in 2016. The petition also noted that capacity utilization for CSPV cell operations had fallen from 81.7% in 2014 to 28.9% in 2016, and CSPV module production utilization had declined from 66.7% in 2013 to 32.9% in 2016. The petition cited information on serious injury and threat of serious injury to the domestic industry. The petition also stated that Suniva, Inc. and SolarWorld AG, two large domestic producers in the United States, had reported operating losses between 2012 and 2016, that 1,200 manufacturing jobs in the United States had been lost, and wages had fallen by 27% in the same period. The petitioner did not allege critical circumstances in the petition.[94]

On 22 September 2017, the USITC determined that imports of CSPV cells (whether or not partially or fully assembled into other products) are being imported into the United States in such increased quantities as to be a substantial cause of serious injury to the domestic industry.[95] The investigation was concluded, and the USITC forwarded its report containing its determination and the separate recommendations of the Commissioners, with an explanation of the basis thereof, to the President on 13 November 2017.[96] On 27 November 2017, USTR requested additional information from the USITC to assist him in making a determination. The USITC's supplemental report was forwarded to USTR on 27 December 2017.[97] On 23 January 2018, the President signed a proclamation applying a safeguard measure on imports of CSPV products.[98] The measure was notified to the WTO.[99] In

addition, the United States notified the non-application of the safeguard measure to developing countries under Article 9.1 of the Safeguards Agreement.[100] The following CSPV products are covered by the safeguard measure: (a) solar cells, whether or not assembled into modules or made up into panels, provided for in HTSUS subheading 8541.40.60; (b) parts or subassemblies of solar cells, provided for in subheadings 8501.31.80, 8501.61.00, and 8507.20.80; (c) inverters or batteries with CSPV cells attached, provided for in subheadings 8501.61.00 and 8507.20.80; and (d) DC generators with CSPV cells attached, provided for in subheading 8501.31.80.

The measure, to be in effect for four years, became effective on 7 February 2018, and took the form of: (a) a tariff rate quota on imports of solar cells not partially or fully assembled into other products, with unchanging within-quota quantities and annual reductions in the rates of duty applicable to goods entered in excess of those quantities in the second, third, and fourth years (Table 3.9); and (b) an increase in duties on imports of modules, with annual reductions in the rates of duty in the second, third, and fourth years. The safeguard measure was applied to imports from all countries, except for the developing countries mentioned above.[101] Both NAFTA partners were included in the scope of the measure. The in-quota quantity in each year under the tariff rate quota is allocated among all countries to which the measure applies. The following temporary HTSUS subheadings were created for the goods subject to the measure: subheading 9903.45.21 (CSPV cell imports originating in covered countries, within the tariff rate quota (i.e., not exceeding 2.5 gigawatts)); subheading 9903.45.22 (CSPV cell out-of-quota imports); and subheading 9903.45.25 (imports of CSPV modules).

China; the Republic of Korea; and Japan notified to the WTO proposed suspensions of substantially equivalent concessions from 7 February 2021, or from the date of a decision by the WTO Dispute Settlement Body that the safeguard measure imposed by the United States is incompatible with the WTO Agreements, whichever is the earlier date.[102]

Large Residential Washers

The second investigation, regarding large residential washers (LRWs) and certain parts thereof, was initiated on 5 June 2017.[103] The investigation was initiated following the receipt of a petition filed by Whirlpool Corporation (Whirlpool), a producer of LRWs in the United States, which alleged that LRWs and certain parts (covered parts) are being imported into the United States in such increased quantities as to be a substantial cause of serious injury, or threat thereof, to the domestic industry producing an article like, or directly competitive with, the imported article. The petition cited information demonstrating that these increased imports seriously injured and threatened further serious injury to the domestic LRW industry. On 5 October 2017, the USITC determined that LRWs and certain parts are being imported into the United States

Table 3.9 Safeguard measures applied on imports of crystalline silicon photovoltaic cells, 2018-22

HTSUS subheading	Applied rate before the increase	Year 1 7 February 2018- 6 February 2019	Year 2 7 February 2019- 6 February 2020	Year 3 7 February 2020- 6 February 2021	Year 4 7 February 2021- 6 February 2022
9903.45.21 (in-quota CSPV cells)	0%	0%	0%	0%	0%
9903.45.22 (out-of-quota CSPV cells)	0%	30%	25%	20%	15%
9903.45.25 (CSPV modules)	0%	30%	25%	20%	15%

Source: WTO documents G/SG/N/8/USA/9/Supp.3, 8 January 2018; and G//SG/N/8/USA/9/Supp.4, 26 January 2018; and Presidential Proclamation 9693 of 23 January 2018.

Table 3.10 Safeguard measures applied on large residential washers, 2018-21

HTSUS subheading	Applied rate before the increase	Year 1 7 February 2018 6 February 2019	Year 2 7 February 2019 6 February 2020	Year 3 7 February 2020 6 February 2021
9903.45.01 (in-quota LRWs)	1.4% (8450.11.00) 1% (8450.20.00)	1.4% + 20% (8450.11.00) 1% + 20% (8450.20.00)	1.4% + 18% (8450.11.00) 1% + 18% (8450.20.00)	1.4% + 16% (8450.11.00) 1% + 16% (8450.20.00)
9903.45.02 (out-of-quota LRWs)	1.4% (8450.11.00) 1% (8450.20.00)	1.4% + 50% (8450.11.00) 1% + 50% (8450.20.00)	1.4% + 45% (8450.11.00 1% + 45% (8450.20.00)	1.4% + 40% (8450.11.00) 1% + 40% (8450.20.00)
9903.45.05 (in-quota covered parts of LRWs)	2.6%	2.6% for 50,000 units (tariff quota)	2.6% for 70,000 units (tariff quota)	2.6% for 90,000 units (tariff quota)
9903.45.06 (out-of-quota covered parts of LRWs)	2.6%	2.6% + 50%	2.6% + 45%	2.6% + 40%

Source: WTO document G/SG/N/8/USA/10 Supp.3., 26 January 2018; and Presidential Proclamation 9694, 23 January 2018.

Part B
Report by the WTO Secretariat

in such increased quantities as to be a substantial cause of serious injury to the domestic industry. The USITC forwarded its report to the President on 4 December 2017.[104] On 23 January 2018, the President signed a proclamation applying a safeguard measure to imports of LRWs and certain parts. The measure was notified to the WTO.[105] The following products are covered by it: (a) washers, provided for in HTSUS subheadings 8450.11.00 and 8450.20.00; (b) all cabinets, or portions thereof, designed for use in washers, and all assembled baskets designed for use in washers that incorporate, at a minimum, a side wrapper, a base, and a drive hub, provided for in HTSUS subheading 8450.90.60; (c) all assembled tubs designed for use in washers that incorporate, at a minimum, a tub and a seal, provided for in HTSUS subheading 8450.90.20; and (d) any combination of the foregoing parts or subassemblies, provided for in HTSUS subheadings 8450.90.20 or 8450.90.60.[106]

The measure, approved for three years and one day, took effect on 7 February 2018, and took the form of: (a) a tariff rate quota on imported finished washers, with unchanging within-quota quantities, annual reductions in the rates of duty for goods entered within those quantities in the second and third years, and annual reductions in

the rates of duty applicable to goods entered in excess of those quantities in the second and third years; and (b) a tariff rate quota on imports of covered washer parts, with increasing within-quota quantities and annual reductions in the rates of duty applicable to goods entered in excess of those quantities in the second and third years (Table 3.10). The safeguard measure was applied to imports from all countries, except for Canada and the same list of developing countries excluded from the CSPV safeguard. For the application of the measure, new temporary HTSUS subheadings were created: subheading 9903.45.01 (imports of finished washers within the tariff-rate quota (i.e., not exceeding 1.2 million units); subheading 9903.45.02 (out-of-quota imports of finished washers)[107]; subheading 9903.45.05 (in-quota imports of washing-machine parts as described in HTSUS subheadings 8450.90.20 or 8450.90.60); and 9903.45.06 (out-of-quota imports of covered parts).

China and the Republic of Korea notified to the WTO proposed suspensions of substantially equivalent concessions from 7 February 2021, or from the date of a decision by the WTO Dispute Settlement Body that the safeguard measure imposed by the United States is incompatible with the WTO Agreements, whichever is the earlier date.[108]

Other measures affecting imports

The current administration has emphasized its "commitment to trading regimes that are free, fair, and reciprocal."[109] In this sense, it considers that U.S. trade policy should be based on the recognition that U.S. economic security is critical to its national security. The current trade agenda aims to accelerate U.S. exports, including through the renegotiation and modernization of its trade agreements, as well as stepping up enforcement of its trade laws and seeking the elimination of foreign barriers to its products and services. Some of the trade enforcement tools available that have an impact on imports and have been utilized during the review period include investigations under Section 232 of the Trade Expansion Act of 1962, and Section 301 of the Trade Act of 1974. According to the U.S. authorities, these investigations, which can lead to the adoption of measures affecting imports, are meant to address U.S. concerns such as forced transfer of technology, excessive capacity build-up, and threatened impairment of national security.

Section 232 investigations

Legal and administrative framework

Under Section 232 of the Trade Expansion Act of 1962 (19 U.S.C. §1862), the Secretary of Commerce is granted authority to conduct investigations to determine the effects of imports of any article on the national security of the United States. Investigations may be initiated based on an application from an interested party, on a request from the head of any department or agency, or may be self-initiated by the Secretary of Commerce. Section 232 requires that the Secretary of Commerce notify the Secretary of Defense that an investigation has been initiated. Under Section 232 procedures, the Secretary of Commerce must also consult with the Secretary of Defense regarding methodological and policy questions raised in the investigation, and seek information and advice from, and consult with, other appropriate officials. The USDOC may, "if it is appropriate and after reasonable notice", hold public hearings or afford interested parties an opportunity to present information and advice relevant to the investigation.[110] This usually takes place through a notice in the Federal Register.

The Secretary of Commerce has 270 days to present a report of the USDOC's findings and recommendations to the President. This report must address whether the importation of the article in question is in such quantities, or under such circumstances, as to threaten to impair U.S. national security. If the Secretary finds that the imports threaten to impair national security, the President has 90 days to determine whether he agrees with the Secretary's findings, and to determine whether to use his statutory authority to adjust the imports. The Secretary of Commerce can recommend, and the President can take, actions other than the adjustment of imports to address the threat. No later than 30 days after the date on which the President makes a determination,

he must submit to Congress a written statement of the reasons for it; such statement shall be included in a report required to be published under the statute.[111]

Requests for a Section 232 investigation must be submitted in writing; they must describe how the quantity, availability, character, and uses of a particular imported article, or other circumstances related to its import, affect national security, and must contain, among other things, a description of the domestic industry affected, including information regarding companies and their plants, locations, capacity and current output of the industry; statistics on imports and domestic production, showing the quantities and values of the article; the nature, sources, and degree of the competition created by imports of the article; and the effect that imports of the article may have upon the restoration of domestic production capacity in the event of national emergency.[112] Requests must also contain information about the extent to which the economy, employment, investment, specialized skills, and productive capacity is, or will be, adversely affected; revenues of federal, state, or local governments which are, or may be, adversely affected; and national security supporting uses of the article, including data on applicable contracts or sub-contracts.

Some of the specific factors taken into account when conducting a Section 232 investigation for determining the effect of imports on national security include: (a) the importation of goods in terms of their quantities and use; (b) the domestic production needed for projected national defense requirements[113]; (c) the domestic industry's capacity to meet those requirements; (d) related human and material resources; (e) the close relation of national economic welfare to U.S. national security; (f) the loss of skills or investment, substantial unemployment and decrease in government revenue; and (g) the impact of foreign competition on specific domestic industries and the impact of displacement of any domestic products by excessive imports.[114]

The USDOC has conducted 16 Section 232 investigations since 1980; of these 14 were concluded before or in 2001.[115] In six cases, the USDOC found no threat to national security, and in eight it recommended the President to take action due to the finding of a threat to national security; in three cases, the President decided to take action.[116] Apart from the decision to apply tariff surcharges on aluminium and steel products in 2018, action was taken with respect to crude oil from Libya (1982), consisting of an oil embargo.[117] In 2018, two new investigations were initiated (see below).

Steel investigation

An investigation under Section 232 of the Trade Expansion Act of 1962, as amended (19 U.S.C. 1862), to determine the effect of imported steel on national security was initiated on 19 April 2017. As mandated by Section 232(b)(1)(B), the USDOC notified the Department of Defense the same day. A Presidential Memorandum was issued on 20 April 2017, directing the

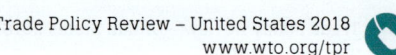

Secretary of Commerce to proceed expeditiously in the conduct for the investigation, and submit a report on his findings to the President. A notice regarding the initiation of this investigation to determine the effect of imports of steel on national security was published in the Federal Register on 21 April 2017. The notice also announced the opening of the public comment period, which ended on 31 May 2017.[118] The USDOC received 201 written public comment submissions concerning this investigation, which were reviewed and factored into the investigation process.

Following previous practice, the Secretary of Commerce in this investigation determined that "national security" for purposes of Section 232 includes the "general security and welfare of certain industries, beyond those necessary to satisfy national defense requirements, which are critical to minimum operations of the economy and government." The Secretary of Commerce submitted to the President a report with the main findings resulting from the investigation. Some of these findings include the following: (a) the United States is the world's largest importer of steel, with imports nearly four times exports; (b) six basic oxygen furnaces and four electric furnaces have closed since 2000, and employment has dropped by 35% since 1998; (c) world steelmaking capacity is 2.4 billion metric tons, up 127% from 2000, while steel demand grew at a slower rate; (d) the recent global excess capacity is 700 million tons, almost seven times the annual total of U.S. steel consumption; (e) China was identified as the largest producer and exporter of steel, and the largest source of excess steel capacity; and (f) for certain types of steel, such as for electrical transformers, only one U.S. producer remains.

The USDOC report concluded that the quantities and circumstances of steel imports threatened to impair national security, and recommended to the President that he consider the following alternative remedies to address the problem: (a) a global tariff of at least 24% on all steel imports from all countries, or a tariff of at least 53% on all steel imports from 12 countries (Brazil; China; Costa Rica; Egypt; India; Malaysia; Korea, Republic of; Russia; South Africa; Thailand; Turkey; and Viet Nam), with a quota by product on steel imports from all other countries equal to 100% of their 2017 exports to the United States; or (b) a quota on all steel products from all countries equal to 63% of each country's 2017 exports to the United States.[119] Each of these remedies was intended to increase domestic steel production from its present 73% of capacity, as calculated by the USDOC, to 80%, the minimum rate considered necessary for the long-term viability of the industry. Each remedy applies measures to all countries and all steel products, to prevent circumvention. The tariffs and quotas would be in addition to any duties already in place. The report recommends putting in place a process to allow the Secretary of Commerce to grant requests from U.S. companies to exclude specific products if the United States lacks sufficient domestic capacity, or for national security considerations.

In a response making reference to both the steel and aluminium (see below) Section 232 investigations, the Department of Defense (DoD), stated that it concurred with the USDOC's conclusion that imports of foreign steel and aluminium based on unfair trading practices impair the national security. The DoD expressed its concern about the negative impact on U.S. key allies regarding the recommended options within the reports, but stated that, among the reports' alternatives, it considered that "targeted tariffs were preferable than a global quota or global tariff", and recommended that "an inter-agency group further refine the targeted tariffs, so as to create incentives for trade partners to work with the United States on addressing the underlying issue of Chinese transshipment".[120]

Following the recommendation made by the Secretary of Commerce in the steel case, and exercising the authority granted by Section 232 of the Trade Expansion Act of 1962 (19 U.S.C. 1862) and Section 604 of the Trade Act of 1974, as amended (19 U.S.C. 2483), which "authorizes the President to embody in the Harmonized Tariff Schedule of the United States (HTSUS) the substance of acts affecting import treatment, and actions thereunder, including the removal, modification, continuance, or imposition of any rate of duty or other import restriction", the President proclaimed adjustments to the imports of steel articles by imposing, as from 23 March 2018, an additional 25% *ad valorem* tariff on steel articles, defined as those included in USHTS six-digit subheadings 7206.10 through 7216.50, 7216.99 through 7301.10, 7302.10, 7302.40 through 7302.90, and 7304.10[121] through 7306.90[122], including any subsequent revisions to these HTS classifications, imported from all countries except Canada and Mexico. The President stated that he considered this tariff necessary and appropriate to address the threat that imports of steel articles pose to national security as defined in Section 232. In adopting the tariff, the President recognized that the United States and certain other countries share a concern about global excess capacity, a circumstance that is contributing to the threatened impairment of national security.[123] He noted that the United States was ready to discuss with countries with which it has a security relationship alternative means to address the threat to national security which could lead to the removal or modification of the restriction on steel articles imports from that country.

On 22 March 2018, the President amended some aspects of Proclamation 9705 to exempt Australia; Argentina; Korea, Republic of; Brazil; and the member countries of the European Union from the measure until 1 May 2018.[124] On 30 April 2018, a new Proclamation was issued, in which the President noted that the United States had successfully concluded discussions with the Republic of Korea on alternative means to address the threatened impairment to its national security posed by steel article imports from the Republic of Korea. The measures agreed include a quota that restricts the quantity of steel articles imported into the United States from the Republic of Korea. In light of the measures, steel article imports from the Republic of Korea would be excluded from the tariff proclaimed in Proclamation 9705. The Proclamation also mentioned that the United States had agreed in principle with Argentina, Australia, and Brazil on satisfactory alternative means to address the threatened impairment to its national security posed by steel articles imported from these countries, and that these countries would remain exempt from the tariff proclaimed in Proclamation 9705, until the details could be finalized and implemented by proclamation. Canada, Mexico, and the European Union would be exempted from the measure until 1 June 2018.[125]

The measures were applied to Canada, Mexico, and the European Union as from 1 June 2018. As a result, on 6 June 2018, the European Union and Canada requested WTO dispute consultations with the United States regarding the U.S. duties on certain imported steel and aluminium products; other Members also requested dispute settlement consultations with the United States.[126] Subsequently, several WTO Members, including China, the European Union, India, Japan, the Russian Federation and Turkey, notified to the WTO proposed suspensions of substantially equivalent concessions, as they considered the measures as safeguards.[127] The United States responded by stating that tariffs imposed pursuant to Section 232 are not safeguard measures but rather measures taken pursuant to Article XXI of the GATT, and that the United States did not take action pursuant Section 201 of the Trade Act of 1974, which is the law under which the United States imposes safeguard measures; the United States did not consider the suspension of concessions justified, as, in its view, the measures adopted were not safeguard measures.[128] On 16 July 2018, the United States requested consultations with Canada, China, the European Union, Mexico and Turkey regarding additional duties imposed by these Members in response to the additional duties imposed by the United States on steel and aluminium products.[129]

In the case of the Republic of Korea, annual import quotas have been fixed for the steel products subject to the Section 232 investigation. Annual aggregate limits have been set for the different HTSUS subheadings covered (all in HTSUS Chapters 72 and 73) to apply for the period starting with calendar year 2018 and for subsequent years, unless modified or terminated.[130] Quarterly imports in an aggregate quantity under any of the subheadings covered by the agreement cannot exceed 30% of the total quota or 500 tons, whichever is greater.[131] Also, once the quota is filled, imports cannot take place under any condition: in accordance with U.S. regulations (19 CFR 132.5), merchandise subject to an absolute quota may not be imported for consumption after the quota limit is reached; options after the quota limit is reached include warehousing, FTZs, exportation or destruction. The status of quotas may be viewed in the CBP website.[132]

Aluminium investigation

The Secretary of Commerce initiated an investigation to determine the effect of imported aluminium on national security under Section 232 of the Trade Expansion Act of 1962, as amended (19 U.S.C. 1862), on 26 April 2017. Pursuant to the requirements of Section 232, the Secretary of Commerce notified the Defense Secretary of this investigation. A public hearing to elicit further information concerning this investigation was held on 22 June 2017. The public comment period ended on 23 June 2017; the USDOC received 91 written submissions concerning this investigation.[133] The investigation covered the following products: unwrought aluminium (HSTSUS 7601), aluminium bars, rods and profiles (7604); aluminium wire (7605); aluminium plates, sheets, and strip, of a thickness exceeding 0.2mm (7606); aluminium foil (whether or not printed, or backed with paper, paperboard, plastics or similar backing materials) of a thickness (excluding any backing) not exceeding 0.2mm (7607); aluminium tubes and pipes (7608); aluminium tube and pipe fittings (7609); other articles of aluminium: castings (7616.99.51.60); and other articles of aluminium: forgings (7616.99.51.70).[134]

Some of the main findings in the USDOC's report include: (a) aluminium is essential to U.S. national security, as it is needed to satisfy requirements for the U.S. Department of Defense (DoD) for maintaining effective military capabilities, and requirements for critical infrastructure sectors that are central to the operation of the U.S. economy and Government, including power transmissions, transportation systems, manufacturing industries, construction, and others; (b) the U.S. Government does not maintain any strategic stockpile of bauxite, alumina, aluminium ingots, billets or any semi-finished aluminium products; (c) in 2016, the United States imported five times as much primary aluminium on a tonnage basis as it produced; the import penetration level was about 90%, up from 66% in 2012; (d) employment has fallen by 58% between 2013 and 2016 (from about 13,000 to 5,000 employees); (e) since 2012, six smelters have been permanently shut down: in 2017, the United States had five smelters, which were producing at 43% of capacity; only one of these produces the high-purity aluminium required for critical infrastructure and defense aerospace applications; (f) the impact so far has been greatest on the primary (unwrought) aluminium sector, but the downstream aluminium sector is also threatened by overcapacity and surging imports; (g) imports accounted for 64% of total consumption of aluminium in 2016; (h) imports in the aluminium categories subject to this investigation totaled 5.9 million metric tons in 2016, up 34% from 4.4 million metric tons in 2013; (i) in the downstream aluminium sector, imports rose 33% from 1.2 million metric tons in 2013 to 1.6 million metric tons in 2016; (j) in 2016, for the aluminium product categories covered by this investigation, the United States ran a trade deficit of US$7.2 billion; and (k) global excess aluminium capacity contributes to the weakening of the U.S. aluminium industry and the U.S. economy.[135]

The Secretary of Commerce recommended to the President three alternative remedies for dealing with excessive imports of aluminium: (a) a tariff of at least 7.7% on all aluminium imports from all countries; (b) a tariff of 23.6% on all products from: China; Hong Kong, China; the Russian Federation; the Bolivarian Republic of Venezuela; and Viet Nam, with all other countries subject to quotas equal to 100% of their 2017 exports to the United States; or (c) a quota on all imports from all countries equal to a maximum of 86.7% of their 2017 exports to the United States. Each of the three proposals was intended to raise production of aluminium from the present 48% average capacity to 80%, a level considered to provide the industry with long-term viability. The tariffs and quotas would be in addition to any duties already in place.

Following the recommendation made by the Secretary of Commerce, the President decided to adjust the imports of aluminium articles by imposing, as from 23 March 2018, an additional 10% *ad valorem* tariff on certain aluminium articles imported from all countries except Canada and Mexico, through Proclamation 9704.[136] On 22 March 2018, the President issued a new proclamation to exempt Australia; Argentina; Korea, Republic of; Brazil; and the member countries of the European Union from the measure until 1 May 2018.[137] On 30 April 2018, a further proclamation was issued, which noted that the United States had agreed in principle with Argentina, Australia, and Brazil on satisfactory alternative means to address the threatened impairment to its national security posed by aluminium articles imported from these countries.[138] It was thus decided to extend the temporary exemption of these countries from the tariff proclaimed in Proclamation 9704, in order to finalize the details in this respect. The United States also announced the extension of the exemption for Canada, Mexico and members of the European Union until 1 June 2018.

On 31 May 2018, a new Proclamation was issued, in which the President noted that the United States had agreed on a range of measures with Argentina to address the threatened impairment to its national security posed by aluminium articles imports from Argentina. A quota was fixed, capping unwrought aluminium exports provided for in HTSUS heading 7601 at 169,658,877 kg, and wrought aluminium, provided for in headings 7604, 7605, 7606, 7607, 7608, 7609, and castings and forgings of aluminium, provided for in subheading 7616.99.51, at 11,279,691 kg.[139]

Aluminium and steel products that are subject to Section 232 duties are not eligible for preferential tariff treatment under the Generalized System of Preferences (GSP) or the African Growth and Opportunity Act (AGOA). They are subject to the MFN tariff rate plus the additional tariff. Trade preference claims under FTAs apply for steel and aluminium products that are subject to Section 232, but Section 232 duties must be paid on those imports even if trade preferences apply. Also, they may be subject to AD and CV duties. Imports of any steel or aluminium article subject to Section 232 duties admitted into U.S. FTZs on or after 23 March 2018, enter with a "privileged foreign status"[140], except those articles eligible for admission under "domestic status"[141], and will be subject, upon entry for consumption, to any *ad valorem* rates of duty related to the classification under the applicable HTSUS subheading. No duty drawback claims may be made with respect to the Section 232 duties imposed on any aluminium or steel article.

Investigation into auto imports

On 23 May 2018, the USDOC initiated a Section 232 investigation into auto imports. The aim of the investigation is to determine whether imports of automobiles, including SUVs, vans and light trucks, and automotive parts into the United States threaten to impair the national security as defined in Section 232. Considerations taken into account to initiate the investigation include the increase of the share of imports of passenger vehicles sold in the United States from 32% to 48% in the last 20 years; a 22% decline in employment in motor vehicle production between 1990 and 2017; the low share of R&D represented by U.S. vehicle manufacturers in the United States (20% of the total); and the fact that U.S. auto part manufacturers account for only 7% of that industry in the United States. The points analyzed in the investigation include: whether the decline of domestic automobile and automotive parts production threatens to weaken the internal economy of the United States, including by potentially reducing R&D and jobs for skilled workers in cutting-edge technologies.[142] In July 2018, the USDOC held a public hearing on the investigation.[143]

Investigation into uranium imports

On 17 January 2018, two U.S. uranium mining companies, UR-Energy and Energy Fuels, filed a petition requesting that the USDOC initiate a Section 232 investigation into imports of uranium ore and products. On 18 July 2018, the USDOC announced the initiation of an investigation into whether the present quantity and circumstances of uranium ore and product imports into the United States threaten to impair national security. The investigation covers the entire uranium sector, from the mining industry through enrichment, defense, and industrial consumption. Some of the considerations taken into account to initiate the investigation include: (a) uranium powers 99 U.S. commercial nuclear reactors that produce 20% of the electricity for the electric grid; (b) uranium is a required component of the U.S. nuclear arsenal, and is used to power the Navy's nuclear fleet of submarines and aircraft carriers; (c) U.S. uranium production dropped from covering 49% of U.S. requirements in 1987 to 5% in 2017; (d) three U.S. companies with uranium mining operations have been idle in recent years; (e) two U.S. petitioners, accounting for over half of all uranium mined in the United States, have laid off over half their workforce over the last two years, and operate at roughly 9% and 13% of capacity, respectively; and (f) shuttered mines would take years to reopen under current environmental permitting regulations.[144]

Section 301 of the Trade Act of 1974

Section 301 procedures

Under Section 301 of the Trade Act of 1974, as amended (19 U.S.C. Section 2411), the United States may impose trade measures on foreign countries that maintain an act, policy or practice that violates, or denies U.S. rights or benefits under trade agreements; or is unjustifiable, unreasonable, or discriminatory, and burdens or restricts U.S. commerce. Under the statute, these acts, policies and practices include those which deny MFN or national treatment to U.S. exports, curtail the right of establishment of U.S. enterprises, and violate intellectual property rights. Section 301 investigations may be initiated following a petition by an interested party to USTR, or may be self-initiated by the USTR. If USTR receives a petition to initiate an investigation, it must determine, within 45 days, whether to initiate an investigation, based on considerations of the effectiveness of an action under Section 301 in addressing the act, policy or practice involved. After this period, USTR must publish in the Federal Register a determination to initiate an investigation, in cases where it finds merits in the petition, or provide reasons for not initiating one.

If an investigation is initiated, the process is open to comment from the public, and may include a public hearing if requested by the petitioner or an interested person. USTR requests consultations with the foreign government or governments involved. Where the investigation involves an alleged violation of a multilateral trade agreement or of a regional economic agreement with dispute settlement provisions, USTR must follow the consultation and dispute settlement provisions set out in that agreement.

Under Section 301 proceedings, USTR must terminate investigations involving a trade agreement with dispute settlement provisions within 18 months after initiation, or 30 days after the conclusion of dispute settlement procedures, whichever comes first. If the investigation does not involve a trade agreement with a dispute settlement mechanism, it must be concluded 12 months after its initiation. Investigations concerning intellectual property rights (IPRs) must lead to a determination within six months of initiation of the investigation, or nine months if the investigation involves complicated issues, or the foreign country involved is making substantial progress in legal and administrative reform in IPRs or undertaking IPR enforcement measures.

USTR may be assisted in Section 301 investigations by a Section 301 Committee, a subordinate body of the Trade Policy Staff Committee (TPSC). USTR designates the Section 301 Committee Chairman. The Committee consists of the Chairman and, with respect to each complaint, members as designated by agencies which have an interest in the issues raised by the particular complaint. The Section 301 Committee performs the following functions: (a) reviews complaints received pursuant to Section 301 of the Trade Act of 1974; (b) provides an opportunity, by the holding of public hearings upon request by a complainant or an interested party, for any interested party to present his views concerning foreign restrictions, acts, policies, and practices affecting U.S. commerce, and United States actions in response thereto, as provided for in Section 301 of the Trade Act (P.L. 93-618, 88 Stat. 1978); (c) reports to the TPSC the results of reviews and hearings conducted with respect to complaints received pursuant to Section 301 of the Trade Act; and (d) on the basis of its review of petitions filed under Section 301 and of the views received through hearings or otherwise on such petitions, makes recommendations to the TPSC for review by that Committee.

The TPEA amended the 1974 Trade Act to confirm that the Trade Representative may reinstate a previously terminated Section 301 action in order to exercise a WTO authorization to suspend trade concessions.[145] In particular, the Act amended relevant provisions of Section 306 of the 1974 Trade Act by adding a next section (c), that permits the Trade Representative to reinstate a Section 301 action following: (a) a request from the petitioner or any representative of the domestic industry that would benefit from the reinstatement of the action; (b) consultations under Section 306(d) of the Trade Act; and (c) a review under Section 307(c) of the Trade Act.[146] The Act does not contain dates of application for any of these amendments.[147]

Section 301 determinations

Under Section 301 (a) of the Trade Act of 1974, if, as a result of the investigation, USTR finds that a foreign government is violating or denying U.S. rights or benefits under a trade agreement, or its acts, policies or practices are unjustifiable and burden or restrict U.S. trade, it is required to take action. This is unless the WTO Dispute Settlement Body (DSB) has adopted a report dealing with a dispute regarding the matter covered in the investigation concerned which finds no violation or denial of U.S. rights, or if a NAFTA panel finds no violation to the agreement or that U.S. rights under the agreement are not being denied. USTR is not required to take action if it is found that the foreign country is taking satisfactory measures to grant U.S. rights under a trade agreement, or has agreed to eliminate or phase out the act, policy or practice or to provide any other satisfactory solution for the United States or, if this is not possible, to provide the United States with compensatory trade benefits.

Section 301 identifies three categories of acts, policies, or practices of a foreign country that are potentially actionable: (i) trade agreement violations; (ii) acts, policies or practices that are unjustifiable (defined as those that are inconsistent with U.S. international legal rights) and that burden or restrict U.S. commerce; and (iii) acts, policies or practices that are unreasonable or discriminatory, and that burden or restrict U.S. commerce. Section 301 defines "discriminatory" to include, when appropriate, any act, policy, and practice which denies national or MFN treatment to U.S. goods, services, or investment. An "unreasonable" act, policy, or practice is one that "while not necessarily in violation of, or inconsistent with, the international legal rights of the United States is otherwise unfair and inequitable." Section 301 further provides that, in determining if a foreign country's practices are unreasonable, reciprocal opportunities to those denied U.S. firms shall be taken into account, to the extent appropriate. Under Section 301(b), unreasonable practices include the denial of: (i) fair opportunities for the establishment of enterprises; (ii) adequate and effective IPR protection; (iii) fair and equitable market access opportunities for U.S. persons that rely on IP protection; (iv) fair and equitable market opportunities, including a foreign government's toleration of anti-competitive activities that restrict access of U.S. goods or services to a foreign market; and (v) worker rights. They may also include export targeting.

After making an affirmative determination under Section 301(a) or 301(b), USTR may reach a binding agreement with a foreign country to eliminate or phase out the act, policy or practice, eliminate any restriction on U.S. trade resulting from it, or provide compensatory trade benefits. In cases where an agreement is not reached, USTR may decide to: suspend or withdraw trade agreement concessions; impose duties or other import restrictions on goods (preference must be given to duties); impose fees or restrict the terms and conditions or deny issuance of authorizations to provide services, prior consultation with the relevant federal agency or state; and withdraw, limit or suspend duty-free treatment under the GSP or any other preferential scheme.

If USTR determines that the Section 301 investigation involves a trade agreement, and if this agreement includes formal dispute settlement procedures, USTR may pursue the investigation through consultations and dispute settlement under the trade agreement. Otherwise, USTR conducts the investigation without recourse to formal dispute settlement. The measure adopted by USTR may be directed at any economic sector, without regard to whether the good or sector was involved in the act, policy or practice subject to the determination. Similarly, the action may be taken on either a non-discriminatory basis or solely against the foreign country involved, but must be limited to a value equivalent to the burden or restriction imposed on U.S. commerce by the foreign country. Unless it considers that expeditious action is required, USTR must provide an opportunity for public comment on any proposed action. Actions must generally be implemented within 30 days of a determination, but may be delayed by not more than 180 days at the petitioner's request, or if USTR determines that substantial progress is being made in negotiations with the foreign country, or if a delay is deemed necessary or convenient to obtain a satisfactory solution to the issue. Section 306 of the Trade Act of 1974 mandates that USTR monitor the implementation of each measure taken and agreement entered resulting from a Section 301 investigation or

from a dispute settlement proceeding under a trade agreement or the WTO. If, as result of a Section 306 monitoring, and prior consultations with the petitioner in the original investigation or with the affected domestic industry or other interested persons, USTR considers that the foreign country is not satisfactorily implementing a measure or agreement, it must make a determination for further action.

Section 301 cases

China technology transfer regime

On 18 August 2017, USTR initiated an investigation under Section 301 of the Trade Act of 1974 into the Government of China's acts, policies, and practices related to technology transfer, intellectual property, and innovation. The notice of initiation identified four specific elements of China's technology transfer regime for investigation, linked to: administrative approval processes, joint venture requirements and foreign equity limitations; the ability to set market-based terms in technology-related negotiations; facilitation of outbound Chinese investment targeting U.S. companies and assets in key industry sectors; and protection of trade secrets and other proprietary information. The notice also requested information on other acts, policies, and practices of the Chinese Government related to technology transfer, IP, and innovation.[148] USTR held a public hearing in October 2017, consulted with the private sector, initiated two rounds of public written comment periods, and received approximately 70 written submissions.

Subsequently, USTR, with the assistance of the interagency Section 301 Committee, prepared a report that concluded that the acts, policies, and practices of the Chinese Government related to technology transfer, IP, and innovation are unreasonable or discriminatory, and burden or restrict U.S. commerce.[149] USTR estimated that China's policies had resulted in harm to the U.S. economy of at least US$50 billion per year.

In a Memorandum signed on 22 March 2018, the President directed his Administration to take a range of actions responding to China's acts, policies, and practices involving the matter investigated, including preparing a list of proposed additional tariffs within 15 days.[150] USTR proposed additional 25% tariffs on certain products of China, with an annual trade value commensurate with the harm caused to the U.S. economy resulting from China's unfair policies. The proposed product list subject to the tariffs included aerospace, information and communication technology (ICT), and machinery.[151] The President also directed USTR to present a complaint with respect to China's technology licensing practices before the WTO's DSB. On 23 March 2018, the United States requested consultations with China concerning certain measures pertaining to the protection of IPRs. The United States claimed that the measures appear to be inconsistent with Articles 3, 28.1(a) and (b) and 28.2 of the TRIPS Agreement.[152] In early April 2018, Japan,

Part B
Report by the WTO Secretariat

the European Union, Ukraine, Saudi Arabia and Chinese Taipei requested to join the consultations.

In the WTO Council for Goods, China expressed concerns over the final conclusions of the Section 301 investigation of China's IP regime, released on 22 March 2018. The United States referred Members to the USTR website for more information about the Section 301 actions, and noted that, according to the USTR report, China's technology transfer policies and practices were causing "billions of dollars in losses annually" to U.S. businesses and individuals, and that the United States had requested consultations with China under the WTO's DSU with respect to one of the four matters covered in the investigation.[153]

On 15 June 2018, USTR issued a list of products covering 1,102 separate U.S. tariff lines valued at approximately US$50 billion in 2018 trade values. The list included products from industrial sectors that contribute to, or benefit from, the "Made in China 2025" industrial policy, which include industries such as aerospace, ICT, robotics, industrial machinery, new materials, and automobiles. This list consists of two sets of U.S tariff lines: the first contains 818 lines of the original 1,333 lines that were included on the proposed list published on the Federal Register on 6 April. It comprises mostly products classified under HS Chapters 84 to 90, and covers approximately US$34 billion worth of imports from China.[154] CBP was instructed to begin to collect the additional duties on 6 July 2018.[155] The second set contains 284 proposed tariff lines identified by the interagency Section 301 Committee as benefiting from Chinese industrial policies, including the "Made in China 2025" industrial policy, covering some US$16 billion worth of imports from China; these would undergo further review in a public notice and comment process, including a public hearing.[156]

On 15 June, China announced it would take countermeasures for US$50 billion in the form of additional 25% tariffs. Tariffs on about US$34 billion of those products would start on 6 July, and be applied to soybeans, corn, wheat, rice, sorghum, beef, pork, poultry, fish, dairy products, nuts and vegetables, autos, etc. On 18 June, the President directed the USTR to identify US$200 billion worth of Chinese goods for additional tariffs at a rate of 10%, that would go into effect after the appropriate legal process if China refused to change its practices, and insisted on going forward with the new tariffs announced.[157]

On 20 June 2018 (83 FR 28710), the USTR provided notice of an initial action in the Section 301 investigation, consisting of the imposition of an additional 25% *ad valorem* duty on products of China with an annual trade value of approximately US$34 billion, effective 6 July 2018. The notice also sought public comment on another proposed action, in the form of an additional 25% *ad valorem* duty on products of China with an annual trade value of approximately US$16 billion. The public comment process in connection with the

proposed additional action was completed on 31 July 2018. On 6 July 2018, China responded to the initial action by imposing increased duties on goods of the United States. In response, the USTR proposed a modification of the action taken in the investigation, to maintain the original US$34 billion and the proposed US$16 billion actions, and to take further action in the form of an additional 10% *ad valorem* duty on products of China covered in 6,031 tariff subheadings with an annual trade value of approximately US$200 billion.[158] In developing the list of tariff subheadings included in this proposed supplemental action, USTR considered products from across all sectors of the Chinese economy. Subheadings identified as likely to cause disruptions to the U.S. economy, and tariff lines subject to legal or administrative constraints, were not included in the list. To ensure enforcement, merchandises subject to the increased tariffs admitted into a U.S. FTZ on or after the effective date of the increased tariffs, except those eligible for admission under domestic status (as defined in 19 CFR 146.43), are to be admitted as "privileged foreign status" and would be subject to the additional duty upon entry for consumption.[159]

EU beef trade

On 9 December 2016, representatives of the beef industry invoked the new Section 306(c) of the 1974 Trade Act, which allows the USTR to reinstate a previously terminated Section 301 action in order to exercise a WTO authorization to suspend trade concessions, by filing a written request for reinstatement of action.[160] A list of products under consideration for the imposition of increased duties in accordance with the WTO DSB authorization in the 1999 EU-Beef dispute was published in the Federal Register. No further action has been taken under Section 306(c); the matter is currently being handled bilaterally with the European Union.[161]

MEASURES DIRECTLY AFFECTING EXPORTS

Export procedures and requirements

CBP is responsible for ensuring that goods leaving the United States do so in conformity with all applicable U.S. laws, regulations, and rules relating to exports. It also acts on behalf of other relevant government agencies in enforcing the rules. Online filing of export data is required prior to the departure of cargo for security purposes and for the conduct of risk assessment by CBP.[162] Licence applications, if needed, for the export, reexport or transfer (in-country) of dual-use and less sensitive military items are submitted electronically to the BIS. BIS reviews the application and then requests review and recommendation from the other agencies (Departments of State, Defense, and Energy).[163]

Commodity information for all export shipments valued over US$2,500 is submitted through the Automated Export System (AES) or AESDirect, a portal within the single-window Automated Commercial Environment (ACE).[164]

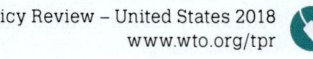

Commodity information for all export shipments that require a licence or licence exemption must be filed in the AES regardless of value. Although the Trade Act of 2002 (P.L. 107-210) stipulates the use of electronic export manifests in all modes of transport, no regulatory requirement has been established to enforce electronic filing, and paper copies continue to be accepted. CBP has deployed export manifest filing capabilities in ACE and has published Federal Register notices announcing electronic manifest pilots for air, ocean, and rail modes of transport. Some carriers are currently submitting electronic export manifest data and bills of lading on a voluntary basis. CBP's Office of Field Operations is expanding the electronic export manifest pilots for air, ocean and rail conveyances, and participation by carriers is encouraged. Federal Register notices expanding the pilots were announced in August 2017. Documentation pertinent to export shipments must be kept for five years by the exporter or those acting on his/her behalf.

Export taxes, charges, and levies

Article I, Section 9 of the Constitution bans the use of export taxes. On various occasions in the past, general export levies or fees have been found unconstitutional when examined by the courts and consequently revoked. However, Article I, Section 10 of the Constitution authorizes fees to be charged for specific services rendered such as inspection and certification fees for agricultural exports.

Export prohibitions, restrictions, and licensing

The United States maintains export restrictions, including prohibitions, licensing requirements or additional controls on a variety of exports and re-exports for reasons of national security, foreign policy considerations, the non-proliferation of nuclear materials, and other temporary objectives. The measures may be based on domestic legislation, policy decisions, UN Security Council resolutions, international agreements, or U.S. participation in non-binding arrangements such as the Wassenaar Arrangement, the Missile Technology Control Regime, the Treaty on the Non-Proliferation of Nuclear Weapons and the Exporters Committee (Zangger Committee), the Nuclear Suppliers Group, and the Australia Group. The Departments of State, Commerce, Homeland Security, Treasury, Defense, and Energy are all involved in export control and non-proliferation activities in the United States and abroad. The enforcement of export controls is shared between the Departments of Homeland Security, Justice, and Commerce.

The Export Administration Act (EAA) of 1979, as amended, was until recently the principal implementing statute for export controls of dual-use and less militarily significant items. The EAA expired on 21 August 2001, after which date the BIS carried out its provisions pursuant to Executive Order 13222 of 17 August 2001 (authorized under the International Emergency Economic Powers Act (IEEPA)) as amended by Executive Order 13637 of 8 March 2013. The EAA was largely repealed by the Export Control Reform Act of 2018 (P.L. 115-232) (ECRA). The ECRA is now the principal implementing statute for the export controls BIS had administered pursuant to the Executive Order issued under the IEEPA. All administrative actions, including licences, orders, and regulations made, issued, conducted, or allowed to become effective under the EAA while it was in effect continue to be in effect under the ECRA. The Atomic Energy Act of 1954, as amended, constitutes the legal basis for export controls on nuclear materials, facilities, and equipment for civilian purposes. These controls are administered by the U.S. Nuclear Regulatory Commission. Other departments and agencies have also been assigned responsibilities for export controls (Table 3.11), and their controls may in some instances (foreign policy or national security considerations) overlap with the functions carried out by the USDOC.

As a starting point, it is the duty of the exporter to determine whether an export licence is needed due to the nature of the product, its destination, or possible end-uses.[165] Every item subject to the Export Administration Regulations (EAR), administered by the BIS, has either an assigned Export Control Classification Number (ECCN) or is designated as EAR99. The classification is derived from the technical parameters of the item, and all ECCNs are listed on the Commerce Control List (CCL) for dual use and certain munitions goods. Items not on the CCL, i.e. EAR99 items, may be exported or re-exported without a licence unless the destination is: (i) an embargoed or sanctioned country; (ii) a party of concern; or (iii) in support of a prohibited end-use (Chart 3.2). Countryspecific embargoes or other special controls primarily affect trade with Cuba, the Democratic People's Republic of Korea, the Russian Federation, Iran, Sudan, and Syria. The BIS maintains a Denied Persons List comprising persons and entities denied export privileges and with whom any dealings are prohibited; an Unverified List, a list of end-users the BIS has been unable to verify in prior transactions; and an Entity List, i.e. parties whose presence in a transaction may trigger a supplementary licence requirement.[166] For destinations posing a low risk of non-authorized or impermissible uses (37 countries), exports, re-exports or in-country transfers may be authorized under "Licence Exception Strategic Trade Authorization (STA)". The determination of criminal acts and penalties for infringement of export controls vary depending on the product and the relevant agency or law.[167]

Changes in the export control regime occur at regular intervals, reflecting, for example, the outcomes of meetings in the non-binding arrangements in which the United States participates; results of review efforts, new entries, deletions, or modified entries in the list of persons and entities of concern; or modifications of sanctions and embargoes applicable to specific countries or institutions (Table A3.4).

Table 3.11 Items subject to export controls, including licensing

Product category	Responsible agencies	Legal reference
Dual-use items, certain munitions and military items, and items controlled for short supply	USDOC, BIS	ECRA EAA IEEPA
Defence services and defence articles	Department of State, Directorate of Defense Trade Controls	22 CFR parts 120 through 130
Controlled substances and listed chemicals used in the production of controlled substances	Drug Enforcement Administration, Office of Diversion Control, Import-Export Unit (chemicals and controlled substances) Food and Drug Administration, Import/Export (drugs and biologics) Food and Drug Administration, International Affairs (investigational drugs permitted)	21 CFR parts 1311 through 1313 21 U.S.C. 301 et seq. 21 CFR 312.1106
Fish and wildlife controls; endangered species	Department of the Interior, Chief Office of Management Authority	50 CFR 17.21, 17.22, 17.31, 17.32
Foreign assets and transaction controls	Department of Treasury, Office of Foreign Assets Control, Licensing	31 CFR parts 500 through 590
Medical devices	Food and Drug Administration, Office of Compliance	21 U.S.C. et seq.
Natural gas and electric power	Department of Energy, Office of Fuels Programs	10 CFR 205.300 through 205.379 and 590
Nuclear materials and equipment	Nuclear Regulatory Commission, Office of International Programs	10 CFR part 110
Nuclear technology; technical data for nuclear weapons, and special nuclear materials	Department of Energy, Office of Export Control Policy and Cooperation (NA-24)	10 CFR part 810
Ocean freight forwarders	Federal Maritime Commission, Office of Freight Forwarders	46 CFR part 510
Patent filing data sent abroad	Department of Commerce, Patent and Trademark Office, Licensing and Review	35 U.S.C. 184 et seq. 37 CFR part 5
U.S. flagged or U.S. manufactured vessels over 1,000 gross tonnes	U.S. Maritime Administration, Division of Vessel Transfer and Disposal	46 CFR part 221
Hazardous waste	Environmental Protection Agency, Office of Resource Conservation and Recovery	40 CFR part 262, subpart E 40 CFR section 263.20 40 CFR section 263.22(d)

Source: WTO Secretariat, based on information contained in Supplement No. 3 to Part 730 of the Export Administration Regulations and BIS online information. Viewed at: https://www.bis.doc.gov/index.php/about-bis/resource-links.

Recognizing that the export control system had become overly complex, fragmented, and needed updating, an export control reform was launched by Presidential initiative in 2009 and the establishment of an Export Enforcement Coordination Center was announced in 2010.[168] The Center is currently managed by Homeland Security Investigations (HSI) as part of the Department of Homeland Security. A major component in the reform work has been the rationalization of the two export control lists for dual-use (military/civilian) goods, including services, technology and data, certain military items, and munitions, i.e. the U.S. Munitions List (USML) maintained by the Department of State, and the CCL of the USDOC (Table 3.12).[169] The regulatory changes led to the migration of less sensitive items from the USML to the CCL. Revisions of 18 of the 21 categories on the USML were completed in 2016. For the three remaining categories, the public comments on the proposed changes are currently under interagency review.[170]

Regarding export controls on energy, the Natural Gas Act of 1938, as amended, requires any person wishing to export or import natural gas to obtain authorization from the Department of Energy (DOE).[171] Permission is granted in the form of short-term or long-term authorizations.[172] Applications to import or export liquefied natural gas (LNG) to countries that have concluded FTAs with the United States are granted without modification or delay as the FTAs stipulate national treatment and such trade is deemed consistent with public interest. The DOE also authorizes natural gas exports to non-FTA countries unless the proposed exports are deemed inconsistent with public interest or explicitly prohibited by law or policy. The first major shipment of U.S. LNG occurred in February 2016. In 2017, exports of LNG totalled almost 2 billion cubic feet per day, a volume four times higher than in 2016.[173] Restrictions on crude oil exports, effectively banned from 1975 to 2015 (except for minor quantities sold to Canada and Mexico), were lifted in December 2015.[174]

Export support and promotion

The Trade Promotion Coordinating Committee (TPCC), created in the early 1990s, brings together 20 federal government agencies with export-related programmes to ensure alignment among federal trade promotion

Chart 3.2 Export control decision tree

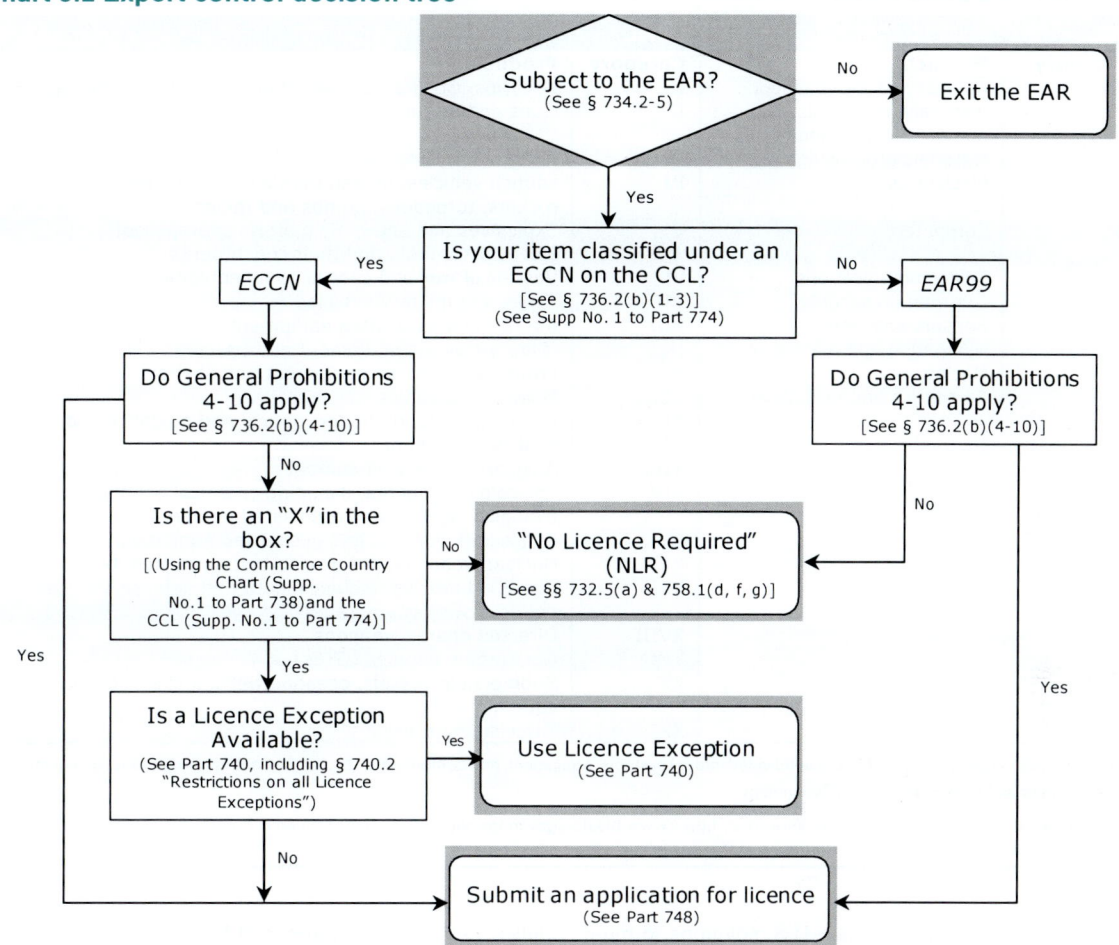

Source: Export Administration Regulations, Supplement No. 1 to Part 732, published in Federal Register, Vol. 82, No. 247, 27 December 2017.

Part B
Report by the WTO Secretariat

activities and to better assist exporters. Trade promotion agencies or programmes also exist at the state and local level. The Trade Facilitation and Trade Enforcement Act of 2015 accordingly instructed the TPCC to work with representatives of state agencies to devise a strategy for the coordination of state and federal resources. The TPCC established a State and Local Working Group, to enhance coordination and created a Federal-State Export Strategic Plan template that federal and state trade offices use to share information and coordinate activities on an annual basis within each state. The TPCC is, in principle, required to publish an annual National Export Strategy, to outline government priorities and report on the effectiveness of existing export promotion efforts. However, after the 2012 report, which focused on export promotion priorities and reducing foreign trade barriers, no new report was issued until December 2016.[175] According to that latest report, federal agency efforts *inter alia* helped U.S. enterprises win US$239 billion in U.S. content on major projects over eight years, counselled several thousand new clients to support US$55 billion in exports of goods and services, and provided significant new market opportunities through the WTO and regional or bilateral instruments. The results were achieved despite strong

economic headwinds. The next National Export Strategy is expected to be published in late 2018.

Although the mandate of the President's Export Council (PEC), an advisory body created in 1979 by Executive Order 12131, has been extended until 30 September 2019[176], the PEC has not met since 14 September 2016. Members of the PEC are appointed by the President, and no appointments have been made in the current Administration.

The U.S. Trade and Development Agency (USTDA) is an independent agency that links U.S. businesses to overseas opportunities by funding project preparation and partnership-building activities that develop sustainable infrastructure in emerging economies. USTDA's funding brings in U.S. industry experts to perform feasibility studies, launch pilot projects, or provide a diverse array of technical assistance. The Agency also connects project sponsors with U.S. businesses through its reverse trade missions, which bring overseas decision-makers to the United States to introduce them to the design, manufacture, and operation of U.S. goods and services. The Agency's programming provides "win-win" results: U.S. companies gain access to high-level decision makers, while overseas partners gain insights

Table 3.12 CCL and USML

CCL		USML	
Category	**Products**	**Category**	**Products**
0	Nuclear and miscellaneous	I	Firearms, close assault weapons, and combat shotguns
1	Materials, chemicals, microorganisms and toxins	II	Guns and armament
2	Materials processing	III	Ammunition/Ordnance
3	Electronics	IV	Launch vehicles, guided missiles, ballistic missiles, rockets, torpedoes, bombs and mines
4	Computers	V	Explosives and energetic materials, propellants, incendiary agents and their constituents
5 Part 1	Telecommunications	VI	Vessels of war and special naval equipment
5 Part 2	Information security	VII	Tanks and military vehicles
6	Sensors and lasers	VIII	Aircraft and associated equipment
7	Navigation and avionics	IX	Military training equipment and training
8	Marine	X	Protective personal equipment and shelters
9	Aerospace and propulsion	XI	Military electronics
		XII	Fire control, range finder, optical and guidance and control equipment
		XIII	Auxiliary military equipment
		XIV	Toxicological agents, including chemical agents, biological agents, and associated equipment
		XV	Spacecraft systems and associated equipment
		XVI	Nuclear weapons, design and testing related items
		XVII	Classified articles, technical data and defense services not otherwise enumerated
		XVIII	Directed energy weapons
		XIX	Gas turbine engines (GTEs)
		XX	Submersible vessels, oceanographic and associated equipment
		XXI	Miscellaneous articles

Note: Each broad category on the CCL is subdivided into (a) systems, equipment, and components; (b) test, inspection, and production equipment; (c) material; (d) software; and (e) Technology.

Source: USDOC, BIS online information. Viewed at: http://www.bis.doc.gov/index.php/regulations/commerce-control-list-ccl and 22 CFR Part 121 viewed at: https://www.ecfr.gov/cgi-bin/text-idx?node=pt22.1.121.

into the latest, most appropriate U.S. solutions to meet their infrastructure needs. The USTDA becomes involved strategically in industry sectors where U.S. businesses are most competitive – energy, transportation, and ICT – and has prioritized its funding in the fastest-growing emerging economies where U.S. goods and services are most in demand. According to the U.S. authorities, the USTDA is unique among federal agencies in that it is mandated to engage the private sector in infrastructure projects at the critical early stages when the projects' technology options and requirements are being defined, with the objective of creating a level, fair playing field for U.S. companies. The Agency's Global Procurement Initiative: Understanding Best Value (GPI) assists in this endeavour by helping public procurement officials in emerging economies establish practices and policies that integrate life-cycle cost analysis and best-value determination in a fair, transparent manner.

Drawback regime

The refund of customs duty paid on imported articles subsequently exported, destroyed, or incorporated in products that are exported (or destroyed) may be requested under the United States Code (19 U.S.C. 1313). According to the provisions of the old legislation ("core drawback") drawback on unused imported merchandise, exported or destroyed under CBP supervision should generally be filed within three years of exportation or destruction of the articles. The drawback usually amounts to 99% of customs duties, certain excise taxes, and fees lawfully collected at importation, including the merchandise processing fee and the harbour maintenance tax.

The Trade Facilitation and Trade Enforcement Act (TFTEA) of 2015 (P.L. 114-125), Section 906, introduced a number of changes in the duty drawback programme. It extended the deadline for the exportation or destruction of imported articles under the unused merchandise drawback programme from three to five years, and increased the overall data inputs required, including mandating the eight-digit classification number when describing the merchandise. For transfers of imported merchandise from importer to manufacturer or claimant, the Act relaxed the documentation requirements, by eliminating the need to obtain a Certificate of Delivery for the drawback claim. Henceforth, business records kept in the normal course of business should suffice to document the transfer of merchandise. The Act provided a two-year transitional period for CBP to implement the new provisions in full, i.e. until 24 February 2018, including a requirement that all drawback claims be filed and processed electronically. As from that date, all Automated Broker Interface (ABI) filings of drawback have been required to use ACE. A further transition period applies until 24 February 2019, during which claimants may opt to file requests for duty drawback according to CORE drawback or the new legislation ("TFTEA drawback"). During this period, claims for CORE drawback may still be submitted in hard copy to one of the four CBP drawback offices, but priority will be given to the processing of electronic filings. The Act mandated the Secretary of the Treasury to elaborate new regulations for the calculation of duty drawback by December 2017. The Notice of Proposed Rule Making for Modernized Drawback was published in the Federal Register on 2 August 2018.

Export finance, insurance, guarantees

The Export-Import Bank (EXIM)

EXIM Bank is the official export credit agency of the United States. As such, it may assume credit and country risks that commercial lenders are unwilling or unable to accept. Nevertheless, the Bank's charter requires all authorized transactions to demonstrate a reasonable assurance of repayment, and to comply with the Bank's policies and practices as directed by statute, the EXIM Bank board, and international agreements. EXIM Bank's Country Limitation Schedule details limitations the bank imposes on itself with respect to the acceptance of commercial and political risks in individual countries.[177] Support to trade with the Plurinational State of Bolivia, Cuba, Iran, the Democratic People's Republic of Korea, and Syria is legally prohibited. Private sector lenders normally act as partners in EXIM Bank transactions.

EXIM Bank is an independent executive branch agency as well as a wholly-owned government corporation, first organized as a District of Columbia banking corporation in 1934. It is financially self-sustained, and its profits have allowed an accumulated US$9.5 billion to be transferred to the Treasury since 1992. EXIM Bank has exposure in 166 countries. Measured by the volume of exposure, the Bank's most important markets are Mexico, Saudi Arabia, China, Australia, and India. Long-term project finance has traditionally been its most profitable business. However, in recent years its operations have been severely constrained by prolonged domestic political disagreement (Table 3.13).

Although EXIM Bank is independent from the Government in day-to-day operations, its lending authority is established by Congress. In 2015, the Bank experienced an unprecedented five-month period during which its authority to approve transactions had lapsed and, as a result, all involvement in new business opportunities was

curtailed. As new legislation reauthorizing EXIM Bank until 30 September 2019 entered into force in December 2015, its lending authority was capped (at US$135 billion), while its small business lending target was raised from 20% to 25%.[178] In FY2017, more than 90% of its authorizations concerned small businesses, which made up more than 63% of the total dollar value of the authorizations and nearly 76% of the direct export value supported by the Bank. However, the Bank's overall financial exposure as of August 2018 (about US$64 billion) is well below the established ceiling and is steadily declining, as a further key operational roadblock persists.

EXIM Bank's charter stipulates a five-member Board of Directors charged with the approval of individual transactions, Bank policies, and other matters that may arise. The Board members are appointed by the President of the United States, with the advice and consent of the Senate. Small loans and certain medium-term loans may be authorized by EXIM Bank staff, but all medium- and long-term authorizations above US$10 million must be approved by the Board of Directors. The Board has lacked a quorum of three members to take such decisions since 20 July 2015, as the confirmation of the President's nominees for vacant positions have been consistently held up in the Senate.

The 2015 legislation reauthorizing EXIM Bank includes provisions (Section 55002) mandating the United States to initiate and pursue negotiations with other major exporting countries to reduce substantially, and with a view to possibly eliminating (by 2025), subsidized export-financing programmes and other forms of export subsidies. In addition, the United States is to initiate and pursue negotiations with countries that are not OECD members, to bring them into a multilateral agreement with rules and limitations on officially supported export credits. Each year, the Department of the Treasury delivers a report to Congress which provides an update on the progress achieved in implementing the instructions set forth in Section 55002.

Small Business Administration (SBA) export loan programmes

The SBA, created by Congress in 1953 to "aid, counsel, assist, and protect, insofar as is possible, the interests

Table 3.13 EXIM Bank authorizations, 2014-17

	2014		2015		2016		2017	
	No.	US$ million	No.	US$ million	No.	US$ million	No.	US$ million
Loans	69	1,947.8	41	72.7	0	0	12	5.6
Long term	14	1,927.6	4	57.7	0	0	0	0
Medium term	0	0	0	0	0	0	0	0
Working capital	55	20.2	37	15.0	0	0	12	5.6
Guarantees	540	13,314.1	344	9,068.1	265	1,229.8	221	961.1
Long term	51	10,786.7	42	7,917.3	0	0	1	2.6
Medium term	58	137.5	41	149.8	28	123.3	25	119.5
Working capital	431	2,389.8	261	1,001.0	237	1,106.5	195	839.0
Credit Insurance	3,137	5,206.1	2,245	3,242.2	2,634	3,807.3	2,228	2,464.3
Short term	3,078	5,107.3	2,216	3,196.5	2,625	3,797.1	2,186	2,414.3
Medium term	59	98.8	29	45.7	9	10.2	42	50.0

Source: EXIM Bank, *Annual Reports*, 2015, 2016, and 2017. Viewed at: https://www.exim.gov/news/reports/annual-reports.

of small business concerns", administers three broad programmes through its Office of International Trade that offer export financing for small businesses exporting or planning to export (Table 3.14). In addition, it provides grants to states to assist small businesses with information and tools to succeed in exporting through its State Trade and Export Promotion Program (STEP).[179] It also contributes staff to the U.S. Export Assistance Centers (USEACs), a joint effort with the USDOC and EXIM Bank to provide export marketing and finance assistance to small and medium sized U.S. businesses.

The SBA as such is not a bank. The specific loan terms are, therefore, negotiated between the qualified borrower and an SBA-approved lender. Applicants for SBA export loans must provide export business plans, including historical data, projections, and written information supporting the likelihood of increased export sales. No minimum borrowed amount is required, and the SBA guarantees loans up to US$5 million. The fee the SBA charges for its guarantee depends on the loan's maturity and the guaranteed amount (up to 90% for most loans), and is initially paid by the lender.

The most streamlined export financing provided with the assistance of the SBA is the Express Loan Program, which allows lenders to use their own forms and procedures. Export Express loans can be up to US$500,000, with an SBA loan guaranty of either 75% or 90%. The Export Working Capital Program provides working capital financing to support an exporter's transactions, from purchase order to final payment, with a US$5 million maximum loan amount and 90% guaranty. Finally, the International Trade Loan Program offers a combination of fixed asset, working capital financing, and debt refinancing up to US$5 million, with the SBA guaranteeing 90% of the total loan amount.

Overseas Private Investment Corporation (OPIC)

Operating since 1971, the OPIC is the Government's development finance institution. It mobilizes private capital to help address critical development challenges by providing investor financing, political risk insurance, and support for private equity investment funds when such funding is not forthcoming from normal commercial sources. The OPIC does not compete with private commercial lenders. It is a financially self-sustaining, independent government corporation. Since its inception, it has realized net collections from its operations totalling US$8 billion.

The OPIC is authorized to do business in more than 160 developing and post-conflict countries.[180] It is mandated by law to prioritize investment in low-income countries. It also sets limits to its exposure in various countries to maintain a balanced portfolio. Its domestic clients must be U.S. citizens, permanent residents, or U.S. companies, or the projects must imply a "meaningful involvement" of the U.S. private sector, defined as a minimum 25% stake in the project or in the project company.[181] The OPIC has a statutory requirement to ensure that its supported projects are established and maintained in accordance with internationally recognized worker rights standards. It has also elaborated an Environmental and Social Policy Statement, designed to ensure that supported projects are environmentally and socially sustainable.[182]

The OPIC provides medium- to long-term loans (up to 30 years), typically ranging from US$5 million to US$50 million, primarily to cover the capital costs of a project's establishment or expansion.[183] It will not consider requests related solely to the need for working capital or the financing of acquisitions, and it does not provide trade finance. Political-risk insurance covers possible

Table 3.14 Approved applications and loan amounts under SBA export loan programmes, 2014-17

Program title	2014		2015		2016		2017	
	No.	US$ million	No.	US$ million	No.	US$ million	No.	US$ million
Export Express	124	23.5	156	28.0	101	22.0	53	15.0
Export Working Capital	185	307.4	176	307.5	167	313.0	166	337.0
International Trade Loan	193	285.4	215	394.3	215	375.0	192	308.0

Source: SBA (2016 & 2017), *Summary of Performance and Financial Information – Fiscal Years 2016 and 2017*. Viewed at: https://www.sba.gov/sites/default/files/aboutsbaarticle/FINAL_SBA_FY_2018_CBJ_May_22_2017c.pdf and https://www.sba.gov/sites/default/files/aboutsbaarticle/SBA_FY_19_508-Final-FINAL.PDF.

Table 3.15 Overview of OPIC activities, FY2015-17

(US$ billion)

New commitments	FY2015	FY2016	FY2017
Financing	3.84	3.02	1.65
Investment funds	0.39	0.56	0.59
Insurance	0.16	0.10	1.51
Total	4.39	3.69	3.76
U.S. exports projected	0.26	0.10	3.09
Total portfolio	19.93	21.48	23.21
Active countries	96	95	90

Source: OPIC, Annual Reports 2015-17. Viewed at: https://www.opic.gov/media-events/annual-reports; and information provided by the authorities.

loss of tangible assets, investment value, and earnings. Since 1987, the OPIC has committed US$5.3 billion to 82 private equity funds in emerging markets. The funds, in turn, have invested US$10.4 billion in more than 670 companies across more than 65 countries. The OPIC is typically one of the first fund sponsors to enter an unproven market.

OPIC operations have been growing over the years. At the end of September 2017, OPIC's combined total exposure stood at US$23.21 billion, the largest portfolio in its history (Table 3.15). Its authorized exposure limit is US$29 billion. At present, it is operating under the Fiscal Year 2018 Consolidated Appropriations Act (P.L. 115-141).

MEASURES AFFECTING PRODUCTION AND TRADE

Incentives

The United States encourages private enterprise and competition based on free market economic principles.

It has no overarching legal framework governing subsidies at federal and sub-federal levels. Traditionally, federal subsidies have been in the form of grants, tax concessions, loan guarantees, and direct payments. The Catalog of Federal Domestic Assistance (CFDA) lists all federal financial (and non-financial) assistance programmes – many, if not most, related to public health and safety, the environment, education, infrastructure, community assistance, and research and development - using a five-digit classification to identify and sort around 2,300 programmes. On 23 May 2018, the CFDA was migrated to the website https://beta.SAM.gov, where the search engine is now referred to as "Assistance Listings". According to a database maintained by SelectUSA, some 108 federal programmes and incentives exist specifically to promote small businesses, provide support to existing or prospective exporters, and assist enterprises with regulatory compliance.[184]

State, territorial and local governments also provide support and incentives, particularly in relation to business start-ups or the expansion of existing operations. A database developed by the Council for Community and Economic Research (C2ER), accessible at: http://selectusa.stateincentives.org/?referrer=selectusa, includes information on 1,790 programmes enacted in the 50 states. Such support is provided in the form of tax credits, tax exemptions, grants, loans or loan participation, or other forms of assistance.

Led by the Department of Commerce, SelectUSA was created in 2011 as a government-wide programme to promote and facilitate business investment by foreign companies. In addition to its databases on federal and state incentives, it offers services such as a public, self-service data visualization tool that provides insights into FDI trends (SelectUSA Stats), and the Cluster Mapping Tool (https://www.clustermapping.us/) allowing users to identify regional concentrations of specific industries

and potential partners. SelectUSA chairs the Federal Interagency Investment Working Group (IIWG), a body that brings together more than 20 federal agencies and bureaus to enhance coordination, provide guidance and information, and respond to broad-based or more limited issues that affect investment decisions. Through its ombudsman services, SelectUSA collaborates with IIWG agency partners to help address investor questions and concerns relating to a wide range of federal regulatory issues.

The SBA supports small businesses and entrepreneurs. It provides its services through partnerships with private and public institutions and via an extensive network of field offices throughout the United States, Puerto Rico, the U.S. Virgin Islands, and Guam. It offers loan guarantees, counselling, and other forms of assistance, while loans are made available through partner financial institutions. According to the Agency, loans with SBA approval totalling more than US$30 billion were provided to small businesses in FY2017, and the loans supported nearly 630,000 jobs.[185] The SBA does not offer grants for business start-ups, but such support may be available from state or local government sources. It is responsible for determining whether the government-wide procurement goal for small businesses[186] is met, and that the achievements of the reporting agencies relate to their individual goals negotiated with the SBA.[187] The SBA publishes the annual goals for the 24 federal agencies that are subject to the Chief Financial Officers Act, and the agencies report their outcomes to the SBA's Office of Government Contracting and Business Development though the Federal Procurement Data System Next Generation.[188]

Among the federal programmes, trade adjustment assistance programmes have been established for enterprises and workers. The Trade Adjustment Assistance for Firms (TAAF) provides technical assistance to eligible domestic manufacturers affected by import competition without regard to the nature of the industry. Support is provided on a cost-sharing basis for the development of business recovery plans, and projects outlined in them, to expand markets, strengthen operations, and increase competitiveness. The TAAF is administered by the Economic Development Administration at the USDOC, and assistance is disseminated through 11 non-profit or universityaffiliated centres serving firms in the 50 states. No funds are provided directly to firms. The FY2017 budget for TAAF was US$13 million, and the value of the technical assistance that firms received amounted to US$6.9 million.[189] Workers losing their jobs or facing cuts in pay or hours worked due to increased imports are eligible for federal assistance under the Trade Adjustment Assistance for Workers programme. The programme is administered by the Employment and Training Administration at the Department of Labor. The programme was reauthorized in 2015, and is ongoing. Trade adjustment assistance for farmers, administered by the Department of Agriculture, is authorized under PL 114-27 to receive US$90 million annually for FY2015 through FY2021, subject to annual appropriations. However, Congress has not appropriated funding since the first quarter of FY2011, and as a result, the programme is inactive.

Like other WTO Members, the United States notifies subsidy programmes to the WTO without prejudice to their legal status regarding specificity, or being actionable (or otherwise) under the Agreement on Subsidies and Countervailing Measures. The most recent subsidy notification, circulated in March 2018, covers fiscal years 2015 and 2016. Aside from agriculture, federal-level subsidies are primarily directed towards the energy sector (Table 3.16). The notification also provides information on 671 subsidy programmes maintained at state level. Data on programme costs in this latest notification has been provided for a significantly higher number of programmes than previously, but not all programmes include an estimated cost.

Standards and other technical requirements

The development of standards is decentralized and demand-driven. The private sector addresses the needs or concerns expressed by industry, Government, and consumers, through the development of voluntary consensus standards (VCSs). The actual work to develop these VCSs is undertaken by standards developing organizations (SDOs). A private, non-profit organization, the American National Standards Institute (ANSI), coordinates and administers the VCS system. ANSI is the sole U.S. member body to the International Organization for Standardization (ISO) and, through the U.S. National Committee, to the International Electrotechnical Commission (IEC).

Some 240 ANSI-accredited standards developers (ASDs) prepare American National Standards (ANSs), a type of VCS.[190] Currently, ASDs sponsor more than 11,000 ANSs. ASDs are obliged to adhere to due process requirements for the preparation, approval, revision, reaffirmation, or withdrawal of ANSs (the "ANSI Essential Requirements") to maintain their accreditation with ANSI.[191] In essence, suitable media should be used to facilitate broad participation; the process should be open to all those affected directly and materially by the activity; the ASD should balance the interests of stakeholders, and guard against the dominance by any single interest category, individual, or organization; exercise coordination and harmonization to resolve potential conflicts; have a readily available procedural appeals mechanism; reach decisions by consensus; and comply with ANSI's patent policy. ANSs may relate to products, processes, services, systems, or personnel. The majority of the standards developed are voluntary consensus standards, but there are also a growing number of consortia standards being developed in the technology space, which may have more narrow participation and work on an accelerated development time frame to meet market needs.

The basic legal framework for the preparation and adoption of standards and technical regulations includes the Trade Agreements Act of 1979, the Administrative Procedure Act (APA) of 1947, the National Technology Transfer and Advancement Act (NTTAA) of 1995 (PL 104-113), U.S. Office of Management and Budget (OMB) Circular A-119, and Executive Orders 12866 (Regulatory Planning and Review), 13563 (Improving Regulation and Regulatory Review), 13609 (Promoting International Regulatory Cooperation), 13610 (Identifying and Reducing Regulatory Burdens), 13771 (Reducing Regulation and Controlling Regulatory Costs), and 13777 (Enforcing the Regulatory Reform Agenda).

Federal law specifically prohibits any government agency from engaging in any standards-related activity that creates unnecessary obstacles to the foreign commerce of the United States.[192] Federal agencies are obliged to ensure that imported goods are treated no less favourably than like domestic products in the application of standards-related activities. The NTTAA directs federal agencies to rely on the output of voluntary consensus standards bodies to meet their objectives, and codifies guidance provided in Circular A-119 whereby federal agencies are directed to rely on VCSs, rather than government unique standards in the elaboration of technical regulations or in their procurement, unless such an approach would be inconsistent with law or otherwise impractical.[193] Circular A-119 encourages federal regulatory agencies to participate in SDOs.[194]

In the elaboration of final rules, including those referencing or mandating standards, the APA, which generally provides for participation in agency rulemaking through a system of public notice and comment, requires agencies to apply the notice-and-comment process for rulemakings and to address substantive comments received from the public, domestic as well as foreign. In addition, Executive Order 12866 directs most federal agencies to present draft regulations that are significant to the Office of Information and Regulatory Affairs (OIRA) for review prior to publication. An assessment of the costs and benefits of the regulatory action must be presented, together with the draft regulation. For regulations deemed economically significant by the OIRA or the agency itself, the requirement includes in-depth cost-benefit analysis of alternative regulatory approaches.[195]

Part of the USDOC, the National Institute of Standards and Technology (NIST) is a nonregulatory federal agency promoting U.S. innovation and industrial competitiveness by advancing measurement science, standards, and technology in ways that enhance economic security and improve quality of life. The NTTAA directs the NIST to coordinate public and private sector conformity assessment activities, to eliminate unnecessary duplication. Procedures for accreditation of conformity assessment bodies vary according to the particular standard or technical regulation. U.S. requirements generally follow the ISO Council Committee on Conformity Assessment (CASCO) standards.

Table 3.16 Federal subsidy programmes (non-agriculture), 2015-16

(US$ million)

Programmes	Type of subsidy	Expenditure FY2015	FY2016
Energy and fuels			
Advanced Research Projects	Annual Congressional appropriations	76.5	56.9
Cybersecurity for Energy Delivery Systems	Co-financing	0	24.6
Smart Grid R&D	Co-financing	0	0.5
Nuclear Energy: Small Modular Reactor Licensing Technical Support	Co-financing	57.4	57.1
Nuclear Energy: Supercritical Transformational Electric Power	Co-financing	0.3	1.5
Nuclear Energy: Fuel Cycle R&D	Co-financing	7.6	22.4
Nuclear Energy Enabling Technologies – Crosscutting Technology Development	Co-financing	1.4	1.0
Nuclear Energy: Reactor Concepts R&D and Demonstration – Advanced Reactor Technologies	Co-financing	7.3	7.4
Renewable Energy Resources	Co-financing	105.7	56.7
Energy Conservation Programs – Transportation Sector	Co-financing	120.0	127.8
Energy Conservation Programs – Building Technologies Office	Co-financing	17.1	19.6
Energy Conservation – Advanced Manufacturing	Co-financing	56.0	51.0
Fossil Energy R&D	Cost-shared contracts	147.6	115.9
Innovative Technology Loan Guarantee Program	Loan guarantees	17.0	17.0
Advanced Technology Vehicles Manufacturing Loan Program (ATVM)	Direct loans	4.0	6.0
Other energy and fuels			
Expensing of Exploration and Development (E&D) Costs for Oil, Gas and other Fuels	Income tax concession	660.0	450.0
Excess of Percentage over Cost Depletion for Oil, Gas and Other Fuels	Income tax concession	650.0	410.0
Capital Gains Treatment of Royalties on Coal	Income tax concession	110.0	150.0
Second Generation Biofuel Credit	Income tax concession	Not yet available	Not yet available
Biodiesel and Renewable Diesel Credit	Income and excise tax concession and direct payments	1,940.0	2,680.0
Alternative Fuel Mixture Credit	Excise tax concession	630.0	590.0
Credits for Investment in Advanced Coal Facilities and Advanced Gasification Facilities	Income tax concession	40.0	160.0
Advanced Energy Property Credit	Income tax concession	60.0	10.0
Two-year Amortization of Geological and Geophysical Expenditures	Income tax concession	90.0	70.0
Energy Production Credit	Income tax concession	1,550.0	1,400.0
Energy Investment Credit	Income tax concession	1,010.0	1,190.0
Energy Grant in lieu of the Energy Production Credit or the Energy Investment Credit	Direct payment	2,009.0	94.0
Credit for Holding New Clean Renewable Energy Bonds	Income tax concession	100.0	100.0
Credit for Holding Qualified Energy Conservation Bonds	Income tax concession	70.0	70.0
Fisheries			
Columbia River Fishery Development Program	Operating grants	13.7	16.2
Fisheries Finance Program (FFP)	Collateralized loans	a	a
Sea Grant College Program	Direct grants	67.3	72.4
Saltonstall-Kennedy Grant Program: Fisheries R&D	Competitive grants	25.0	11.0
Lumber and timber			
Capital Gains Treatment of Certain Timber Income	Income tax concession	110.0	150.0
Expensing of Multi-period Timber Growing Costs		320.0	330.0
Expensing and Seven-Year Amortization for Reforestation Expenditures		50.0	60.0
Medical			
Office of Nuclear Physics, Isotope Development and Production for Research and Applications Program	Annual Congressional appropriations	19.9	21.6
Orphan Drug Tax Credit	Income tax concession	1,460.0	1,720.0
Non-fuel minerals, metals			
Excess of percentage over Cost Depletion for Non-fuel Minerals	Income tax concession	520.0	430.0
Expensing of Exploration and Development Costs for Non-fuel Minerals		10.0	20.0

Part B
Report by the WTO Secretariat

Programmes	Type of subsidy	Expenditure	
		FY2015	FY2016
Shipyards			
Assistance to Small Shipyards Grant Program	Grants	0	5.0
Regional programs			
Empowerment Zones	Income tax concession	100.0	140.0
New Markets Tax Credit		1,200.0	1,290.0

a   The amount of the loans and the general terms of the loans are provided but the subsidy benefit, if any, is not estimated.

Source: WTO document G/SCM/N/315/USA, 14 March 2018.

The Standards Coordination Office (SCO) of the NIST serves as the enquiry point and notification authority for the United States under the WTO Agreement on Technical Barriers to Trade (TBT Agreement). All notifications of other WTO Members are disseminated to domestic stakeholders, and they are provided opportunities to review and comment on proposed foreign technical regulations and conformity assessment procedures via Notify U.S., a free, web-based email registration service. Comments and queries received from other WTO Members on notified proposed U.S. measures are forwarded to the relevant domestic regulatory authority within three business days. The SCO received 60 information requests in 2017, and a further 36 in the first seven months of 2018.

The United States provided 442 TBT notifications concerning proposed and final measures to the WTO in 2016, and 295 in 2017. They cover federal measures as well as technical regulations and conformity assessment procedures proposed at the state level consistent with U.S. obligations under the TBT Agreement. The United States submitted 58 regular notifications (88 overall) concerning technical regulations of state-level authorities in 2016, and 9 regular (60 overall) notifications in 2017. In the first six months of 2018, the United States provided 31 notifications relating to the activities of state bodies (Article 3.2 of the TBT Agreement), 6 of whom related to proposed conformity assessment procedures (Article 7.2). No dispute settlement proceedings were initiated against the United States with reference to the TBT Agreement during the period under review. A total of four specific trade concerns relating to measures maintained by the United States were raised in the TBT Committee during the period under review. During the same period, the United States used the TBT Committee to raise or support 67 new specific trade concerns regarding measures maintained by other Members, in areas such as: labelling, particularly for consumer goods; restrictive conformity assessment practices; and requirements for information technology and cybersecurity products.

The NIST also operates the U.S. inquiry point for NAFTA and provides technical background for the resolution of potential issues related to standards and conformity assessment between Canada, Mexico, and the United States.

The Asia-Pacific Economic Cooperation (APEC)'s Sub-Committee on Standards and Conformance (SCSC) and numerous Specialist Regional Bodies (SRBs) work closely with the 21 member economies to promote APEC's agenda for the liberalization and facilitation of trade and investment, including the design of practical programmes to promote the development of technical infrastructure.[196] Many bilateral FTAs concluded by the United States incorporate provisions reaffirming the adherence to obligations under the TBT Agreement as well as the Decision of the TBT Committee of 13 November 2000; acceptance of conformity assessment procedures; joint work on standards, technical regulations, and conformity assessment procedures; and information exchange.

The United States has concluded mutual recognition agreements (MRAs) with numerous foreign partners. In the area of telecommunications equipment, MRAs have been signed with Australia; Canada; Chinese Taipei; Europe (EU/EFTA); Hong Kong, China; Israel; Japan; Korea, Republic of; Malaysia; Mexico; New Zealand; Singapore; and Viet Nam. These telecom MRAs establish procedures enabling the Parties to recognize each other's competent conformity assessment bodies (CABs), and then to accept the conformity assessment results of those CABs for regulatory purposes. Foreign MRA partners designate their qualified accredited CABs (testing laboratories and/or certification bodies) to the Federal Communication Commission (FCC). In the United States, the NIST (through the MRA Program Office) designates qualified U.S. CABs (testing laboratories, certification bodies, and/or Notified Bodies in the case of the European Union) to the relevant MRA partners for recognition.[197] The United States has signed separate MRAs with the EU (2004) and EFTA States (2006) for marine safety equipment.

Sanitary and phytosanitary (SPS) requirements

The United States has numerous laws and regulations pertaining to food safety, animal health, and plant health. The promulgation of the Food and Drug Administration (FDA) Food Safety Modernization Act (FSMA) in 2011 (P.L. 111-353) represented a major and long-awaited update in the oversight of food safety.[198] The FSMA was accompanied by the issuance of seven key implementing regulations during 2015 and 2016, as well as four supplementary regulations, following a period of extensive public comment and review. Other major long-standing pieces of SPS legislation include the Federal Food, Drug and Cosmetic Act (including the FSMA amendments), the Federal Meat Inspection Act, the Poultry Products Inspection Act, the Egg Products

Inspection Act, the Plant Protection Act, the Animal Health Protection Act, and the Federal Insecticide, Fungicide, and Rodenticide Act.

Responsibilities for SPS matters are allocated among several federal agencies depending on the nature of the product and the element of risk. Food is generally regulated by the FDA, except for meat, poultry, Siluriformes fish and fish products (catfish), and processed egg products, which fall under the responsibility of the U.S. Department of Agriculture (USDA) Food and Safety Inspection Service (FSIS). Other areas of FDA supervision and authority include food additives, dietary supplements, human and veterinary drugs, medical devices, human biologics, tobacco, and cosmetics. Within the USDA, the FSIS ensures that commercial supplies, including imports, of meat, Siluriformes fish and fish products (catfish), poultry, and egg products are wholesome, safe, and properly labelled and packaged. Imported goods are required to be produced under conditions equivalent to the level of protection applicable in the United States. The Animal and Plant Health Inspection Service (APHIS) at the USDA promotes and defends agricultural health, including protection against plant and animal diseases and pests. While both APHIS and FSIS responsibilities apply to imported goods, the APHIS safeguards against animal and plant health risks, whereas the FSIS ensures that food safety requirements are enforced. The Environmental Protection Agency (EPA) is responsible, *inter alia*, for the registration of pesticides (including herbicides and fungicides), and the establishment of tolerances, i.e. maximum residue limits, for pesticides in food. Other federal agencies involved in SPS issues include CBP, the Agricultural Marketing Service, the Agricultural Research Service, the National Institute of Food and Agriculture (USDA), the Centers for Disease Control and Prevention (Department of Health and Human Services), the National Marine Fisheries Service (Department of Commerce), and the Alcohol and Tobacco Tax and Trade Bureau (Department of Treasury).

The International Regulations and Standards Division at the USDA Foreign Agricultural Service operates the national enquiry point and notification authority under the WTO SPS Agreement. The United States submitted 159 regular SPS notifications to the WTO in 2016; 88 in 2017; and 41 in the first half of 2018 (including addenda or corrigenda to earlier regular notifications). During the period under review, a total of two new specific trade concerns have been raised in the WTO Committee on Sanitary and Phytosanitary Measures relating to measures maintained by the United States. During the same period, the United States used the SPS Committee to raise five new specific trade concerns regarding measures maintained by other Members, in areas such as hazard-based pesticide regulations; delays in premarket approvals for the products of biotechnology; and, import bans on animals and animal products deemed inconsistent with OIE international standards.

Under the FSMA, the Foreign Supplier Verification Program (FSVP) Rule requires U.S.-based food importers to establish FSVPs for the products (human or animal food) that they bring into the United States.[199] An FSVP must be developed for each type of product and each foreign supplier, to confirm that the imported food is produced with the same level of health protection as that provided by the United States, which includes preventive controls and produce safety regulations, and that the goods have not been adulterated or misbranded. Risk-based supplier verification may be effected by various means, including annual on-site audits, sampling and testing, or verification of the supplier's food safety records. As of June 2018, the FSVP Importer List, maintained by the FDA, contained more than 46,000 entries. However, the inclusion of an establishment in the List does not constitute approval or endorsement by the FDA of the listed importer.

The FDA published its final rule regarding the Accreditation of Third-Party Certification Bodies to Conduct Food Safety Audits and to Issue Certifications ("Accreditation Third-Party Certification Rule") in November 2015.[200] A voluntary certification programme allows "accreditation bodies", which may be foreign government agencies or private entities, to seek recognition by the FDA to obtain the authority to accredit third-party "certification bodies", also known as third-party auditors. The certification bodies, in turn, conduct consultative and/or regulatory food safety audits, and issue certifications to eligible food producing entities. The FDA issued a guidance document describing the standards for the accreditation of third-party certification bodies ("Model Accreditation Standards") in December 2016.[201] The FDA launched a website where organizations could apply for recognition as accreditation bodies on 21 June 2017.[202] To date, the FDA has recognized three accreditation bodies: ANSI; the American National Accreditation Bureau (ANAB); and the National Bureau of Agricultural Commodity and Food Standard (ACFS).

U.S. importers may use facility certifications of foreign suppliers to make them eligible for participation in the Voluntary Qualified Importer Program (VQIP), an expedited review and entry programme for food.[203] Although the FDA opened its VQIP application portal in January 2018, no applications were received before the end of this year's application period (31 May), as the process to issue accreditations to third-party auditors (who could then begin the certification of facilities) was still ongoing.

On 9 March 2018, the FDA announced a proposal to recognize as equivalent the shellfish control systems of Spain and the Netherlands, based on those countries' implementation of EU food safety controls for bivalve molluscan shellfish.[204] The determinations would conclude that the control systems in Spain and the Netherlands achieve at least the same level of public health protection provided by U.S. controls for bivalve molluscan shellfish, administered through the National

Shellfish Sanitation Program. Following the FDA's announcement, it received 25 comments which will be taken into account as the FDA prepares its final equivalence determination to be published in a second Federal Register notice.

The FDA is working with the food safety authorities of Mexico to ensure the safety of fresh and minimally processed produce. A progress report on the USFDA-Mexico Produce Safety Partnership was released in June 2018.[205]

Competition policy

Competition policy framework

The competition policy framework has been well established in the United States for many years. The federal competition (antitrust) legislation consists of three core laws: the Sherman Act (1890), which limits agreements in restraint of trade, and bars abuse of monopoly; the Clayton Act (1914), which prohibits mergers and acquisitions that lessen competition; and the Federal Trade Commission Act (1914, FTC Act), which prohibits mainly unfair methods of competition and unfair or deceptive acts in or affecting commerce.[206] In addition, under the Hart-Scott-Rodino Antitrust Improvements Act of 1976 (HSR), parties to certain mergers and acquisitions must file pre-merger notifications and await government review before closing their deals. The HSR provides the federal agencies the opportunity to review the antitrust issues presented by certain acquisitions of assets, non-corporate interests or voting securities.[207]

Federal antitrust laws apply to foreign conduct that has a substantial and intended effect in the United States. Title IV of the Export Trading Company Act (1982), also known as the Foreign Trade Antitrust Improvement Act of 1982 or the FTAIA, clarifies the application of the Sherman Act and the FTC Act to conduct involving non-import foreign commerce. Under the FTAIA, these laws are not applicable to conduct involving foreign trade (other than import trade) unless such conduct has a direct, substantial, and reasonably foreseeable effect: (a) on trade, which is not with foreign nations; (b) on import trade with foreign nations; or (c) on export trade with foreign nations, of a person engaged in such trade or commerce in the United States; and such effect gives rise to a claim under the provisions of the Sherman Act or the FTC Act.

Government institutions, including those engaging in commercial activity, are exempted from federal antitrust legislation unless statute clearly provides otherwise.[208] Limited immunity also applies, by way of example, to specific aspects of agriculture, fisheries, shipping, and insurance. In relation to international trade, the Webb-Pomerene Export Trade Act may allow associations of otherwise competing businesses to engage in the collective exports of goods, provided there are no anti-competitive effects or injury to competitors within the United States. The Export Trading Company Act (1982)

also creates a procedure whereby persons engaged in export may obtain, under certain circumstances, an export trading certificate of review (ETCR) providing, *inter alia,* for limited antitrust immunity.[209] The Shipping Act (1984) allows international ocean carriers to engage in pricing arrangements (liner conferences) that are filed with the Federal Maritime Commission, unless these are contested by that Commission.

Enforcement of federal antitrust laws is entrusted to the Antitrust Division of the Department of Justice (DOJ) and Federal Trade Commission (FTC).[210] Private parties, typically acting on their own behalf or on behalf of an affected group, can also bring actions by seeking damages for harms resulting from anti-competitive conduct (see below). Overall, public and private enforcement work in a complementary manner.[211] State antitrust enforcement is normally done under specific state statutes.

The DOJ prosecutes violations of the antitrust laws by: (i) filing criminal information or indictment for *per se* violations, such as price fixing, bid rigging, and market allocation, that can lead to large fines or jail sentences; and (ii) suing to forbid future violations of the law and/or requiring steps to remedy the anti-competitive effects of past violations.[212] The FTC has exclusive responsibility for pursuing anti-competitive conduct that violates Section 5 of the FTC Act, and joint authority (with the Antitrust Division) over the enforcement of the Clayton Act and its amendment by the Robinson-Patman Act. While both agencies have jurisdiction to enforce antitrust laws in relation to merger control, only one will review a particular transaction, and the choice of agency will depend on the basis of the agency's relative familiarity with the industry or companies involved.[213] A well-established system of cooperation exists, where competencies overlap between the two agencies.

Private enforcement in the United States plays a bigger role than in other jurisdictions. Private plaintiffs can seek treble damages for violations of antitrust laws under Section 4 of the Clayton Act, which creates an economic incentive for private parties to undertake antitrust litigation.[214] Federal law limits standing to bring a private lawsuit to direct purchasers and rivals who suffer antitrust injury. Indirect purchasers may seek injunctive relief, but may not bring private antitrust suits for damages under federal law. Though some state antitrust claims can be heard in state courts, they may be removed to a federal court if they supplement a federal claim.[215] In recent years, private antitrust litigation in the United States has declined.[216]

Enforcement developments during the review period

According to the 2016 Annual Report of the Director of the Administrative Office of the U.S. Courts, 853 new civil antitrust actions - both government and private - were filed in the federal district courts in FY2016.[217] In that same time period, the Antitrust Division charged 52 individuals, including 11 auto parts executives and

Table 3.17 Sherman Act violations yielding a corporate fine of US$10 million or more in FY2016, 2017 and 2018

FY	Defendant	Product	Fine (US$ million)	Country
2016	Nishikawa Rubber Co., Ltd.	Automotive body sealing brake [fluid] hoses for automobiles	130	Japan
2016	Wallenius Wilhelmsen Logistics AS	Ocean shipping roll on, roll off cargo – deep sea freight transportation	98.9	Norway
2016	Corning International Kabushiki Kaisha	Ceramic substrates used in the emission control systems of automobiles	66.5	Japan
2016	NGK Insulators, Ltd.	Automobile parts	65.3	Japan
2016	Kayaba Industry Co., Ltd, d/b/a KYB Corporation	Automobile parts - shock absorbers	62	Japan
2016	NEC Tokin Corporation	Capacitors	13.8	Japan
2017	Citicorp	Foreign currency exchange	925	United States
2017	Barclays, PLC	Foreign currency exchange	650	United Kingdom
2017	JP Morgan Chase and Co.	Foreign currency exchange	550	United States
2017	Royal Bank of Scotland	Foreign currency exchange	395	Scotland (United Kingdom)
2017	Hitachi Automotive Systems, Ltd.	Automobile parts - shock absorbers	55.4	Japan
2017	Bumble Bee Foods, LLC	Packaged seafood	25	United States
2017	Rubycon Corporation	Capacitors	12	Japan
2018	BNP Paribas USA, Inc.	Foreign currency exchange	90	United States
2018	Nichicon Corporation	Capacitors	54.6	Japan
2018	Hoegh Autoliners AS	Ocean shipping roll on, roll off cargo – deep sea freight transportation	21	Norway
2018	Maruyasu Industries Co., Ltd.	Automobile parts – steel tubes	12	Japan

Source: Antitrust Division, Sherman Act Violations Yielding a Corporate Fine of US$10 Million or More. Viewed at: https://www.justice.gov/atr/sherman-act-violations-yielding-corporate-fine-10-million-or-more.

16 real estate investors, with criminal antitrust offenses. Twenty-two individuals were sentenced to serve time in jail for an average of 11 months. The Division also obtained more than US$399 million in criminal fines and penalties.[218] For additional information on corporate fines, see Table 3.17.

The Antitrust Division has also devoted substantial resources to individual prosecutions and sentencings in criminal antitrust proceedings, resulting in 30 individuals sentenced to prison terms in 2017, the highest number of individual prison terms imposed since 2012. Many of the Division's individual convictions were the result of investigations into anti-competitive conduct at public real estate foreclosure auctions.[219] Nine criminal cases went to trial, the largest number of criminal Antitrust Division trials in modern criminal antitrust enforcement.

With regard to merger review, in FY2017, 2,052 transactions were reported under the Hart-Scott-Rodino Act, representing about a 12.0% increase from the 1,832 transactions reported in FY2016.[220] Moreover, the FTC's Premerger Notification Office (PNO) continued to respond to thousands of questions seeking information about the reportability of transactions under the Hart-Scott-Rodino Act, and the details involved in completing and filing the Notification and Report Form, a trend that follows from FY2016.[221]

During 2017, the FTC brought 21 merger enforcement challenges, including: 14 in which it accepted consent orders for public comment, all of which resulted in final orders; 6 in which the transaction was abandoned or restructured as a result of antitrust concerns raised during the investigation; and 1 in which the FTC initiated administrative or federal court litigation. In the same year, the Antitrust Division challenged 18 merger transactions, including 11 cases in which it filed complaints in U.S. District Court. In nine of these cases, the Division simultaneously filed a proposed settlement. In six of the challenges not subject to court proceedings, the parties abandoned the proposed transaction, and in one case, the parties restructured the transaction to resolve the Division's concerns.[222]

DOJ public merger investigations and challenges during the review period included, among others, the Anheuser-Busch InBev/SABMiller USm107 billion acquisition - the biggest beer merger in history - cleared in July 2016 following a settlement; and the DOW/DuPont merger, cleared in June 2017 after the parties reached an agreement to divest multiple crop protection assets and two petrochemical products.[223]

In November 2017, the DOJ filed a lawsuit challenging AT&T's acquisition of Time Warner, valued at US$106 billion, arguing that the proposed merger could have significant anti-competitive effects.[224] In June 2018, the District Court allowed the merger without conditions.[225] Although the Court accepted the Government's proposed product and

Part B
Report by the WTO Secretariat

geographic markets, it held that the Government had not shown that the merger was reasonably likely to harm competition. The Government appealed this decision.

In May 2018, the DOJ secured a negotiated merger divestiture in connection with Bayer's Acquisition of Monsanto. Besides divestiture of certain businesses, the settlement also required the divestiture of certain IP and research capabilities, including "pipeline" R&D projects, in order to resolve horizontal and vertical competition concerns.[226]

In civil non-merger enforcement cases, in October 2016, the DOJ announced that, from that point forward, it intended to proceed criminally against naked no-poach and wage-fixing agreements between employers.[227] In this regard, on 3 April 2018, the Antitrust Division filed a civil antitrust lawsuit, simultaneously with a civil settlement, against Knorr-Bremse AG and Westinghouse Air Brake Technologies Corp. The complaint alleges that these and a third company, Faiveley, reached naked no-poach agreements, in violation of Section 1 of the Sherman Act.[228] The conduct in that matter was resolved by civil action because the companies withdrew from the no-poach agreements before October 2016.

In March 2017, the DOJ reached a settlement prohibiting DirecTV and its parent corporation, AT&T, from sharing confidential, forward-looking information with competitors.[229]

During the review period, the U.S. Courts of Appeals heard and decided antitrust cases related to pharmaceutical reverse patent settlements. In 2016, the First Circuit decided, in *In re Loestrin 24 FE Antitrust Litigation,* that non-monetary reverse payments made by a patent owner to generic manufacturers to settle patent litigation are also subject to antitrust scrutiny.[230] In *In re Nexium (Esomeprazole) Antitrust Litigation,* the Court re-affirmed the decision that reverse payments may take the form of non-monetary conveyances.[231]

Policy developments

According to recent official statements, when the DOJ challenges a merger, it requires structural remedies, not behavioural remedies, to ensure the Federal Government does not have an inappropriate role in market place competition.[232] The Antitrust Division's approach on behavioural remedies will be to accept such commitments, particularly in merger cases, only when a high degree of confidence exists that the remedy itself does not usurp regulatory functions for law enforcement, in addition to fully protecting U.S. consumers and the competitive process. This reflects a view that behavioural remedies should not supplant competition with regulation.[233]

The interface of antitrust with IP will be a particular focus of attention.[234] With respect to IP, the current approach to competition enforcement is shaped by, and places a particularly strong emphasis on, the dynamic power of innovation. The DOJ has pledged to seek a more symmetric balance between IP and competition law by which, while the application of competition laws to the exercise of IP rights is to be supported, enforcers should give particular attention and weight to the forces that drive innovation, including by allowing innovators to reap the full rewards of their investments in R&D.[235] A new approach has been proposed in relation to standard essential patents, the so-called "New Madison" approach. This approach aims at ensuring that: (i) patent holders have adequate incentives to innovate and create new technologies; and (ii) licensees have the appropriate incentives to implement them. In addition, the Antitrust Division will adopt an evidence-based approach in applying antitrust law equally to both innovators who develop and implementers who use technological standards in innovation industries.[236]

As part of a larger effort to streamline and improve the Antitrust Division's use of consent decrees, the Division

Box 3.1 The New Madison approach

"The New Madison approach [...] has four basic premises that are aimed at ensuring that patent holders have adequate incentives to innovate and create new technologies, and that licensees have appropriate incentives to implement those technologies.

First, the approach holds that antitrust law should not be used as a tool to police FRAND commitments that patent-holders make to standard setting organizations[a].

Second, standard setting organizations should not become vehicles for concerted actions by market participants to skew conditions for patented technologies' incorporation into a standard in favour of implementers because this can reduce incentives to innovate and encourage patent hold-out.

Third, because a key feature of patent rights is the right to exclude, standard setting organizations and courts should have a very high burden of proof before they adopt rules that severely restrict that right or amount to a *de facto* compulsory licensing scheme.

Fourth, consistent with the fundamental right to exclude, from the perspective of the antitrust laws, a unilateral and unconditional refusal to license a patent should be considered *per se* legal."

a   Fair, reasonable, and non-discriminatory (FRAND) commitments are voluntary licensing agreements between a standards organization and the owner of an IPR, usually a patent, that is, or may become, essential to practice a technical standard (standard-essential patents).

Source: Assistant Attorney General Makan Delrahim Keynote Address at University of Pennsylvania Law School, The "New Madison" Approach to Antitrust and Intellectual Property Law, DOJ News Release, 16 March 2018. Viewed at: https://www.justice.gov/opa/speech/assistant-attorney-general-makan-delrahim-delivers-keynote-address-university.

has identified nearly 1,300 longstanding judgments still in effect. It has announced that it is currently reviewing these decrees, and addressing any that no longer serve the public interest and are appropriate for termination.[237]

The FTC and the DOJ have undertaken to promote international cooperation and convergence toward best practices in antitrust enforcement and policy. This includes work in the multilateral fora (in coordination with the International Competition Network) as well as further efforts to develop strong bilateral relationships with other competition agencies, emphasizing consumer welfare-based enforcement, good policies and practices regarding the application of antitrust rules to IP, the territorial scope of remedies, and procedural fairness.[238]

In a further important development, recently, the United States, in partnership with leading antitrust agencies around the world, has put forward a new instrument to promote procedural fairness and related values in competition law enforcement, namely the Multilateral Framework on Procedures in Competition Law Investigation and Enforcement (MFP). The Framework (jointly sponsored by the DOJ and the FTC) includes procedural commitments that reflect fundamental due process rights and considerations. Specifically, it commits participating jurisdictions to important due process requirements relating to non-discrimination, transparency, timely resolution, confidentiality, conflicts of interest, proper notice, opportunity to defend, access to counsel, and judicial review.[239]

Legislative and institutional framework developments

In October 2016, antitrust guidance for human resource (HR) professionals was issued for the first time.[240] This guidance aims at alerting HR professionals, and others involved in hiring and/or compensation decisions, about potential violations of antitrust law, e.g. in the implementation of "no-poaching" agreements. It also discusses how antitrust laws apply to firms' decisions to share sensitive information, such as compensation information, with competing employers, either directly or through third-party entities.[241]

In January 2017, the Antitrust Division, together with the FTC, released revised Antitrust Guidelines for International Enforcement and Cooperation. These now include a new chapter detailing the Agencies' policies and practices regarding case cooperation, investigative tools, confidentiality safeguards, and waivers of confidentiality.[242] The Guidelines updated the discussion of the application of U.S. antitrust law to conduct involving foreign commerce, the Foreign Trade Antitrust Improvements Act (FTAIA) of 1982, foreign sovereign immunity, foreign sovereign compulsion, the act of state doctrine and petitioning of sovereigns, in light of developments in both the law and the Agencies' practice. In addition, the Guidelines stress that the Agencies have championed, and will continue to promote, policy engagement that focuses

on substantive law, enforcement and due process standards that advance consumer welfare based on sound economics, procedural fairness, transparency, and non-discriminatory treatment of parties.

Another significant development during the review period was the 2017 update of the Antitrust Guidelines for the Licensing of Intellectual Property, issued jointly by the Antitrust Division and the FTC. This new version of the IP Guidelines highlights the benefits of robust IP protection, and the importance of innovation incentives. The Guidelines deal with technology transfer and innovation-related issues that typically arise with respect to patents, copyrights, trade secrets, and know-how agreements; they do not cover the antitrust treatment of trademarks, which is characterized primarily by product-differentiation issues. The updated Guidelines support three principles: (i) that for the purpose of antitrust analysis, the Agencies apply the same analysis to conduct involving IP as to conduct involving other forms of property, taking into account the specific characteristics of a particular property right; (ii) the Agencies do not presume that IP creates market power in the antitrust context; and (iii) the Agencies recognize that IP licensing allows firms to combine complementary factors of production, and is generally procompetitive.[243]

In January 2017, the Antitrust Division also issued an updated version of the Frequently Asked Questions About the Antitrust Division's Leniency Program and Model Leniency Letters. This update, besides clarifying some answers in light of previous experiences, describes leniency application procedure; the criteria for receiving leniency under both the corporate and individual policies; the potential revocation of the conditional leniency letter; the issuance of the final unconditional leniency letter; and confidentiality for the leniency applicant. A new feature is the description of the Antitrust Division's approach to "Penalty Plus", a situation where a company pleads guilty to an antitrust offense but fails to report additional antitrust crimes it was also involved in.[244]

During the review period, the threshold for premerger notification was adjusted. On 26 January 2017, the FTC published a notice to reflect adjustment of the reporting thresholds as required by the amendments to Section 7A of the Clayton Act effected in 2000. The size of transaction threshold was raised from US$78.2 million to US$80.8 million, effective 27 February 2017.[245]

Sectoral coverage

Antitrust activities during the review period have covered a number of sectors/industries. In the healthcare sector, the Antitrust Division, both individually and jointly in coordination with the FTC, has raised awareness, through competition advocacy, of the importance of antitrust enforcement in the industry, and encouraged federal, state and local governments to consider the competitive impact of various healthcare-related legislative and regulatory proposals.[246] Additionally, FTC actions have sought to promote competition among health care providers, as well as encourage cost containment. The Antitrust Division was successful in blocking two proposed mergers that would have reduced the number of large health insurance providers in the United States from five to three.[247] In the first of these two cases, in April 2017, the U.S. Court of Appeals affirmed the decision by the U.S. District Court for the District of Columbia to block health insurer Anthem, Inc.'s acquisition of Cigna Corp. Anthem abandoned its planned acquisition in May 2017. In the second case, *United States v. Aetna*, et al., the D.C. District Court enjoined the proposed merger of Aetna and Humana, after concluding that it would likely substantially lessen competition in the market for individual Medicare Advantage plans.[248]

In 2016, the FTC brought its first case challenging an agreement not to market an authorized generic against Endo Pharmaceuticals Inc. In 2017, Endo Pharmaceuticals agreed to abandon the pay-for-delay agreements[249], and to settle the allegations that it violated antitrust laws by using these agreements to block consumers' access to lower-cost generic versions of its top-selling branded drugs. In a related matter, the FTC refiled charges against Watson Laboratories, Inc. and its former parent, Allergan plc, for illegally blocking a lower-cost generic version of Lidoderm when it entered into a pay-for-delay agreement also with Endo.[250] The

FTC also filed an administrative complaint against Impax Laboratories, Inc. for engaging in similar conduct.[251]

With the aim of promoting competitive energy markets, the FTC required structural divestitures to resolve charges that the proposed merger of energy infrastructure companies Enbridge, Inc. and Spectra Energy Corporation would likely reduce natural gas pipeline competition in three offshore natural gas producing areas in the Gulf of Mexico, leading to higher prices for natural gas pipeline transportation from those areas. A settlement was reached between the parties in 2017.[252]

State trading, state-owned enterprises, and privatization

The incidence of governmental authorities owning or controlling enterprises that engage in commercial activities is fairly limited. At the federal level, a number of government corporations or government-sponsored enterprises generally fulfil public policy objectives or governmental functions and their intended purpose is not to compete with private enterprises (Table 3.18). While U.S. states possess a general incorporation statute, the Federal Government does not have such powers, and each government corporation is chartered through an act of Congress to perform a public purpose with a clear and transparent mandate. Government corporations

Table 3.18 Government corporations, 2018

Government corporation	Legal reference	Area of operation
Commodity Credit Corporation	15 U.S.C. 714	Commodity credit financing
Community Development Financial Institutions Fund	12 U.S.C. 4701	Banking
Corporation for National and Community Service	42 U.S.C. 12651	National and community services
EXIM Bank	12 U.S.C. 635	Export financing
Federal Crop Insurance Corporation	7 U.S.C. 1501	Agricultural insurance
Federal Deposit Insurance Corporation	12 U.S.C. 1811	Bank resolution and deposit insurance
Federal Financing Bank	12 U.S.C. 2281	Financing
Federal Home Loan Banks	12 U.S.C. Ch. 11	Banking
Federal Prison Industries (UNICOR)	18 U.S.C. 4121	Prison services
Financing Corporation[a]	12 U.S.C. 1441	Financing
Government National Mortgage Association	12 U.S.C. 1717	Mortgages
International Clean Energy Foundation	42 U.S.C. 17352	Foreign assistance for greenhouse gas reduction
Millennium Challenge Corporation	22 U.S.C. 7703	Foreign assistance
National Credit Union Administration Central Liquidity Facility	12 U.S.C. 1795b	Credit unions
National Railroad Passenger Corporation (AMTRAK)	49 U.S.C. 241	Passenger rail services
Overseas Private Investment Corporation	22 U.S.C. 2191	International investment and financing
Pension Benefit Guaranty Corporation	29 U.S.C. 1301	Pensions
Presidio Trust of San Francisco	16 U.S.C. 460bb	Parks and recreation
Resolution Funding Corporation	12 U.S.C. 1441(b)	Financing and bonds for debt created by the former Resolution Trust Corporation
St. Lawrence Seaway Development Corporation	33 U.S.C. 981	Marine transport
Tennessee Valley Authority	16 U.S.C. 831	Navigation, flood control, electricity, certain manufacturing and economic development
U.S. Postal Service[b]	39 U.S.C. 101	Mail services
Valles Caldera Trust	16 U.S.C. 698-v4	Historical preservation

a   No longer writing new business; current outstanding obligations expire by 2019.

b   Only partially a government corporation.

Source: Kosar, K. (2011), *Federal Government Corporations: An Overview*, Congressional Research Service Publication RL30365, 8 June. Viewed at: http://www.fas.org/sgp/crs/misc/RL30365.pdf; Government Corporation Control Act, 31 U.S.C. 9101; and information provided by the authorities.

Table 3.19 Government-sponsored enterprises

(US$ million)

GSE	Area of operation	Total assets (end 2017)
Federal National Mortgage Association (Fannie Mae)[a]	Residential and multi-family mortgages	3,345,529
Federal Home Loan Mortgage Corporation (Freddie Mac)[a]	Residential and multi-family mortgages	2,049,776
Federal Agricultural Mortgage Corporation (Farmer Mac)	Creates a secondary market for agricultural, rural housing, and rural utility loans	17,792
Federal Home Loan Bank System	Provides funding to member banks so they can provide community development credit	1,103,451
Farm Credit System[b]	Guarantees payments as to principal and interest on securities issued by member banks	329,518

a   In conservatorship since 6 September 2008; the U.S. Department of the Treasury entered into a Senior Preferred Stock Purchase Agreement (PSPA) to make investments in senior preferred stock to maintain positive equity. Fannie Mae has not received funds from Treasury since the first quarter of 2012.

b   The Farm Credit System banks are AgFirst Farm Credit Bank, AgriBank, CoBank, and Farm Credit Bank of Texas.

Source: Financial Statements. Viewed at: http://www.fanniemae.com/resources/file/ir/pdf/quarterly-annual-results/2017/10k_2017.pdf; http://www.freddiemac.com/investors/financials/pdf/10k_021518.pdf; https://www.farmermac.com/wp-content/uploads/2018-Q1-10-Q-Final.pdf; http://www.fhlb-of.com/ofweb_userWeb/resources/2017Q4CFR.pdf; and https://www.farmcreditfunding.com/ffcb_live/financialInformation.html.

have a separate legal personality, and may receive federal allocations, but they may also have their own sources of revenue.[253]

Government-sponsored enterprises (GSEs) operate exclusively in the financial sector. GSEs are quasi-governmental, private corporations structured and regulated by the Government to enhance their ability to borrow money (Table 3.19). As GSEs are private companies, they are not included in the Federal Budget, and their debt is not fully backed by the Federal Government.

The United States provides notifications on its state trading enterprises (STEs) to the WTO on a regular basis pursuant to Article XVII:4(a) of the GATT 1994 and Paragraph 1 of the Understanding on the Interpretation of Article XVII. As in previous years, the most recent notification (June 2018) covered the activities of the Commodity Credit Corporation, the Isotopes Production and Distribution Program within the Department of Energy, the marketing of electricity by certain power administrations, and the Strategic Petroleum Reserve.[254] In September 2017, the United States also updated the information on its STEs provided in earlier notifications.[255]

Government procurement

Institutional and legal framework

No major institutional or legal changes with respect to Government procurement have taken place since the last Review in 2016. Procurement at the federal level is decentralized, and is carried out through the procurement systems of the various executive agencies'. Procurement at the state level is also decentralized.

Although decentralized, federal procurement follows general guidelines. Procurement at the federal level is overseen and coordinated by the Office of Management and Budget (OMB) through the Office of Federal Procurement Policy (OFPP)., which reviews proposed regulations for compliance with policy guidance. The OFPP, headed by an Administrator appointed by the President and confirmed by the Senate, provides overall direction for government-wide procurement policies and plays a central role in shaping the policies and practices used by federal agencies to acquire goods and services.[256] The OFPP Administrator may prescribe Government-wide procurement policies and may issue policy letters stating principles that must be followed by the agencies; implementation takes place through the Federal Acquisition Regulation (FAR).[257]

Several federal agencies, such as the National Aeronautics and Space Administration (NASA), the Department of Health and Human Services have been designated by the OFPP to manage government-wide acquisition contracts that leverage federal buying of common goods and services.

The General Services Administration (GSA) develops evidence-based governmentwide regulations to encourage federal agencies to use cost-effective management practices, and works with them in their procurement processes.[258] The GSA maintains a General Services Administration Acquisition Manual (GSAM) that provides procurement guidelines.[259] The GSA also manages Federal Supply Schedules, also known as Multiple Award Schedules (MAS), or more commonly, as GSA Schedules, which are long-term governmentwide contracts with commercial firms. GSA Schedules are organized by specific supply and service types. Each Schedule is then divided into more specific supply and service subcategories called Special Item Numbers (SINs).[260] The schedules include both national and foreign suppliers from parties to the GPA or other international agreements. Interested suppliers can apply for inclusion on the Schedules at any time. The list of Federal Supply Schedule contractors is available publicly on "GSA Advantage!".[261] Only authorized users may purchase directly from the Federal Supply Schedules. Authorized users are outlined in GSA Order 4800.2I.

The Department of Defense (DoD) has its own procurement regulations. The DoD's Defense Pricing and Contracting (DPC) is responsible for all pricing, contracting, and procurement policy matters. DPC executes policy through the update of the Defense Federal Acquisition Regulation Supplement (DFARS) and Procedures, Guidance, and Information (PGI).[262] The Defense Acquisition Regulations System (DARS) creates and maintains develops and maintains DoD acquisition regulations. The DPC utilizes the DARS office to create and maintain the Federal Acquisition Regulation (FAR) (see below) and the Defense Federal Acquisition Regulation Supplement (DFARS).[263]

The United States is a party to the WTO Agreement on Government Procurement (GPA). Annex 1 of Appendix I of the GPA contains the list of central government agencies covered by it, while Annexes 2 and 3 list the 37 states and other entities applying the GPA.[264] The Protocol amending the Agreement on Government Procurement entered into force for the United States on 6 April 2014. U.S. threshold values as expressed in Special Drawing Rights (SDR) are the same under the revised and the 1994 Agreements; USTR revises GPA thresholds in U.S. dollars every two years. The United States notified to the WTO its basic procurement legislation and GPA-implementing legislation in 1998.[265] The GPA is implemented at the federal level primarily through the Trade Agreements Act (TAA) of 1979, as amended; it is implemented at the state level through laws and regulations in each of the 37 states participating in it.

The Buy American Act (BAA, 1933) and the TAA remain the main laws regarding government procurement. Other laws containing legislation on procurement include the Federal Property and Administrative Services Act of 1949 (FPASA), the Competition in Contracting Act of 1984 (CICA), the Federal Acquisition Streamlining Act of 1994 (FASA), the Clinger-Cohen Act of 1996, the Small Business Act of 1985, and the Services Acquisition Reform Act. The BAA requires the Federal Government to purchase domestic goods, while the TAA provides authority for the President to waive purchasing requirements, such as those contained in the BAA, designate eligible countries, and bar procurement from non-designated countries. Federal agencies may waive domestic procurement requirements in U.S. law under certain conditions.[266]

The FAR, found at Chapter 1 of title 48 of the Code of Federal Regulations, regulates federal government agencies' acquisitions of supplies and services with appropriated funds. The Department of Defense (DoD), the GSA, and NASA jointly issue the FAR for use by executive agencies in acquiring goods and services. The FAR system allows executive agencies and their sub-agencies to develop their own specific internal guidelines. It is updated regularly through Federal Acquisition Circulars (FACs) to reflect changes in procurement procedures, the effect of trade agreements, and other changes. Proposed regulations are published in the Federal Register, and are open to public comments, which are considered when drafting the final rules. The FAR regulates the procurement process in detail. Heads of major purchasing entities, i.e. the Secretary of Defense, the Administrator of General Services, and the Administrator of NASA, have the authority to issue regulations in the context of the FAR, following approval by the OMB, specifically the Administrator of the OFPP and the Office of Information and Regulatory Affairs. In 2016, the DoD established an 18-person panel, created in Section 809 of the FY2016 National Defense Authorization Act (NDAA) and amended by Section 863(d) of the NDAA for FY2017 and Sections 803(c) and 883 of the NDAA for FY2018, tasked with finding ways to streamline and improve the defense acquisition process.[267]

On 18 April 2017, Executive Order No. 13788, Buy American and Hire American[268], was issued in relation to the implementation of Buy American laws.[269] The Order instructs federal agencies to prioritize procurement of domestically produced goods, specifically referencing U.S. iron and steel products. The Order states that nothing in the Order shall be construed to impair or otherwise affect existing rights or obligations under international agreements which includes the GPA. In the course of the WTO Committee on Government Procurement October 2017 formal meeting, a discussion was held on current developments concerning buy-national initiatives in the United States.[270]

On 16 June 2018, new cybersecurity rules[271] for defence contractors went into effect, requiring contractors to meet certain minimum standards, or have a plan in place to meet those standards.[272] In December 2016, the FAR Council finalized a rule aimed at protecting small business subcontractors.[273] Under the rule, contracting officers will be required to track contractors who make late or reduced payments to subcontractors. The FAR Council also recently finalized a rule requiring contractors to undergo training relating to privacy rules, with the aim of protecting personally identifiable information to which they have access.[274]

In order to standardize procurement transactions across the Federal Government, the FAR Subpart 4.16 has been amended to implement a uniform award identification system, referred to as the Procurement Instrument Identifiers (PIID) - a unique identifier for each solicitation, contract, agreement, order or related procurement instrument. Beginning 1 October 2017, agencies are required to have in place a process that ensures that each PIID used to identify a solicitation or contract action is unique government-wide, and will remain so for at least 20 years from the date of contract award. The PIID will be used to identify all solicitation, contract, agreement, order or related procurement instruments, and will also be used to identify solicitation and contract actions in designated support and reporting systems (e.g., the Federal Procurement Data System, the System for Award Management), in accordance with regulations, applicable authorities, and agency policies and procedures.[275]

Rules and regulations with respect to government procurement are also contained in agency supplements to the FAR. For example, as mentioned above, the General Services Acquisition Manual (GSAM) consolidates GSA agency acquisition rules and guidance. The GSAM incorporates the General Services Administration Acquisition Regulation (GSAAR) and the internal agency acquisition policy.

The publication of notices of proposed procurement in Federal Business Opportunities (FedBizOpps) is required for federal government agency contracts in excess of the simplified acquisition threshold (currently US$25,000), with some exceptions. These notices must be published at least 15 days before a request for bids, and prospective suppliers have at least 30 days from that date to submit bids. Shorter timeframes and simplified procedures may be established for procurement valued at or below the simplified acquisition threshold. For procurement falling within the scope of the GPA or an FTA, a period of not less than 40 days must generally be granted. States covered by the GPA are required to publish invitations to tender in their own publications, and must conform to GPA deadlines.

As provided for under the CICA, procurement must take place through full and open competitive procedures; there are only a limited number of exceptions to this rule.[276] The use sole-source procurement is not allowed unless the written authorization of the Agency head is obtained and specific statutory or regulatory authority exists for sole source or limited competition. Deviations from the requirement for full and open competition must be documented in writing and authorized. The competitive procedures defined in the CICA are mainly "sealed bidding" and "competitive proposals" (see below).[277] Awards must be generally made on the basis of price, although there are some exceptions. The CICA provides for simplified procedures for small purchases.

The FASA establishes a threshold, the Simplified Acquisition Threshold (SAT), which provides simplified procedures in cases of new acquisitions valued below the SAT. It also exempts purchases valued below the micro-purchase threshold, from Buy American Act requirements and allows them to be made without obtaining competitive quotations if the contracting officer determines that the purchase price is reasonable.[278] The National Defense Authorization Act (NDAA) for FY2018 (P.L. 115-91, 12 December 2017) (NDAA 2018), raises the micropurchase and simplified acquisition thresholds for federal acquisitions. Section 806 of NDAA 2018 increases the micro-purchase threshold, for products only, from US$3,500 to US$10,000. The micro-purchase threshold for services remains at US$2,500 (Service Contract Labor Standards—formerly the Service Contract Act of 1965), and at US$2,000 for construction services (Construction Wage Rate Requirements Statute — formerly the Davis-Bacon Act).[279] On 16 February 2018, the Civilian Agency Acquisition Council (CAAC) issued CAAC Letter No. 2018-02 to federal agencies, regarding a class deviation to the FAR to implement the new increased micro-purchase and SATs, raising them from US$150,000 to US$250,000. The Notice and comment rulemaking are to follow.

Registration online in the System for Award Management (SAM), an official website of the Government, is required to do business with the Federal Government. Both domestic and foreign entities may register. A unique nine-digit identification number (D-U-N-S Number) is required for each physical location of a business required to register with the Federal government for contracts or grants.[280] The use of Commercial and Government Entity (CAGE) codes, including North Atlantic Treaty Organization (NATO) CAGE (NCAGE) codes is required for foreign entities, for awards valued at greater than the micro-purchase threshold. Since June 2018, entities registering in SAM must submit a notarized letter appointing their authorized Entity Administrator.

Procurement at the sub-federal level is governed by state or other sub-federal government laws and procurement regulations. Where procurement is funded with federal money, states must comply with certain federal statutory requirements. Local governments have their own procurement agencies, as well as their own procurement policies. The Cooperative Purchasing Program allows state, local, and tribal governments to purchase IT, security, and law enforcement products and services offered through specific Schedule contracts. Cooperative Purchasing allows eligible entities to purchase from approved industry partners, at any time, for any reason, using any funds available.[281]

Efforts to increase transparency in U.S. federal procurement includes the introduction of changes to ensure that the unique identifier used in federal procurement (the Procurement Instrument Identifier (PIID)) is both unique and uniform across the Federal Government, capturing information on bidder affiliation, and requirements to make public expenditures under federal contracts in addition to existing obligations. These requirements are being implemented through regulatory, process, and information technology changes, and will be completed by 2018.

U.S. government procurement market

USAspending.gov, a website which provides for the public dissemination of federal contract, grant, loan, and financial assistance data, as required by the Federal Funding Accountability and Transparency Act of 2006, provides information on total federal government spending, principally in relation to federal contracts, grants, loans, and other financial assistance awards of more than US$25,000, and excluding tax credits and assistance for housing, rent, food, or personal expenses. For this purpose, federal agencies submit contract,

Trade Policy Review – United States 2018
www.wto.org/tpr

grant, loan, direct payment, and other award data at least twice a month, to be published on USAspending. gov. Data is also pulled or derived from other government systems, e.g. from the Federal Procurement Data System Next Generation (FPDS-NG).[282] In FY2017, total federal spending was US$4.9 trillion. Contract spending accounted for US$507.9 billion, with the Departments of Defense, Energy, Veterans Affairs, Health and Human Services, and Homeland Security as the top five contracting agencies.[283] In FY2018, total government spending was in excess of US$3.2 trillion as at 31 March 2018.[284]

Statistics on the procurement activities of the main agencies at the federal level are contained in the United States' Federal Procurement Data System – Next Generation (FPDS-NG), maintained by the GSA under the direction of the OFPP. The GSA operates multiple e-procurement systems that support collection and dissemination of information on federal procurements, to include awards, contractor performance and integrity, and a single point-of-entry for contracting opportunities, known as Federal Business Opportunities (Geobios's).[285] In November 2017, the United States notified certain statistics for FY2015 under Article XIV:4 of the revised GPA. For federal procurement, the notified values are broken down in open and limited procedures for goods, services, and construction services; the partial total notified reached US$142.2 billion (Table 3.20). For sub-central entities, namely the 37 states implementing the GPA, the estimated procurement was US$510.95 billion; and for the other entities covered in Annex 3, the total expenditure amounted to US$14.94 billion.

Market access conditions

U.S. policy with respect to market access for government procurement continues to be based on reciprocity, and is governed by specific trade agreements, including the GPA. Domestic purchasing requirements are maintained for procurement not covered by the GPA, the

WTO plurilateral Agreement on Trade in Civil Aircraft, or preferential trade agreements. The Trade Agreements Act of 1979 generally prohibits federal agencies from purchasing goods and services from countries that are not a party to the GPA or other trade agreements that cover government procurement (non-designated countries).

The United States Trade Representative is required by Executive Order 12260 to set the U.S. dollar thresholds for the WTO GPA and other FTAs.[286] In December 2017, the United States notified its latest threshold values, in the national currency, for the GPA (Table 3.21) and other procurement agreements (Table 3.22).[287] The threshold levels provided apply to the period starting on 1 January 2018 and ending on 31 December 2019.[288]

Under the Buy American Act of 1933 (BAA), the purchase of supplies and construction materials by government agencies is limited to those defined as "domestic end-products", in accordance with a two-part test that must establish that the article is manufactured in the United States, and that the cost of domestic components exceeds 50% of the cost of all the components. The BAA does not apply to services. As a way of monitoring enforcement of the BAA, the Independent Agencies Appropriations Act of 2006 (P.L. No. 109-115) requires the head of each federal agency to submit a report to Congress relating to acquisitions of articles, materials, or supplies manufactured outside the United States. Federal domestic preference requirements are also sometimes included in annual appropriation and authorization bills.

Under the Trade Agreements Act of 1979, the President may grant waivers from the BAA and other procurement restrictions; this authority has been delegated to the USTR. The Act waives the application of the BAA to the end-products of designated countries, which include the parties to the GPA, bilateral agreements that cover government procurement, CBERA beneficiaries,

Table 3.20 Reported statistics for open procedures, limited procedures, and small and minority owned enterprise set-asides at the federal government level, FY2015

(Number and US$)

Number of actions and values	Open procedures	Limited procedures	Small and minority owned enterprise set-asides
Goods and services: number of contracts awarded below threshold	359,894	147,968	111,514
Goods and services: number of contracts awarded equal to or above threshold	1,453,368	125,074	73,350
Goods and services: total US$ obligated below threshold	3,514,520,173.82	2,546,913,713.01	1,999,896,467.19
Goods and services: total US$ obligated equal to or above threshold	61,638,746,737.08	30,787,313,504.57	23,782,447,591.17
Construction services: number of contracts awarded below threshold	5,969	3,011	16,216
Construction services: number of contracts awarded equal to or above threshold	1,298	155	3,940
Construction services: total US$ obligated below threshold	1,436,773,738.09	418,018,015.77	4,797,345,480.94
Construction services: total US$ obligated equal to or above threshold	8,954,716,931.33	540,664,162.04	3,974,520,764.47

Source: WTO document GPA/137/Add.8, 28 November 2017, Annex I.

and LDCs. CBERA and LDCs face GPA thresholds. For the other trading partners that are beneficiaries of a preferential agreement, the thresholds are as shown in Table 3.22. Eligible products are granted non-discriminatory treatment. There are few other situations in which procurement may be exempt from BAA requirements. Exceptions to the BAA can be granted if it is determined that the domestic preference is inconsistent with the public interest, in case of U.S. non-availability of a supply or material, or for reasonableness of cost. Public interest determinations may be made on individual procurements or as a blanket for a set of procurements. Non-availability may be determined following FAR 25.104, which contains a list of articles that have been determined to be non-available, which must go through public notice and comment every five years, or on an individual basis. The cost of the domestic offer is understood to be unreasonable if the cost of the foreign (non-eligible) product, inclusive of import duty and a 6% added margin, is below the lowest domestic offer when this offer is from a large business concern. If the lowest domestic offer is from a small business concern, the added margin considered is 12%. For purchases by the DoD, the price difference must be at least 50%. The provisions of the BAA are also waived for civil aircraft and related articles that meet the substantial transformation test of the Act and originate in parties to the WTO Agreement on Trade in Civil Aircraft.

The Balance of Payments Program allows the DoD the application of provisions similar to those required under the BAA, to contracts over the SAT for end-products for use outside the United States.[289] The DoD waives the restrictions of the BAA/Balance of Payments Program for eligible goods (i.e. those covered by the United States under the WTO GPA or an FTA). For other goods, the DoD waives the restrictions for equipment produced in a "qualifying country" (with which there is a reciprocal procurement agreement or MoU).

The FAR provides that imported supplies for use by government agencies may be exempted from customs duties in certain cases. Agencies must use these exemptions when the anticipated savings to appropriated funds will outweigh the administrative costs associated with processing required documentation. Subchapters VIII and X of Chapter 98 of the HTSUS (19 U.S.C. 1202) list supplies for which exemptions from duty may be obtained when imported into the customs territory of the United States under a government contract. For certain of these supplies, the contracting agency must certify that they are for the purpose stated in the HTSUS. Supplies (excluding equipment) for government-operated vessels

Table 3.21 U.S. thresholds in Appendix I of the GPA, expressed in SDR and in the national currency, 2018-19

Level of government	Goods		Services		Construction	
	SDR	US$	SDR	US$	SDR	US$
Annex 1 – Central Government	130,000	180,000	130,000	180,000	5,000,000	6,932,000
Annex 2 – Sub-central government	355,000	492,000	355,000	492,000	5,000,000	6,932,000
Annex 3 – Other entities	400,000	555,000	400,000	555,000	5,000,000	6,932,000

Source: WTO document, GPA/THR/USA/1, 20 December 2017.

Table 3.22 Central Government thresholds for the application of other trade agreements, in national currency, 2018-19

(US$)

Trade agreement	Procurement of goods and services	Procurement of construction services
U.S.-Bahrain FTA	180,000	10,441,216
U.S.-Chile FTA	80,317	6,932,000
U.S.-Colombia FTA	80,317	6,932,000
Dominican Republic-Central America-U.S. FTA	80,317	6,932,000
U.S.-Israel FTA	50,000 (goods only)	n.a.
U.S.-Korea FTA	100,000	6,932,000
U.S.-Morocco FTA	180,000	6,932,000
NAFTA		
Canada	25,000 (goods), 80,137 (services)	10,441,216
Mexico	80,137	10,441,216
U.S.-Oman FTA	180,000	10,441,216
U.S.-Panama FTA	180,000	6,932,000
U.S.-Peru FTA	180,000	6,932,000
U.S.-Singapore FTA	80,137	6,932,000

n.a. Not applicable.

Source: Federal Register, Vol. 82, No. 236, Monday, 11 December 2017, Notices. Viewed at: https://ustr.gov/issue-areas/government-procurement/thresholds.

or aircraft may be imported free of duties; they are also free from internal revenue tax.[290]

Under Title III of Public Law 111-347, a federal excise tax of 2% is applied to government purchases of goods and services from foreign entities not party to an international procurement agreement, entered on or after 2 January 2011. Payments for purchases under the simplified acquisition procedures that do not exceed the SAT, as are emergency acquisitions and certain foreign humanitarian assistance contracts are exempted from the tax. Final regulations implementing the Title were issued in August 2016.[291].

Bidding procedures

Two commonly used types of bidding procedures are sealed bidding and contracting by negotiation. Sealed bidding requires that the final decision by agencies be based only on price and the price-related factors included in the invitation. The contract is awarded to the lowest bidder meeting all the contract requirements. A two-step sealed bidding process may be applied in cases where more information from suppliers is needed before the sealed bidding process is initiated. Contracting by negotiation is used when sealed bidding is not applicable, for instance, when consideration of evaluation factors other than price and price-related factors is required.

Government agencies are generally required to publish all contracts exceeding US$25,000 in www.fedbizopps. gov 15 days before solicitations begin.[292] They must allow for a 30-day response time, or a 40-day response time for procurements covered under an international trade agreement. Agencies must give consideration first to "required sources" for their supplies and services' needs. The list of required sources is made up of various sources, including excess (left over) from other agencies, and supplies from the Federal Prison Industries, Inc..[293] Required sources take priority over all other sources, including the programmes authorized by the SBA.

A simplified acquisition procedure is used for purchases below the SAT, and there are normally set-asides for the small business categories when there is a reasonable expectation that a minimum of two small businesses are able to provide the product/service competitively in terms of market prices, quality, and delivery. Where there is a repetitive need for supplies or services, the FAR allows for blanket purchase agreements (BPAs),

which establish regular "charge accounts" with suppliers found after a competitive bidding process.

Set-asides and preferences

U.S. procurement policy makes use of set-aside programmes to foster the participation of small businesses, veteran owned small businesses, small disadvantaged business (SDBs), Historically Underutilized Business Zone (HUBZone) businesses, and women-owned small businesses in the procurement process.[294] Relevant set-aside programmes are referenced in the U.S. schedules under the GPA.[295] The Federal Government determines specified annual prime contracting goals for designated small businesses. Under the Small Business Act (PL 85-536), as amended, government purchases with an anticipated value above the micro-purchase threshold of US$10,000, and up to the SAT of US$250,000, are to be automatically and exclusively set aside for small businesses, provided there are at least two or more (Rule of Two) small business concerns that are competitive in terms of market prices, quality, and delivery. Contract opportunities above US$250,000 must also be set aside for small businesses if the Rule of Two is met. Contract opportunities over US$700,000, or US$1.5 million for construction projects, awarded to Other than Small Businesses (OTSBs) must include small business subcontracting plans to the extent there are subcontracting opportunities.

The Small Business Administration (SBA) is responsible for defining the specific size standards for each industry, to determine which businesses qualify as small. This information is contained in a table published by the SBA, and most recently updated in 2016. Size may be defined in U.S. dollars or according to the number of employees.[296] SBA programmes seek to promote the ability of small businesses to compete for federal procurement contracts. They are: the Women-Owned Small Business (WOSB) Federal Contract programmes; the 8(a) Business Development Program; the Historically Underutilized Business Zones (HUBZone) Program; and the Service-Disabled Veteran-Owned Small Business Concerns (SDVOSBC) Program.[297]

There is a government-wide procurement goal that stipulates that at least 23% of all federal government contracting dollars should be awarded to small businesses. As part of this general goal, there are targeted subgoals for the following small business categories: WOSB: 5%;

Table 3.23 Government-wide procurement goals and results, FY2017

Goal category	Goal %	Actual %
Small business	23%	23.9%
8(a) Business Development Program (SDBs)	5%	9.1%
WOSB	5%	4.72%
SDVOSBC	3%	4.03%
Certified HUBZone small business	3%	1.65%

Source: Small Business Dashboard, *Small Business Goaling Report, FY2017 and FY2018*. Viewed at: https://smallbusiness.data.gov/explore? carryfilters=on&fromfiscal=yes&tab=By+Performance+Goal&fiscal_year=2018&tab=By+Performance+Goal&fiscal_year=2017&fromfiscal= yes&carryfilters=on&Submit=Go.

small disadvantaged business: 5%; SDVOSBC: 3%; and HUBZone: 3%. These sub-goals are not in addition to the 23% but are counted as part of the overall goals. The goals set were met, overall in FY2017, with the exception of women-owned and HUBZone, which were below the desired percentage.

Some contracting rules and limitations apply to set-asides. Under the non-manufacturer rule, a small business prime contractor that does not itself manufacture the products or materials provided to the Government under a set-aside contract for supplies, must supply the product of a small business, unless the SBA has granted a waiver, or the contract is a small business set-aside under the SAT. Waivers to the nonmanufacturer rule may be granted by the SBA if it is determined that there are an insufficient number of small businesses with the required manufacturing capabilities. Some subcontracting limitations also apply when a contract amount exceeds the SAT and for all other set-aside or sole-source contracts under the 8(a), HUBZone, SDVOSB or WOSB programmes. In these cases, under set-aside award conditions, small businesses are required to limit the amounts they spend on subcontractors that are not similarly situated: (a) in the case of service contracts, the small business prime contractor may not pay subcontractors more than 50% of the amount paid to the prime under the contract; (b) for supply contracts, the prime contractor may not pay subcontractors more than 50% of the amount, less the cost of materials, paid to the prime under the contract; and (c) the small business prime contractor may not pay more than 85% of the amount paid to it by the Government to subcontractors, not including the cost of materials, for general construction contracts, and may not pay more than 75% of the amount paid by the Government to it to subcontractors, not including the cost of materials, for specialty construction contracts.

Benefits are subject to eligibility conditions that vary according to the programme. In the case of the HUBZone Program, where benefits include a 10% price evaluation preference in full and open contract competitions, as well as subcontracting opportunities, for eligibility the business must be: (a) a small business by SBA standards; (b) at least 51% owned and controlled by U.S. citizens, or a Community Development Corporation, an agricultural cooperative, or an Native American tribe; (c) at least 35% of its employees must reside in a HUBZone; and (d) its principal office must be located within a HUBZone.

The WOSB Program (P.L. 106-554) allows Contracting Officers (COs) to set aside contracts for WOSBs under certain conditions, and to grant them contracts under sole-source authority in specific circumstances.[298] To be eligible for the WOSB Program, a business must: (a) be a small business; (b) be at least 51% owned and controlled by women who are U.S. citizens; and (c) have women manage day-to-day operations and make long-term decisions. Additionally, to qualify as an economically disadvantaged business within the WOSB Program, the business must meet all the requirements of the WOSB Contracting Program, and be owned and controlled by one or more women, each with a personal net worth less than US$750,000, adjusted gross income averaged over the previous three years of US$350,000 or less, and with personal assets of US$6 million or less. The qualifying North American Industry Classification System (NAICS) codes for the WOSB Contracting Program were last revised in October 2017.[299]

To benefit from the 8(a) Business Development Program and be considered small disadvantaged businesses (SDBs), businesses must be at least 51% owned and controlled by socially and economically disadvantaged individuals; they must be owned by someone whose personal net worth is US$250,000 or less, and have an average adjusted gross income for three years of US$250,000 or less and assets of US$4 million or less. Participation in this program by an SDB is limited to nine years. Sole-source contracts can be granted for up to a ceiling of US$4 million for goods and services and US$6.5 million for manufacturing, with a cumulative limit by recipient of US$100 million per recipient while in the program.

The SDVOSBC Program is a procurement programme that allows federal contracting officers, certain criteria are met, to restrict competition to SDVOSBCs and award a sole-source or set-aside contract. To qualify for the program, a business must be small, at least 51% owned and controlled by one or more service-disabled veterans, and have one or more service-disabled veterans manage day-to-day operations and make long-term decisions. Sole-source contracts may be awarded only if the CO does not have a reasonable expectation that at least two responsible SDVOSBCs will submit offers, the anticipated award price of the contract is not expected to exceed US$4 million for manufacturing requirements and US$6.5 million for all other requirements, and the award can be made at a fair market price. If the requirement is at or below the SAT, the CO may set aside the requirement for consideration among SDVOSBCs using simplified acquisition procedures, or may award a sole-source contract to a SDVOSBC. These sole-source benefits mirror those in the WOSB and HUBZone programmes, except HUBZone programme thresholds for manufacturing requirements are capped at US$7 million as outlined in FAR 19.1306.

Enforcement

Bid protests (before awards) are governed by federal statutes, including the Competition in Contracting Act of 1984 and the Federal Courts Improvement Act of 1982. They may be taken to the Government Accountability Office (GAO) or the U.S. Court of Federal Claims (COFC). A party dissatisfied with a decision by the GAO may file a new protest with the COFC, whose decisions may be appealed to the U.S. Court of Appeals for the Federal Circuit.

Part B
Report by the WTO Secretariat

According to statistics maintained by the U.S. General Accountability Office (GAO), during FY2016, 2,789 total cases were filed at the GAO, including 2,621 protests, 80 cost claims, and 88 requests for reconsideration. This reflects a 6% increase, year-to-year. The GAO reported further that, while more than 22% of those cases filed were sustained, 46% of the cases filed resulted in some form of relief being obtained by the protestor, referred to as an overall "effectiveness rate".[300] In FY2017, 2,596 bid protest cases were filed with the GAO, and 39 bid protests were filed with the COFC. Contract disputes on actions and events that occur after a contract is awarded are dealt with under the Contract Disputes Act of 1978. The parties may file contract dispute claims to either an agency board of contract appeals or the COFC, whose decisions may be appealed to the Court of Appeals for the Federal Circuit. In FY2017, 89 contract dispute cases were filed with the COFC, and 26 were appealed to the U.S. Court of Appeals for the Federal Circuit.

Intellectual property rights

Overview

The United States is one of main producers and exporters of goods and services that embody intellectual property (IP). IP is present in some 60% of U.S. goods exports and IP-intensive industries account for over one third of U.S. GDP (see below).[301] In 2016, the United States accounted for 31% of global commercial knowledge and technology intensive services, i.e., business, financial and information: in that year, U.S. exports of information and communications technology ICT)-enabled services exports (excluding digital goods) reached US$404 billion.[302] The United States has also been the largest global producer of high-technology manufactures with a global share of 31%, over the last decade.[303] During the period under review, the United States has continued to post its traditional balance-of-payments surplus in IP-related payments, as measured by the category "charges for the use of IP". In 2017, net receipts were US$79.5 billion, with receipts totalling US$127.9 billion and payments reaching US$48.4 billion.[304]

In 2016, the USDOC designated 81 industries, out of a total of 313 (25.9% of the total), as IP-intensive, which, in 2014, collectively accounted for US$6.6 trillion in value added, or 38.2% of 2014 GDP.[305] In 2014, IP-intensive industries directly accounted for 27.9 million jobs, and indirectly supported an additional 17.6 million, representing almost one in three jobs. Also in 2014, IP workers in IP-intensive industries earned 46% higher weekly wages than other workers. More particularly, trademark-intensive industries accounted for 23.7 million jobs in 2014; copyright-intensive industries accounted for 5.6 million; and patent-intensive industries accounted for 3.9 million.[306]

Regulations with respect to innovation, including in IP issues and funding of research and development (R&D), are contained in the Bayh-Dole and Stevenson Wydler

Acts.[307] The Bayh-Dole Act allows universities, non-profit institutions, and small businesses to obtain rights to patents arising from research funded by the Federal Government. The Stevenson-Wydler Act requires the establishment of an Office of Research and Technology Applications within each federal laboratory and agency. These offices work to transfer technology, including through the licensing of IP developed by the U.S. Government at its laboratories. The federal technology transfer policy is currently under review: IP issues, including the licensing of technology developed using federal funds, are an important factor in the review. The National Institute for Standards and Technology (NIST) is currently working with stakeholders on prioritizing technology transfer issues and improving the process to enhance innovation, technology commercialization and partnerships. Innovative partnership models involving state and local governments, the private sector, academia and international partners are seen as vehicles to maximize the utilization of underused facilities and share the costs of new R&D facilities.[308]

Government expenditures on R&D reached US$139.7 billion in 2016 across all federal R&D programmes. The Department of Defense receives some 49% of the funding. Other important recipients are the National Institutes of Health (22%), the National Aeronautics and Space Administration (8.2%), and the National Science Foundation (4.3%).[309] Government expenditure on R&D is estimated to have reached US$145 billion in 2017.[310]

Digital trade has raised new challenges for the U.S. Administration, such as how to best address new and emerging trade barriers created by other countries. According to a study by the USITC, the most cited policy measure impeding digital trade cited by industry representatives was data localization, while the U.S. content industry reported that ineffective enforcement procedures of IP affected them the most.[311]

The adequate and effective protection and enforcement of IP rights (IPRs) has remained a top trade policy priority for the U.S. Administration, as reflected in the 2017 and 2018 Special 301 Reports. The stated objectives are to encourage and maintain enabling environments for innovation, including effective IP protection and enforcement, in markets worldwide, which would benefit U.S. exporters and domestic IP-intensive industries in those markets as well.[312] IP is considered critical for economic growth and high-quality jobs for the United States. As noted in the 2018 Special 301 Report of the USTR, a top trade priority for the Administration is to use all possible sources of leverage to encourage other countries to provide adequate and effective protection and enforcement of U.S. IPRs.[313] Also, as stated in the 2018 National Trade Estimate Report, the Administration is maintaining a focus on the removal of barriers to digital trade, including restrictions to cross-border data flows, digital products, Internet-enabled services and other restrictive technology requirements.[314]

General regulatory framework

As a member of the World Intellectual Property Organization (WIPO), the United States participates in a large number of international conventions and treaties related to IPRs, including 19 instruments administered by the WIPO.[315] On 17 December 2005, the United States accepted the Protocol Amending the TRIPS Agreement adopted by the General Council on 6 December 2005 (WT/L/641).

The United States has systematically notified to the WTO its laws and regulations on traderelated aspects of IPRs, including amendments to legislation or regulations. The most recent updates were made in 2016. Recent amendments to legislation notified to the WTO include: the Consolidated Patent Laws, which entered into force on 1 August 2012[316]; the Patent Law Treaty, which entered into force with respect to the United States on 18 December 2013[317]; the Act to implement the provisions of the Geneva Act of the Hague Agreement Concerning the International Registration of Industrial Designs, which entered into force for the United States on 13 May 2015; and the Defend Trade Secrets Act of 2016, which entered into force on 5 November 2016, and amended the Economic Espionage Act, to create a private civil cause of action for trade secret misappropriation.[318]

The United States addresses IP protection and enforcement issues with its trading partners through several mechanisms at the bilateral, plurilateral or multilateral levels. In addition to securing binding IPR-related commitments as part of bilateral and plurilateral FTAs, the United States has addressed IPR issues through bilateral agreements and MOUs, bilateral investment treaties, and trade and investment framework agreements. The United States has also actively pursued enhanced standards of IP protection through its engagement with countries seeking accession to the WTO. Other instruments used by the United States for IPR protection and enforcement include: the annual "Special 301" review and report (see below) and IP dialogues with trading partners; multilateral engagement on IP issues through the WTO, the WIPO, the Asia-Pacific Economic Cooperation (APEC), and other organizations; implementation of trade policy in support of U.S. innovations; and providing interagency trade policy leadership.[319]

The Under Secretary of Commerce for Intellectual Property and Director of the United States Patent and Trademark Office (USPTO), among other duties, advises the President, through the Secretary of Commerce, on national and certain international IP policy issues; advises federal departments and agencies on matters of IP policy in the United States and IP protection in other countries; provides guidance, as appropriate, with respect to proposals by agencies to assist foreign governments and international intergovernmental organizations on matters of IP protection; and conducts programmes, studies, or exchanges of items or services regarding domestic and international IP law and the effectiveness of IP protection domestically and throughout the world.[320]

The USPTO Office of Policy and International Affairs (OPIA) leads agency efforts to formulate and execute U.S. domestic and international policy regarding protection and enforcement of IPRs, including the promotion of the development of IP systems, nationally and internationally, and advocating improved and more effective means of obtaining and enforcing the IPRs of U.S. nationals, domestically and internationally. Recent cooperative projects to improve the efficiency and quality of patent examination include technical training through the USPTO's Global IP Academy, exchanging best practices with counterpart offices, the Patent Prosecution Highway work sharing framework, the Cooperative Patent Classification system, and the Global Dossier Initiative. The OPIA coordinates its work with the USPTO's Patent Operations, including the Office of International Patent Cooperation, in implementing these and other cooperative projects.

Table 3.24 provides a snapshot of IPR protection in the United States as of mid-2018.

Patents

Patents are protected by the Patent Law of the United States, as incorporated in Title 35 of the U.S. Code. The Leahy-Smith America Invents Act (AIA), passed in 2011[321], significantly reformed U.S. patent law. In particular: (a) it transitioned the United States to a first-inventor-to-file system; (b) it provided an enhanced grace period for inventors to safeguard patent rights against disclosures made by inventors made one year or less before the effective filing date; (c) it modified the definition of prior art to include non-printed disclosures, including oral disclosures, made available to the public anywhere in the world; (d) it provided prior art effect to U.S. patent applications as of their foreign priority dates; (e) it eliminated the requirement for inventors to set forth the best mode to carry out the invention as a defense in infringement actions or in post grant review; and (f) it provided a 75% discount for patent fees to all applicants that qualify as micro entities.[322] No major changes to patent law have been introduced since then.

Inventions that are new, useful, and non-obvious are patentable.[323] Patents may be granted for a process, machine, manufacture or composition of matter, or improvements thereof. The term of protection is 20 years from the filing date.

The United States Patent and Trademark Office (USPTO), an agency of the USDOC, is in charge of granting patents and registering trademarks. The USPTO is responsible for examining applications, and granting patents on inventions when applicants are entitled to them; and it publishes and disseminates patent information, records assignments of patents,

Table 3.24 Summary of IP protection, June 2018

Form	Main legislation	Coverage	Duration
Copyright and related rights	Copyright Act of the United States (1976), as amended, and as incorporated in Title 17 of the U.S. Code	Authors' economic rights in the artistic, literary and scientific domains. The Act also provides rights of attribution and integrity for authors of works of visual art. Other federal and state laws address protection for the attribution and integrity of other works and authors. To benefit from copyright protection, a work must be an original creation. Registration is not required for protection.	Life of author plus 70 years for works created on or after 1 January 1978. Anonymous and pseudonymous works and works made for hire are protected for 95 years after publication or 120 years after creation, whichever is the shorter
Patents	Patent Law of the United States, as incorporated in Title 35 of the U.S. Code Leahy-Smith America Invents Act (AIA) of 2011. Patent Law Treaties Implementation Act of 2012	Inventions that are new, useful, and non-obvious are patentable. Patents may be granted for a process, machine, manufacture or composition of matter, or improvements thereof.	20 years from filing date
Industrial designs	Patent Law of the United States, as incorporated in Title 35 of the U.S. Code Patent Law Treaties Implementation Act of 2012	Any new, original and ornamental design for an article of manufacture	For applications filed before 13 May 2015, 14 years from the date of grant; for applications filed on or after 13 May 2015, 15 years from the date of grant
Trademarks	The Lanham Act of 1946, as amended (15 U.S.C. 1051 et seq.) and state laws	Any sign used to identify and distinguish goods or services of one enterprise from those of another enterprise	10 years from registration date; renewable indefinitely as long as the trademark is in use in commerce that is lawfully regulated by Congress
Geographical indications	The Lanham Act of 1946, as amended (15 U.S.C. 105 et seq.) and state laws, and supplemented with the Federal Alcohol Administration Act of 1935	Geographic signs and names of viticultural significance	10 years from registration date; renewable indefinitely as long as the trademark is in use in commerce that is lawfully regulated by Congress
New plant varieties	Plant Variety Protection Act Amendments of 1994 (7 U.S.C. 2321 et seq.)	Protection is granted to new plant varieties reproduced by seed or tuber-propagated, not previously sold in the United States for purposes of exploitation of the variety, more than 1 year prior to the date of filing; or in any area outside of the United States more than 4 years prior to the filing date, or, in the case of a tree or vine, over 6 years prior to the filing date	20 years from date of issue of the certificate in the United States
Layout designs of integrated circuits	Semiconductor Chip Protection Act of 1984 (17. U.S.C. 901 et seq.)	Topography of microelectronic semiconductor products, provided it is original (the result of its creator's own intellectual effort) and is not staple, commonplace or familiar in the industry at the time of its creation	10 years from filing date (or, if earlier, from first use)
Trade secrets	Economic Espionage Act of 1996 and state laws. Defend Trade Secrets Act, Public Law No. 114-153, 2016 amended the Economic Espionage Act.	Any information, not generally known to the relevant portion of the public, that provides an economic benefit to its holder, and is the subject of reasonable efforts to maintain its secrecy	Indefinite

Source: WIPO; USDOC; and notifications to the WTO.

maintains search databases of U.S. and foreign patents, and keeps a search room for public use in examining issued patents and records. The USPTO administers the patent laws as they relate to the granting of patents for inventions, and performs other duties relating to patents. The USPTO has no jurisdiction over questions of infringement and enforcement of patents.

Applications for patents are examined by the USPTO to determine if the applicants are entitled to patents under the law, and patents are granted when applicants are so entitled. The filing date of an application for patent is the date on which a specification, and any drawings necessary to understand the subject matter sought to be patented, are received in the USPTO; or the date on which the last part completing the application is received, in the case of a previously incomplete or defective application. The application for a patent is not forwarded for examination until all required parts, complying with the rules related thereto, are received. The USPTO publishes issued patents and most patent applications 18 months from the earliest effective application filing date, and makes various other publications concerning patents. The USPTO also records assignments of patents. Similar functions are performed with respect to the registration of trademarks.[324]

U.S. law provides for the possibility of submitting a provisional application for a patent.[325] The purpose is to provide a lower-cost first patent filing in the United States, and to give U.S. applicants parity with foreign applicants. A provisional application provides the means to establish an early effective filing date in a patent application and permits the term "Patent Pending" to be applied in connection with the invention.[326] The applicant would then have up to 12 months to file a non-provisional application for patent. A provisional application is not examined on its merits. The 12-month pendency for a provisional application is not counted toward the 20-year term of a patent granted on a subsequently filed non-provisional application. Provisional applications may not be filed for design inventions.

In accordance with the American Inventors Protection Act (AIPA) of 1999, publication of patent applications is required for most plant and utility patent applications filed on or after 29 November 2000. A patent applicant may request that the application not be published, but only if the invention has not been, and will not be, the subject of an application filed in a foreign country that requires publication 18 months after filing (or earlier claimed priority date) or under the Patent Cooperation Treaty.[327] Under U.S. law, a person who is not the owner of a patent may challenge the validity of an issued patent by filing a petition to institute an *inter partes* review of the patent before the Patent Trial and Appeal Board (PTAB), an administrative court of the USPTO. Two options for challenging validity before the PTAB may be Post-Grant Reviews (limited to within nine months of issuance), or *inter partes* reviews (any time after nine months of issuance, or the conclusion of a post-grant proceeding).

The petitioner may request to cancel as unpatentable one or more claims of a patent, on certain grounds. A petition for *inter partes* review must be filed after the later of either the date that is nine months after the grant of a patent, or the issuance of a reissue of a patent. The Patent Trial and Appeal Board (PTAB) is in charge of conducting *inter partes* reviews, which can be appealed.

As reported in the previous Review, the USPTO's Strategic Plan for 2014-18 continues to include the main elements with respect to current IP policy. The Plan sets out three goals for the 2014-18 period: optimizing patent quality and timeliness; optimizing trademark quality and timeliness; and providing domestic and global leadership to improve IP policy, protection, and enforcement.[328] In its overall Strategic Plan for 2018-22, the USDOC identified a role for the USPTO in accelerating U.S. leadership in the strengthening of IP protection, both in the United States and abroad, so as to strengthen U.S. economic and national security.[329]

The USPTO received 647,388 patent applications in FY2017, slightly down from the 650,411 received in FY2016 (Table 3.26).[330] During the review period, the USPTO has continued to make progress towards addressing some of the concerns identified in previous years, with respect to the pendency period for patent applications and the need to improve the quality of patent applications. In this respect, it has made Optimizing Patent Quality and Timeliness its Strategic Goal I within its Strategic Performance Framework, aimed at reducing the average time from filing until an examiner's initial determination on patentability to 10 months, and average total pendency (average time from filing until the application is issued as a patent or abandoned) to 20 months. During the period under review, the pendency time has continued to decrease. In FY2017, total pendency time was 24.2 months, down from 25.2 months in FY2016 and 26.6 months in FY2015.[331] The unexamined patent application backlog fell from 537,655 at the end of FY2016 to 526,579 at the end of FY2017. Also in FY2017, average first action pendency was 16.3 months.[332]

During the period under review, the number of patents granted by the UPSTO increased. In FY2017, it granted a total of 315,367 utility patents, up from 304,568 in FY2016. The number of industrial design patents also rose, from 27,830 in FY2016, to 30,637 in FY2017. The number of plant patents remained stable between FY2016 and FY2017, but increased with respect to previous years. The number of patent reissues continued to decline (Table 3.26).

The share of patents of foreign origin issued by the USPTO during the review period continued to be larger than the share of patents of domestic origin. Patents issued by the United States to residents of foreign countries represented almost 52% of total patents issued in FY2017.[333] Among foreign countries, the largest share was held by Japan (28.7% of patents issued to foreign residents), followed by the Republic

Table 3.25 Number of patent and trademark filings and pendencies, FY2013-17

Filings and pendencies	FY2013	FY2014	FY2015	FY2016	FY2017
Patent filings	601,464	618,457	618,062	650,411	647,388
% change in patent filings	6.3	2.8	-0.1	5.2	-0.5
Patent first action pendency (months)	18.2	18.4	17.3	16.2	16.3
% change in patent first action pendency	-16.9	1.1	-6.0	-6.4	0.6
Total patent pendency (months)	29.1	27.4	26.6	25.3	24.2
% change in total patent pendency	-10.2	-5.8	-2.9	-4.9	-4.3
Trademark filings	433,654	455,017	503,889	530,270	594,107
% change in trademark filings	4.5	4.9	10.7	5.2	12.0
Trademark first action pendency (months)	3.1	3.0	2.9	3.1	2.7
% change in trademark first action pendency	-3.1	-3.2	-3.3	6.9	-12.9
Total trademark average pendency (months)	10.0	9.8	10.1	9.8	9.5
% change in total trademark average pendency	-2.0	-2.0	3.1	-3.0	-3.1

Source: USPTO.

Table 3.26 Patents issued FY2010-FY2017

Year	Utility	Design	Plant	Re-issue	Total
FY2010	207,915	23,373	978	861	233,127
FY2011	221,350	21,295	816	969	244,430
FY2012	246,464	21,953	920	921	270,258
FY2013	265,979	22,453	842	809	290,083
FY2014	303,930	24,008	1,013	661	329,612
FY2015	295,460	25,438	1,020	531	322,448
FY2016	304,568	27,830	1,250	459	334,107
FY2017	315,367	30,637	1,246	392	347,243

Source: USPTO.

Table 3.27 Patents issued by the United States to residents of foreign countries and territories, FY2013–17

Residence	FY2013	FY2014	FY2015	FY2016	FY2017
Total	**150,014**	**167,937**	**168,050**	**173,650**	**180,275**
Australia	1,878	2,062	1,937	1,888	1,964
Austria	1,065	1,296	1,248	1,416	1,613
Belgium	1,111	1,267	1,234	1,315	1,359
Canada	6,915	7,922	7,487	7,258	7,532
China	6,181	7,715	8,598	10,988	14,147
Denmark	1,009	1,309	1,186	1,221	1,248
Finland	1,205	1,499	1,437	1,604	1,727
France	6,245	7,144	7,034	6,907	7,365
Germany	15,798	17,926	17,485	17,568	17,998
India	2,222	2,937	3,328	3,685	4,206
Israel	2,948	3,561	3,839	3,820	4,306
Italy	2,834	3,043	3,060	3,158	3,212
Japan	53,359	56,639	54,487	53,046	51,743
Korea, Republic of	15,058	17,815	19,615	21,865	22,687
Netherlands	2,391	2,883	2,732	2,941	3,133
Sweden	2,309	2,905	2,828	3,044	3,328
Switzerland	2,278	2,660	2,745	2,905	3,022
Chinese Taipei	12,168	12,271	12,317	12,738	12,540
United Kingdom	6,292	7,232	7,143	7,289	7,633

Source: USPTO.

of Korea (12.6%), Germany (10.0%), and China (7.8%) (Table 3.27).

As indicated above, the PTAB oversees validity challenges, which include post-grant review and *inter partes* reviews. It also oversees appeals during the course of patent examination (*ex partes* appeals), and implements the patent dispute resolution portions of the AIA. In FY2018, it decided 14,118 *ex partes* appeals. Also, in FY2018, it had a total of 66 post-grant review cases, and 3,303 *inter partes* review cases. Statistics with respect to appeals show that 11,650 appeal cases were filed, and 14,118 cases were decided, during FY2017. At the end of FY2017, there were 12,998 appeal cases pending, compared to 15,449 at the end of FY2016.[334]

Industrial designs

Industrial designs, understood as any new, original and ornamental design for an article of manufacture, are protected in the United States by the Patent Law, as incorporated in Title 35 of the U.S. Code. The specific legal instruments for protecting industrial designs are known as "design patents". The Patent Law Treaties Implementation Act of 2012 introduced modifications to this law, and established the legal basis to implement the Geneva Act of The Hague Agreement Concerning the International Registration of Industrial Designs (the Hague Agreement), which entered into force with respect to the United States on 13 May 2015. This also enabled the United States to join the WIPO-administered system.

As a result of the implementation of the Patent Law Treaties Implementation Act of 2012, U.S. applicants can file international design applications through the USPTO as an office of indirect filing, and applicants filing international design applications can designate the United States for design protection. The term of protection for applications filed on or after 13 May 2015 is 15 years from the date of grant; applications filed before 13 May 2015 have a term of protection of 14 years from the date of grant.

The number of patents granted for industrial designs has followed an upward trend since FY2013. Specifically, the USPTO issued 30,270 design patents in FY2017, up from 27,830 granted in FY2016.[335]

Trademarks

Trademarks are governed by the Lanham Act of 1946 (Trademark Act), as amended (15 U.S.C. 1051 et seq.), the Trademark Rules (37 CFR Part 2), the Trademark Manual of Examining Procedures, and state laws. Trademark protection arises from federal registration with the USPTO, from the actual use of the mark in commerce, and from federal unfair competition laws. Federal registration of a mark is not a requisite to establish rights to it, nor is it required in order to use it. However, federal registration grants the holder additional rights, such as the legal presumption of ownership, validity, and the entitlement to use the mark in connection with the goods or services identified in the registration. Trademark protection has a renewable term of 10 years, for as a long as the mark is in use. The protection granted to a mark may be cancelled if an affidavit of use is not provided between the fifth and sixth year of use.

Applications for federal trademark registration are filed with the USPTO. They can be based on use of the mark in the ordinary course of U.S. trade; a bona fide intention to use the mark in the ordinary course of U.S. trade; the Paris Convention or the Madrid Protocol. The first to use the mark in commerce can prevent registration of a mark with a later filing date or later use in commerce. The USPTO determines the right to register, but not the right to use a mark, which must be determined by a court. In the case of applications

filed by U.S. applicants, the trademark must be used in U.S. commerce before federal registration is issued. Applications filed by foreign applicants under the Paris Convention or the Madrid Protocol do not require use of the mark in U.S. commerce before registration, but must include a declaration of bona fide intention to use the mark in commerce. Pursuant to the Madrid Protocol, a trademark owner with an application filed with, or a registration issued by, the USPTO and who is a national of, has domicile in, or has an industrial or commercial establishment in, the United States may also file an international application with the USPTO. Holders of international registrations based on U.S. applications or registrations may request extensions of protection in other Madrid Protocol member states.

For applications filed pursuant to the Paris Convention and the Madrid Protocol, use is not required for registration, but is required to maintain the registration.[336] Use of a mark in promotion or advertising before the product or service is actually provided under the mark does not qualify as use in commerce. Notices of marks entitled to registration are published in the USPTO's Official Gazette. A trademark registration can be cancelled at any time if there is evidence of non-use or if it has been discontinued. Registration with the USPTO provides protection for the mark only in the United States and its territories. Foreigners registering a mark with the USPTO, if not represented by an attorney in the United States, must designate a U.S. representative under Section 1(e) of the Trademark Act of 1946.

The United States has legislation to deal with dilution of a mark. Under the Trademark Dilution Revision Act of 2006 (P.L. 109-312), which revised and clarified the Federal Trademark Dilution Act, enacted in 1996, an owner of a famous mark is entitled to obtain an injunction against the use of a mark or trade name in a manner that is likely to cause dilution by blurring or tarnishment, as well as to oppose applications or cancel registrations that are likely to cause dilution with the famous mark. Marks are also protected against dilution at the state level.

Disputes regarding trademark registrability may be settled in the USPTO's Trademark Trial and Appeal Board (TTAB) through an opposition or cancellation proceeding, or may be taken to court. Opposition to a mark's registration may be filed up to 30 days after publication; this period may be extended for up to six months. In cases of conflict between two marks, the USPTO determines the likelihood of confusion as a result of the use of the marks at issue by both parties. The main factors considered in determining the likelihood of confusion are the similarity of the marks and the commercial relationship between the goods and services identified by the marks. The likelihood of confusion is generally presumed if the marks are identical and the goods or services are identical. Fame of a mark is also taken into account when determining likelihood of confusion. However, there are no lists of famous marks. The TTAB's amended Rules of Practice

Part B
Report by the WTO Secretariat

in Trademark Cases became effective in January 2017. This is the first amendment to the rules since 2007, and aims at streamlining trial proceedings by promoting the efficient and cost-effective use of resources of both the Board and the parties to the proceedings. The USPTO has also issued several orders that clarify and interpret certain aspects of the rules.

Trademark application filings increased by 12% in FY2017, to 594,107, continuing a trend that began in FY2013. Trade mark registrations totalled 327,314 in FY2017, of which 242,709 were new registrations, and 84,727 were renewals of existing trademarks (Table 3.28). The average pendency time for processing a new trademark application FY2017 was 9.5 months.[337] The trademark renewal rate was 31.5% in FY2017, somewhat below the 32.1% rate posted in FY2016. Earned revenue for trademark filings increased from US$146.1 million in FY2016 to US$159.1 million in FY2017.[338]

There were 65,636 trademarks registered to residents of foreign countries in FY2017, up 28.7% from FY2016

(Table 3.29), and accounting for 20.1% of all trademark registrations in FY2017. Residents of China accounted for 36.4% of the registrations, followed by residents from Canada (7.2%), the United Kingdom (6.9%), Germany (6.1%), Japan (4.2%), and France (3.7%).

As part of its mission to optimize trademark quality and timeliness, the USPTO continued to encourage electronic filing through the Trademark Electronic Application System (TEAS) and discourage paper filing during the review period. Following the introduction of the TEAS Reduced Fee (TEAS RF) application option in January 2015, the USPTO implemented additional fee changes communicated in the Federal Register, 81 Fed. Reg. 72694 in October 2016, to raise fees for paper filings. The fees were adjusted to be better aligned with the full cost of relevant products and services, and to encourage the use of electronic filing options, which reduce the USPTO's examination costs. First and final action compliance rates, which measure trademark quality, exceeded 97% and 98%, respectively in FY2017. The number of trademark applications processed

Table 3.28 Trademarks registered, renewed, and published, FY2010–17

Fiscal year	Certificates of registration issued	Renewed	Registrations (incl. classes)
2010	164,330	46,734	221,090
2011	177,661	44,873	237,586
2012	182,761	59,871	243,459
2013	193,121	63,709	259,681
2014	206,555	56,166	279,282
2015	208,660	58,284	282,091
2016	227,407	62,604	309,188
2017	242,709	84,727	327,314

Source: USPTO.

Table 3.29 Trademarks issued by the United States to residents of foreign countries and territories, FY2013–17

Residence	FY2013	FY2014	FY2015	FY2016	FY2017
Total	36,916	38,498	40,864	50,980	65,636
Australia	1,385	1,564	1,445	1,940	2,016
Austria	361	369	305	406	467
Belgium	362	408	161	372	398
British Virgin Islands	396	295	445	286	426
Canada	3,944	4,010	6,420	4,288	4,739
China	2,444	2,901	4,016	10,582	23,893
Denmark	377	393	275	472	442
France	2,390	2,338	1,488	2,358	2,455
Germany	3,641	3,702	2,478	3,875	3,978
Hong Kong, China	775	883	1,472	1,268	1,504
India	294	249	364	315	386
Israel	462	443	470	596	574
Italy	1,821	1,843	730	1,994	1,928
Japan	2,568	2,770	2,433	2,982	2,763
Korea, Republic of	1,153	1,272	1,997	1,724	2,316
Luxembourg	271	312	343	375	388
Mexico	1,040	921	1,123	1,005	982
Netherlands	810	891	582	1,017	951
Singapore	324	277	311	385	431
Spain	965	914	786	1,151	1,086
Sweden	661	636	604	744	749
Switzerland	1,623	1,735	1,268	2,060	1,775
Chinese Taipei	957	926	1,172	902	921
United Kingdom	3,092	3,607	4,836	4,299	4,552

Source: USPTO (2018).

completely electronically increased to 86.5% in FY2017, and the number of paper application filings declined to 425 from 1,189 in FY2016.[339]

Geographical indications

The United States provides protection to foreign and domestic geographical indications (GIs) through its trademark system for all classes of goods and services, usually as certification marks and collective marks with indications of regional origin.[340] The U.S. system provides that an interested party may assert grounds (such as those described below) to oppose an application to register, or to cancel a registered mark, if that party believes that it will be damaged by the registration or continued existence of the registration. The USPTO examines applications for trademarks, including certification marks and collective marks with indications of regional origin. Protection is not granted to geographic terms or signs that are generic for goods or services. Under the system, the owner of a mark has the exclusive right to prevent its use by unauthorized parties when such use would likely cause consumer confusion, mistake or deception as to the source of the goods/ services. A prior right holder has priority and exclusivity over any later users of the same or similar sign on the same, similar, related, or in some cases unrelated goods/ services where consumers would likely be confused by the two uses. Complementary protection is provided under the Federal Alcohol Administration Act and its implementing regulations for wine and distilled spirits of both domestic and foreign origin.

The Trademark Act differentiates certification marks with indications of regional origin from trademarks by two characteristics: (a) a certification mark is not used by its owner; and (b) a certification mark does not indicate the commercial source nor distinguish the goods or services of one person from those of another person. Any entity, which meets the certifying standards, is entitled to use the certification mark. Certification marks identify the nature and quality of the goods, and affirm that these goods have met certain defined standards.

Geographic names or signs may also be registered as collective marks or as trademarks. However, the geographic term must not be deceptive; and the applicant must either show acquired distinctiveness in the geographic term, or disclaim exclusive right to use the geographic term. Although registration is preferable because of notice to the public and other benefits, GIs may also be protected through common law without being registered by the USPTO if they are a valid common law regional certification or collective mark (not a generic term).[341]

Trade secret protection

The main legislation with respect to the protection of trade secrets in the United States is contained in the Economic Espionage Act (EEA) of 1996 (as amended by the Theft of Trade Secrets Clarification Act of 2012) and the Defend Trade Secrets Act (DTSA) of 2016, P.L. No. 114-153, 2016, as well as state laws. The EEA defines as trade secret tangible or intangible information in all forms and types regarding a number of areas (financial, business, scientific, technical, economic, or engineering) whether it is stored, compiled, or memorialized physically, electronically, graphically, photographically, or in writing, provided: (a) the owner thereof has taken reasonable measures to keep such information secret; and (b) the information derives independent economic value, actual or potential, from not being generally known to, and not being readily ascertainable through proper means by, the public. Until 2016, U.S. federal trade secret protection legislation was focused on criminal acts, while civil enforcement of trade secret protection was addressed through state law; however, the passage of the DTSA added a federal civil cause of action for trade secret misappropriation.

The Theft of Trade Secrets Clarification Act of 2012 expanded the scope of the EEA, so that it now applies to products or services that are used, or intended for use, in interstate or foreign commerce. The provisions of the EEA do not apply to lawful activity by government entities. The EEA has extraterritorial jurisdiction in cases where the offender is a U.S. citizen or permanent resident, or if the offender is an organization organized under the laws of the United States or any U.S. state, or if the offense was committed in the United States.

The DTSA, signed into P.L. No. 114-153 in May 2016, created federal civil cause of action by amending the Federal Criminal Code to establish a private civil cause of action for trade secret misappropriation. The DTSA authorizes a trade secret owner to file a civil action in a district court seeking relief for trade secret misappropriation related to a product or service in interstate or foreign commerce. The Act provides for private civil remedies, including *ex parte* orders for the seizure of property necessary to prevent the propagation or dissemination of the trade secret that is the subject of the action. The DTSA also gives the choice to parties between localized disputes under state laws or disputes under federal law, heard in federal courts. State laws differ somewhat, but there is similarity among them because almost all states have adopted the Uniform Trade Secrets Act (UTSA), with modifications.[342] The DTSA also provides for whistle-blower protection for an individual who makes a confidential disclosure to a government official in cases of a suspected violation of the law, or files a sealed document to the court with respect to an anti-retaliation lawsuit. It establishes injunctive and damages remedies. Under the Act, a trade secret owner may apply for, and a court may grant, a seizure order to prevent dissemination of the trade secret if the court makes specific findings, including that an immediate and irreparable injury will occur if seizure is not ordered. The court must take custody of the seized materials, and hold a seizure hearing within seven days.[343]

Under the EEA, economic espionage for a foreign power, and the theft or misappropriation of a trade secret, are federal crimes. For economic espionage, the EEA sets fines of up to US$500,000 per offense and imprisonment of up to 15 years for individuals, and fines of up to US$10 million for organizations. In the case of theft of trade secrets, penalties for violation are imprisonment for up to 10 years for individuals (no fines) and fines of up to US$5 million for organizations. The amount of these fines was extended in 2013, in the case of individuals, from US$500,000 to US$5 million, and in the case of organizations, from US$10 million to the greater of US$10 million or three times the value of the stolen trade secret to the affected organization. Amendments to maximum fines were also introduced in 2016 with the passage of the DTSA. This Act amended the EEA, to provide for criminal fines for individuals to be the greater of US$5 million or three times the trade secret's value (including any reproduction costs that the holder of the trade secret has avoided).

Section 1637 of the National Defense Authorization Act (NDAA) of 2015 (50 U.S.C. 1708), Actions to Address Economic or Industrial Espionage in Cyberspace, directs the President to submit to Congress, not later than 180 days after 19 December 2014, and annually thereafter through 2020, a report on foreign economic and industrial espionage in cyberspace during the 12month period preceding the submission of the report, that identifies: (a) foreign countries that engage in economic or industrial espionage in cyberspace with respect to trade secrets or proprietary information owned by U.S. persons; (b) foreign countries identified under clause (a) that the President determines engage in the most egregious economic or industrial espionage in cyberspace with respect to such trade secrets or proprietary information (to be known as "priority foreign countries"); and (c) categories of technologies or proprietary information developed by U.S. persons that are targeted for economic or industrial espionage in cyberspace and, to the extent practicable, have been appropriated through such espionage. The report must also identify the actions taken by the President to "decrease the prevalence of economic or industrial espionage in cyberspace." The NDAA also authorizes the President to prohibit all transactions in property of any (foreign) person who the President determines knowingly engages in economic or industrial espionage in cyberspace. This authority is an expansion of the long-standing International Emergency Economic Powers Act (IEEPA), and does not include the authority to impose sanctions on the importation of goods.

Table 3.30 Main Amendments to the Copyright Act since 1995

Act	Coverage
Digital Performance Right in Sound Recordings Act of 1995	Amended the Copyright Act to provide an exclusive public performance right for sound recordings that extends to digital performances.
Legislative Branch Appropriations Act of 1997 (Public Law 104-197)	Introduced amendments concerning the exception for reproducing literary works in specialized format for the blind and disabled.
Digital Millennium Copyright Act of 1998 (Public Law 105–304)	Amended U.S. copyright law to comply with the WIPO Copyright Treaty and the WIPO Performances and Phonograms Treaty, including the introduction of anti-circumvention provisions. Also established a legal framework limiting online infringement liability for Internet service providers.
Sonny Bono Copyright Term Extension (P.L. 105-298)	Extended by 20 years the overall term of copyright protection.
Digital Theft Deterrence and Copyright Damages Improvement Act of 1999 (P.L. 106-160)	Increased the possible civil penalties for copyright infringement.
Copyright Royalty and Distribution Reform Act of 2004 (P.L. 108.419, 118 Stat. 2341)	Amended copyright law to replace copyright arbitration royalty panels with Copyright Royalty Judges.
Family Entertainment and Copyright Act of 2005 (P.L. 109-119 Stat. 218)	Increased penalties for copyright infringement, and introduced penalties against unauthorized camcording.
Copyright Royalty Judges Program Technical Corrections Act (2006) (P.L. 109-303)	Makes technical corrections relating to copyright royalty judges.
Copyright Cleanup, Clarification, and Corrections Act of 2010 (P.L. 111-295)	Makes some technical corrections to the Copyright Act.
STELA Reauthorization Act of 2014 (P.L. 113-200)	Amended Title 17, to extend, until 31 December 2019, the statutory license under which satellite carriers retransmit distant television broadcast stations to viewers who are unable to receive signals for such stations in their local market.
Unlocking Consumer Choice and Wireless Competition Act of 2014 (Public Law 113-144)	Re-establishes a limited exemption to prohibitions on circumvention of certain technological protection measures for the purposes of "unlocking" wireless telephone handsets to allow cell phone owners to connect to different wireless network providers.

Source: WIPO; Government Publishing Office (GPO). Viewed at: https://www.gpo.gov/; and U.S. Copyright Office, Preface to Circular 92. Viewed at: https://www.copyright.gov/title17/preface.pdf.

Copyright

In accordance with the Constitution, the Federal Government has jurisdiction over copyright protection. Copyright is protected under the Copyright Act of 1976, as amended, which took effect on 1 January 1978. The Act, embodied in Title 17 of the U.S. Code (17 U.S.C.), pre-empts any state law that provides equivalent rights in copyrightable subject matter. Since its enactment in 1976, the Copyright Act has been amended on several occasions (Table 3.30).

The United States is a party to the Berne Convention for the Protection of Literary and Artistic Works (1989), the WIPO Copyright Treaty (2002), the WIPO Performances and Phonograms Treaty (2002), the Brussels Convention Relating to the Distribution of Program-Carrying Signals Transmitted by Satellite (1985), and the Convention for the Protection of Producers of Phonograms Against Unauthorized Duplication of their Phonograms (1974). The United States is not a party to the Rome Convention.[344]

The United States grants automatic protection to copyrighted works, including computer programs, from all WTO Members and Berne Convention signatories. To be eligible for copyright protection, a work must be an original creation. Copyright protection covers an author's economic rights in artistic, literary and scientific works. The period of protection is the lifetime of the author, plus 70 years for works created on or after 1 January 1978. Anonymous and pseudonymous works and works made for hire, are protected for 95 years after publication or 120 years after creation, whichever is shorter. Copyright owners who have registered their copyright with the Copyright Office may also choose to record their registration with CBP for protection against the importation of infringing copies.

The U.S. Copyright Office administers the Copyright Act, and the duties of the Office and the Register of Copyrights are prescribed in, and governed by, the Copyright Act and the related chapter of Title 17 of the U.S. Code.[345] The Office: examines and registers copyright claims and administers deposit requirements; records transfers, assignments, licenses and other transactions; and administers regulations, practices and programmes that explain the provisions of the law. Registration is not required for protection, although, in addition to establishing a public record of the copyright claim, there are additional benefits that accrue with timely registration, including the availability of statutory damages.[346] The Copyright Office advises Congress, the judiciary and executive branch agencies on national and international issues relating to copyright. The Copyright office may also undertake studies on U.S. copyright law at the request of Congress, and also under its own initiative.[347] Recent reports have included: (a) a report on Section 1201 (exemption to non-circumvention rules) (June 2017)[348]; (b) a software-enabled consumer products study (December 2016)[349]; (c) a Proposed Schedule and Analysis of Copyright Recordation Fee to

go into Effect on or about 18 December 2017 (submitted to Congress on 18 August 2017)[350]; and (d) a discussion document on revising the Section 108 exceptions for libraries and archives.[351]

The Copyright Office registered 452,122 claims to copyright in FY2017.[352] In September 2017, it released an updated version of the Third Edition of its Compendium of U.S. Copyright Office Practices, a technical manual on registration practices that serves as a guidebook for authors, copyright licensees, practitioners, scholars, the courts, and members of the general public.[353] This update was effective as of 29 September 2017, and it is the governing administrative manual for registrations and recordations issued by the Copyright Office on or after that date.[354]

In U.S. copyright legislation, the approach is based on copyright and authors' rights; there is no concept of neighbouring rights (certain elements of the rights of performers, producers of sound recordings and broadcasters) separate from copyright. Those parties may receive protection under copyright, via contract law, including collective bargaining rights, and under telecommunications law. The United States is a party to the Geneva Phonograms Convention, which is used to provide a point of attachment for U.S. sound recordings in foreign countries, as does the WTO TRIPS Agreement. Sound recordings are considered works of authorship under the Copyright Act, but have a more limited scope of rights than other categories of works. Federal law provides protection against unauthorized recordings of live musical performances.[355] The Audio Home Recording Act of 1992 requires that manufacturers and importers of digital audio recorders and digital recording media pay fees that are distributed to recording artists and copyright owners on a national treatment basis. The Copyright Royalty and Distribution Reform Act of 2004 and the amendments contained in the Copyright Royalty Judges Program Technical Corrections Act of 2006 replaced the Copyright Arbitration Royalty Panels with Copyright Royalty Judges (CRJs), who serve on the Copyright Royalty Board which is part of the Library of Congress.

U.S. copyright law does not grant retransmission rights for broadcast organizations, but U.S. telecommunications law provides protections for broadcast signals and technical measures used in connection with the signals.[356] Additionally, U.S. copyright law protects the copyrighted content contained within broadcast signals.[357] Computer programs and compilations of data that constitute original works of authorship are protected as literary works. Owners of copyrighted works enjoy an exclusive right to create derivative works based on the copyrighted works.

Statutory licences consistent with the Berne Convention may be applied for certain types of copyrighted products, for example for secondary transmissions by cable and satellite, and for the use of certain works in connection with non-commercial broadcasting. In this respect,

Part B
Report by the WTO Secretariat

the Copyright Act provides for several types of statutory licences. Generally, interested parties are given the opportunity to negotiate the terms of the licence; a rate is set by the authorities only if they fail to agree. Statutory licensing provisions in the Copyright Act govern the retransmission of distant and local television broadcast signals by cable operators and satellite carriers to those who cannot receive broadcast signals. The STELA Reauthorization Act of 2014 (P.L. 113-200), signed into law on 4 December 2014, amended Title 17, to extend, until 31 December 2019, the statutory license under which satellite carriers retransmit distant television broadcast stations to viewers who are unable to receive signals for such stations in their local market.[358]

U.S. copyright law has anti-circumvention rules as those contained in the Digital Millennium Copyright Act (DMCA). The DMCA also allows possible temporary exemptions to the DMCA's prohibition against circumvention of technological measures that control access to, or unauthorized use of, copyrighted works. Under Section 1201 of Title 17 of the U.S. Code, the Copyright Office conducts a public rulemaking every three years, so it can advise the Librarian of Congress on any proposed exemptions to the prohibition on circumventing technological protection measures.[359] Petitioners submit evidence and arguments for the Copyright Office to consider when evaluating whether to recommend an exemption to the Librarian. The rulemaking has several phases: the petition phase, the public comment phase, which has multiple rounds, and the public hearings phase. After these phases are completed, the Register, after consulting with the National Telecommunications and Information Administration at the USDOC, presents his or her recommendation to the Librarian. The primary responsibility of the Register and the Librarian of Congress in the rulemaking proceeding is to assess whether the implementation of technological protection measures impairs the ability of individuals to make non-infringing use of copyrighted works within the meaning of Section 1201(a)(1). The Librarian will review the recommendation before issuing any exemptions.[360]

The U.S. Copyright Office initiated its seventh triennial rulemaking proceeding under the DMCA in 2017.[361] In this proceeding, the Copyright Office established a streamlined procedure for the renewal of exemptions that were granted during the sixth triennial rulemaking and considered petitions for new exemptions to engage in activities not permitted by existing exemptions. In June 2017, the Copyright Office published a Notice of Inquiry requesting petitions to renew existing exemptions and comments in response to those petitions, as well as petitions for new exemptions to engage in activities not currently permitted by existing exemptions. Subsequently, in October 2017, the Copyright Office issued a Notice of Proposed Rulemaking, in which it stated its intention to recommend each of the existing exemptions for re-adoption, and through which it initiated three rounds of public comment on the newly-proposed exemptions.[362] Final rules will be issued in the fall of 2018.

Also with respect to exemptions to anti-circumvention policies, the Unlocking Consumer Choice and Wireless Competition Act of 2014 re-established a limited exemption to prohibitions on circumvention of certain technological protection measures for the purposes of "unlocking" wireless telephone handsets to allow cell phone owners to connect to different wireless network providers.

The USDOC's Internet Policy Task Force (IPTF or Task Force), created in 2010, is responsible for identifying leading public policy and operational issues impacting the private sector's ability to realize the potential for economic growth and job creation through the Internet. The IPTF draws expertise from several bureaus, including those responsible for domestic and international ICT policy, international trade, cyber security standards and best practices, IP, business advocacy, and export control.[363] The Task Force issued a comprehensive Green Paper on "Copyright Policy, Creativity, and Innovation in the Digital Economy" in 2013[364], and a follow-on White Paper on "Remixes, First Sale, and Statutory Damages" in 2016.[365]

Enforcement

Main provisions, institutions and actions

All main IP laws contain provisions with respect to enforcement. The Stop Counterfeiting in Manufactured Goods Act of 2006 (P.L. 109-181) prohibits the trafficking in counterfeit goods and services, including trafficking in labels or similar packaging of any type or nature bearing a counterfeit mark and that are intended to be used on, or in connection with, the goods or services for which the genuine mark is registered.

There are several agencies involved in the enforcement of IPRs, including the Departments of Commerce, Justice, Treasury, Homeland Security, State, Agriculture, Health and Human Services, the Copyright Office, and the Office of the U.S. Intellectual Property Enforcement Coordinator (IPEC).

The IPEC, like other Executive Branch agencies and departments, engages with stakeholders and international partners to address IP issues, impacting infringement, market access, competition, digital trade, cybersecurity, and rule of law concerns around the world. The IPEC also works to expand IP law enforcement cooperation. Under Section 304 of the PRO IP Act of 2008 (15 U.S.C. § 8114), the IPEC must present an annual report focusing on the IP enforcement activities of the Federal Government. The FY2017 Section 304 Report noted that the current Administration's efforts have focused on coordinating and developing overall IP enforcement policy and strategy, to promote innovation and creativity, and to ensure effective IP protection and enforcement, domestically and abroad. The IPEC's IP strategy calls for the coordinated participation of a broad range of Executive Branch agencies and departments. Its strategic approach has four parts: (a) engagement with U.S. trading partners; (b) effective use of all U.S. legal authorities, including trade tools; (c) expanded law enforcement action and cooperation; and (d) engagement and partnership with the private sector and other stakeholders.[366]

With a view to fostering greater intra-agency coordination, the IPEC established the White House Intellectual Property Strategy Group, that brings together the National Economic Council (NEC), the National Security Council (NSC), the Office of Science and Technology Policy (OSTP), the Council of Economic Advisors (CEA), the Office of the Vice President (OVP), USTR, other relevant White House offices, and departments and agencies. Additionally, the IPEC chairs: (i) a Senior IP Enforcement Advisory Committee; and (ii) an IP Enforcement Advisory Committee in connection with the formation of the Joint Strategic Plan.

The IPEC and the interagency IP Enforcement Advisory Committee issued the new threeyear Joint Strategic Plan on IP Enforcement for 2017-19, in December 2016. The objectives of the Plan, are summarized as follows:

- Reduce counterfeit and infringing goods in domestic and international supply chains;

- Identify unjustified impediments to effective enforcement action against the financing, production, trafficking, or sale of counterfeit or infringing goods;

- Support the sharing of information to curb illicit trade;

- Disrupt domestic and international counterfeiting and infringement networks;

- Strengthen the capacity of other countries to protect and enforce IPRs;

- Establish with other governments international standards and policies for effective IPR protection and enforcement; and

- Protect IPRs overseas by enhancing international collaboration and public-private partnerships.[367]

The Department of Justice (DOJ) plays a key role in the enforcement of IPRs, both at the criminal and civil levels. It is in charge of investigating and prosecuting a wide range of IP crimes, including those involving copyright piracy, trademark counterfeiting, and trade secret theft. Primary investigative and prosecutorial responsibility within the DOJ rests with the Federal Bureau of Investigation (FBI), the United States Attorneys' Offices, the Computer Crime and Intellectual Property Section (CCIPS) in the Criminal Division, the Counterintelligence and Export Control Section (CES) in the National Security Division, and the Consumer Protection Branch of the Civil Division with regard to offenses arising under the Food, Drug, and Cosmetic Act. The DOJ also maintains a Computer Hacking and Intellectual Property (CHIP) Network, which consists of prosecutors who are specially trained in the investigation and prosecution of IP and computer crimes. IP enforcement is also an integral part of the mission of three sections of the DOJ's Civil Division: the IP Section, which brings affirmative cases when U.S. IP is infringed; the National Courts Section, which initiates civil actions to recover various penalties or customs duties arising from negligent or fraudulent import transactions, and defends CBP enforcement of the USITC's exclusion orders under Section 337 of the Tariff Act of 1930, as amended (19 U.S.C. 1337); and the Consumer Protection Branch, which conducts civil and criminal litigation under the Food, Drug, and Cosmetic Act.

The U.S. Immigration and Customs Enforcement (ICE) - Homeland Security Investigations (HSI)-led National Intellectual Property Rights Coordination Center (IPR Center), officially recognized by the TFTEA of 2015 (P.L. 144-125) Sec. 305, plays an important role in the Government's response to global IP theft and enforcement of international trade laws.[368] The IPR Center, headed by an ICE-HSI Director, with Deputy Directors from the FBI and CBP, has as its mission to stop predatory and unfair trade practices that threaten the global economy. To accomplish this goal, the Center brings together 19 key federal agencies, and four international entities: Interpol, Europol and the Governments of Canada and Mexico, in a task-force setting. The Center combats IP theft through a three-pronged approach, comprising of: (a) investigation: identifying, disrupting, prosecuting and dismantling criminal organizations involved in the manufacture and distribution of counterfeit products; (b) interdiction: using focused targeting and inspections to keep counterfeit and pirated goods out of U.S. supply chains, markets and streets; and (c) outreach and training: providing training for domestic and international law enforcement, and stakeholders to build stronger enforcement capabilities worldwide. The IPR Center's Outreach and Training Section engages in partnerships with the public and private sectors to combat IP theft through its Operation Joint Venture initiative, designed to increase information sharing with public and private sectors to combat the illegal importation and distribution of counterfeit, substandard and tainted goods.

Estimates of the annual cost of IP theft to the economy in counterfeit goods, pirated software, and theft of trade secrets, including cyber-enabled trade secrets, range between US$225 billion and US$600 billion. The estimated cost of trade secret theft alone to U.S. firms is between US$180 billion, or 1% of U.S. GDP, and US$540 billion, 3% of GDP.[369] The Council of Economic Advisers has estimated that malicious cyber activity cost the economy between US$57 billion and US$109 billion in 2016.[370]

CBP reported seizing US$1.38 billion of counterfeit goods in FY2016 (valued at suggested retail price had they been genuine). In FY2017, the number of IPR seizures increased 8% to 34,143, from 31,560 in FY2016; however, the total estimated value of the seized goods decreased to US$1.21 billion.[371] In partnership with the Express Association of America and its members, CBP continued in FY2017 the Voluntary Abandonment Pilot Program, which resulted in 5,588 voluntary abandonments of detained goods. Also, in FY2017, CBP completed 115 exclusion order enforcement actions (shipments seized and shipments excluded). CBP seized 297 shipments of circumvention devices for violations of the DMCA, a 324% increase from FY2016. Among the products seized in FY2017, 15% were apparel and accessories, 15% watches and jewellery, 13% consumer electronics, 12% footwear, 11% consumer products, 10% handbags and wallets, 8% pharmaceuticals and personal care products, 3% optical media, 2% computers and accessories, 2% labels and tags, 1% toys, and the remaining 15% other products.[372] The combined total number of all IPR border enforcement actions in FY2017 increased 12% over FY2016.

CBP also conducted 12 national level IPR-mitigating trade operations in FY2017, which targeted high-risk shipments at seaports, airports, international mail facilities, and express carrier hubs across the United States, and resulted in 1,845 seizures of IPR-infringing goods with an estimated (if genuine) value of US$44 million. CBP also seized 123 shipments of semiconductor devices affixed with counterfeit trademarks in FY2017. In total, 49 trademarks were discovered to be counterfeits in these seizures.

In FY2017, ICE/HSI initiated 713 IP investigations, arrested 457 individuals, obtained 288 indictments, and received 240 convictions related to IP crimes. At the end of FY2017, the FBI had 228 pending IPR investigations. The largest number of investigations dealt with the theft of trade secrets (79), copyright infringement (79), and trademark infringement (64). During FY2017, the FBI initiated 44 new investigations, made 31 arrests and got 23 convictions. In FY2017, the IPR Center examined 27,856 investigative leads; of these 16,030 were referred to law enforcement partners.[373]

The DOJ continues to prioritize IP investigations and prosecutions that involve health and safety issues, trade secret theft or economic espionage, and large-scale commercial counterfeiting and online piracy. The DOJ has also increased focus on IP crimes that are committed or facilitated by use of the Internet, or perpetrated by organized criminal networks.[374]

Special 301

Under "Special 301" provisions (Section 182 of the Trade Act of 1974, as amended), USTR conducts annual reviews of the state of IPR protection and enforcement in U.S. trading partners around the world.

In the Special 301 Annual Review, a trading partner may be identified as a "Priority Foreign Country" (PFC) if it is found that it has the most onerous or egregious acts, policies, or practices that deny adequate and effective IPRs, or deny fair and equitable market access to U.S. persons that rely on IP protection, whose acts, policies, or practices have the greatest adverse impact (actual or potential) on the relevant U.S. products, and is not "entering into good faith negotiations or making significant progress in bilateral or multilateral

negotiations." Trading partners may also be identified on a Priority Watch List, if they meet some, but not all, of the criteria for designation as a PFC, or on a "Watch List", in the case of trading partners with which the United States has significant IPR concerns. For certain countries identified in USTR's Priority Watch List, the USTR is required to develop an action plan containing benchmarks designed to assist the foreign country to achieve adequate and effective IPR protection and fair and equitable market access for U.S. persons that reply upon IPR protection.[375]

PFC is a statutory category. In cases where a trading partner has been identified as a PFC, the USTR is required to initiate a Section 301 investigation within 30 days of when the country was identified, unless the USTR determines that the initiation of such an investigation would be detrimental to U.S. economic interests, or where the act, policy, or practice identified as the basis for the PFC identification is the subject of any other investigation or action under Section 301. If the case involves the TRIPS Agreement or another trade agreement, a determination must be made within 18 months of initiating the investigation. In other cases, the USTR must make a determination of unfairness and decide what action to take, if any, within six months of the initiation of the investigation, or nine months under certain specific conditions.[376]

In its 2018 Special 301 report, released on 30 April 2018, the USTR identified 36 trading partners as failing to provide adequate and effective IP protection, and fair and equitable market access to persons that rely on such protection.[377] No trading partner was identified as a PFC as a result of the review. Twelve trading partners were placed on the Priority Watch List. In addition to identifying 36 countries on the Priority Watch List and the Watch List, the report also mentioned areas of concern in several countries. The Report also identified a wide range of cross-cutting IP concerns with regard to adequate and effective IP protection and enforcement worldwide, including: (a) concerns related to IP protection and enforcement and market access barriers with respect to pharmaceuticals and medical devices; (b) lack of adequate or effective border enforcement against counterfeit and pirated goods, and lack of authority to take ex officio action to seize and destroy such goods at the border or to take such action for goods in transit; (c) failure to address the continuing and emerging challenges of copyright piracy; (d) online piracy; (e) restrictive patentability criteria and lack of adequate and effective protection for regulatory test or other data submitted by pharmaceutical and agricultural chemical producers; and (f) inadequate protection for trade secrets in a number of countries.[378]

USTR also conducts Out-of-Cycle Reviews that focus on identified IP challenges in specific trading partner markets, and can lead to a positive change in a trading partner's Special 301 status outside of the annual review. In 2017, USTR closed four such reviews.

The Notorious Markets List identifies selected markets, including those on the Internet, that engage in and facilitate copyright piracy and trademark counterfeiting. The List includes markets where owners, operators, and governments have failed to address concerns. The List is not an exhaustive account of all physical and online markets worldwide in which IP infringement may take place. The List does not make findings of legal violations, nor does it reflect the U.S. Government's analysis of the general IP protection and enforcement climate in the countries connected with the listed markets.[379] The 2017 Out-of-Cycle Review of Notorious Markets, published in December 2017, highlighted 25 online markets based in 13 trading partners, and 18 physical markets in 12 trading partners, around the world that are reported to be engaging in and facilitating substantial copyright piracy and trademark counterfeiting. USTR plans to conduct its next Out-of-Cycle Review of Notorious Markets in the fall of 2018.

Section 337 investigations

Section 337 of the Tariff Act of 1930 (19 U.S.C. Section 1337) declares unlawful "unfair methods of competition and unfair acts in the importation and sale" of articles subject to satisfaction of a domestic industry test. For some unfair acts, depending on the type of unfair method of competition or act at issue, a showing of injury or threat of injury must also be made.

Upon receipt of a complaint alleging a violation of Section 337, the USITC determines whether the complaint satisfies the requirements of its rules, and if an investigation should be instituted. The USITC is required to conclude its investigation at the earliest practicable time, and must, within 45 days after an investigation is instituted, establish a target date for issuing its final determination.[380] If, at the completion of the investigation, the USITC determines that Section 337 has been violated, the USITC may issue orders excluding the articles from entry into the United States (exclusion orders) and/or directing the violating parties to cease and desist from certain actions. USITC orders are effective when issued, although imports are often allowed to continue subject to a bonding requirement; they become final 60 days after issuance unless disapproved for policy reasons by the USTR within that 60-day period.

Exclusion orders direct CBP either to bar entry into the United States of infringing goods from whatever source (general exclusion orders) or to bar entry to imports from specifically identified entities (limited exclusion orders). The USITC may issue a general exclusion order applicable to imports from all countries if a violation of Section 337 is established by substantial, reliable, and probative evidence and either a general exclusion order is necessary to prevent circumvention of an exclusion order limited to products of named persons, or there is a pattern of violation of Section 337 and it is difficult to identify the source of infringing products.[381] Instead of, or in addition to, exclusion orders, the USITC may

issue cease and desist orders against named importers and other persons engaged in unfair acts that violate Section 337.[382] Also, the USITC may refuse to issue an exclusion or cease and desist order after taking into account statutory public interest factors. In this respect, the USITC must consider the effects of a remedial order on: public health and welfare; competitive conditions in the U.S. economy; the production of like or directly competitive articles in the United States; and U.S. consumers.[383]

Between 1 January 2016 and 23 May 2018, 182 new Section 337 complaints were received by the USITC, and 137 investigations were instituted.[384] The majority of the cases (87% in 2017) dealt with patent infringement; a few cases dealt with copyright, trade secrets and trademarks or with several IPRs combined. Investigations covered products from 37 trading partners and from the United States. In the same period, the USITC issued 27 exclusion orders, of which 20 were limited exclusion orders, and 7 were general exclusions, together with 33 cease and desist orders.[385] Almost two thirds of the investigations ended in a settlement, or consent order, or the complaint was withdrawn. As of 31 December 2017, 109 active exclusion orders were in effect, of which 20 were general exclusion orders affecting imports of a range of products, including automotive/manufacturing/transportation products; chemical compositions; computer and telecommunications products; consumer electronics products; integrated circuits; LCD/TV; lighting products; memory chips and related products; pharmaceuticals and medical devices; printing products; and other consumer items.

CBP is in charge of the enforcement of Section 337 exclusion orders that affect trading partners. The DOJ is responsible for defending CBP actions linked to these orders in the case of a dispute.

IP and technology transfer

In September 2017, the United States updated the TRIPS Council on its implementation of Article 66.2 of the TRIPS Agreement, noting that it is committed to continually enhancing its activities pursuant to it, and reporting those activities.[386] The report noted that much of the Government's research conducted by federally operated laboratories and federally funded R&D centres results in inventions or findings that contribute to the development of new technologies and processes. Commercialization of these outputs can yield economic and social benefits that increase returns on the investment in federal R&D.[387] The report noted that the United States continues to believe that the effective functioning of Article 66.2 of the TRIPS Agreement requires a robust dialogue between developed country and LDC Members, in order to target incentives in a way that is most responsive to the self-identified technology transfer interests and needs of LDC Members.

The Bayh-Dole Act of 1980 directs that inventions that result from federally funded research be used to promote commercialization and public access through practical application. To this end, the United States conducts a number of technology transfer programmes, incentives, and partnerships. The National Science and Technology Council (NSTC) Workgroup on Lab to Market coordinates federal initiatives on technology transfer, and federal agencies implement these initiatives. The Federal Laboratory Consortium for Technology Transfer (FLC), a national network of approximately 300 U.S. federal laboratories and centres, plays a key role in providing information about technologies that are available for licensing, and the availability of laboratories for collaboration and partnership. The FLC encourages technology transfer and, through its member laboratories, seeks partners around the world.

The United States Government also conducts a number of technology transfer programmes through, or with the support of, USAID. The Partnerships for Enhanced Engagement in Research (PEER) programme supports scientists in developing countries through institutional research awards ranging up to US$300,000. It aims to build capacity among local scientists and research institutions, strengthen research partnerships world-wide, and better translate data and evidence into policy. Under this programme, U.S. scientific agencies, as well as universities and research institutes around the world, have partnered with scientists in developing countries

through PEER awards. Since its launch in 2011, PEER has supported more than 250 projects in 50 countries.[388] The Research and Innovation Fellowship Program connects early-career U.S. researchers and scientists to hosting organizations in the developing world, to conduct collaborative research projects of up to a year, funded by USAID and its partners. Other initiatives include the Global Innovation Exchange platform, a network that connects innovators, donors, academia, and the private sector to innovative devices, data, technologies, approaches, processes and funding opportunities. Under this initiative, USAID both provides funds and facilitates. Under the Development Innovation Ventures (DIV) programme, a year-round grant competition, open to nearly any individual or organization for any sector in any country where USAID operates, grants are awarded based on cost-effectiveness, evidence of impact, and the potential to scale.

The United States also utilizes science and technology (S&T) agreements as frameworks for increased international collaboration, by facilitating cooperation between U.S. technical agencies and foreign counterparts, on topics including public health, watershed management, agriculture, environment and biodiversity protection, biotechnology, earth sciences, marine science, and alternative energy.

Endnotes

1   WTO document G/TFA/N/USA/1, 13 June 2017. The notification regarding resources for technical assistance and capacity building is available in WTO document G/TFA/N/USA/2, 12 June 2017. Updated information has been provided in WTO document G/TFA/N/USA/2/Add.1, 14 June 2018.

2   WTO document G/TFA/W/5, 4 April 2018.

3   Executive Order 13659 on "Streamlining the Export/Import Process for America's Businesses", 19 February 2014.

4   Reconciliation refers to the opportunity for importers to update the information provided to CBP at the time of entry. The final amounts of duties, fees, and taxes due to CBP are determined during liquidation. Until February 2019, the drawback function in ACE allows the users to file either for drawback in accordance with existing legislation or under a new drawback procedure required by the Trade Facilitation and Trade Enforcement Act of 2015.

5   The 22 partner agencies have signed memoranda of understanding with CBP that grant them access to ACE and detail the information they are entitled to receive from the system.

6   CBP online information. Viewed at: https://www.cbp.gov/newsroom/national-media-release/cbp-reaches-historic-milestone-final-core-trade-processing. For ACE in isolation, savings are difficult to calculate in the absence of a reliable baseline, i.e. an environment without ACE.

7   ACE also imposes costs on the trade community, as brokers, importers, and exporters may need to invest in software compatible with ACE.

8   GAO, *Customs and Border Protection, Automated Trade Data System Yields Benefits, but Interagency Management Approach is Needed*, GAO-18-271, March 2018. The report was required according to the Trade Facilitation and Trade Enforcement Act of 2015.

9   81 FR 92978.

10 Only manufacturers in Canada and Mexico are eligible to participate in C-TPAT.

11 CROSS contains approximately 200,000 searchable rulings.

12 The requirement does not apply to cargo arriving by other modes of transportation.

13 Foreign-Trade Zones Board (2017), *78th Annual Report to the Congress of the United States*, November. Viewed at: https://enforcement.trade.gov/ftzpage/annualreport/ar-2016.pdf.

14 Domestic status merchandise may include goods of foreign origin imported into the customs territory of the United States (with duty paid) before being admitted into an FTZ.

15 The export figures are based on material inputs only, and do not take into account value added in FTZs.

16 The operations of bonded warehouses are covered by Regulations 19 CFR Part 19.

17 WTO document G/VAL/N/1/USA/1, 1 April 1996.

18 The main marking provisions are set out in Section 304 of the Tariff Act of 1930, 19 U.S.C. §1304 (2018).

19 WTO documents G/RO/N/1, 9 May 1995; G/RO/N/1/Add.1, 22 June 1995; G/RO/N/6, 19 December 1995; and G/RO/N/12, 1 October 1996.

 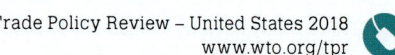

20 WTO documents G/RO/N/1/Add.1, 22 June 1995; and G/RO/N/88, 18 January 2013. The 2013 notification covered the rules in the FTAs with Chile; Singapore; Australia; Morocco; Bahrain; Central America-Dominican Republic; Oman; and Korea, Republic of; and the Trade Promotion Agreements with Peru, Colombia, and Panama.

21 WTO General Council Decision of 7 December 2016, circulated in WTO document WT/L/999, 12 December 2016.

22 83 FR 37993.

23 WTO document G/MA/TAR/RS/440/Rev.1, 10 August 2016 and its Addendum 1, 11 November 2016. The modifications were certified in WTO document WT/Let/1213, 29 November 2016.

24 WTO document WT/L/969, 2 December 2015.

25 The current applied rates are 5.25 cents and 10.5 cents per barrel respectively.

26 The preferential trading partners are indicated in each instance.

27 Cuba and the Democratic People's Republic of Korea are the only countries falling in the latter category.

28 Annual fluctuations, for example the observed moderate increase in agricultural tariffs, are due to changes in import prices. Leaving specific and compound duty rates unchanged, lower import prices will raise their estimated *ad valorem* equivalents.

29 The high incidence of zero MFN duty is a reflection of close U.S. involvement in WTO initiatives and agreements such as the ITA, the Agreement on Trade in Civil Aircraft, and zero-for-zero tariff outcomes in the Uruguay Round.

30 The tariff suspensions for two tariff lines were in effect until the end of 2014.

31 The final report is available at: https://www.usitc.gov/documents/mtbps/pub4712_introduction.pdf.

32 TRQ allocation methods are described in WTO document G/AG/N/USA/2/Add.3, 5 October 2001.

33 A surcharge of US$3.08 is applied for manual processing of declarations.

34 The threshold was raised from US$200 in March 2016.

35 CBP has compiled an informal overview of such exempt or non-exempt agreements and arrangements. Viewed at: https://www.cbp.gov/sites/default/files/assets/documents/2017-Nov/B%20MPF% 20Table%2C%2011%2724%2717.pdf.

36 Decals are stickers placed on private aircraft and vessels (longer than 30 feet) proving that the annual user fee has been paid. Affixed to the inside of windscreens of vehicles, transponders contain radio frequency identification chips transmitting information about the vehicle and its user fee status. The transponder is updated as the user fee is paid and may have a life span of 10 years. If the annual fee has not been acquitted, the transponder will continue to transmit, and a per-crossing fee will be applied.

37 Thus, the budget resources made available to the Secretary from the HMTF for fiscal year 2018 corresponds to 74% of the total amount of harbour maintenance taxes received in fiscal year 2017.

38 OMB Circular No. A-25 requires user charges to match the full cost to the Federal Government. Viewed at: https://www.whitehouse.gov/wp-content/uploads/2017/11/Circular-025.pdf.

39 The fee covers only the cost of APHIS supervision. The charge for the required treatment is paid separately.

40 Fifty years ago, excise taxes represented close to 10% of federal government revenue. Joint Committee on Taxation (2018), *Overview of the Federal Tax System as in Effect for 2018 (JCX-3-18)*, 7 February. Viewed at: https://www.jct.gov/publications.html?func=startdown&id=5060.

41 Regarding the taxation of alcoholic beverages, reduced tax rates apply to small brewers and wineries, and there is an exemption on limited production for own consumption. A portion of the distilled spirits excise tax on rum (US$10.50 per proof gallon) is remitted to Puerto Rico and the U.S. Virgin Islands.

42 The annual fee has been set at US$13.9 billion for calendar year 2017 and US$14.3 billion for 2018. It is to be indexed to the rate of premium growth after 2018. However, H.R. 195 "Making further continuing appropriations for the fiscal year ending September 30, 2018, and for other purposes." (P.L. 115-120) has suspended the annual fee for the year 2019.

43 The original two-year moratorium introduced through the Consolidated Appropriations Act, 2016 (P.L. 114-113) was extended for another two years through H.R. 195 (PL 115-120).

44 The formal title is "An Act to Provide for Reconciliation Pursuant to Titles II and V of the Concurrent Resolution on the Budget for Fiscal Year 2018".

45 81 FR 88975.

46 NOAA Fisheries online information. Viewed at: https://www.iuufishing.noaa.gov/Portals/33/SIMPComplianceGuide2017.pdf.

47 According to NOAA Fisheries, the initial phase of SIMP affects approximately 215,000 customs entries per year, filed by around 2,000 importers and 600 customs brokers.

48 The report to Congress released in January 2017 contained positive certifications for five countries identified in the previous report (Colombia, Ecuador, Nicaragua, Nigeria, and Portugal). NOAA Fisheries addressed a negative certification in a formal communication to the authorities of Mexico on 18 January 2017. Further evidence of action taken provided by the Government of Mexico resulted in a positive certification announced in April 2018 (Addendum to the Biennial Report), for Mexico's 2015 IUU fishing identification. For the next biennial report (June 2019), consultations are ongoing with Ecuador, the Russian Federation, and Mexico regarding the activities of some of their fishing vessels. Viewed at: https://www.fisheries.noaa.gov/foreign/international-affairs/identification-iuu-fishing-activities#magnuson-steven-reauthorization-act-biennial-reports-to-congress.

49 WTO documents G/LIC/N/3/USA/13, 8 November 2016; and G/LIC/N/3/USA/14, 22 January 2018.

50 78 FR 11090.

51 82 FR 1183. The decision has also been notified to the WTO (document G/LIC/N/1/USA/7, 20 March 2017).

52 All official actions of OFAC are published as soon as practicable in the Federal Register under the index heading "Foreign Assets Control".

53 The European Union, China, France, Germany, the Russian Federation, and the United Kingdom.

54 Strengthening the Policy of the United States Toward Cuba, A Notice by the State Department on 20 October 2017, FR Doc. 2017-22928. Viewed at: https://www.federalregister.gov/documents/2017/10/20/2017-22928/strengthening-the-policy-of-the-united-states-toward-cuba.

55 Notified to the WTO in WTO documents G/ADP/N/1/USA/1/Suppl.24, 1 April 2016; and G/SCM/N/1/USA/1/Suppl.24, 26 August 2016, respectively.

56 Notified to the WTO in WTO document G/ADP/N/1/USA/1/ Suppl.20-G/SCM/N/1/USA/1/Suppl.20, 16 July 2015.

57 See Notice of Determination for the Dates of Application of Amendments to the Anti-dumping and Countervailing Duty Laws Made by the Trade Preferences Extension Act of 2015. 80 Fed. Reg. 46793 (6 August 2015). Notified to the WTO in WTO document G/ADP/N/1/Suppl.21-G/SCM/N/1/USA/1/Suppl.20, 13 August 2015.

58 See, e.g., *Heavy Walled Rectangular Welded Carbon Steel Pipes and Tubes from Korea, Mexico, and Turkey*, Inv. Nos. 701-TA-539 and 731-1280-1282 (Preliminary), USITC Publication 4563, September 2015.

59 WTO documents G/ADP/N/1/USA/1/Suppl.23 and G/SCM/N/1/ USA/1/Suppl.23, 1 April 2016.

60 CBP online information. Viewed at: https://eallegations.cbp.gov/ Home/Index.

61 CBP online information. Viewed at: https://www.cbp.gov/sites/default/ files/assets/documents/2017-Apr/EAPA%20Investigation%20 Process%20Overview_FINAL%20%28002%29.PDF.

62 CBP online information. Viewed at: https://www.cbp.gov/trade/ trade-enforcement/tftea/enforce-and-protect-act-eapa.

63 Section 1592 of the Tariff Act of 1930 is the main customs penalty provision regarding the importation of goods. The Section is the enforcement tool used by CBP to ensure customs laws concerning tariff classification, customs valuation, and others are followed when importing into the United States; it gives CBP authority to impose penalties for customs laws violations. Section 1592 prohibits the importation of, or attempt to import, merchandise by means of false and material documents or electronic data or material omissions; it also prohibits aiding or abetting any other person to violate the statute.

64 The interim regulations (Investigation of Claims of Evasion of Anti-dumping and Countervailing Duties, U.S. Customs and Border Protection, Department of Homeland), effective 22 August 2016, are contained in Federal Register Volume 81, Number 162 (Monday, 22 August 2016), Rules and Regulations, pp. 56477-56490. They were notified to the WTO in WTO document G/ADP/N/1/USA/1/ Suppl.25-G/SCM/N/1/USA/1/Suppl.24, 26 August 2016.

65 Section 421 of the EAPA requires that regulations be prescribed as necessary and, within 180 days of TFTEA's enactment, to implement the provisions of the EAPA that establish procedures for investigating claims of evasion of AD/CVD orders. WTO documents G/ADP/N/1/USA/1/Suppl.25 and G/SCM/N/1/ USA/1/Suppl.24, 26 August 2016.

66 Whitehouse online information. Viewed at: https://www. whitehouse.gov/search/?s=residential+executive+order+ establishing+enhanced+collection+enforcement+antidumping+ countervailing+duties+violations+trade+customs+laws.

67 WTO document G/ADP/N/1/USA/1/Suppl.15-G/SCM/N/1/ USA/1/Suppl.15, 10 October 2013.

68 WTO document G/ADP/N/1/USA/1/Suppl.24, 1 April 2016.

69 WTO document G/ADP/M/52, 28 July 2017.

70 USDOC online information. Viewed at: http://trade.gov/ enforcement/operations/.

71 USITC online information. Viewed at: https://www.usitc.gov/ press_room/usad.htm.

72 In some cases, the determination can be postponed, in accordance with 19 CFR 351.205.

73 The *de minimis* threshold is 2% for AD investigations (0.5% for reviews) and, in the case of countervailable subsidies, 1% for developed countries, 2% for developing countries.

74 A determination of critical circumstances results from a history of dumping and material injury, knowledge of dumping, presumed to exist when there is a margin of dumping of 25% or more for export price sales, and a margin of 15% or more for constructed export price sales, together with massive imports over a short period of time (normally, when imports increase by 15% or more in the three months following the petition as compared to the three-month period prior to the petition).

75 An affirmative determination of injury requires that at least half of the participating USITC commissioners find injury; if there is a tie in the vote, it is deemed to be an affirmative determination, and final duties are imposed.

76 In cases where a suspension agreement is interrupted, the investigation resumes where it was left.

77 USDOC Regulations, 19 CFR 351.213.

78 USDOC Regulations, 19 CFR 351.213(b).

79 WTO online information. Viewed at: https://www.wto.org/english/ tratop_e/adp_e/AD_InitiationsByRepMem.pdf.

80 USITC online information. Viewed at: https://www.usitc.gov/sites/ default/files/trade_remedy/documents/orders.xls.

81 USITC online information. Viewed at: https://www.usitc.gov/sites/ default/files/trade_remedy/ documents/orders.xls.

82 DHS online information. Viewed at: https://www.dhs.gov/ news/2017/03/31/fact-sheet-enhanced-collection-and-enforcement-antidumping-and-countervailing-duties.

83 According to information from the USITC, 114 AD orders were revoked between 1 January 2006 and end-April 2018. USITC online information. Viewed at: http://www.usitc.gov/trade_remedy/ documents/orders.xls.

84 USDOC online information. Viewed at: http://ia.ita.doc.gov/ sunset/; and WTO documents G/ADP/N/294/USA, 9 March 2017; and G/ADP/N/300/USA, 6 September 2017.

85 Some of these measures were applied in the first half of 2016. WTO documents G/SCM/N/298/USA, 11 March 2016; and G/ SCM/N/305, 26 September 2016.

86 The trading partners affected were: Argentina (1); Brazil (4); Canada (2); China (50); India (18); Indonesia (5); Iran (2); Italy (3); Korea, Republic of (7); Mexico (1); Oman (1); Sri Lanka (1); South Africa (1); Chinese Taipei (1); Thailand (1); Turkey (8); and Viet Nam (3).

87 CBP online information. Viewed at: https://eallegations.cbp.gov/ Home/Index2.

88 On 5 September 2017, CBP initiated its EAPA investigation based on a properly filed allegation that reasonably suggested that LM Supply had entered merchandise into the customs territory of the United States through evasion of the AD Order. CBP was unable to determine whether the imported merchandise was subject to the AD Order. Accordingly, pursuant to the EAPA, CBP referred this matter to the USDOC for a determination as to whether the merchandise at issue was within the scope of the AD Order. CBP Notice of Scope Referral, 4 December 2017. Viewed at: https:// www.cbp.gov/trade/eapa-investigation-number-7212-lm-supply-inc-notice-scope-referral-december-4-2017.

89 USITC online information. Viewed at: https://www.usitc.gov/ press_room/us_safeguard.htm.

90 USITC (2014), *Summary of Statutory Provisions Related to Import Relief*, USITC Publication 4468, August 2014. Viewed at: https://www.usitc.gov/oig/documents/pub4468_2014.pdf.

91 USITC online information. Viewed at: https://www.usitc.gov/press_room/us_safeguard.htm.

92 These comprise: CSPV cells assembled into modules or panels (HTSUS 8541.40.6020); CSPV cells not assembled into modules (8541.40.6030); inverters or batteries with CSPV cells attached (8501.61.00 and 8507.20.80, respectively); and DC generators (8501.31.80).

93 Also excluded from the investigation were certain thin film photovoltaic cells and CSPV cells not exceeding 10,000 mm2 permanently integrated into a consumer good whose function was other than power generation and that consumed electricity generated by the integrated CSPV cell.

94 WTO document G/SG/N/6/USA/11, 29 May 2017.

95 WTO document G/SG/N/8/USA/9, 4 October 2017.

96 WTO documents G/SG/N/8/USA/9, 4 October 2017, and G/SG/N/8/USA/9/Supp.2, Supp.2, 4 December 2017. The USITC report may be viewed at: https://usitc.gov/trade_remedy/publications/safeguard_pubs.htm.

97 WTO document G/SG/N/8/USA/9/Suppl.3, 8 January 2018.

98 Proclamation 9693 of 23 January 2018, To Facilitate Positive Adjustment to Competition From Imports of Certain Crystalline Silicon Photovoltaic Cells (Whether or Not Partially or Fully Assembled into Other Products) and for Other Purposes, 542 Federal Register, Vol. 83, No. 17, Thursday, 25 January 2018, Presidential Documents.

99 WTO document G/SG/N/8/USA/9/Suppl.4, 26 January 2018.

100 Afghanistan, Albania, Angola, Armenia, Azerbaijan, Belize, Benin, Bhutan, Plurinational State of Bolivia, Bosnia and Herzegovina, Botswana, Brazil, Burkina Faso, Burma (Myanmar), Burundi, Cambodia, Cameroon, Cabo Verde, Central African Republic, Chad, Congo (Brazzaville), Côte d'Ivoire, Djibouti, Dominica, Ecuador, Egypt, Fiji, Gabon, The Gambia, Georgia, Ghana, Grenada, Guinea, Guinea-Bissau, Guyana, Haiti, India, Indonesia, Jamaica, Jordan, Kazakhstan, Kenya, Kyrgyzstan (Kyrgyz Republic), Lesotho, Liberia, Madagascar, Malawi, Maldives, Mali, Mauritania, Mauritius, Republic of Moldova, Mongolia, Montenegro, Mozambique, Namibia, Nepal, Niger, Nigeria, Pakistan, Papua New Guinea, Paraguay, Rwanda, Saint Lucia, St. Vincent and the Grenadines, Samoa, Senegal, Sierra Leone, Solomon Island, South Africa, Sri Lanka, Suriname, Eswatini, Tanzania, Togo, Tonga, Tunisia, Turkey, Uganda, Ukraine, Vanuatu, Yemen, Zambia, and Zimbabwe. The measure will not be applied either to the following developing countries which are not WTO Members: Algeria, Azerbaijan, Comoros, Congo (Kinshasa), Eritrea, Ethiopia, Iraq, Kiribati, Kosovo, Lebanon, Macedonia, Sao Tomé and Principe, Serbia, Somalia, South Sudan, Timor-Leste, Tuvalu, and Uzbekistan.

101 As long as such a developing country's share of total imports of the product, based on imports during a recent representative period, does not exceed 3%, and provided that imports that are the product of all such countries collectively account for not more than 9% of total imports, as specified in the Safeguards Agreement.

102 WTO documents G/L/1220 and G/SG/N/12/CHN/2, 5 April 2018; G/L/1224 and G/SG/N/12/KOR/3, 6 April 2018; and G/L/1226 and G/SG/N/12/JPN/3, 6 April 2018, respectively.

103 For the investigation, the term LRWs denoted all automatic clothes washing machines, regardless of the orientation of the rotational axis, with a cabinet width (measured from its widest point) of at least 24.5 inches (62.23 cm) and no more than 32.0 inches (81.28 cm). Also covered were certain parts used in LRWs, namely: all cabinets, or portions thereof, designed for use in LRWs; all assembled tubs designed for use in LRWs; all assembled baskets designed for use in LRWs; and any combination of the foregoing parts or sub-assemblies. WTO document G/SG/N/6/USA/12, 12 June 2017.

104 WTO documents G/SG/N/8/USA/10, 13 October 2017; and G/SG/N/8/USA/10/Supp.2, 11 December 2017. The USITC report may be viewed at: https://usitc.gov/trade_remedy/publications/safeguard_pubs.htm.

105 WTO document G/SG/N/8/USA/10/Suppl.3, 26 January 2018.

106 Proclamation 9694 of 23 January 2018, To Facilitate Positive Adjustment to Competition From Imports of Large Residential Washers. 3554 Federal Register, Vol. 83, No. 17, Thursday, 25 January 2018, Presidential Documents.

107 For the purposes of subheadings 9903.45.01 and 9903.45.02,"household-type (residential) washing machines, including machines which both wash and dry, whether or not with a dry linen capacity exceeding 10 kg" (goods provided for in subheadings 8450.11.00 and 8450.20.00 and reported under statistical reporting numbers 8450.11.0040, 8450.11.0080, 8450.20.0040 and 8450.20.0080, respectively) include automatic clothes washing machines, regardless of the orientation of the rotational axis, each with a cabinet width (measured from its widest point) of at least 62.23 cm and no more than 81.28 cm.

108 WTO documents G/L/1221 and G/SG/N/12/CHN/3, 5 April 2018; and G/L/1223 and G/SG/N/12/KOR/2, 6 April 2018, respectively.

109 *President Donald J. Trump Proclaims May 20 through May 26, 2018, as World Trade Week.* Viewed at: https://www.whitehouse.gov/presidential-actions/president-donald-j-trump-proclaims-may-20-may-26-2018-world-trade-week/.

110 19 U.S.C. § 1862(b)2A(iii).

111 Bureau of Industry and Security (BIS), Office of Technology Evaluation (2007), *Section 232 Investigations Program Guide: The Effect of Imports on the National Security - Investigations conducted under the Trade Expansion Act of 1962, as amended.* Viewed at: https://www.bis.doc.gov/index.php/forms-documents/section-232-investigations/86-section-232-booklet.

112 15 CFR 705.5.

113 15 CFR 705.4.

114 USDOC online information. Viewed at: https://www.commerce.gov/page/section-232-investigation-effect-imports-steel-us-national-security#factsheet232.

115 Past investigations and remedies have included the following: Steel (2018); Aluminium (2018); Iron Ore and Semi-Finished Steel (2001); the Effect of Imports of Crude Oil on National Security (1999); Crude Oil and Petroleum Products (1994); Ceramic Semiconductor Packaging (1993); Gears and Gearing Products (1992); Crude Oil and Petroleum Products (1989); Plastic Injection Molding (1989); Uranium (1989); Antifriction Bearings (1988); Crude Oil from Libya (1982);Chromium, Manganese and Silicon Ferroalloys and Related Materials (1981); the Effect of Imports of Nuts, Bolts, and Large Screws on the National Security (1983); Metal-Cutting and Metal-Forming Machine Tools (1983); and Glass-Lined Chemical Processing Equipment (1981). Bureau of Industry and Security (BIS) online information. Viewed at: https://www.bis.doc.gov/232.

116 BIS, Office of Technology Evaluation (2007), *Section 232 Investigations Program Guide: The Effect of Imports on the National Security Investigations conducted under the Trade Expansion Act of 1962, as amended.* Viewed at: https://www.bis.doc.gov/index.php/forms-documents/section-232-investigations/86-section-232-booklet.

117 BIS online information. Viewed at: https://www.bis.doc.gov/index.php/forms-documents?task=doc_download&gid=1669.

118 BIS, Office of Technology Evaluation, *The Effect of Imports of Steel on the National Security. An Investigation Conducted under Section 232 of the Trade Expansion Act of 1962, as amended.* 11 January 2018. Viewed at: https://www.commerce.gov/sites/commerce.gov/files/the_effect_of_imports_of_steel_on_the_national_security_-_with_redactions_-_20180111.pdf.

119 BIS, Office of Technology Evaluation, *The Effect of Imports of Steel on the National Security. An Investigation Conducted under Section 232 of the Trade Expansion Act of 1962, as amended.* 11 January 2018. Viewed at: https://www.commerce.gov/sites/commerce.gov/files/the_effect_of_imports_of_steel_on_the_national_security_-_with_redactions_-_20180111.pdf.

120 Secretary of Defense, Memorandum for Secretary of Commerce. Subject: Response to Steel and Aluminium Policy Recommendations. Viewed at: https://www.commerce.gov/sites/commerce.gov/files/department_of_defense_memo_response_to_steel_and_aluminium_policy_recommendations.pdf.

121 Amended to HTSUS 731011 by Presidential Proclamation 9711 on Adjusting Imports of Steel into the United States, of 22 March 2018. Federal Register, Vol. 83, No. 60, Wednesday, 8 March 2018. Viewed at: https://www.whitehouse.gov/presidential-actions/presidential-proclamation-adjusting-imports-steel-united-states/.

122 The current MFN tariff rate for all products affected by the measure is 0%.

123 Presidential Proclamation on Adjusting Imports of Steel into the United States, issued on 8 March 2018. Viewed at: https://www.whitehouse.gov/presidential-actions/presidential-proclamation-adjusting-imports-steel-united-states/.

124 Presidential Proclamation on Adjusting Imports of Steel into the United States, issued on 22 March 2018. Viewed at: https://www.whitehouse.gov/presidential-actions/presidential-proclamation-adjusting-imports-steel-united-states-2/.

125 *Presidential Proclamation on Adjusting Imports of Steel into the United States.* Issued on 30 April 2018. Viewed at: https://www.whitehouse.gov/presidential-actions/presidential-proclamation-adjusting-imports-steel-united-states-3/.

126 WTO documents WT/DS548/1 and WT/DS550/1, 6 June 2018, respectively.

127 WTO documents G/L/1218 and G/SG/N/12/CHN/1, 3 April 2018; G/L/1237 and G/SG/N/12/EU/1, 18 May 2018; G/L/1239 and G/SG/N/12/IND/1, 18 May 2018; G/L/1240 and G/SG/N/12/JPN/4, 22 May 2018; G/L/1241 and G/SG/N/12/RUS/2, 22 May 2018; and G/L/1242 and G/SG/N/12/TUR/6, 22 May 2018, respectively.

128 WTO document WT/DS548/13, 6 July 2018.

129 WTO documents WT/DS557/1, WT/DS558/1, WT/DS559/1, WT/DS560/1 and WT/DS561/1, 19 July 2018.

130 83 Federal Register 20683, 7 May 2018. Viewed at: https://www.federalregister.gov/documents/2018/05/07/2018-09841/adjusting-imports-of-steel-into-the-united-states.

131 See clause (3) of Proclamation 9759, viewed at: https://www.whitehouse.gov/presidential-actions/presidential-proclamation-adjusting-imports-steel-united-states-4/.

132 CBP online information. Viewed at: https://www.cbp.gov/trade/quota/tariff-rate-quotas.

133 BIS, Office of Technology Evaluation, *The Effect of Imports of Aluminum on the National Security. An Investigation Conducted under Section 232 of the Trade Expansion Act of 1962, as amended,* 17 January 2018. Viewed at: https://www.commerce.gov/sites/commerce.gov/files/the_effect_of_imports_of_aluminium_on_the_national_security_-_with_redactions_-_20180117.pdf.

134 The MFN tariff rates for the products affected by the investigation are: 76011060, 76012090, 76072050: 0%; 76042100: 1.5%; 76012060: 2.1%; 7616.99.51.60: 2.5%; 76011030, 76012030, 76041030, 76042930, 76051100, 76052100: 2.6%; 76069160: 2.7%; 76041050, 76042950, 76061130, 76061230, 76069130, 76069230, 76071190, 76071960: 3%; 76072010: 3.7%; 76051900, 76052900: 4.2%; 76041010, 76042910: 5%; 76071160, 76071910: 5.3%;76071930, 76081000, 76082000, 76090000, 76081000, 76082000, 76090000: 5.7%; 76071130: 5.8%; and 76061160, 76061260, 76069260: 6.5%.

135 BIS, Office of Technology Evaluation, *The Effect of Imports of Aluminum on the National Security. An Investigation Conducted under Section 232 of the Trade Expansion Act of 1962, as amended,* 17 January 2018. Viewed at: https://www.commerce.gov/sites/commerce.gov/files/the_effect_of_imports_of_aluminium_on_the_national_security_-_with_redactions_-_20180117.pdf.

136 *Presidential Proclamation on Adjusting Imports of Aluminum into the United States.* Issued on 8 March 2018. Viewed at: https://www.whitehouse.gov/presidential-actions/presidential-proclamation-adjusting-imports-aluminum-united-states/. 83 Federal Register 11619, 15 March 2018. Viewed at: https://www.federalregister.gov/documents/2018/03/15/2018-05477/adjusting-imports-of-aluminum-into-the-united-states. 83 Federal Register 13355, 28 March 2018. Viewed at: https://www.federalregister.gov/documents/2018/03/28/2018-06420/adjusting-imports-of-aluminum-into-the-united-states.

137 *Presidential Proclamation on Adjusting Imports of Aluminum into the United States* (2), 22 March 2018. Viewed at: https://www.whitehouse.gov/presidential-actions/presidential-proclamation-adjusting-imports-aluminum-united-states-2/. 83 Federal Register 20677, 7 May 2018. Viewed at: https://www.federalregister.gov/documents/2018/05/07/2018-09840/adjusting-imports-of-aluminum-into-the-united-states.

138 *Presidential Proclamation on Adjusting Imports of Aluminum into the United States* (3), 30 April 2018. Viewed at: https://www.whitehouse.gov/presidential-actions/presidential-proclamation-adjusting-imports-aluminum-united-states-3/.

139 Annex to Proclamation 9758 *Adjusting Imports of Aluminum Into the United States* of 31 May 2018. Federal Register Vol. 83, No. 108, Tuesday, 5 June 2018. Viewed at: https://www.gpo.gov/fdsys/pkg/FR-2018-06-05/pdf/2018-12137.pdf.

140 In 19 CFR 146.41, merchandise having a privileged foreign status is defined as foreign merchandise which has not been manipulated or manufactured so as to effect a change in tariff classification; it will be given status as privileged foreign merchandise on proper application to the port director.

141 As per 19 CFR 146.43, domestic status may be granted to merchandise: (a) which is the growth, product, or manufacture of the United States on which all internal revenue taxes, if applicable, have been paid; (b) previously imported and on which duty and tax has been paid; or (c) previously entered free of duty and tax.

142 USDOC online information. Viewed at: https://www.commerce.gov/news/press-releases/2018/05/us-department-commerce-initiates-section-232-investigation-auto-imports.

143 USDOC online information. Viewed at: https://www.commerce. gov/news/press-releases/2018/07/us-department-commerce-host-public-hearing-section-232-national-security.

144 USDOC online information. Viewed at: https://www.commerce. gov/news/press-releases/2018/07/us-department-commerce-initiates-section-232-investigation-uranium.

145 P.L. 114-25, SEC. 602. Exercise of WTO Authorization to Suspend Concessions or other Obligations under Trade Agreements. Viewed at: https://ustr.gov/sites/default/files/301/Section%20 301%20Beef%20FR%20Notice.pdf.

146 Section 306(d) of the 1974 Trade Act requires the Trade Representative to consult with the petitioner involved in the initial investigation and with representatives of the domestic industry concerned, and provide an opportunity for the presentation of views by interested parties. Section 307(c) requires the Trade Representative to conduct a review of the effectiveness of such an action, and of other actions that could be taken (including actions against other products), in achieving the objectives of Section 301 of this title (19 U.S.C. 2411) and the effects of such actions on the U.S. economy, including consumers.

147 The full text of P.L. 114-27 may be viewed at: https://www.congress. gov/bill/114th-congress/house-bill/1295?q=%7B%22search%22 %3A%5B%22antidumping%22%5D%7D&resultIndex=18.

148 USTR (2018), *Findings of the Investigation into China's Acts, Policies, and Practices related to Technology Transfer, Intellectual Property, and Innovation under Section 301 of the Trade Act of 1974*, Executive Summary.

149 USTR (2018), Executive Office of the President, *Findings of the Investigation into China's Acts, Policies, and Practices related to Technology Transfer, Intellectual Property, and Innovation under Section 301 of the Trade Act of 1974*, 22 March 2018. Viewed at: https://ustr.gov/sites/default/files/Section%20301%20FINAL.PDF.

150 USTR (2018), Section 301 Fact Sheet. Viewed at: https://ustr.gov/ sites/default/files/USTR%20301%20Fact%20Sheet.pdf.

151 The full list may be found in: Federal Register, Vol. 83, No. 67, Friday, 6 April 2018, Notices.

152 WTO document WT/DS542/4, 6 April 2018.

153 WTO online information. Viewed at: https://www.wto.org/english/ news_e/news18_e/good_28mar18_e.htm.

154 The full list may be viewed at: https://ustr.gov/sites/default/files/ enforcement/301Investigations/List%201.pdf.

155 USTR (2018), *USTR Issues Tariffs on Chinese Products in Response to Unfair Trade Practices*, USTR Press Release, 15 June 2018. Viewed at: https://ustr.gov/about-us/policy-offices/press-office/press-releases/2018/june/ustr-issues-tariffs-chinese-products.

156 Products included in this list are classified under Chapters 27, 34, 38, 39, 70, 73, 76, 84, 85, 86, 87, 89 and 90, of the HTSUS. The full list may be viewed at: https://ustr.gov/sites/default/files/ enforcement/301Investigations/List%202.pdf.

157 *Statement from the President Regarding Trade with China*, 18 June 2018. Viewed at: https://www.whitehouse.gov/briefings-statements/statement-president-regarding-trade-china-2/.

158 The full list of products was published in the Federal Register on 17 July 2018, Federal Register, Vol. 83, No. 137, Tuesday, 17 July 2018, Notices, and may be viewed at: https://ustr.gov/sites/ default/files/enforcement/301Investigations/2018-0026%20 China%20FRN%207-10-2018_0.pdf.

159 As defined in 19 CFR 146.41, foreign merchandise which has not been manipulated or manufactured so as to effect a change in tariff classification.

160 USTR online information. Viewed at: https://ustr.gov/sites/default/ files/301/Section%20301%20Beef%20FR%20Notice.pdf.

161 Federal Register, Vol. 81, No. 249, Wednesday, 28 December 2016, Notices.

162 Around 3,000 exporters have the option to file data post departure with CBP, though only 150-200 of them avail of this opportunity.

163 The Departments of State, Energy, and/or Defense frequently make applications subject to interagency review. The Departments of Commerce, State, and Treasury established an interagency working group in March 2016 to develop a Single Trade Application and Reporting System (STARS) to create a landing page to consolidate access points for the existing systems maintained by control agencies within these departments, i.e. DTRADE, SNAP-R, and OASIS. The page is currently available at: https://2016.export. gov/ecr/eg_main_100285.asp.

164 AESDirect is a free internet application developed jointly by CBP and the U.S. Census Bureau.

165 The USDOC has developed a basic user guide for export controls maintained by the BIS. Viewed at: https://www.bis.doc.gov/index. php/forms-documents/regulations-docs/142-eccn-pdf/file

166 The Specially Designated Nationals and Blocked Persons (SDN) List is maintained by the Department of the Treasury, OFAC.

167 In addition to the lists maintained by the BIS, the Department of the Treasury, OFAC has elaborated lists with respect to specially designated nationals, foreign sanctions evaders, sectoral sanctions identifications, the Palestinian Legislative Council, foreign financial institutions subject to Part 561, and non-SDN Iranian sanctions. The Arms Export Control Act (AECA) Debarred List (Department of State, Directorate and Defence Trade Controls) enumerates entities and persons prohibited from participating, directly or indirectly, in the export of defence articles. Although the Department of State, Bureau of International Security and Non-proliferation, identifies parties sanctioned under various statutes, the Federal Register is the only complete official source for non-proliferation sanctions determinations.

168 Executive Order 13558, 9 November 2010.

169 The USML identifies items controlled and regulated by the International Traffic in Arms Regulations (ITAR) and the CCL implements the Export Administration Regulations (EAR).

170 83 FR 24166.

171 The requirement applies to natural gas in any form, including LNG, compressed natural gas, and compressed gas liquids.

172 A short term authorization enables the holder to import or export natural gas for up to two years on a spot basis or similar short arrangement. Long-term authorizations are granted to companies having concluded tolling agreements or sales/purchase contracts of more than two years duration.

173 All exports originated from the Sabine Pass liquefaction terminal in Louisiana. U.S. Energy Information Administration online information. Viewed at: https://www.eia.gov/todayinenergy/detail. php?d=35512.

174 Export licences may be reintroduced in limited circumstances, e.g. a national emergency declared by the President or due to a sustained material shortage. Although crude oil is now classified as EAR99 and no licence is required, permission is still needed for exports to embargoed or sanctioned countries or persons, or sales to entities and persons on the Denied Persons List.

175 Trade Promotion Coordinating Committee, *Helping U.S. Businesses Increase Global Sales to Support Local Jobs, National Export Strategy 2016,* Washington D.C., December 2016. Viewed at: https://www.trade. gov/publications/pdfs/nes2016.pdf.

176 Presidential Executive Order on the Continuance of Certain Federal Advisory Committees, 29 September 2017.

177 The Schedule is updated regularly. The country limitation schedule applicable as from 27 March 2018 was viewed at: https://www. exim.gov/sites/default/files/tools/countrylimitationschedule/CLSMarch2018.pdf.

178 Fixing America's Surface Transportation Act (PL 114-94), Division E - The Export-Import Bank Reform and Reauthorization Act of 2015 (12 U.S.C. 635), 4 December 2015.

179 Activities include participation in foreign trade missions, sales trips, international marketing campaigns, export trade shows, and training sessions.

180 The list of authorized countries is available at: https://www.opic. gov/doing-business-us/OPIC-policies/where-we-operate. The consideration of new financing and insurance transactions in the Russian Federation and Venezuela is currently suspended.

181 OPIC may also take into consideration other forms of participation, such as franchise or long-term management contracts.

182 Following a review initiated in 2015, OPIC management approved a revised Environmental and Social Policy Statement on 7 January 2017. The Statement is available at: https://www.opic.gov/sites/default/files/files/final%20revised%20ESPS%2001132017(1).pdf.

183 Loans may range from US$500,000 to US$350 million per project.

184 SelectUSA online information. Viewed at: https://www.selectusa. gov/federal_incentives.

185 SBA online information. Viewed at: https://www.sba.gov/sites/default/files/aboutsbaarticle/SBA_FY_2017_AFR_.pdf.

186 Section 15(g) of the Small Business Act (PL 85-536).

187 The combined federal target is that 23% of the total contract dollars should be awarded to small businesses, including secondary-level goals for prime and subcontracts awarded to women-owned small businesses, small disadvantaged businesses, HUBZone small businesses, and service-disabled veteran-owned small businesses (Section 3.3.6.5).

188 The final goals for FY2018 are available at: https://www.sba. gov/sites/default/files/2018-02/FY2018_Final_Agency_Goals_Spreadsheet_20171220.pdf.

189 USDOC, Economic Development Administration online information. Viewed at: https://www.eda.gov/files/annual-reports/taaf/FY17-TAAF-Annual-Report-to-Congress.pdf.

190 A listing of ASDs as of 8 June 2018 is available at: https://share. ansi.org/Shared%20Documents/Standards%20Activities/American%20National%20Standards/ANSI%20Accredited%20Standards%20Developers/JUNE2018ASD.pdf.

191 The ANSI Essential Requirements embrace globally-accepted principles of standardization as they are implemented, *inter alia,* by the International Telecommunications Union, the ISO, and the IEC. The 27-page document setting out the Requirements is available online at: https://share.ansi.org/Shared%20Documents/Standards%20Activities/American%20National%20Standards/Procedures%2C%20Guides%2C%20and%20Forms/ANSI-Essential-Requirements-2018.pdf.

192 19 USC 2532.

193 25 federal agencies report annually on their use of government unique standards in lieu of voluntary consensus standards to the USDOC which, in turn, provides a summary to the OMB. The 20th Annual Report, summarizing developments in FY2016, is available at: https://nvlpubs.nist.gov/nistpubs/ir/2017/NIST.IR.8189.pdf.

194 The OMB published a revision of Circular A-119 in January 2016. The revision took account of regulatory developments since 1998, including the increasingly easy access to and online availability of information, and the timely updating of standards using a retrospective review mechanism (as set out in Executive Orders 13563 and 13610).

195 Executive Order 12866 defines economically significant regulatory action as any regulatory action likely to result in a rule that may "have an annual effect on the economy of US$100 million or more or adversely affect in a material way the economy, a sector of the economy, productivity, competition, jobs, the environment, public health or safety, or State, local, or tribal governments or communities." Federal Register online information. Viewed at: http://www.archives. gov/federal-register/executive-orders/pdf/12866.pdf.

196 These SRBs include the Asia-Pacific Laboratory Accreditation Cooperation (APLAC), the Asia-Pacific Legal Metrology Forum (APLMF), the Asia-Pacific Metrology Program (APMP), the Pacific Accreditation Cooperation (PAC), and the Pacific Area Standards Congress (PASC).

197 Further details regarding these agreements and arrangements are available at: https://www.nist.gov/standardsgov/requirements-nist-designation-us-conformity-assessment-bodies.

198 Box III.1 in WTO document WT/TPR/S/275/Rev.1, 12 February 2013, provides an overview of the principal elements of the Act.

199 FSVPs for Importers of Food for Humans and Animals, 80 FR 74225. Notified to the WTO (document G/SPS/N/USA/2569/Add.3, 16 November 2015).

200 80 FR 74569. The notification to the WTO was circulated in document G/SPS/N/USA/2570/Add.4, 16 November 2015.

201 81 FR 88099.

202 Applications are received through the FDA Industry Systems. Viewed at: https://www.access.fda.gov/.

203 Importers need to meet certain eligibility criteria and pay a user fee to participate in the program. The fee is collected to cover the FDA's costs in administering the VQIP.

204 83 FR 10487.

205 FDA online information. Viewed at: https://www.fda.gov/Food/InternationalInteragencyCoordination/InternationalCooperation/ucm610841.htm.

206 Section 5 of the Federal Trade Commission Act (1914) 15 USC. Viewed at: https://www.law.cornell.edu/uscode/text/15/45.

207 Getting the Deal Through, *United States: Merger Control* (2018). Viewed at: https://gettingthedealthrough.com/area/20/jurisdiction/23/merger-control-united-states/.

208 Additionally, the judicially-created "state action doctrine" exempts anti-competitive conduct by state bodies and municipalities authorized by a clearly articulated state policy or law, as well as private parties as long as they have legal authorization and are actively supervised by the State. For a recent case involving questions of foreign state action, see Supreme Court of the United States, *Animal Science Products, Inc. et al, v. Hebei Welcome Pharmaceutical Co. Ltd., et al.* (2018). Decided on 14 June 2018. Viewed at: https://www.supremecourt.gov/opinions/17pdf/16-1220_3e04.pdf.

209 Persons named in the ETCR obtain limited immunity from suit, under both federal and state antitrust laws, for activities that are specified in the certificate and that comply with the terms of the certificate. To obtain an ETCR, an applicant must show that proposed export conduct will: (a) result in neither a substantial lessening of competition or restraint of trade within the United States, nor a substantial restraint of the export trade of any competitor of the applicant; (b) not unreasonably enhance, stabilize, or depress prices in the United States of the class of goods or services covered by the application; (c) not constitute unfair methods of competition against competitors engaged in the export of the class of goods or services exported by the applicant; and (d) not include any act that may reasonably be expected to result in the sale for consumption or resale in the United States of such goods or services. As of September 2016, 47 certificate groups were reporting information to the USDOC.

210 Federal Trade Commission (FTC) official webpage. Viewed at: https://www.ftc.gov/reports/annual-highlights-2017/introduction.

211 OECD (2015), Working Party No. 3 on Co-operation and Enforcement, *Relationship between public and private antitrust enforcement*. Viewed at https://www.ftc.gov/system/files/attachments/us-submissions-oecd-other-international-competition-fora/publicprivate_united_states.pdf.

212 United States Department of Justice (DOJ), Antitrust Division: Mission. Viewed at: https://www.justice.gov/atr/mission.

213 Getting the Deal Through, *United States: Merger Control* (2018). Viewed at: https://gettingthedealthrough.com/area/20/jurisdiction/23/merger-control-united-states/.

214 Hawaii v. Standard Oil Co., 405 U.S. 251, 262 (1972).

215 Getting the Deal Through, *United States: Private Antitrust Litigation* (2018). Viewed at: https://gettingthedealthrough.com/area/27/jurisdiction/23/private-antitrust-litigation-united-states/.

216 Getting the Deal Through, *United States: Private Antitrust Litigation* (2018). Viewed at: https://gettingthedealthrough.com/area/27/jurisdiction/23/private-antitrust-litigation-united-states/.

217 United States Courts (2017), *2016 Annual Report of the Director of the Administrative Office of the U.S. Courts*, Table C-2A. Viewed at: http://www.uscourts.gov/statistics/table/c-2a/judicial-business/ 2016/09/30.

218 United States Courts (2017), *2016 Annual Report of the Director of the Administrative Office of the U.S. Courts*, table C-2A. Viewed at: http://www.uscourts.gov/statistics/table/c-2a/judicial-business/ 2016/09/30.

219 DOJ Antitrust Division, *Division Update Spring 2018*, p. 17. Viewed at: https://www.justice.gov/file/1053036/download.

220 FTC Bureau of Competition and DOJ Antitrust Division (2018), *Hart-Scott-Rodino Annual Report Fiscal Year 2017*. Viewed at: https://www.ftc.gov/system/files/documents/reports/federal-trade-commission-bureau-competition-department-justice-antitrust-division-hart-scott-rodino/p110014_fy_2017_hsr_report_final_april_2018.pdf.

221 FTC Bureau of Competition and DOJ Antitrust Division (2018), *Hart-Scott-Rodino Annual Report Fiscal Year 2017*. Viewed at: https://www.ftc.gov/system/files/documents/reports/federal-trade-commission-bureau-competition-department-justice-antitrust-division-hart-scott-rodino/p110014_fy_2017_hsr_report_final_april_2018.pdf.

222 FTC and DOJ Antitrust Division (2017), *Hart-Scott-Rodino Annual Report Fiscal Year 2016*, p. 3. Viewed at: https://www.ftc.gov/system/files/documents/reports/federal-trade-commission-bureau-competition-department-justice-antitrust-division-hart-scott-rodino/p110014_fy_2016_hsr_report_final_october_2017.pdf.

223 "Justice Department Requires Divestiture of Certain Herbicides, Insecticides, and Plastics Businesses in Order to Proceed with Dow-DuPont Merger". DOJ News Release, 15 June 2017. Viewed at: https://www.justice.gov/opa/pr/justice-department-requires-divestiture-certain-herbicides-insecticides-and-plastics.

224 "Justice Department Challenges AT&T/DirecTV's Acquisition of Time Warner". DOJ News Release, 20 November 2017. Viewed at: https://www.justice.gov/opa/pr/justice-department-challenges-attdirectv-s-acquisition-time-warner.

225 U.S. District Court Judge Richard Leon Opinion, 12 June 2018. Viewed at: http://www.dcd.uscourts.gov/sites/dcd/files/17-2511opinion.pdf.

226 "Justice Department Secures Largest Negotiated Merger Divestiture Ever to Preserve Competition Threatened by Bayer's Acquisition of Monsanto". DOJ News Release, 29 May 2018. Viewed at: https://www.justice.gov/opa/pr/justice-department-secures-largest-merger-divestiture-ever-preserve-competition-threatened.

227 A no-poach agreement involves an agreement with another company not to compete for each other's employees, such as by not soliciting or hiring them. A wage-fixing agreement involves an agreement with another company regarding employees' salaries or other terms of compensation, either at a specific level or within a range. No-poach agreements are naked if they are not reasonably necessary to any separate, legitimate business collaboration between the employers. Naked no-poach and wage-fixing agreements are *per se* unlawful because they eliminate competition in the same way as agreements to fix product prices or allocate customers. DOJ online information. Viewed at: https://www.justice.gov/atr/division-operations/division-update-spring-2018/antitrust-division-continues-investigate-and-prosecute-no-poach-and-wage-fixing-agreements.

228 DOJ Antitrust Division, *Division Update Spring 2018*. Viewed at: https://www.justice.gov/file/1053036/download.

229 OECD, Directorate for Financial and Enterprise Affairs Competition Committee (2017), *Annual Report on Competition Policy Developments in the United States*, pp. 6-9. Viewed at: https://www.ftc.gov/system/files/attachments/us-submissions-oecd-other-international-competition-fora/annual_report_united_states.pdf.

230 Thereby following the Supreme Court's decision in *FTC v. Actavis, Inc.*, 570 U.S. ___, 133 S. Ct. 2223 (2013).

231 OECD, Directorate for Financial and Enterprise Affairs Competition Committee (2017), *Annual Report on Competition Policy Developments in the United States*, p. 9. Viewed at: https://www.ftc.gov/system/files/attachments/us-submissions-oecd-other-international-competition-fora/annual_report_united_states.pdf, p. 9.

232 "Assistant Attorney General Makan Delrahim Keynote Address at the American Bar Association's Antitrust Fall Forum, DOJ News Release, 16 November 2017. Viewed at: https://www.justice.gov/opa/speech/assistant-attorney-general-makan-delrahim-delivers-keynote-address-american-bar.

233 "Assistant Attorney General Makan Delrahim Keynote Address at the American Bar Association's Antitrust Fall Forum", DOJ News Release, 16 November 2017. Viewed at: https://www.justice.gov/opa/speech/assistant-attorney-general-makan-delrahim-delivers-keynote-address-american-bar.

234 Assistant Attorney General Makan Delrahim Keynote Address at University of Pennsylvania Law School, The "New Madison" Approach to Antitrust and Intellectual Property Law, DOJ News Release, 16 March 2018. Viewed at: https://www.justice.gov/opa/speech/assistant-attorney-general-makan-delrahim-delivers-keynote-address-university.

235 Assistant Attorney General Makan Delrahim Delivers Remarks at the U.S. Embassy in Beijing, Competition, Intellectual Property, and Economic Prosperity. DOJ News Release, 1 February 2018. Viewed at: https://www.justice.gov/opa/speech/assistant-attorney-general-makan-delrahim-delivers-remarks-us-embassy-beijing.

236 Assistant Attorney General Makan Delrahim Delivers Keynote Address at University of Pennsylvania Law School, The "New Madison" Approach to Antitrust and Intellectual Property Law, DOJ News Release, 16 March 2018. Viewed at: https://www.justice.gov/opa/speech/assistant-attorney-general-makan-delrahim-delivers-keynote-address-university.

237 "Assistant Attorney General Makan Delrahim Delivers Remarks at the Antitrust Division's Second Roundtable on Competition and Deregulation", DOJ News Release, 26 April 2018. Viewed at: https://www.justice.gov/opa/speech/assistant-attorney-general-makan-delrahim-delivers-remarks-antitrust-divisions-second.

238 Acting Chairman Maureen K. Ohlhausen, "Guidelines for Global Antitrust: The Three Cs – Cooperation, Comity, and Constraints", International Bar Association, 21st Annual Competition Conference, Florence, Italy, 8 September 2017. Viewed at: https://www.ftc.gov/system/files/documents/public_statements/1252733/iba_keynote_address-international_guidelines_2017.pdf.

239 "Assistant Attorney General Makan Delrahim Delivers Remarks on Global Antitrust Enforcement at the Council on Foreign Relations", DOJ News Release, 1 June 2018. Viewed at: https://www.justice.gov/opa/speech/assistant-attorney-general-makan-delrahim-delivers-remarks-global-antitrust-enforcement.

240 DOJ Antitrust Division, FTC (2016), *The Antitrust Guidance for Human Resource Professionals*, October 2016. Viewed at: https://www.justice.gov/atr/file/903511/download.

241 *FTC and DOJ Release Guidance for Human Resource Professionals on How Antitrust Law Applies to Employee Hiring and Compensation*, (2016). Viewed at: https://www.ftc.gov/news-events/press-releases/2016/10/ftc-doj-release-guidance-human-resource-professionals-how.

242 DOJ and FTC (2017), *Antitrust Guidelines for International Enforcement and Cooperation*, 13 January. Viewed at: https://www.justice.gov/atr/guidelines-and-policy-statements-0/antitrust-guidelines-international-enforcement-and-cooperation-2017.

243 DOJ and FTC (2017), *Antitrust Guidelines for the Licensing of Intellectual Property*, 12 January. Viewed at: https://www.justice.gov/atr/IPguidelines/download.

244 DOJ (2017), *Updated FAQs Provide Answers to the Antitrust Division's Leniency Program and Model Leniency Letters*. Viewed at: https://www.justice.gov/archives/opa/blog/updated-faqs-provide-answers-antitrust-division-s-leniency-program-and-model-leniency.

245 FTC Bureau of Competition and DOJ Antitrust Division (2018), *Hart-Scott-Rodino Annual Report Fiscal Year 2017*, p. 8. Viewed at: https://www.ftc.gov/system/files/documents/reports/federal-trade-commission-bureau-competition-department-justice-antitrust-division-hart-scott-rodino/p110014_fy_2017_hsr_report_final_april_2018.pdf.

246 "Deputy Assistant Attorney General Barry Nigro Delivers Keynote Remarks at the American Bar Association's Antitrust in Healthcare Conference", DOJ News Release, 17 May 2018. Viewed at: https://www.justice.gov/opa/speech/deputy-assistant-attorney-general-barry-nigro-delivers-keynote-remarks-american-bar.

247 DOJ Antitrust Division, *Division Update Spring 2017*. Viewed at: https://www.justice.gov/atr/division-operations/division-update-spring-2017/spotlight-litigation.

248 OECD, Directorate for Financial and Enterprise Affairs, Competition Committee (2017), *Annual Report on Competition Policy Developments in the United States*, pp. 6-9. Viewed at: https://www.ftc.gov/system/files/attachments/us-submissions-oecd-other-international-competition-fora/annual_report_united_states.pdf.

249 Pay-for-delay agreements are arrangement to settle patent infringement litigation, in which the company that has brought the suit (patentee) for patent infringement agrees to pay the company it sued (the alleged infringer) to stop challenging the validity of the disputed patent.

250 FTC (2018), *Annual Highlights 2017, Enforcement*. Viewed at: https://www.ftc.gov/reports/annual-highlights-2017/enforcement.

251 In May 2018, the Administrative Law Judge (ALJ), after balancing the anti-competitive harm and procompetitive benefits posed by the agreement, dismissed the antitrust charges against Impax. The FTC filed an appeal. FTC online information. Viewed at: https://www.ftc.gov/news-events/press-releases/2018/05/administrative-law-judge-dismisses-ftc-antitrust-complaint.

252 FTC online information. Viewed at: https://www.ftc.gov/enforcement/cases-proceedings/161-0215/enbridge-spectra-energy.

253 Title 5 of the US Code (5 U.S.C. 103) defines a government corporation as a corporation owned or controlled by the Government of the United States. The Government Corporation Control Act (31 U.S.C. 9101 10) distinguishes between mixed-ownership government corporations and wholly-owned government corporations.

254 WTO documents G/STR/N/17/USA, 19 June 2018, and G/STR/N/17/USA/Corr.1, 2 July 2018.

255 Revisions 1 to WTO documents G/STR/N/11/USA/Rev.1 (notification for 2006); G/STR/N/12/USA/Rev.1 (2008); G/STR/N/13/USA/Rev.1 (2010); G/STR/N/14/USA/Rev.1 (2012); G/STR/N/15/USA/Rev.1 (2014); and G/STR/N/16/USA/Rev.2 (for 2016); all documents circulated on 11 October 2017.

256 OFPP online information. Viewed at: https://www.whitehouse.gov/omb/management/office-federal-procurement-policy/.

257 Government Publishing Office (GPO) online information. Viewed at: https://www.gpo.gov/fdsys/pkg/USCODE-2011-title41/pdf/USCODE-2011-title41-subtitleI-divsnB-chap11-subchapI-sec1101.pdf.

258 GSA online information. Viewed at: https://www.gsa.gov/policy-regulations.

259 GSA online information. Viewed at: https://www.acquisition.gov/browsegsam.

260 The available categories of supplies and services are: facilities and construction, human capital; industrial products and services; information technology; medical; office management; professional services; security and protection; and travel, transportation, and logistics. The full list of GSA schedules may be found at: http://www.gsaelibrary.gsa.gov/ElibMain/scheduleList.do.

261 See GSA online information. Viewed at: www.gsa.gov/schedules.

262 DoD online information. Viewed at: https://www.acq.osd.mil/dpap/dars/dfarspgi/current/index.html.

263 DoD online information. Viewed at: https://www.acq.osd.mil/dpap/dars/about.html.

264 WTO document GPA/113, 2 April 2012.

265 WTO document GPA/23, 15 July 1998.

266 Presidential Executive Order on Buy American and Hire American, Sec. 4.(c) Judicious Use of Waivers, 18 April 2017. Viewed at: https://www.whitehouse.gov/presidential-actions/presidential-executive-order-buy-american-hire-american.

267 Section 809 online information. Viewed at: https://section809panel.org/about/.

268 82 Fed. Reg. 18837 (21 April 2017).

269 "Buy American Laws" means all statutes, regulations, rules, and Executive Orders relating to federal procurement or federal grants, including those that refer to "Buy America" or "Buy American" that require, or provide a preference for, the purchase or acquisition of goods, products, or materials produced in the United States, including iron, steel, and manufactured goods. See also the Presidential Executive Order on Buy American and Hire American, 18 April 2017. Viewed at: https://www.whitehouse.gov/presidential-actions/presidential-executive-order-buy-american-hire-american/.

270 For further detail, see GPA/145 of 16 November 2017.

271 DFARS 252.204-7008 and DFARS 252.204-7012.

272 International Comparative Legal Guides, "Public Procurement 2018, USA". Viewed at: https://iclg.com/practice-areas/public-procurement-laws-and-regulations/usa.

273 Federal Register Vol. 81, No. 244, Tuesday, 20 December 2016, Rules and Regulations.

274 Federal Register Volume 81, Number 244, pp. 93476-93481.

275 Acquisition.gov, 'Subpart 4.16—Unique Procurement Instrument Identifiers'. Viewed at: https://www.acquisition.gov/far/html/Subpart%204_16.html.

276 Under the FAR, subpart 6.3, the following statutory authorities permit contracting without providing for full and open competition: (a) only one responsible source will satisfy agency requirements; (b) unusual and compelling urgency; (c) industrial mobilization; engineering, developmental, or research capability; or expert services; (d) international agreement; (e) authorized or required by statute; (f) national security; and (g) public interest.

277 Under the FAR, subpart 6.1, the competitive procedures available for use in fulfilling the requirement for full and open competition are as follows: (a) Sealed bids, (b) Competitive proposals, when sealed bids are not appropriate; (c) Combination of competitive procedures, such as two-step sealed bidding); (d) Other competitive procedures.

278 The threshold adjustment process is governed by statute 41 U.S.C. 1908, which requires mandatory review and adjustment of certain statutory acquisition-related thresholds for inflation using the Consumer Price Index (CPI).

279 Centre Law and Consulting online information. Viewed at: http://www.centrelawgroup.com/increased-micropurchase-simplified-acquisition-thresholds-may-implemented-sooner-later/.

280 SAM online information. Viewed at: https://sam.gov/portal/SAM/#1.

281 GSA online information. Viewed at: https://www.gsa.gov/acquisition/purchasing-programs/gsa-schedules/schedule-buyers/state-and-local-governments/cooperative-purchasing.

282 "About Usaspending.gov". Viewed at: https://www.usaspending.gov/#/about.

283 USAspending.gov, DataLab. Viewed at: https://datalab.usaspending.gov/contract-explorer.html?search=Contract%20spending%20in%20Fiscal%20Year%202017.

284 USAspending.gov, Spending Explorer: FY2018. Viewed at: https://www.usaspending.gov/#/explorer/agency.

285 FedBizOpps website is: https://www.fbo.gov/?s=main&mode=list&tab=list.

286 U.S. obligations under these agreements apply to covered procurement valued at or above the specified U.S. dollar thresholds, which are adjusted every two years.

287 WTO document, GPA/THR/USA/1, 20 December 2017.

288 USTR online information. Viewed at: https://ustr.gov/issue-areas/government-procurement/thresholds.

289 FAR Subpart 225.75. Viewed at: https://www.acq.osd.mil/dpap/dars/dfars/html/r20051114/225_75.htm.

290 FAR Subpart 25.9. Viewed at: https://www.acquisition.gov/far/html/Subpart%2025_9.html.

291 Federal Register 81 FR 55133. Viewed at: https://www.gpo.gov/fdsys/pkg/FR-2016-08-18/pdf/2016-19452.pdf.

292 FAR 5.202 identifies 15 exceptions to this posting requirement. See: https://www.acquisition.gov/far/html/Subpart%205_2.html.

293 In accordance with FAR Part 8, agencies shall satisfy requirements for supplies and services from or through the following sources and publications, in descending order of priority: (1) supplies: (i) inventories of the requiring agency; (ii) excess from other agencies; (iii) Federal Prison Industries, Inc.; (iv) supplies which are on the Procurement List maintained by the Committee for Purchase from People Who Are Blind or Severely Disabled; and (v) wholesale supply sources, such as stock programmes of the GSA; and (2) services: services that are on the Procurement List maintained by the Committee for Purchase From People Who Are Blind or Severely Disabled.

294 SBA online information. Viewed at: https://www.sba.gov/contracting/government-contracting-programs/what-small-business-set-aside.

295 Online information. Viewed at: https://www.wto.org/english/tratop_e/gproc_e/rev_usa7e.doc.

296 SBA online information. Viewed at: http://www.sba.gov/sites/default/files/files/Size_Standards_Table.pdf.

297 SBA online information. Viewed at: https://www.sba.gov/contracting/government-contracting-programs/what-small-business-set-aside.

298 SBA online information. Viewed at: http://www.sba.gov/federal-contracting/contracting-assistance-programs/women-owned-small-business-federal-contracting-program.

299 SBA online information. Viewed at: https://www.sba.gov/sites/default/files/2018-02/FY17-EDWOSB-NAICS-Codes.pdf.

300 Getting the Deal Through, Public Procurement US (2017). Viewed at: https://gettingthedealthrough.com/area/33/jurisdiction/23/public-procurement-united-states/.

301 Economic and Statistics Administration (ESA) and U.S. Patent and Trademark Office (USPTO) (2016), Intellectual Property and the U.S. Economy: 2016 Update. Viewed at: https://www.uspto.gov/sites/default/files/documents/IPandtheUSEconomySept2016.pdf.

302 Bureau of Economic Analysis (BEA) online information. Viewed at: https://www.bea.gov/iTable/iTable.cfm?ReqID=62&step=1#reqid=62&step=9&isuri=1&6210=4.

303 National Science Foundation, *Science and Engineering Indicators 2018*. Viewed at: https://www.nsf.gov/statistics/2018/nsb20181/report/sections/industry-technology-and-the-global-marketplace/highlights.

304 BEA online information. Viewed at: http://www.bea.gov/iTable/iTable.cfm?ReqID=62&step=1#reqid=62&step=6&isuri=1&6210=1&6200=2.

305 United States Intellectual Property Enforcement Coordinator (2018), *Annual Intellectual Property Report to Congress, March 2018*. Viewed at: https://www.whitehouse.gov/wp-content/uploads/2017/11/2018 Annual_IPEC_Report_to_Congress.pdf.

306 Economic and Statistics Administration (ESA) and USPTO (2016), *Intellectual Property and the U.S. Economy: 2016 Update*. Viewed at: https://www.uspto.gov/sites/default/files/documents/IPandtheUSEconomy Sept2016.pdf.

307 The Patent and Trademark Law Amendments Act (Bayh-Dole Act, PL 96-517) and the Stevenson-Wydler Technology Innovation Act of 1980 (PL 96−480).

308 Executive Office of the President, *Memorandum for the Heads of Executive Departments and Agencies, 31 July 2018, FY2020 Administration Research and Development Budget Priorities*. Viewed at: https://www.whitehouse.gov/wp-content/uploads/2018/07/M-18-22.pdf.

309 National Science Foundation online information. Viewed at: https://ncsesdata.nsf.gov/fedfunds/2014/html/FFS2014_DST_003.html.

310 National Science Foundation online information. Viewed at: https://ncsesdata.nsf.gov/fedfunds/2015/html/FFS2015_DST_001.html.

311 USITC (2017), *Global Digital Trade 1: Market Opportunities and Key Foreign Trade Restrictions*, August 2017. Viewed at: https://www.usitc.gov/publications/industry_econ_analysis_332/2017/global_digital_trade_1_market_opportunities_and.htm.

312 USTR online information. Viewed at: https://ustr.gov/issue-areas/intellectual-property/Special-301.

313 USTR (2018), *2018 Special 301 Report*. Viewed at: https://ustr.gov/sites/default/files/files/Press/Reports/2018%20Special%20301.pdf.

314 USTR online information. Viewed at: https://ustr.gov/about-us/policy-offices/press-office/fact-sheets/2018/march/ustr-releases-2018-national-trade.

315 The full list may be found at WIPO's website, at: http://www.wipo.org.

316 WTO documents IP/N/1/USA/D/6, IP/N/1/USA/P/11, 6 May 2013.

317 WTO documents IP/N/1/USA/D/8, IP/N/1/USA/P/13, 6 May 2013.

318 WTO documents IP/N/1/USA/7 and IP/N/1/USA/U/3, 7 December 2016.

319 USTR online information. Viewed at: https://ustr.gov/issue-areas/intellectual-property.

320 35 USC Sections 2(b)(8)-(13); and 35 USC Section 3.

321 P.L. No. 112-29. Viewed at: http://www.gpo.gov/fdsys/pkg/PLAW-112publ29/content-detail.html.

322 USPTO online information "Global Impacts of the AIA". Viewed at: http://www.uspto.gov/patent/laws-and-regulations/america-invents-act-aia/global-impacts-aia.

323 The term "useful" refers to the condition that the subject matter has a useful purpose, and also includes operativeness.

324 USPTO online information. Viewed at: https://www.uspto.gov/patents-getting-started/general-information-concerning-patents#heading-1.

325 In a non-provisional patent application, the specification must conclude with a claim or claims, particularly pointing out and distinctly claiming the subject matter that the applicant regards as the invention. This is not required in the case of a provisional application.

326 The filing date of a provisional application is the date on which a written description of the invention, and drawings if necessary, are received in the USPTO.

327 USPTO online information. Viewed at: https://www.uspto.gov/patents-getting-started/general-information-concerning-patents#heading-1.

328 USPTO (2014), *Strategic Plan 2014-2018*. Viewed at: http://www.uspto.gov/about/stratplan/.

329 USDOC (2018), *Helping the American Economy Grow, Strategic Plan for Fiscal Years 2018 2022*. Viewed at: https://www.commerce.gov/news/blog/2018/02/helping-american-economy-grow-2018-2022-strategic-plan.

330 USPTO online information. Viewed at: http://www.uspto.gov/web/offices/ac/ido/oeip/taf/us_stat.htm.

331 USPTO (2018), *United States Patent and Trademark Office Performance and Accountability Report for FY2017*. Viewed at: http://www.uspto.gov/sites/default/files/documents/USPTOFY17PAR.pdf.

332 First action pendency measures the time from when an application is filed until it receives an initial determination of patentability by the patent examiner. Total pendency measures the time from filing until an application is either issued as a patent or abandoned.

333 USPTO online information. Viewed at: http://www.uspto.gov/web/offices/ac/ido/oeip/taf/us_stat.htm.

334 USPTO (2018), *United States Patent and Trademark Office Performance and Accountability Report for FY2017*. Viewed at: http://www.uspto.gov/sites/default/files/documents/USPTOFY17PAR.pdf.

335 USPTO (2018), United States Patent and Trademark Office Performance and Accountability Report for FY2017. Viewed at: http://www.uspto.gov/sites/default/files/documents/USPTOFY17PAR.pdf.

336 This benefit, which originally applied only to non-U.S. individuals or firms from countries that are parties to the Paris Convention, was extended to U.S. citizens and firms by the Trademark Law Revision Act of 1988 which, since November 1989, has allowed the filing of applications based on the bona fide intention to use the mark commercially, and not necessarily on the basis of actual use.

337 USPTO (2018), *Performance and Accountability Report FY2017*. Viewed at: http://www.uspto.gov/sites/default/files/documents/USPTOFY17PAR.pdf.

338 USPTO (2018), *Performance and Accountability Report FY2017*. Viewed at: http://www.uspto.gov/sites/default/files/documents/USPTOFY17PAR.pdf.

339 USPTO (2018), *Performance and Accountability Report FY2017*. Viewed at: http://www.uspto.gov/sites/default/files/documents/USPTOFY17PAR.pdf.

340 USPTO, *Geographical Indication Protection in the United States*. Viewed at: http://www.uspto.gov/sites/default/files/web/offices/dcom/olia/globalip/pdf/gi_system.pdf.

341 USPTO, *Geographical Indication Protection in the United States*. Viewed at: http://www.uspto.gov/sites/default/files/web/offices/dcom/olia/globalip/pdf/gi_system.pdf.

342 The UTSA, passed in 1979 and amended in 1985, is a model civil trade secrets law drafted by the National Conference of Commissioners on Uniform State Laws, with the goal of making the state laws governing trade secrets uniform. The UTSA does not pre-empt state trade secrets law, and its adoption by states is not mandatory, and, when and if adopted, it can be modified by the state adopting it. The UTSA has been adopted by 47 states (the exceptions are Massachusetts, New York and North Carolina), the District of Columbia, Puerto Rico and the U.S. Virgin Islands. States that have not adopted a version of the UTSA protect trade secrets by statute, common law, or a combination.

343 DTSA 2016. Viewed at: https://www.congress.gov/bill/114th-congress/senate-bill/1890?q=%7B%22search%22%3A%5B%22trade+secret%22%5D%7D&resultIndex=1.

344 U.S. Copyright Office, Circular 38A, *International Copyright Relations of the United States,* June 2018. Viewed at: https://www.copyright.gov/circs/circ38a.pdf.

345 See 17 U.S.C. Secs 701 and 702.

346 See U.S. Copyright Office, Circular 1, Copyright Basics 5 (2017) at: https://www.copyright.gov/circs/circ01.pdf. Such benefits include the following. Registration establishes *prima facie* evidence of the validity of the copyright, and of the facts stated in the certificate when registration is made before or within five years of publication. When registration is made prior to infringement, or within three months after publication of a work, the copyright owner is eligible for statutory damages, attorneys' fees, and costs. Before an infringement suit may be filed in court, registration (or refusal) is necessary for works of U.S. origin (this is not required for works of foreign origin).

347 17 U.S.C. Sec. 701(b).

348 U.S. Copyright Office (2017), *Section 1201 of Title 17.* Viewed at: http://www.copyright.gov/policy/1201/section-1201-full-report.pdf.

349 U.S. Copyright Office (2016), *Software-Enabled Consumer Products.* Viewed at: http://www.copyright.gov/policy/software/software-full-report.pdf.

350 U.S. Copyright Office (2017), *Proposed Schedule and Analysis of Copyright Recordation Fee to go into Effect on or about December 18, 2017.* Viewed at: http://www.copyright.gov/policy/feestudy2017/fee-study-2017.pdf.

351 U.S. Copyright Office (2017), *Section 108 of Title 17: A Discussion Document of the Register of Copyrights.* Viewed at: https://www.copyright.gov/policy/section108/discussion-document.pdf.

352 U.S. Copyright Office (2018), *Fiscal 2017 Annual Report.* Viewed at: http://www.copyright.gov/reports/annual/2016/ar2016.pdf; and http://www.copyright.gov/reports/annual/2017/ar2017.pdf.

353 U.S. Copyright Office, *Compendium of U.S. Copyright Office Practices, Third Edition.* Viewed at: http://www.copyright.gov/comp3/docs/introduction.pdf.

354 See U.S. Copyright Office, *Compendium of U.S. Copyright Office Practices.* Viewed at: https://www.copyright.gov/comp3/.

355 17 U.S.C. Section 1101.

356 47 U.S.C. Sections 325, 553, 605; see also 18 U.S.C. Section 2511.

357 17 U.S.C. 106; 18 U.S.C. Section 2511; and 47 U.S.C. Sections 553 and 605.

358 U.S. Copyright Office information online. Viewed at: http://www.copyright.gov/title17/.

359 Section 1201 of Title 17 is the part of the DMCA that encourages copyright owners to provide greater access to their digital works, by providing them with legal protections against unauthorized access to their works.

360 U.S. Copyright Office, *Section 1201 of Title 17. The Triennial Rulemaking Process.* Viewed at: https://www.copyright.gov/1201/1201_rulemaking_slides.pdf.

361 Federal Register, Vol. 82, No. 206, Thursday, 26 October 2017, Proposed Rules. https://www.gpo.gov/fdsys/pkg/FR-2017-10-26/pdf/2017-23038.pdf.

362 Federal Register, Vol. 82, No. 206, Thursday, 26 October 2017, Proposed Rules. https://www.gpo.gov/fdsys/pkg/FR-2017-10-26/pdf/2017-23038.pdf.

363 USPTO online information. Viewed at https://www.uspto.gov/learning-and-resources/ip-policy/copyright/internet-policy-task-force.

364 The Green Paper is available at: https://www.uspto.gov/learning-and-resources/ip-policy/copyright/green-paper-copyright-policy-creativity-and-innovation.

365 The White Paper is available at: https://www.uspto.gov/learning-and-resources/ip-policy/copyright/white-paper-remixes-first-sale-and-statutory-damages.

366 Office of the U.S. Intellectual Property Enforcement Coordinator (IPEC)(2018), *Annual Report for Fiscal Year 2017.* Viewed at: https://www.whitehouse.gov/wpcontent/uploads/2017/11/2018Annual_IPEC_Report_to_Congress.pdf.

367 IPEC (2016), *U.S. Joint Strategic Plan on Intellectual Property Enforcement FY2017 – 2019.* Viewed at: https://www.whitehouse.gov/sites/whitehouse.gov/files/omb/IPEC/2016jointstrategicplan.pdf.

368 IPR Center online information. Viewed at: https://www.iprcenter.gov/about-us.

369 Commission on the Theft of American Intellectual Property (IP Commission (2017), *The Theft of American Intellectual Property: Reassessments of the Challenge and United States Policy.* 2017. Update to the IP Commission Report. Viewed at: http://ipcommission.org/report/IP_Commission_Report_Update_2017.pdf.

370 Council of Economic Advisers (2018), *The Cost of Malicious Cyber Activity to the U.S. Economy,* February. Viewed at: https://www.whitehouse.gov/wp-content/uploads/2018/03/The-Cost-of-Malicious-Cyber-Activity-to-the-U.S.-Economy.pdf.

371 CBP (2018), *Intellectual Property Rights Seizure Statistics. Fiscal Year 2017.* Viewed at: https://www.cbp.gov/sites/default/files/assets/documents/2018-Apr/ipr-seizure-stats-fy2017.pdf.

372 CBP (2018), *Intellectual Property Rights Seizure Statistics. Fiscal Year 2017.* Viewed at: https://www.cbp.gov/sites/default/files/assets/documents/2018-Apr/ipr-seizure-stats-fy2017.pdf.

373 IPEC, *Annual Intellectual Property Report to Congress,* March 2018. Viewed at: https://www.whitehouse.gov/wp-content/uploads/2017/11/2018Annual_IPEC_Report_to_Congress.pdf.

374 IPEC, *Annual Intellectual Property Report to Congress,* March 2018. Viewed at: https://www.whitehouse.gov/wp-content/uploads/2017/11/2018Annual_IPEC_Report_to_Congress.pdf.

375 The report is prepared pursuant to Section 182 of the Trade Act of 1974, as amended by the Omnibus Trade and Competitiveness Act of 1988, the Uruguay Round Agreements Act, and the TFTEA of 2015 (19 U.S.C. §2242).

376 This period may be extended to nine months if: the issues involved are complex; the foreign country is making substantial progress in drafting or implementing legislation or administrative measures that will provide adequate and effective IPR protection; or it is undertaking enforcement measures to this end.

377 USTR, *2018 Special 301 Report*. Viewed at: https://ustr.gov/sites/default/files/files/Press/Reports/2018%20Special%20301.pdf.

378 USTR, *2018 Special 301 Report*. Viewed at: https://ustr.gov/sites/default/files/files/Press/Reports/2018%20Special%20301.pdf.

379 USTR (2018), *2017 Out-of-Cycle Review of Notorious Markets*. Viewed at: https://ustr.gov/sites/default/files/files/Press/Reports/2017%20Notorious%20Markets%20List%201.11.18.pdf.

380 USITC online information. Viewed at: https://www.usitc.gov/intellectual_property/about_section_337.htm.

381 USITC, *Summary of Statutory Provisions Related to Import Relief, Investigations of Unfair Practices in Import Trade, Including Infringement of Patents, Trademarks, Copyrights, Mask Works, or Boat Hull Designs*. USITC Publication 4468, August 2014. Viewed at: https://www.usitc.gov/oig/documents/pub4468_2014.pdf.

382 USITC online information. Viewed at: https://www.usitc.gov/intellectual_property/about_section_337.htm.

383 USITC, *Summary of Statutory Provisions Related to Import Relief, Investigations of Unfair Practices in Import Trade, Including Infringement of Patents, Trademarks, Copyrights, Mask Works, or Boat Hull Designs*. USITC Publication 4468, August 2014. Viewed at: https://www.usitc.gov/oig/documents/pub4468_2014.pdf.

384 USITC online information. Viewed at: https://pubapps2.usitc.gov/337external/.

385 Online information. Viewed at: https://www.usitc.gov/intellectual_property/337_statistics_remedial_orders_issued_leo_v_geo.htm.

386 In accordance with the TRIPS Council's Decision of 20 February 2003, contained in WTO document IP/C/28, developed country members shall provide yearly reports to LDC Members on actions taken or planned in the pursuance of the commitments of developed countries under Article 66.2 to provide incentives to enterprises and institutions in their territories for the purpose of promoting and encouraging technology transfer to LDC members, in order to enable them to create a sound and viable technological base.

387 WTO document IP/C/W/631/Add.2, 28 September 2017.

388 WTO document IP/C/W/631/Add.2, 28 September 2017.

Trade policies by sector

AGRICULTURE

Main features

The U.S. agricultural sector is among the largest in the world, even though agriculture and other primary activities (forestry, fisheries and hunting) account for less than 1% of GDP (Chart 1.1) and about 1.5% of employment. Agricultural activities are very important to the local economy in certain parts of the United States. Significant differences in landscape and climate within the United States provide opportunities not only for large-scale agriculture but also for highly diversified agricultural output. The United States is a major world exporter of many agricultural commodities and a net exporter of food.

The slightly more than 2 million farms generated a combined value of agricultural production of US$372.7 billion in 2017 (Table 4.1).[1] The decline of US$50 billion in the production value since 2014 was primarily due to lower prices for key commodities. Measured by value, agricultural production is split roughly equally between crops and livestock, the principal crops being maize, soybeans, hay (including alfalfa), and wheat. Cattle (beef and dairy), milk, poultry, and eggs dominate in animal production. The United States is the world's largest producer of soybeans, maize, beef, chicken, and turkey, and ranks third in the world in the production of pig meat and cotton. Market developments in the United States therefore have a considerable influence on the world market prices for many commodities.

Despite a sizable domestic market, much of agriculture is highly export oriented, particularly in the production of soybeans, maize, wheat, cotton, and chicken. The United States is the world's leading exporter of most of these commodities. However, for maize and wheat, and to some extent for poultry, U.S. shares in world trade have been declining over the years, as other countries have been expanding their production faster than the United States (Table 4.2). In beef, the United States is both a major exporter and major importer of bovine meat (Table 4.3).

Except in 2005 and 2006, when imports almost matched exports, the United States has been a significant net exporter of agricultural products since 2000, although the trade surplus has declined since the peak period 2012-14 (Chart 4.1).

Major support programmes

General legal framework

Support to agriculture is primarily authorized by the so-called "farm bills", i.e. multi-year omnibus legislation covering a wide array of agricultural and food programmes. While some of the programmes have permanent authorization (e.g. crop insurance), others are authorized only for the life of the farm bill, and their authorization will lapse unless they are continued in a subsequent farm bill. While the first versions of farm legislation (in the 1930s) focused on support to producers of staple commodities (maize, soybeans, wheat, cotton, sugar, rice, and dairy), modern farm bills are much wider in scope, and address a range of issues such as revenue and price support, crop insurance, credit, disaster relief, conservation, research, bioenergy, horticulture and organic farming, rural development, nutrition, food aid, and trade. The farm bills are renewed approximately every five years.

Authorization for most programmes under the Agricultural Act of 2014 (PL 113-79), signed into law

Table 4.1 Value of production, 2010-17

(US$ billion and %)

	2010	2011	2012	2013	2014	2015	2016	2017	% of total[a]
Total	**334.9**	**379.5**	**396.6**	**394.3**	**406.4**	**376.2**	**355.5**	**372.7**	**100.0**
Maize for grain	64.5	76.7	74.2	61.9	53.0	49.3	51.3	48.5	13.0
Soybeans for beans	37.6	38.5	43.7	43.6	39.5	35.2	40.7	41.0	11.0
Hay	14.6	18.1	18.6	19.8	19.1	16.5	15.6	16.2	4.4
Wheat	12.6	14.3	17.4	14.6	11.9	10.0	9.2	8.1	2.2
Cotton	7.3	7.0	6.3	5.2	5.1	4.0	5.8	7.2	1.9
Milk	31.5	39.7	37.2	40.5	49.6	35.9	34.7	38.1	10.2
Cattle and calves	36.9	45.1	48.1	48.5	59.9	59.8	48.6	50.2	13.5
Poultry and eggs	34.7	35.3	38.2	44.4	48.4	48.1	38.7	42.7	11.5
Hogs	16.0	20.0	20.3	21.7	24.2	18.9	17.4	19.2	5.2
Crops total (excl. horticulture)	**191.1**	**211.4**	**223.9**	**210.2**	**194.8**	**179.2**	**185.7**	**185.2**	**49.7**

a   Percentage of total for the year 2016.

Source: USDA National Agricultural Statistics Service online. Viewed at: https://quickstats.nass.usda.gov/; USDA National Agricultural Statistics Service online information, "Poultry Production and Value", different bulletins, viewed at: http://usda.mannlib.cornell.edu/MannUsda/viewDocumentInfo.do?documentID=1130; and OECD Stats, Agriculture Policy Indicators, 2017 Monitoring and Evaluation: Reference Tables.

Part B
Report by the WTO Secretariat

Table 4.2 U.S. and world production and trade of selected commodities, 2010-19

('000 tonnes, unless otherwise indicated)

	Marketing year	2010/ 11	2011/ 12	2012/ 13	2013/ 14	2014/ 15	2015/ 16	2016/ 17	2017/ 18	2018/ 19
Maize										
Production	United States	315,618	312,789	273,192	351,272	361,091	345,506	384,778	370,960	370,514
	% of world	37.8	35.1	31.3	35.3	35.3	35.5	35.7	35.9	34.9
Exports	United States	46,508	39,096	18,545	48,790	47,421	48,229	58,270	60,963	59,693
	% of world	50.8	33.4	19.4	37.1	33.3	40.3	36.4	41.3	37.4
Wheat										
Production	United States	58,868	54,244	61,298	58,105	55,147	56,117	62,833	47,371	51,078
	% of world	9.1	7.8	9.3	8.1	7.6	7.6	8.4	6.2	7.0
Exports	United States	35,147	28,606	27,544	32,012	23,523	21,168	28,602	24,524	27,896
	% of world	26.4	18.1	19.9	19.3	14.3	12.2	15.6	13.4	15.2
Cotton (thousand 480 lb. bales)										
Production	United States	18,102	15,573	17,314	12,909	16,319	12,888	17,170	20,923	19,235
	% of world	15.4	12.2	14.0	10.7	13.7	13.4	16.1	16.9	16.0
Exports	United States	14,376	11,714	13,026	10,530	11,246	9,153	14,917	15,847	15,500
	% of world	41.2	25.5	28.0	25.8	31.7	26.2	39.6	38.8	37.0
Soybean, oilseed										
Production	United States	90,663	84,291	82,791	91,389	106,878	106,857	116,920	119,518	124,808
	% of world	34.3	35.1	30.8	32.3	33.4	33.9	33.6	35.5	34.0
Exports	United States	40,959	37,186	36,129	44,594	50,136	52,870	58,960	57,425	56,064
	% of world	44.7	40.5	36.0	39.6	39.7	39.9	40.0	37.4	35.5
	Calendar year	**2010**	**2011**	**2012**	**2013**	**2014**	**2015**	**2016**	**2017**	**2018**
Beef and veal										
Production	United States	12,034	11,978	11,845	11,751	11,075	10,817	11,507	11,938	12,601
	% of world	20.3	20.3	19.9	19.4	18.2	18.1	19.0	19.4	20.0
Exports	United States	1,043	1,263	1,112	1,174	1,167	1,028	1,159	1,298	1,372
	% of world	13.4	15.7	13.6	12.7	11.7	10.7	12.3	13.0	13.1
Poultry meat										
Production	United States	16,563	16,694	16,621	16,976	17,306	17,971	18,262	18,696	19,004
	% of world	21.2	20.6	19.9	20.1	19.9	20.2	20.5	20.6	20.6
Exports	United States	3,067	3,165	3,299	3,332	3,310	2,867	3,014	3,075	3,152
	% of world	34.4	33.0	32.7	32.4	31.6	27.9	28.2	27.9	28.0

Source: USDA Foreign Agricultural Service, Production, Supply and Distribution database. Viewed at: https://apps.fas.usda.gov/psdonline/app/index.html#/app/advQuery.

on 7 February 2014, will expire on 30 September 2018. The 2014 Farm Bill introduced numerous changes in the system of support to agriculture. A system of direct payments to crop producers, in place since 1996, was discontinued. Countercyclical payments on historical base were replaced by the option to enrol in one of two programmes tied to historical base, either a price-based countercyclical income support programme – the Price Loss Coverage (PLC) – or a revenue-based countercyclical income support programme – the Agricultural Risk Coverage (ARC).[2] Market price support for dairy products was replaced by a margin protection programme for dairy farmers. Disaster aid programmes for livestock producers were modified and reauthorized. Federal crop insurance programmes were expanded. A new programme, the Supplemental Coverage Option (SCO), which requires producers to have an underlying insurance policy, allowed them to add an area-based plan on top of individual farm coverage. Producers with historical upland cotton base were not eligible to elect PLC or ARC for cotton, but cotton producers were offered a supplemental crop insurance programme: the Stacked Income Protection Plan (STAX). The Farm Bill also sought to rationalize various conservation programmes.

Based on expected and actual outlays, the 2014 Farm Bill has been dominated by the Supplemental Nutrition Assistance Program (SNAP), providing food assistance to low-income households. Nearly 80% of the projected expenditure concerned the funding of SNAP. At the time of enactment, the estimated cost of the 2014 Farm Bill was US$489 billion for its entire duration, of which SNAP accounted for US$391 billion, and three other main titles in the bill (crop insurance, conservation, and commodities and disaster) a further US$93 billion. Revised projections released by the Congressional Budget Office of the United States in January 2017, based on actual expenditures on SNAP and the other major programmes during FY2014 through FY2016, indicated a reduced level of spending of some US$28 billion, including nearly US$26 billion less spent on SNAP. At the same time, while lower commodity prices had boosted the cost of countercyclical farm support programmes relative to the initial projections, these higher costs had been almost fully balanced by the lower insured crop value, and hence reduced costs, for federal crop insurance.[3]

The 2014 Farm Bill was amended in early 2018, through the passage of the Bipartisan Budget Act of 2018 (PL 115-123). As part of the revision, "seed cotton" has now become a covered commodity under the PLC and ARC programmes from the 2018 crop year. Changes were also made to the Margin Protection Program for dairy farmers, to make it more attractive for small and averagesized farms. In addition, an indemnity programme was created to help offset losses due to hurricanes and wildfires in 2017, and changes were made in some of the existing disaster relief programmes.

Table 4.3 Exports and imports of selected products, 2012-July 18[a]

			2012	2013	2014	2015	2016	2017	July 2018
Total exports		**US$ million**	**145,933**	**148,499**	**154,554**	**137,229**	**138,909**	**142,905**	**85,925**
1201	Soybeans	US$ million	24,804	21,605	23,917	18,909	22,885	21,518	9,715
		'000 tonnes	43,655	39,400	49,622	48,203	57,848	55,324	25,117
1005	Maize	US$ million	9,686	6,839	11,102	8,664	10,260	9,555	8,043
		'000 tonnes	31,477	24,065	49,706	44,703	55,893	53,044	43,746
0802	Other nuts, fresh or dried	US$ million	6,011	7,043	7,464	7,622	7,312	7,907	4,102
		'000 tonnes	1,116	1,118	1,053	1,048	1,252	1,334	615
0201 + 0202[a]	Meat of bovine animals fresh and frozen	US$ million	4,628	5,216	6,015	5,159	5,237	6,171	4,134
		'000 tonnes	773	814	812	716	814	913	579
1001	Wheat and meslin	US$ million	8,169	10,445	7,715	5,632	5,366	6,082	2,986
		'000 tonnes	25,767	32,882	25,449	21,266	23,956	27,243	12,366
5201	Cotton	US$ million	6,225	5,592	4,396	3,889	3,959	5,828	4,995
		'000 tonnes	2,752	2,790	2,167	2,396	2,469	3,253	2,756
2106	Food preparations not elsewhere specified	US$ million	4,763	5,406	5,568	5,372	5,703	5,468	3,264
		'000 tonnes	791	850	842	815	827	764	424
0203	Meat of swine	US$ million	4,836	4,426	4,966	4,030	4,199	4,558	2,738
		'000 tonnes	1,645	1,488	1,545	1,526	1,601	1,722	1,068
0207	Meat and edible offal poultry	US$ million	5,015	4,977	4,924	3,466	3,309	3,629	2,116
		'000 tonnes	3,926	3,859	3,855	3,179	3,334	3,429	1,983
2304	Oil-cake and solid residues, from extraction of soybean oil	US$ million	3,474	4,002	4,229	3,886	3,297	3,122	2,573
		'000 tonnes	6,747	7,539	7,843	9,306	8,607	8,618	6,752
2309	Preparations of a kind used in animal feeding.	US$ million	2,703	2,911	2,811	2,658	2,819	2,943	1,770
		'000 tonnes	2,016	2,032	1,858	1,826	2,061	2,091	1,190
2303	Residues of starch manufacture and similar residues, beet-pulp, bagasse and other waste of sugar manufacture	US$ million	3,005	4,009	3,989	3,796	2,889	2,614	1,826
		'000 tonnes	9,750	12,089	18,862	14,750	13,641	13,480	8,060
Total imports		**US$ million**	**109,640**	**111,979**	**119,629**	**122,021**	**123,324**	**129.976**	**82,497**
2208	Spirits, liqueurs and other spirituous beverages	US$ million	6,509	6,918	7,076	7,232	7,642	7,831	4,619
		'000 tonnes	686	698	666	670	705	720	419
0901	Coffee	US$ million	6,534	5,324	5,889	5,903	5,621	6,182	3,381
		'000 tonnes	1,446	1,493	1,525	1,539	1,604	1,624	941
2204	Wine of fresh grapes	US$ million	5,059	5,245	5,370	5,380	5,541	5,913	3,608
		'000 tonnes	1,168	1,097	1,077	1,104	1,114	1,209	681
2203	Beer made from malt	US$ million	3,706	3,709	4,154	4,550	4,869	5,087	3,255
		'000 tonnes	3,252	3,231	3,462	3,675	3,914	4,038	2,546
1905	Bread, pastry, cakes, biscuits and other bakers' wares	US$ million	3,232	3,397	3,566	3,961	4,511	4,955	2,895
		'000 tonnes	980	1,019	1,059	1,203	1,420	1,564	937
0201 + 0202[a]	Meat of bovine animals fresh and frozen	US$ million	3,372	3,434	5,296	6,251	4,850	4,912	3,173
		'000 tonnes	715	717	957	1,078	957	973	590
0804	Dates, figs, pineapples, avocados, guavas, mangoes and mangosteens, fresh or dried	US$ million	1,799	2,135	2,654	2,796	3,156	3,960	2,245
		'000 tonnes	1,833	2,017	2,206	2,342	2,441	2,593	1,560
2202	Waters, including mineral waters and aerated waters, containing added sugar or other sweetening matter or flavoured, and other non-alcoholic	US$ million	2,024	2,208	2,363	2,694	2,901	3,185	1,855

Trade Policy Review – United States 2018
www.wto.org/tpr

Part B
Report by the WTO Secretariat

			2012	2013	2014	2015	2016	2017	July 2018
	beverages, not including fruit or vegetable juices of heading 20.09								
0709	Other vegetables, fresh or chilled	'000 tonnes	1,535	1,570	1,636	1,853	2,052	2,204	1,239
		US$ million	2,195	2,566	2,586	2,626	3,033	2,984	1,927
2008	Fruit, nuts and other edible parts of plants, otherwise prepared or preserved	'000 tonnes	1,842	1,903	2,044	2,031	2,305	2,371	1,516
		US$ million	2,250	2,341	2,394	2,666	2,706	2,888	1,816
		'000 tonnes	1,298	1,399	1,352	1,477	1,487	1,518	927

a   HS headings 0201 (meat of bovine animals, fresh and chilled) and 0202 (meat of bovine animals, frozen) have been added together so that trade in meat of bovine animals is comparable to HS headings 0203 (meat of swine) and 0207 (meat and edible offal of poultry), which both include fresh, chilled, and frozen meat under the same HS heading.

Source: UNSD Comtrade database.

Chart 4.1 Exports and imports of agricultural products, 2000-17

(US$ billion)

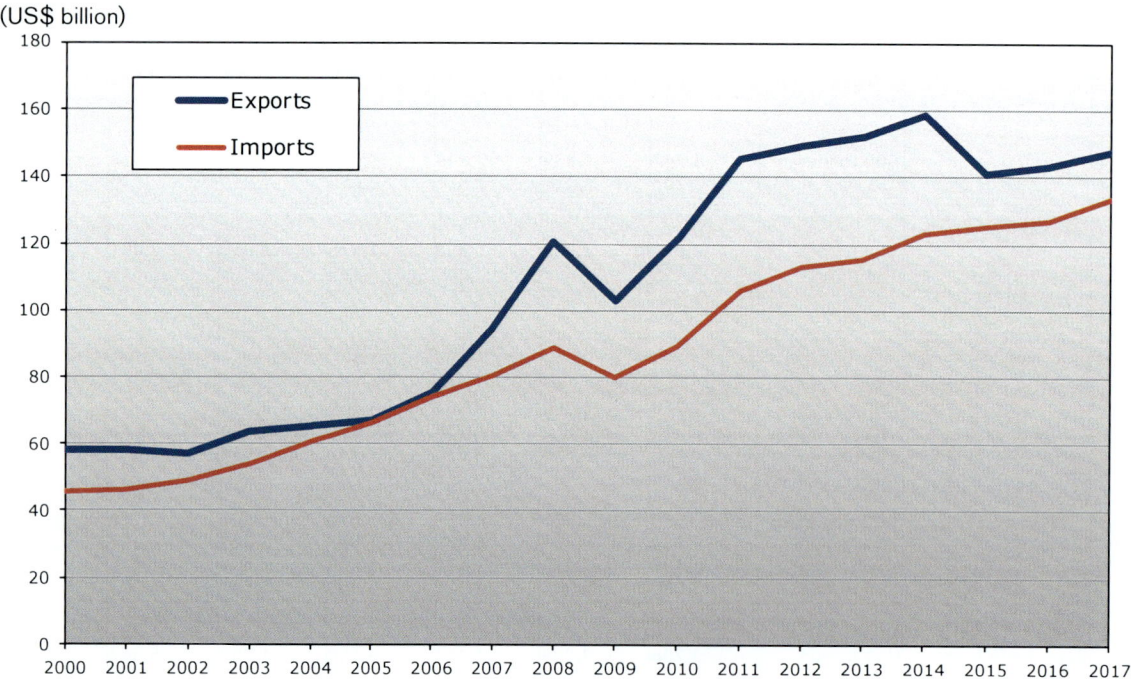

Source: UNSD Comtrade database.

In July 2018, the Department of Agriculture announced its intention to provide a short-term aid package designed to assist agricultural producers with market disruptions caused by retaliatory tariffs.[4]

Preparations for a new farm bill began in 2016. A number of hearings were held in 2017, and the legislative process has been underway throughout the reporting period in 2018.

Price Loss Coverage (PLC)

PLC covers historical base (i.e. historical area and yield) of maize, soybeans, wheat, other feed grains, other oilseeds, peanuts, pulses, rice, and - from the 2018 crop year - seed cotton. When the current average market year price falls below the reference price set in the

2014 Farm Bill, PLC payments are made on 85% of the historical base for each covered commodity on a farm. Farmers were obliged to make a one-time choice (for the duration of the 2014 Farm Bill) whether to elect PLC for historical base of each covered commodity on the farm. PLC is decoupled from current production as it relies on historical base without any requirement to produce[5], but it is triggered by current prices.

The payment the farmer receives, no earlier than 1 October after the end of the applicable marketing year for the covered commodity, equals the difference between the higher of the national average market price or loan rate and the reference price multiplied by the eligible base. According to the USDA Farm Service Agency, PLC payments for the 2016 crop year totalled nearly US$3.25 billion, primarily for historical base acres of wheat (US$1,273 million), long grain rice (US$736 million), peanuts (US$528 million), sorghum (US$342 million), and maize (US$208 million).

Agricultural Risk Coverage (ARC)

Farmers have had the choice to enrol their historical base in PLC or ARC for the covered commodities. ARC is a revenue-based income support programme tied to county-level benchmark revenue guarantees. Although the ARC revenue guarantee may also be determined at the farm level (individual ARC or ARC-IC), most farmers opting for ARC have chosen the version that establishes the revenue guarantee on a commodity-by-commodity basis at the county level (ARC-CO). This solution has allowed producers to select the ARC-CO revenue guarantee for some crops and PLC for others.[6] However, once a choice has been made, no switching back and forth between the two programmes is permitted.

ARC-CO establishes benchmark revenue for each covered commodity corresponding to 86% of the five-year (Olympic) average national market price multiplied by the five-year (Olympic) average county yield. When the actual county revenue (based on current prices and current county yields) falls below the county benchmark, farmers with a historical base of those commodities may be paid up to 10% of the difference.[7] Payments are limited to 85% of the enrolled historical base. Like for PLC, landowners have been allowed to reallocate, but not increase, their ARC base acres according to planted acres in 2009-12.

Data from the USDA Farm Service Agency (FSA) indicates that payments under ARC-CO amounted to US$3.76 billion for the 2016 crop year, mainly for historical base acres of maize (US$2.8 billion), wheat (US$651 million), and soybeans (US$201 million). The selection of PLC or ARC has varied by region and by crop. Overall, about 76% of the historical base acres were enrolled in ARC-CO and 23% in PLC in 2014. The preference for ARC may have been influenced by favourable price and revenue data over 2011-13 - particularly for maize, soybeans, and wheat – and correspondingly attractive benchmark revenue for the 2014-16 crop years.[8]

Marketing Loan Programme

The USDA Commodity Credit Corporation (CCC) provides interim financing to eligible producers of 28 commodities (Table A4.1).[9] Marketing loans are fully coupled to current prices and current production. Support is provided only for harvested commodity; no benefits are provided under this programme in the event of a crop loss.

The interim financing allows farmers to delay sales from normal harvest time until market conditions are favourable. At the end of the loan term (typically nine months), or at any time before that, the producer is expected to repay the loan. Alternatively, when market prices fall below the

statutorily fixed loan rates, the farmer has four options, either (i) to repay the loan at a rate determined by county market conditions and keep the difference between the repayment rate and the original loan rate (marketing loan gain (MLG)), while retaining ownership of the commodity for later sale; (ii) instead of taking a loan, to request a loan deficiency payment (LDP) when the posted county price is below the fixed marketing loan rate; (iii) to purchase commodity certificates at the lower market price and exchange for the crop provided as collateral to the CCC; or (iv) to forfeit the crop provided as collateral to the CCC and keep the difference between the value of the loan and the value of the commodity forfeited. As with all commodity and crop insurance programmes, producers must comply with conservation and wetland protection requirements and report all crop acreage planted to be eligible for LDP or marketing loans; gross income and payment limitations also apply.[10]

The 2014 Farm Bill fixed the statutory marketing loan rates for crop years 2014-18.[11] The rates, which are below the PLC reference prices, observed market prices, and actual production costs, in recent years, are designed to provide income support at times of low commodity prices. Marketing loan benefits have been modest in recent years. In the agriculture support notifications for marketing years 2014 and 2015, benefits reported under the marketing loan programme amounted to US$444 million and US$357 million, respectively.[12]

Crop insurance

Federal multi-peril insurance was introduced in 1938 (for wheat), but the policies sold by the Federal Crop Insurance Corporation (FCIC) remained limited in both geographical scope and covered crops, for many years. The 1980 Crop Insurance Act expanded federal crop insurance to new crops and regions, and introduced subsidized insurance premiums to encourage farmer participation.[13] Subsequent legislation in 1994 and 2000 increased subsidy rates, and expanded the role of the private sector in programme delivery.

At present, the insurance products on offer include revenue or yield-based plans as well as whole-farm policies. Some 130 crops are covered, including specialty crops (fruit, vegetables, nursery crops, and tree nuts), although four major crops – maize, soybeans, wheat, and cotton – dominate in terms of area enrolled (75%) and claims paid (80%). The USDA Risk Management Agency (RMA) sets the premium rates and other contract provisions, and the policies are sold to farmers by private insurance companies and private insurance agents.[14] Under a Standard Reinsurance Agreement (SRA) that is renegotiated periodically, private insurers are reimbursed for their administrative and operating expenses related to the policies, and they share the risks (i.e. losses or gains) with the Federal Government through reinsurance.

Farmers may generally choose between the minimum "catastrophic" coverage and additional ("buy-up")

Part B
Report by the WTO Secretariat

coverage.[15] The Federal Government pays the entire premium for catastrophic coverage, while participants pay an annual US$300 administrative fee for each crop insured in each county. Buy-up plans are also subsidized, although levels vary according to the type of plan and coverage selected. The 2014 Farm Bill introduced an additional area-based policy – the Supplemental Coverage Option (SCO)[16] – that allows participants to purchase area-based policies on top of their individual farm coverage to a level of 86% of expected yield or revenue. The first 14% of the loss (actual versus expected revenue) is always borne by the participant. The premium subsidy for the SCO is 65%. Producers who have elected ARC for historical base of covered commodities may not purchase SCO policies for current production of those same commodities.[17]

The growth in crop insurance has been significant since the 1990s. In 2018, crops on more than 300 million acres were insured, and nearly 95% of the policies provided coverage beyond the minimum "catastrophic" level.[18] Boosted by higher commodity prices, particularly from 2006 to 2012, the insured liabilities have also risen sharply. Federal Government costs for crop insurance, which averaged US$3 billion annually between 1997 and 2006, reached US$7 billion per year on average in the most recent 10-year period. Although the federal crop insurance programme may be the largest agricultural insurance programme in the world, the U.S. experience has also shown that farmers have been reluctant to take on such insurance without the strong support of the Government. On average, 62% of insurance premiums were paid by the Federal Government over the period 2012-17.[19] Total premiums (from farmers and the Government combined) need to exceed claim payments over time, to maintain the viability and actuarial soundness of the insurance programmes. On average, the crop insurance programme has paid out around US$0.85 in indemnities per dollar of total premium over the last 20 years. The federal premium subsidies reduce the share of total premium paid by producers so that, in aggregate, total indemnities will exceed total producer-paid share of premiums. Since 2008, the federal crop insurance programme has been required to operate the programme to achieve a loss ratio of 1.0, which means that producer premium subsidies represent the full subsidy provided by the programme to producers.

The federal crop insurance system has been subject to numerous studies, evaluating its effectiveness and possible options to reduce its costs to the Government. A recent study by the Congressional Budget Office (CBO)[20] suggested that modification of loss-calculation provisions could offer the highest potential savings. At present, most farmers purchase flexible revenue policies that calculate losses either against the projected commodity price at the time of purchase or the actual price at harvest, whichever is higher.[21] Removing the harvest price option according to the CBO, would reduce projected outlays by US$19.2 billion over the period 2018-27. Other major savings could be attained

by dropping the reimbursement of administrative and operational costs of the private insurers (US$10.2 billion), or a 15-percentage point cut in average premium subsidies (US$8.1 billion). The expected budgetary effects of other measures, such as changes in the terms of the SRA, caps on premium subsidies, or reduced ability for producers to adjust their actual production history, would be less pronounced.

Cotton

According to the 2012 Census, there were 18,155 cotton farms, down from more than 1 million farms in the 1940s. Nevertheless, the United States is the world's third largest producer, and the number one exporter, of cotton. Cotton has always been an important export crop, and exports have continued to rise with the decline in textile production in the United States.

The 2014 Farm Bill did not include upland cotton as a covered commodity under the PLC or ARC programmes, but introduced a subsidized Stacked Income Protection Plan (STAX), a cottonspecific supplemental crop insurance programme. STAX, which provides coverage for losses of up to 20% of the expected county revenue, could be bought on its own or in conjunction with an underlying (companion) policy.[22] STAX, which triggers indemnities when area revenue declines below 90% of the expected level, could cover a maximum 30% of the expected revenue or the difference between 90% and the loss level under the companion policy. The grower also chooses the effective coverage under STAX by electing a multiplier (protection factor), ranging from 80% to 120%. However, even with most of the premium (80%) paid by the Federal Government, cotton farmers were reluctant to sign up to STAX, particularly in the southern plains. Nationwide, only 30% of the eligible acreage was enrolled in STAX the first year the plan was offered and, though there were differing regional trends, overall participation rates declined further to 26% in 2016 and 23.9% in 2017.[23]

While upland cotton was not included as a covered commodity under the PLC and ARC programmes, former upland cotton base became "generic acres", and farmers with generic acres could qualify for PLC and ARC payments by planting those lands with crops eligible for ARC or the PLC. Payments would accordingly be based on current planting decisions, and not on historical production, for the crops planted on generic acres. Of the 17.6 million generic acres in total, some 8.66 million acres were planted with ARC- and PLC-eligible crops in the 2016 crop year, resulting in payments amounting to US$505 million. The most commonly planted crops were peanuts enrolled in PLC, planted on 1 million acres, with US$186 million paid, and maize enrolled in ARC-CO, planted on 2 million acres, with US$114 million paid.[24]

The Bipartisan Budget Act of 2018 revised the ARC and PLC support programmes, with the introduction of seed cotton, defined as unginned upland cotton including both lint and seed, as a covered commodity under ARC

and PLC for the 2018 crop year. Producers with generic base acres have the option to allocate those base acres to seed cotton or other covered commodities, based on 2009-12 plantings. Generic acres without the required 2009-12 plantings of either cotton or other covered commodities become unassigned base acres.[25] Either ARC or PLC may be selected for the seed cotton acres, with a one-time opportunity to update the PLC yield for seed cotton. The reference price (PLC) is set at US$0.367 per pound, and the marketing loan rate for seed cotton at US$0.25 per pound (for use only in the PLC programme; marketing assistance loans are not authorized for seed cotton). Farmers who choose to enrol historical seed cotton base acres in ARC or PLC will not be eligible to enrol in STAX for current cotton production as from the 2019 crop year.

As a temporary measure to support cotton producers, the U.S. Department of Agriculture (USDA) announced a second Cotton Ginning Cost Share (CGCS) programme in March 2018. Producers were invited to sign up by 31 May 2018 to receive a one-time payment equal to 20% of the average ginning costs, based on their cotton planted acres reported to the FSA for 2016.[26] The cost-sharing payment is limited to US$40,000 per person or legal entity.[27]

Sugar

The United States ranks fourth in the world for sugar consumption, and is the world's sixth largest sugar producer, producing both beet and cane sugar. The CCC of the USDA offers nonrecourse marketing loans to the processors of domestically grown sugarcane and sugar beet, and the processors, in turn, pay the growers at a rate proportional to the loan. At the end of the loan term (maximum nine months), or any time before, borrowers may sell the sugar on the domestic market and repay the loans in full or, should prices be too low, forfeit the sugar collateral to the USDA and thus redeem the loans. However, the second option rarely occurs, as U.S. sugar prices have exceeded world market levels since the early 1980s.

The marketing loans are administered in combination with a market allotment mechanism, designed to manage supplies in such a way that the price of sugar does not fall to levels that would trigger forfeitures.[28] The allotments are based on production history, and established at state level (sugarcane) or processor level (beet sugar). Overall, the sugar allotments equal at least 85% of the estimated domestic demand for human consumption. Excess sugar may not be sold on the market for human consumption, and remains in storage at the owner's expense. Depending on market conditions, the USDA may permit more sugar to be released into the market by adjusting the allotments upwards in the course of the marketing year. Furthermore, the Feedstock Flexibility Program (FFP) may be mobilized to divert sugar from human consumption towards the production of ethanol, in excess supply situations.

Since 2000, imports of raw and refined sugar (raw value) have averaged 1.48 million short tons per year.[29] Nearly all imports of raw cane sugar, refined sugars (certain sugars, syrups and molasses), and sugar-containing products take place under a system of tariff rate quotas (TRQs). Above-quota imports are normally neither practical nor economical, due to relatively high MFN tariffs. The annual WTO quota amounts to 1,117,200 metric tons of raw sugar and 22,000 metric tons of refined sugar. The USDA determines the overall TRQ quantities for each fiscal year, while USTR allocates the volumes.[30] The TRQ for raw cane sugar is allocated among 40 countries, based on patterns observed at a time when trade was relatively unrestricted (1975-81), resulting in the largest portions being allocated to the Dominican Republic (17%), Brazil (14%), and the Philippines (13%).[31] The Dominican Republic-Central American Free Trade Agreement (DR-CAFTA) and certain other FTAs (Chile, Colombia, Morocco, Panama, and Peru) provide additional TRQs for sugar and syrup goods and sugar-containing products, as long as these countries have a trade surplus in these goods based on the most recent data available. The NAFTA made U.S. imports of sugar from Mexico duty-free and quota-free from 1 January 2008. However, following the initiation of anti-dumping and countervailing duty proceedings by the United States in 2014, sugar exports from Mexico have been limited under a suspension agreement since 2015. Agreed amendments to this Agreement entered into force on 30 June 2017.[32]

Outside of the TRQ system, two re-export programs help sugar refiners and manufacturers of sugar-containing products compete in global markets. The Refined Sugar Re-Export Program allows refiners to import sugar at world market prices, refine it for export, or sell the refined sugar to licensed manufacturers of sugar-containing products. Under the Sugar-Containing Products Re-Export Program, U.S. participants may buy sugar from any refiner participant and use it in products for export. In addition, the Polyhydric Alcohol Program ensures that participating manufacturers may obtain sugar at world market prices from licensed refiners or their agents for the production of polyhydric alcohols, except for polyhydric alcohols used as sugar substitutes in human food consumption. Imports under these three programs average approximately 400,000 short tons (raw value) annually.

Dairy sector

The 2014 Farm Bill eliminated market price support, deficiency payments for dairy producers, and dairy export subsidies.[33] It introduced the Margin Protection Program for Dairy (MPP-Dairy), which is a voluntary risk management programme for dairy producers, and the Dairy Product Donation Program (DPDP). The DPDP allows the CCC to purchase dairy products at prevailing market prices when milk margins are depressed, and subsequently distribute the products among low income households.

MPP-Dairy insures milk farmers against falling margins, calculated as the difference between the national "all-milk" price and average feed costs.[34] The production margin was calculated bimonthly, until amendments to the programme under the Bipartisan Budget Act in 2018 required it be calculated monthly. Enrolled dairy producers receive a monthly payment when the margin stays below their chosen insured levels (US$4-US$8 per hundredweight) for the percentage of eligible production they have selected for coverage. For each dairy farm, historical (i.e. eligible) production is determined according to the average annual milk sales during calendar years 2011, 2012, and 2013.[35] The USDA has the possibility to adjust individual historical production levels to reflect increases in overall national milk production in future years. Otherwise, no change in production history is allowed. Producers were not required to enrol in MPP-Dairy immediately upon its establishment in 2014 but, once they signed up, they have been required to stay in it until the expiry of the 2014 Farm Bill.

MPP-Dairy guarantees all participating producers a US$4 margin (per hundredweight (cwt) of milk) for 90% of the historical production volume at no cost, other than an annual US$100 administrative fee paid to the USDA Farm Service Agency.[36] Additional coverage up to a US$8 margin is available with the payment of premiums. MPP-Dairy was revised in early 2018, with retroactive coverage applicable from 1 January 2018, to make it more attractive for small and average-sized dairy producers (Tier 1 farms). The lower premiums already applicable to these producers under the original programme were cut further (by up to 80%), and the production ceiling applicable to these lower rates was raised from 4 million pounds of annual historical production to 5 million pounds. For larger dairy producers, i.e. Tier 2 farms with historical production exceeding 5 million pounds per year, there were no changes in the offered conditions.

The changes made in MPP Dairy for 2018 imply that the participants are guaranteed catastrophic coverage for 90% of the established production history, should the margin fall below US$4 for Tier 2 producers and US$5

for Tier 1 farmers. Milk producers may continue to opt for higher margin protection against the payment of an annual premium (Table 4.4). At the same time, they must also choose the coverage level (25%-90% of historical production) for the higher margin.[37] MPP-Dairy does not cap compensation payments or limit eligibility according to farm size. Payments may nonetheless be subject to sequestration pursuant to the Balanced Budget and Emergency Deficit Control Act of 1985. At the outset, the CBO estimated the annual cost of MPP-Dairy to be in the order of US$30-190 million per year. The premiums collected from producers in 2015 and 2016 were higher than the compensation paid in both years.[38] No payments were made in 2017.

The DPDP has been set up to use CCC funds to purchase dairy products during periods of low production margins, for donation to public and private non-profit organizations that provide nutrition assistance to low-income households.[39] The DPDP is administered by the FSA and the Food and Nutrition Service (FNS). DPDP purchases would be triggered should the FSA determine that the national production margin had fallen below US$4 (per cwt) for two consecutive months.[40] The DPDP is authorized until the end of 2018, but no purchases have been made so far, as the production margin has stayed consistently above the trigger level.

Federal Milk Marketing Orders provide classified pricing and price pooling. The 2014 Farm Bill maintained this system without change, and also extended the Dairy Forward Pricing Program, the Dairy Indemnity Program, and the Dairy Promotion and Research Program through 2018. The latter authorizes the collection of a levy equal to US$0.15 per cwt on domestically-produced milk and US$0.075 per cwt (milk equivalent) on imported dairy products.[41]

Other programmes

About 80% of the projected outlays under the 2014 Farm Bill concerned the Supplemental Nutrition Assistance Program (SNAP), a programme that offers assistance to eligible, low-income individuals and families. Although the average monthly benefit has remained roughly stable,

Table 4.4 MPP-Dairy, premium payments in 2018

(US$)

Coverage level (margin) per cwt.	Tier 1 – premium for 2018 Covered production history < 5 million lbs.	Tier 2 – premium for 2018 Covered production history > 5 million lbs.
4.00	None	None
4.50	None	0.020
5.00	None	0.040
5.50	0.009	0.100
6.00	0.016	0.155
6.50	0.040	0.290
7.00	0.063	0.830
7.50	0.087	1.060
8.00	0.142	1.360

Source: USDA FSA (2018), *Margin Protection Program for Dairy (MPP-Dairy) Fact Sheet*, April. Viewed at: https://www.fsa.usda.gov/Assets/ USDA-FSA-Public/usdafiles/FactSheets/ 2018/mpp_dairyprogram_april_ 2018.pdf.

at US$125 per person and US$255 per household, in recent years, expenditures on SNAP have been declining due to a lower number of participants. In April 2018, just under 40 million persons received payments under SNAP, down from nearly 46 million in FY2015.[42] While changes in the benefit calculations may account for some of this reduction, the main contribution appears to be a firmer job market that has improved earnings for the low-income segment.

The 2014 Farm Bill retained the three main conservation programmes, maintained some smaller programmes in the Agricultural Conservation Easement Program, and created a new Regional Conservation Partnership Program (Title II). The Biomass Crop Assistance Program and the Rural Energy for America Program were continued (Title IX), and US$30 million per year was earmarked for the Farmers Market and Local Food Promotion Program. The 2014 Farm Bill also reauthorized the Non-insured Crop Disaster Assistance Program (NAP), which compensates for natural disaster damage to crops where crop insurance is not available, and allowed producers eligible for NAP to pay a premium to increase coverage.

The Bipartisan Budget Act introduced new disaster relief measures in response to losses stemming from natural disasters in 2017. The 2017 Wildfires and Hurricanes Indemnity Program (2017 WHIP) covered crop, tree vine, and bush losses in area hit by wildfires and hurricanes, compensating producers for their individual losses up to 95% (for those with crop insurance) or 65% (for non-insured farmers), retroactively from 1 January 2017. In return, the beneficiaries are obliged to purchase insurance for the next two available crop years. The expenditure cap for the Emergency Assistance for Livestock, Honeybees and Farm-Raised Fish Program (ELAP), which compensates for losses due to disease or certain adverse weather conditions as determined by the Secretary of Agriculture, was lifted. Changes were also made in the Livestock Indemnity Program (LIP) and the Tree Assistance Program (TAP) to make them more flexible, including the elimination of an annual cap (US$125,000) on individual indemnities. Finally, the Act authorized US$400 million to fund the Emergency Conservation Program, a programme providing assistance for repairs due to natural disasters or water conservation measures in response to severe drought.

Trade measures

Imports

Agricultural import duties are low compared with many other countries, and are applied on a reduced base (f.o.b. value) relative to imports elsewhere (c.i.f. value). With no change in the underlying tariff policy, the slight increase in the average applied MFN tariff on agricultural products (WTO definition) from 2016 to 2018, 9.1% compared with 9.4%, is entirely due to the effect that easing commodity prices have for the (higher) AVEs of specific and compound duties. Over the last two years,

the estimated average MFN duties have increased for dairy products and sugars and confectionary, whereas the estimated average rates are unchanged or slightly lower for other agricultural product categories. The highest average applied MFN rates are found in dairy (30.1%) and beverages, spirits, and tobacco (22.6%).

The tariff quota regime covers 54 bound TRQs, corresponding to approximately 200 tariff lines at present. It mainly affects imports of beef, cheese and other dairy products, sugar and sugar-containing products, tobacco, and cotton. Fill rates vary considerably among the commodities subject to TRQs. As outlined in p. 127, the sugar TRQs are country-specific and linked to a domestic market allocation mechanism, which means that quotas may be adjusted in the light of developments in the U.S. sugar market. The United States notifies the Committee on Agriculture regarding the administration of its WTO tariff quota commitments on a regular basis. The most recent notification, circulated in April 2018, covered imports under tariff quotas during the calendar year 2015.[43] Arrangements applicable to TRQ imports of sugar and sugar-containing products for FY2018 were notified in September 2017.[44]

The United States has reserved the right to apply the Special Agricultural Safeguard (SSG) on imports from other WTO Members on 189 tariff lines, mainly dairy, sugar/sugar-containing products, and cotton. SSGs may be based on price or volume, but the United States has generally opted to apply price-based SSGs. Such measures were applied on 44 tariff lines in 2014, and on 60 tariff lines in 2015. As price-based SSGs are applied on a shipment-by-shipment basis, and triggered automatically when the declared price for an item is below a pre-established price range, some of the SSGs may affect very small quantities of trade. In October 2015, the United States switched from a price-based SSG on butter to a volume-based action, the first such SSG since 2003.[45]

Exports

The Foreign Agricultural Service (FAS) of the USDA administers the Export Credit Guarantee Program (GSM-102) on behalf of the CCC. For exports of agricultural commodities financed through normal commercial channels or by the exporters themselves, the programme offers guarantees to approved U.S. exporters for sales to eligible countries, principally developing countries. The guarantees, issued by the CCC, insure payments under U.S. dollar denominated irrevocable letters of credit, and typically cover 98% of the principal and a portion of the interest payments. The maximum credit term is 18 months, but the limit may vary according to the obligor country. The CCC determines the product coverage of GSM-102 based on the market potential of the commodities and applicable legislative and regulatory requirements. Although most guarantees are issued for bulk commodities, intermediate goods (such as wood chips and pulp) and high-value processed consumer goods may also be covered. In FY2017, registered guarantees totalled US$1.58 billion in value, principally for exports of yellow maize (US$541 million), soybeans (US$421 million), wheat (US$243 million), soybean meal (US$228 million), rice (US$48 million), and soybean oil (US$11 million).[46] About one third of the guarantees available in FY2018 (US$4.9 billion) had been used by 10 August 2018.[47]

Four export promotion programmes, among which the Market Access Program (MAP) is the most important, were reauthorized in the 2014 Farm Bill.[48] MAP provides co-funding for the overseas marketing and promotional activities of agricultural trade associations, cooperatives, state regional trade groups, and small businesses. Participants must put up a minimum of 10% of the funding for generic marketing and promotion, while 50/50 cost-sharing is required for the promotion of branded products. Applicants for export promotion and market development funding managed by the FAS access the programmes through a single portal - the Unified Export Strategy (UES).

Food aid

The United States has been providing international food assistance for more than 60 years, principally in the form of agricultural commodities procured by the USDA and made available to developing countries in response to emergency or chronic food shortages. USDA data indicate that the Government shipped 8,140,420 metric tonnes of food aid commodities between 2012 and 2017. The 2014 Farm Bill reauthorized the programmes that govern U.S. international food assistance, including the Food for Peace Act (PL 480), the Food for Progress Act of 1985; the McGovern-Dole International Food for Education and Child Nutrition Program; and the Bill Emerson Humanitarian Trust. The new Emergency Food Security Program (EFSP) was codified through the 2016 Global Food Security Act (PL 114-195), with no change in the programmes authorized under the Farm Bill.

Food for Peace Title II (Emergency and Private Assistance Programs), which is the dominant programme with annual expenditures averaging around US$1.8 billion, is administered by USAID. It regulates U.S. donations of agricultural commodities to international organizations (such as the World Food Programme) and nongovernmental organizations. U.S. laws subject in-kind food aid to numerous conditions, notably that the food donations must be sourced in the United States and shipped on U.S.-flag vessels (at least 50%). Moreover, 20%30% of the aid funded under Food for Peace (minimum US$350 million per year) should be non-emergency food aid, of which a minimum of 75% should be processed, fortified, or bagged. At least 50% of bagged food transfers should be whole-grain commodities bagged in the United States. Non-governmental recipients are also required to subject at least 15% of U.S. non-emergency food donations to monetization, i.e. the sale of donated

food in recipient-country markets to generate cash for development programmes. The FAS administers the other international food assistance programmes authorized under the Farm Bill. Expenditures under these programmes averaged nearly US$400 million during FY2006 to FY2015.[49]

The international food assistance programmes have been subject to extensive debate in Congress over the years, and the discussions are continuing. Among the issues that resurface are whether to change requirements on where commodities are purchased, how food aid is transported, and the pros and cons of monetization. Although the EFSP operates without restrictions on sourcing or shipping, and cash-based food assistance is increasing through programmes such as the EFSP and the Local and Regional Procurement Projects programme, most U.S. international food aid is still provided in kind.

Levels of support

The OECD notes that the United States has reduced its producer support and border protection substantially since 1986-88, and support levels to agricultural producers have remained consistently below the OECD average. The share of the potentially most distorting support is also lower than the OECD average. Market price support has declined in importance over the years relative to budgetary support that requires production. As many of the present programmes are counter-cyclical by design, the levels of budgetary support move inversely with developments in market prices. The OECD's Producer Support Estimate (PSE) for the United States is currently around US$40 billion per year, or close to 10% of gross farm receipts (Table 4.5).

With few exceptions, producer prices are largely aligned with border prices. Among the main commodities tracked by the OECD, the highest single commodity transfers (as a percentage of gross farm receipts) occur to sugar, milk, and cotton. The OECD essentially sees the U.S. emphasis on insurance and risk management as a good approach to farm support policy. Noting that the programmes remain commodity-specific, the OECD advocates all farm revenue as an alternative approach, pointing to opportunities to exploit differences in price and yield variability, the elimination of distortions across commodity sectors, and lower costs to the Government. The OECD also recommends that the risk management instruments should be reviewed, to ensure that risks that should be borne by farmers do not end up in the public budget.

At the WTO, the United States provides information on support to agriculture to the Committee on Subsidies and Countervailing Measures as well as to the Committee on Agriculture. The most recent subsidy notification to the SCM Committee covers FY2015 and FY2016, and reports payments under the new ARC and PLC programmes of US$4.5 billion and US$779 million, respectively (Table 4.6). Disaster payments for livestock

Table 4.5 Total PSE and single commodity transfer values for selected commodities, 2008-17

(US$ million or % of gross farm receipts for respective products)

	2008	2009	2010	2011	2012	2013	2014	2015	2016	2017[a]
Producer support estimate										
US$ million	29,954	31,535	30,774	32,684	36,040	29,056	40,517	38,225	36,485	39,606
PSE as % gross farm receipts	8.6	10.1	8.6	8.0	8.5	6.9	9.3	9.5	9.6	9.9
Single commodity transfers										
Wheat										
US$ million	940	1,610	802	1,140	1,117	1,318	920	813	905	632
SCT as % gross farm receipts	5.2	13.0	6.1	7.3	6.0	8.2	7.0	7.5	9.1	7.3
Maize										
US$ million	2,147	2,167	1,771	2,894	2,846	2,998	2,203	2,258	2,213	2,160
SCT as % gross farm receipts	4.2	4.5	2.7	3.6	3.7	4.6	4.0	4.4	4.2	4.3
Soybeans										
US$ million	1,483	1,198	1,076	1,597	1,536	1,540	1,396	1,313	1,168	1,618
SCT as % gross farm receipts	4.8	3.6	2.8	4.0	3.4	3.4	3.4	3.6	2.8	3.8
Cotton										
US$ million	1,313	252	339	813	591	529	889	852	518	712
SCT as % gross farm receipts	30.1	6.2	4.4	10.4	8.6	9.4	14.9	17.9	8.2	9.6
Milk										
US$ million	8	2,947	4,581	2,637	5,125	2,296	6,646	6,557	6,902	7,497
SCT as % gross farm receipts	0.0	11.9	14.5	6.7	13.7	5.7	13.5	18.4	19.9	19.7
Beef and veal										
US$ million	0	0	0	0	0	230	1	1	1	1
SCT as % gross farm receipts	0.0	0.0	0.0	0.0	0.0	0.4	0.0	0.0	0.0	0.0
Refined sugar										
US$ million	718	557	1,157	990	656	193	1,576	1,918	1,545	1,676
SCT as % gross farm receipts	33.6	21.3	35.0	29.0	17.6	7.6	46.1	55.2	50.6	56.1

a   Preliminary data.

Source: OECD Stats.

Table 4.6 Federal subsidy programmes for agriculture, FY2015-16

(US$ million)

Programmes	Expenditure	
	FY2015	FY2016
Agriculture Income Support and Marketing Assistance for Covered Commodities		
Direct payments	24.0	0.3
Average Crop Revenue Election (ACRE)	279.0	0.8
MILC	1.8	0
PLC	0	779.0
ARC	0	4,500.0
Cotton Transition Assistance Payment (CTAP)	484.0	2.9
MPP-Dairy	0	0
DPDP	0	0
Non-recourse Marketing Assistance Loans and Loan Deficiency Payments	361.0	400.0
Price support		
Sugar	0	0
Extra-long staple (ELS) cotton	0	0
Upland cotton	49.0	47.0
Tobacco	35.0	0
Disaster and risk management assistance		
Livestock indemnity payments	45.0	41.0
Livestock Forage Disaster Program	2,500.0	452.0
ELAP	49.0	24.0
TAP	11.0	13.0
NAP	125.0	137.0
Crop insurance	6,000.0	5,900.0
Other programmes		
Grazing livestock on federal land	47.0	43.0
Reimbursement of transportation costs	2.0	2.0
Biorefinery, renewable chemical, and biobased product manufacturing assistance	0	0
Repowering Assistance Program	4.0	0
Other agricultural programmes		
Expensing of Multi-period Livestock and Crop Production Costs	350.0	370.0
Treatment of Loans Forgiven Solvent Farmers as if Insolvent	40.0	40.0
Capital Gains Treatment of Certain Agricultural Income	1,150.0	1,470.0

Source: WTO document G/SCM/N/315/USA, 14 March 2018.

forage were particularly important in FY2015. This notification includes programmes that are not in the DS:1 notification to the Committee on Agriculture.

The U.S. notifications to the Committee on Agriculture classify support according to the definitions of the Agreement on Agriculture. Green Box expenditures dominate (Charts 4.2 and 4.3) due to the importance of SNAP and child nutrition programmes. Overall, Green Box support declined from US$124.5 billion in 2014

to US$121.5 billion in 2015, reflecting the elimination of direct payments to producers and landowners, and increased spending on child nutrition programmes. As for Amber Box support, the United States notified product and non-product specific support totalling US$13.6 billion (including *de minimis* subsidies) for the marketing year 2014 and US$17.2 billion for 2015. Excluding *de minimis* support, the current total AMS reported was US$3.8 billion in both 2014 and 2015.

Chart 4.2 Green Box support, 2001-15

(US$ million)

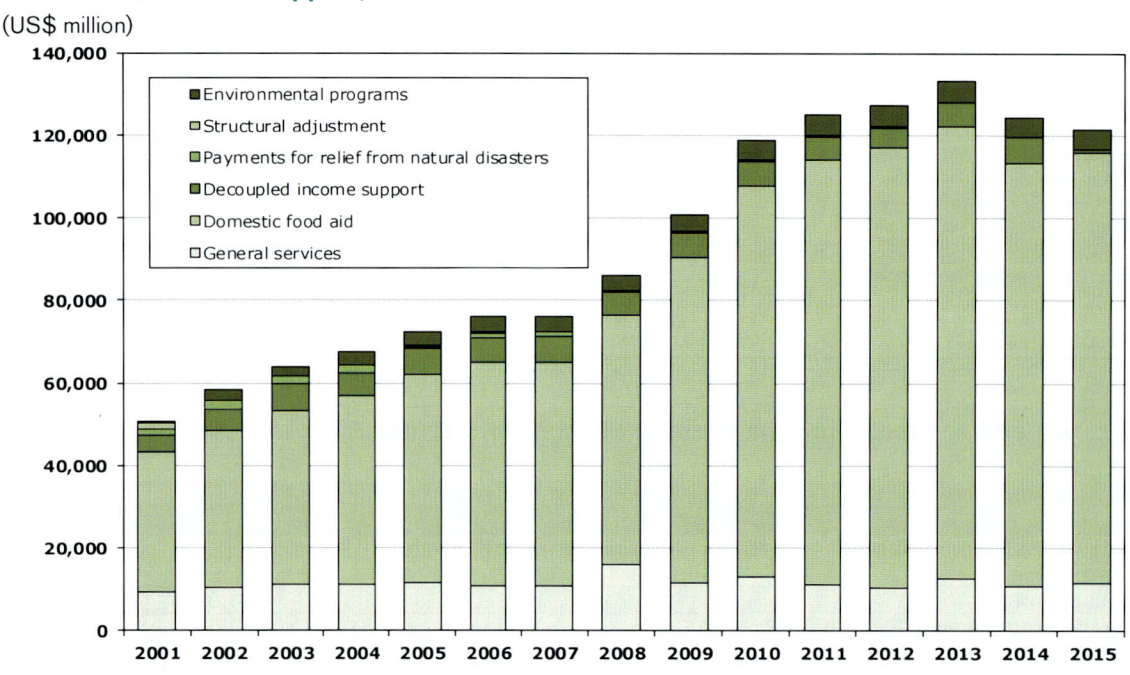

Source: WTO notifications.

Chart 4.3 Amber Box support, 2001-15

(US$ million)

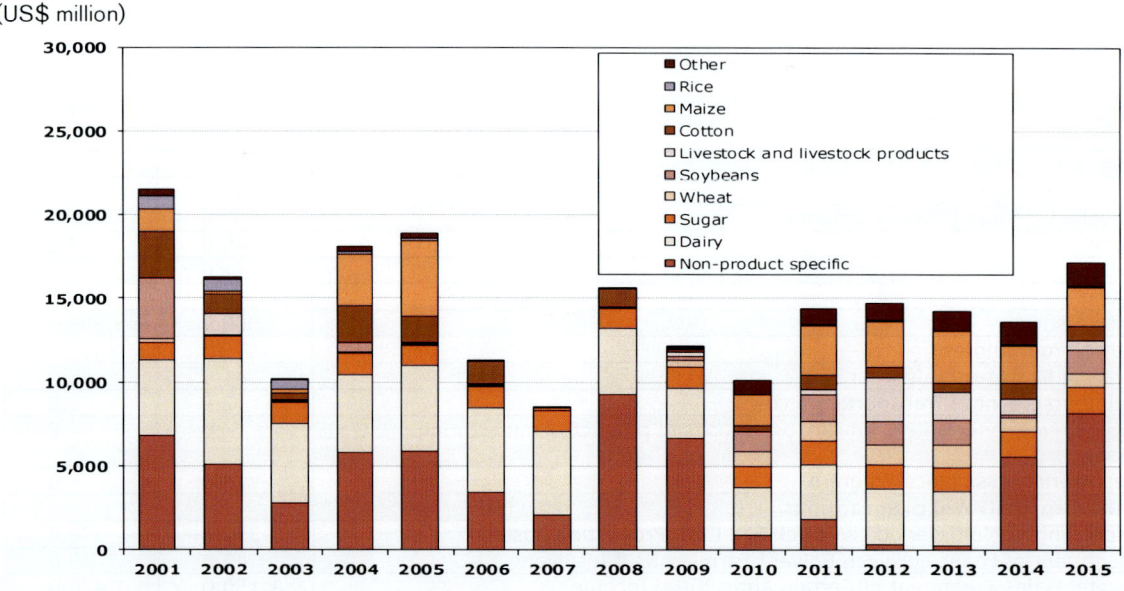

Source: WTO notifications.

ENERGY

General

Primary energy consumption amounted to nearly 98 quadrillion British thermal units (Btu) in 2017 (Chart 4.4). About 80% of the demand was covered by the combustion of fossil fuels, while 20% was met by renewable energy or nuclear electric power. Domestic energy production could have covered approximately 90% of the energy consumption. However, as some of this production was exported, approximately 71% of consumption was derived from domestically-produced energy in 2017. Fossil fuels have dominated the energy mix for more than 100 years. Among such fuels, the most significant trends over the last 50 years have been a steady rise in the production of natural gas and, from 2008, a decline in the consumption of coal. Primary energy consumption peaked in 2007, and then fell as a result of the economic downturn. However, the subsequent economic recovery has not led to a similar rebound in energy demand, as the economy has become ever more energy efficient. The energy intensity of the economy declined by 2% per year on average between 1980 and 2010.[50]

About 38% of the primary energy resources consumed are used for the production of electricity (Chart 4.5). The demand from transportation, the second most important primary energy consumption sector, is predominantly (92%) met by petroleum products. U.S. industries use a wider variety of energy sources, whereas households and commercial establishments primarily consume electricity, natural gas, or natural gas liquids (such as propane) for space heating and cooking.

Energy is relatively lightly taxed in the United States compared with other industrialized countries, even though taxes may be levied at federal and state levels, and the taxes are cumulative.[51] The main revenue earner is the federal tax on petrol and diesel, which brings in more than US$10 billion per year for the Highway Trust Fund (Table 3.4). In addition, all states collect taxes on petrol and diesel, but these taxes are also modest compared with the levels of taxation in other members of the International Energy Agency (IEA).

The Federal Government receives royalties, rents, and other income from the sales of federal leases of oil, natural gas and coal.

Federal and state agencies manage a range of incentives, notably tax credits, to encourage investment in renewable energy. Tax credits have also been available for purchases of energy-efficient appliances and for energy efficiency upgrades of residential buildings since 1978.

Crude oil

The United States is the world's third largest producer of crude oil (after the Russian Federation and Saudi Arabia), though it has been a net importer since the 1950s. As domestic demand consistently outstrips domestic supply, the United States accounts for a major portion of world oil trade, and current and projected changes in net U.S. demand may have a significant impact on the price outlook for crude oil. Although the anticipated impact of the 2009 recession in the United States may have been exaggerated, and thus short lived, the decline in world market prices for crude oil from mid-2014 came in direct response to a significant increase in U.S. production of light tight (shale) oil. As prices have recovered,

Chart 4.4 Primary energy consumption by major sources, 1950-2017

(Quadrillion Btu)

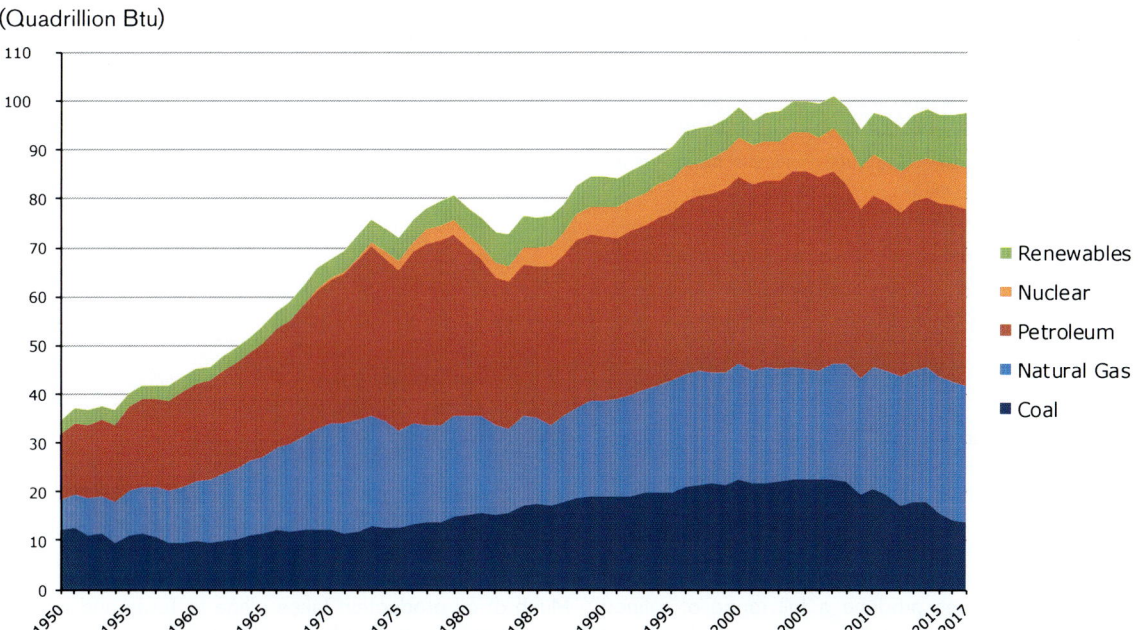

Note: Petroleum products exclude biofuels; biofuels are included in renewables.

Source: U.S. Energy Information Administration, *Monthly Energy Review*, Table 1.3.

Chart 4.5 Primary energy consumption by source and sector, 2017

(Total=97.7 quadrillion British thermal units)

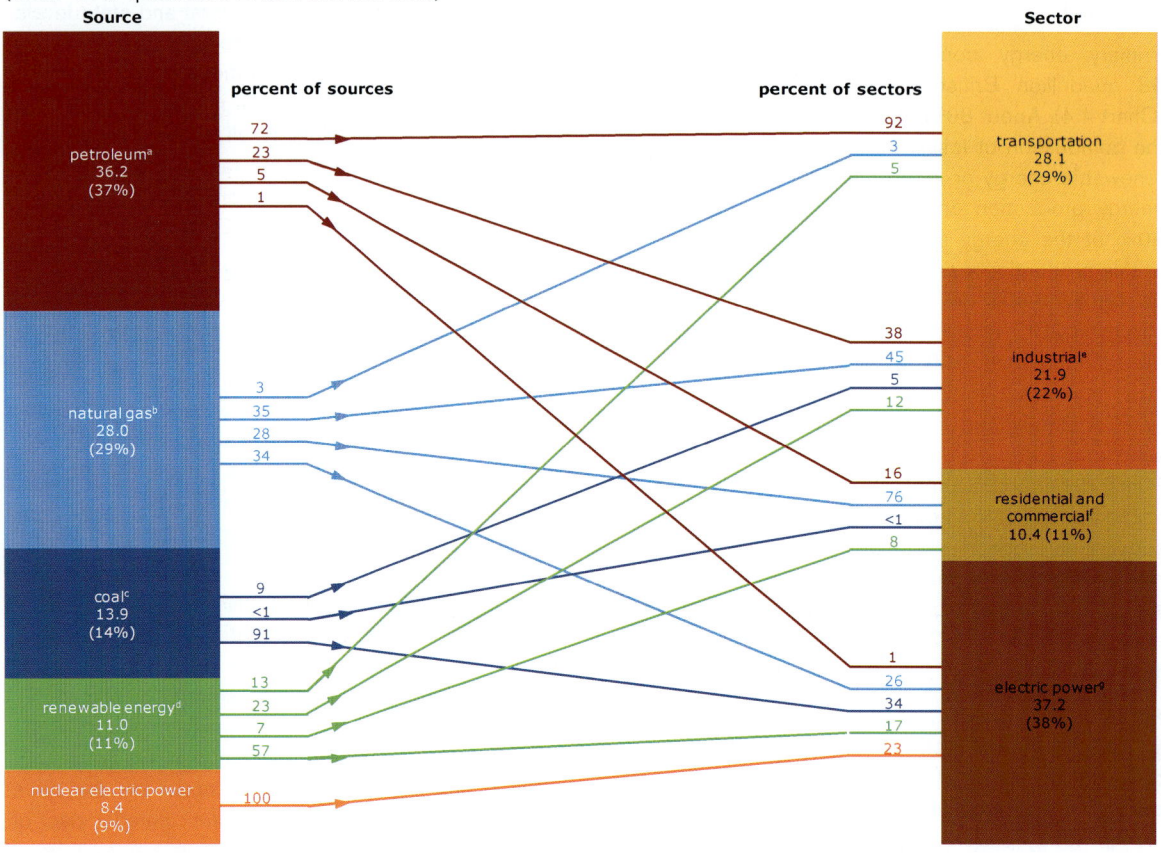

a   Does not include biofuels that have been blended with petroleum – biofuels are included in "renewable energy".

b   Excludes supplemental gaseous fuels.

c   Includes -0.03 quadrillion Btu of coal coke net imports.

d   Conventional hydroelectric power, geothermal, solar, wind, and biomass.

e   Includes industrial combined-heat-and-power (CHP) and industrial electricity-only plants.

f   Includes commercial CHP and commercial electricity-only plants.

g   Electricity-only and CHP plants whose primary business is to sell electricity, or electricity and heat, to the public. Includes 0.17 quadrillion Btu of electricity net imports not shown under "source".

Note: Primary energy is energy in the form that it is accounted for in statistical energy balance, before any transformation to secondary or tertiary forms of energy occurs (for example, coal is used to generate electricity).

The source total may not equal the sector total because of differences in the heat contents of total, end-use, and electric power sector consumption of natural gas.

Data are preliminary.

Values are derived from source data prior to rounding.

Sum of components may not equal total, due to independent rounding.

Source: U.S. Energy Information Administration, Monthly Energy Review (April 2018), Tables 1.3, 1.4a, 1.4b, and 2.1-2.6.

shale production - negligible as late as 2005 - has continued to expand. In July 2018, overall U.S. production of crude oil reached 11 million barrels per day for the first time in history.[52]

About one fifth of the world's refining capacity is located in the United States. The many modern and sophisticated facilities produce a full range of refined output, including high value light products, and the United States is currently the world's second largest exporter of petroleum products. It is now a net exporter, having been a net importer for decades prior to 2011. The surge in domestic refining was partly a response to the surge in shale oil production at a time when crude oil exports were effectively banned under the Energy Policy and Conservation Act of 1975 and other statutes. However, these export restrictions were lifted in December 2015.

Much of oil production takes place in Texas and in and around the Gulf of Mexico, which is close to major refineries, or in Alaska or North Dakota, from where crude oil is shipped to refineries elsewhere. A network

of oil pipelines links inland refineries with the Gulf of Mexico. Four major pipelines also ship oil from Canada to the northern United States. Shale oil produced in areas outside of (or constrained by the capacity of) the existing pipeline network has so far been transported by railroad or truck. Further expansion of shale oil production may require major investments in new pipeline or local refining capacity.[53]

Natural gas

The United States is the world's largest consumer and producer of natural gas. Technological breakthroughs in the exploitation of shale gas, which made it a relatively inexpensive energy resource, sparked a 500% increase in shale gas production between 2007 and 2013, and it currently represents about 67% of the domestic gas supply. Weaker prices have slowed the growth in the production of natural gas, including shale gas. About three quarters of the currently produced shale gas is extracted from four plays (Marcellus, Barnett, Fayetteville, and Haynesville). The electric power industry has been a major driver of domestic demand for natural gas, as it has been retiring coal-fired generation capacity.

The United States is now a net exporter of natural gas. It principally imports gas from Canada to areas that are either impossible or uneconomical to serve with domestic gas. Net imports represent about 5% of the total gas supply. Exports of gas to Canada and Mexico occur for similar economic reasons in those countries. Exportation of LNG is an attractive option, and export volumes are on the rise. As detailed in p. 71, all imports or exports of natural gas require authorization from the Department of Energy.

Coal

The United States holds the world's largest estimated recoverable reserves of coal. Coal is mined in 25 states, although about 70% of it takes place in only five of them (Wyoming, West Virginia, Pennsylvania, Illinois, and Kentucky). Steam coal represents more than 90% of the output, followed by coking coal. About 93% of the domestic demand for coal comes from power generation. Competition from cheap natural gas has weakened this demand considerably, and the coal industry also experienced a significant fall in domestic demand from the 2009 economic downturn. By contrast, exports of hard coal have grown steadily, and accounted for 25% of the coal industry's total earnings in 2012.[54]

The amount of CO_2 emitted from the burning of coal is significantly higher than for other fossil fuels.[55] Federal and state funds continue to be allocated to projects to develop cleaner coal technologies, including for the capture and sequestration of CO_2 emissions from industrial sources.

Renewable energy

Hydropower and solid biomass generate the majority of renewable power. However, biofuels, wind, and solar energy have become important additional resources. Consumption of biofuels and other renewable energy resources (other than hydropower) more than doubled between 2000 and 2017, mainly in response to federal and state requirements or incentives. The surge in production was particularly sharp for wind power, and to some extent also for solar power. As the reliance on renewable energy forms an essential part of efforts to reduce greenhouse gas emissions, further expansion of the renewable energy supply is expected in coming years.

Renewable energy resources accounted for approximately 17% of the electricity generated in 2017. The United States does not have a national target for renewable energy or an explicit federal support mechanism.[56] However, various federal programmes support research and development projects related to renewable energies, and regulations encourage their use, for example by requiring transportation fuel to include a minimum level of renewable fuel. At the state level, 29 states and the District of Columbia have "renewable portfolio standards" or similar binding targets for renewable energy, and eight states and one territory have set non-binding targets. States apply numerous measures, including tax credit schemes, energy metering, and certification programmes, to promote the development and use of renewable energy sources.[57]

Nuclear energy

The United States pioneered the development of nuclear power technology, and its nuclear power industry is the largest in the world. Nuclear electricity is currently produced in 30 states at 61 nuclear power plants, comprising 99 reactors. Two new reactors are expected to come online in 2021 or 2022. The share of nuclear power in electricity production has been consistently around 20% since the early 1990s. The relatively high capital costs for nuclear reactors make investment decisions vulnerable to low gas prices and, consequently, low wholesale electricity rates.

The Nuclear Regulatory Commission issues 40-year licences for nuclear power plants. The licences may be extended for additional 20-year periods. At present, the average age of the nuclear power reactors is 37 years. In all, 12 plants were retired in the 1980s and 1990s, primarily for economic reasons. A further six reactors have been shut down since 2013, but high capacity utilization and power plant uprates have kept the overall electricity output stable. The United States is highly reliant on imported mined uranium concentrates, and converted or enriched uranium, for the nuclear fuel supply. Many services and other inputs are also imported. The fuel fabrication requirements are largely met by domestic suppliers.

The management of used fuel, including the disposal of high-level waste, is the responsibility of the Federal Government. A charge has been levied on sales of electricity generated by nuclear power since 1982. The proceeds have been accumulated in the Nuclear Waste

Part B
Report by the WTO Secretariat

Fund, which was set up to finance the permanent and safe disposal of highly radioactive waste. The Fund was valued at US$44.5 billion at the end of September 2017. At present, public utilities store their waste on-site, in specially designed pools or in steel and concrete casks, while agreement on a long-term storage site remains pending.

Electricity

In 2017, electricity end-use consumption amounted to approximately 3.82 trillion kWh, 96% of which was sold by retail and 4% consumed directly by end-users. Electricity use rose 13-fold between 1950 and 2005, but the economic downturn in 2009 and subsequent energy economies have led to a levelling off of electricity consumption. Energy-efficiency standards and other improvements should slow future growth. The residential sector and the commercial sector are the largest users of electricity as a percent of retail sales, each with a share of around 37%, followed by industries (26%). The use of electricity in transportation is still modest (less than 0.3%), and primarily concerns the running of some public transit systems. Air conditioning/cooling, water heating, lighting, refrigeration, and space heating were estimated to be slightly more than 50% of residential uses, while computers and office equipment (15.3%), refrigeration (14%), ventilation (11.2%), lighting (10.6%), and space cooling (10.6%) were the most important uses in the commercial sector in 2017.

The use of natural gas in steam turbines was the principal source of electricity generation in 2017, accounting for 32% of the supply. Coal-fired power plants, which historically have been the dominant source (Chart 4.6), delivered 30% of the electricity produced, followed by nuclear energy (20%), and renewable energy sources

(17%). Petroleum, which, depending on the type of product, may be used as fuel in gas turbines, steam turbines, or diesel-engine generators, was the source of less than 1% of the electricity generated in 2017. Electricity trade with other countries, in practice Canada and to a minor extent Mexico, is marginal, and normally accounts for no more than 2% of the domestic demand. The United States is a net importer of electricity.

Among the renewables, the hydroelectric capacity expanded rapidly until the 1970s. Since then, production has varied substantially in line with fluctuations in annual rainfall. Among other types of renewable energy, wind power currently dominates. Biomass, solar energy, and geothermal power plants still account for no more than 4% of the electricity supply. Even though the construction costs for solar and wind energy production capacity have fallen in recent years, the average construction cost of new wind power capacity was still 80% higher than for new natural gas generators in 2016.[58]

The electricity industry is, with few exceptions, subject to regulatory regimes at municipal, state, and federal levels. It is diverse, and comprises more than 3,000 public, private, and co-operative utilities, including almost 2,600 independent power producers (as of May 2018). The Energy Policy Act of 2005 built on the Energy Policy Act of 1992 to enhance competition in the wholesale electricity market. Among its provisions, it allows the Federal Energy Regulatory Commission (FERC) to order utilities to make transmission services available to requesting wholesale generators. State Public Utility Commissions deal with regulatory issues that fall outside the legal jurisdiction of the FERC, including the regulation of retail sales to customers, the approval of generation facilities, and distinct reliability issues.

Chart 4.6 Electricity net generation by major sources, 1950-2017

(Billion kWh)

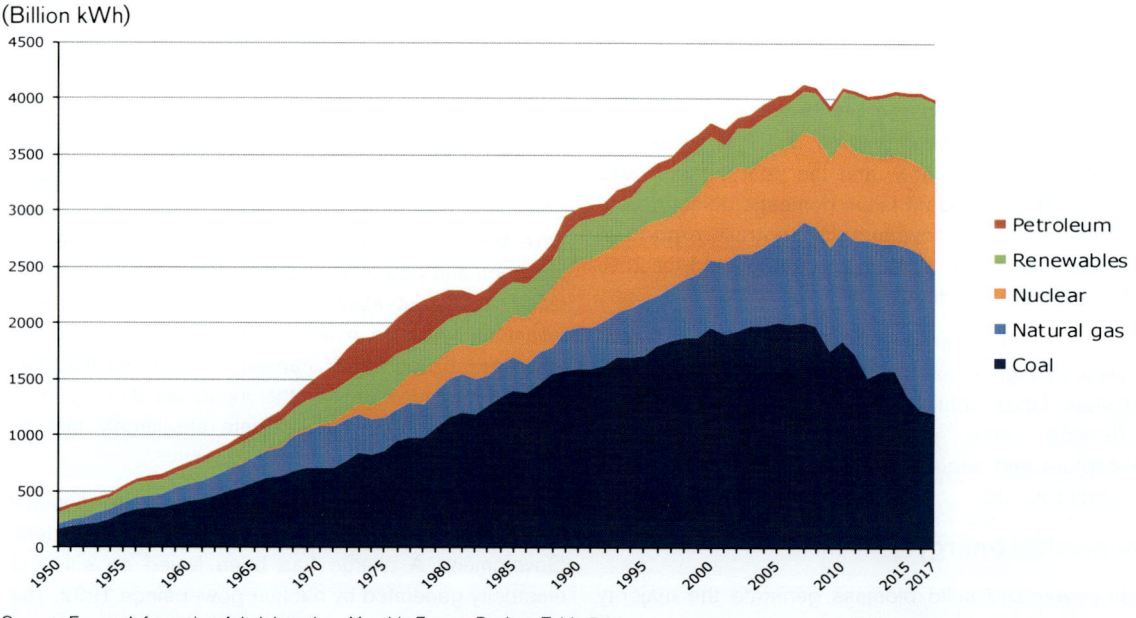

Source: Energy Information Administration, *Monthly Energy Review, Table 7.2a.*

Table 4.7 Value added by the manufacturing sector as a percentage of GDP, 2013-18

	2013	2014	2015	2016	2017	2018[a]
Manufacturing sector (US$ billion)	2,035.2	2,111.5	2,185.0	2,183.0	2,244.3	2,330.2
			(% of GDP)			
Manufacturing sector	12.2	12.1	12.1	11.7	11.6	11.7
Durable goods	6.5	6.5	6.5	6.3	6.3	6.3
Wood products	0.2	0.2	0.2	0.2	0.2	0.2
Non-metallic mineral products	0.3	0.3	0.3	0.3	0.3	0.3
Primary metals	0.3	0.3	0.3	0.3	0.3	0.3
Fabricated metal products	0.8	0.8	0.8	0.8	0.8	0.8
Machinery	0.9	0.9	0.8	0.8	0.8	0.8
Computer and electronic products	1.6	1.5	1.5	1.5	1.5	1.5
Electrical equipment, appliances, and components	0.3	0.3	0.3	0.3	0.3	0.3
Motor vehicles, bodies and trailers, and parts	0.8	0.8	0.9	0.9	0.9	0.9
Other transportation equipment	0.7	0.7	0.7	0.7	0.7	0.7
Furniture and related products	0.1	0.2	0.2	0.2	0.2	0.2
Miscellaneous manufacturing	0.5	0.5	0.5	0.4	0.4	0.4
Non-durable goods	5.7	5.6	5.6	5.4	5.3	5.4
Food and beverage and tobacco products	1.4	1.4	1.5	1.5	1.5	1.4
Textile mills and textile product mills	0.1	0.1	0.1	0.1	0.1	0.1
Apparel and leather and allied products	0.1	0.1	0.1	0.1	0.0	0.1
Paper products	0.3	0.3	0.3	0.3	0.3	0.3
Printing and related support activities	0.2	0.2	0.2	0.2	0.2	0.2
Petroleum and coal products	1.0	1.0	0.9	0.7	0.7	0.8
Chemical products	2.1	2.1	2.1	2.1	2.0	2.0
Plastics and rubber products	0.4	0.4	0.4	0.4	0.4	0.4

a   The first quarter of 2018 at seasonally adjusted annual rates.

Source: U.S. Bureau of Economic Analysis.

MANUFACTURING

The manufacturing sector's contribution to GDP has declined in the past few years. It represented 11.6% of GDP in 2017, down from 12.2% in 2013.[59] Durable goods accounted for 6.3% of GDP in 2017, down from 6.5% in 2013, while non-durable goods represented 5.3% of GDP, down from 5.7%. Considering individual subsectors, the largest contribution to GDP came from chemical products, which represented 2% of GDP in 2017 (2.1% in 2013), followed by the computer and electronic goods subsector, which accounted for 1.5% of GDP in 2017 (1.6% in 2013), motor vehicles and parts (0.9% of GDP in 2017), machinery, fabricated metal products, and petroleum and coal products (0.8% of GDP each in 2017) (Table 4.7).

Manufacturing is the fourth largest employer in the United States. In July of 2018, according to Bureau of Labor Statistics data, manufacturing employed 12.75 million people.[60] Durable-goods industries employed 7.98 million people, and non-durable goods industries 4.77 million. The manufacturing industries that employed more people were transportation equipment, with 1.68 million, of which 972,000 were employed in the automobile and auto parts industry; food manufacturing, with 1.64 million employees; fabricated metal products, 1.49 million; machinery, 1.13 million; and computers and electronic equipment, 1.08 million.[61]

Despite having lost market share in recent years, the United States remains a large producer of many manufacturing

products. For example, it is the world's second largest producer of motor vehicles, with a production of some 11.8 million vehicles in 2017. Also in 2017, it was the fourth largest producer of steel and the second largest exporter of pharmaceutical products. Foreign investment plays an important role in U.S. manufacturing. Foreign affiliates' production represented slightly over 20% of total manufacturing production in 2015. In the same year, affiliates in manufacturing accounted for 45.8% of affiliate value added. Within manufacturing, chemicals, which include pharmaceuticals, accounted for the largest share of affiliate value added, followed by transportation equipment.[62] In 2015, manufacturing accounted for the largest share of affiliate employment by industry of sales (30.4%), of which motor vehicles, bodies and trailers, and parts accounted for 5.9%, chemicals for 4.0% (half of which was in pharmaceuticals), and food products for 3.7%.

The United States does not have policies specifically targeted to manufacturing, at the federal level. Its main policy thrust is to create the framework for market forces to act in a fair and competitive environment. However, at the state level, there are programmes to attract investment in manufacturing.[63] There is also a policy of encouraging small businesses, including those in manufacturing, through government procurement set-asides and preferences (p. 87). In addition, the USDOC provides a national advanced manufacturing portal and information clearinghouse, found at https://www.manufacturing. gov/ to provide general information on federal policy regarding advanced manufacturing. Formally authorized by Congress in 2014, Manufacturing USA brings together industry, academia and federal partners within a growing network of advanced manufacturing institutes, for collaborative research in innovations in manufacturing technology of benefit to broad industrial sectors, with the overall goal of increasing manufacturing competitiveness, and promoting a robust and sustainable national manufacturing R&D infrastructure.

USTR's Office of Small Business, Market Access, and Industrial Competitiveness (SBMAIC) is responsible for manufactured goods trade policy, and for addressing market access, competitiveness, and small business issues facing exports of manufactured goods. The SBMAIC office acts as a focal point for dealing with key tariff and non-tariff barriers for, and developing creative approaches to, minimizing future barriers and divergences through regulatory cooperation. The SBMAIC office also leads USTR's trade policy efforts to address the challenges facing smaller exporters and promote the global export opportunities that these businesses need to create jobs.[64]

Through its trade policy, the Administration aims to advance and defend the interests of manufacturers and their workers, by expanding export opportunities and strengthening enforcement of trade rules. USTR works to level the playing field for U.S. manufacturers by: (a) eliminating tariff and non-tariff barriers; (b) negotiating WTO rules to benefit U.S. manufacturers; (c) countering foreign trade distorting practices; and d) enforcing trade agreements.[65] In this respect, the President's Trade Policy Agenda stresses that U.S. trade remedy laws and other trade laws must be vigorously enforced to ensure fair trade for U.S. manufacturers and their workers.[66]

SERVICES

Financial services

Overview

The United States has one of the most evolved and deepest financial systems in the world. In addition to being a substantial contributor to the U.S. economy, the U.S. financial system has considerable bearing on the global financial system and architecture. There are eight U.S. banks which are considered global systemically-important banks. The United States is the largest insurance market in the world, being responsible for nearly 30% of the gross insurance premiums worldwide, which amounted to US$5.02 trillion in 2016. The combined market capitalization of the U.S. stock market, based on the Russell 3000 index, crossed US$30 trillion threshold in January 2018.

In 2017, the share of financial services in GDP was 7.5%, the same as in 2016. Banking services generated 2.9% of GDP, insurance and related services 3.1%, securities, commodity contracts and investment 1.3%, and funds trusts and other financial vehicles 0.3%.[67]

The United States continues to run a significant surplus in trade in financial services (Box 4.1). In 2016, exports of financial services excluding insurance services were US$98 billion, a decline from 2015 and 2014 levels, while imports amounted to US$25.6 billion. Exports of insurance services were US$16.3 billion compared with imports of US$48.1 billion in 2016.[68]

As a response to the financial crisis, the Government put in place the Troubled Asset Relief Program (TARP). As part of the TARP, the Treasury put in place the Capital Purchase Program (CPP), a preferred stock and subordinated debenture purchase programme. As of 30 June 2018, only four banks remained under the TARP.[69] Out of the 707 institutions that received funds, 264 banks had fully repaid their entire principal with interest, 137 institutions resorted to Small Business Lending Fund (SBLF) repayments, 28 to Community Development Capital Initiative (CDCI) conversions, 47 sold investments, 190 auctioned investments, 33 were in bankruptcy or receivership, and 4 had merged.[70] As at 30 June 2018, the Treasury had recovered US$226.8 billion from the CPP through repayments, dividends, interest, and other income, compared to the US$204.9 billion initially invested under the programme.[71] The Federal National Mortgage Association (Fannie Mae) and Federal Home Loan Mortgage Corp (Freddie Mac) continue to be under conservatorship.

At the end of March 2018, there were 1,812 "large" commercial banks in the United States, each with consolidated assets of US$300 million or more. At the same date, total banking system assets were US$16.7 trillion.[72]

Legislation and regulation

The main legislation regulating the financial sector, that was promulgated in the aftermath of the 2008 global financial crisis, is the Dodd-Frank Wall Street Reform and Consumer Protection Act of 2010 (DFA). The objective of the DFA is to promote the financial stability of the United States by: improving accountability and transparency in the financial system, ending "too big to fail" practices; protecting the U.S. taxpayer by ending bailouts; and protecting consumers from abusive financial services practices, among other considerations. In pursuit of the above, the DFA established a new and comprehensive regulatory framework, which included bringing previously unregulated markets, entities, and activities under the regulatory sphere. Additionally, the DFA also established a framework for the orderly resolution of large, complex and systemically important financial institutions. The largest bank holding companies (BHC) and the designated non-bank financial companies are required to submit resolution plans to the Federal Reserve and the Federal Deposit Insurance Corporation (FDIC).

Under the DFA, the Office of Thrift Supervision was abolished, and its responsibilities were reassigned to the Federal Reserve, the FDIC, and the Office of the Comptroller of Currency (OCC). The Act created the

Financial Stability Oversight Council (FSOC) and the Consumer Financial Protection Bureau (CFPB). The responsibilities of the FSOC include: (i) identifying risks to the financial stability of the United States that could arise from material financial distress, failure or ongoing activities of large, interconnected bank holding companies or non-bank financial companies; (ii) promoting market discipline; and (iii) responding to emerging threats to the stability of the financial system. The CFPB (an independent bureau of the Federal Reserve System) is mandated to regulate the offering and provision of consumer financial products and services under federal consumer financial protection laws. The CFPB supervises insured depository institutions and credit unions with assets greater than US$10 billion, and non-bank mortgage originators and servicers, payday lenders, and private student lenders of all sizes, to ensure compliance with federal consumer financial protection laws and regulations, and may take appropriate enforcement action to address violations (see Table 4.10 in previous report).[73]

The DFA also established the Treasury's Federal Insurance Office (FIO). The FIO, among other things, advises the Secretary of the Treasury on major domestic and prudential international insurance policy issues, and its Director serves as a non-voting member of the FSOC. In addition, the FIO assists the Secretary in the administration of the Terrorism Risk Insurance Program (TRIP). It also monitors all aspects of the insurance sector, and represents the United States on prudential aspects pertaining to international insurance matters. The DFA also granted the SEC and the CFTC authority to regulate over-the-counter derivatives.

Section 113 of the DFA authorizes the FSOC to determine whether a non-bank financial company shall be supervised by the Board of Governors of the Federal Reserve System, and be subject to enhanced prudential standards if material financial distress at the company, or the nature, scope, size, scale, concentration, interconnectedness, or mix of the activities of the company, could pose a threat to the financial stability of the United States.[74] The FSOC issued a rule and interpretive guidance regarding its determinations authority, and later also adopted supplemental procedures related to non-bank financial company determinations. The FSOC established a three-stage process for identifying and analyzing companies for a determination. In the first stage of the process, the FSOC applies six quantitative thresholds to a broad group of non-bank financial companies, to identify a set of companies that merit further evaluation; these are: US$50 billion in total consolidated assets[75]; US$30 billion in gross notional credit default swaps (CDSs) outstanding for which a non-bank financial company is the reference entity; US$3.5 billion of derivative liabilities; US$20 billion in total debt outstanding; a 15 to 1 leverage ratio (ratio of total consolidated assets to total equity); and a 10% short-term debt ratio (ratio of total debt outstanding with a maturity of less than 12 months to total consolidated assets).[76]

The DFA also authorized the FSOC to designate a Financial Market Utility (FMU) as systemically important if it determines that the failure of, or a disruption to the functioning of, the FMU could threaten the stability of the U.S. financial system. Designated FMUs are subject to heightened prudential and supervisory provisions, must provide advance notice and review of changes to their rules, procedures, and operations, and are subject to relevant examination and enforcement provisions. In July 2012, the FSOC designated eight FMUs as systemically important under the DFA.[77]

One of the most significant changes brought about by the DFA was the introduction of the "Volcker Rule", which came into force in July 2015. The objective of the Rule is to reduce the amount of speculative investments in insured banks and any company affiliated with an insured bank. To achieve this, the Volcker Rule prohibits banking entities from proprietary trading of any securities, derivatives or certain other financial instruments for a banking entity's own account. There are certain exemptions to the definitions of proprietary trading and permitted activity exemptions.[78] Banking entities are also prohibited from acquiring or retaining any equity, partnership or other ownership interest in, or from sponsoring, a hedge fund or private equity fund (covered fund), under the Rule. However, these are also subject to exceptions and exemptions, depending on the definition of covered funds and certain permitted activities.[79]

With a view to promoting the short-term resilience of internationally active banking organizations, and in line with the liquidity coverage ratio (LCR) stipulated under Basel III standards, the U.S. banking regulators issued a final rule to implement the LCR in the United States in September 2014.[80] The LCR is the ratio of highquality, liquid assets (central bank reserves and government and corporate debt that can be converted quickly and easily into cash) to a banking organization's projected net cash outflows over a 30-day period. The rule requires that companies have an LCR of 100% or more. Implementation of the rule started in 2015, and companies were expected to be fully compliant by 2017. Banking organizations with less than US$50 billion in assets are generally exempt from the final rule, while minimum liquidity requirements for FSOC-designated systemically important, non-bank financial companies were to be established at a later date.[81]

In July 2013, the Federal Reserve issued a final rule to implement Basel III capital rules in the United States. The rule was designed to help ensure that banks maintain strong capital positions that will enable them to continue lending to creditworthy households and businesses, even after unforeseen losses and during severe economic downturns.[82] The rule stipulates a minimum ratio of common equity tier 1 capital to risk-weighted assets of 4.5%, and a common equity Tier 1 capital conservation buffer of 2.5% of risk-weighted assets that will apply to all banking organizations. Under the rule, the minimum ratio of Tier 1 capital to riskweighted assets was raised from 4% to 6%, and included a minimum leverage ratio of 4% for all banking organizations, as well as a ratio of total capital to risk-weighted assets (total capital ratio) of 8%. Furthermore, in September 2016, the Federal Reserve Board issued a final policy statement, allowing implementation of a countercyclical capital buffer, to range from 0% to 2.5% of risk-weighted assets, when authorities determine credit growth is resulting in unacceptable systemic risk. This capital buffer, currently set at 0% of risk-weighted assets, is to be phased in by 2019.

In response to Executive Order 13772, the U.S. Department of the Treasury issued a series of reports, in 2017, on Banking and Credit Unions, Capital Markets, and Asset Management and Insurance. On 24 May 2018, the President signed into law the Economic Growth, Regulatory Relief and Consumer Protection Act, which included several recommendations that were contained in the Treasury reports. The legislation contains several provisions encompassing: consumer access to mortgage credit; regulatory relief; protection for student borrowers, veterans, consumers and home owners; and regulations for bank holding companies and for encouraging capital formation (Box 4.1).

The most noteworthy changes include: allowing banks with between US$50 billion and US$250 billion in assets to be run with less regulatory oversight; exempt banks with less than US$10 billion from the Volcker Rule; requiring the Federal Reserve to tailor regulations with respect to bank size rather than "one size fits all", and enabling large foreign banks to avoid regulations by allowing them to tally their U.S. assets in certain ways that keeps them below the US$250 billion threshold (Table 4.8).

Consolidated financial sector regulation

There has been no change in legislation governing financial sector consolidation. The Gramm-Leach-Bliley Act (Financial Services Modernization Act) of 1999 (GLBA) allows domestic and foreign banks to affiliate with entities that engage in financial activities or provide services that are incidental, or complementary to, a financial activity, provided certain capital and managerial standards are met. The Act allowed commercial banks, investment banks, securities firms and insurance companies to consolidate and create a financial holding company (FHC). In July 2018, there were 534 FHCs, which included 42 foreign banks. As at 31 March 2018, there were 130 large FHCs, with assets of above US$10 billion each.[83]

Overall regulation and supervision of large consolidated banking institutions, including FHCs, is the responsibility of the Federal Reserve, while the FSOC monitors the risks to financial stability posed by such institutions or by non-bank financial companies. The FSOC is empowered to determine that certain financial companies should be subject to supervision by the Federal Reserve, and to make recommendations concerning prudential standards

that should apply to those companies. Furthermore, the activities of subsidiaries of FHCs are regulated by the appropriate regulator: the OCC in the case of national banks; a state banking agency and the Federal Reserve or the FDIC in the case of state-chartered banks; the SEC in the case of securities firms; and a state insurance commission in the case of insurance companies.

Banking services

Due to the fragmented nature of the sector, a number of federal and state regulators are responsible for the supervision of the banking sector. The Federal Reserve is responsible for supervising bank holding companies (BHCs), saving and loans holding companies, domestic and foreign financial holding companies, foreign banks operating in the United States, state member banks, foreign branches, Edge Act and agreement corporations[84], and designated financial market utilities.[85]

The OCC charters, regulates, and supervises all national banks and federally-chartered savings associations, and supervises the federal branches and agencies of foreign banks, as well as the international activities of U.S. national banks. The FDIC insures deposits, and is the primary federal regulator for state-chartered institutions that are not members of the Federal Reserve System. State regulators are organized in the Conference of State Bank Supervisors (CSBS).[86] The federal banking regulators are members of the FSOC, as are other financial service regulators and representatives.

The United States provides national treatment with respect to all banking services, except that branches of foreign banks are not allowed to accept FDIC insured deposits unless grandfathered, and agencies of foreign banks are not permitted to accept deposits from U.S. citizens and residents.

The United States made GATS commitments in market access and national treatment for all subsectors included in the Annex on Financial Services, and in line with the Understanding on Commitments in Financial Services.[87] Although geographic and other limitations are applied to foreign banks and foreign-owned bank subsidiaries generally on a national treatment basis, the U.S. GATS Schedule has reserved against national treatment for some measures. For example, foreign banks cannot be members of the Federal Reserve System, although foreign-owned U.S. bank subsidiaries are not subject to this limitation. Also, foreign ownership of Edge corporations is limited to foreign banks and U.S. subsidiaries of foreign banks, while domestic nonbank firms may own such corporations.

The FDIC provides a maximum deposit insurance amount of US$250,000 per depositor, per insured bank, for each account ownership category.[88] Foreign banks in the United States can be insured by the FDIC.

Under the International Banking Act of 1978, foreign banks can establish a commercial presence in the United States by setting up federal or state licensed branches

Box 4.1 Main provisions of the Economic Growth, Regulatory Relief and Consumer Protection Act, Public Law 115-174, of 24 May 2018

Title II - Regulatory relief and protecting consumer access to credit

- Federal banking agencies must develop a specified Community Bank Leverage Ratio (the ratio of a bank's equity capital to its consolidated assets) for banks with assets of less than US$10 billion. Banks that exceed this ratio shall be deemed to be in compliance with all other capital and leverage requirements.

- Amends the Federal Deposit Insurance Act to exclude reciprocal deposits (deposits that banks make with each other in equal amounts) of an insured depository institution from certain limitations on prohibited broker deposits, if the total reciprocal deposits of the institution do not exceed the lesser of US$5 billion or 20% of its total liabilities.

- Amends the Bank Holding Company Act of 1956, to exempt from the Volcker Rule banks with:total (1) assets valued at less than US$10 billion; and (2) trading assets and liabilities comprising not more than 5% of total assets (Table 4.8).

- Volcker Rule restrictions on entity name sharing are eased, in specified circumstances.

- Amends the Federal Deposit Insurance Act, to require federal banking agencies to issue regulations allowing certain small depository institutions to satisfy reporting requirements with a reduced Report of Condition and Income.

- Amends the Home Owners' Loan Act, to permit certain federal savings associations to elect to operate, subject to supervision by the OCC, with the same rights and duties as national banks.

- The Federal Reserve Board (FRB) must increase, from US$1 billion to US$3 billion, the consolidated asset threshold (i.e. permissible debt level) for a bank holding company (BHC) or savings and loan holding company that: (1) is not engaged in significant non-banking activities; (2) does not conduct significant off-balance-sheet activities; and (3) does not have a material amount of debt or equity securities, other than trust-preferred securities, outstanding (Table 4.8).

- Amends the Federal Deposit Insurance Act, to increase the asset limit below which certain depository institutions are eligible for an 18-month, instead of a 12-month, examination cycle.

- Creates the Insurance Policy Advisory Committee on International Capital Standards and Other Insurance Issues at the FRB.

- Amends the Federal Deposit Insurance Act, to specify that a federal banking agency may not subject a depository institution to higher capital standards with respect to a high-volatility commercial real-estate (HVCRE) exposure, unless the exposure is a HVCRE acquisition, development, or construction (ADC) loan.

- Amends the Federal Reserve Act, to lower the maximum allowable amount of surplus funds of the Federal Reserve banks.

Title IV - Tailoring regulations for certain bank holding companies

- Amends the Financial Stability Act of 2010, with respect to non-bank financial companies supervised by the FRB and certain bank holding companies, to (a) increase the asset threshold at which certain enhanced prudential standards shall apply, from US$50 billion to US$250 billion, while allowing the FRB discretion in determining whether a financial institution with assets equal to or greater than US$100 billion must be subject to such standards; (b) increase the asset threshold at which company-run stress tests are required, from US$10 billion to US$250 billion; and (c) increase the asset threshold for mandatory risk committees, from US$10 billion to US$50 billion (Table 4.8).

- Requires federal banking agencies to exclude, for the purposes of calculating a custodial bank's supplementary leverage ratio, funds of a custodial bank that are deposited with a central bank.

- Amends the Federal Deposit Insurance Act, to require certain municipal obligations to be treated as level 2B liquid assets if they are investment grade, liquid, and readily marketable.

Title V - Encouraging capital formation

- Amends the Securities Act of 1933, to exempt from state registration securities qualified for national trading by the SEC and authorized to be listed on a national securities exchange.

- Amends the Investment Company Act of 1940, to exempt from the definition of an "investment company", for purposes of specified limitations applicable to such a company under the Act, a qualifying venture capital fund that has no more than 250 investors.

- Amends the Investment Company Act of 1940, to apply the Act to investment companies created under the laws of Puerto Rico, the U.S. Virgin Islands, or any other U.S. possession.

- Requires the SEC to increase, from US$5 million to US$10 million, the 12-month sales threshold beyond which an issuer is required to provide investors with additional disclosures related to compensatory benefit plans.

- Expands the applicability to issuers of "Regulation A+" (which exempts certain smaller offerings from securities registration requirements).

- Directs the SEC to revise registration rules to allow a closed-end company (publicly traded investment management company that sells a limited number of shares to investors in an initial public offering) to use offering and proxy rules currently available to other issuers of securities.

Source: Online information. Viewed at: https://www.congress.gov/bill/115th-congress/senate-bill/2155.

Table 4.8 Asset size and other thresholds in P.L. 115-174

P.L. 115-174 section number	New size threshold	Former size threshold	Provision description
Asset size threshold			
207	US$3 billion	US$1 billion	BHCs below this threshold, subject to other requirements, are not subject to the same capital requirement as depository subsidiaries, and are permitted to take on more debt to acquire other banks.
210	US$3 billion	US$1 billion	Banks below this threshold, subject to other requirements, are eligible for less frequent examination.
205	US$5 billion	None	Banks below this threshold are eligible for reduced reporting requirements to federal regulators.
101	US$10 billion	US$2 billion	Mortgages originated and retained by banks or credit unions below this threshold, subject to other requirements, are considered "qualified mortgages" for the purposes of the Ability-to-Repay Rule.
109	US$10 billion	US$2 billion	Banks or credit unions below this threshold, subject to other requirements, are exempt from certain escrow requirements.
201	US$10 billion	None	Banks below this threshold, possibly subject to other regulatory requirements, are considered as meeting all capital and leverage requirements if they maintain at least a minimum Community Bank Leverage Ratio.
203	US$10 billion	None	Banking organizations below this threshold are exempt from the Volcker Rule, provided their trading assets and liabilities are less than 5% of total assets.
206	US$20 billion	None	Federal savings associations below this threshold, subject to other requirements, can opt in to the national bank charter regulatory regime.
401	US$50 billion	US$10 billion	Publicly traded BHCs below this threshold are exempt from certain risk committee requirements.
401	US$100 billion	US$50 billion	BHCs below this threshold are exempt from Dodd-Frank enhanced prudential regulation (except for the risk committee requirement).
401	US$100 billion - US$250 billion	US$50 billion	Regulatory discretion to apply Dodd-Frank enhanced prudential regulation to BHCs in this range, except supervisory stress testing requirements to which these BHCs would still be subject.
401	US$250 billion or G-SIB	US$10 billion for company-run stress tests; US$50 billion for others	BHCs above this threshold would be automatically subject to Dodd-Frank enhanced prudential standards.
209	550-unit public housing agency	None	An agency of small size is subject to less frequent inspection, provided it predominately operates in a rural area.
504	US$10 million in invested capital and 250 beneficial owners	100 beneficial owners	The new threshold applies to when a qualifying venture capital fund must register with the SEC as an investment company.
507	US$10 million in aggregate sales of company securities to employees	US$5 million in aggregate sales of company securities to employees.	Certain companies that are exempt from registering their securities with the SEC are subject to a higher threshold before they would be required to give employee-investors additional investor disclosures.
Product/activity limitations			
202	Lesser of US$5 billion or 20% of total liabilities	None	Reciprocal deposits below this threshold are not considered brokered deposits for the purposes of prohibitions from accepting brokered deposits facing banks that are not well capitalized.
103	US$400,000 mortgage	US$250,000 mortgage	Loans below this threshold, subject to other requirements, do not require an appraisal of the property in rural areas.

Note: BHC = bank holding company. Some existing thresholds are statutory, whereas others are applied through regulation.

Source: Congressional Research Service.

and agencies, representative offices, or through the acquisition of a national or state subsidiary bank. These are accorded national treatment. If a foreign bank that poses a threat to the stability of the U.S. financial system applies to set up an office in the United States, the DFA requires that the Federal Reserve consider whether the home country of the foreign bank has adopted, or is in the process of adopting, regulation that would minimize such risk. In the absence of such criteria, the DFA gives the Federal Reserve powers to shut down the offices of foreign banks.

Under U.S. law, interstate banking is allowed; this can be done either through a merger or through the establishment of new branches, subject to certain restrictions. With regard to mergers, size limitations apply on a non-discriminatory basis, whereby the merged bank cannot control more than 10% of the total deposits of insured depository institutions in the United States. Additionally, limits on the total deposits of the merged bank within a state apply as well.

A foreign person is permitted to establish or acquire a nationally chartered bank subsidiary in all states, subject to commercial presence requirements. Initial entry or expansion by a foreign person through the acquisition or establishment of a state-chartered commercial bank subsidiary is prohibited or limited in 22 states; other limitations also apply at the state level.[89]

Insurance services

Structure and performance

The insurance sector in the United States is divided into three segments: life and health (L&H) insurers, property and casualty (P&C) insurers, and health insurers. Companies in the L&H sector offer life insurance and annuities, and accident and health (A&H) products. At the end of 2016, there were 780 L&H firms. The 2,655 P&C insurers offer personal lines, which protect individuals and families against the risk of financial loss associated with damage to property or exposure to liability. They also provide commercial lines, which protect against the risk of financial loss for businesses. There are 1,095 companies licensed solely as health insurers or Health Maintenance Organizations. There has been considerable consolidation in the insurance industry in recent years. There were 91 merger and acquisition (M&A) deals worth US$21.6 billion in 2016, and 77 deals worth US$143 billion in 2015.

In 2016, net premiums for approximately US$600 billion were written for the L&H sector, accounting for 34% of total net premiums, while, for the P&C segment, net premiums written were around US$534 billion (30% of total net written premiums). Net premiums written for the health sector were US$631 billion, or 36% of the combined total for the three sectors. In terms of total assets, the L&H sector dominates, with US$6.6 trillion at the end of 2016, followed by the P&C sector, with around US$1.9 trillion, and US$377 billion by health insurance companies. The L&H sector continues to be

noticeably concentrated in the United States. In 2016, the top 10 firms in the life and annuities subsector were responsible for nearly 53% of the direct premiums written, a slight decline from nearly 55% in 2015. The A&H subsector is even more concentrated, with the top 10 firms being responsible for over 74% of the direct premiums written in 2016, an increase from around 72% in 2015 (Table A4.2).

The P&C insurance sector is less concentrated than the other two: the top 10 companies were responsible for 46.5% of direct premiums written in 2016, a small increase from 2015 (Tables A4.2). Within P&C, the commercial lines segment is even less concentrated, with the top 10 firms being responsible for 38.2% of direct premiums written in 2016. The top 10 firms in the health insurance sector wrote 52% of the direct premiums in 2016.

The U.S. insurance industry continues to be in a sound financial state; however, in 2016, the sector reported a mixed financial performance. In 2016, the aggregate net premiums written in the L&H sector declined to US$600 billion, compared with US$638 billion in 2015, contributing to a decline in net income to US$39 billion in 2016, from US$40 billion a year earlier. Net income primarily raised capital and surplus of the L&H sector to a record level of US$380.7 billion at the end of 2016. In contrast, net written premiums rose by 2.5% in 2016 for the P&C sector, to reach US$534 billion; however, net income declined to US$44 billion in 2016, less than the US$58 billion posted in 2015, and US$65 billion in 2014. Underwriting losses of US$2 billion in 2016 compared to gains of US$11 billion in 2015 was the main reason for the decline in income. Positive earnings in 2016 largely resulted in policyholder surplus for the sector, rising to US$712.3 billion at the end of the year.

Legislation and regulation

During the period under review, there has been no change to the regulation of the insurance sector. Under the McCarran-Ferguson Act of 1945 and the GLBA, the insurance sector is regulated mainly at the state level. The Treasury's Federal Insurance Office (FIO) monitors the insurance sector, and represents the United States on prudential aspects of international insurance matters; however, the FIO wields no regulatory powers. Additionally, the FSOC has general oversight responsibilities.

To be able to offer insurance services, insurance companies, agents and brokers need to be licensed in the state where they plan to provide services. Licensing requirements vary across states. Furthermore, insurance premium rates for many types of coverage need to be approved by the state regulators.

With respect to foreign participation in the insurance sector, foreign firms can access the direct insurance market by acquiring a licensed insurance company, or through a subsidiary or a branch office. Furthermore, the majority of states prohibit the conduct of business by

Part B
Report by the WTO Secretariat

governmentcontrolled or government-owned insurance companies. A foreign company operating as a branch is only permitted to write premiums based on the capital it has deposited in the state where it is conducting business. However, this condition is usually waived, particularly if the company has a deposit in another state. Foreign companies in the sector are liable for the full amount of their assets in the United States. In certain cases, such as large industrial placements, marine, aviation, or transport (MAT) insurance or "surplus lines" insurance, exemptions from the state residency requirements exist; these vary across states.

Foreign reinsurers that are permitted to conduct cross-border business with U.S. companies, even when not licensed in a particular state, are required to post collateral for some or all of their liabilities to the U.S. ceding insurer.

Insurance premiums covering U.S. risks paid to companies not incorporated in the United States, or in countries with which the United States has a double taxation treaty, are subject to a federal tax of 1% on life insurance and reinsurance, and 4% on non-life insurance premiums. This was listed as a national treatment exemption in the U.S. GATS schedule.

With a view to reinforcing state coordination, state officials participate in the National Conference of State Insurance Legislators (NCOIL) and the National Association of Insurance Commissioners (NAIC). The NCOIL is composed of state legislators, whose purpose is "to help legislators make informed decisions on insurance issues that affect their constituents and to declare opposition to federal encroachment of state authority to oversee the business of insurance, as authorized under the McCarran-Ferguson Act of 1945". The NAIC is composed of the chief insurance regulators from the 50 states, the District of Columbia and five U.S. territories. It provides a forum for policy coordination, establishing standards and best practices, conducting peer reviews and coordinating regulatory oversight.[90]

On 12 January 2015, the Terrorism Risk Insurance Program Reauthorization Act of 2015 (Reauthorization Act) was enacted. The Act, *inter alia*, extends the Terrorism Risk Insurance Program (TRIP) to 31 December 2020. Under the TRIP, the U.S. Government currently pays 82% of the insured losses of an insurer resulting from acts of terrorism[91], subject to prior payment of a deductible by each participating insurer.[92] All payments by participating insurers that have satisfied their deductibles and by the Government, combined, are capped at an annual aggregate maximum of US$100 billion. Also, the Government does not share in any losses if industry-wide insured losses do not first exceed US$160 million (increasing to US$200 million by 2020).[93]

On 22 September 2017, the United States and the European Union signed a covered agreement, which addresses important areas of regulatory cooperation between the two as regards the insurance business, including: group supervision, reinsurance (including collateral and local presence requirements), and exchange of information between the respective regulatory authorities. The agreement entered into force on 4 April 2018. According to the FIO, the covered agreement allows U.S. insurers with EU operations to avoid burdensome worldwide group capital, governance, and reporting requirements under the European Union's "Solvency II" prudential regulatory system for insurers, as well as EU local presence and collateral requirements for U.S. reinsurers. The FIO also reports that the covered agreement builds on NAIC initiatives underway at the state level, by committing the United States to eliminating state-based reinsurance collateral requirements as applied to cessions to EU reinsurers that meet the consumer protection standards specified in the agreement.[94]

As mentioned in the previous TPR report, in the aftermath of the financial crisis, the Financial Stability Board (FSB) and the International Association of Insurance Supervisors (IAIS) developed a process to assess insurers' systemic risk, and recommend policy measures that would prevent failures in the sector. Following on from this, in January 2017, the IAIS established the Systemic Risk Assessment Task Force (SRATF), with responsibility to assess and measure systemically-risky activities, improve cross-sectoral consistency in systemic risk management, and make improvements to the Global Systemically Important Banks and Global Systemically Important Insurers (G-SII) assessment methodology. Unlike an entity-based approach to assessing systemic risk, which focuses on the extent to which any single insurance company poses a threat to the broader financial system, the SRATF will explore an activity-based approach that examines risk across insurers to assess vulnerabilities that may be relevant to financial stability.

Additionally, in conjunction with the Basel Committee on Banking Supervision, the IAIS established a Task Force on Systemically Important Banks and Insurers (TFBI) in 2017. The purpose of the TFBI is to address inconsistencies between the Globally Systemically Important Banks' (GSIB) framework and the Globally Systemically Important Insurers' (GSII) assessment methodology. The FSB, in consultation with the IAIS and national authorities, decided not to publish a new list for 2017. The FSB also welcomed and encouraged the work being done by the IAIS to develop an activities-based approach to systemic risk in the insurance sector.[95]

Securities market regulation

During the period under review, there has been very little change to the legislation governing the securities market in the United States. Under the provisions of the Securities Act of 1933, a full disclosure of securities being offered for sale is required, and such securities need to be registered if offered for sale in the United States.[96]

The Securities and Exchange Commission (SEC), set up under the Securities Exchange Act of 1934 (SEA), is the principal regulator of the securities sector in the United States.[97] The Act provides the SEC with disciplinary powers; furthermore, companies with more than US$10 million in assets, and whose securities are held by more than 500 owners, are required to file annual and other periodic reports. An amendment to the SEA, by the enactment of the Financial Services Regulatory Relief Act of 2006, exempted savings associations from the investment adviser and broker-dealer registration requirements in place for banks. The DFA also introduced amendments to the SEA.

Debt securities, such as bonds, debentures and notes, need to be registered under the Securities Act of 1933. However, if such securities are offered for public sale, a formal agreement between the bond issuer and the bond holder known as a "trust indenture" is needed. The trust indenture needs to conform to the provisions of the Trust Indenture Act of 1939.

Companies which engage in investing, reinvesting, and trading in securities, and whose own securities are offered to investors, are regulated under the Investment Company Act of 1940 (ICA). Under the provisions of the Act, companies are required to disclose their financial condition and investment policies to investors, when the stock is initially offered for sale, and subsequently on a regular basis. However, the Act does not permit the SEC to supervise the companies' investment decisions or policies.

Investment advisors, which are firms or individuals engaged in advising others about securities investment for compensation, are regulated under the Investment Advisors Act of 1940 (IAA). Under the provisions of the Act and its amendments, advisors who manage US$100 million or more, or advise a registered investment company, need to register with the SEC. As per the national treatment exemption undertaken by the United States in GATS, domestic banks involved in securities advisory and investment management services are exempt from registration under the IAA, while foreign banks are required to register. The registration requirement involves maintenance of records, inspections, submission of reports and the payment of a fee.

The Sarbanes-Oxley Act of 2002 (SOA), the Dodd Frank Wall Street Reform and Consumer Protection Act of 2010 (DFA), the Jumpstart Our Business Start-ups (JOBS) Act of 2012, and the Economic Growth, Regulatory Relief and Consumer Protection Act of 2018 introduced further changes and reforms to the regulation of the securities sector. The SOA increased corporate responsibility, enhanced financial disclosures and improved combating corporate and accounting fraud. The SOA also created the Public Company Accounting Oversight Board to oversee auditing activities.

The DFA of 2010 amended the SEA Act of 1934, whereby the SEC, when considering the application of a foreign person, or an affiliate of a foreign person, to register in the United States as a broker or a dealer, has to take into account whether the applicant poses a risk to the stability of the U.S. financial system, and whether the applicant's home country has legislation in place that would mitigate such risk. Furthermore, the SEC is authorized to revoke the authorization of foreign brokers and dealers if their home country has not taken appropriate steps to mitigate risk. The DFA also amended the SEA Act to require that each nationally recognized statistical rating organization set up, enforce and document an effective internal control structure, to determine policies, procedures and framework for assigning credit ratings. The DFA also amended the IAA, by abolishing the private advisor exemption.[98] Advisors subject to registration requirements were required to register by end-March 2012. Registration requires significant regulatory and compliance undertakings. Additionally, the DFA established a comprehensive regulatory framework for swaps and security-based swaps. Swap dealers and major swap participants are required to register with the CFTC, while security-based swap dealers and major security-based swap participants need to register with the SEC. Certain swaps and security-based swap transactions need to take place in an exchange and be cleared through a central counterparty, so as to reduce systemic risk. In addition, companies that use swaps are now subject to new regulatory, business, and operational requirements.

The JOBS Act was passed in 2012, with a goal of enabling businesses to raise funds in public capital markets, by easing regulatory requirements. It is designed to facilitate capital formation, and help innovative, emerging growth companies access the capital they need to grow and create jobs. It also allows for an exemption for up to five years from the SOA Section 404 requirement to obtain an annual verification report from a registered public accounting firm.

Section 501 of the Economic Growth, Regulatory Relief and Consumer Protection Act signed into law on 24 May 2018, amended the Securities Act of 1933, exempting from the obligation of state registration securities approved by the SEC for national trading and authorized to be listed on a national securities exchange. It also directs the SEC to report on the risks and benefits of algorithmic trading in capital markets. Section 504 of the Act creates a new subset of venture capital funds, called qualifying venture capital funds (QVCFs), that cannot be defined as an investment company as stipulated in the ICA. Being exempt from the ICA definition reduces the QVCF's registration and disclosure requirements. To qualify as a QVCF, a venture capital fund needs to have less than 250 beneficial investors and less than US$10 million in invested capital.

Section 506 of the Economic Growth, Regulatory Relief and Consumer Protection Act now requires mutual funds organized in domestic territories, such as Puerto Rico, the U.S. Virgin Islands and Guam, to be compliant with the provisions of the ICA, such as SEC enforcement and regulatory oversight, and disclosure requirements. The Act also increased the threshold amount of stock that a company can sell to its corporate employees in a year, without being subject to additional disclosure requirements, from US$5 million to US$10 million. The Act requires that the SEC offset future fees and assessments, which are due from a national securities exchange or association that has previously overpaid such fees and assessments, and informs the SEC of the overpayment within 10 years.

The Act increases the coverage of Regulation A+, which allows certain "fully reporting" companies to be eligible for certain exemptions from disclosure requirements. Section 509 of the Act allows closed-end funds to use certain streamlined reporting procedures, which are available through the well-known seasoned issuer status. This would include self-registration, communications with potential investors before and during the offering period, and being allowed to deliver electronic prospectuses.

Telecommunications

The United States has the largest telecommunications market in the world in terms of revenue (US$601.8 billion in 2015).[99] It ranked 16th out of 176 economies in 2017 in the ICT Development Index compiled by the International Telecommunications Union (ITU).[100] In 2017, the United States recorded a trade surplus in telecommunications, computer, and information services of US$6.5 billion, with exports totalling US$36.5 billion, and imports reaching US$29.0 billion.[101]

The number of mobile phone subscriptions in the United States reached 396 million in 2016, with a penetration rate of 122.9%. Fixed telephone subscriptions decreased until 2016, to 122 million subscriptions, or 37.7 subscriptions per 100 inhabitants. Fixed-broadband subscriptions per 100 inhabitants increased from 32.0 in 2015 to 33.0 in 2016, and wireless-broadband subscriptions per 100 inhabitants reached 127 in 2016. In 2016, 76.2% of individuals had Internet access (Table 4.9).

In its latest (2017) report, "Measuring the Information Society", the ITU noted the high level of penetration and competitive tariffs of the U.S. telecommunications market. The ITU also highlighted that operators are engaged in upgrading technology, and that the 5G service is expected to be available beginning in 2019.

The report also notes that fixed broadband is an affordable and fast service, but that challenges remain with respect to the provision of high-speed broadband to rural areas. The report recognizes the role played by the Federal Communications Commission (FCC) in the development of the sector.[102]

The Communications Act of 1934, as amended, continues to be the main law governing the sector. The FCC, an independent government agency whose five members are appointed by the President subject to confirmation by the Senate, is the federal agency responsible for implementing and enforcing communications law and regulations. It regulates interstate telecommunications carriers and others transmitting by wire or radio, including wireline[103] and wireless companies, radio and TV broadcasters, cable providers, and satellite companies. The FCC regulatory oversight covers interstate and international communications in all 50 states, the District of Columbia and U.S. territories.[104] The FCC has rulemaking authority, and may initiate a rulemaking proceeding when, for example, Congress specifically requires it to do so; when the FCC itself identifies an issue that is within its authority to address; or when a petition for rulemaking concerning an area within the FCC's authority is filed by a member of the public.[105] The National Telecommunications and Information Administration (NTIA), under the USDOC, is the principal advisor to the President on telecommunications and information policy issues. The International Communication and Information Policy (CIP) Office under the Department of State, and the USTR play an active role in developing and coordinating telecommunications policy in international fora, including in the negotiation of bilateral and multilateral agreements.

The FCC is in charge of assigning licences and authorizations under the Communications Act, including broadcast radio and television licences, licences used by wireless companies, satellite authorizations, and authorizations to provide landline telephone service. The FCC must also approve the transfer of those licences or authorizations, or when control of the company holding that licence or authorization is transferred.[106] The FCC reviews most mergers involving a telecommunications company.

Table 4.9 Selected telecommunications indicators, 2011–16

	2011	2012	2013	2014	2015	2016
Fixed telephone subscriptions (million)	143	139	133	128	125	122
Fixed telephone subscriptions per 100 inhabitants	46.1	44.2	42.2	340.4	39.0	37.7
Mobile-cellular telephone subscriptions (million)	297	305	311	356	382	396
Mobile-cellular telephones per 100 inhabitants	95.6	97.3	98.5	111.9	119.5	122.9
Internet users (%)	69.7	74.7	71.4	73.0	74.6	76.2
Fixed-broadband subscriptions (million)	88	93	96	98	102	106
Fixed-broadband subscriptions per 100 inhabitants	28.4	29.5	30.4	30.8	32.0	33.0
Wireless-broadband total subscriptions (million)	242.6	282.9	313.7	331.4	375.5	409.2
Wireless-broadband total subscriptions per 100 inhabitants	78.0	90.3	99.4	104.3	117.4	127.0

Source: ITU World Telecommunication/ICT Database (WTID), June 2018 Edition. Viewed at: https://www.itu.int/en/ITU-D/Statistics/Pages/publications/wtid.aspx.

Before granting an application for a new licence/authorization or for approval of a transfer, the FCC must determine whether the public interest, convenience, and necessity would be served by granting the application. The FCC may assess the competitive impact of granting the licence/authorization or transfer, analysing not only whether competition would be harmed by approving the licence or its transfer, but also if it would be enhanced. Depending on the type of licence/authorization involved, the FCC may also examine the possible effects of the transfer on the private sector deployment of advanced services, the diversity of licence holders, and the diversity of information sources and services available to the public. The FCC will typically review the evidence and hear the views of the public before it issues its decision: it may approve the application unconditionally, or with conditions designed to ensure that the public interest is served or that any potential harms identified by the FCC are eliminated or mitigated. If the evidence in the record presents a substantial and material question of fact or if the FCC for any reason is unable to make an affirmative finding that the public interest will be served by approving a transaction involving wireless or broadcast licenses, the FCC must designate the application for a hearing. (If there are no such questions in dispute, the FCC will deny the application.) The FCC endeavours to complete its review of all transactions and issue an order within 180 days of accepting the application for filing.[107]

The FCC is responsible for managing and licensing the electromagnetic spectrum for commercial users and for non-commercial users, including state, county and local governments. This includes public safety, commercial and non-commercial fixed and mobile wireless services, broadcast television and radio, satellite, and other services. To obtain a licence it is necessary to register with the FCC's Commission Registration System (CORES).[108] The FCC has several licensing systems. The Universal Licensing System (ULS) allows electronic filing of terrestrial wireless licence applications, and provides the ability to search for applications by providing information such as a file number, applicant name or application purpose, or to search for licences by providing information such as a call sign, licensee name or radio service. The Broadcast Radio and Television Electronic Filing System (CDBS) permits electronic filing of broadcast radio and television applications with the FCC. Public Internet access to these electronic filings, as well as station, application, and authorization information is available. The Cable Operations and Licensing System (COALS) permits electronic filing of Cable Operator and Multichannel Video Programming Distributor (MVPD) forms with the FCC. Filers can obtain COALS system log-ins, submit cable community registrations, and make operator information changes. The International Bureau Electronic Filing System (MyIBFS) allows for electronic filing of the following types of applications, requests and notifications: space station, earth station, Section 214, cable landing licence, Section 310(b) foreign ownership petitions, recognized operating agency, international

signaling point code (ISPC), data network identification code (DNIC), foreign carrier affiliation notification filings, and milestone/bond filings.

In general, common carriers, which are subject to Title II of the Communications Act, have a duty to interconnect with each other, either directly or through other common carriers' facilities.[109] Interconnection agreements may be regulated at both the state and federal levels.[110] The FCC has the authority to address interconnection issues for such common carriers.[111]

The FCC maintains regulatory safeguards to deter conduct by a foreign carrier that could result in harm to competition in the U.S. telecommunications market. These safeguards include the "no special concessions" rule, the benchmark settlement rates policy, and dominant carrier requirements. Under the no special concessions rule, U.S. international carriers are prohibited from agreeing to enter into exclusive arrangements with foreign carriers that have sufficient market power to affect competition adversely in the U.S. market. The Foreign Participation Order adopted a presumption that carriers with less than a 50% market share in the foreign market lack such market power.

The provision of a number of services is not subject to any foreign ownership limitation. This is the case, for example, of the provision of wireline broadband Internet access service. In other cases, there are foreign ownership limitations only under certain circumstances. For example, wireline based carriers, as well as submarine cable landing licensees, are not generally subject to any foreign ownership restrictions beyond the FCC's general obligations and qualifications for ownership of such entities. Some other telecom services, however, are subject to restrictions. Under Section 310 of the Communications Act of 1934, common carrier wireless licences cannot be granted to, or held by, non-U.S. citizens, corporations not organized under the laws of the United States, or foreign governments, nor can they be granted to U.S. corporations of which more than 20% of the capital stock is owned of record or voted by any of these entities without prior FCC approval.[112] Licences may be granted to companies set up in the United States that are controlled by holding companies set up in the United States and in which foreign individuals, corporations, or governments own of record or vote more than 25% of the capital stock, unless the FCC finds that such ownership is inconsistent with the public interest. Under the Communications Act, the FCC must conduct a public interest analysis when evaluating applications to receive authorization to exceed the 25% foreign-ownership benchmark.[113] Since the inception of the WTO, no foreign applicant has ever been denied a common carrier wireless licence under the FCC's public interest analysis of foreign ownership. During the review period, in 2016, the FCC revisited its prior policies with respect to broadcast applicants and licensees involving more than 25% foreign ownership, and incorporated them into the existing streamlined rules and procedures that apply to common carrier applicants and licensees, with certain modifications.[114]

A major regulatory change that occurred during the review period was the FCC's decision to end public-utility style regulation of the Internet, which had been introduced by the Title II Order in 2015, and to return to the light-touch regulatory framework that had been in place for nearly 20 years.

Under the new Open Internet Order, now commonly referred to as the Title II Order, adopted by the FCC on 26 February 2015, and effective on 12 June 2015[115], fixed and mobile broadband Internet access service were reclassified as a telecommunication service under Title II of the Communication Act (hence the name Title II Order).[116] As a result, providers of broadband Internet access service were made subject to some of the same statutory provisions that apply to common carriers, including a prohibition on unjust or unreasonable practices or unreasonable discrimination.[117] The provisions applied to both fixed and mobile broadband service. The Title II Order prohibited the blocking of lawful content, applications, services, or non-harmful devices; throttling (impairing or degrading lawful Internet traffic on the basis of Internet content, application, service, or use of a non-harmful device); and paid prioritization (management of a broadband provider's network to directly or indirectly favour some traffic over other traffic, in exchange for consideration (monetary or otherwise) from a third party, or to benefit an affiliated entity).[118] Additionally, the Title II Order established a general no unreasonable interference/disadvantage Internet conduct standard for conduct falling outside of the blocking, throttling, and paid prioritization prohibitions above.[119] The *Title II Order* also added additional reporting requirements to the FCC's transparency rule for broadband Internet access service.[120] It did not apply to enterprise services, virtual private network services, hosting, or data storage services. The Order was challenged by several groups, including the United States Telecom Association. In 2016, a D.C. Circuit Court upheld the Title II Order in *United States Telecom Association v. FCC*, concluding that the FCC's classification of broadband Internet access service was permissible.[121]

The FCC started work in 2017 to review the Title II Order. In May 2017, it adopted a Notice of Proposed Rulemaking (Internet Freedom NPRM), in which it proposed to reinstate the classification of broadband Internet access service as an information service under Title I of the Communications Act.[122] The Internet Freedom NPRM also proposed to reinstate the determination that mobile broadband Internet access service is not a commercial mobile service, and to re-evaluate the FCC's rules and enforcement regime to analyse whether *ex ante* regulatory intervention in the market was necessary. In this respect, the Internet Freedom NPRM proposed to eliminate the Internet conduct standard and the non-exhaustive list of factors intended to guide application of that rule.[123] It also sought comment on whether to keep,

modify, or eliminate the blocking, throttling, and paid prioritization prohibitions, and the transparency rule.[124]

In December 2017, the FCC issued a new Order reverting to the practices in place before the Title II Order was implemented. The 2017 Restoring Internet Freedom Order reversed the FCC's shift in 2015 to heavier regulation of broadband Internet access service, and returned to the lightertouch framework that had been in place during almost two decades of rapid Internet growth.[125] The main points of the Restoring Internet Freedom Order may be summarized as follows:

- Ending utility-style regulation of the Internet in favour of market-based policies;

- Reversing the 2015 Title II Order that had reclassified broadband Internet access service as a telecommunications service subject to several regulatory obligations under Title II of the Communications Act of 1934, as amended, and restoring broadband Internet access service to its Title I information service classification;

- Reinstating the private mobile service classification of mobile broadband Internet access service, and returning to the FCC's definition of interconnected service that existed prior to 2015;

- Restoring the authority of the Federal Trade Commission (FTC) to police the privacy practices of Internet Service Providers (ISPs);

- Requiring ISPs to be transparent, through the disclosure of network management practices, performance, and commercial terms of service, so as to help consumers' choice. This is a return to the transparency rule the FCC adopted in 2010, with certain limited modifications to promote additional transparency;

- Eliminating certain reporting requirements adopted in the Title II Order found to be unnecessary and unduly burdensome; and

- Eliminating the FCC's conduct rules, considered a costly burden on innovation and investment, and unnecessary because of the transparency requirement adopted, together with antitrust and consumer protection laws.

The FCC expects, through these actions, to promote broadband deployment in rural areas and infrastructure investment throughout the country, and to move closer to the goal of eliminating the digital divide.

During the review period, following the submission of public comments responding to the Internet Freedom NPRM, the FCC released its 2018 Broadband Deployment Report[126], prepared under Section 706 of the Telecommunications Act of 1996[127], which requires the FCC to report annually on whether advanced telecommunications capability "is being deployed to all Americans in a reasonable and timely fashion", and to take "immediate action" if it is not. The FCC found that there are both fixed and mobile services capable of meeting

the statutory definition of advanced telecommunications capability, but that mobile services are not currently full substitutes for fixed services.[128] The Report also found that, in the wake of the 2015 Title II Order, the deployment of advanced telecommunications capability had slowed dramatically, with new deployments falling by 55%. Further, although the number of people without access to both fixed terrestrial broadband and mobile broadband had continued to fall, it had done so at a pace three times slower after the adoption of the 2015 Title II Order. The Report also noted that, as of end 2016, 92.3% of the population had access to fixed terrestrial broadband at speeds of 25 Mbps/3 Mbps, up from 89.4% in 2014 and 81.2% in 2012; however, over 24 million people still lack fixed terrestrial broadband at these speeds. While approximately 92% (85.3%) of the population had access to both fixed terrestrial services at 25 Mbps/3 Mbps and mobile LTE at speeds of 5 Mbps/1 Mbps (10 Mbps/3 Mbps), in rural areas only 68.6% (61%) of the people had access to both services, as opposed to 97.9% (89.8%) in urban areas. Also, the United States ranked 10th out of 28 countries for download speed. Closing the digital divide and furthering the deployment of advanced telecommunications capabilities remains the top priorities for the FCC, and the Report concludes there is much work still to be done.[129]

To respond to the slowdown in deployment (both actual and predicted) in the wake of the 2015 Title II Order, the FCC has taken action, beginning in 2017, including by removing barriers to infrastructure investment, promoting competition in the telecommunications market, and by restoring the previous light-touch regulatory framework for broadband Internet access services.

In this respect, the FCC's Strategic Plan, as revised for FY2018 to 2022, set a number of priorities in order to "bring the benefits of the digital age to all Americans". These include:

- Closing the digital divide, by bringing down the cost of deploying broadband and creating incentives for providers to connect consumers in hard-to-serve areas;

- Promoting innovation, by ensuring that the FCC's actions and regulations reflect the realities of the current marketplace, promote entrepreneurship, expand economic opportunity, and remove barriers to entry and investment;

- Protecting consumers and public safety, by combatting unwanted and unlawful robocalls[130], which intrude into consumers' lives; making communications accessible for people with disabilities; and taking steps to assist and safeguard the communications of law enforcement officers and first responders; and

- Reforming the FCC's processes, to make the work of the FCC more transparent, open, and accountable, by modernizing and streamlining the FCC's operations and programmes to improve decision-making, build consensus, reduce regulatory burdens, and simplify the public's interactions with the Commission.[131]

The United States has made commitments on basic telecommunications under the GATS, and made an MFN exemption to allow for "differential treatment of countries due to application of reciprocity measures or through international agreements guaranteeing market access or national treatment" for direct-to-home (DTH) services, direct broadcast satellite (DBS) television services, and digital audio services (DARS).[132] The United States has also made both regulatory and market access commitments on telecommunications in its FTAs. In the telecommunications chapters of its FTAs, rules have been agreed with regard to access to telecommunication networks, the provision of enhanced or value-added services, and the adoption of telecommunications standards.

Postal and courier services

Postal services market overview

Postal and courier services are competitive activities, except for the services reserved for the United States Postal Service (USPS), the designated operator for universal service (see below). The USPS is an independent agency of the executive branch of the Federal Government. Private carriers may accept and deliver any item which does not fall within the reserved category, including items not considered letters, such as merchandise, newspapers, and periodicals.[133] However, under "the mailbox rule" (see below), delivery must be made by means that do not involve access to mailboxes or post office boxes in USPS retail units, unless postage is affixed to the privately carried matter.

The USPS delivered 149 billion pieces of mail in FY2017, serving 157 million delivery points via 31,377 post offices, stations and branches and 3,628 additional contracted partners.[134] In FY2017, the USPS recorded total revenue of US$69.7 billion, and total expenses of US$72.4 billion; both revenue and expenses were lower than in FY2016, and the net loss was halved, to US$2.7 billion.[135] The USPS has a statutory borrowing ceiling of US$15 billion from the Treasury. As the USPS reached this ceiling at the end of FY2012,[136] it has limited its expenditures on capital investments, and has cut operational costs. For the past three fiscal years (FY2017, FY2016, and FY2015), the USPS has generated net cash from operations of US$3.8 billion, US$2.7 billion, and US$2.9 billion, respectively. Revenue from First-Class Mail products amounted to US$25.6 billion; revenue from USPS Marketing Mail to US$16.6 billion; revenue from shipping and packaging to US$19.5 billion; revenue from international mail to US$2.7 billion; revenue from Periodicals to US$1.4 billion; and the rest corresponded to revenue from other sources.[137] Some 62.6% of revenue stems from market-dominant products (see below). According to Title 39 of the U.S.C., the USPS "shall be operated as a basic and fundamental service."[138]

USPS rates and fees are established by its 11-seat Board of Governors, and are subject to a review process by the Postal Regulatory Commission (PRC). The USPS offers two categories of products: market-dominant products, and competitive products. Market-dominant products include: First-Class Mail, USPS Marketing Mail, and Periodicals. Price increases for these products are subject to a cap based on the Consumer Price Index (CPI). The Postal Accountability and Enhancement Act of 2006 (PAEA) requires the USPS to provide notice of proposed rate adjustments for market-dominant products at least 45 days before the proposed effective date.[139] These proposed prices must be reviewed and approved by the Commission before they go into effect. Competitive products include Priority Mail, Priority Mail Express, First-Class Package Service, Parcel Select, Parcel Return Service, and some types of international mail. Competitive products are subject to greater price flexibility, but prices are also set by the Board of Governors, and reviewed by the PRC for legal compliance. The PAEA requires the USPS to provide notice of proposed rate adjustments of general applicability for competitive products at least 30 days before the proposed effective date.[140] Prices for these products must cover direct and indirect costs, may not be subsidized by market-dominant products, and must contribute an appropriate share of the USPS' institutional costs. This amount is currently 5.5%.

The volume and value of USPS activities have been affected by competition from electronic transmission means and private competition. However, the growth of the parcels activity has partially offset the decline of the letters and printed matter activities.

The "Postal Service" subsector (491) in the North American Industry Classification System (NAICS)

comprises establishments primarily engaged in providing mail services under a universal service obligation, and includes the activities of the National Post Office and its subcontractors operating under a universal service obligation to provide mail services, and using the infrastructure required to fulfil that obligation. These services include delivering letters and small parcels. Although not explicitly defined, the USPS's universal service obligation (USO) is broadly outlined in multiple statutes. In its 2008 Report on the Universal Postal Service and Value of the Postal Monopoly, the PRC identified seven aspects of universal service: geographic scope, range of products, access to services and facilities, delivery frequency, affordable and uniform pricing, service quality, and security of the mail.[141] The Postal Service is the only carrier obligated to provide all aspects of universal service. Some USPS activities are classified under NAICS 492 "courier and messenger services" (see below). Publicly available U.S. official statistics do not isolate the value added of postal services, nor do they provide figures for FDI or Foreign Affiliate Trade Statistics (FATS) for the subsector.

Postal and courier activities combined employed 547,500 persons in 2017[142], of which, 503,103 were USPS "career employees". The USPS also employed at that date 141,021 "non-career employees". The United States has posted a surplus in cross-border trade of postal services since 2015, as shown in Chart 4.7. Before 2015, the trade balance in post services was in deficit. The trade surplus increased substantially in 2016, to US$207 million, compared to US$65 million the previous year. This was due to a strong increase in receipts (exports) and decline in payments (imports).

Chart 4.7 Postal services trade, 2009-16

(US$ million)

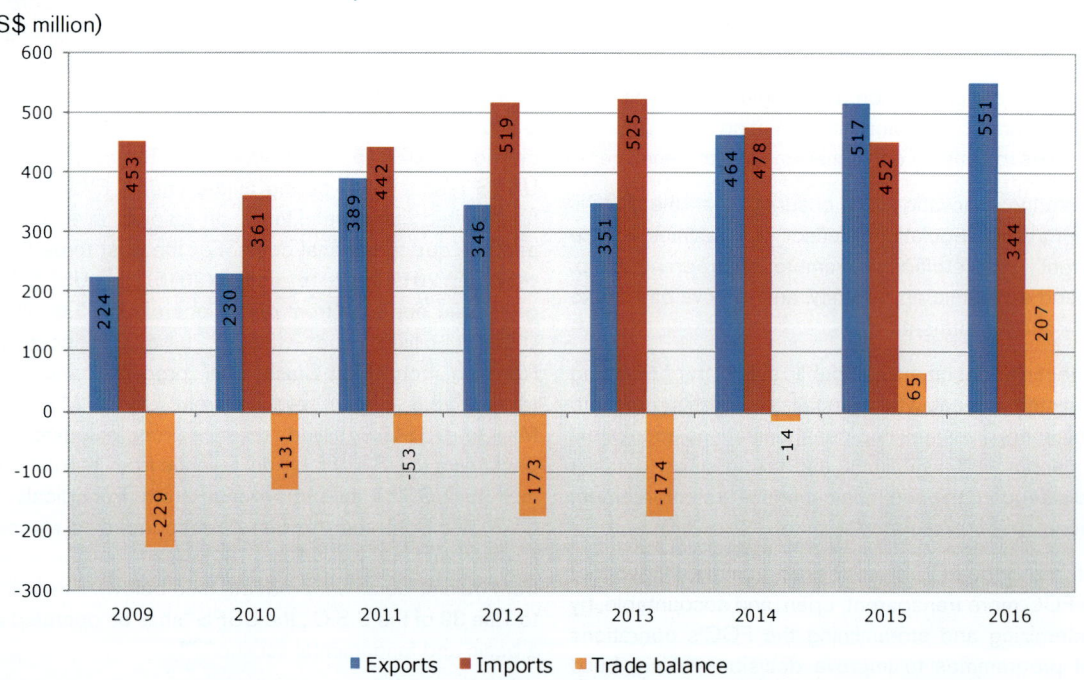

Source: Bureau of Economic Analysis.

Courier and express services market overview

Courier and express services firms have developed alongside the postal service. The sector can be divided into five sub-segments: standard courier services, overnight courier services, same-day express services, international courier services, and pallet courier services. The industry is composed essentially of two types of actors: very large express companies, such as Fedex, UPS, DHL and TNT, collecting and dispatching courier nationally and internationally through vans, trucks and planes via hub systems and hand courier, messengers and local delivery firms using vans, trucks, bicycles, or other means to deliver documents and parcels within a given metropolitan area (e.g. A1Express, Courier Express, LaserShip and Last Mile Logistics Group). Hauliers, air cargo carriers and freight forwarders are also present to various degrees in the sector. With the growing importance of e–commerce, the competitive landscape is rapidly changing. Regional carriers, such as OnTrac and Eastern Connection in the Western and North-Eastern states, are emerging, while start-ups, such as Shyp, PostMates, and Uber, and prominent companies, such as Amazon and Google, are trying to make a mark in this industry. Delivery by drone is now being tried by some companies.

"Couriers and messengers" are classified as a subsector within the category of transportation services under the NAICS. In accordance with the NAICS definition, industries in the couriers and messengers' subsector provide intercity and/or local delivery of parcels and documents (including express delivery services) without operating under a universal service obligation (USO). Under the NAICS classification, the restriction to small parcels partly distinguishes courier and messenger establishments from those in the transportation industries. The complete network of courier services establishments also distinguishes these transportation services from local messenger and delivery establishments in this subsector. This includes the establishments that perform intercity transportation as well as establishments that, under contract, perform local pick-up and delivery.

According to the Bureau of Labor Statistics, the courier and messenger subsector employed 719,000 persons in the first quarter of 2018, and there were 17,405 establishments in the first quarter of 2017 (Table 4.10).[143]

According to private observers' information, the revenues of the courier and messenger industry was US$93 billion in 2017; according to the same source, the subsector posted an annual average growth rate of 3.2% during the 2012-17 period.[144] Regarding value added, official statistics do not isolate courier and messenger services; they are included in the category "other transportation and support activities". The value added of this type of services reached US$130 billion in 2017, accounting for some 0.7% of GDP (Table 4.11).

Cross-border trade data pertaining exclusively to express delivery is lacking. However, following on the methodology used by the USITC for its 2004 enquiry on the subsector, one can approximate these flows by measuring air freight transport data, which include express delivery air freight.[145] The United States has traditionally run a trade surplus in air freight trade services, including courier and messenger services (Chart 4.8). This surplus peaked in 2013, at US$7,996 million, and has decreased since. However, at US$5,522 million in 2016, it remains substantial. A considerable share of this surplus is generated by carriers such as UPS, FedEx and the USPS. The United States is home to three of the four largest courier carriers in the world. UPS, the largest company, had revenue of US$66 billion in 2017, and employed 454,000 people worldwide, of which 374,000 were in the United States.[146] FedEx had revenues of US$60.3 billion in FY2017 (including TNT operations).[147]

Table 4.10 Employment and number of establishments in courier and messenger services, 2010-18Q1

NAICS code		2010	2011	2012	2013	2014	2015	2016	2017	2018[a]
492	Number of employees ('000)	528	531	534	544	574	611	643	683	719
492	Establishments	16,428	17,911	17,969	17,722	17,765	17,886	17,659	17,405[b]	..

.. Not available.

a Data for the first quarter of 2018.

b Data for the first quarter of 2017.

Source: WTO Secretariat calculations, based on data from the Bureau of Labour Statistics.

Table 4.11 Value added in other transportation and support activities, 2010-17

(US$ billion and % of total GDP)

	2010	2011	2012	2013	2014	2015	2016	2017
Value (US$ billion)	96	102	105	108	110	117	122	130
Share of total GDP (%)	0.6	0.7	0.6	0.6	0.6	0.6	0.7	0.7

Source: Bureau of Economic Analysis.

Chart 4.8 Air freight services trade, 2009-16

(US$ million)

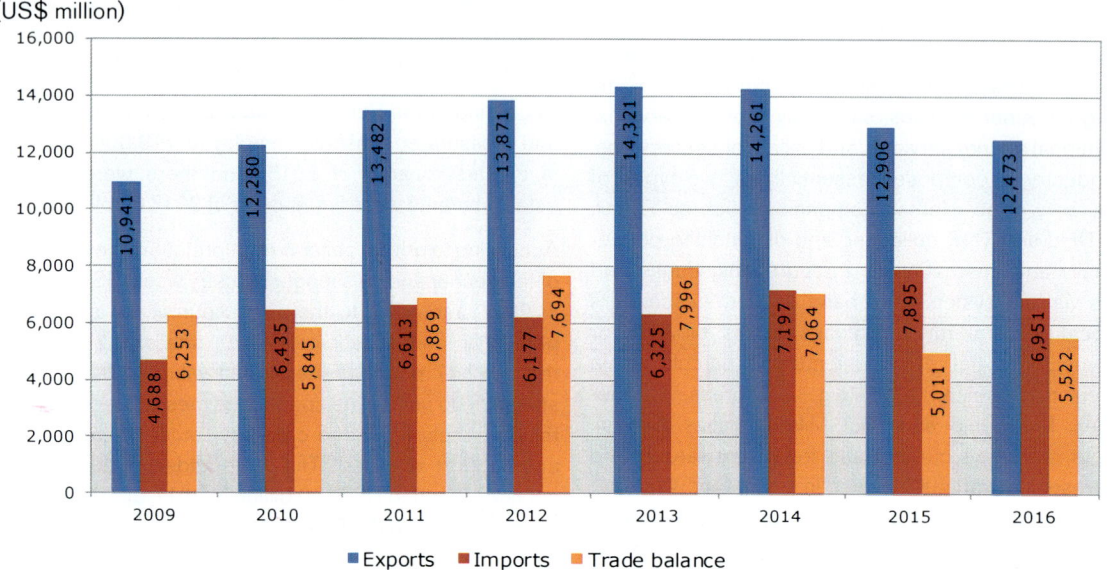

Note: Courier services are included in "Air transport, freight" but are not separately identifiable.

Source: Bureau of Economic Analysis.

Chart 4.9 Air freight services: cross-border exports, imports, and trade balance, by major trading partners, 2016

(US$ million)

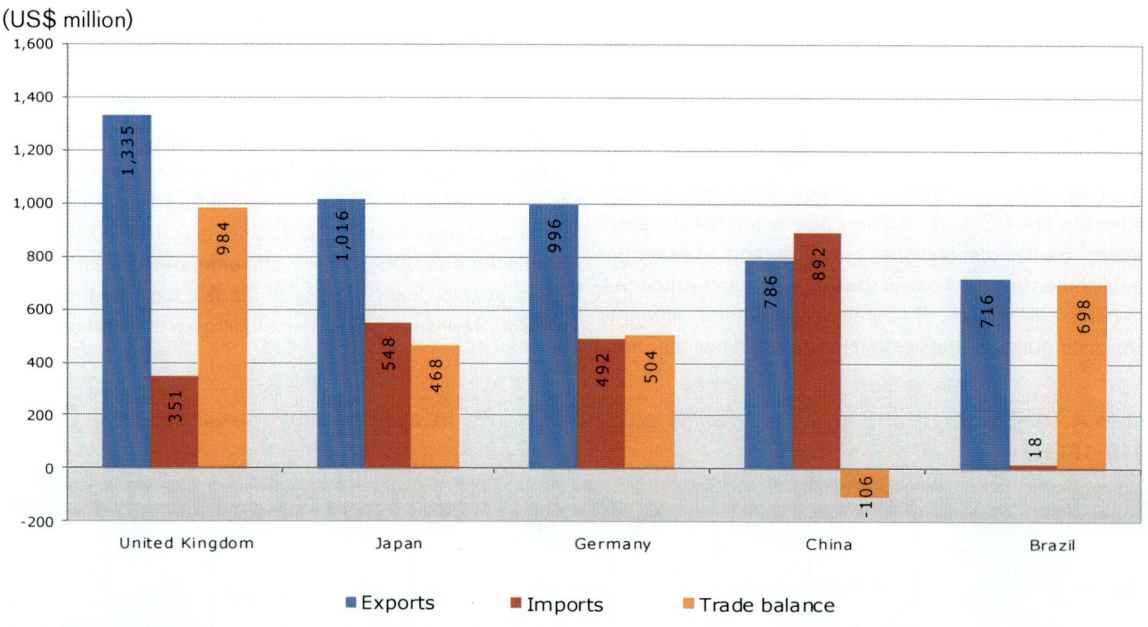

Source: Bureau of Economic Analysis.

In 2016, the United States ran a large trade surplus in air freight services with most of its main trading partners, except China, with whom it exhibits a small deficit (Chart 4.9).

The last available figures, for 2015, indicate that there were seven U.S. majority owned affiliates of foreign multinational enterprises of courier and messenger services with assets, sales or net income over US$20 million. The amount of total assets is not disclosed due to confidentiality issues; they had between 25,000 and 49,999 employees in 2015.

Regulatory regime

The USPS is regulated by the Postal Regulatory Commission (PRC), established under the Postal Accountability and Enhancement Act (PAEA) of 2006 (P.L. 109-435), and which replaced the Postal Rate Commission. The PRC does not regulate the postal services activities of the private sector. The PRC's responsibilities include, *inter alia:* developing a rate setting system; consulting with the USPS on service standards quality, targets and measurement; hearing complaints on rate and service issues; providing an annual report to the U.S. Congress on its activities; analysing the USPS' annual financial and operational results and their consistency with postal laws, in order to issue an annual compliance determination; issuing advisory opinions on nationwide service changes; approving new rates and classifications; approving market tests; and engaging in international postal policy to support the U.S. Department of State. The USPS enjoys immunity from antitrust laws for products covered by the postal monopoly; products that are not covered by the postal monopoly are subject to antitrust laws (39 U.S.C. § 409(e)).

The main U.S. provisions with respect to postal services are included in Title 39 of the U.S.C. The Postal Reorganization Act of 1970 (P.L. 91-375) created the USPS as a basic and fundamental service.[148] The provisions specifying the USPS' reserved area are contained in the Private Express Statutes (PES) (18 U.S.C. §§ 1693–1699; 39 U.S.C. §§ 601–606), which make it unlawful for any entity other than the USPS to send or carry letters over post routes for compensation, unless applicable postage has been paid and the letter has been prepared according to certain requirements, or the carriage qualifies as an exception. Exceptions under the Statutes include carriage prior, or subsequent, to mailing, letters of the carrier, letters accompanying and relating to cargo, carriage without compensation, and carriage of fewer than 25 letters by special messenger.

The 2007 PAEA added two new exceptions to the reserved-area provisions, which became effective on 10 December 2007. Under these exceptions, a letter may be carried privately if the amount paid for the private carriage of the letter is six times the rate currently charged for the first ounce (28.25 g) of a single-piece first class letter, or the letter weighs at least 12½ ounces (354 grams).[149] The PAEA also codified as exceptions those circumstances in which, under previous statutory authority, the USPS suspended enforcement of the PES as of 1 July 2005. These suspensions cover data processing materials, letters of bona fide college and university organizations carried within a campus mail system, international ocean carrier-related documents, extremely urgent letters, advertisements accompanying parcels or periodicals, and international remailing. The USPS no longer has the authority to promulgate new suspensions to allow for private carriage. The PAEA also removed provisions empowering the USPS to provide non-postal services, except those delivered prior to 1 January 2006, subject to specified review by the PRC. In accordance with the PAEA, the PRC is also in charge of determining whether a service should be considered market-dominant or competitive.[150] The Act also requires the PRC to establish a system of regulated rates, and

to promulgate regulations forbidding the subsidization of competitive products by marketdominant products; the PRC must also ensure that each competitive product covers costs and its share of USPS institutional costs (as described above). The PAEA also directs the USPS to establish in the Treasury a revolving Postal Service Competitive Products Fund, to be devoted to meeting the cost of competitive products. The PAEA introduced greater transparency and accountability into the U.S. postal system.

The mailbox rule (18 U.S.C. § 1725) prohibits private carriers from delivering mailable matter to most types of mail receptacles installed at residences and businesses, unless postage is paid. The mailbox rule applies regardless of content. Private carriers can hang mailable matter on doorknobs, place articles under doors, leave articles in doorways, use receptacles designated for receipt of newspapers or circulars, arrange to have the recipient retrieve articles at a designated location, or deliver in person to the recipient. Postal regulations also limit access to post office boxes in USPS retail units.

GATS and bilateral commitments

The classification used by the United States for its GATS commitments follows the structure of document MTN/GNS/W/120, which distinguishes postal services from courier services by the ownership nature of the entity providing those identical services: public for postal services, private for courier services. The United States did not schedule any commitments regarding postal services under the GATS, but made a full commitment for the first three modes regarding market access, and for all four modes for national treatment for land-based courier services (with the exception of courier services involving any prior or subsequent movement by air). The Mode 4 commitment for market access cross-refers to the horizontal section of the (GATS) Schedule. The commitments are the same in the United States-Jordan FTA, which has a positive listing structure.

In its other FTAs, the United States maintains its GATS-level market access commitment through cross-reference, except for Korea, where it was improved; there are no sector-specific limitations listed for the other obligations, taken on a negative-list basis.

Distribution services

Wholesale trade market overview

In 2017, there were 611,036 establishments devoted to wholesale activities; over 40% of them were dedicated to the wholesale of durable goods. Some 5.96 million people were employed in wholesale activities, more than half of which were in the area of durable goods (Table 4.12). The value added of wholesale services reached US$1.15 trillion in 2017, and the share of GDP was 5.9% in the same year.

FDI in wholesale services has increased steadily in the past few years. As a result, the FDI stock in wholesale

Table 4.12 Employment, number of establishments and value added in wholesale trade, 2010-18Q1

NAICS code/ description	2010	2011	2012	2013	2014	2015	2016	2017	2018[a]
	Number of employees ('000)								
42 Wholesale trade	5,476	5,605	5,704	5,763	5,844	5,851	5,874	5,942	5,955
423 Durable goods	2,725	2,802	2,852	2,871	2,924	2,930	2,940	2,995	3,004
424 Non-durable goods	1,929	1,949	1,978	1,998	2,017	2,031	2,043	2,055	2,052
425 Electronic markets and agents and brokers	823	855	874	893	903	890	892	892	899
	Number of establishments[b]								
42 Wholesale trade	613,944	613,907	615,897	619,209	620,944	619,446	615,605	611,036	..
423 Durable goods	249,366	248,221	248,883	250,248	251,433	252,188	253,194	254,293	..
424 Non-durable goods	136,284	135,385	135,670	136,538	138,168	138,376	138,849	139,925	..
425 Electronic markets and agents and brokers	228,293	230,303	231,345	232,423	231,342	228,884	223,563	216,818	..
	Value added in wholesale trade								
Value (US$ billion)	868	907	963	1,002	1,055	1,098	1,103	1,154	..
Share of GDP	5.8	5.8	6.0	6.0	6.1	6.1	5.9	5.9	..

..   Not available.

a   Data for the first quarter on 2018.

b   Data for the first quarter on 2017.

Source: WTO Secretariat calculations, based on data from the Bureau of Labour Statistics and the Bureau of Economic Analysis.

services reached US$425.4 billion in 2017, up from US$282.2 billion in 2011 (Table 4.13).

Most FDI in wholesale services in 2017 originated in trading partners in Asia, which represented 43.9% of the total; of particular importance is investment originating in Japan, which represented 28.1% of total investment in wholesale services in 2017. FDI from Europe represented 35.0% of the total (Chart 4.10).

While the number of majority-owned U.S. affiliates of foreign multinational enterprises operating in the sector of wholesale trade with assets, sales or net income greater than US$20 million has remained largely stable, both the total assets and the employment by majorityowned U.S. affiliates of foreign multinational enterprises operating in the sector of wholesale trade have increased during the same period (Table 4.14).

Wholesale trade services supplied to U.S. persons by multi-national enterprises (MNEs) through their majority-owned U.S. affiliates (MOUSAs) increased between 2010 and 2015, particularly in the areas of motor vehicles and parts, and electrical and electronic goods (Table 4.15).

Chart 4.11 shows services supplied by MOUSAs of the United States' main trading partners, and their respective shares, in 2015: Japan, with 35.0% of the total, had the largest share, followed by the Republic of Korea (13.1%), Germany (8.4%), the United Kingdom (5.1%), and Canada (4.6%).

Retail trade market overview

The value added of retail trade reached US$1.14 trillion in 2017, representing 5.9% of GDP. Although the value of trade has risen in nominal terms in recent years, its contribution to GDP has remained relatively stable.

Retail trade in motor vehicles, and food and beverages represents, combining both categories, one third of the total (Table 4.16).

Some 15.9 million people were employed in retail trade activities in 2017; there were 1.04 million establishments at the same date. Some 15% of establishments were food and beverage retailers, while 12% dealt with motor vehicles and parts (Table 4.17).

Table 4.18 shows that FDI stocks in the retail sector almost doubled over the 2010-17 period, when they reached US$88.6 billion. Some 39.4% of the FDI stock in retail trade that year was in the food and beverage stores area, and 18.5% in clothing and clothing accessories stores.

Chart 4.12 describes the respective shares in 2017 of trading partners' FDI stock in retail services in the United States. Europe accounts for some two thirds of this stock, with Germany, the Netherlands, the United Kingdom, and France being the main investors. Another important investor is Canada, with 23.5% of the total.

While the number of majority-owned U.S. affiliates of foreign multinational enterprises operating in the sector of retail trade with assets, sales or net income greater than US$20 million has remained largely stable, both the total assets and the employment by majority-owned U.S. affiliates of foreign multinational enterprises operating in the sector of retail trade have increased during the same period (Table 4.19).

Table 4.20 provides detailed data on retail trade services supplied to U.S. persons by MNEs through their MOUSAs between 2010 and 2015, and shows a regular and considerable increase of the value of services provided, which reached US$55.3 billion in 2015, the last year for which information is available.

Table 4.13 FDI position, 2010-17

(US$ million)

	2010	2011	2012	2013	2014	2015	2016	2017
Wholesale trade	255,045	282,221	293,406	324,284	332,424	369,535	374,110	425,403
Motor vehicles and motor vehicle parts and supplies	44,244	49,308	50,589	57,620	59,790	63,227	50,296	45,313
Electrical goods	32,126	39,079	45,758	50,598	46,468	57,254	59,015	72,299
Petroleum and petroleum products	34,087	51,178	57,365	58,455	56,604	65,882	65,479	99,176
Other	144,588	142,657	139,693	157,611	169,562	183,171	199,321	208,616
Other durable goods	79,462	77,698	74,551	77,899	82,655	81,770	86,869	94,171
Furniture and home furnishings	865	658	917	2,478	2,210	2,199	2,102	1,601
Lumber and other construction materials	1,060	711	642	757	931	997	979	1,031
Professional and commercial equipment and supplies	28,404	29,084	26,201	25,520	29,139	28,562	30,576	33,006
Metals and minerals (except petroleum)	10,565	12,239	12,491	11,280	11,686	9,868	9,850	10,382
Hardware, and plumbing and heating equipment and supplies	6,956	7,810	8,474	7,670	5,797	7,268	8,418	9,195
Machinery, equipment, and supplies merchant wholesalers	20,161	17,051	16,430	20,809	22,631	22,852	24,034	26,903
Miscellaneous durable goods	11,452	10,143	9,394	9,385	10,261	10,024	10,908	12,054
Other non-durable goods	(D)	63,922	64,451	79,023	(D)	(D)	(D)	(D)
Paper and paper products	2,378	2,256	2,682	2,714	2,756	1,979	2,810	2,879
Drugs and druggists' sundries	31,573	28,262	27,774	30,484	36,588	52,546	44,677	38,964
Apparel, piece goods, and notions	10,089	13,721	14,532	16,327	16,080	13,722	13,209	12,694
Groceries and related products	4,839	4,068	4,713	6,654	8,040	6,660	7,716	8,589
Farm product raw materials	918	-647	-2,406	3,999	5,241	7,542	7,344	7,224
Chemical and allied products	6,883	7,999	8,583	9,943	7,162	7,249	23,493	27,298
Beer, wine, and distilled alcoholic beverages	2,719	(D)	(D)	(D)	(D)	4,910	5,619	5,865
Miscellaneous non-durable goods	(D)	(D)	(D)	(D)	4,545	(D)	(D)	(D)
Wholesale electronic markets and agents and brokers	(D)	1,037	692	690	(D)	(D)	(D)	(D)

(D) Suppressed to avoid disclosure of data of individual companies.

Source: Bureau of Economic Analysis.

Chart 4.13 describes the respective shares in 2015 of trading partners that are the home countries of MNEs providing retail services in the United States through their MOUSAs. Europe accounts for some 62% of the total, with the Netherlands, Germany, the United Kingdom, and France being the main investors. Other important investors are Canada and Japan, with some 21% and 11% of the total, respectively.

Regulatory regime

Save for some sub-federal and local non-discriminatory limitations on the sales of alcohol and firearms, the applied regime for distribution services does not contain any market access or national treatment limitations.

GATS and bilateral commitments

The U.S. GATS commitments on distribution services are very extensive and liberal. They cover all the subsectors of the MTN/GNS/W120 nomenclature (namely 4.A commission agents' services, 4.B wholesale trade services, 4.C retailing, and 4.D franchising) except for the undefined 4.E "other" category. There are full market access commitments for modes 1, 2 and 3, and full national treatment commitments for all four modes for commission agents' services and for franchising services, as well as for wholesale and retail trade services except wholesale trade of alcoholic beverages, firearms and military equipment. The wholesale trade

Part B
Report by the WTO Secretariat

Chart 4.10 Foreign Direct Investment in wholesale trade in the United States, by country of ultimate beneficiary owner, 2017

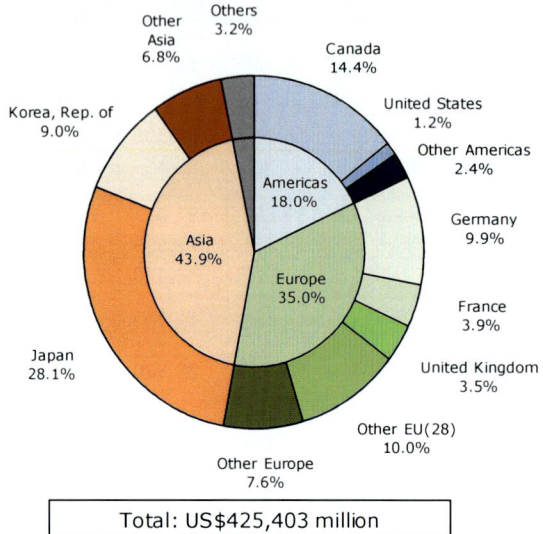

Total: US$425,403 million

Source: WTO Secretariat calculations, based on data from the Bureau of Economic Analysis.

of alcoholic beverages is unbound for the three first modes for market access but is fully bound for national treatment. Mode 4 commitments for the four subsectors for market access make a cross-reference to the horizontal commitment limitations on the temporary entry and stay of natural persons. There are no sectorspecific MFN exemptions regarding distribution services.

The commitments are the same in the United States-Jordan FTA, which has a positive listing structure. In its other FTAs the United States maintains its GATS market access commitments through cross-reference; there are no sector-specific limitations listed for the other obligations, taken on a negative-list basis.

Restrictions at the sub-federal and local levels, if any, are covered by standard provisions that appeared first in the NAFTA. The most significant of these is, with respect to five obligations (market access, national treatment, local presence, performances requirements and senior management and composition of the board), applying a standstill and ratchet to all existing restrictions by the states, the District of Columbia and Puerto Rico through an Annex I reservation.

Franchising

Market overview

Franchising is an important activity in the United States. The USDOC estimates that it accounts for 50% of all retail sales across 75 industries, and that it is responsible for one in seven jobs in the United States.[151] The International Franchise Association estimates that there were over 745,000 franchise businesses directly employing almost 7.9 million people in 2017. The Association's report also notes that franchise establishments are set to grow by 1.9% to 759,000 locations in 2018, while employment is expected to increase by 3.7% to 8.1 million. The sector's

GDP is expected to reach US$451 billion, up 6.1% from 2017, representing approximately 3% of nominal GDP.[152] The United States is a major net exporter of franchising services. The surplus in franchise fees reached US$5.2 billion in 2017, resulting from exports totaling US$5,268 million and imports of US$62 million (Chart 4.14). There is no publicly available official information on the share of FDI and the participation of foreign affiliates in these franchised activities.

Regulatory regime

There is no federal law governing franchising; however, there are both federal regulations and state laws regulating it. State laws are not uniform; they vary from state to state (see below). Franchising is regulated by the Federal Trade Commission (FTC) and by various state agencies. The pre-sale disclosure requirements of the FTC Franchise Rule apply everywhere, in the United States and overrule any state law or regulation that does not provide greater protection to prospective franchisees. In general terms, a state's franchise disclosure laws apply only if: (a) the offer or sale of a franchise is made in the state, regardless of where the franchise will be located; (b) the business to be franchised will be located in the state; or (c) the person benefitting from the franchise (the franchisee) is a resident of the state. The original Franchise Rule went into effect on 21 October 1979.[153] The FTC approved amendments to the Franchise Rule on 22 January 2007.[154] Since 1 July 2008, franchisors must comply with the FTC's disclosure requirements, by using the Franchise Disclosure Document (FDD), a disclosure format specified by the Franchise Rule.

Under the Franchise Rule, a commercial business arrangement is defined as a "franchise" if it satisfies three elements: (a) the franchisor must promise to provide a trademark or other commercial symbol; (b) the franchisor must promise to exercise significant control

Table 4.14 Selected data for majority-owned U.S. affiliates of foreign multinational enterprises, 2010, 2012 and 2015

	Number of affiliates with assets, sales, or net income (+/-) greater than $20 million			Total assets (US$ million)			Number of employees ('000)		
	2010[a]	2012	2015	2010	2012	2015	2010	2012	2015
Wholesale trade	**1,049**	**988**	**1,010**	**590,975**	**685,794**	**830,211**	**542**	**561**	**632**
Motor vehicles and motor vehicle parts and supplies	75	73	66	201,742	239,399	308,644	81	90	103
Electrical goods	133	130	136	56,569	73,334	78,673	81	93	102
Petroleum and petroleum products	37	33	33	83,851	10,6862	118,816	18	17	17
Other	804	752	775	248,813	26,6199	324,077	363	362	410
Other durable goods	514	479	486	136,398	135,270	150,051	245	234	262
Furniture and home furnishings	27	23	24	1,783	1,636	6,378	5	4	7
Lumber and other construction materials	24	18	18	1,687	1,469	3,028	7	7	11
Professional and commercial equipment and supplies	106	100	95	48,326	44,172	45,234	106	100	106
Metals and minerals (except petroleum)	59	54	54	23,193	26,329	23,538	22	25	28
Hardware, and plumbing and heating equipment and supplies	28	24	27	11,472	14,006	10,862	26	27	32
Machinery, equipment, and supplies	181	175	172	33,170	31,652	41,808	52	43	48
Miscellaneous durable goods	89	85	96	16,766	16,006	19,203	27	27	31
Other non-durable goods	285	267	283	111,575	13,0142	173,098	117	M	148
Paper and paper products	17	15	16	3,426	4,123	4,778	6	7	10
Drugs and druggists' sundries	42	37	39	40,324	43,280	68,347	33	34	41
Apparel, piece goods, and notions	42	40	42	14,893	19,747	22,129	20	24	24
Grocery and related products	72	62	63	6,745	8,272	13,748	14	15	14
Farm product raw materials	15	17	23	11,274	13,930	22,887	7	7	11
Chemical and allied products	43	39	41	12,312	10,448	10,869	15	9	10
Beer, wine, and distilled alcoholic beverages	13	16	19	11,543	16,415	15,875	H	H	5
Miscellaneous non-durable goods	41	41	40	11,059	13,928	14,464	J	K	33
Wholesale electronic markets and agents and brokers	5	6	6	840	787	928	0	A	1

a   For the year 2010, affiliates with assets, sales, or net income (+/-) greater than US$15 million.

Note: Letters in the employment cells correspond to the following ranges of employees: A-1 to 499; F-500 to 999; G-1,000 to 2,499; H-2,500 to 4,999; I-5,000 to 9,999; J-10,000 to 24,999; K-25,000 to 49,999; L-50,000 to 99,999; and M-100,000 or more.

Source: Bureau of Economic Analysis.

Part B
Report by the WTO Secretariat

Table 4.15 Wholesale trade services supplied to U.S. persons by foreign MNEs through their MOUSAs, 2010-15

(US$ million)

	2010	2011	2012	2013	2014	2015
Wholesale trade	119,409	133,989	141,586	147,282	168,300	172,618
Motor vehicles and motor vehicle parts and supplies	25,402	30,334	31,355	34,358	34,701	36,403
Professional and commercial equipment and supplies	16,482	16,471	17,153	16,811	19,619	19,419
Electrical and electronic goods	15,135	18,382	18,330	20,732	29,899	32,871
Petroleum and petroleum products	7,652	11,693	13,103	12,937	20,983	20,988
Drugs and druggists' sundries	..	..	..	..	12,767	13,094
Other wholesale trade	..	..	..	..	50,330	49,843
As a share of total wholesale trade services supplied to U.S. persons supplied by MOUSAs[a]	17.1	18.1	18.0	18.1	19.9	20.0

.. Not available.

a   Calculated by dividing the total supply of services by U.S. affiliates of foreign MNEs by the total services products used, as derived from input/output tables. The supply of services by U.S. affiliates is given for each industry (the industry of each affiliate's primary industry), covering the total supply of services from primary or secondary activities. On the other hand, uses in input-output tables cover the total services corresponding to a particular activity (services produced as secondary activities are reallocated to their respective service activity). Although both sets of data are not entirely comparable, this methodology allows an approximation of the share of the supply of services via mode 3 in total services consumed in the United States.

MNEs: Multinational enterprises; MOUSAs: Majority-owned U.S. affiliates.

Source: Bureau of Economic Analysis.

Chart 4.11 Wholesale services supplied to U.S. persons by foreign MNEs through their MOUSAs, by country, 2015

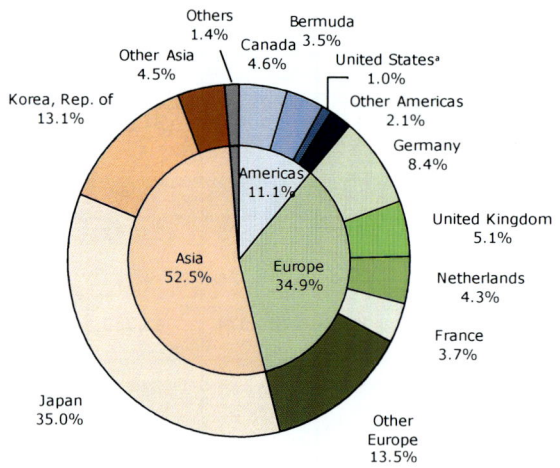

Total: US$172,618 million

a   Contains data for U.S. affiliates that have a foreign parent but whose ultimate beneficial owner is a U.S. person.

Source: WTO Secretariat calculations, based on data from the Bureau of Economic Analysis.

Table 4.16 Value added in retail trade, 2010-17

(US$ billion and % of total GDP)

	2010	2011	2012	2013	2014	2015	2016	2017
Value (US$ billion)								
Retail trade	**869**	**892**	**933**	**969**	**1,003**	**1,058**	**1,097**	**1,137**
Motor vehicle and parts dealers	148	155	167	177	185	197	205	212
Food and beverage stores	137	138	143	145	149	158	163	167
General merchandise stores	133	137	138	143	147	153	156	161
Other retail	451	462	485	504	521	550	573	597
Share of total GDP (%)								
Retail trade	**5.8**	**5.7**	**5.8**	**5.8**	**5.8**	**5.8**	**5.9**	**5.9**
Motor vehicle and parts dealers	1.0	1.0	1.0	1.1	1.1	1.1	1.1	1.1
Food and beverage stores	0.9	0.9	0.9	0.9	0.9	0.9	0.9	0.9
General merchandise stores	0.9	0.9	0.9	0.9	0.8	0.8	0.8	0.8
Other retail	3.0	3.0	3.0	3.0	3.0	3.0	3.1	3.1

Source: Bureau of Economic Analysis.

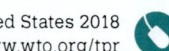

Table 4.17 Employment and number of establishments in retail trade, 2010-18Q1

NAICS code/description	2010	2011	2012	2013	2014	2015	2016	2017	2018[a]
	Number of employees ('000)								
44-45 Retail trade	14,445	14,670	14,838	15,071	15,357	15,607	15,832	15,864	15,906
441 Motor vehicle and parts dealers	1,630	1,691	1,737	1,793	1,862	1,929	1,980	2,008	2,024
442 Furniture and home furnishings stores	438	439	439	445	456	467	472	476	482
443 Electronics and appliance stores	522	528	507	496	497	522	522	505	497
444 Building material and garden supply stores	1,132	1,146	1,174	1,208	1,228	1,234	1,267	1,277	1,312
445 Food and beverage stores	2,809	2,823	2,861	2,930	3,004	3,063	3,090	3,090	3,096
446 Health and personal care stores	980	981	998	1,016	1,022	1,033	1,054	1,065	1,059
447 Gasoline stations	819	831	844	867	882	905	923	931	937
448 Clothing and clothing accessories stores	1,355	1,362	1,390	1,388	1,370	1,355	1,362	1,375	1,365
451 Sporting goods, hobby, book, and music stores	579	578	582	602	619	623	621	604	593
452 General merchandise stores	2,998	3,085	3,066	3,057	3,102	3,133	3,172	3,135	3,127
453 Miscellaneous store retailers	761	772	794	803	818	827	832	827	826
454 Non-store retailers	421	434	447	467	497	515	539	571	588
	Number of establishments[b]								
44-45 Retail trade	1,028,260	1,025,424	1,029,979	1,037,013	1,041,710	1,042,470	1,044,935	1,043,133	..
441 Motor vehicle and parts dealers	114,495	113,932	114,542	115,303	116,105	116,067	116,569	117,024	..
442 Furniture and home furnishings stores	52,739	51,020	49,947	49,040	48,332	47,752	47,448	47,058	..
443 Electronics and appliance stores	49,818	53,332	52,729	50,398	48,819	48,099	47,599	46,839	..
444 Building material and garden supply stores	74,326	73,029	71,717	71,049	70,463	69,979	69,906	69,054	..
445 Food and beverage stores	141,982	143,027	144,468	145,831	146,758	146,907	146,990	147,047	..
446 Health and personal care stores	96,999	97,687	100,428	105,691	107,514	108,254	109,764	109,710	..
447 Gasoline stations	103,858	104,099	104,929	104,946	104,781	105,057	104,984	105,581	..
448 Clothing and clothing accessories stores	130,127	128,734	129,510	129,653	129,147	127,591	126,874	126,585	..
451 Sporting goods, hobby, book, and music stores	58,033	53,937	53,177	53,010	53,042	52,793	52,078	51,044	..
452 General merchandise stores	52,752	54,792	56,083	58,027	60,052	61,250	62,352	62,156	..
453 Miscellaneous store retailers	114,968	112,738	111,816	111,815	112,896	113,199	113,142	112,479	..
454 Non-store retailers	38,069	39,097	40,634	42,252	43,802	45,523	47,227	48,555	..

..   Not available.

a   Data for the first quarter of 2018.

b   Data for the first quarter of 2017.

Source: WTO Secretariat calculations, based on data from the Bureau of Labour Statistics.

Table 4.18 FDI position in retail trade, 2010-17

(US$ million)

	2010	2011	2012	2013	2014	2015	2016	2017
Retail trade	44,770	46,540	48,965	52,634	58,911	64,610	75,554	88,640
Food and beverage stores	21,405	21,682	22,690	24,631	27,433	28,497	31,071	34,888
Other	23,365	24,858	26,275	28,003	31,479	36,113	44,483	53,752
Motor vehicle and parts dealers	478	511	388	422	466	569	577	648
Furniture and home furnishings stores	2,027	(D)	1,936	1,820	1,700	1,032	4,715	4,713
Electronics and appliance stores	84	24	41	86	129	133	155	185
Building material and garden equipment and supplies dealers	(D)	(D)	(D)	(D)	(D)	(D)	(D)	(D)
Health and personal care stores	2,784	3,004	3,244	(D)	6,487	7,913	10,250	10,404
Gasoline stations	(D)	(D)	(D)	(D)	(D)	(D)	(D)	(D)
Clothing and clothing accessories stores	8,972	9,567	9,065	8,982	10,288	13,922	15,731	17,002
Sporting goods, hobby, book, and music stores	17	16	12	-16	-85	(D)	-116	-119
General merchandise stores	2	(D)	(D)	(D)	(D)	(D)	(D)	(D)
Miscellaneous store retailers	5,416	(D)	(D)	(D)	(D)	(D)	6,668	9,046
Non-store retailers	1,161	1,488	1,232	835	1,522	1,228	1,003	642

(D) Suppressed to avoid disclosure of data of individual companies.

Source: Bureau of Economic Analysis.

Part B
Report by the WTO Secretariat

Chart 4.12 FDI in retail trade in the United States, by country of ultimate beneficiary owner, 2017

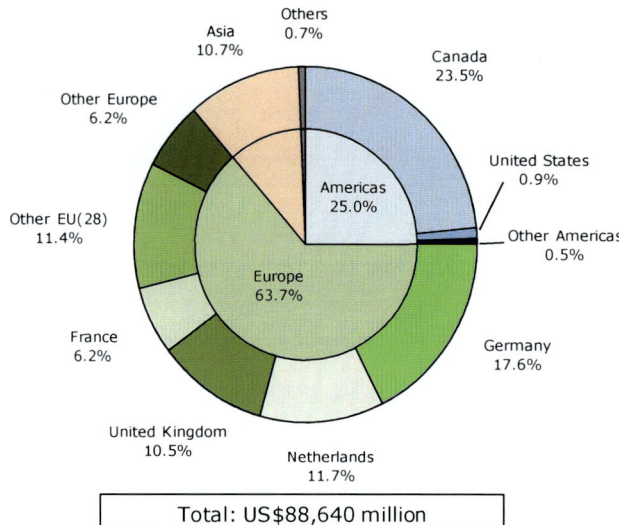

Total: US$88,640 million

Source: WTO Secretariat calculations, based on data from the Bureau of Economic Analysis.

Table 4.19 Selected data for majority-owned U.S. affiliates of foreign multinational enterprises, 2010, 2012 and 2015

	Number of affiliates with assets, sales, or net income (+/-) greater than US$20 million			Total assets (US$ million)			Number of employees ('000)		
	2010ᵃ	2012	2015	2010	2012	2015	2010	2012	2015
Retail trade	**104**	**101**	**113**	**81,841**	**90,101**	**115,816**	**485**	**527**	**614**
Food and beverage stores	16	17	16	35,405	39,315	41,243	280	302	305
Other	88	84	97	46,436	50,787	74,573	206	225	309
Motor vehicle and parts dealers	7	7	9	1,343	1,482	1,659	4	4	3
Furniture and home furnishings stores	3	3	5	(D)	4,009	4,777	J	24	29
Electronics and appliance stores	4	3	4	191	196	832	1	1	2
Building material and garden equipment and supplies dealers	3	2	2	(D)	(D)	(D)	1	1	1
Health and personal care stores	4	5	6	(D)	(D)	(D)	K	K	K
Gasoline stations	4	5	4	4,235	4,035	(D)	K	K	K
Clothing and clothing accessories stores	39	31	37	19,556	20,448	30,751	77	87	142
Sporting goods, hobby, book, and music stores	2	2	2	53	360	364	0	1	2
General merchandise stores	3	1	2	52	(D)	(D)	0	I	J
Miscellaneous store retailers	7	6	7	8,067	(D)	11,594	16	16	20
Non-store retailers	12	19	19	1,935	1,934	1,576	10	7	5

a   For 2010, number of affiliates with assets, sales, or net income (+/-) greater than US$15 million.

(D) Suppressed to avoid the disclosure of data of individual companies.

Note: Letters in the employment cells correspond to the following ranges of employees: A-1 to 499; F-500 to 999; G-1,000 to 2,499; H-2,500 to 4,999; I-5,000 to 9,999; J-10,000 to 24,999; K-25,000 to 49,999; L-50,000 to 99,999; and M-100,000 or more.

Source: Bureau of Economic Analysis.

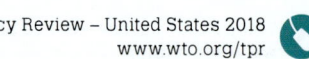

Table 4.20 Retail trade services supplied to U.S. persons by foreign MNEs through their MOUSAs, 2010-15

(US$ million)

	2010	2011	2012	2013	2014	2015
Retail trade	37,432	41,040	44,535	46,427	52,055	55,266
General merchandise stores	..	..	..	..	1,593	1,645
Clothing and clothing accessories stores	..	..	..	..	11,702	12,981
Food and beverage stores	19,296	20,382	21,241	22,050	24,034	25,087
Non-store retailers	..	..	..	..	1,128	990
Other retail trade	..	..	..	..	13,599	14,563
As a share of the total of retail trade services supplied to U.S. persons by MOUSAs[a]	7.5	8.1	8.4	8.5	9.6	9.7

.. Not available.

a See note "a" in Table 4.22.

MNEs: Multinational enterprises; MOUSAs: Majority-owned U.S. affiliates.

Source: Bureau of Economic Analysis.

Chart 4.13 Retail services supplied to U.S. persons by foreign MNEs through their MOUSAs, by country, 2015

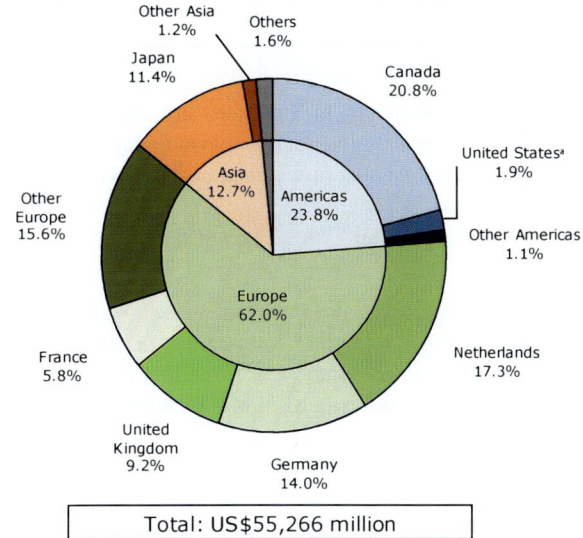

Other Asia 1.2%
Others 1.6%
Japan 11.4%
Canada 20.8%
Asia 12.7%
Americas 23.8%
United States[a] 1.9%
Other Europe 15.6%
Other Americas 1.1%
Europe 62.0%
France 5.8%
Netherlands 17.3%
United Kingdom 9.2%
Germany 14.0%

Total: US$55,266 million

a Contains data for U.S. affiliates that have a foreign parent but whose ultimate beneficial owner is a U.S. person.

Source: WTO Secretariat calculations, based on data from the Bureau of Economic Analysis.

or provide significant assistance in the operation of the business; and (c) the franchisor requires a minimum payment of at least US$500, adjusted every four years (US$570 effective 1 July 2016), during the first six months of operations. The Rule covers only the offer or sale of franchises to be located in the United States and its territories.

Concerning the trademark element, a franchise must grant the right to operate a business that is identified or associated with the franchisor's trademark, or to offer, sell, or distribute goods, services, or commodities that are identified or associated with the franchisor's trademark. With respect to the significant control and assistance elements, the franchisor's control

or assistance must relate to the franchisee's overall method of operation. Significant types of control include: (a) site approval for new businesses; (b) site design or appearance requirements; (c) hours of operation; (d) production techniques; (e) accounting practices; (f) personnel policies; (g) promotional campaigns requiring franchisee participation or financial contribution; (h) restrictions on customers; and (i) locale or area of operation.[155] Significant types of assistance include: (a) formal sales, repair, or business training programmes; (b) establishing accounting systems; (c) furnishing management, marketing, or personnel advice; (d) selecting site locations; (e) furnishing system wide networks and websites; and (f) furnishing a detailed operating manual.[156] Regarding the minimum payment

Chart 4.14 Franchise services trade, 2009-16

(US$ million)

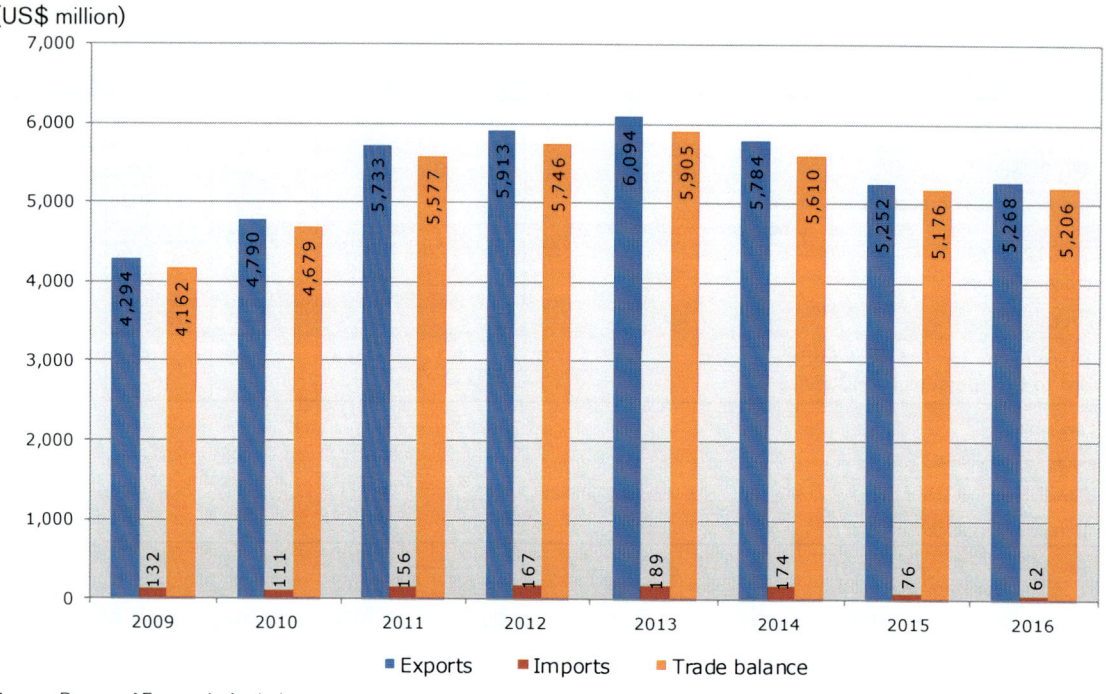

Source: Bureau of Economic Analysis.

requirement, it may include: (a) the initial franchise fee; (b) rent; (c) advertising assistance; (d) equipment and supplies; (e) training; (f) security deposits; (g) escrow deposits; (h) nonrefundable bookkeeping charges; (i) promotional literature; (j) equipment rental; and (k) continuing royalties on sales.[157]

There are a number of exemptions to the scope of the Franchise Rule.[158] The fractional franchise exemption applies when, at the start of the relationship: i) the franchisee, or its directors or officers, has more than two years of experience in the same type of business; and ii) the parties anticipate that the sales arising from the relationship will not exceed 20% of the franchisee's total sales during the first year of operation. The Rule also exempts from its coverage leased department arrangements, in which an independent retailer sells its own goods and services from premises leased from a larger retailer in that retailer's store. The amended Rule expressly exempts petroleum marketers and resellers covered by the Petroleum Marketing Practices Act (PMPA). The Rule exempts franchise offers and sales where the initial investment is at least US$1 million, to be updated every four years (US$1,143,100 effective 1 July 2016), excluding the cost of unimproved land and any franchisor (or affiliate) financing. Additionally, the Franchise Rule exempts franchise offers and sales to large entities that have been in business for at least five years and have a net worth of at least US$5 million, also to be updated every four years (US$5,715,500 effective 1 July 2016). The 2007 amended Rule added a new exemption for franchise sales to the officers, directors, general partners, managers, and owners of a franchisor.

There are also exclusions to the Rule that apply to employeremployee relationships, general partner relationships, cooperative associations, and certification and testing services. The Rule also excludes trademark licensing arrangements in which a single licensee is granted the right to use the trademark.

Under the Rule, franchisors are responsible for preparing disclosure documents, and furnishing them to prospective franchisees at least 14 calendar days before a buyer signs a binding agreement, or makes any payment to the franchisor in connection with a proposed franchise sale. The disclosure document must contain information on a number of legal and financial issues. It must also provide information on each of the franchisor's principal trademarks and their registration with the USPTO, as well as on ownership rights or licences in other types of intellectual property (IP), and on any legal proceedings, settlements, and restrictions that may impact the franchisee's ability to use such IP.[159]

There is no federal registration of franchises, as the Franchise Rule does not provide for any registration of a franchise with the FTC.[160] However, several states require that franchises register before operating in the state; registrations are generally valid for one year.[161] In several of these states, registration involves a review of the FDD by a franchise regulator. Some states require that all advertising for the sale of franchises must be filed with the state before they are published.[162] The transfer of a franchise is allowed in all states; in some states it is even illegal for a franchisor to refuse to allow a transfer of the franchise without good cause.[163]

Construction services

Market overview

The construction sector (NAICS 23) includes establishments primarily engaged in the construction of buildings or engineering projects (highways and utility systems). It also comprises establishments primarily engaged in the preparation of sites for new construction, and establishments primarily engaged in subdividing land for sale as building sites. The share of GDP represented by construction and related services has been increasing in recent years. Construction services accounted for 4.3% of GDP in 2017, up from 3.6% in 2010 (Table 4.21). Construction activities, especially residential construction, were severely affected in the aftermath of the subprime crisis, but have resumed growing since, as the economy recovered and employment increased. This progression also benefitted from the quantitative easing policy and the consequent low interest rates in the aftermath of the crisis.

Construction is an important employer. In the first quarter of 2018, it employed an estimated 7.14 million people, 64% of which were specialty (construction) trade contractors (Table 4.22).[164] The number of construction companies declined in the wake of the subprime crisis, and reached a minimum in 2013; however, it has been increasing ever since. The sector is constituted by a large number of medium and small enterprises, alongside very large companies. Table 4.22 describes, for various subsectors of construction services, the evolution of employment and of the number of establishments between 2010 and 2018.

The United States ran a surplus in construction services from 2009 to 2011; the balance turned into a deficit in the 2012-2016 period, with the lowest point in 2013, but the gap between exports and imports has been closing since then, and in 2016 the deficit shrank to US$148 million (Chart 4.15). This has been accompanied, however, by a substantial decline in trade flows.

Despite running an overall trade deficit in construction services, the United States runs a surplus with some of its major trading partners, as shown in Chart 4.16.

The FDI position in the U.S. construction sector more than doubled between 2010 and 2017, when it reached US$23,290 million; about half of the investment was in the construction of buildings (Table 4.23).

While the number of majority-owned U.S. affiliates of foreign multinational enterprises with assets, sales or net income greater than US$20 million in the construction sector has declined between 2010 and 2015, both the total assets and the total employment of majority-owned U.S. affiliates of foreign multinational enterprises have increased (Table 4.24).

The supply of construction services by MNEs through their MOUSAs has being increasing in recent years. Table 4.25 provides detailed data on construction services supplied between 2010 and 2015.

Table 4.21 Value added in construction, 2010-17

(US$ billion and % of total GDP)

	2010	2011	2012	2013	2014	2015	2016	2017
Value (US$ billion)	542	547	584	621	674	740	793	826
Share of total GDP (%)	3.6	3.5	3.6	3.7	3.9	4.1	4.3	4.3

Source: Bureau of Economic Analysis.

Table 4.22 Employment and number of establishments in construction, 2010-18Q1

	2010	2011	2012	2013	2014	2015	2016	2017	2018[a]
NAICS code/description	Number of employees ('000)								
23 Construction	5,518	5,530	5,646	5,857	6,149	6,459	6,726	6,954	7,141
236 Construction of buildings	1,229	1,221	1,240	1,287	1,359	1,424	1,492	1,538	1,578
237 Heavy and civil engineering construction	825	836	868	885	911	937	952	988	1,003
238 Specialty trade contractors	3,464	3,473	3,537	3,685	3,878	4,097	4,281	4,429	4,561
	Number of establishments[b]								
23 Construction	798,962	769,450	753,279	749,728	757,846	768,112	780,970	787,840	..
236 Construction of buildings	235,888	225,167	220,049	219,747	223,464	228,044	233,368	236,657	..
237 Heavy and civil engineering construction	58,997	57,610	56,847	56,673	56,681	56,486	56,591	56,293	..
238 Specialty trade contractors	504,077	486,674	476,383	473,309	477,702	483,582	491,011	494,890	..

.. Not available.

a Data for the first quarter of 2018.

b Data for the first quarter of 2017.

Source: WTO Secretariat calculations, based on data from the Bureau of Labour Statistics.

Chart 4.15 Construction services trade, 2009-16

(US$ million)

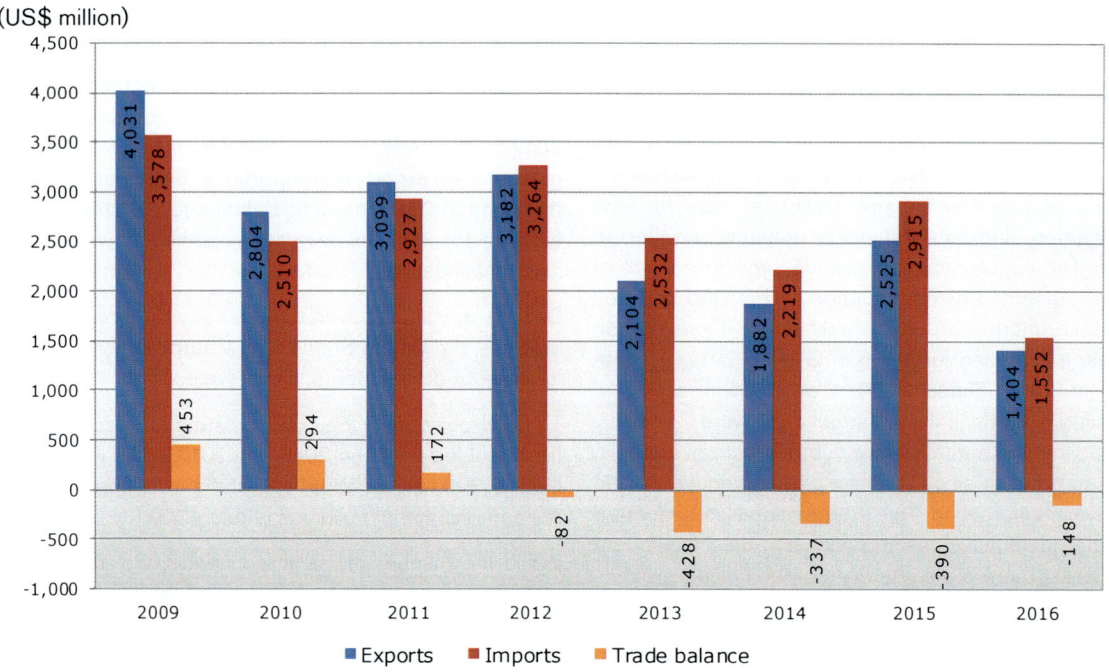

Source: Bureau of Economic Analysis.

Chart 4.16 Construction: cross-border exports, imports, and trade balance, by major trading partners, 2016

(US$ million)

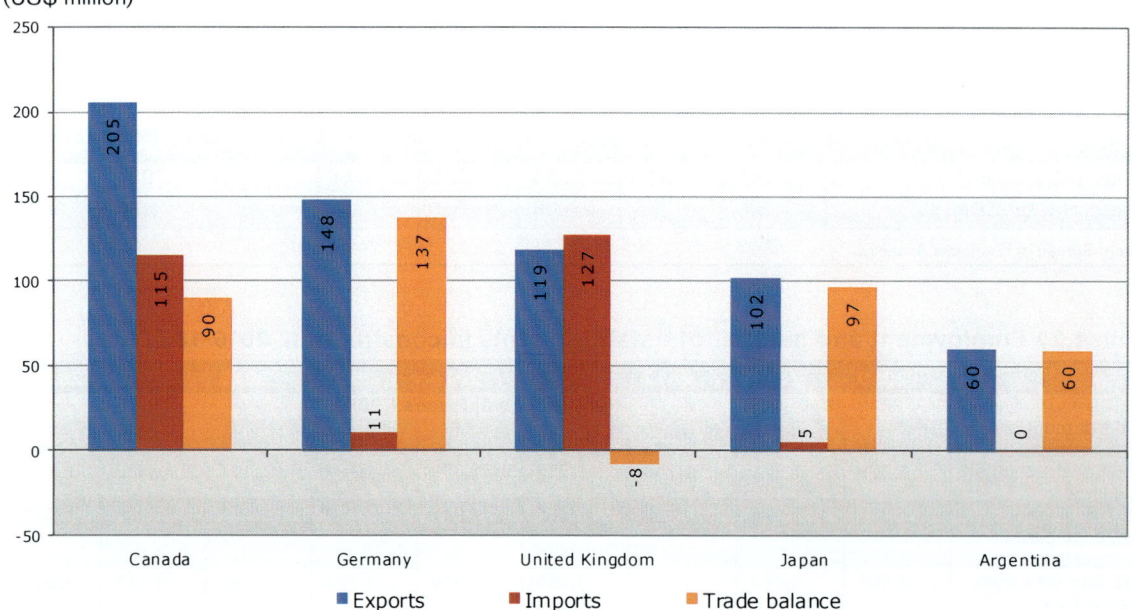

Note: In the case of Argentina, U.S. imports are between zero and US$500,000.

Source: Bureau of Economic Analysis.

Regulatory regime

The construction industry in the United States is regulated by a number of public agencies; however, there is no central body that oversees this regulation. There is no federal construction licensing in the United States. Contractors are licensed in most, but not all, states. The licensing requirement in most states concentrates on the business entity undertaking the construction work. In some states, however, workers conducting certain specific tasks where there can be safety concerns are subject to regulation, and hence licensing requirements. Contractor licensing varies from state to state. In several

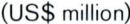

Table 4.23 Foreign Direct Investment position in construction in the United States, 2010-17

(US$ million)

	2010	2011	2012	2013	2014	2015	2016	2017
Construction	10,359	10,015	12,320	18,032	20,970	23,178	24,299	23,290
Construction of buildings	4,360	3,750	5,100	8,249	9,444	10,527	12,094	12,798
Heavy and civil engineering construction	5,250	5,299	6,365	8,809	10,260	11,509	10,854	9,079
Special trade contractors	750	965	855	974	1,265	1,142	1,350	1,414

Source: Bureau of Economic Analysis.

Table 4.24 Selected data for MOUSAs of foreign MNEs in construction, 2010, 2012 and 2015

	No. of affiliates with assets, sales, or net income (+/-) greater than US$20 million			Total assets (US$ million)			Number of employees ('000)		
	2010[a]	2012	2015	2010	2012	2015	2010	2012	2015
Construction	104	88	94	32,117	35,853	60,282	70	68	92
Construction of buildings	47	40	45	18,153	22,255	29,382	37	37	41
Heavy and civil engineering construction	40	34	35	11,883	12,062	29,014	26	24	42
Special trade contractors	17	14	14	2,081	1,535	1,886	8	7	9

a   For 2010, affiliates with assets, sales, or net income (+/-) greater than US$15 million.

Source: Bureau of Economic Analysis.

Table 4.25 Construction services supplied to U.S. persons by foreign MNEs through their MOUSAs, 2010-15

(US$ million and %)

	2010	2011	2012	2013	2014	2015
Construction services[a]	1,969	2,058	2,122	3,338	5,012	5,365
As a share of total services supplied to U.S. persons in the construction sector by foreign MNEs[b]	0.2	0.2	0.2	0.3	0.5	0.5

a   Because sales resulting from construction activities are recorded as sales of goods rather than sales of services, the sales of services through MOUSAs in construction represent sales in secondary, non-construction industries.

b   See note "a" in Table 4.22.

MNEs: Multinational enterprises; MOUSAs: Majority-owned U.S. affiliates.

Source: Bureau of Economic Analysis.

states, not abiding by licensing requirements may result in a civil or even penal action. Also, not abiding by licensing laws may result in unlicensed contractors not being able to sue in court for payments they are owed.

Although construction *per se* is not federally regulated, safety issues are. Safety regulations concerning the construction industry are enforced by the Occupational Safety and Health Administration at the federal level, or by equivalent state agencies. All states require contractors to have workers' compensation insurance. There are also a number of environment-related laws that must be followed, including those related to asbestos, lead, and industrial waste.[165]

The construction industry has few economic barriers to entry, and there are no restrictions on the repatriation of capital or profits. Market access conditions vary somewhat, depending on whether the project is public or private. Private construction activities are open to foreigners with few limitations, while public construction

activities are subject to Buy American provisions and to the provisions of the GPA and FTAs (p. 43).

Private construction projects are market-driven. Construction services are priced freely, usually following a cost-plus scheme, where the contractor is paid for all of its costs plus an additional percentage for overhead and profit. An alternative pricing method is the cost-plus Gmax, where the price may not exceed a guaranteed maximum price. Larger infrastructure projects are often undertaken by joint ventures of major contractors, in order to diversify risk.

GATS and bilateral commitments

The United States made full commitments for modes 2 (consumption abroad) and 3 (commercial presence), for both market access and national treatment, for construction and related engineering services, except marine dredging. Mode 1 is scheduled as technically unfeasible, and hence unbound. The mode 4 market access commitments refer to the horizontal section of the schedule, and include a reservation for an in-state office requirement for contractors in Michigan.

The commitments are the same in the United States-Jordan FTA which has a positive listing structure. In its other FTAs, the United States maintains its GATS-level market access commitments through cross reference; there are no sector-specific limitations listed for other obligations, taken on a negative-list basis.

Transport

Air transport and airports

Air transport

Air transport policy formulation is the responsibility of the Office of the Assistant Secretary for Aviation and International Affairs under the United States Department of Transportation (USDOT). The Department of State conducts the negotiation of international air transport agreements, in consultation with the Departments of Transportation and Commerce. The Federal Aviation Administration (FAA) is responsible for safety issues, regulating U.S. commercial space aviation, and monitoring U.S. and foreign air carriers operating in U.S. territory. The Air Traffic Organization (ATO), under the FAA, provides air navigation services in the airspace of the United States and large portions of the Atlantic and Pacific Oceans and the Gulf of Mexico.[166] The Department of Homeland Security Transportation Security Administration is responsible for the regulation and oversight of air transport security in the United States, at U.S. airports, and for all aircraft operations to, from, and within the United States.

Aviation accounted for 10.6 million jobs, with earnings of US$446.8 billion, contributed US$1.6 trillion annually to the U.S. economy, and was responsible for 5.1% of GDP in 2014.[167] The FAA guides approximately 26 million flights every year, consisting of 15.6 million instrument flight rule flights (radar assisted) and 10.4 million visual flight rule flights (low flying planes). It manages 517 control towers and 24 air route traffic control centres, with 14,050 air traffic controllers. After a number of mergers in the industry, American Airlines, Delta Air Lines, Southwest Airlines, and United Airlines are the four largest passenger carriers in the domestic market. Scheduled U.S. passenger airlines reported an after-tax net profit of US$15.5 billion in 2017, up from US$14 billion in 2016.[168]

Air freight is generally used for perishable and/or high value goods. Although air freight accounted for less than 0.1% of total freight in terms of volume, it represented 6.2% of total freight value in 2015. In 2015, total freight transported by air reached US$1.18 trillion in value terms, with international trade via air freight accounting for 88% of that figure (at US$1.03 trillion). The share of exports and imports carried via air was 26.9% (US$459 billion) and 23.4% (US$573 billion), respectively. The Bureau of Transportation Statistics estimates that the total value of air freight may reach US$5.09 trillion in 2045.[169] UPS and FedEx are the world's two largest air cargo carriers (p. 149).

Regulations concerning air transport have not been substantially modified since the last Review; they are contained in Title 14 of the Code of Federal Regulations.[170] Statutory requirements, like cabotage, remain in place so that domestic air services can be provided only by U.S. carriers, which are required to be owned and controlled by U.S. citizens. Non-U.S. citizens are allowed to hold up to 25% of the voting interest of any airline providing domestic services. Additionally, there are nationality requirements for the management: the airline's president and at least two thirds of the Board of Directors and other managing officers must be U.S. citizens. Over time, USDOT precedent has allowed for up to 49% equity, or non-voting stock, if an Open Skies air services agreement is in effect between the United States and the foreign investor's country of origin. Crews engaged in domestic air passenger and freight service must be U.S. nationals or U.S. residents.

Two separate authorizations from the USDOT are required to provide air transport services as a U.S. air carrier. The first one is an economic authorization from the Office of the Secretary of Transportation, and the second one is a safety authorization from the FAA. Any authorization granted by the Secretary of Transportation is conditional on the operator satisfying safety and security requirements.

Government-financed transportation of passengers or cargo must be provided by U.S. air carriers or a U.S. carrier code-share on a foreign airline, as mandated by the Fly America Act (49 U.S.C. 40118). This restriction may be waived when the United States has entered into bilateral or multilateral agreements that allow the provision of such services by foreign air carriers. Currently, five bilateral agreements (outside code-shares), those with Australia, the European Union, Japan, Saudi Arabia (cargo only) and Switzerland, allow federally funded transportation services for travel and cargo movements to use foreign carriers under certain circumstances.[171] Government-financed transportation is permitted on foreign carriers operating without a U.S. carrier code when no U.S. carrier is serving the market. For the last 25 years, the U.S. has adopted the policy to engage with international aviation partners to achieve Open Skies Agreements (OSAs).[172] The United States currently has OSAs, as defined by the USDOT[173], with 125 trading partners.[174] These OSAs cover, among other issues, market access, pricing, and commercial opportunities (i.e. including codesharing, self-handling, user charges, fair competition, and intermodal rights).

In order to ensure the provision of air transport services to areas of the country where it would not otherwise be profitable to do so, the USDOT implements one subsidy programme and one grant programme: the Essential Air Service (EAS) Program and the Small Community Air Service Development Program (SCASDP), respectively. The EAS, codified at 49 U.S.C. §§ 41731–41748, is a programme that aims at guaranteeing a minimum level of scheduled air services to a limited universe of eligible small communities that were generally served by certificated air carriers before deregulation in 1978.[175] This generally entails subsidizing two round-trips a day with 50-seat aircraft, or additional frequencies with aircraft with nine or fewer seats, usually to large or mediumhub airports in the 48 contiguous states, Hawaii, and Puerto Rico, and varying service levels, from once per month to daily services, within Alaska. As of May 2018, there were 111 subsidized EAS communities in the 48 contiguous states, Hawaii, and Puerto Rico, with annual contract subsidy rates totalling US$288.526 million.[176] The Department of Transportation provides the subsidy directly to air carriers on a per-flight-completed basis.

To remain eligible for EASs, communities must meet various eligibility criteria, including subsidy caps and other requirements. Under the Department of Transportation and Related Agencies Appropriations Act of 2000, the USDOT may not provide an EAS subsidy that exceeds US$200 per passenger to communities located within the 48 contiguous states, unless these communities are located more than 210 miles from the nearest large- or medium-hub airport. A Final Notice of Enforcement Policy on the US$200 cap was issued in October 2014, whereby all communities receiving subsidized EASs had until 30 September 2015 to ensure compliance with the US$200 subsidy cap or possibly face termination of subsidy eligibility.[177] The FAA Modernization and Reform Act of 2012 amended 49 U.S.C. § 41731(a)(1)(B), to change the definition of eligible place for the purpose of receiving an EAS. According to the amendment, to be eligible, a community must maintain an average of 10 enplanements or more per service day, as determined by the Secretary of Transportation, during the most recent fiscal year beginning after 30 September 2012.[178] The Act exempts locations in Alaska and Hawaii, and communities that are more than 175 driving miles from the nearest large- or medium-hub airport.[179] The Secretary of Transportation also has the authority to waive the 10-enplanement standard, on an annual basis, if the community can demonstrate that the reason the location averages fewer than 10 enplanements per day is due to a temporary decline in enplanements.

The Alternate Essential Air Service Program (AEAS) provides more flexibility to communities to craft their own air service, typically with public charter operators, through a grant of specified funds, for a defined period of time.[180]

The SCASDP, a grant programme designed to help small communities address air service and airfare issues, has a broader eligibility scope than the EAS. In particular, applicants for SCASDP grants self-identify their air service deficiencies, and propose appropriate solutions. In general, an applicant cannot be larger than a small-hub airport. Assistance under the SCASDP is provided in the form of a reimbursable grant to the benefiting community. The programme can involve, among other things, revenue guarantees, financial assistance for marketing programmes, start-up costs and studies. The SCASDP program is limited to a maximum of 40 grant awards, with no more than 4 grants per state, in each year the programme is funded. There are no limits on the amounts of individual awards: the amounts awarded vary according to the merits of the proposals selected. In past years, the USDOT's individual grant sizes have ranged from US$20,000 to nearly US$1.6 million.[181] In FY2017, the SCASDP offered a total of US$10 million in grants to 16 local communities.

Airports

There were 19,576 airports in the United States in 2016; of these, 5,116 were public airports and 14,168 were private, generally smaller, airports; the rest were mostly military airports.[182] Most public-use airports with commercial services are publicly owned, either by state or local governments, or local authorities. There were 9.44 million scheduled flights in 2016, and 41.4 billion pounds (18.8 billion kilograms) of freight was transported.

Airport ownership in the United States may be private or public. However, general legal complexities at the federal, state, and local levels, plus restrictions on the use of revenues, have meant that there has been little incentive for the private sector to own an airport.[183] The United States offers grants for the planning and development of public-use airports included in the National Plan of Integrated Airport Systems (NPIAS)[184] through the Airport Improvement Program (AIP).[185] The share of costs covered by grants from the AIP depends on the type of work and the size of the airport: it can be up to 93.75% of eligible costs[186] for small primary and general aviation airports. In FY2017, a total of US$3.75 billion was authorized for the AIP in the Federal Aviation Administration Reauthorization Act of 2016.[187]

Airport infrastructure projects that are funded under the AIP remain subject to Buy American provisions.[188] (49 U.S.C. § 50101) which require that all steel and manufactured goods used in AIP-funded projects be produced in the United States. However, under 49 U.S.C. 50101, the FAA may grant a discretionary waiver when: 60% domestic content is reached and final assembly of the facility or equipment has occurred in the United States; the steel and goods produced in the United States are not produced in a sufficient and reasonably available amount or are not of a satisfactory quality; or when using domestic products increases the cost of the overall project by more than 25%.[189]

Although policies to promote airport privatization have been in place for years, the results so far have been modest. In 1997, Congress established the Airport Privatization Pilot Program (APPP) through the Federal Aviation Reauthorization Act of 1996 (49 U.S.C. 47134, P.L. 104-264), to increase private participation in airport operations and development. The APPP allows private companies to own, manage, lease and develop public airports. The APPP also permits airport sponsors to be exempted from certain federal requirements, such as

Part B
Report by the WTO Secretariat

repayment of federal grants, return of property acquired with federal assistance, and the use of proceeds from airport's sale or lease to be used exclusively for airport purposes.

The FAA Modernization and Reform Act of 2012 (P.L. 112-95) increased the number of airports participating in the APPP from 5 to 10 in 2012; of these, only 1 large-hub commercial airport may participate in the programme, and that airport may only be leased but not sold. Also, one of the participating airports must be a general aviation airport.[190] The APPP has had very limited success in increasing the number of privately-run airports.[191] As of April 2017, among 10 participating airports, 4 had been privatized (as compared to 2 in July 2016), namely: the Luis Muñoz Marin International Airport (San Juan, Puerto Rico), for which the privatization had been approved; and the Hendry County Airglades Airport (Clewiston, FL), St. Louis Lambert International Airport (St. Louis, MO) and Westchester County Airport (White Plains, NY), for all of which a preliminary application had been accepted.[192]

The operation and management of airports may be fully carried out by the airports' owners, or partly or wholly by a third party through outsourcing and management contracts including for specific facilities.

The United States has GATS commitments with respect to aircraft repairs and maintenance, and has scheduled MFN exemptions with regard to the sale and marketing of air transport services and the operation and regulation of Computer Reservation System (CRS) services.

The United States is a contracting party to the WTO Plurilateral Agreement on Civil Aircraft. Thus, national treatment is granted to the acquisition of civil aircraft and related articles originating from other parties of the Agreement.

Maritime transport, port services, and shipbuilding

Maritime transport

Waterborne trade in the United States amounted to 2.08 billion metric tons in 2016 (up from 1,75 billion in 2015). International waterborne trade totalled 1.28 billion metric tons, while domestic waterborne trade was 800 million metric tons, including intraport and intra-territory traffic.[193] The size of the U.S. flag privately-owned fleet of self-propelled, cargo-carrying vessels of 1,000 gross tons and above has slightly increased: as of early June 2018, there were a total of 181 privatelyowned vessels (as compared to 171 in 2016) with a capacity of 8.2 million deadweight tons (as compared to 7.9 in 2016).[194] Some 72% of the volume and 44% of the value of goods that the United States imports and exports move by water transportation.[195]

The Maritime Administration (MARAD), under the Department of Transportation, is the agency responsible for developing commercial maritime regulations and programmes that ensure the viability of the U.S. Merchant Marine, and promote the use of waterborne transportation

and its integration with other segments of the transportation system. MARAD is charged with carrying out the national policies established by the Merchant Marine Act of 1936 (see below). MARAD's mission is to improve, strengthen and promote the maritime transportation system to meet economic, environmental, and security needs. MARAD also advocates for the maritime industry; manages assets in support of the Department of Defense (USDOD), including maintaining a fleet of government-owned cargo vessels; administers, in partnership with USDOD, the Voluntary Intermodal Sealift Agreement (VISA) emergency preparedness programme; administers and funds the Maritime Security Program (MSP); operates the U.S. Merchant Marine Academy (USMMA); provides training ships, funding and other support for the six State Maritime Academies (SMAs) (Maine, Massachusetts, New York, Texas, California and Michigan); and administers the Federal Ship Financing Program (Title XI).[196]

The Federal Maritime Commission (FMC) is responsible for regulating ocean-borne liner transport, including ocean transportation intermediaries, and for supervising the collective activities of shipping lines that are not subject to U.S. anti-trust laws for both U.S. and foreign operators of liner shipping services with fixed schedules. The U.S. Coast Guard (USCG), under the Department of Homeland Security, is in charge of regulating maritime transport, including vessel safety and security, and environmental protection, and of licensing mariners.

The Merchant Marine Act of 1936, as amended, is one of the principal laws governing maritime transport. The Act provides for the U.S. government's support of the U.S. Merchant Marine. It defines maritime transport policy by declaring it necessary for the national defense and the development of the domestic and foreign commerce of the United States to have a merchant marine:

- Sufficient to carry the waterborne domestic commerce and a substantial part of the waterborne export and import foreign commerce of the United States, and to provide a shipping service essential for maintaining the flow of the waterborne domestic and foreign commerce at all times;

- Capable of serving as a naval and military auxiliary in time of war or national emergency;

- Owned and operated as vessels of the United States by citizens of the United States;

- Composed of the best-equipped, safest, and most suitable types of vessels constructed in the United States, and manned with a trained and efficient citizen personnel; and

- Supplemented by efficient facilities for building and repairing vessels.

Restrictions to cabotage services of both goods and passengers remain in place, under the coastwise trade laws. Section 27 of the Merchant Marine Act of 1920, commonly referred to as the Jones Act (46 U.S.C. § 55102), reserves cargo service between two points in

the United States (including most of its territories and possessions)[197], either directly or via a foreign port, for ships that are registered and built (or repaired) in the United States, and that are at least 75% owned by a U.S. corporation, and on which 100% of the officers and 75% of the crew are U.S. citizens.[198] In general, the same requirements apply to the domestic passenger service under the Passenger Vessel Service Act of 1886 (46 U.S.C. § 55103). As of 1 June 2018, 99 ocean-going, self-propelled, cargocarrying and privately-owned vessels of 1,000 gross tons and above, with a dead weight of 4.9 billion deadweight tons (DWT), qualified as coastwise-eligible Jones Act vessels.[199] Although the Jones Act places limitations on cargo services, it does not prevent foreign companies from establishing shipping companies in the United States, as long as they meet the Act's requirements regarding citizenship, crew and operation of domestic-built vessels.[200] Foreign-owned U.S. companies may also own and operate ships flying the U.S. flag in international service.

Cargo carried on routes covered by the Jones Act, including coastwise, intercoastal, Great Lakes, and inland shipping, reached 795 metric tons in 2016. Coastwise trade accounted for 19.2% of the Jones Act trade on a tonnage basis in 2016; 93% of coastwise trade was petroleum.[201] Some 119 million passengers were also transported on domestic routes in 2016.[202]

Requests for waivers of the provisions of the coastwise laws are made to the Commissioner of the U.S. Customs and Border Protection (CBP). With the exception of waivers requested by the Secretary of Defense, CBP is required to consult with MARAD and, as a matter of practice, also consults with other interested agencies before a waiver is granted or denied. Waivers of the Jones Act are granted by the Secretary of Homeland Security only "in the interest of national defence", and, consequently, only in "extremely rare" cases. One such waiver was granted in the wake of Hurricane Sandy. Under the Defense Authorization Act of 2013, MARAD is required to publish Jones Act vessel availability determinations not later than 48 hours after the determination is made.

MARAD has responsibility for the Small Passenger Vessels Waiver Program, under which it grants approximately 75 waivers of the U.S. build requirement each year to foreign vessels, or vessels of unknown build, to operate in the United States as commercial passenger vessels.[203] To qualify for the Program, the vessel must be at least three years old, and must carry no more than 12 passengers. Activities such as carriage of cargo, commercial fishing, towing, dredging and salvage do not qualify for this Program. The vessel must be owned by a U.S. citizen. The intended use of the vessel must be published in the Federal Register; after the publication, MARAD will determine if the issuance of the waiver will cause an "undue adverse effect" on existing operators and shipbuilders. If that is not the case, the waiver is approved. Most waiver requests are approved.[204]

Once obtained, the waiver stays with the vessel, even if it is sold. The waiver does not apply to any vessel documentation, vessel manning or vessel inspection requirements. Once a waiver is received, the applicant should file for a Coastwise Trade Endorsement for the passenger trade with the U.S. Coast Guard (USCG). MARAD no longer issues waivers for all coasts of the United States: the waiver request must list all states of intended operation.

U.S. law (46 U.S.C. § 55108) allows MARAD to make determinations permitting the use of foreign-built launch barges under specific circumstances (i.e. when the launch of an exceptionally large oil rig or offshore platform requires the use of a foreign-built launch barge), and after an application and review process. This is done under the Launch Barge Program. Regulations require that the platform owner or operator notify MARAD at least 21 months prior to the contemplated use of a foreign-built launch barge.[205] MARAD is also authorized to make determinations under P.L. 111281 allowing the use of foreign anchor handling vessels (used to position mobile offshore drilling units) if no U.S.-flag vessels are available, and if the companies wanting to use foreign vessels have contracts in place to bring in replacement U.S.-flag vessels. This applies to operations in the Beaufort Sea and the Chukchi Sea adjacent to Alaska. Since the provision was passed in 2006, MARAD has issued decision letters allowing three foreign-flag vessels into service for a limited length of time.[206]

Preferences are accorded to U.S.-flag vessels under certain acts to provide a revenue base that will retain and encourage a privately owned and operated U.S.-flag merchant marine.[207] Public Resolution No. 17 of 1934 requires that exports of goods that benefit from export loans or credit guarantees from EXIM Bank be carried in U.S-flag vessels, although the vessels of a recipient country may be granted access to 50% of those cargoes, where there is no discriminatory treatment against U.S.-flag carriers. Waivers may be granted, subject to reciprocal treatment for U.S-flag vessels by the recipient country. In practice, a sizeable number of foreign-owned vessels have been allowed to transport government-generated cargo in the past few years.[208] Under the Military Cargo Preference Act of 1904, 100% of military cargo must be transported in U.S.-flag carriers at rates that are not excessive or otherwise unreasonable; and cargo preference applies not only to the end product but also to component parts.[209] The Cargo Preference Act of 1954 requires that at least 50% of the gross tonnage of all government-generated cargo be transported on privately owned, domestically flagged commercial vessels, to the extent that such vessels are available at fair and reasonable rates. The Act also requires that shipments from or to the Strategic Petroleum Reserve use domestically flagged tankers for at least 50% of oil transport.

The United States also administers two maritime transport programmes related to national defense:

The Maritime Security Program (MSP) and the Voluntary Intermodal Sealift Agreement (VISA) program.

The Maritime Security Program (MSP), created by the Maritime Security Act of 1996 to replace the operating-differential subsidy (ODS), supports the U.S.-flag merchant marine by providing fixed payments to U.S.-flag vessel operators.[210] The Program was originally established to run from FY1996 through FY2005, and provide funding of up to US$100 million annually for up to 47 vessels. The stated purpose of the MSP is assuring that a limited number of militarily useful vessels from the international commercial fleet are available to meet the nation's sealift requirements in time of war or national emergencies. The National Defense Authorization Act (NDAA), which contained the Maritime Security Act of 2003, reauthorized the MSP for FY2006 through FY2015, and increased the size of the Maritime Security Fleet receiving stipend payments to 60 vessels. In January 2013, the President signed the NDAA of 2013 (P.L. 112-239), extending the MSP to the period from FY2016 through FY2025.[211] Section 3504 of the National Defense Authorization Act for FY2016 (P.L. 114-92) and Division O, Title 1, Section 101(e) of the Consolidated Appropriations Act 2016 (P.L. 114-113) revised the annual MSP payment schedule for FY2016 through FY2021. The authorized funding for FY2017 was just short of US$300 million, while that for FY2018-20 is US$300 million per FY. All MSP dry cargo ships are enrolled in the Voluntary Intermodal Sealift Agreement (VISA), while MSP tankers are enrolled in the Voluntary Tanker Agreement.[212]

The Voluntary Intermodal Sealift Agreement (VISA) program, introduced in January 1997 and sponsored by MARAD, is a partnership between the U.S. Government and the maritime industry to provide the Department of Defense (DOD) with "assured access" to commercial sealift, and intermodal capacity to support the emergency deployment and sustainment of U.S. military forces. The VISA program is authorized under the Defense Production Act of 1950, and the Maritime Security Act of 2003. The VISA program provides for a time-phased activation of state-of-the-art commercial intermodal equipment to coincide with the DOD requirements, while minimizing disruption to U.S. commercial operations.[213] The VISA program can be activated in three stages, as determined by the DOD, with each stage representing a higher level of capacity commitment. By Stage III, participants must commit at least 50% of their capacity, with the exception of participants in the MSP, who must commit 100%. Enrollment in the VISA programme is conducted on a year-round basis.[214] VISA participants get priority preference when bidding on USDOD peacetime cargo.

As of 1 June 2018, there were 100 ocean-going, self-propelled, cargo-carrying vessels of 1,000 gross tons and above in the VISA programme, with 3,706,884 DWT. MSP participants' vessel capacity made up 72.6% of the VISA capacity at the same date.[215]

U.S. and foreign operators of liner shipping services and marine terminal operators in the United States are exempt from certain antitrust laws, including the Sherman and Clayton Acts, with respect to their operations in U.S.-foreign ocean-borne trade. Under the Shipping Act of 1984, as amended by the Ocean Shipping Reform Act (OSRA) of 1998, agreements among liner operators and marine terminal operators (MTOs) to discuss, fix, or regulate transportation rates, and other conditions of service, or cooperate on operational matters, must be filed with, and examined by, the FMC. Also under the Shipping Act of 1984, ocean carriers must publish tariff rates and charges for carriage for trade with foreign countries. These rates are reviewed by the FMC, which also reviews the rates of government-controlled ocean carriers, to ensure that their rates and contracts are not unreasonably low.

Under the American Fisheries Act (AFA) of 1998, incorporated in the Omnibus Consolidated and Emergency Supplemental Appropriations Act, 1999 (P.L. 105-277), MARAD was designated as the agency responsible for ensuring compliance with the U.S. citizen ownership and control requirements for U.S.-flag fishing industry vessels of 100 feet and greater in registered length. Under the AFA, foreign investment in the fisheries of the United States is limited: in order to document a vessel with a fishery endorsement, the AFA and its implementing regulations (46 C.F.R. Part 356) require that 75% of the ownership and control of the vessel be vested in U.S. citizens, at each tier and in the aggregate. MARAD is charged with determining whether vessels of 100 feet or greater in length are owned and controlled by U.S. citizens and eligible for documentation with a fishery endorsement. In addition, MARAD must determine whether lenders are qualified to hold a preferred mortgage on fishing industry vessels; if that is not the case, the lender must utilize an approved mortgage trustee to hold the preferred mortgage for its benefit, and MARAD must review the transaction to determine whether it results in an impermissible transfer of control to a non-citizen.[216]

Under the Foreign Shipping Practices Act (FSPA, 46 U.S. Code § 42302) of 1988, the FMC is required to investigate, and take action in response to, conditions arising from foreign government measures or business practices in the U.S.-foreign shipping trades that adversely affect U.S. carriers but do not apply to foreign carriers in the United States. Section 19 of the Merchant Marine Act of 1920 authorizes the FMC to investigate, and take action to address, "unfavourable shipping conditions in U.S. foreign commerce and may impose penalties". No action was taken during the period under review.

In response to challenges identified by MARAD, a medium-run strategy was launched, in particular to meet the challenge posed by ageing ships and infrastructure, and to face foreign competition. The FMC is also engaged in a regulatory reform to evaluate existing FMC regulations and in making recommendations regarding their repeal, replacement, or modification.[217]

The United States has no maritime transport commitments under the GATS. It maintains an MFN exemption under the GATS covering restrictions on performance of longshore work by crews of foreign vessels owned and flagged in countries that similarly restrict U.S. crews on U.S.-flag vessels from longshore work.

The United States has bilateral agreements with Brazil; China; Japan; Korea, the Republic of; the Philippines; the Russian Federation; and Viet Nam.[218]

Port services

The United States has over 300 ports; they may be operated by a state, a county, a municipality, a private corporation, or a combination of these. The top 50 ports account for roughly 85% of total waterborne cargo tonnage. Port congestion, particularly in the west coast ports, continues to be a challenge, requiring an improvement in infrastructure.

MARAD, through its Strong-Ports programme, provides expertise on port finance and infrastructure, and has assisted major ports in their recent redevelopment plans. MARAD's Office of Port Infrastructure Development and Congestion Mitigation is responsible for assisting with port, terminal, waterway, and transportation network development issues, including: coordinating and managing port infrastructure projects for a variety of entities, including state, local, and territorial authorities; promoting the use of waterways and ports; and coordinating and directing studies for recommending improvements in port operation and facilities.[219]

The United States does not grant domestic preferential treatment with respect to the use of port and harbour facilities. The United States maintains an MFN exemption covering restrictions on performance of longshore work by crews of foreign vessels owned and flagged in countries that similarly restrict U.S. crews on U.S.-flag vessels from longshore work. The Immigration and Nationality Act of 1952, as amended, prohibits non-U.S.-national crewmembers from performing longshore work in the United States, but provides a reciprocity exception.

Under Title I of the Maritime Transportation Security Act of 2002 (P.L. 107-295), commercial vessels arriving in the United States from a foreign port are required to transmit electronically, in advance, information on passengers, crew, and cargo. The Maritime Transportation Security Act of 2004 amended federal shipping law to grant U.S. district courts jurisdiction to restrain violations of certain port security requirements, and authorized the Secretary of Transportation to refuse or revoke port clearance to any owner, agent, master, officer, or person in charge of a vessel that is liable for a penalty or fine for violation of such requirements.

The Deepwater Port Act of 1974, as amended (DWPA) (P.L. 93–627, 33 U.S.C. 1501 *et seq.*), and its regulations (68 FR 36496) establish a licensing system for

ownership, construction, operation and decommissioning of deepwater port structures located beyond U.S. territorial waters, for the import and export of oil and natural gas. The Act sets out conditions that applicants must meet and detailed procedures for the issuance of licences by the Secretary of Transportation, and prohibits the issuance of a licence without the approval of the Governors of the adjacent coastal states. MARAD is responsible for determining the financial capability of potential licensees, the citizenship of the applicant, and for issuing or denying the deepwater port licence. The DWPA establishes a specific timeframe of 330 days from the date of publication in the Federal Register for approval or denial of the deepwater port licence.[220]

Shipbuilding and ship repairs

Under U.S. law, only U.S.-built ships qualify for domestic service; the United States was granted an exemption from GATT rules for measures prohibiting the use, sale, or lease of foreign-built or foreign-reconstructed vessels in commercial applications between points in national waters or the waters of an exclusive economic zone. There are no restrictions on foreign investment in U.S. shipyards or ship-repair facilities, but floating dry-docks are eligible for loan guarantees under the Federal Ship Financing Program only if owned by U.S. citizens.[221]

MARAD provides financial assistance to ship-owners and U.S. shipyards through the Federal Ship Financing Program (Title XI), established pursuant to Title XI of the Merchant Marine Act of 1936, as amended. The aim of the Title XI Program is to promote the growth and modernization of the U.S. merchant marine and U.S. shipyards. The Program, authorized pursuant to 46 U.S.C. Chapter 537, provides U.S. Government-guaranteed debt issued by: (a) U.S. or foreign ship-owners for the purpose of financing or refinancing either U.S.-flag vessels or eligible export vessels constructed, reconstructed or reconditioned in U.S. shipyards; and (b) U.S. shipyards for the purpose of financing advanced shipbuilding technology and modern shipbuilding technology of a privately-owned, general shipyard facility located in the United States.[222] Under the Federal Credit Reform Act of 1990, appropriations to cover the estimated costs of a project must be obtained prior to the issuance of any letter of commitment for debt guarantees.

Title XI encourages U.S. ship-owners to obtain new vessels from U.S. shipyards by offering long-term debt repayment guarantees; the Program also allows vessels to be built in U.S. shipyards for foreign ship-owners. It also assists U.S. shipyards with modernizing their facilities for building and repairing vessels. Since the obligations are guaranteed by the U.S. Government, the repayment term allowed is longer, and the interest rates lower, than those available from the commercial lending market.[223] The guarantee is based on the "actual cost" of the vessels or the technology used in shipbuilding, which generally includes the cost of construction, reconstruction, or reconditioning of the vessel, together with construction-period interest and the guarantee fee. The guarantees are up to 87.5% of the value of the project, for up to 25 years, depending on the type of project. Amortization in equal payments of principal is usually required. However, other amortization methods, such as level debt (equal payments of principal and interest), may be approved if sufficient security is offered. In FY2016, one new application for a project totalling US$451 million was approved, representing US$394 million in guarantees; no guarantees were issued in FY2017 or, up to this point, in FY2018. As of the end-June 2018, Title XI guarantees totalling US$1.34 billion were outstanding.[224]

The Capital Construction Fund (CCF) and the Construction Reserve Fund (CRF) allow U.S. citizens owning or leasing vessels to obtain tax benefits for the construction, reconstruction, or acquisition of vessels. CCF vessels must be U.S.-built and documented under U.S. laws for operation in the nation's foreign, Great Lakes, short-sea shipping, or non-contiguous domestic trade or its fisheries. Participants must meet U.S. citizenship requirements. The CCF provides tax-deferral benefits to vessel operators in the foreign or domestic trade of the United States and U.S. fisheries. The CCF aims to make up for the competitive disadvantage operators of U.S.-flag vessels face in the construction and replacement of their vessels, relative to foreignflag operators whose vessels are registered in countries that do not tax shipping income. The CRF is a financial assistance scheme that provides tax-deferral benefits to U.S.-flag, operators with respect to gains attributable to the sale or loss of a vessel, provided the proceeds are used to expand or modernize the U.S. merchant fleet.

The Manufacturing Extension Program, Section 8062 of P.L. No. 108-87 makes naval shipyards eligible to participate in any manufacturing extension programme financed by funds appropriated by any Act.

As of mid-2018, there were 124 shipyards and ship-repair facilities in the United States. The order book was estimated at US$1.6 billion. U.S.-flag vessels repaired in most foreign countries face a 50% ad valorem duty[225], assessed on the cost of equipment and nonemergency

repairs in foreign countries, although exemptions apply under certain circumstances. U.S.-owned foreign-flag vessels are not subject to any duty.

Tourism services

Market overview

General

Tourism services are divided, in the MTN/GNS/W120 nomenclature used for U.S. GATS commitments, into four categories, namely: 9.A hotels and restaurants (including catering); 9.B travel agencies and tour operators; 9.C tour guide services; and the undefined 9.D "other" category. There are no available official figures on cross-border exchanges of tourism services according to this classification, because, by construction, balance of payments statistics for tourism are based on types of consumer rather than on types of services purchased. Table 4.26, which describes the exchanges of travel and tourism services between 2011 and 2017, illustrates that point, while Chart 4.17 describes the evolution of the balance of trade for the same years.

Both the previous table and the chart below show that the United States is running a substantial surplus in tourism services, which reached US$77.4 billion in 2017.

The United States runs a structurally large surplus in tourism services, a considerable part of it is linked to transport activities and not to tourism activities *per se,* and it is not currently possible to distinguish the contribution of each tourism activity in these results.

Table 4.27 describes the evolution of employment and of the number of establishment in accommodation, food services and drinking places between 2011 and 2018. It shows a constant growth of these two parameters in the two subsectors during the period under review.

Table 4.28 shows an upward trend over the 2011-17 period with respect to value added in accommodation and food services, not only in absolute terms but also in terms of relative share of total GDP. It also shows an increase in the sector's foreign investment position in the United States, which reached US$19.3 billion in 2016,

Table 4.26 Trade balance in the tourism sector, 2011-17

(US$ million, seasonally adjusted)

	2011	2012	2013	2014	2015	2016	2017
Exports (receipts)							
Total travel and tourism-related exports	187,630	200,996	218,497	235,989	249,183	246,173	251,360
Travel receipts (for all purposes, including education)	150,867	161,632	177,484	191,918	206,936	206,902	210,747
Travel spending	118,645	126,745	139,453	149,754	159,942	155,606	155,807
Medical/education/workers' spending	32,222	34,887	38,031	42,164	46,994	51,296	54,940
Passenger fare receipts	36,763	39,364	41,013	44,071	42,247	39,271	40,613
Imports (payments)							
Total travel and tourism-related imports	116,447	129,903	130,149	140,558	150,042	160,936	173,921
Travel receipts (for all purposes, including education)	89,700	100,338	98,120	105,668	114,548	123,569	135,024
Travel spending	81,663	91,789	88,980	95,831	104,254	112,500	123,067
Medical/education/workers' spending	8,037	8,549	9,140	9,837	10,294	11,069	11,957
Passenger fare receipts	26,747	29,565	32,029	34,890	35,494	37,367	38,897
Balance of trade (surplus/deficit)	71,183	71,093	88,348	95,431	99,141	85,237	77,439

Source: Bureau of Economic Analysis and the National Travel and Tourism Office.

Chart 4.17 Tourism services trade, 2011-17

(US$ million)

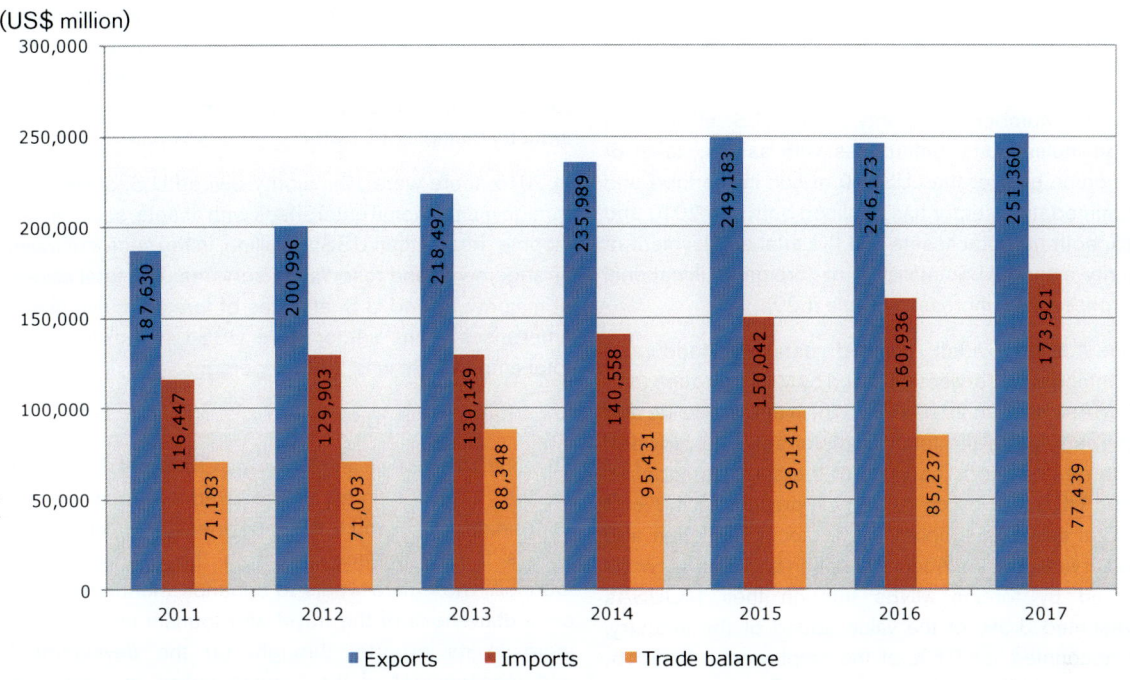

Source: Bureau of Economic Analysis, and National Travel and Tourism Office.

Table 4.27 Accommodation and food services, number of employees and establishments, 2011-18Q1

('000 and numbers)

NAICS code/description	2010	2011	2012	2013	2014	2015	2016	2017	2018[a]
	Number of employees ('000)								
721 Accommodation	1,760	1,801	1,825	1,865	1,894	1,923	1,960	2,003	2,019
722 Food services and drinking places	9,373	9,633	9,976	10,361	10,696	11,066	11,444	11,726	11,877
	Number of establishments[b]								
721 Accommodation	65,122	65,534	65,976	66,650	67,301	67,953	68,832	69,729[b]	..
722 Food services and drinking places	556,524	566,471	578,095	585,642	594,103	603,061	613,784	626,599[b]	..

.. Not available.

a Data for the first quarter of 2018.

b Data for the first quarter of 2017.

Source: WTO Secretariat calculations, based on data from the Bureau of Labour Statistics.

Table 4.28 Value added and Foreign Direct Investment in accommodation and food services, 2010-17

(US$ billion and % of total GDP)

	2010	2011	2012	2013	2014	2015	2016	2017
Value added (US$ billion)								
Accommodation and food services	**396**	**414**	**440**	**463**	**491**	**530**	**559**	**583**
Accommodation	111	120	126	134	141	152	159	164
Food services and drinking places	286	294	314	329	351	377	401	419
Share of total GDP (%)								
Accommodation and food services	**2.6**	**2.7**	**2.7**	**2.8**	**2.8**	**2.9**	**3.0**	**3.0**
Accommodation	0.7	0.8	0.8	0.8	0.8	0.8	0.9	0.8
Food services and drinking places	1.9	1.9	1.9	2.0	2.0	2.1	2.2	2.2
Foreign Direct Investment position in the United States (US$ million)								
Accommodation and food services	**14,550**	**17,656**	**15,463**	**14,811**	**15,059**	**17,766**	**19,774**	**31,389**
Accommodation	6,710	6,728	4,919	5,398	6,213	7,886	8,546	9,272
Food services and drinking places	7,840	10,928	10,545	9,413	8,846	9,880	11,229	22,117

Source: Bureau of Economic Analysis.

of which 44.5% was in accommodation, and 55.5% in food services and drinking places. There are no detailed statistics available on individual trade partners' FDI in the industry.

While the number of majority-owned U.S. affiliates of foreign multinational enterprises with assets, sales or net income greater than US$20 million in the food and accommodation sector has declined between 2010 and 2015, both the total assets and the total employment of majority-owned U.S. affiliates of foreign multinational enterprises have increased (Table 4.29).

Table 4.30 provides detailed data on food and accommodation services supplied by MNEs through their MOUSAs between 2010 and 2015, in terms of value and as percentage of the total supply of services provided by the retail sector. The value of the services supplied totaled US$33.9 billion in 2015, representing 4.3% of the total services supplied in the accommodation and food services sector. Accommodation and food services supplied by foreign MNEs through their MOUSAs represented 3.5% of the value added of the industry, and accounted for 9.6% of the employment. In 2015, some 81% of MNEs in the sector were European, 10.2% from Asia, and the rest from other regions.

Travel agencies and tour operators

According to information by the BEA, based on travel and tourism satellite accounts, the direct output of travel arrangements and reservation services reached US$51.1 billion in 2016. Total tourism-related output, including indirect output (a statistical concept corresponding to the supply of services) totalled US$78.0 billion in 2016, resulting from a commodity output multiplier of 1.53. Direct employment in the industry reached 193,000 in the same year, and total tourism-related employment was 260,000, with a total industry multiplier of 1.35.

In 2015, there were 19 majority-owned U.S. affiliates of foreign multinational enterprises with assets, sales, or net income greater than US$20 million, in the sector of travel arrangements and reservation services. The total assets of majority-owned U.S. affiliates of foreign multinational enterprises in the sector were US$4,484 million, and total employment was 23,000 persons.

Regulatory regime

The National Travel and Tourism Office (NTTO), part of the USDOC International Trade Administration, coordinates travel and tourism policies and programmes across federal agencies through the Tourism Policy Council. The Office works to enhance the international competitiveness of the travel and tourism industry and increase its exports, through: (a) the development and management of the tourism policy, strategy and advocacy; (b) the design and administration of export expansion activities; (c) the management of the travel and tourism statistical system for assessing the economic contribution of the industry; and (d) technical assistance for expanding international tourism.[226] The NTTO serves as the liaison with Brand USA, the destination marketing organization for the United States. The USDOC appoints the Brand USA Board of Directors, approves Brand

Table 4.29 Selected data for majority-owned U.S. affiliates of foreign multinational enterprises, 2010, 2012 and 2015

	Number of affiliates with assets, sales, or net income (+/-) greater than US$20 million[a]			Total assets (US$ million)			Number of employees ('000)		
	2010[a]	2012	2015	2010	2012	2015	2010	2012	2015
Accommodation and food services	**127**	**107**	**113**	**30,821**	**37,377**	**38,453**	**377**	**419**	**489**
Accommodation	108	86	92	15,765	14,539	17,670	51	41	47
Food services and drinking places	19	21	21	15,056	22,838	20,783	326	378	442

a   For 2010, affiliates with assets, sales, or net income (+/-) greater than US$15 million.

Source: Bureau of Economic Analysis.

Table 4.30 Accommodation and food services supplied by foreign MNEs through their MOUSAs, 2010-15

(US$ million and %)

	2010	2011	2012	20103	2014	2015
US$ million						
Accommodation and food services	25,429	27,130	29,743	30,215	33,586	33,865
Accommodation	5,537	5,673	5,208	5,545	5,992	6,025
Food services and drinking places	19,893	21,457	24,535	24,670	27,594	27,840
As a share of total services supplied to U.S. persons in the accommodation and food services sector[a]						
Accommodation and food services	4.0	4.2	4.4	4.3	4.5	4.3
Accommodation	5.9	5.6	4.8	4.9	4.9	4.7
Food services and drinking places	3.9	4.0	4.3	4.2	4.4	4.2

a   See note "a" in Table 4.22.

Source: Bureau of Economic Analysis.

USA's annual objectives, and approves matching funds of up to US$100 million for the international promotion of the United States as a travel destination.

The United States Travel and Tourism Advisory Board (Board) is the principal private sector advisory body to the Secretary of Commerce on matters relating to the travel and tourism industry. The Board advises the Secretary on government policies and programmes that affect the travel and tourism industry, offers counsel on current and emerging issues, and provides a forum for discussing and proposing solutions to industry-related problems. Advice may be given on a range of policies and issues, including travel facilitation, visa policy, infrastructure, aviation security, research, and economic sustainability. The Board is comprised of up to 32 members, representing companies and organizations in the travel and tourism industry; they are appointed by the Secretary of Commerce. Members are appointed for a two-year term. The Deputy Assistant Secretary for Travel and Tourism serves as the Board's Executive Director. The National Travel and Tourism Office (NTTO) serves as the Executive Secretariat for the Board.[227]

The NTTO plays an active role in domestic and international policy issues related to the U.S. travel and tourism industry. The NTTO fosters the development of policies that encourage the growth of travel and tourism to the United States by: (a) promoting the growth of U.S. travel exports through bilateral agreements with countries of strategic importance, including, for instance, the MoU with China to allow packaged leisure travel from China to the United States; (b) representing U.S. tourism interests in intergovernmental organizations, to lead the global efforts for travel and tourism policy concerns and issues, including the Tourism Committee for the OECD and the APEC Tourism Working Group; (c) serving as the Secretariat for the interagency Tourism Policy Council; and (d) serving as the official U.S. Government observer and participant on committees and activities of the United Nations World Tourism Organization.

The NTTO offers export assistance services to U.S. travel and tourism industry suppliers. For instance, the NTTO provides research reports and analysis, as well as market intelligence, to the U.S. travel and tourism industry, to help identify international markets where their goods and services would be well received. The Corporation for Travel Promotion (doing business as Brand USA) has a multi-language website (https://www.visittheusa.com/), whose primary purpose is to provide international travellers with a "one-stop shop" for travel information about the United States. This website covers all 50 states, the District of Columbia, the five U.S. territories and hundreds of U.S. destinations.

The National Travel and Tourism Strategy, launched in 2012, aims at attracting 100 million international visitors, with an estimated expenditure of US$250 billion annually, by the end of 2021. A new goal is under development as the United States has achieved its financial target. The five strategies of the Strategy are (a) promoting the

United States; (b) enabling and enhancing travel and tourism to, and within, the United States; (c) providing world-class customer service; (d) coordinating across government; and e) conducting research and measuring results.[228]

GATS and bilateral commitments

The U.S. GATS commitments on tourism services are very extensive and liberal. They cover all the subsectors of the MTN/GNS/W120 nomenclature, namely 9.A Hotels and Restaurants (including Catering); 9.B Travel agencies and Tour operators; 9.C Tour guide services; and the undefined 9.D "Other" category.

There are full ("none") market access commitments for modes 1, 2 and 3, and full national treatment commitments for all four modes for all four sectors. The only exceptions are a restriction in mode 3 for market access for travel agencies and tour operators, that states that "official tourism offices with diplomatic or official status are not permitted to operate on a commercial basis in the United States or to act as agents or principals in commercial transactions", and another restriction for modes 2 and 3 for market access for tour guide services that states that "the number of concessions available for commercial operations in federal, state and local facilities is limited". Mode 4 market access commitments for the four subsectors make cross-reference to the horizontal commitment limitations, which concern limitations on the temporary entry and stay of natural persons. There are no sector-specific MFN exemptions regarding tourism services.

The commitments are the same in the United States-Jordan FTA which has a positive listing structure. In its other FTAs, the United States maintains its GATS-level market access commitments through cross reference; there are no sector-specific limitations listed for other obligations, taken on a negative-list basis.

E-COMMERCE

The United States does not have a general e-commerce law; however, e-commerce is subject to a number of federal and state measures that address various aspects of e-commerce. Current U.S. laws, regulations and orders affecting e-commerce address, among other things, the use of personal information, advertising, IP, cybercrime, taxation, and online speech (Table 4.31).

Two federal agencies oversee different aspects of e-commerce: the Federal Trade Commission (FTC) and the Federal Communications Commission (FCC). The FTC's authority over unfair and deceptive practices in commerce extends to various aspects of e-commerce, including online advertising, mobile and in-app payments, online medical claims, and consumer privacy. The FTC has enforcement authority: up to July 2018, it had brought some 60 enforcement actions for alleged unfair or deceptive data security practices. In 2017, the FTC announced nine privacy and three data security cases. The FTC's authority also extends to when

Trade Policy Review – United States 2018
www.wto.org/tpr

Table 4.31 Selected measures affecting e-commerce

Act	Main provisions
Federal Trade Commission Act of 1914 (FTCA), 15 U.S.C. §§ 41-58, as amended	Applies to advertising on the Internet. Prevents unfair methods of competition and unfair or deceptive acts or practices affecting interstate commerce.
Electronic Communications Privacy Act (ECPA) of 1986, P.L. 99-508	Regulates the interception of electronic communications, and provides for federal criminal penalties for anyone who improperly accesses, uses, intercepts or discloses electronic communications that affect interstate or foreign commerce.
Health Insurance Portability and Accountability Act (HIPAA) of 1996, P.L. 104-191	Applies to healthcare providers, data processors, pharmacies, and other entities that handle medical information, and sets out standards that apply to the electronic transmission of medical data.
Section 230 of the Communications Decency Act of 1996 (Title V of the Telecommunications Act of 1996), 47 U.S.C. § 230	Section 230(c)(1) provides immunity from non-IP, civil liability for providers and users of an "interactive computer service" who publish information provided by third-party users. It specifies that no provider or user of an interactive computer service shall be treated as the publisher or speaker of any information provided by another information content provider.
Online Copyright Infringement Liability Limitation Act of the Digital Millennium Copyright Act of 1998 (DMCA), P.L. 105-304	Contains provisions and procedural requirements that, in certain circumstances, insulate internet service providers (ISPs) from copyright infringement claims based on actions by users of their services.
Gramm-Leach-Bliley Act of 1999 (GLBA), P.L. 106–102	Regulates the collection, use, protection and disclosure of non-public personal information by financial institutions. Requires financial institutions to explain their information-sharing practices to their customers.
Anticybersquatting Consumer Protection Act of 1999 (ACPA), 15 U.S.C. § 1125(d)	Established a civil cause of action for owners of trademarks and service marks against a person who (i) registers, traffics in or uses a domain name that is identical or confusingly similar to the mark; or (ii) in the case of a famous mark, dilutes the mark and has a bad faith intent to profit from the use of the mark.
Controlling the Assault of Non-Solicited Pornography and Marketing Act of 2003 (the CAN-SPAM Act), P.L. 108-187	Governs unsolicited email communications, and prohibits false or misleading email header information and deceptive subject lines.
Computer Fraud and Abuse Act (CFAA), 18 U.S.C. § 1030	Governs computer hacking, and makes unlawful certain computer-related activities involving the unauthorized access of a computer. The CFAA criminalizes the following general conduct: •Knowingly accessing a computer without authorization, or by exceeding authorized access, and obtaining protected information; •Knowingly, and with intent to defraud, accessing a protected computer without authorization, or by exceeding authorized access, and obtaining anything with a value of more than US$5,000 in a one-year period; •Knowingly causing the transmission of a program, information, code, or command, and thereby intentionally causing unauthorized damage to a protected computer; •Intentionally accessing a protected computer without authorization and recklessly causing damage; •Knowingly, and with intent to defraud, trafficking in passwords or access information; and •Extortion involving computers. Federal law provides for potential imprisonment of up to 10 years for a violation of the CFAA, and up to 20 years for a second offense.
Electronic Signatures in Global and National Commerce Act of 2000 (the ESIGN Act)	Main law regarding the enforceability of contracts formed over the Internet, and the enforceability of electronic signatures
Restore Online Shoppers' Confidence Act (ROSCA), P.L. 111-345	Places restrictions on third-party data passing from initial merchant. Under ROSCA, a third-party seller is prohibited from charging a consumer for any goods or services sold on the Internet, unless it has disclosed clearly all material terms of the transaction, and has obtained the consumer's express informed consent to the charge. Initial merchants are prohibited from disclosing to third-party sellers any billing information used to charge consumers post-transaction, except for subsidiaries, corporate affiliates or successors to the initial merchant.
Unlawful Internet Gambling Enforcement Act of 2006 (UIGEA), P.L. 109-347	Regulates online gambling. Prohibits any person, including gambling businesses, from knowingly accepting payments in connection with the participation of another person in a bet or wager that involves the use of the Internet and that is unlawful under any federal or state law.
Broadband Data Improvement Act of 2008 (BDIA), P.L. 110-385	Geared at improving the quality of data regarding the availability and quality of broadband services to promote the availability of broadband Internet
Prioritizing Resources and Organization for Intellectual Property Act of 2008 (PRO IP), P.L. 110-403	Increased both civil and criminal penalties for trademark and copyright infringement, including online infringement.

Act	Main provisions
Internet Tax Freedom Act, P.L. 105-277	Forbids federal, state and local governments from taxing Internet access and from imposing discriminatory Internet-only taxes. It also prohibits multiple taxes on electronic commerce.

Source: Kirkland & Ellis International LLP online information. Viewed at: https://gettingthedealthrough.com/area/11/e-commerce/; and information provided by the authorities.

broadband providers engage in anti-competitive, unfair, or deceptive acts or practices. To date, no enforcement actions have been taken under this authority.

The Federal Communications Commission (FCC) regulates interstate and international communications by radio, television, wire, satellite and cable. The FCC's authority is discussed in the Telecommunications section of this report (p. 146).

Electronic contracts are governed by the Electronic Signatures in Global and National Commerce Act of 2000 (the ESIGN Act), as well as by state laws that meet the requirements in the ESIGN Act. Most state laws are based upon a model law, the Uniform Electronic Transactions Act (UETA), which has been adopted by 47 states, the District of Columbia, Puerto Rico and the U.S. Virgin Islands.[229]

The United States has no overarching federal cybersecurity law. Protection of cybersecurity is regulated mainly by state laws and federal regulations, which provide industry-specific mandates with respect to data security. The Federal Government has, however, through its National Institute of Standards and Technology, developed a Cybersecurity Framework, which seeks to support the development of better cybersecurity practices by both governmental and non-governmental actors.

Although not as popular as generic top-level domains such as .com and .org, the United States has a country code top-level domain (ccTLD), ".us". To be granted the ccTLD ".us", the registrant must be a U.S. citizen, a U.S. permanent resident or have its primary domicile in the United States (if a natural person); or be incorporated in the United States or have a bona fide presence in the country (if an entity or organization).

Advertising on the Internet is subject to the same measures as conventional advertising. In addition, the CAN-SPAM Act contains restrictions on senders of commercial email messages that, if violated, may lead to civil or penal action. Misleading online advertisements are subject to the same FTC regulations, enforcement procedures and penalties as conventional advertisements. There are no regulations prohibiting the advertisement of specific goods and services online.

Providers of interactive computer services are generally not liable for content provided by third-party users. Section 230 of the Communications Decency Act of 1996 provides immunity from civil liability to providers and users of any interactive computer service that publishes information provided by third parties. If the interactive service provider has had a substantive role in the creation or modification of content, it may be held liable for civil infractions arising from the content. This Act does not address liability arising from IP infringement.

Rules on taxation on sales online were recently changed by a Supreme Court ruling. Under rules applied since 1992, in general terms, if an online retailer maintained a physical presence in, or had a nexus (personnel, etc.) within, a state that charges a sales tax on most purchases, then that online retailer was obliged to charge sales tax on any items sold to customers within the home state. In practice, that meant that most small businesses, which generally do not have a presence in several states, were not obliged to charge sales tax on sales to customers located in states other than their own. In the South Dakota v. Wayfair Inc. case, the Supreme Court ruled that states may compel online retailers to charge sales tax regardless of whether the retailer has a physical presence in the state.[230]

Endnotes

1   Crop farms have been getting larger over the last 30 years, the midpoint size increasing from 589 acres in 1982 to more than 1,200 acres in 2012.

2   The 2014 Farm Bill eliminated the Counter-Cyclical Payments (CCP) Programme and the Average Crop Revenue Election (ACRE) Programme.

3   Congressional Research Service, *Previewing a 2018 Farm Bill*, Washington D.C., 15 March 2017.

4   For more information, see: https://www.usda.gov/media/press-releases/2018/09/04/usda-launches-trade-mitigation-programs.

5   Land owners had a one-time option to reallocate, but not to increase, their base acres using average planted acreage during 2009-12. They could also choose to retain the payment yield under the previous CCP programme or update it to 90% of the average commodity yield for the crop years 2008-12.

6   The revenue guarantee under ARC-IC automatically requires enrolment of all covered commodities on the farm, and may therefore not be used in combination with PLC.

7   ARC payments are capped at 10% of the benchmark revenue.

8   Congressional Research Service (2018), *U.S. Farm Commodity Support: An Overview of Selected Programs*, 17 April.

9   The interest rate is set at the CCC cost of borrowing from the Treasury, plus one percentage point, at the time the loan is made.

10 Persons or legal entities are not eligible for MLGs or LDPs if their average adjusted gross income exceeds US$900,000, but remain eligible for marketing loans repaid at principal plus interest. Accumulated payments for PLC, ARC, MLGs, and LDPs may not exceed US$125,000 per person or legal entity per year. A separate and additional US$125,000 annual payment limit applies to programme benefits for peanuts.

11 The loan rates were generally the same as in crop years 2010-13.

12 The United States reports MLGs, LDPs, and certificate exchange gains under non-exempt direct payments in supporting table DS:6, and commodity loan interest subsidies and forfeiture benefits under other product-specific support in supporting table DS:7.

13 The aim was to reduce the reliance on federal disaster relief programmes.

14 In practice, the RMA or third parties propose the premium rates and other conditions, which are then reviewed by independent experts on behalf of the FCIC board. The FCIC board approves or rejects the proposed rates. The RMA manages the FCIC.

15 Catastrophic coverage insures 50% of the normal yield and 55% of the estimated market price of the crop. A buy-up plan may increase the coverage to 50%-85% of normal yield and 100% of the estimated market price.

16 The SCO takes on the characteristics of the underlying policy, i.e. if it is a yield policy, the SCO will generate a guarantee for yields, or a guarantee for revenue for underlying revenue policies. As the SCO is area-based, a producer may experience an individual loss that does not give rise to compensation if his/her revenue or yield is poorly correlated with the outcome at the county level.

17 CBO, *Options to Reduce the Budgetary Costs of the Federal Crop Insurance Program*, Washington D.C., December 2017.

18 Land allocated to crops is reported every five years. The most recent report from 2012 indicated 340 million acres of cropland in the United States. Principal crop acreage, reported annually, has been relatively stable at 319-326 million acres between 2012 and 2018.

19 CBO, *Options to Reduce the Budgetary Costs of the Federal Crop Insurance Program*, Washington D.C., December 2017.

20 CBO, *Options to Reduce the Budgetary Costs of the Federal Crop Insurance Program*, Washington D.C., December 2017.

21 Policies with this built-in flexibility accounted for 98% of the revenue policies sold in 2016.

22 Examples of such policies are Yield Protection, Revenue Protection, Revenue Protection with the Harvest Price Exclusion, and any Area Risk Protection.

23 Glauber, Joseph, W. *Unraveling Reform? Cotton in the 2018 Farm Bill*, American Enterprise Institute, January 2018. The author bases his calculations on data from the USDA Risk Management Agency.

24 USDA FSA online information. Viewed at: https://www.fsa.usda.gov/Assets/USDA-FSA-Public/usdafiles/arc-plc/pdf/2016%20ARC%20PLC%20payments%20April%202018.pdf.

25 Unassigned base acres are not eligible for payments. A farm owner that did not plant any covered commodities (including seed cotton) on the generic base acres during the 2009-16 crop years would now have an unassigned crop base.

26 The ginning costs are averaged for four production regions, and range from US$19.65 in the Southwest (Kansas, Oklahoma and Texas) to US$48.02 in the West (Arizona, California and New Mexico). USDA FSA online information. Viewed at: https://www.fsa.usda.gov/Assets/USDA-FSA-Public/usdafiles/cotton-ginning-cost-share/cgcs_program_fact_sheet_march_2018.pdf.

27 Conditions also apply, i.e. compliance with conservation measures, active engagement in farming, and that the producer's average adjusted gross income (in the preceding three tax years) must not exceed US$900,000.

28 The 2014 Farm Bill set the marketing loan rates at 18.75 cents per pound for raw sugar and 24.09 cents per pound for refined beet sugar. These rates are national average rates.

29 USDA online information. Viewed at: https://www.ers.usda.gov/topics/crops/sugar-sweeteners/trade .aspx.

30 The total amounts for FY2018 were published in the Federal Register on 30 June 2017 (82 FR 29822).

31 For 10 small suppliers, each allocation is limited to 7,258 metric tons, which corresponds to a minimum boatload of sugar.

32 The amendments were published in full in the Federal Register on 11 July 2017 (82 FR 31945).

33 The programmes that were terminated were the Dairy Product Price Support Program, the Milk Income Loss Contract (MILC) Program, and the Dairy Export Incentive Program.

34 The National Agricultural Statistics Service reports the average price of milk marketed in the United States. The average feed cost for the production of 1 cwt of milk is derived from the sum of (i) 1.0728 times the price of maize (per bushel); (ii) 0.00735 times the price of soybean meal (per ton); and (iii) 0.0137 times the price of alfalfa hay (per ton).

35 Separate provisions govern intergenerational transfers and new dairy operations.

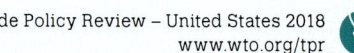

36 Beginning farmers, socially disadvantaged farmers and ranchers, and farmers with limited resources may apply to be exempted from the fee.

37 For example, a producer selecting a US$7 margin for 50% of his historical production (3 million lbs=30,000 cwt) would pay a premium of US$0.063x30,000x0.5=US$945 for one year. Should the actual margin be US$6 during one of these months, he would receive an indemnity of US$(7-6)x30,000x0.5/12= US$1,250 for that month.

38 Payments to producers under MPP-Dairy amounted to US$0.5 million in 2015 and US$11 million in 2016 (WTO document G/SCM/N/315/USA, 14 March 2018).

39 Products are purchased for immediate distribution, and may not be stored or resold in commercial markets.

40 The DPDP production margin is calculated in the same manner as the margin under MPP-Dairy.

41 Farmers and importers may receive a credit against the levy if they contribute to quality programmes, authorized by federal or state laws, conducting dairy product promotion, research, or nutrition education.

42 USDA FNS online information. Viewed at: http://www.fns.usda. gov/sites/default/files/pd/34SNAPmonthly.pdf.

43 WTO document G/AG/N/USA/120, 24 April 2018.

44 WTO document G/AG/N/USA/117, 4 October 2017.

45 WTO document G/AG/N/USA/111, 2 March 2017.

46 USDA online information. Viewed at: https://www.fas.usda.gov/ sites/default/files/2016-10/2016_5.pdf.

47 USDA online information. Viewed at: https://www.fas.usda.gov/ programs/export-credit-guarantee-program-gsm-102/gsm-102- allocations.

48 The other programmes are the Foreign Market Development Program, the Emerging Markets Program, and the Technical Assistance for Specialty Crops Program. The Federal Budget for FY2018 allocated US$173.8 million for MAP, and US$26.5 million for the Foreign Market Development Program.

49 Congressional Research Service, *Previewing a 2018 Farm Bill*, Washington, D.C., March 2017.

50 International Energy Agency, *Energy Policies of IEA Countries, the United States*, Paris, 2014.

51 IEA, *Energy Policies of IEA Countries, the United States*, Paris, 2014.

52 U.S. Energy Information Administration online information. Viewed at: https://www.eia.gov/dnav/pet/PET_SUM_SNDW_A_EPC0_ FPF_MBBLPD_W.htm.

53 The Green River Formation, which stretches across Colorado, Utah and Wyoming, is by far the largest currently known shale oil deposit in the world. However, further technological advance is needed to make the extraction of this resource commercially viable.

54 IEA, *Energy Policies of IEA Countries, the United States*, Paris, 2014.

55 Energy Information Administration online information. Viewed at: https://www.eia.gov/tools/faqs/faq.php?id=73&t=11.

56 Among the federal tax incentives, the Federal Renewable Energy Production Tax Credit (PTC) was introduced in 1992 and subsequently reauthorized and expanded. However, except for wind facilities, the PTC is no longer available for projects commenced after 1 January 2018.

57 According to the North Carolina Clean Energy Technology Center, its DSIRE database is the most comprehensive source available on state incentives and policies that support renewables and energy efficiency in the United States. Viewed at: http://www.dsireusa.org/.

58 Energy Information Administration online information. Viewed at: https://www.eia.gov/todayinenergy/detail.php?id=36813.

59 BEA (2018), Gross Domestic Product by Industry: First Quarter 2018. Viewed at: https://www.bea.gov/system/files/2018-07/ gdpind118_3.pdf.

60 Department of Labor, Bureau of Labor Statistics, The Employment Situation - July 2018. News Release, 3 August 2018. Viewed at: https://www.bls.gov/news.release/archives/empsit_08032018.pdf.

61 Department of Labor, Bureau of Labor Statistics, The Employment Situation- July 2018. News Release, 3 August 2018. Viewed at: https://www.bls.gov/news.release/archives/empsit_08032018.pdf.

62 BEA (2017, August), *Activities of U.S. Affiliates of Foreign Multinational Enterprises in 2015*. Viewed at: https://www.bea. gov/scb/pdf/2017/08-August/0817-activities-of-us-affiliates-of- foreign-multinational-enterprises.pdf.

63 These programmes may be consulted in the Council for Community and Economic Research's (C2ER) State Business Incentives Database, at: http://selectusa.stateincentives.org/Programs/?State.

64 USTR online information. Viewed at: https://ustr.gov/issue-areas/ industry-manufacturing.

65 USTR online information. Viewed at: https://ustr.gov/issue-areas/ industry-manufacturing/industrial-competitiveness.

66 USTR (2018), *2018 Trade Policy Agenda and 2017 Annual Report of the President of the United States on the Trade Agreements Program*. Viewed at: https://ustr.gov/sites/default/files/files/Press/ Reports/2018/AR/2018%20Annual%20Report%20FINAL.PDF.

67 BEA online statistics. Viewed at: https://www.bea.gov/iTable/iTable. cfm?ReqID=51&step=1#reqid=51&step=51&isuri=1&5114=a& 5102=5.

68 BEA online statistics. Viewed at: www.bea.gov/scb/pdf/2017/10- October/1017-international-services-tables.pdf.

69 Department of the Treasury (2018), *Troubled Asset Relief Program, Monthly Report to Congress, June 2018*, issued on 10 July. Viewed at: https://www.treasury.gov/initiatives/financial-stability/reports/ Documents/2018.06%20June%20Monthly%20Report%20 to%20Congress.pdf.

70 SBLF repayments refer to investments refinanced under the Small Business Lending Fund (SBLF), a programme created by Congress outside of the TARP under which certain CPP institutions were allowed to repay TARP funds by borrowing under that programme. CDCI conversions refer to exchanges of CPP investments into the Community Development Capital Initiative (CDCI), as permitted under the terms of that programme. Auctions refer to net proceeds from all auctions of CPP preferred and note securities where cash has settled with the Treasury Department's Office of Financial Stability (OFS) as of 30 June 2018.

71 Department of Treasury online information. Viewed at: https:// www.treasury.gov/initiatives/financial-stability/TARP-Programs/ bank-investment-programs/cap/Pages/payments.aspx.

72 Federal Reserve online information. Viewed at: https://www. federalreserve.gov/releases/h8/current/default.htm.

73 WTO document WT/TPR/S/350/Rev.1, 28 March 2017.

74 More information can be found at: https://www.treasury.gov/ initiatives/fsoc/designations/Pages/nonbank-faq.aspx.

75 For a U.S. non-bank financial company, the global assets of the company and its consolidated subsidiaries are included in the calculation of this threshold. For a foreign non-bank financial company, only the U.S. assets of the company and its consolidated subsidiaries are included.

76 FSOC (2015), *Staff Guidance. Methodologies Relating to Stage 1 Thresholds*, 8 June. Viewed at: https://www.treasury.gov/initiatives/fsoc/designations/Documents/FSOC%20Staff%20Guidance%20-%20Stage%201%20Thresholds.pdf.

77 These are: the Clearing House Payments Company L.L.C. on the basis of its role as operator of the Clearing House Interbank Payments System; CLS Bank International; Chicago Mercantile Exchange, Inc.; the Depository Trust Company; Fixed Income Clearing Corporation; ICE Clear Credit LLC; National Securities Clearing Corporation; and the Options Clearing Corporation. Department of the Treasury online information. Viewed at: https://www.treasury.gov/initiatives/fsoc/designations/Pages/default.aspx.

78 The definition of "banking entities" includes insured depository institutions, bank holding companies, and their subsidiaries or affiliates. It also includes foreign banks that maintain branches or agencies in the United States or that own U.S. banks or commercial lending companies in the United States. The exemptions to the ban on proprietary trading include trading transactions in government securities; and transactions in connection with underwriting or market-making, on behalf of customers by an insurance company solely for the general account of the company. Additionally, certain risk-mitigating hedging is allowed under the Act, as well as proprietary trading occurring solely outside of the United States and conducted by a banking entity not directly or indirectly controlled by a banking entity organized under U.S. federal or state laws.

79 Despite the general prohibition, a banking entity may make a *de minimis* investment in a fund it advises, to provide the fund sufficient initial equity to attract unaffiliated investors. This investment may not exceed 3% of the total ownership interest of the fund within one year of the date of its establishment, and the aggregate of all of the interests of the banking entity in all such funds may not exceed 3% of its Tier 1 capital.

80 The final rule applies to internationally active banking organizations, generally those with US$250 billion or more in total consolidated assets or US$10 billion or more in on-balance-sheet foreign exposure. Less stringent, modified LCR requirements for bank holding companies and savings and loan holding companies without significant insurance, or commercial operations that, in each case, have US$50 billion or more in total consolidated assets but are not internationally active, were adopted.

81 Federal Reserve online information. Viewed at: http://www.federalreserve.gov/newsevents/press/bcreg/20131024a.htm.

82 Board of Governors of the Federal Reserve System online information. Viewed at: http://www.federalreserve.gov/bankinforeg/basel/default.htm.

83 Federal Financial Institutions Examination Council, National Information Center (NIC) online information. Viewed at: https://www.ffiec.gov/npw/Institution/TopHoldings.

84 Edge Act and agreement corporations are subsidiaries of banks or bank holding companies, organized to allow international banking and financial business.

85 Financial market utilities are multilateral systems that provide the essential infrastructure for transferring, clearing and settling payments, securities and other financial transactions among financial institutions.

86 CSBS online information. Viewed at: https://www.csbs.org.

87 WTO document GATS/EL/90/Suppl.3, 26 February 1998.

88 FDIC online information. Viewed at: https://www.fdic.gov/deposit/deposits/.

89 Branch licences for foreign banks are not permitted in Georgia, Louisiana, Missouri, and Oklahoma. Representative offices of foreign banks are not permitted in 12 states, and are subject to limitations in Oklahoma, while some states require the incorporation of representative offices. Some states also place limitations on the acquisition by a foreign person of savings banks or loan associations (Tennessee and Washington).

90 For further details of the NAIC's role, see WTO document WT/TPR/S/350/Rev.1., 28 March 2017.

91 The Government's contribution would decrease by 1% per year, until it is 80% by 2020.

92 The deductible for each insurer is 20% of its prior year's earned premiums in commercial lines of insurance subject to the TRIP.

93 For further details concerning the TRIP and its operation, see FIO (2018), *Report on the Effectiveness of the Terrorism Risk Insurance Program.* Completed pursuant to the Terrorism Risk Insurance Program Reauthorization Act of 2015. Viewed at: https://www.treasury.gov/initiatives/fio/reports-and-notices/Documents/2018_TRIP_Effectiveness_Report.pdf.

94 FIO (2017), *U.S. Department of the Treasury, Annual Report on the Insurance Industry.* Completed pursuant to Title V of the Dodd-Frank Wall Street Reform and Consumer Protection Act, September 2017. Viewed at: https://www.treasury.gov/initiatives/fio/reports-and-notices/Documents/2017_FIO_Annual_ Report.pdf.

95 FSB online information. Viewed at: http://www.fsb.org/wp-content/uploads/P211117-2.pdf.

96 Private offerings to a limited number of persons or institutions; offerings of limited size; intrastate offerings; and securities of municipal, state, and federal governments are exempt from registration requirements. Furthermore, foreign issuers can opt to use different registration and periodic reporting forms than those used by domestic users.

97 This includes the power to register, regulate, and oversee brokerage firms, transfer agents, and clearing agencies, as well as securities self-regulatory organizations (SROs).

98 Exemptions from the Advisers Act registration requirements apply, *inter alia,* to: (i) advisers solely to venture capital funds; (ii) advisers solely to private funds with less than US$150 million in assets under management in the United States; and (iii) certain foreign advisers without a place of business in the United States, having less than 15 clients and investors in the United States in private funds, and less than US$25 million in aggregate assets under management attributable to clients.

99 OECD (2018), *Digital Economy Outlook 2017.* Viewed at: http://www.oecd.org/sti/oecd-digital-economy-outlook-2017-9789264232440-en.htm.

100 The ICT Development Index comprises 11 indicators covering ICT access, use, and skills. ITU online information. Viewed at: https://read.itu-ilibrary.org/science-and-technology/measuring-the-information-society-report-2017_pub/80f52533-en#page44; and https://www.itu.int/net4/ITU-D/idi/2017/index.html.

101 BEA online information, *International Transactions, International Services, and International Investment Position Tables.* Viewed at: https://www.bea.gov/iTable/iTable.cfm?ReqID=62&step=1#reqid=62&step=9&isuri=1&6210=4.

102 ITU (2018), *Measuring the Information Society Report 2017.* Viewed at: https://read.itu-ilibrary.org/science-and-technology/measuring-the-information-society-report-2017_pub/80f52533-en#page1.

103 Intrastate wireline telecommunications providers are primarily regulated by a public utility commission (PUC) in each state, and some PUCs also lightly regulate wireless companies and/or interconnected Voice over Internet Protocol (VoIP) providers. Cable operators are licensed by cable franchising authorities at the local or state level, and regulatory power over these operators is shared by such local/state authorities and the FCC.

104 FCC online information. Viewed at: https://www.fcc.gov/about/overview.

105 FCC online information. Viewed at: https://www.fcc.gov/about-fcc/rulemaking-process.

106 FCC online information. Viewed at: https://www.fcc.gov/reports-research/guides/review-of-significant-transactions.

107 FCC online information. Viewed at: https://www.fcc.gov/reports-research/guides/review-of-significant-transactions.

108 FCC online information. Viewed at: https://www.fcc.gov/licensing-databases/licensing.

109 47 U.S.C. 251. Viewed at: https://www.law.cornell.edu/uscode/text/47/251. See also the definition of "telecommunications carrier" and "telecommunications service" in 47 U.S.C. 153 for the requirement that the service must be offered to the public. Viewed at: https://www.law.cornell.edu/uscode/text/47/153.

110 47 U.S.C. 252. Viewed at: https://www.law.cornell.edu.uscode/text/47/252.

111 47 U.S.C. 201 et seq. Viewed at: https://www.law.cornell.edu/uscode/text/47/chapter-5/subchapter-II.

112 Non-common carrier wireless licensees, including most satellite licensees, are not subject to foreign ownership restrictions.

113 The public interest analysis conducted to review an application by a supplier from a WTO Member relies on an "open entry" standard, whereby the FCC starts from a presumption (subject to rebuttal) that foreign entry does not threaten competition in the U.S. telecommunications market. It also involves a consideration of policy concerns raised by federal government agencies in relation to national security, law enforcement, foreign policy, or trade policy issues.

114 FCC (2016), *Review of Foreign Ownership Policies for Broadcast, Common Carrier and Aeronautical Radio Licensees under Section 310(b)(4) of the Communications Act of 1934, as Amended*, FCC 16-128. Adopted on 29 September 2016. Viewed at: https://docs.fcc.gov/public/attachments/FCC-16-128A1.pdf.

115 FCC (2015), *Report and Order on Remand, Declaratory Ruling, and Order in the Matter of Protecting and Promoting the Open Internet*, GN Docket No. 14-28. Adopted on 26 February 2015; released on 12 March 2015. Viewed at: https://apps.fcc.gov/edocs_public/attachmatch/FCC-15-24A1.pdf (Title II Order).

116 FCC (2015), *Title II Order*, paras. 41-50.

117 FCC (2015), *Title II Order*, paras. 283-284.

118 FCC (2015), *Title II Order*, paras. 14-19.

119 FCC (2015), *Title II Order*, paras. 20-22. Under this standard, a broadband Internet access service provider was not allowed to unreasonably interfere with, or unreasonably disadvantage, end users' ability to select, access, and use broadband Internet access service or the lawful Internet content, applications, services, or devices of their choice.

120 FCC (2015), *Title II Order*, paras. 23-24.

121 *United States Telecom Ass'n v. FCC*, 825 F.3d 674 (D.C. Cir. 2016). Viewed at: https://www.cadc.uscourts.gov/internet/opinions.nsf/3F95E49183E6F8AF85257FD200505A3A/$file/15-1063-1619173.pdf.

122 FCC (2017), *Notice of Proposed Rulemaking in the Matter of Restoring Internet Freedom*, WC Docket No. 17-108. Adopted on 18 May 2017; released on 23 May 2017. Viewed at: https://docs.fcc.gov/public/attachments/FCC-17-60A1.pdf (Internet Freedom NPRM).

123 FCC (2017), *Internet Freedom NPRM*, para. 73.

124 FCC (2017), *Internet Freedom NPRM*, para. 76.

125 FCC (2017), *Declaratory Ruling, Report and Order, and Order in the Matter of Restoring Internet Freedom*, WC Docket No. 17-108. Adopted on 14 December 2017; released on 4 January 2018. Viewed at: https://docs.fcc.gov/public/attachments/FCC-17-166A1.pdf (Restoring Internet Freedom Order).

126 FCC (2018), *2018 Broadband Deployment Report*. Adopted on 2 February 2018. Viewed at: https://docs.fcc.gov/public/attachments/FCC-18-10A1.pdf. See also https://www.fcc.gov/reports-research/reports/broadband-progress-reports/2018-broadband-deployment-report.

127 Section 706 is codified in 47 U.S.C. § 1302. Section 706(d)(1) defines advanced telecommunications capability "without regard to any transmission media or technology, as high-speed, switched, broadband telecommunications capability that enables users to originate and receive high-quality voice, data, graphics, and video telecommunications using any technology." Viewed at: https://www.law.cornell.edu/uscode/text/47/1302.

128 FCC (2018). *2018 Broadband Deployment Report*, paras. 14-19. The FCC found that, beyond the most obvious distinction that mobile services permit their users mobility, there are clear variations in consumer preferences and demands for fixed and mobile services.

129 FCC (2018), *2018 Broadband Deployment Report*. Viewed at: https://docs.fcc.gov/public/attachments/FCC-18-10A1.pdf.

130 Robocalls are calls made with an autodialer or that contain a message made with a pre-recorded or artificial voice. See https://www.fcc.gov/consumers/guides/stop-unwanted-robocalls-and-texts.

131 FCC (2018), *Strategic Plan 2018-2022*. Viewed at: https://docs.fcc.gov/public/attachments/DOC-349143A1.pdf.

132 WTO document WT/TPR/S/307/Rev.1, 13 March 2015.

133 See 39 U.S.C. §§ 601-606 and 18 U.S.C. §§ 1693-1699.

134 Including Contract Postal Units, Village Post Offices, and Community Post Offices.

135 United States Postal Regulatory Commission (2018), *FY 2017 Report on Form 10-K*. Viewed at: https://about.usps.com/who-we-are/financials/10k-reports/fy2017.pdf.

136 United States Postal Regulatory Commission (2018), *FY 2017 Report on Form 10-K*. Viewed at: https://about.usps.com/who-we-are/financials/10k-reports/fy2017.pdf.

137 USPS (2018), *FY 2017 Annual Report to Congress*. Viewed at: http://about.usps.com/who-we-are/financials/annual-reports/fy2017.pdf.

138 See 39 U.S.C. § 101(a).

139 See 39 U.S.C. § 3622(d)(1)(C).

140 See 39 U.S.C. § 3632(b)(2).

141 United States Postal Regulatory Commission (2008), *Report on Universal Postal Service and the Postal Monopoly*, 19 December. Viewed at: https://www.prc.gov/docs/61/61628/USO%20Report.pdf.

142 Bureau of Labor Statistics online information. Viewed at: https://www.bls.gov/iag/tgs/iag491.htm.

143 Bureau of Labor Statistics online information. Viewed at: https://www.bls.gov/iag/tgs/iag492.htm.

144 IBIS World online information. Viewed at: https://www.ibisworld.com/industry-trends/market-research-reports/transportation-warehousing/couriers-messengers/couriers-local-delivery-services.html.

145 USITC (2004), *Express Delivery Services: Competitive Conditions Facing U.S.-based Firms in Foreign Markets*. Investigation No. 332-456, USITC publication 3678, April. Viewed at: https://www.usitc.gov/publications/332/pub3678.pdf.

146 UPS Fact Sheet. Viewed at: https://pressroom.ups.com/pressroom/ContentDetailsViewer.page?ConceptType=FactSheets&id=1426321563187-193.

147 FedEx Annual Report 2017. Viewed at: http://s1.q4cdn.com/714383399/files/oar/2017/AnnualReport2017/AnnualReport2017flat/docs/FedEx_2017_Annual_Report.pdf.

148 For a detailed description of the status and structure of the USPS, see the Universal Postal Union's profile of the USPS, on a questionnaire filled by the U.S. authorities. Viewed at: http://www.upu.int/fileadmin/documentsFiles/theUpu/statusOfPostalEntities/usaEn.pdf.

149 Parcels weighing over 354 grams fall outside the scope of the reserved area.

150 The Act provides that, when reviewing every non-postal service, the PRC must take into account: (a) the public need for the service; and (b) the ability of the private sector to meet the public need for the service.

151 USDOC, International Trade Administration, *2016 Top Markets Report Franchising*. https://www.trade.gov/topmarkets/pdf/Franchising_Executive_Summary.pdf.

152 International Franchise Association (2018), *Franchise Business Economic Outlook for 2018, January Forecast*. Prepared by IHS Markit for the International Franchise Association, and the Franchise Education and Research Foundation. Viewed at: https://www.franchise.org/sites/default/files/Franchise_Business_Outlook_Jan_2018.pdf.

153 FTC (2008), *Franchise Rule 16 C.F.R. Part 436 Compliance Guide*, May 2008. Viewed at: https://www.ftc.gov/system/files/documents/plain-language/bus70-franchise-rule-compliance-guide.pdf.

154 Franchise Rule (16 CFR Part 436 and 437, Federal Register, Vol. 72, No. 61, Friday, 30 March 2007, Rules and Regulations) may be viewed at: https://www.ftc.gov/sites/default/files/070330franchiserulefrnotice.pdf.

155 FTC (2008), *Franchise Rule 16 C.F.R. Part 436 Compliance Guide*, May 2008. Viewed at: https://www.ftc.gov/system/files/documents/plain-language/bus70-franchise-rule-compliance-guide.pdf.

156 FTC (2008), *Franchise Rule 16 C.F.R. Part 436 Compliance Guide,* May 2008. Viewed at: https://www.ftc.gov/system/files/documents/plain-language/bus70-franchise-rule-compliance-guide.pdf.

157 FTC (2008), *Franchise Rule 16 C.F.R. Part 436 Compliance Guide*, May 2008. Viewed at: https://www.ftc.gov/system/files/documents/plain-language/bus70-franchise-rule-compliance-guide.pdf.

158 These exemptions from federal Franchise Rule coverage may not be available in state franchise disclosure laws, which also may have their own exemptions with no counterpart in the Franchise Rule.

159 The details of the requirements to be included in a disclosure document are found in: FTC (2008), *Franchise Rule 16 C.F.R. Part 436 Compliance Guide*, May 2008. Viewed at: https://www.ftc.gov/system/files/documents/plain-language/bus70-franchise-rule-compliance-guide.pdf.

160 Vinson Franchise Law online information. Viewed at: http://franchiselaw.net/startups/usfranchiselawbasics.html.

161 California, Hawaii, Illinois, Indiana, Maryland, Michigan, Minnesota, New York, North Dakota, Rhode Island, South Dakota, Virginia, Washington and Wisconsin.

162 These states include: California, Indiana, Maryland, Minnesota, New York, North Dakota, Rhode Island, South Dakota and Washington.

163 Arkansas, California, Hawaii, Indiana, Iowa, Michigan, Minnesota, Nebraska, New Jersey and Washington. The substantive franchise relationship laws in these states also require good cause for termination and non-renewal of a franchise. See: Vinson Franchise Law online information. Viewed at: http://franchiselaw.net/startups/usfranchiselawbasics.html.

164 Special trade contractors undertake activities that are specialized either to building construction, including work on mobile homes, or to both building and non-building projects. These activities include painting (including bridge painting and traffic lane painting), electrical work (including work on bridges, power lines, and power plants), carpentry work, plumbing, heating, air-conditioning, roofing, and sheet metal work.

165 Environmental Protection Agency (EPA) online information. Viewed at: https://www.epa.gov/regulatory-information-sector/construction-sector-naics-23.

166 FAA online information, *Air Traffic Organization*. Viewed at: http://www.faa.gov/about/office_org/headquarters_offices/ato/.

167 FAA (2017), *Performance and Accountability Report*. Viewed at: https://www.faa.gov/about/plans_reports/media/2017_FAA_PAR.pdf.

168 Bureau of Transportation Statistics online information, "Airline Financial Data". Viewed at: https://www.bts.gov/event/behind-numbers-airline-financial-data.

169 Bureau of Transportation Statistics (2018), *Freight Facts and Figures 2017*. Viewed at: https://www.bts.gov/newsroom/freight-facts-and-figures-2017.

170 Title 14 of the CFR may be viewed at: http://www.ecfr.gov/cgi-bin/text-idx?c=ecfr&tpl=/ecfrbrowse/ Title14/14tab_02.tpl.

171 The rights granted to foreign airlines concerning U.S. government procured transportation under Open Skies Agreements (OSAs) do not apply to transportation obtained or funded by the Secretary of Defense or the Secretary of a military department.

172 Department of Transportation, "Statement of United States International Air Transportation Policy". 60 Federal Register 21841 (3 May 1995).

173 An OSA is defined by USDOT Order 92-8-13.

174 The full list and status of all the OSAs signed by the United States may be viewed at: http://www.state.gov/e/eb/rls/othr/ata/270724.htm.

175 The Airline Deregulation Act (ADA), passed in 1978, gave air carriers almost total freedom to determine which markets to serve domestically, and what fares to charge for that service.

176 USDOT (2018), *Subsidized EAS report for Non-Alaska communities - May 2018*. Viewed at: https://cms.dot.gov/office-policy/aviation-policy/subsidized-eas-report-non-alaska-communities-may-2018-pdf.

177 USDOT online information. Viewed at: https://www.transportation.gov/policy/aviation-policy/small-community-rural-air-service/essential-air-service.

178 Among other things, 49 U.S.C. § 41731 states that, to be eligible, a community must have had an average subsidy per passenger of less than US$1,000 during the most recent fiscal year, as determined by the Secretary of Transportation, or face termination of subsidy eligibility, regardless of distance to a hub airport.

179 USDOT online information. Viewed at: https://www.transportation.gov/policy/aviation-policy/small-community-rural-air-service/essential-air-service.

180 USDOT online information, *Alternate Essential Air Service*. Viewed at: https://cms.dot.gov/office-policy/aviation-policy/alternate-essential-air-service.

181 USDOT online information. Viewed at: https://cms.dot.gov/policy/aviation-policy/small-community-rural-air-service/SCASDP.

182 FAA (2018), *Administrator's Fact Book, September 2018*. Viewed at: https://www.faa.gov/news/media/2018_Administrators_Fact_Book.pdf.

183 For example, a federally-funded airport may not use proceeds from the sale of the airport for non-airport purposes, i.e. the airport revenue must be used for the capital and operating costs of the airport.

184 There are nearly 3,400 airports covered in the National Plan of Integrated Airport System (NPIAS). Viewed at: http://www.faa.gov/airports/planning_capacity/npias/.

185 The Airport Improvement Program (AIP) was established by the Airport and Airway Improvement Act of 1982 (49 U.S.C. 471). The AIP is funded through taxes on passenger ticket sales and on aviation fuel.

186 In limited cases, 95% of eligible costs may be covered by the AIP.

187 U.S. Senate Committee on Commerce, Science, and Transportation (2016), *Federal Aviation Administration Reauthorization Section-by-Section Analysis*. Viewed at: http://www.commerce.senate.gov/public/_cache/files/ae9d5486-e1fa-4456-97f4-c993b7997742/EC864F25A5CC519BA632299E860F6D29.faa-section-by-section-handout.pdf.

188 Department of Transportation online information, *Buy America Provisions*. Viewed at: https://www.transportation.gov/highlights/buyamerica. See also FAA online information, *AIP Buy American Preference Requirements*. Viewed at: http://www.faa.gov/airports/aip/buy_american/.

189 When procuring a facility or equipment, the cost of components and subcomponents produced in the United States must be more than 60% of the cost of all components, and final assembly must be in the United States.

190 Only general aviation airports can be sold under the Airport Privatization Pilot Program (APPP).

191 Tang, R., Y. (2017), *Airport Privatization: Issues and Options for Congress*, Congressional Research Service Report. Viewed at: https://www.fas.org/sgp/crs/misc/R43545.pdf.

192 FAA online information. Viewed at: https://www.faa.gov/airports/airport_compliance/privatization/.

193 Institute for Water Resources (2017), *Final Waterborne Commerce Statistics for Calendar Year 2016*. Viewed at: http://cwbi-ndc-nav.s3-website-us-east-1.amazonaws.com/files/wcsc/pdf/2016-Final.pdf.

194 MARAD online information, "MARAD Open Data Portal". Viewed at: http://www.marad.dot.gov/resources/data-statistics/. All the numbers referring to vessels in this section only reflect ocean-going, self-propelled, cargo-carrying vessels of 1,000 gross tons and above.

195 MARAD (2017), *Maritime Administration Strategic Plan, Navigating the Future, 2017-2021*. Viewed at: https://www.marad.dot.gov/wp-content/uploads/pdf/MARAD-Strategic-Plan-2017-2021-20170119-Final-signed.pdf.

196 MARAD (2017), *Maritime Administration Strategic Plan, Navigating the Future, 2017-2021*. Viewed at: https://www.marad.dot.gov/wp-content/uploads/pdf/MARAD-Strategic-Plan-2017-2021-20170119-Final-signed.pdf.

197 The U.S. Virgin Islands are exempt from the Jones Act, and certain Pacific islands (Guam, etc.) are dual-status ports.

198 Under 46 U.S.C. 8103(b)(B), not more than 25% of the total number of unlicensed seamen on the vessel may be aliens lawfully admitted to the United States for permanent residence.

199 MARAD online information, "MARAD Open Data Portal". Viewed at: https://www.marad.dot.gov/wp-content/uploads/pdf/Consolidated_Summary_20180601-June.pdf.

200 46 U.S.C. § 50501 requires 75% U.S. citizen voting and stock control.

201 Institute for Water Resources, Navigation and Civil Works Decision Support Center, U.S. Army Corps of Engineers, Waterborne Commerce Statistics Center (2017), *Final Waterborne Commerce Statistics for Calendar Year 2016, Waterborne Commerce National Totals and Selected Inland Waterways for Multiple Years*. Viewed at: https://usace.contentdm.oclc.org/utils/getfile/collection/p16021coll2/id/1655.

202 Department of Transportation, Bureau of Transportation Statistics, *2016 Highlights of Ferry Operators in the United States*. Viewed at: https://www.bts.gov/sites/bts.dot.gov/files/docs/browse-statistical-products-and-data/surveys/national-census-ferry-operators-ncfo/210441/ferry-operators-highlights-2016.pdf.

203 MARAD online information, "Small Passenger Vessel Waiver Program". Viewed at: http://www.marad.dot.gov/ships-and-shipping/domestic-shipping/.

204 MARAD online information, *Small Vessel Waiver Program*. Viewed at: https://www.marad.dot.gov/ships-and-shipping/domestic-shipping/small-vessel-waiver-program/.

205 MARAD online information. Viewed at: https://www.marad.dot.gov/ships-and-shipping/domestic-shipping/launch-barge-program/.

206 MARAD online information. Viewed at: https://www.marad.dot.gov/ships-and-shipping/domestic-shipping/.

207 MARAD online information, *Cargo Preference*. Viewed at: http://www.marad.dot.gov/ships-and-shipping/cargo-preference/.

208 A complete list of eligible foreign-owned vessels, as of 12 April 2018, may be viewed at: https://www.marad.dot.gov/wp-content/uploads/pdf/180412-MAR730_Foreign-Flag-Vessel-List-NEW-2.pdf.

209 MARAD online information. Viewed at: https://www.marad.dot.gov/ships-and-shipping/cargo-preference/laws-and-regulations/.

210 The ODS, granted on a 20-year contract basis, was provided for U.S.-flag vessels operating on international trade routes, in order to compensate for cost differences between U.S. and foreign operators. WTO document S/NGMTS/W/2/Add.11, 31 January 1995.

211 MARAD online information, "Maritime Security Program". Viewed at: http://www.marad.dot.gov/search/maritime+security+program/.

212 As at 1 June 2018, there were the following MSP operators and vessels: American International Shipping, LLC (1), APL Marine Services, Ltd. (8), APL Maritime, Ltd. (1), Argent Marine Operations, Inc. (1), Central Gulf Lines, Inc. (4), Farrell Lines Incorporated (5), Fidelio Limited Partnership (8), Hapag-Lloyd USA, LLC (5), Liberty Global Logistics, LLC (3), Mykonos Tanker Corporation (1), Maersk Line, Ltd. (18), Santorini Tanker Corporation (1), Patriot Shipping, LLC (2), and Waterman Steamship Corporation (2). See: *The Maritime Security Program*, at https://www.marad.dot.gov/wp-content/uploads/pdf/MSP-Brochure-7-1-2017.pdf.

213 MARAD online information, "VISA Program". Viewed at: http://www.marad.dot.gov/search/VISA+program/.

214 See Voluntary Intermodal Sealift Agreement, Changes to the Open Season Enrolment Period, 83 Fed. Reg. 4552 (31 January 2018).

215 Based on tonnage, see: MARAD (2018), *Consolidated Fleet Summary and Change List*

United States Flag Privately-Owned Merchant Fleet, 1 June 2018. Viewed at: https://www.marad.dot.gov/wp-content/uploads/pdf/Consolidated_Summary_20180601-June.pdf.

216 MARAD online information. Viewed at: https://www.marad.dot.gov/ships-and-shipping/american-fisheries-act/.

217 FMC online information. Viewed at: https://www.fmc.gov/regulatory_reform.aspx.

218 MARAD online information, *International Agreements*. Viewed at: http://www.marad.dot.gov/about-us/international-activities/international-agreements/.

219 MARAD online information. Viewed at: https://www.marad.dot.gov/ports/office-of-port-infrastructure-development-and-congestion-mitigation/.

220 MARAD online information. Viewed at: https://www.marad.dot.gov/ports/office-of-deepwater-ports-and-offshore-activities/about-the-deepwater-port-act/.

221 See 46 U.S.C. 53701 and 46 U.S.C. 53706.

222 MARAD online information. Viewed at: https://www.marad.dot.gov/ships-and-shipping/federal-ship-financing-title-xi-program-homepage/.

223 MARAD online information, *Federal Ship Financing Program (Title XI)*. Viewed at: http://www.marad.dot.gov/ships-and-shipping/federal-ship-financing-title-xi-program-homepage/.

224 MARAD online information. Viewed at: https://www.marad.dot.gov/ships-and-shipping/federal-ship-financing-title-xi-program-homepage/outstanding-guarantees/.

225 Exemptions are applied to certain countries in accordance with the bilateral agreements between the United States and the countries.

226 USDOC online information. Viewed at: https://www.commerce.gov/tags/travel-and-tourism.

227 ITA online information. Viewed at: https://www.trade.gov/ttab/.

228 *National Travel and Tourism Strategy - Task Force on Travel and Competitiveness (2012)*. Viewed at: https://travel.trade.gov/pdf/national-travel-and-tourism-strategy.pdf.

229 Kirchhoefer, Gregg; Bond, P., Daniel; Eisenberg, Ashley; and Mitrani, Adine, *e-commerce: United States*, August 2018. Kirkland & Ellis International LLP online information. Viewed at: https://gettingthedealthrough.com/area/11/jurisdiction/23/e-commerce-2018-united-states/%20-%20link-32.

230 Supreme Court of the United States, Syllabus, *South Dakota v. Wayfair, Inc., Et Al., Certiorari to the Supreme Court of South Dakota, No. 17–494*. Argued 17 April 2018, decided 21 June 2018. Viewed at: https://www.supremecourt.gov/opinions/17pdf/17-494_j4el.pdf.

Appendix tables

Table A1.1 Merchandise exports by HS sections and main chapters, 2012-17

(US$ million and %)

Description	2012	2013	2014	2015	2016	2017
Total exports	1,544,932	1,577,587	1,619,743	1,501,846	1,450,457	1,545,609
	(% of total exports)					
1 - Live animals; animal products	1.8	1.9	1.9	1.7	1.7	1.8
02. Meat and edible meat offal	1.0	1.0	1.1	1.0	1.0	1.1
03. Fish and crustaceans, molluscs and other aquatic invertebrates	0.3	0.3	0.3	0.3	0.3	0.3
04. Dairy produce; birds' eggs; natural honey; edible products of animal origin	0.3	0.4	0.4	0.3	0.3	0.3
2 - Vegetable products	4.6	4.4	4.6	4.3	4.7	4.4
12. Oil seeds and oleaginous fruits; miscellaneous grains, seeds and fruit	1.9	1.7	1.8	1.6	1.9	1.7
10. Cereals	1.3	1.3	1.4	1.3	1.3	1.2
08. Edible fruit and nuts; peel of citrus fruit or melons	0.9	0.9	0.9	1.0	1.0	1.0
3 - Animal or vegetable fats and oils; prepared edible fats	0.3	0.2	0.2	0.2	0.2	0.2
4 - Prepared foodstuffs; beverages, spirits and vinegar; tobacco	2.6	2.8	2.8	3.0	3.0	2.8
23. Residues and waste from the food industries	0.6	0.7	0.7	0.7	0.7	0.6
21. Miscellaneous edible preparations	0.5	0.5	0.5	0.5	0.6	0.6
22. Beverages, spirits and vinegar	0.4	0.4	0.5	0.5	0.5	0.5
5 - Mineral products	9.5	10.1	10.3	7.6	7.0	9.6
27. Mineral fuels, mineral oils and products of their distillation	8.9	9.4	9.6	6.9	6.5	9.0
6 - Products of the chemical or allied industries	10.5	10.4	10.2	10.8	10.6	10.3
30. Pharmaceutical products	2.6	2.5	2.7	3.1	3.2	2.9
29. Organic chemicals	3.0	3.0	2.6	2.6	2.3	2.3
38. Miscellaneous chemical products	1.6	1.7	1.7	1.7	1.7	1.8
33. Essential oils and resinoids; perfumery, cosmetic or toilet preparations	0.7	0.7	0.7	0.8	0.8	0.8
28. Inorganic chemicals; organic or inorganic compounds of precious metals	0.9	0.8	0.8	0.8	0.8	0.8
7 - Plastics and articles thereof; rubber and articles thereof	4.8	4.8	4.8	4.9	4.9	4.9
39. Plastics and articles thereof	3.8	3.9	3.9	4.0	4.0	4.0
8 - Raw hides and skins, leather, furskins and articles thereof; travel goods, handbags; articles of animal gut	0.3	0.4	0.4	0.4	0.3	0.3
9 - Wood and articles of wood; wood charcoal; cork and articles of cork	0.5	0.6	0.6	0.6	0.6	0.6
10 - Pulp of wood or of other fibrous cellulosic material; paper and paperboard and articles thereof	2.0	2.0	1.9	1.9	1.9	1.9
48. Paper and paperboard; articles of paper pulp, of paper or of paperboard	1.0	1.0	1.0	1.0	1.0	1.0
47. Pulp of wood or of other fibrous cellulosic material; recovered paper	0.6	0.6	0.6	0.6	0.6	0.6
11 - Textiles and textile articles	1.7	1.7	1.6	1.7	1.6	1.7
52. Cotton	0.5	0.5	0.4	0.4	0.4	0.5
61. Articles of apparel and clothing accessories, knitted or crocheted	0.2	0.2	0.2	0.2	0.2	0.2
56. Wadding, felt and non-woven; special yarns	0.1	0.2	0.2	0.2	0.2	0.2
12 - Footwear, headgear, umbrellas; prepared feathers and articles; artificial flowers	0.1	0.1	0.1	0.1	0.1	0.1
13 - Articles of stone, plaster, cement, etc.; ceramic products; glass and glassware	0.7	0.7	0.7	0.8	0.8	0.8
14 - Natural or cultured pearls, precious or semi-precious stones, precious metals	4.7	4.5	4.0	3.9	3.9	3.9
15 - Base metals and articles of base metal	5.3	5.0	4.9	4.6	4.4	4.4
73. Articles of iron or steel	1.4	1.4	1.4	1.3	1.2	1.2
72. Iron and steel	1.5	1.2	1.1	1.0	0.9	1.0
76. Aluminium and articles thereof	0.8	0.8	0.8	0.8	0.8	0.7
74. Copper and articles thereof	0.6	0.6	0.5	0.5	0.4	0.5

Part B
Report by the WTO Secretariat

Description	2012	2013	2014	2015	2016	2017
16 - Machinery and mechanical appliances; electrical equipment; television image and sound recorders	24.4	24.0	24.2	25.0	24.7	24.4
84. Nuclear reactors, boilers, machinery and mechanical appliances	13.9	13.5	13.6	13.7	13.1	13.1
85. Electrical machinery and equipment; sound recorders and reproducers	10.5	10.5	10.6	11.3	11.5	11.3
17 - Vehicles, aircraft, vessels and associated transport equipment	15,9	16.2	16.6	17.7	18.3	17.3
87. Vehicles other than railway or tramway rolling-stock, parts and accessories	8.6	8.5	8.4	8.5	8.6	8.4
88. Aircraft, spacecraft, and parts thereof	6.8	7.3	7.7	8.8	9.3	8.5
18 - Optical, photographic, precision, medical or surgical instruments; clocks and watched; musical instruments	5.5	5.5	5.4	5.7	5.8	5.5
90. Optical, photographic, cinematographic, measuring, precision, medical or surgical instruments and apparatus	5.4	5.3	5.2	5.6	5.7	5.4
19 - Arms and ammunition	0.3	0.3	0.3	0.3	0.4	0.3
20 - Miscellaneous manufactured articles	1.3	1.3	1.3	1.3	1.4	1.3
94. Furniture; bedding, mattresses, mattress supports, cushions and similar stuffed furnishings	0.7	0.7	0.7	0.8	0.8	0.7
21 - Works of art, collectors' pieces and antiques	0.5	0.5	0.6	0.7	0.8	0.8
Other	2.6	2.7	2.7	2.8	2.8	2.7

Source: UNSD, Comtrade database.

Table A1.2 Merchandise imports by HS sections and main HS chapters, 2012–17

(US$ million and %)

Description	2012	2013	2014	2015	2016	2017
Total	2,334,678	2,326,590	2,410,855	2,313,425	2,248,209	2,407,390
	(% of total imports)					
1 - Live animals; animal products	1.1	1.1	1.3	1.4	1.4	1.4
03. Fish and crustaceans, molluscs and other aquatic invertebrates	0.6	0.6	0.7	0.7	0.7	0.7
02. Meat and edible meat offal	0.2	0.3	0.3	0.4	0.4	0.3
2 - Vegetable products	1.8	1.8	1.8	1.9	2.0	2.0
08. Edible fruit and nuts; peel of citrus fruit or melons	0.5	0.5	0.6	0.7	0.7	0.8
07. Edible vegetables and certain roots and tubers	0.3	0.4	0.4	0.4	0.5	0.4
09. Coffee, tea, maté and spices	0.4	0.3	0.3	0.4	0.4	0.4
3 - Animal or vegetable fats and oils; prepared edible fats	0.3	0.3	0.3	0.3	0.3	0.3
4 - Prepared foodstuffs; beverages, spirits and vinegar; tobacco	2.4	2.4	2.4	2.6	2.8	2.7
22. Beverages, spirits and vinegar	0.9	0.9	0.9	1.0	1.0	1.0
20. Preparations of vegetables, fruit, nuts or other parts of plants	0.3	0.3	0.3	0.3	0.4	0.4
5 - Mineral products	18.9	17.0	15.2	9.0	7.5	8.7
27. Mineral fuels, mineral oils and products of their distillation	18.5	16.7	14.9	8.7	7.3	8.5
6 - Products of the chemical or allied industries	7.6	7.6	7.8	8.5	8.8	8.3
30. Pharmaceutical products	2.8	2.7	3.0	3.7	4.1	4.0
29. Organic chemicals	2.3	2.3	2.3	2.2	2.2	1.9
38. Miscellaneous chemical products	0.5	0.5	0.5	0.6	0.6	0.6
33. Essential oils and resinoids; perfumery, cosmetic or toilet preparations	0.4	0.5	0.5	0.5	0.6	0.6
28. Inorganic chemicals; organic or inorganic compounds of precious metals	0.7	0.7	0.6	0.6	0.5	0.5
7 - Plastics and articles thereof; rubber and articles thereof	3.2	3.2	3.3	3.4	3.4	3.4
39. Plastics and articles thereof	1.9	2.0	2.1	2.2	2.2	2.3
40. Rubber and articles thereof	1.3	1.2	1.2	1.2	1.2	1.2
8 - Raw hides and skins, leather, furskins and articles thereof; travel goods, handbags; articles of animal gut	0.6	0.6	0.6	0.7	0.6	0.6
42. Articles of leather; travel goods, handbags; articles of animal gut	0.5	0.6	0.6	0.6	0.6	0.6
9 - Wood and articles of wood; wood charcoal; cork and articles of cork	0.6	0.7	0.8	0.8	0.9	0.9
10 - Pulp of wood or of other fibrous cellulosic material; paper and paperboard and articles thereof	1.0	1.1	1.0	1.1	1.1	1.0
48. Paper and paperboard; articles of paper pulp, of paper or of paperboard	0.7	0.7	0.7	0.7	0.7	0.7
11 - Textiles and textile articles	4.6	4.8	4.8	5.2	5.1	4.7
61. Articles of apparel and clothing accessories, knitted or crocheted	1.8	1.9	1.9	2.1	2.0	1.9
62. Articles of apparel and clothing accessories, not knitted or crocheted	1.6	1.7	1.6	1.8	1.7	1.6
63. Other made up textile articles	0.5	0.6	0.6	0.6	0.7	0.6
12 - Footwear, headgear, umbrellas; prepared feathers and articles; artificial flowers	1.3	1.3	1.3	1.5	1.4	1.3
64. Footwear, gaiters and the like; parts of such articles	1.1	1.1	1.1	1.2	1.2	1.1
13 - Articles of stone, plaster, cement, etc.; ceramic products; glass and glassware	0.8	0.8	0.9	1.0	1.0	1.0
68. Articles of stone, plaster, cement, asbestos, mica or similar materials	0.3	0.3	0.3	0.3	0.3	0.3
70. Glass and glassware	0.3	0.3	0.3	0.3	0.3	0.3
69. Ceramic products	0.2	0.3	0.3	0.3	0.3	0.3
14 - Natural or cultured pearls, precious or semi-precious stones, precious metals	2.7	2.8	2.7	2.5	2.9	2.4
15 - Base metals and articles of base metal	5.3	5.1	5.5	5.3	4.9	5.5
73. Articles of iron or steel	1.7	1.6	1.6	1.7	1.5	1.6
72. Iron and steel	1.3	1.1	1.5	1.2	1.0	1.2
76. Aluminium and articles thereof	0.7	0.7	0.7	0.8	0.8	1.0
83. Miscellaneous articles of base metal	0.4	0.4	0.4	0.5	0.5	0.5

Description	2012	2013	2014	2015	2016	2017
16 - Machinery and mechanical appliances; electrical equipment; television image and sound recorders	26.2	26.4	27.0	28.7	29.0	29.3
85. Electrical machinery and equipment; sound recorders and reproducers	12.7	13.0	13.3	14.4	14.9	14.8
84. Nuclear reactors, boilers, machinery and mechanical appliances	13.5	13.4	13.7	14.3	14.0	14.5
17 - Vehicles, aircraft, vessels and associated transport equipment	11.7	12.3	12.6	14.0	14.2	13.7
87. Vehicles other than railway or tramway rolling-stock, parts and accessories	10.5	10.9	11.0	12.3	12.7	12.2
88. Aircraft, spacecraft, and parts thereof	1.0	1.3	1.4	1.5	1.4	1.3
18 - Optical, photographic, precision, medical or surgical instruments; clocks and watched; musical instruments	3.3	3.4	3.4	3.7	3.9	3.8
90. Optical, photographic, cinematographic, measuring, precision, medical or surgical instruments and apparatus	3.0	3.1	3.2	3.4	3.6	3.6
19 - Arms and ammunition	0.1	0.2	0.1	0.1	0.2	0.1
20 - Miscellaneous manufactured articles	3.5	3.6	3.8	4.3	4.5	4.4
94. Furniture; bedding, mattresses, mattress supports, cushions and similar stuffed furnishings	2.0	2.2	2.3	2.6	2.8	2.8
95. Toys, games and sports requisites; parts and accessories thereof	1.2	1.2	1.2	1.4	1.4	1.4
21 - Works of art, collectors' pieces and antiques	0.3	0.4	0.4	0.5	0.4	0.4
Other	2.9	3.0	3.1	3.7	3.8	3.8

Source: UNSD, Comtrade database.

Table A1.3 Merchandise exports by trading partner, 2012-17

(US$ million and %)

Description	2012	2013	2014	2015	2016	2017
Total exports	1,544,932	1,577,587	1,619,743	1,501,846	1,450,457	1,545,609
	(% of exports)					
Americas	44.7	45.0	45.4	44.4	43.5	43.7
Canada	18.9	19.1	19.3	18.7	18.4	18.3
Mexico	14.0	14.3	14.8	15.7	15.8	15.7
Brazil	2.8	2.8	2.6	2.1	2.1	2.4
Chile	1.2	1.1	1.0	1.0	0.9	0.9
Colombia	1.1	1.2	1.2	1.1	0.9	0.9
Argentina	0.7	0.7	0.7	0.6	0.6	0.6
Peru	0.6	0.6	0.6	0.6	0.5	0.6
Dominican Republic	0.5	0.5	0.5	0.5	0.5	0.5
Guatemala	0.4	0.4	0.4	0.4	0.4	0.4
Panama	0.6	0.7	0.6	0.5	0.4	0.4
Costa Rica	0.5	0.5	0.4	0.4	0.4	0.4
Europe	20.3	19.7	19.6	20.7	21.3	20.8
EU-28	17.6	16.9	17.2	18.3	18.8	18.4
United Kingdom	3.6	3.0	3.3	3.7	3.8	3.6
Germany	3.1	3.0	3.0	3.3	3.4	3.5
Netherlands	2.6	2.7	2.7	2.7	2.7	2.7
France	2.1	2.1	2.0	2.1	2.2	2.2
Belgium	1.9	2.0	2.1	2.3	2.2	1.9
EFTA	2.0	2.0	1.7	1.7	1.9	1.8
Switzerland	1.7	1.7	1.4	1.5	1.6	1.4
Norway	0.2	0.3	0.3	0.2	0.3	0.4
Other Europe	0.8	0.8	0.7	0.6	0.7	0.6
Turkey	0.8	0.8	0.7	0.6	0.6	0.6
Commonwealth of Independent States (CIS)	1.0	1.0	1.0	0.6	0.7	0.7
Russian Federation	0.7	0.7	0.7	0.5	0.4	0.5
Ukraine	0.1	0.1	0.1	0.1	0.1	0.1
Africa	2.1	2.2	2.3	1.8	1.5	1.4
South Africa	0.5	0.5	0.4	0.4	0.3	0.3
Egypt	0.4	0.3	0.4	0.3	0.2	0.3
Nigeria	0.3	0.4	0.4	0.2	0.1	0.1
Middle East	4.5	4.6	4.6	4.8	4.7	4.2
United Arab Emirates	1.5	1.5	1.4	1.5	1.5	1.3
Saudi Arabia, Kingdom of	1.2	1.2	1.2	1.3	1.2	1.1
Israel	0.9	0.9	0.9	0.9	0.9	0.8
Asia	27.3	27.4	27.1	27.6	28.2	29.2
China	7.2	7.7	7.6	7.7	8.0	8.4
Japan	4.5	4.1	4.1	4.2	4.4	4.4
Other Asia	15.6	15.5	15.3	15.7	15.9	16.4
Korea, Republic of	2.7	2.6	2.7	2.9	2.9	3.1
Hong Kong, China	2.4	2.7	2.5	2.5	2.4	2.6
Singapore	2.0	1.9	1.9	1.9	1.8	1.9
Chinese Taipei	1.6	1.6	1.6	1.7	1.8	1.7
India	1.4	1.4	1.3	1.4	1.5	1.7
Australia	2.0	1.7	1.6	1.7	1.5	1.6
Malaysia	0.8	0.8	0.8	0.8	0.8	0.8
Thailand	0.7	0.7	0.7	0.7	0.7	0.7
Other	0.0	0.0	0.0	0.0	0.0	0.0

Source: UNSD, Comtrade database.

Part B
Report by the WTO Secretariat

Table A1.4 Merchandise imports by trading partner, 2012–17

(US$ million and %)

Description	2012	2013	2014	2015	2016	2017
Total imports	2,334,678	2,326,590	2,410,855	2,313,425	2,248,209	2,407,390
	(% of imports)					
Americas	33.6	33.7	33.5	31.2	30.8	30.9
Mexico	12.0	12.2	12.3	12.9	13.2	13.2
Canada	14.0	14.5	14.7	13.1	12.6	12.7
Brazil	1.4	1.2	1.3	1.2	1.2	1.3
Colombia	1.1	1.0	0.8	0.6	0.6	0.6
Venezuela, Bolivarian Republic of	1.7	1.4	1.3	0.7	0.5	0.5
Chile	0.4	0.5	0.4	0.4	0.4	0.5
Peru	0.3	0.4	0.3	0.2	0.3	0.3
Ecuador	0.4	0.5	0.5	0.3	0.3	0.3
Argentina	0.2	0.2	0.2	0.2	0.2	0.2
Dominican Republic	0.2	0.2	0.2	0.2	0.2	0.2
Costa Rica	0.5	0.5	0.4	0.2	0.2	0.2
Honduras	0.2	0.2	0.2	0.2	0.2	0.2
Guatemala	0.2	0.2	0.2	0.2	0.2	0.2
Europe	18.5	18.8	19.6	20.9	21.2	20.7
EU-28	16.7	17.0	17.7	18.9	18.9	18.5
Germany	4.8	5.0	5.2	5.5	5.2	5.0
United Kingdom	2.4	2.3	2.3	2.5	2.5	2.2
Italy	1.6	1.7	1.8	2.0	2.1	2.1
France	1.8	2.0	2.0	2.1	2.1	2.1
Ireland	1.4	1.4	1.4	1.7	2.0	2.0
EFTA	1.4	1.5	1.6	1.6	1.9	1.8
Switzerland	1.1	1.2	1.3	1.4	1.6	1.5
Norway	0.3	0.2	0.2	0.2	0.2	0.2
Other Europe	0.3	0.3	0.4	0.4	0.4	0.4
Turkey	0.3	0.3	0.3	0.4	0.4	0.4
Commonwealth of Independent States (CIS)	1.5	1.4	1.2	0.9	0.8	0.8
Russian Federation	1.3	1.2	1.0	0.7	0.7	0.7
Africa	2.9	2.2	1.5	1.1	1.2	1.4
South Africa	0.4	0.4	0.4	0.3	0.3	0.3
Nigeria	0.8	0.5	0.2	0.1	0.2	0.3
Algeria	0.4	0.2	0.2	0.2	0.2	0.2
Middle East	5.1	4.7	4.4	2.8	2.6	2.7
Israel	1.0	1.0	1.0	1.1	1.0	0.9
Saudi Arabia, Kingdom of	2.5	2.3	2.0	1.0	0.8	0.8
Iraq	0.8	0.6	0.6	0.2	0.3	0.5
United Arab Emirates	0.1	0.1	0.1	0.1	0.2	0.2
Asia	38.4	39.2	39.8	43.0	43.4	43.4
China	19.0	19.7	20.2	21.8	21.4	21.9
Japan	6.4	6.1	5.7	5.8	6.0	5.8
Other Asia	12.9	13.3	14.0	15.4	15.9	15.7
Korea, Republic of	2.6	2.8	3.0	3.2	3.2	3.1
India	1.8	1.9	1.9	2.0	2.1	2.1
Viet Nam	0.9	1.1	1.3	1.7	1.9	2.0
Chinese Taipei	1.7	1.7	1.7	1.8	1.8	1.8
Malaysia	1.1	1.2	1.3	1.5	1.7	1.6
Thailand	1.2	1.2	1.2	1.3	1.4	1.3
Indonesia	0.8	0.8	0.8	0.9	0.9	0.9
Singapore	0.9	0.8	0.7	0.8	0.8	0.8
Philippines	0.4	0.4	0.4	0.5	0.5	0.5
Other	0.0	0.0	0.0	0.0	0.0	0.0

Source: UNSD, Comtrade database.

Table A2.1 Selected U.S. notifications to the WTO, August 2016-July 2018

WTO Agreement	Description	Document symbol	Date
Agreement on Agriculture			
Articles 10 and 18.2 (ES:1 and ES:2)	Export subsidies commitments: budgetary outlays and quantity reduction commitments; and notification of total exports	G/AG/N/USA/118 G/AG/N/USA/112	29/11/2017 30/03/2017
Article 16.2 NF:1 (1)-(4)	Net-Food Importing Developing Country (NFIDC) Decision: food and other assistance; and other specific actions	G/AG/N/USA/119 G/AG/N/USA/116 G/AG/N/USA/113	25/01/2018 04/10/2017 30/03/2017
Article 18.2 (DS:1)	Domestic support	G/AG/N/USA/121 G/AG/N/USA/80/Rev.2/Corr.1 G/AG/N/USA/109 G/AG/N/USA/108/Rev.1 G/AG/N/USA/100/Rev.1 G/AG/N/USA/93/Rev.1 G/AG/N/USA/89/Rev.2 G/AG/N/USA/80/Rev.2 G/AG/N/USA/77/Rev.2	01/05/2018 06/03/2017 19/01/2017 03/02/2017 03/02/2017 31/01/2017 31/01/2017 27/01/2017 12/01/2017
Article 18.3 (DS:2)	Domestic support	G/AG/N/USA/110	19/01/2017
Article 18.2 (MA:1)	Administration of tariff and other quota commitments	G/AG/N/USA/114/Add.1 G/AG/N/USA/117	04/09/2017 04/10/2017
Articles 5.7 and 18.2 (MA:4)	Special safeguard provisions	G/AG/N/USA/111	02/03/2017
Article 18.2 (MA:5)	Tariff rate quotas	G/AG/N/USA/120 G/AG/N/USA/115 G/AG/N/USA/102/Corr.1	24/04/2018 30/03/2017 30/03/2017
Agreement on the Implementation of Article VI of the GATT 1994 (Anti-dumping Agreement)			
Article 16.4 – semi annual	Anti-dumping actions (taken within the preceding six months)	G/ADP/N/286/USA G/ADP/N/294/USA G/ADP/N/300/USA G/ADP/N/308/USA	07/09/2016 09/03/2017 06/09/2017 21/03/2018
Article 16.4 – ad hoc	Anti-dumping actions (preliminary and final)	G/ADP/N/315 G/ADP/N/313 G/ADP/N/312 G/ADP/N/311 G/ADP/N/310 G/ADP/N/309 G/ADP/N/307 G/ADP/N/306 G/ADP/N/305 G/ADP/N/304 G/ADP/N/303 G/ADP/N/302 G/ADP/N/301 G/ADP/N/299 G/ADP/N/298 G/ADP/N/297 G/ADP/N/296 G/ADP/N/295 G/ADP/N/293 G/ADP/N/292 G/ADP/N/291 G/ADP/N/290	29/06/2018 30/05/2018 12/04/2018 26/03/2018 22/02/2018 24/01/2018 20/12/2017 14/12/2017 19/10/2017 20/09/2017 30/08/2017 18/07/2017 28/06/2017 31/05/2017 20/04/2017 23/03/2017 24/02/2017 30/01/2017 13/12/2016 29/11/2016 18/10/2016 22/09/2016
Article 18.5	Laws and regulations, and changes thereto, including changes in the administration of such laws	G/ADP/N/1/USA/1/Suppl.25/corr.1 G/ADP/N/1/USA/1/Suppl.24/corr.1 G/ADP/N/1/USA/1/Suppl.25 G/ADP/N/1/USA/1/Suppl.24	13/09/2016 13/09/2016 26/08/2016 26/08/2016

WTO Agreement	Description	Document symbol	Date
GATT 1994			
Article XVII:4(a) and Paragraph 1 of the Understanding on the Interpretation of Article XVII	State-trading activities	G/STR/N/17/USA/Corr.1 G/STR/N/17/USA G/STR/N/16/USA/Rev.2 G/STR/N/15/USA/Rev.1 G/STR/N/14/USA/Rev.1 G/STR/N/13/USA/Rev.1 G/STR/N/12/USA/Rev.1 G/STR/N/11/USA/Rev.1 G/STR/N/16/USA/Rev.1	02/07/2018 19/06/2018 11/10/2017 11/10/2017 11/10/2017 11/10/2017 11/10/2017 11/10/2017 13/04/2017
Paragraph 3(c)	Notification and statistical data	WT/L/1020 WT/L/948	14/11/2017 05/01/2017
Agreement on Government Procurement			
Appendix I	Procurement thresholds	GPA/THR/USA/1	20/12/2017
Article XIX:5	Statistical submissions	GPA/108/Add.9 GPA/114/Add.8 GPA/137/Add.8	13/09/2016 21/11/2017 28/11/2017
Agreement on Import Licensing			
Article 1.4(a)	Licensing procedures	G/LIC/N/1/USA/7	20/03/2018
Article 7.3	Replies to the questionnaire	G/LIC/N/3/USA/13 G/LIC/N/3/USA/14	08/11/2016 22/01/2018
Article 8.2(b)	Changes in Laws/regulations and administrative arrangements	G/LIC/N/1/USA/7	20/03/2017
Decision on Notification Procedures for Quantitative Restrictions			
G/L/59/Rev.1	Notification of QRs	G/MA/QR/N/USA/3	07/10/2016
Agreement on Rules of Origin			
Paragraph 4 of Annex II	Preferential rules of origin	G/RO/LDC/N/USA/1 G/RO/LDC/N/USA/2 G/RO/LDC/N/USA/3	11/07/2017 11/07/2017 11/07/2017
Agreement on Subsidies and Countervailing Measures			
Article 25.1 and GATT 1994 Article XVI:1	Subsidies	G/SCM/N/315/USA	14/03/2018
Article 25.11 – ad hoc	Countervailing duty actions (preliminary and final)	G/SCM/N/336 G/SCM/N/335 G/SCM/N/333 G/SCM/N/332 G/SCM/N/331 G/SCM/N/330 G/SCM/N/329/rev.1 G/SCM/N/327 G/SCM/N/326 G/SCM/N/325 G/SCM/N/324 G/SCM/N/323 G/SCM/N/322 G/SCM/N/320 G/SCM/N/319 G/SCM/N/318 G/SCM/N/317 G/SCM/N/316 G/SCM/N/314 G/SCM/N/312 G/SCM/N/311 G/SCM/N/310 G/SCM/N/309 G/SCM/N/308	24/07/2018 19/06/2018 25/05/2018 12/04/2018 16/03/2018 22/02/2018 05/02/2018 15/12/2017 09/11/2017 12/10/2017 14/09/2017 04/08/2017 13/07/2017 13/06/2017 12/05/2017 13/04/2017 14/03/2017 21/02/2017 12/01/2017 13/12/2016 11/11/2016 12/10/2016 27/09/2016 25/08/2016
Article 25.11 – semi-annual	Countervailing duty actions (taken within the preceding six months)	G/SCM/N/328/USA G/SCM/N/305/USA/corr.1 G/SCM/N/321/USA G/SCM/N/313/USA G/SCM/N/305/USA	22/02/2018 10/11/2017 03/10/2017 14/03/2018 26/09/2016

WTO Agreement	Description	Document symbol	Date
Article 32.6	Laws/regulations and changes thereto, including changes in administration of such laws	G/SCM/N/1/USA/1/Suppl.24/Corr1 G/SCM/N/1/USA/1/Suppl.24	13/09/2016 26/08/2016
Agreement on Sanitary and Phytosanitary Measures			
Article 7 Annex B	Sanitary and phytosanitary regulations	Some 200 notifications (series G/SPS/N/USA/) 138 new notifications G/SPS/N/USA/2876- G/SPS/N/USA/3014	
Agreement on Technical Barriers to Trade			
Article 2.9	Technical regulations	Several notifications (series G/TBT/N/USA/)	
Articles 2.9 and 5.6	Technical regulations and conformity assessment procedures	G/TBT/N/USA/1143/Add.2 G/TBT/N/USA/1209 G/TBT/N/USA/1267 G/TBT/N/USA/1273 G/TBT/N/USA/1273/Add.1 G/TBT/N/USA/1143/Add.3 G/TBT/N/USA/1316 G/TBT/N/USA/1205/Rev.1 G/TBT/N/USA/1326 G/TBT/N/USA/1337 G/TBT/N/USA/1273/Add.3 G/TBT/N/USA/1364 G/TBT/N/USA/1364/Add.1 G/TBT/N/USA/1364/Corr.1 G/TBT/N/USA/1367 G/TBT/N/USA/1367/Add.1 G/TBT/N/USA/1369 G/TBT/N/USA/1375 G/TBT/N/USA/1379	11/08/2016 26/10/2016 31/01/2017 06/02/2017 13/11/2017 26/09/2017 10/11/2017 10/01/2018 09/01/2018 05/02/2018 12/02/2018 07/05/2018 28/05/2018 26/06/2018 17/05/2018 10/07/2018 23/05/2018 27/06/2018 16/07/2018
Article 3.2	Technical regulations (local government)	Many notifications received, see: http://tbtims.wto.org/	

Source: WTO Secretariat.

Table A2.2 United States as a complainant in WTO disputes 2016-July 2018

Subject	DS No./WTO document series	Respondent	Request date	Status (as at 26 July 2018)
Turkey - Additional Duties on Certain Products from the United States	561 WT/DS561/	Turkey	16 July 2018	Consultations
Mexico - Additional Duties on Certain Products from the United States	560 WT/DS560/	Mexico	16 July 2018	Consultations
European Union - Additional Duties on Certain Products from the United States	559 WT/DS559/	European Union	16 July 2018	Consultations
China - Additional Duties on Certain Products from the United States	558 WT/DS558/	China	16 July 2018	Consultations
Canada - Additional Duties on Certain Products from the United States	557 WT/DS557/	Canada	16 July 2018	Consultations
China - Certain Measures Concerning the Protection of Intellectual Property Rights	542 WT/DS542/	China	23 March 2018	Consultations
India - Export Related Measures	541 WT/DS541/	India	14 March 2018	Panel composed on 23 July 2018 (WT/DS541/5)
Canada - Measures Governing the Sale of Wine in Grocery Stores (Second Complaint)	531 WT/DS531/	Canada	28 September 2017	Panel established, but not yet composed
Canada - Measures Governing the Sale of Wine in Grocery Stores	520 WT/DS520/	Canada	18 January 2017	Consultations
China - Subsidies to Producers of Primary Aluminum	519 WT/DS519/	China	12 January 2017	Consultations
China - Tariff Rate Quotas for Certain Agricultural Products	517 WT/DS517/	China	15 December 2016	Panel composed on 12 February 2018
China - Domestic Support for Agricultural Producers	511 WT/DS511/	China	13 September 2016	Panel composed on 24 June 2017
China - Export Duties on Certain Raw Materials	508 WT/DS508/	China	13 July 2016	Panel established, but not yet composed

Source: WTO Secretariat.

Table A2.3 United States as a respondent in WTO disputes 2016-July 2018

Subject	DS No. WTO document series	Complainant(s)	Request date	Status (as at 26 July 2018)
United States - Certain Measures on Steel and Aluminium Products	556 WT/DS556/	Switzerland	9 July 2018	Consultations
United States - Certain Measures on Steel and Aluminium Products	554 WT/DS554/	Russia	29 June 2018	Consultations
United States - Certain Measures on Steel and Aluminium Products	552 WT/DS552/	Norway	12 June 2018	Consultations
United States - Certain Measures on Steel and Aluminium Products	551 WT/DS551/	Mexico	5 June 2018	Consultations
United States - Certain Measures on Steel and Aluminium Products	550 WT/DS550/	Canada	1 June 2018	Consultations
United States - Certain Measures on Steel and Aluminium Products	548 WT/DS548/	European Union	1 June 2018	Consultations
United States - Certain Measures on Steel and Aluminium Products	547 WT/DS547/	India	18 May 2018	Consultations
United States - Safeguard Measure on Imports of Large Residential Washers	546 WT/DS546/	Korea	14 May 2018	Consultations
United States - Safeguard Measure on Imports of Crystalline Silicon Photovoltaic Products	545 WT/DS545/6	Korea	14 May 2018	Consultations
United States - Certain Measures on Steel and Aluminium Products	544 WT/DS544/	China	5 April 2018	Consultations
United States - Tariff Measures on Certain Goods from China	543 WT/DS543/	China	4 April 2018	Consultations
United States - Certain Measures Concerning Pangasius Seafood Products from Viet Nam	540 WT/DS540/	Viet Nam	22 February 2018	Consultations
United States - Anti-Dumping and Countervailing Duties on Certain Products and the Use of Facts Available	539 WT/DS539/	Korea	14 February 2018	Panel established, but not yet composed
United States - Anti-Dumping Measures on Fish Fillets from Viet Nam	536 WT/DS536/	Viet Nam	8 January 2018	Panel established, but not yet composed
United States - Certain Systemic Trade Remedies Measures	535 WT/DS535/	Canada	20 December 2017	Consultations
United States - Anti-Dumping Measures Applying Differential Pricing Methodology to Softwood Lumber from Canada	534 WT/DS534/	Canada	28 November 2017	Panel composed on 22 May 2018
United States - Countervailing Measures on Softwood Lumber from Canada	533 WT/DS533/	Canada	28 November 2017	Panel composed on 6 July 2018
United States - Countervailing Measures on Certain Pipe and Tube Products from Turkey	523 WT/DS523/	Turkey	8 March 2017	Panel composed on 14 September 2017
United States - Measures Related to Price Comparison Methodologies	515 WT/DS515/	China	12 December 2016	Consultations
United States - Countervailing Measures on Cold- and Hot-Rolled Steel Flat Products from Brazil	514 WT/DS514/	Brazil	11 November 2016	Consultations
United States - Certain Measures Relating to the Renewable Energy Sector	510 WT/DS510/	India	9 September 2016	Panel composed on 24 April 2018

Source: WTO Secretariat.

Part B
Report by the WTO Secretariat

Table A3.1 Analysis of United States MFN tariff, 2018

Description	No. of lines	Average (%)	Range (%)	Coefficient of variation (CV)	Final bound average[a] (%)
Total	**10,878**	**4.8**	**0 - 439.9**	**2.8**	**4.8**
HS 01-24	1,928	8.4	0 - 439.9	3.5	8.6
HS 25-97	8,950	4.1	0 - 57.1	1.3	4.0
By WTO category					
WTO Agriculture	1,707	9.4	0 - 439.9	3.3	9.4
- Animals and products thereof	162	3.0	0 - 26.4	1.8	3.0
- Dairy products	167	30.1	0 - 354.8	1.5	30.1
- Fruit, vegetables and plants	532	5.4	0 - 131.8	2.1	5.5
- Coffee and tea	82	8.0	0 - 27.9	0.8	8.0
- Cereals and preparations	190	9.5	0 - 246.6	2.3	9.4
- Oil seeds, fats and oils and their Products	107	7.0	0 - 163.8	3.4	7.0
- Sugars and confectionary	53	9.4	0 - 30	0.9	9.4
- Beverages, spirits and tobacco	152	22.6	0 - 439.9	3.6	23.0
- Cotton	16	5.9	0 - 34.8	1.6	4.7
- Other agricultural products n.e.s.	246	1.6	0 - 41.2	2.5	1.7
WTO Non-agriculture (incl. petroleum)	9,171	4.0	0 - 57.1	1.4	3.9
- WTO Non-agriculture (excl. petroleum)	9,139	4.0	0 - 57.1	1.4	3.9
- - Fish and fishery products	369	1.4	0 - 35	2.5	1.5
- - Minerals and metals	1,567	2.5	0 - 38	1.6	2.5
- - Chemicals and photographic supplies	1,941	3.7	0 - 6.5	0.7	3.7
- - Wood, pulp, paper and furniture	579	1.1	0 - 16	2.4	1.0
- - Textiles	1,098	7.9	0 - 38.9	0.7	7.8
- - Clothing	647	11.3	0 - 32	0.7	11.5
- - Leather, rubber, footwear and travel goods	421	7.5	0 - 57.1	1.5	7.3
- - Non-electric machinery	820	1.3	0 - 9.9	1.4	1.3
- - Electric machinery	543	1.8	0 - 15	1.2	1.8
- - Transport equipment	261	2.4	0 - 25	1.9	2.5
- - Non-agriculture articles n.e.s.	893	2.8	0 - 42.7	1.3	2.8
- Petroleum	32	2.0	0.03 - 10.5	1.5	2.1
By ISIC sector[b]					
Agriculture and fisheries	598	5.8	0 - 439.9	6.1	5.9
Mining	115	0.4	0 - 10.5	3.1	0.4
Manufacturing	10,164	4.8	0 - 354.8	2.3	4.8
By HS section					
01 Live animals & products	605	9.4	0 - 354.8	2.9	9.9
02 Vegetable products	563	3.9	0 - 163.8	2.9	3.9
03 Fats & oils	69	3.8	0 - 19.5	1.3	3.8
04 Prepared food etc.	691	11.7	0 - 439.9	3.5	11.7
05 Minerals	204	0.6	0 - 13.7	2.8	0.6
06 Chemical & products	1,804	3.5	0 - 15.8	0.8	3.5
07 Plastics & rubber	376	3.7	0 - 14	0.7	3.7
08 Hides & skins	231	4.9	0 - 20	1.1	4.3
09 Wood & articles	273	2.4	0 - 18	1.4	2.4
10 Pulp, paper etc.	275	0.0	0 - 0	n.a.	0.0
11 Textile & articles	1,674	9.0	0 - 34.8	0.8	9.0
12 Footwear, headgear	197	13.4	0 - 57.1	1.1	13.3
13 Articles of stone	317	5.5	0 - 38	1.1	5.2
14 Precious stones, etc.	105	3.0	0 - 13.5	1.1	3.1
15 Base metals & products	988	1.9	0 - 20.5	1.4	1.9
16 Machinery	1,383	1.5	0 - 15	1.4	1.5
17 Transport equipment	272	2.3	0 - 25	1.9	2.4
18 Precision equipment	518	2.5	0 - 27.7	1.3	2.5
19 Arms and ammunition	33	2.0	0 - 13.6	1.4	2.0
20 Miscellaneous manufactures	293	3.6	0 - 42.7	1.3	3.6
21 Works of art, etc.	7	0.0	0 - 0	n.a.	0.0
By stage of processing					
First stage of processing	1,122	3.9	0 - 439.9	6.7	4.0
Semi-processed products	3,536	4.2	0 - 27.5	1.0	4.2
Fully-processed products	6,220	5.4	0 - 354.8	2.5	5.3

n.a. Not applicable.

a   Bound rates are provided in HS2012 classification and applied rates in HS2017; therefore, there is a difference between the number of lines included in the calculation. In some circumstances, a higher applied MFN tariff average than the bound average is due to the change in nomenclature.

b   ISIC (Rev.2) classification, excluding electricity (1 line).

Source: WTO Secretariat estimates, based on data provided by the authorities.

Table A3.2 Prohibitions, restrictions or other special requirements

Product	Prohibition, restriction, or requirement
Art materials	Conform to the provisions of the Labeling of Hazardous Art Materials Act
Bicycles and bicycle helmets	Bicycles to meet regulations issued under the Federal Hazardous Substances Act and helmets must meet CPSC's Safety Standard
Biological drugs	Domestic as well as foreign manufacturers of such products must obtain a U.S. licence for both the manufacturing establishment and for the product intended to be produced or imported
Biological materials and vectors	Prohibited unless they have been propagated or prepared at an establishment with a U.S. licence for such manufacturing issued by the Secretary of the Department of Health and Human Services
Cheese, milk, and dairy products	Subject to requirements of the Food and Drug Administration and the Department of Agriculture
Cigarette lighters and multi-purpose lighters	Compliance with the child-resistant safety standard
Commercial and industrial equipment	Energy performance standards to be met
Counterfeit articles	Articles bearing facsimiles or replicas of coins or securities of the United States or of any foreign country cannot be imported
Dog or cat fur	The importation, exportation, transportation, distribution or sale of any product that consists of any dog fur, cat fur, or both, is prohibited
Fireworks	Labelling requirements and technical specifications to be met
Flammable fabrics	Conform to applicable flammability standard under the Flammable Fabrics Act
Foods, cosmetics, etc.	Prohibits the importation of articles that are adulterated or misbranded and products that are defective, unsafe, filthy, or produced under unsanitary conditions
Foods, drugs, cosmetics, and medical devices	Subject to the requirements of the Public Health Security and Bio-Terrorism Preparedness and Response Act of 2002
Fruits, vegetables, and nuts	Import requirements relating to grade, size, quality, and maturity
Fur	Must be tagged, labelled, or otherwise clearly marked with specific information
Gold and silver	Articles made of gold or alloys thereof are prohibited from importation into the United States if the gold content is one half carat divergence below the indicated fineness
Hazardous substances	Substances must be shipped to the United States in packages suitable for household use
Household appliances	Energy standards to be met, and labelled to indicate expected energy consumption or efficiency
Insects in a live state that are injurious to cultivated crops, and the eggs, pupae, or larvae of such insects	Prohibited from importation, except for scientific purposes, under regulations prescribed by the Secretary of Agriculture
Lead in paint	Banned if they contain more than 0.06% lead by weight of the dried plant film
Livestock and animals	Inspection and quarantine requirements of the Animal and Plant Health Inspection Service (APHIS)
Matches, fireworks, knives	Certain matches, fireworks, and knives are prohibited
Meat, poultry, egg products, and (since 1 March 2016) *Siluriformes* fish and fish products	Subject to USDA regulations and must be inspected by the Food Safety and Inspection Service (FSIS)
Monetary instruments	If a person receives more than US$10,000 at one time from or through a place outside the United States, a report of the transportation (form FINCEN 105) must be filed with CBP
Obscene, immoral, or seditious matter and lottery tickets	Certain books, writings, advertisements, circulars, or pictures containing these are prohibited
Pesticides	The regulations require importers to submit to CBP an EPA Notice of Arrival that the EPA has reviewed and approved before the importation arrives in the United States
Products of convict or forced labour	Merchandise produced, mined, or manufactured, wholly or in part, by means of the use of convict labour, forced labour, or indentured labour under penal sanctions is prohibited from importation
Radiation- and sonic radiation-producing products	Compliance with a radiation performance standard
Radio frequency devices	Subject to radiation performance standards
Refrigerants	The EPA regulates the importation of ozone-depleting substances
Seeds	Provisions of the Federal Seed Act of 1939 and regulations of the Agricultural Marketing Service govern the importation into the United States
Textile products	Must be stamped, tagged, labelled, or otherwise marked with the specific information
Toxic substances	Imports will not be released from CBP custody unless proper certification is presented to CBP indicating that the import "complies with" or "is not subject to" TSCA requirements
Toys and children's articles	Compliance with applicable regulations issued under the Federal Hazardous Substances Act
Wood packing materials	Import regulations require wood packing material to be treated and marked
Wool	Must be tagged, labelled, or otherwise clearly marked with specific information

Source: WTO document WT/TPR/S/307/Rev.1, 13 March 2015, summarizing CBP online information. Viewed at: https://www.cbp.gov/sites/default/files/documents/Importing%20into%20the%20U.S.pdf (document last revised in 2006).

Table A3.3 Products subject to import licensing

Category	Products	Agency	Purpose	Legal reference	Other information
Animals and animal products	Certain animal and animal products	Department of Agriculture	To protect domestic agriculture from the introduction or entry of animal diseases or disease vectors	Title 9 CFR, Parts 92, 94.7, 94.16, 95.4, 95.18, 95.19, 95.20 through 98, 104 and 122; and: 21 U.S.C 102 to 105, 111, 134, 135, 151-159 and 19 U.S.C-1306	All persons, firms and institutions in the United States may apply for permits
Controlled substances and listed chemicals	Controlled substances and listed chemicals	Department of Justice, Drug Enforcement Administration	To restrict the quantity of imports of controlled substances and listed chemicals (not monetary value) and to maintain a monitoring system	Title 21, CFR, Part 1310, 1312, 1313, 21 U.S.C. Sections 822, 823, 826, 953, 957 and 958	Importation only by approved, registered importers
Dairy products	Certain dairy products	Department of Agriculture	An administrative tool that governs importations of certain dairy products subject to TRQs resulting from the Uruguay Round Agreement	CFR 6.20-6.37	Importers or manufacturers of dairy products may apply for import licences if they meet the Import Regulation performance criteria on the quantity of imports entered in a previous 12-month period, and for manufacturers the specified level of dairy production in a previous 12-month period. Manufacturers must be listed in USDA's Dairy Plants Surveyed
Distilled spirits (beverages), wine, and malt beverages	Distilled spirits (beverages), wine, and malt beverages	Department of the Treasury, Alcohol and Tobacco Tax and Trade Bureau	To provide an enforcement mechanism to ensure that importers comply with all requirements of federal law relating to alcohol	Federal Alcohol Administration Act	Any person, firm or institution may apply for a licence
Distilled spirits or alcohol for industrial use	Distilled spirits or alcohol for industrial use, including denatured spirits	Department of the Treasury, Alcohol and Tobacco Tax and Trade Bureau	To prevent tax fraud	26 U.S.C. 5001, 26 U.S.C. 5002(a), 26 U.S.C. 5171, 26 U.S.C. 5181, 27 CFR Part 19	Any person, firm or institution may apply for a licence
Explosives	Explosives, blasting agents and detonators	Department of Justice, Bureau of Alcohol, Tobacco, Firearms and Explosives	To protect against the misuse and unsafe storage of explosive materials	18 U.S.C. Chapter 40; 27 CFR Part 555	All persons, firms, and institutions may apply for a licence
Firearms and ammunition	Firearms and ammunition	Department of Justice, Bureau of Alcohol, Tobacco, Firearms and Explosives	To administer licensing provisions under three statutes	18 U.S.C., Chapter 44 and 27 CFR Part 478	All persons, firms, and institutions may apply for a licence
Firearms, ammunition, and defence articles	Defence articles on the U.S. munitions list	Department of Justice, Bureau of Alcohol, Tobacco, Firearms and Explosives	To regulate international trafficking in arms, consistent with U.S. national security and foreign policy interests	18 U.S.C. Chapter 44, 22 U.S.C. 2778, 26 U.S.C. Chapter 53	All persons, firms, and institutions may apply for a licence

Category	Products	Agency	Purpose	Legal reference	Other information
Fish and wildlife	Fish and wildlife including endangered species	Department of the Interior, U.S. Fish and Wildlife Service	To: identify commercial importers and exporters of wildlife; and require records that fully and correctly disclose each importation or exportation of wildlife and the subsequent disposition of the wildlife by the importer or exporter	50 CFR Part 14	All persons, firms, and institutions may apply for a licence
Natural gas	Natural gas, including LNG and CNG	Department of Energy	To fulfil the requirements of the Natural Gas Act requiring authorization to import	15 U.S.C. 717b	All persons, firms, and institutions may import natural gas
Nuclear facilities and materials	Production and utilization facilities, special nuclear materials, source materials, and by-product materials, including when such materials are contained in radioactive waste	Nuclear Regulatory Commission	To protect public health and safety and the environment, and maintain the common defense and security of the United States, by exercising prudent controls over the possession, use, distribution, and transport of such items	Atomic Energy Act, 10 CFR Part 110	All persons, firms and institutions must have a permanent (physical) address within the United States
Plant and plant products	Certain plant and plant products	Department of Agriculture	To protect against the entry of plant pests and diseases, and to protect endangered plant species	Section 412 of the Plant Protection Act, 7 U.S.C. 7712, the Endangered Species Act, and Title 7 CFR Parts 300-399	Persons, firms, and institutions resident in the United States may apply for a permit
Steel	All basic steel mill products	Department of Commerce, International Trade Administration	To provide fast and reliable statistical information on steel imports to the Government and the public	78 FR 11090 and 82 FR 1183	Only registered users may file steel licences; registration is available to all and is free
Sugar	Raw and refined sugar	Department of Agriculture	To administer the sugar TRQ and the sugar re-export programme	15 CFR 2011, Sub-part A, 15 CFR 2011, Sub-part B.7 CFR 1530	All importers are eligible to apply for certificates for specialty sugars. Only U.S refiners may apply for licences to import quota-exempt sugar
Tobacco products	Tobacco products, processed tobacco, and proprietors of export warehouses	Department of the Treasury, Alcohol and Tobacco Tax and Trade Bureau	Primary purpose is to ensure proper collection of federal excise tax revenue on tobacco products	Title 26 U.S.C. Chapter 52	Any person, firm or institution may apply for a licence

Source: WTO document WT/TPR/S/307/Rev.1, 13 March 2015, based on WTO document G/LIC/N/3/USA/10, 24 September 2013; and WTO document G/LIC/N/3/USA/14, 22 January 2018.

Part B
Report by the WTO Secretariat

Table A3.4 Changes in U.S. export controls, July 2016-June 2018

Date	Title	Citation	Purpose
6/6/2018	Revisions to the Unverified List (UVL)	83 FR 26204	Minor corrections
4/6/2018	Implementation of the February 2017 Australia Group (AG) Intersessional Decisions and the June 2017 AG Plenary Understandings; Addition of India to the AG; Correction	83 FR 25559	Technical corrections to Supplement No. 7 to part 748, identifying eligible ECCN 1C350 items for three PRC validated end-users
5/4/2018	Reclassification of Targets for the Production of Tritium and Related Development and Production Technology Initially Classified Under the 0Y521 Series	83 FR 14580	Implementing new classifications agreed at the Nuclear Suppliers Group in June 2017
2/4/2018	Implementation of the February 2017 Australia Group (AG) Intersessional Decisions and the June 2017 AG Plenary Understandings; Addition of India to the AG	83 FR 13849	ECCNs amended to reflect changes to the AG common control lists. EAR amended to reflect India as new participating country in the AG
22/3/2018	Addition of Certain Persons to the Entity List and Removal of Certain Persons from the Entity List; Correction of Licence Requirements	83 FR 12475	23 persons added to the Entity List (destination Pakistan, Singapore, and South Sudan). Two persons removed from list. Licence requirement corrected for 12 entities (Russian Federation)
16/2/2018	Russian Sanctions: Addition of Certain Entities to the Entity List (final rule)	83 FR 6949	21 entities added, destination Crimea region.
26/1/2018	Addition of Certain Entities; Removal of Certain Entities; and Revisions of Entries on the Entity List (RIN 0694-AH43)	83 FR 3577	21 persons added (destination Bulgaria, China, Kazakhstan, Russian Federation, Syria, and the UAE). Three entities removed, two entries modified
8/1/2018	Revisions, Clarifications, and Technical Corrections to the Export Administration Regulations; Correction	83 FR 709	Textual error corrected
27/12/2017	Revisions, Clarifications, and Technical Corrections to the Export Administration Regulations	82 FR 61153	Editorial corrections
20/12/2017	Addition of Certain Entities to the Entity List (RIN 0694-AG29)	82 FR 60304	Two entities added (destination Russian Federation)
9/11/17	Amendments to Implement United States Policy Toward Cuba (RIN 0694-AH47)	82 FR 51983	Published in conjunction with OFAC amendments to Cuban Assets Control Regulations (31 CFR Part 515) and Department of State notice setting forth the Cuba Restricted List
1/11/17	Clarifications to the Export Administration Regulations for the Use of Licence Exceptions (RIN 0694-AG80)	82 FR 50511	Guidance on existing agency interpretative practice regarding licence exception governments, international organizations, international inspections under the Chemical Weapons Convention, and the International Space Station; and five notes added to the Licence Exception Strategic Trade Authorization (STA)
23/10/17	Amendments to Existing Validated End-User Authorization in the People's Republic of China: Lam Research Service Co., Ltd. (RIN 0694-AH40)	82 FR 48925	Updating the list of eligible destinations (facilities) and items in Supplement No. 7 to part 748 for Lam Research Service Co. Ltd.
3/10/17	Updated Statements of Legal Authority for the Export Administration Regulations	82 FR 45959	Keeping the authority citation paragraphs in the Code of Federal Regulations current
25/9/17	Removal of Certain Entities from the Entity List; and Revisions of Entries on the Entity List (RIN 0694-AH41)	82 FR 44514	Three entities removed. Five entries modified to provide additional or modified addresses
15/8/17	Wassenaar Arrangement 2016 Plenary Agreements Implementation	82 FR 38764	Implementing changes to the Wassenaar Arrangement List of Dual-Use Goods and Technologies (WA List)
7/7/17	Revisions to the Export Administration Regulations Based on the 2016 Missile Technology Control Regime Plenary Agreements (RIN 0694-AH33)	82 FR 31442	Reflecting changes to the Missile Technology Control Regime Annex agreed by member countries during 2016
22/6/17	Russian Sanctions: Addition of Certain Entities to the Entity List	82 FR 28405	Ten entities added (destination Crimea region)
14/6/17	Wassenaar Arrangement 2015 Plenary Agreements Implementation, Removal of Foreign National Review Requirements, and Information Security Updates; Corrections	82 FR 27108	Correcting errors and omissions in "WA15 rule" published on 20 September 2016
26/5/17	Addition of Certain Persons and Revisions to Entries on the Entity List	82 FR 24242	16 persons added to the Entity List (destinations Pakistan, Turkey, and the UAE); modifying two existing entries
18/4/17	Revision to Entry on the Entity List	82 FR 18217	Modifying one existing entry

Date	Title	Citation	Purpose
6/4/17	Revisions to the Unverified List (UVL)	82 FR 16730	Sixteen persons added to the UVL, three addresses revised, one alternate name added
29/3/17	Removal of Certain Persons from the Entity List (RIN 0694-AH28)	82 FR 15461	Seven persons removed from the Entity List
29/3/17	Removal of Certain Persons from the Entity List; Addition of a Person to the Entity List; and EAR Conforming Change (RIN 0694-AH30)	82 FR 15458	Two persons removed from the Entity List (settlement of administrative and criminal enforcement actions against ZTE Corporation and ZTE Kangxun). One person added to the list (destination China)
24/2/17	Temporary General License: Extension of Validity	82 FR 11505	Temporary general licence extended until 29 March (for ZTE Corporation and ZTE Kangxun)
1/2/17	Commerce Control List: Removal of Certain Nuclear Nonproliferation (NP) Column 2 Controls – Additional Delay in Implementation of ECCN 3D991 Controls on Certain Software	82 FR 8893	Continuation of "software" classified and licensed by BIS as EAR99. From 22 March 2017, "software" to be classified and licensed under ECCN 3D991
19/1/17	Amendments to the Export Administration Regulations Implementing an Additional Phase of India-U.S. Export Control Cooperation	82 FR 6218	Implementing joint statement of 7 June 2016
19/1/17	Support Document Requirements with Respect to Hong Kong	82 FR 6216	Import licence to be obtained from the authorities of Hong Kong, China (and export licence for subsequent re-exports), or statement that no licence is required
17/1/17	Revisions to Sudan Licensing Policy	82 FR 4781	Applications to be reviewed under general policy of approval for use in Sudanese civil aviation or railroads.
13/1/17	Increase of Controls: Infrared Detection Items	81 FR 4287	Notice of inquiry requesting comments from the public
10/1/17	Addition of Certain Persons and Revisions to Entries on the Entity List; and Removal of a Person from the Entity List	81 FR 2883	Five persons added to the Entity List (destination Turkey). One entity removed, and five existing entries in the list revised
10/1/17	Revisions to the Export Administration Regulations (EAR): Control of Spacecraft Systems and Related Items the President Determines No Longer Warrant Control under the United States Munitions List (USML)	81 FR 2875	Part of the President's Export Control Reform Initiative, moving certain spacecraft and related items from USML Category XV to the CCL
4/1/17	Addition of Certain Entities to the Entity List	81 FR 722	Five entities added to the Entities List in conjunction with amended Executive Order No. 13694 (significant malicious cyber-enabled activities)
27/12/2016	Commerce Control List: Updates Based on the 2015 and 2016 Nuclear Suppliers Group (NSG) Plenary Meetings; Conforming Changes and Corrections to Certain Nuclear Nonproliferation (NP) Controls.	81 FR 94971	Addressing nuclear nonproliferation controls applicable to certain centrifugal multiplane balancing machines and certain linear displacement measuring systems
27/12/2016	Russian Sanctions: Addition of Certain Entities to the Entity List, and Clarification of License Review Policy	81 FR 94963	23 entities added to the Entities List. U.S. national security interests to be taken into account in the review of licence applications for exports, re-exports, and in-country transfers to the Russian Federation
27/12/2016	Burma: Amendment of the Export Administration Regulations Consistent with an Executive Order that Terminated U.S. Government's Sanctions	81 FR 94962	Terminating sanctions consistent with Executive Order No. 13742 of 7 October 2016
16/12/2016	Implementation of the February 2016 Australia Group (AG) Intersessional Decisions and the June 2016 AG Plenary Understandings	81 FR 90983	Reflecting AG updates
15/12/2016	Addition of Certain Persons to the Entity List	81 FR 90712	Seven persons added to the Entity List (destination Pakistan)
5/12/2016	Amendment to the Export Administration Regulations: Removal of Special Iraq Reconstruction License	81 FR 87424	Streamlining regulations and reducing unnecessary regulatory burdens on the public
5/12/2016	Amendment to the Export Administration Regulations: Removal of Semiconductor Manufacturing International Corporation from the List of Validated End-Users in the People's Republic of China	81 FR 87246	Change made at company's request, and not in response to activities of concern
1/12/2016	Temporary Exports to Mexico Under License Exception TMP	81 FR 86571	Licence exception amended to align with time constraints in Mexican programme
25/11/2016	Commerce Control List: Removal of Certain Nuclear Nonproliferation (NP) Column 2 Controls	81 FR 85138	Revision of EAR controls to make them more consistent with export controls of other participating countries in the Nuclear Suppliers Group

Part B
Report by the WTO Secretariat

Date	Title	Citation	Purpose
21/11/2016	Clarifications and Revisions to Military Aircraft, Gas Turbine Engines and Related Items License Requirements	81 FR 83114	Published simultaneously with related changes to the USML
18/11/2016	Temporary General Licence: Extension of Validity	81 FR 81663	Expiration date extended until 27 February 2017 for ZTE Corporation and ZTE Kangxun
4/11/2016	Amendments to the Export Administration Regulations: Update of Arms Embargoes on Cote d'Ivoire, Liberia, Sri Lanka and Viet Nam, and Recognition of India as Member of the Missile Technology Control Regime	81 FR 76859	Changes in controls on arms and related materiel
17/10/2016	Cuba: Revisions to Licence Exceptions	81 FR 71365	Authorizing License Exception SCP for items sold directly to individuals in Cuba (personal use) and Licence Exception AVS (cargo transiting in Cuba). Published simultaneously with OFAC rule amending the Cuban Assets Control Regulations
14/10/2016	Amendments to the Export Administration Regulations: Reporting Requirements Optional Electronic Filing of Reports of Requests for Restrictive Trade Practice or Boycott	81 FR 70933	Authorizing reports from U.S. persons regarding requests received to take certain actions in furtherance or support of unsanctioned foreign boycott to be submitted in electronic form
12/10/2016	Commerce Cat XII bookend final rule	81 FR 70320	Transfer of articles from the USML (Category XII) to the CCL. Expansion of controls on certain software and technology employed in certain dual-use infrared detection items
20/9/2016	Revisions to the Entity List	81 FR 64694	Licence requirement to apply to all EAR items for 12 Chinese entities. Linked to 2015 Wassenaar Implementation rule
20/9/2016	Wassenaar Arrangement 2015 Plenary Agreements Implementation, Removal of Foreign National Review Requirements, and Information Security Updates	81 FR 64657	Amending the CCL. Raising the Adjusted Peak Performance for high performance computers and related technology and software, updating licence requirements and policies associated with Category 5 – Part 2, and removing Foreign National Review for deemed exports under Licence Exceptions APP and CIV
7/9/2016	Russian Sanctions: Addition of Certain Entities to the Entity List	81 FR 61595	81 entities added to the Entity List.
6/9/2016	Amendments to Existing Validated End-User Authorization in the People's Republic of China: Boeing Tianjin Composites Co. Ltd.	81 FR 61104	Updating the list of eligible destinations (facilities)
1/9/2016	Updated Statements of Legal Authority for the Export Administration Regulations	81 FR 60254	Keeping the authority citation paragraphs in the Code of Federal Regulations current
23/8/2016	Addition of Certain Persons to the Entity List	81 FR 57451	Ten persons added to the Entity List (destinations Iraq, the Philippines, Syria, and Turkey)
23/8/2016	Temporary Exports to Mexico Under License Exception TMP	81 FR 57505	Proposed rule to align licence exception with time constraints in Mexican programme
19/8/2016	Temporary General Licence: Extension of Validity	81 FR 55372	Extending temporary general licence for ZTE Corporation and ZTE Kangxun until 28 November 2016
17/8/2016	Revisions to the Export Administration Regulations (EAR): Harmonization of the Destination Control Statements	81 FR 54721	Harmonizing statement for EAR items with statement required for International Traffic in Arms Regulations (ITAR) items. Part of President's Export Control Reform Initiative
8/8/2016	Amendment to the Export Administration Regulations to Add Targets for the Production of Tritium and Related Development and Production Technology to the List of 0Y521 Series	81 FR 52326	Interim Final Rule making certain items subject to the EAR and imposing a licence requirement to all destinations, except Canada
28/7/2016	Commerce Control List: Addition of Items Determined to No Longer Warrant Control under United States Munitions List Category XIV (Toxicological Agents) or Category XVIII (Directed Energy Weapons)	81 FR 49517	Items transferred from the USML to the CCL
11/7/2016	Updated Statements of Legal Authority for the Export Administration Regulations	81 FR 44770	Keeping the authority citation paragraphs in the Code of Federal Regulations current

Source: WTO Secretariat, based on Bureau of Industry and Security online information. Viewed at: https://www.bis.doc.gov/index.php/federal-register-notices.

Table A4.1 Commodity Loan Rates and Price Loss Coverage Reference Prices, Agricultural Act of 2014 (as amended)

Covered commodities	Marketing loan programme Commodity loan rates		Price loss coverage Reference prices	
		Converted into US$/tonne		Converted into US$/tonne
Wheat (bu.)	2.94	108.0	5.5	202.1
Maize (bu.)	1.95	76.8	3.7	145.7
Grain sorghum (bu.)	1.95	76.8	3.95	155.5
Barley (bu.)	1.95	89.6	4.95	227.3
Oats (bu.)	1.39	95.8	2.4	165.3
Rice long-grain (cwt.)	6.50	143.3	14	308.6
Rice medium-grain (cwt.)	6.50	143.3	14	308.6
Peanuts (ton)	355	391.3	535	589.7
Soybeans (bu.)	5.00	183.7	8.4	308.6
Other oilseeds (cwt)	10.09	222.4	20.15	444.2
Dry peas (cwt.)	5.40	119.0	11	242.5
Lentils (cwt.)	11.28	248.7	19.97	440.3
Small chickpeas (cwt.)	7.43	163.8	19.04	419.8
Large chickpeas (cwt.)	11.28	248.7	21.54	474.9
Graded wool (lb.)	1.15	2535.3	n.a.	n.a.
Non-graded wool (lb.)	0.40	881.8	n.a.	n.a.
Mohair (lb.)	4.20	9259.3	n.a.	n.a.
Honey (lb.)	0.69	1521.2	n.a.	n.a.
Sugar beet, refined (lb.)	0.2409	531.1	n.a.	n.a.
Sugar cane, raw (lb.)	0.1875	413.4	n.a.	n.a.
Extra-long staple cotton (lb.)	0.7977	1758.6	n.a.	n.a.
Seed cotton (lb.)	0.25[a]	551.2[a]	0.367	809.1
Upland cotton	Simple average of the adjusted prevailing world price for the two immediately preceding MYs, but not less than US$0.45/lb. or more than US$0.52/lb. The loan rate for the 2017 crop year was US$0.4949/lb.		n.a.	n.a.

n.a. Not applicable (i.e. not a covered commodity).

a The loan rate is set only for the purposes of determining the effective prices for seed cotton under the Price Loss Coverage programme. Seed cotton is not a covered commodity under the marketing assistance loan programme.

Note: For the conversion factors, see U.S. TPR (2010), Table AIV.1.

Source: The Agricultural Act of 2014, as amended, and information provided by the authorities.

Table A4.2 Insurance: direct premiums written

L&H insurance groups by 2016; U.S. life and annuities subsector direct premiums written

2015 rank	2016 rank	Insurance group	2015 direct premiums written (US$'000)	Share of total (%)	2016 direct premiums written (US$'000)	Share of total (%)
1	1	MetLife Inc.	102,487,074	16.42	95,110,811	15.22
2	2	Prudential Financial Inc.	43,134,670	6.91	45,902,327	7.34
3	3	New York Life Insurance Group	29,647,519	4.75	30,922,462	4.95
7	4	Principal Financial Group Inc.	23,416,059	3.75	28,186,098	4.51
8	5	Massachusetts Mutual Life Insurance Co.	23,117,904	3.70	23,458,883	3.75
6	6	American International Group	24,976,781	4.00	22,463,202	3.59
4	7	Jackson National Life Group	27,457,195	4.40	22,132,278	3.54
10	8	AXA SA	19,478,236	3.12	21,920,627	3.51
5	9	AEGON NV	24,983,201	4.00	21,068,180	3.37
9	10	Lincoln National Corp.	22,676,916	3.63	19,441,555	3.11
		Combined top 10	341,375,555	54.68	330,606,423	52.89
		Combined top 25	497,410,941	79.70	492,133,340	78.74
		Combined top 100	615,636,993	98.62	616,338,749	98.63
		Total U.S. life insurance lines	624,175,403		624,950,037	

L&H insurance groups by 2016; U.S. A&H lines direct premiums written

2015 rank	2016 rank	Insurance group	2015 direct premiums written (US$'000)	Share of total (%)	2016 direct premiums written (US$'000)	Share of total (%)
1	1	UnitedHealth Group Inc.	43,817,056	25.79	46,669,151	26.44
2	2	Aetna Inc.	24,962,250	14.69	28,358,852	16.07
3	3	Cigna Corp.	14,795,932	8.71	15,505,890	8.78
4	4	Aflac Inc.	13,643,143	8.03	14,872,435	8.43
5	5	MetLife Inc.	6,979,479	4.11	7,407,695	4.20
6	6	Unum Group	5,528,316	3.25	5,739,627	3.25
7	7	Mutual of Omaha Insurance Co.	3,473,325	2.04	3,740,570	2.12
8	8	Guardian Life Insurance Co. of America	3,413,472	2.01	3,629,131	2.06
10	9	Genworth Financial Inc.	2,637,316	1.55	2,676,522	1.52
11	10	AEGON NV	2,150,211	1.27	2,079,926	1.18
		Combined top 10	122,308,095	71.98	130,679,799	74.05
		Combined top 25	145,756,216	85.79	153,742,118	87.13
		Combined top 100	164,856,966	97.00	173,688,976	98.41
		Total U.S. A&H lines	169,895,327		176,522,262	

L&H insurance groups by 2016, combined lines direct premiums written

2015 rank	2016 rank	Insurance group	2015 direct premiums written (US$'000)	Share of total (%)	2016 direct premiums written (US$'000)	Share of total (%)
1	1	State Farm Mutual Automobile Insurance	59,361,685	10.03	62,189,311	10.19
3	2	Berkshire Hathaway Inc.	29,967,354	5.06	33,300,439	5.46
4	3	Liberty Mutual Group	29,848,412	5.04	31,077,066	5.09
2	4	Allstate Corp.	30,180,756	5.10	30,875,771	5.06
6	5	Progressive Corp.	21,383,662	3.61	23,951,690	3.93
5	6	Travelers Companies Inc.	23,200,304	3.92	23,918,048	3.92
7	7	Chubb Ltd [a]	20,671,147	3.49	20,728,330	3.40
8	8	Nationwide Mutual Group	19,577,849	3.31	19,756,093	3.24
9	9	Farmers Insurance Group of Cos.	19,050,733	3.22	19,677,601	3.22
11	10	USAA Insurance Group	16,744,764	2.83	18,273,675	2.99
		Combined top 10	271,249,081	45.82	283,748,024	46.50
		Combined top 25	383,385,662	64.76	397,042,076	65.08
		Combined top 100	506,847,957	85.61	524,967,972	86.04
		Total U.S. P&C sector	591,757,790		610,166,276	

a 2015 data for The Chubb Corp. is provided on a combined basis with ACE Ltd. In January 2016, ACE Ltd. acquired The Chubb Corp. and changed the name of the combined insurer to Chubb Ltd. See "ACE Limited acquires Chubb Corporation", SNL Financial.

P&C insurance groups by 2016, commercial lines direct premiums written

2015 rank	2016 rank	Insurance group	2015 direct premiums written (US$'000)	Share of total (%)	2016 direct premiums written (US$'000)	Share of total (%)
1	1	Chubb Ltd.	16,675,155	5.71	16,482,259	5.61
2	2	Travelers Companies Inc.	16,347,492	5.60	16,463,566	5.60
4	3	Liberty Mutual Group	13,801,267	4.73	14,049,356	4.78
3	4	American International Group	15,921,080	5.45	13,080,949	4.45
5	5	Zurich Insurance Group	13,403,445	4.59	12,554,597	4.27
6	6	CNA Financial Corp.	9,203,419	3.15	9,763,122	3.32
7	7	Nationwide Mutual Group	8,401,984	2.88	8,335,275	2.83
8	8	Hartford Financial Services Group Inc.	7,635,701	2.61	7,679,737	2.61
9	9	Berkshire Hathaway Inc.	7,056,856	2.42	7,650,236	2.60
10	10	Tokio Marine Group	5,956,554	2.04	6,248,195	2.13
		Combined top 10	114,402,953	39.18	112,307,292	38.20
		Combined top 25	174,171,894	60.62	174,555,327	59.37
		Combined top 100	249,529,480	85.40	252,269,401	85.81
		Total U.S. P&C commercial lines	291,999,817		294,021,050	

P&C insurance groups by 2016, personal lines direct premiums written

2015 rank	2016 rank	Insurance group	2015 direct premiums written (US$'000)	Share of total (%)	2016 direct premiums written (US$'000)	Share of total (%)
1	1	State Farm Mutual Automobile Insurance	54,340,977	18.53	57,083,833	18.43
2	2	Allstate Corp.	27,963,957	9.54	28,717,388	9.27
3	3	Berkshire Hathaway Inc.	22,828,453	7.78	25,553,714	8.25
4	4	Progressive Corp.	18,463,485	6.30	20,559,851	6.64
6	5	USAA Insurance Group	15,562,507	5.31	17,032,072	5.50
5	6	Liberty Mutual Group	16,039,932	5.47	17,026,207	5.50
7	7	Farmers Insurance Group of Cos.	15,270,479	5.21	15,819,900	5.11
8	8	Nationwide Mutual Group	11,163,343	3.81	11,414,637	3.68
9	9	Travelers Companies Inc.	6,852,414	2.34	7,454,481	2.41
10	10	American Family Insurance Group	6,420,260	2.19	6,980,730	2.25
		Combined top 10	194,905,807	66.48	207,642,813	67.04
		Combined top 25	233,942,544	79.78	249,171,554	80.46
		Combined top 100	273,734,365	93.34	290,588,723	93.79
		Total U.S. P&C personal lines	293,257,615		309,778,137	

P&C health insurance groups by 2016, health lines direct premiums written

2015 rank	2016 rank	Insurance group	2015 direct premiums written (US$'000)	Share of total (%)	2016 direct premiums written (US$'000)	Share of total (%)
1	1	UnitedHealth Group Inc.	68,041,707	11.69	79,473,071	12.46
2	2	Anthem Inc.	54,715,501	9.40	58,748,993	9.21
3	3	Humana Inc.	51,405,175	8.83	53,601,025	8.40
4	4	HealthCare Services Corp. a Mutual	32,644,621	5.61	32,157,585	5.04
5	5	Aetna Inc.	24,417,307	4.19	24,414,237	3.83
6	6	Centene Corp.	20,261,187	3.48	24,070,523	3.77
8	7	Independence Health Group Inc.	13,869,064	2.38	17,013,754	2.67
7	8	Kaiser Foundation Health Plan Inc.	15,155,609	2.60	16,166,834	2.53
10	9	Molina Healthcare Inc.	11,918,163	2.05	15,317,439	2.40
9	10	WellCare Health Plans Inc.	13,072,554	2.25	13,451,891	2.11
		Combined top 10	305,500,887	52.48	334,415,351	52.42
		Combined top 25	421,926,055	72.48	459,615,681	72.05
		Combined top 100	554,167,344	95.20	607,899,577	95.30
		Total U.S. health insurance lines	582,097,176		637,902,483	

Source: Annual Report on the Insurance Industry (September 2017), Federal Insurance Office, Department of the Treasury.

Part B
Report by the WTO Secretariat

Part C

Report by the United States

Part C
Report by the United States

The United States in the global trading system

As the United States Government undergoes its fourteenth Trade Policy Review—more than any other World Trade Organization (WTO) Member—the United States is committed to reforming the global trading system in ways that lead to fairer outcomes for U.S. workers and businesses, and more efficient markets for countries around the world. U.S. trade policy is driven by a pragmatic determination to use the leverage available to the world's largest economy to secure these objectives. Our trade policy is steadfastly focused on the national interest, including retaining and using U.S. sovereign power to act in defense of that interest.

U.S. trade policy rests on five major pillars: supporting U.S. national security, strengthening the U.S. economy, negotiating better trade deals, aggressive enforcement of U.S. trade laws, and reforming the multilateral trading system.

Supporting U.S. National Security

In December 2017, the Administration issued a new National Security Strategy for the United States. The document states that, "A strong economy protects the American people, supports our way of life, and sustains American power." It also makes clear that the United States will not turn a blind eye to violations, cheating, or economic aggression. U.S. trade policy will fulfill these goals by using all possible tools to preserve our national sovereignty and strengthen the U.S. economy.

Strengthening the U.S. Economy

In 2017, the President signed a new tax bill designed to make U.S. companies and workers more competitive with the rest of the world. The Administration also began a determined effort to eliminate wasteful and unnecessary regulations that hamper business. These and other efforts to strengthen the U.S. economy will make it easier for U.S. companies to succeed in global markets.

Negotiating Better Trade Deals

For too long, the rules of global trade have been tilted against U.S. workers and businesses. The United States has demonstrated that it will alter—or terminate—old trade deals that are not in the U.S. national interest. In 2018, the United States completed a comprehensive renegotiation of the North American Free Trade Agreement (NAFTA) and improved the U.S.–Korea Free Trade Agreement to rebalance trade and address implementation concerns. Furthermore, with roughly 80% of the world's economy and 95% of the world's population living outside the United States, the United States is committed to opening foreign markets and is actively pursuing new and better trade deals with potential partners around the world.

Aggressive Enforcement of U.S. Trade Laws

Free and fair trade benefits both the United States and the rest of the world by providing more affordable goods and services, raising living standards, fuelling economic growth, and supporting good jobs. Reducing barriers to trade offers greater product variety, enhances product quality, increases innovation, and raises productivity. In addition, the United States strongly believes that all countries would benefit from adopting policies that promote true market competition. Unfortunately, history shows that not all countries will do so voluntarily. Non-market policies and practices and unfair trade practices, including dumping, discriminatory non-tariff barriers, forced technology transfers, excess capacity, industrial subsidies, and other forms of support by governments and related entities distort markets and damage U.S. workers and businesses.

The United States has an aggressive trade enforcement agenda designed to prevent countries from benefitting from unfair trade practices. The United States will use all tools available—including unilateral action where necessary—to support this effort. More broadly, robust trade enforcement across the spectrum of goods and services remains a central pillar of U.S. trade policy. Vigorous work by the Office of the U.S. Trade Representative (USTR) and sister U.S. agencies, including the Departments of Agriculture, Commerce, Labor, State, Treasury, and others, helps ensure that trade agreements yield the maximum benefits in terms of ensuring market access for Americans, and creating a fair, open, and predictable trading environment. Ensuring full implementation of U.S. trade agreements remains one of the United States' strategic priorities.

Reforming the Multilateral Trading System

The United States wants to help build a better multilateral trading system and will remain active in the WTO. At the same time, the United States recognizes that the WTO has not always worked as expected. Instead of serving as a negotiating forum where Members can develop new and better rules, the ability of Members to negotiate has become increasingly frustrated by an overactive dispute settlement system in which activist "judges" impose their own policy preferences and institutional preferences on Members. Instead of constraining market distorting countries, the WTO has in some cases given them an unfair advantage over the United States and other market-based economies. Instead of promoting more efficient markets, the WTO has been used by some Members as a bulwark in defense of market access barriers, dumping, subsidies, and other market distorting practices. The United States has been drawing the attention of WTO Members to instances where the WTO Appellate Body has disregarded the explicit rules agreed by Members in the WTO Dispute Settlement Understanding. The United States will not allow any multilateral organization to prevent us from taking actions that are essential to the economic well-being of the American people.

At the same time, as the United States demonstrated at the WTO's Eleventh Ministerial Conference, we remain eager to work with like-minded countries to build a global economic system that will lead to higher living standards here and around the world. The United States submitted a proposal in the November 2017 meeting of the General Council to improve compliance with WTO notification requirements and is working with other Members to further develop the proposal. The United States is also interested in working with other Members on improving the functioning of the regular committees of the WTO. In an effort to improve the negotiating arm of the WTO, the United States is encouraging a discussion on development status in the WTO to ensure that a larger proportion of WTO Members will undertake substantive obligations under future WTO agreements.

The United States economic and trade environment

INTRODUCTION

The United States maintains one of the world's most open trade regimes, with the U.S. simple average MFN tariff at 3.4% in 2017 on a bound basis under the WTO. When GSP and other tariff preferences are taken into account, the U.S. trade-weighted average tariff is 1.4% on an applied basis. By comparison, simple average applied tariffs in our top five trading partners range from 4.0% to 9.8% and trade-weighted average tariffs range from 2.5% to 5.2%. In 2017, nearly 70% of all U.S. imports (including under preference programs) entered the United States duty free. The United States also has among the lowest non-tariff barriers of any country in the world. U.S. service markets are open to foreign providers with limited exceptions, and U.S. regulatory processes are transparent, accessible, and open to public input.

ECONOMIC GROWTH

During the period under review, the United States' economy continued to grow. This marked the 9th consecutive year of GDP growth – this expansion will be the longest on record if it continues into the second half of 2019. U.S. real gross domestic product (GDP) increased by 1.6% in 2016 and 2.2% in 2017. For the first half of 2018, real GDP is up 2.7%, on an annual basis, and up 4.2% in the second quarter of 2018 (highest since 3rd quarter 2014 (up 4.9%)). The increase in growth in the first half of 2018 is based on several factors: higher consumer spending (resulting from robust job gains, rising after-tax incomes, and greater consumer confidence), strong business investment, and strong growth in exports and manufacturing output (due to good economic performance in the rest of the world). The Administration is projecting real GDP growth of 3.1% for 2018, and 3.2% and 3.1% for 2019 and 2020, respectively. Since the end of the recession in the 2nd quarter of 2009 through the 2nd quarter of 2018, U.S. GDP has increased at an annual rate of 2.3%.

The primary contributor to growth since 2016 has been consumer spending. Personal consumption expenditures, which account for nearly 70% of U.S. GDP (68.4% in 2017), increased 2.7% in 2016, 2.5% in 2017, and 2.5%, on an annual basis, for the first half of 2018 (with a 4.2% growth in the 2nd quarter of 2018). Consumer spending has contributed roughly 72% of the increase in U.S. real GDP since the end of the recession. Business fixed investment increased 0.5% in 2016 and 5.3% in 2017, and increased 6.7%, on an annual basis, for the first half of 2018. U.S. real exports of goods and services decreased 0.1% in 2016, but have grown since, up 3.0% in 2017, and 5.0% for the first half of 2018). Real imports increased by 1.9% in 2016 and 4.6% in 2017, and have increased by 4.7% so far in 2018. U.S. government expenditures increased 1.4% in 2016, but decreased 0.1% in 2017, before increasing 1.0% through the first half of 2018.

FEDERAL BUDGET DEFICIT

The Federal budget deficit has increased over the period under review in both absolute terms and relative to GDP. The budget deficit increased from US$438.5 billion (2.4% of GDP) in fiscal year 2013 to US$584.7 billion (3.2% of GDP) in fiscal year 2016, and to US$665.4 billion (3.5% of GDP) in fiscal year 2017. The federal deficit in fiscal year 2017, at 3.5% of GDP, was still slightly over one-third of the 9.8% of GDP deficit recorded in 2009 during the depth of the recession. According to the U.S. Office of Management and Budget mid-session review of the FY2019 budget, the federal budget deficit is projected to increase to US$890 billion (4.4% of GDP) in FY2018, and peak at US$1.1 trillion (5.1% of GDP) in FY2019. The deficit is estimated to decline thereafter to US$458 billion (1.4% of GDP) in FY2028. The debt-to-GDP ratio is projected to increase from 78.5% in 2018 to 82.7% in 2022 before declining to 73.8% in 2028.

NOMINAL SAVINGS/INVESTMENT

U.S. gross savings as a percentage of gross national income slightly declined from 19.6% (US$3.66 trillion) in 2015 to 18.3% (US$3.48 trillion) in 2016 before increasing to 18.5% (US$3.68 trillion) in 2017 and 18.7% (US$3.88 trillion) in the second quarter of 2018 (on an annual rate). Although there was a slight increase in gross savings of US$17 billion between 2015 and 2017, this was due to an increase in business savings of US$165 billion, being offset by an increase in government dissaving of US$143 billion. Household and institution savings declined slightly by US$5 billion, as the personal savings rate stayed steady at 6.7% in both 2016 and 2017 (down from 7.6% in 2015, but up from a low of 3.2% in 2005). U.S. gross investment increased by US$178 billion between 2015 and 2017 to US$4.0 trillion.

LABOR MARKETS

U.S. employment continued to increase during the period under review, up 6.2 million net jobs between December 2015 and August 2018 (up 2.3 million between December 2015 and December 2016, up 2.2 million between December 2016 and December 2017, and up 1.7 million between December 2017 and August 2018).

Part C
Report by the United States

The pace of net job growth for the first eight months of 2018 (207,000) remains higher than the average monthly pace in both 2016 (195,000) and 2017 (182,000). U.S. employment has increased for 95 consecutive months from February 2010 through August 2018 (19.6 million), and private employment has increased for 102 consecutive months (up 19.7 million). Manufacturing employment has also increased, up 1.3 million since February 2010, and accounted for one in 10.6 U.S. non-farm jobs in 2017 and one in 10.4 jobs thus far in 2018. Service-providing industries (including government) employed 86% of all U.S. non-farm workers in 2017, and services jobs are up nearly 17.0 million since February 2010.

With the improvement in U.S. employment during the period under review, the unemployment rate has also declined, dropping from a high of 10.0% in October 2009 to 3.9% in August 2018 (3.7% in September). The unemployment rate has been at 5.0% or below for the past 36 months and is well below its pre-recession average of 5.3%. August 2018 marked the fourth time this year that the monthly unemployment rate has been below 4.0%. Prior to this year, unemployment was below 4.0% only five times since 1970. Since December 2015, the unemployment rate has declined by 1.1 percentage points.

The labor market continues to improve. Labor force participation has remained constant at 62.7%, the same rate as in December 2015, though down from the 67.3% peak rate in April 2000. Labor compensation has been increasing. Nominal hourly earnings for all private sector workers are up 2.9% over the past 12 months ending in August 2018, the largest nominal 12 month increase in average hourly earnings since 2009. Real hourly earnings were up 0.2% over the past year. Real median household income in the United States increased 1.8% in 2016 to US$61,372, the third consecutive annual increase, and surpassed the series high of US$58,655 in 1999.

PRODUCTIVITY

Labor productivity, as measured by output per hour worked, has improved in recent years, picking up from the 0.6% average pace from 2011 to 2016. Productivity grew by 1.9% between 4th quarter 2015 and 4th quarter 2017 (up 1.0% in both 2016 and 2017)). Productivity increased sharply in the 2nd quarter 2018 by 2.9% at an annualized rate. With the tight labor market, firms are increasingly turning to capital investment to continue growth, which should support higher productivity growth.

EXPORTS, IMPORTS, AND THE TRADE BALANCE

Nominal U.S. exports of goods and services (on a balance of payments basis) decreased by 2.2% between 2015 and 2016 (the 2nd consecutive annual decline), then increased by 6.1% in 2017. Thus far in 2018 through July, U.S. exports were up 8.6%. Similar to exports, nominal U.S. imports of goods and services declined in 2016 (by 2.2%), and increased in 2017 (up 6.1%) and

thus far in 2018 (up 8.3%). The increase in U.S. trade can be attributed, in part, to stronger economic growth at home and abroad. The stronger dollar in 2018 (up 6% this year) provided some tailwinds on imports and headwinds on exports. As a share of nominal GDP, U.S. goods and services exports was roughly 12% during the period under review, while imports were roughly 15%.

The United States was the recipient of 18.7% of goods and services exports from the rest of the world (excluding intra-European Union (EU) exports) in 2017. The United States supplied 15.1% of goods and services imports to the rest of the world (excluding intra-EU imports).

During the period of review, the U.S. goods and services trade deficit with other countries (on a national income and product accounts basis) increased by 10.9% from US$521 billion in 2015 (2.9% of U.S. GDP) to US$578 billion in 2017 (nearly 3.0% of U.S. GDP). The U.S. deficit in 2017 was significantly down from its all-time high of US$771 billion, or 5.6% of GDP, in 2006. The deficit was even lower in the second quarter 2018 at US$552 billion (2.7% of GDP) on an annual rate.

CHALLENGES TO THE U.S. AND GLOBAL ECONOMY

The U.S. economy has been strong during the period under review, with accelerating growth, low unemployment, and inflation at a sustainable rate. However, growth outside the United States has generally disappointed in 2018: other major advanced economies have seen output growth step down from its 2017 level, while several emerging market economies have come under pressure as rebounding commodity prices, rising U.S. interest rates, and shifts in investor sentiment have interacted with pre-existing weaknesses and led to episodes of financial volatility. Though there are not yet signs that these financial pressures in key emerging markets are leading to broader contagion, a sharp tightening of financial conditions across emerging markets could be a significant drag on global activity and weigh on U.S. growth.

The global economy also remains marked by very large trade and current account imbalances, in part due to persistent trade and investment barriers across many economies. These barriers inhibit the efficient allocation of capital across the global economy and prevent trade from expanding in a way that is fair and reciprocal. Growth across the global economy and in the United States could be stronger and more balanced if these trade and investment barriers were dismantled, and if domestic demand became the sustained engine of expansion for key economies that have maintained large trade surpluses.

Openness and accountability: building support for trade

Support for the United States' active trade agenda – including for actions under domestic trade law,

legislation, bilateral and regional trade agreements, as well as U.S. participation in the WTO – has been built through constant coordination with Congress and extensive outreach to U.S. industry leaders, entrepreneurs, farmers, ranchers, small business owners, workers, state and local government officials, as well as advocates for labor rights, environmental protection, and public health, among others. The United States views consultation with those interested in and affected by trade and investment issues as an important part of any government's responsibility. Consultation and engagement is vital to ensuring that trade policy reflects American interests and American values. Advice from such stakeholders is both a critical and integral part of the trade policy process.

Reflecting Congressional direction, and to draw advice from the widest array of stakeholders, including business, labor, agriculture, civil society, and the general public, USTR has broadened opportunities for public input and worked to ensure transparency of trade policy through various initiatives. USTR works to ensure that timely trade information is available to the public and disseminated widely to stakeholders, and to offer opportunities for public comment on trade issues and for interaction with negotiators during trade negotiations. In addition to public outreach, USTR is responsible for administering the statutory Advisory Committee system, created by the U.S. Congress under the Trade Act of 1974, as amended, as well as facilitating formal consultations with State and local Governments regarding the President's trade priorities and the status of current trade negotiations which may impact them or touch upon state and local government policies.

POLICY COORDINATION

USTR has primary responsibility, with the advice of the interagency trade policy organization, for developing and coordinating the implementation of U.S. trade policy, including on commodity matters (for example, coffee and rubber) and, to the extent they are related to trade, direct investment matters. Under the Trade Expansion Act of 1962, the U.S. Congress established an interagency trade policy mechanism to assist with the implementation of these responsibilities. This organization, as it has evolved, consists of three tiers of committees that constitute the principal mechanism for developing and coordinating U.S. Government positions on international trade and trade-related investment issues.

The Trade Policy Review Group (TPRG) and the Trade Policy Staff Committee (TPSC), both administered and chaired by USTR, are the subcabinet interagency trade policy coordination groups that are central to this process. The TPSC is the first-line operating group, with representation at the senior civil servant level. Supporting the TPSC are more than 100 subcommittees responsible for specialized issues. The TPSC regularly seeks advice from the public on its policy decisions and negotiations through *Federal Register* Notices

and public hearings. During the reporting period, the TPSC held public hearings regarding the China 301 Investigation (October 2017; May 2018), Special 301 Review (February 2017; February 2018), the EU Beef 301 Investigation (February 2017), the Generalized System of Preferences (GSP) product, country and out-of-cycle reviews (October 2016; January 2017; February 2017; July 2017; September 2017; June 2018), the African Growth and Opportunity Act (AGOA) country and out-of-cycle reviews (August 2016; July 2017; August 2017), two Section 201 investigations (December 2017; January 2018), the negotiation of the United States-Mexico-Canada Agreement (June 2017), China's compliance with its WTO Commitments (September 2016; October 2017), and Russia's implementation of its WTO Commitments (October 2016; October 2017).

Through the interagency process, USTR requests input and analysis from members of the appropriate TPSC subcommittee or task force. This group then presents its conclusions and recommendations to the full TPSC and serves as the basis for reaching interagency consensus. On average, the TPSC considers over 250 policy papers and negotiating documents, and holds over 50 TPSC meetings annually. In cases where the TPSC does not reach agreement on a topic, or if the issue under consideration involves particularly significant policy questions, the TPSC refers the issue to the TPRG (whose membership is at the Deputy USTR/Under Secretary level) or to Cabinet Principals.

The member agencies of the TPSC and the TPRG are the U.S. Departments of Commerce, Agriculture, State, Treasury, Labor, Justice, Defense, Interior, Transportation, Energy, Health and Human Services, and Homeland Security; the Environmental Protection Agency; the Office of Management and Budget; the Council of Economic Advisers; the Council on Environmental Quality; the U.S. Agency for International Development; the Small Business Administration; the National Economic Council, and the National Security Council as well as USTR itself. The U.S. International Trade Commission is a non-voting member of the TPSC and an observer at TPRG meetings. Representatives of other agencies also may be invited to attend meetings depending on the specific issues discussed.

PUBLIC ENGAGEMENT AND TRANSPARENCY

USTR works to provide extensive opportunities for public input and works to ensure the transparency of trade policy.

USTR's Office of Intergovernmental Affairs and Public Engagement (IAPE) works with USTR's Offices of Public and Media Affairs and Congressional Affairs, coordinating with the agency's 13 regional and functional offices, the Office of WTO and Multilateral Affairs, Office of General Counsel, and the Office of Trade Policy and Economics to ensure that timely trade information is available to the public and disseminated widely to stakeholders. IAPE uses various tools to accomplish this including USTR's interactive website; online postings of Federal Register Notices soliciting public comment and input and publicizing public hearings held by the Trade Policy Staff Committee (TPSC); offering opportunities for interaction with negotiators during trade negotiations; managing the agency's outreach and engagement to a diverse set of all stakeholders; providing regular data updates to help the public understand and evaluate the role of trade and trade policy in the economy; and participating in discussions of trade policy at major domestic trade events and academic conferences.

USTR officials, including the U.S. Trade Representative, and professional staff from regional, functional, and multilateral offices as well as IAPE, conduct outreach with a broad array of stakeholders, including agricultural commodity groups and farm associations, labor unions, environmental organizations, consumer groups, large and small businesses, trade associations, consumer advocacy groups, faith groups, development and poverty relief organizations, and other public interest groups. USTR also engages with State and local Governments, non-governmental organizations, think tanks, and academics to discuss specific trade policy issues, subject to negotiator availability and scheduling.

USTR goes to great lengths to ensure that the public is actively involved during negotiations and investigations. During the negotiation of the United States-Mexico-Canada Agreement, USTR officials at all levels spent well over 1,500 hours consulting with U.S. stakeholders. Likewise, during the KORUS amendment process, USTR met with over 120 U.S. industry groups and cleared trade advisors. During the review period, USTR has published 33 Federal Register notices to solicit public comment on and provide notice of public hearings concerning negotiations, investigations, and a wide range of issues including the negotiation of the United States-Mexico-Canada Agreement, the China 301 Investigation, and KORUS amendments.

Public comments received in response to Federal Register Notices and transcripts of the public hearings are available for review online.[1]

ADVISORY COMMITTEE PROCESS

The United States continues to rely on its trade advisory committee system as an integral part of its efforts to ensure that U.S. trade policy and trade negotiating objectives adequately reflect U.S. public and private sector interests. The trade advisory committee system, substantially broadened and reformed, consists of 26 advisory committees, with a total membership of approximately 700 advisors. Advisory committee members represent the full span of interests including manufacturing; agriculture; digital trade; intellectual property; services; small businesses; labor; environmental, consumer, and public health organizations; and state and local governments. The system is arranged in three tiers: the President's

Advisory Committee for Trade Policy and Negotiations (ACTPN); five Policy Advisory Committees dealing with environment, labor, agriculture, Africa, and state and local issues; and 20 technical advisory committees in the areas of industry and agriculture.

Tier I: President's Advisory Committee on Trade Policy and Negotiations

The President's Advisory Committee on Trade Policy and Negotiations (ACTPN) consists of not more than 45 members who are broadly representative of the key economic sectors affected by trade. The President appoints ACTPN members to fouryear terms not to exceed the duration of the committee's charter. Members of ACTPN are appointed to represent a variety of interests including non-Federal Governments, labor, industry, agriculture, small business, service industries, retailers, and consumer interests.

Tier II: the Policy Advisory Committees

Members of the five policy advisory committees are appointed by USTR or in conjunction with other Cabinet officers. The Intergovernmental Policy Advisory Committee on Trade (IGPAC), the Trade and Environment Policy Advisory Committee (TEPAC), and the Trade Advisory Committee on Africa (TACA) are appointed and managed by USTR. The Agricultural Policy Advisory Committee for Trade (APAC) is managed jointly with the Department of Agriculture and the Labor Advisory Committee for Trade Negotiations and Trade Policy (LAC) is managed jointly with the Department of Labor. Each committee provides advice based upon the perspective of its specific area, and its members are chosen to represent the diversity of interests in those areas.

Tier III: the Technical and Sectoral Advisory Committee

The 20 technical and sectoral advisory committees are organized into two areas: agriculture and industry. Representatives are appointed jointly by the U.S. Trade Representative and the Secretaries of Agriculture and Commerce, respectively. Each sectoral or technical committee represents a specific sector, commodity group, or functional area and provides specific technical advice concerning the effect that trade policy decisions may have on its sector or issue.

STATE AND LOCAL GOVERNMENT RELATIONS

USTR maintains consultative procedures between Federal trade officials and state and local governments. USTR informs the states, on an ongoing basis, of trade-related matters that directly relate to, or that may have a direct effect on, them. U.S. territories may also participate in this process. USTR also serves as a liaison point in the Executive Branch for state and local government and Federal agencies to transmit information to interested state and local governments, and relay advice and

 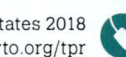

information from the states on trade-related matters. This is accomplished through a number of mechanisms, detailed below.

State Point of Contact System and the Intergovernmental Policy Advisory Committee on Trade

For day-to-day communications, USTR operates State Single Point of Contact (SPOC) system. The Governor's office in each state designates a single contact point to disseminate information received from USTR to relevant state and local offices and assist in relaying specific information and advice from the states to USTR on trade-related matters. Through the SPOC network, state governments are promptly informed of Administration trade initiatives so that they can provide companies and workers with information in order to take full advantage of increased foreign market access and reduced trade barriers. It also enables USTR to consult with states and localities directly on trade matters which may affect them.

Additionally, USTR works closely with the Intergovernmental Policy Advisory Committee on Trade (IGPAC) made up of various state and local officials. The IGPAC makes recommendations to USTR and the Administration on trade policy matters from the perspective of state and local governments. During the review period, the IGPAC was briefed and consulted on trade priorities of interest to states and localities, including the negotiation of the United States–Mexico–Canada Agreement, KORUS modification negotiations, and enforcement actions at the WTO. IGPAC members are also invited to participate in periodic teleconference briefings, similar to teleconference calls held for SPOC and chairs of the advisory committees.

Meetings of State and Local Associations and Local Chambers of Commerce

USTR officials participate frequently in meetings of state and local government associations and local chambers of commerce to apprise them of relevant trade policy issues and solicit their views. USTR senior officials have met with the National Governors Association and with other state and local commissions and organizations. Additionally, USTR officials have addressed gatherings of state and local officials around the country.

Consultations Regarding Specific Trade Issues

USTR consults with particular states and localities on issues arising under the WTO and other U.S. trade agreements and frequently responds to requests for information from state and local governments. Topics of interest include negotiation of the United States–Mexico–Canada Agreement, the Section 301 investigation, enforcement of trade agreements, and consultations with individual states regarding certain trade remedy investigations.

Trade policy developments since 2016

WTO AGREEMENTS AND INITIATIVES

The WTO is an important institution, and the United States has a strong track record of building coalitions of like-minded Members to use the WTO committee system, in particular, to pressure noncomplying economies to bring measures into conformity with WTO rules, to advance transparency and predictability in global trade rules, and to avert the need to resort to dispute settlement.

For the past two decades, the United States has been concerned that the WTO is not operating as the contracting parties envisioned. Multiple administrations have voiced various concerns with the WTO system and the direction in which it has been headed.

First among those concerns is that the WTO dispute settlement system has appropriated to itself powers that the WTO Members never intended to give it. This includes where panels or the Appellate Body have, through their findings, sought to add to or diminish WTO rights and obligations of Members in a broad range of substantive areas. The United States has grown increasingly concerned with the activist approach of the Appellate Body on procedural issues, interpretative approach, and substantive interpretations. These approaches and findings do not respect WTO rules as written and agreed by the United States and other WTO Members. The United States has been drawing the attention of WTO Members to instances where the WTO Appellate Body has disregarded the explicit rules agreed by Members in the WTO Dispute Settlement Understanding (DSU). For example, in the context of meetings of the Dispute Settlement Body, the United States has expressed concerns with respect to the Appellate Body's consistent exceeding of the 90-day deadline for appeals in contravention of DSU Article 17.5, the Appellate Body's review of fact-finding (including of the meaning of a WTO Member's domestic law) in contravention of DSU Article 17.6, and the Appellate Body's decisions pursuant to its Working Procedures for Appellate Review (Rule 15) that purport to "deem" a person whose term of appointment had expired to continue to be an Appellate Body member, in contravention of DSU Article 17.2.

Second, there is also longstanding concern in the United States about the WTO's inability to reach agreements that are of critical importance in the modern global economy. After spending close to 15 years attempting to conclude the Doha Development Agenda (DDA) negotiations, Ministers at the WTO's Tenth Ministerial Conference in December 2015 collectively acknowledged that there was no consensus to reaffirm the DDA's mandates. Consequently, the United States will not negotiate off the basis of the DDA mandates or old DDA texts and considers the Doha Round to be a thing of the past.

For the WTO to be successful going forward, its membership will need to break from the failures of the last two decades, and base future work on lessons learned and, importantly, current data and up-to-date notifications. Members' failure to comply with their notification obligations under the WTO Agreement undermines the negotiating function of the WTO and the credibility of the organization. At the November 2017 meeting of the General Council, the United States put forward a proposal aimed at improving Members' compliance with their notification obligations. In September 2018, the United States, Japan, and the EU agreed to co-sponsor an updated transparency and notification proposal for consideration at the next meeting of the WTO Council on Trade in Goods. The United States stands ready to work with Members to advance this proposal.

It is also vital to focus on issues that are affecting our stakeholders today and into the future. In this regard, the United States seeks to work with those Members who are ready and able to negotiate free, fair, and reciprocal agreements, with the expectation that participants to these agreements will contribute commensurate with their status in the global economy.

At the WTO's Eleventh Ministerial Conference in Buenos Aires in December 2017, Members agreed to several important outcomes, including a Ministerial decision on fisheries subsidies and a joint declaration on electronic commerce. Regarding fisheries subsidies, which is an issue that impacts our oceans and our economies, the United States is working with other Members to finalize a meaningful agreement to prohibit harmful fisheries subsidies, such as those that contribute to overfishing and overcapacity or which support illegal, unreported, and unregulated (IUU) fishing. The United States is also advocating for enhanced transparency and reporting of fisheries support programs. The United States is pleased to partner with 70 WTO Members in advancing exploratory work on potential negotiations on electronic commerce issues in the WTO. The digital economy serves as a critical engine of domestic and global economic growth, and all countries would benefit from the development of strong, market-based rules in this area.

Third, the United States sees an acute need for the WTO to change how it approaches questions of development. While "least-developed countries" (LDCs) are defined in the WTO using the United Nations criteria, there are no WTO criteria for what designates a "developing country." Any country may "self-declare" as a developing country, thus entitling itself to all "special and differential" treatment afforded to developing countries under the WTO agreements, as well as any new flexibilities afforded to developing countries under current or forthcoming negotiations. In practice, this means that more advanced countries receive the same flexibilities as very low-income countries, despite these more advanced countries' very significant role in the global economy. Such disparities, where countries that some institutions categorize as high- or high-middle-income receive the same flexibilities

as low- or low-middle-income, make it challenging to find balance in the application of existing obligations or the development of new commitments.

Finally, there is significant concern that the WTO is unable to manage the rise of countries that pay lip service to the values of free trade but intentionally avoid, circumvent, or violate the commitments accompanying those values.

The United States will work with other like-minded countries to address these concerns.

TRADE ENFORCEMENT ACTIVITIES

Trade enforcement encompasses a broad range of activities, including monitoring of trade agreements, direct engagement with trading partners, use of domestic trade laws, and engagement in multilateral fora such as the WTO. USTR coordinates the U.S. Government's trade enforcement activities. Ensuring full implementation of U.S. trade agreements is one of the strategic priorities of the United States.

The United States has been actively engaged in numerous WTO dispute settlement actions, including important offensive actions related to China's discriminatory regime for technology licensing, agricultural market access in China, India, and Indonesia, China's excessive agricultural domestic support, Indian prohibited export subsidies, and the EU's subsidies benefitting large civil aircraft. The United States has also initiated actions relating to additional duties imposed by certain Members related to the administration's actions under section 232 of the Trade Expansion Act of 1962 to address the threat to national security presented by imports of steel and aluminium, as well as participating in related defensive actions brought by certain Members.

Where appropriate, the United States applies the full range of its trade laws, including section 301 of the Trade Act of 1974 (Trade Act), as amended. Section 301 of the Trade Act is designed to facilitate USTR's examining and addressing foreign unfair practices affecting U.S. commerce. In February 2017, USTR held a public hearing in connection with the request of representatives of the U.S. beef industry to reinstate action against the EU pursuant to Section 301 of the Trade Act. The United States is engaged in discussions with the EU on possible modifications to the operation of a TRQ to address U.S. industry concerns. In addition, in August 2017, USTR initiated an investigation under Section 301 of the Trade Act to determine whether acts, policies, and practices of the Government of China related to technology transfer, intellectual property (IP), and innovation are actionable under Section 301. USTR held a public hearing on October 10, 2017, and two rounds of public written comments. In March 2018, USTR released the findings of its Section 301 investigation on China, determining that the acts, policies, and practices of the Government of China related to technology transfer, IP, and innovation covered in the investigation are unreasonable or discriminatory and burden or restrict U.S. commerce.

Addressing foreign subsidies that affect U.S. businesses is another critical trade enforcement activity. USTR and U.S. Department of Commerce Enforcement and Compliance staff researched foreign subsidies and met with representatives of U.S. industries concerned with the subsidization of foreign competitors.

The United States also actively monitors, evaluates, and where appropriate, participates in ongoing anti-dumping (AD) and countervailing duty (CVD) cases conducted by foreign countries to safeguard the interests of U.S. industry and to ensure that Members abide by their WTO obligations in conducting such proceedings. To this end, the United States works closely with U.S. companies affected by foreign countries' AD and CVD investigations and provides extensive responses to inquiries in foreign CVD investigations. The United States also advocates on behalf of U.S. industry in connection with ongoing investigations, with the goal of obtaining unbiased and objective treatment as is consistent with the WTO Agreements.

USTR is committed to holding foreign countries accountable and exposing the laws, practices, and other measures that fail to provide adequate and effective IP protection and enforcement for U.S. inventors, creators, brands, manufacturers, and service providers. The identification of IP-related market access barriers and steps necessary to address those barriers are a critical component of the administration's aggressive efforts to defend Americans from harmful IP-related trade barriers.

Finally, the United States commits significant resources to identify and confront unjustified barriers stemming from sanitary and phytosanitary (SPS) measures as well as from technical regulations, standards, and conformity assessment procedures (standards-related measures). USTR uses tools, including its Annual Report and the National Trade Estimate Report, to bring greater attention and focus to addressing SPS and standards-related measures that may be inconsistent with international trade agreements to which the United States is a party. USTR's activities in the WTO SPS Committee and the WTO Technical Barriers to Trade (TBT) Committee are at the forefront of these efforts. USTR also engages on these issues with U.S. trading partners through mechanisms established in free trade agreements and through regional and multilateral organizations, such as the Asia-Pacific Economic Cooperation (APEC) forum and the Organization for Economic Cooperation Development (OECD).

FREE TRADE AGREEMENTS AND INITIATIVES

Central America and the Dominican Republic Free Trade Agreement

On 5 August 2004, the United States signed the Dominican Republic–Central America–United States Free Trade Agreement (CAFTA–DR) with five Central American countries (Costa Rica, El Salvador, Guatemala, Honduras, and Nicaragua) and the Dominican Republic. The CAFTA–DR is the first free trade agreement between the United States and a group of smaller developing economies. This agreement created new economic opportunities by eliminating tariffs, opening markets, reducing barriers to services, and promoting transparency. It helped facilitate trade and investment among the seven countries, furthering regional integration.

CAFTA-DR countries represent the third largest U.S. export market in Latin America, behind Mexico and Brazil. U.S. goods exported to the CAFTA-DR countries were valued at US$31 billion in 2017. Combined total two-way trade in 2017 between the United States and Central America and the Dominican Republic was US$54 billion.

The agreement entered into force for the United States and El Salvador, Guatemala, Honduras, and Nicaragua during 2006, for the Dominican Republic on 1 March 2007, and for Costa Rica on 1 January 2009.

North American Free Trade Agreement

On 1 January 1994, the North American Free Trade Agreement between the United States, Canada, and Mexico (NAFTA) entered into force. Under NAFTA, the Parties progressively eliminated tariffs, with tariffs eliminated on all goods (except for dairy, poultry, and eggs products for Canada, and dairy, sugar and egg products for the United States). NAFTA created the world's largest free trade area, linking 494 million people producing roughly US$22.2 trillion worth of goods and services. U.S. goods exports to NAFTA partners increased by 270% between 1993 and 2017, from US$142 billion to an estimated US$526 billion.

In August 2017, the United States began negotiations with Canada and Mexico to address remaining market access barriers, and to modernize and rebalance the obligations between the Parties, including by bringing the labor and environment obligations that had been included in supplemental agreements into the core body of the agreement. On September 30, 2018, the three Parties announced they had reached agreement on the United States–Mexico–Canada Agreement (USMCA).[2]

United States–Australia Free Trade Agreement

The United States–Australia FTA entered into force on 1 January 2005. U.S. two-way goods trade with Australia totalled US$34.6 billion in 2017, up 61% since 2004, the year before the FTA entered into force. U.S. two-way services trade with Australia totalled US$29.8 billion in 2017 (latest data available), an increase of 186% since 2004. The stock of U.S. foreign direct investment in Australia reached US$169 billion in 2017 (latest data available); the United States is the largest foreign investor in Australia, while the United States is the top destination for outbound Australian foreign direct investment.

The United States and Australia continue to closely monitor FTA implementation. The sixth Joint Committee Meeting to review implementation of the FTA and other bilateral issues was held in December 2017, and covered topics including intellectual property, services, autos, and investment. The two countries work closely to further promote trade and investment through WTO, APEC, and other regional initiatives.

United States–Bahrain Free Trade Agreement

The United StatesBahrain FTA entered into force on 1 August 2006. On the first day the agreement took effect, 100% of the twoway trade in industrial and consumer products began to flow without tariffs. In 2016, two-way trade in goods was US$1.9 billion. U.S. exports of goods were US$898 million, and U.S. imports of goods from Bahrain were US$996 million.

The U.S.Bahrain FTA promotes the United States' policy to increase job-supporting trade and investment between the United States and Middle East. The United StatesBahrain Bilateral Investment Treaty (BIT) took effect in May 2001.

United States–Chile Free Trade Agreement

The United StatesChile FTA entered into force on 1 January 2004. The United States-Chile FTA eliminates tariffs and opens markets, reduces barriers to trade in services, provides protection for intellectual property, ensures regulatory transparency, guarantees non-discrimination in the trade of digital products, commits the Parties to maintain competition laws that prohibit anticompetitive business conduct, and requires effective labor and environmental enforcement. Two-way goods trade totalled US$27.8 billion in 2016, with U.S. goods exports to Chile totalling US$17.2 billion. As of 1 January 2015, all products became duty free under the Agreement.

United States–Colombia Trade Promotion Agreement

The United States-Colombia Trade Promotion Agreement (CTPA) entered into force on 15 May 2012. Two-way goods trade totalled US$26.9 billion in 2017, with U.S. goods exports to Colombia totalling US$13.3 billion. "Year 7" tariff cuts occurred on 1 January 2018.

During 2016 and 2017, the United States continued regular engagement with the Colombian government to support its efforts to improve the protection of worker rights and address cases of violence and threats against trade unionists. The United States will continue its engagement with the Government of Colombia to ensure progress on workers' rights, including through cooperative efforts and dialogue regarding the collection of fines for labor law violations, and to increase the number of resolved cases of violence and threats against unionists.

The Agreement established an Environmental Affairs Council (EAC) under the environment chapter. The related U.S.-Colombia Environmental Cooperation Agreement (ECA) established an Environmental Cooperation Commission (ECC). In 2017 and 2018, the United States and Colombia worked on an agreement establishing a secretariat to receive and consider submissions from the public on matters regarding enforcement of environmental laws pursuant to Article 18.8 of the CTPA, which was finalized in July 2018. The secretariat is housed in Colombia and is intended to promote public participation in the identification and resolution of issues regarding each party's enforcement of its environmental laws.

United States–Israel Free Trade Agreement

The United States-Israel Free Trade Agreement is the United States' first FTA. It entered into force in 1985 and continues to serve as the foundation for expanding trade and investment between the United States and Israel by reducing barriers and promoting regulatory transparency. In 2017, U.S. goods exports to Israel were US$15.1 billion.

In February 2016, the United States and Israel sought ways to engage in collaborative efforts to increase bilateral trade and investment. During the meeting, the United States and Israel began discussion of a work plan to address the remaining barriers to bilateral trade, including in agriculture and customs, among other areas. The two sides also made progress on a number of market access issues related to standards, customs classification, and technical regulations. In 2017, the United States and Israel agreed to adopt new procedures making it easier for exporters to gain approvals when claiming duty-free status under the FTA for individual products.

In 1996, the United States and Israel concluded an Agreement Concerning Certain Aspects of Trade in Agricultural Products (ATAP), which provided for duty-free or other preferential treatment for certain agricultural products. The 1996 agreement was extended through 2003, and a new agreement was concluded in 2004. While this Agreement originally ran through 2008, it has been extended annually since then. In February 2016, the United States proposed to Israel that they negotiate a permanent U.S.-Israel ATAP. Each side is reviewing the proposals put forward by the other in preparation for negotiations, tentatively planned for late 2018.

United States–Jordan Free Trade Agreement

The United States-Jordan Free Trade Agreement entered into force on 17 December 2001, and all tariffs were eliminated as of 1 January 2010. U.S. goods exports were an estimated US$2.0 billion in 2017, up 34.5% from 2016.

At the May 2016 meeting of the Joint Committee (JC) established under the FTA, the United States and Jordan agreed to implement an action plan outlining concrete

steps to boost trade and investment bilaterally and between Jordan and other countries in the Middle East region.

Additionally, the United States continues to work with Jordan in the area of labor standards, particularly through ongoing efforts under the Implementation Plan Related to Working and Living Conditions of Workers in Jordan, signed in 2013. The Plan addresses labor concerns in Jordan's garment factories including anti-union discrimination against foreign workers, conditions of accommodations for foreign workers, and gender discrimination and harassment.

United States–Korea Free Trade Agreement

The United States-Korea Free Trade Agreement (KORUS) entered into force on 15 March 2012. Since the Agreement entered into force, the U.S.-Korea goods and services trade increased from US$126.5 billion in 2011 to US$154.8 billion in 2017. However, the U.S. goods deficit with Korea also quickly increased, topping US$23 billion in 2017, with the overall goods and services deficit also reaching nearly US$10 billion.

On July 12, 2017, the United States requested a special session of the KORUS Joint Committee to review the implementation of the agreement and to discuss additional steps to address the significant bilateral trade imbalance, including through possible amendments and modifications. Negotiations to improve the agreement were launched in early 2018, with outcomes announced in March 2018. Following the completion of domestic procedures in the United States, the final texts reflecting the outcomes from these negotiations were signed by the two countries on September 24, 2018. The modernized provisions will then enter into force after completion of applicable procedures by both countries. These outcomes focus on improving automobile trade, in addition to other provisions including on investment. Progress on implementation-related issues also was announced, including in the areas of pharmaceuticals and customs.

There are 21 KORUS committees and working groups, which meet regularly and may also be convened on an ad hoc basis to address issues of concern.

United States–Morocco Free Trade Agreement

The United States-Morocco Free Trade Agreement (FTA) entered into force on 1 January 2006. Since the entry into force of the FTA, two-way U.S.-Morocco trade in goods has grown from US$927 million in 2005 (the year prior to entry into force) to US$3.5 billion in 2016. U.S. goods exports to Morocco in 2017 were US$2.2 billion, up 14.8% from the previous year. U.S. imports from Morocco in 2017 were US$1.2 billion, up nearly 20.7% from 2016.

The United States and Morocco held the fifth meeting of the FTA Joint Committee (JC) on October 18, 2017 in Washington, DC. U.S. and Moroccan officials noted productive bilateral environmental and labor-related cooperation under the Labor and Environment FTA Subcommittees, reviewed recent improvements to Morocco's legislative regime for the protection of intellectual property rights, and decided to further discuss the concerns of some U.S. pharmaceutical companies. In the area of agriculture, the JC reviewed discussions held just prior to the JC's session in combined meetings of the Agriculture and SPS FTA Subcommittees.

United States–Oman Free Trade Agreement

The United States-Oman Free Trade Agreement, which entered into force on 1 January 2009, complements other U.S. FTAs to promote economic reform and openness in the region. In 2017, two-way trade in goods was US$3.1 billion. U.S. exports of goods were US$2.0 billion, and U.S. imports of goods from Oman were US$1.1 billion. As of 1 January 2018, all products became duty free under the Agreement.

United States–Panama Trade Promotion Agreement

The United States-Panama Trade Promotion Agreement (Panama TPA) entered into force on 31 October 2012. The United States' two-way goods trade with Panama was US$6.7 billion in 2017, with U.S. goods exports to Panama totalling US$6.3 billion. "Year 7" tariff cuts occurred on 1 January 2018. The TPA's central oversight body is the United States-Panama Free Trade Commission (FTC), which held its last FTC meeting in November 2016, to review implementation of the Agreement.

The Agreement includes obligations for both countries to protect fundamental labor rights as well as to effectively enforce existing labor laws, which will enable workers and businesses to compete on a level playing field. The Agreement also established a Labor Affairs Council (LAC) under the labor chapter.

The Agreement established an Environmental Affairs Council (EAC) under the environment chapter. The related U.S.-Panama Environmental Cooperation Agreement (ECA) established an Environmental Cooperation Commission (ECC). In August 2016, the agreement establishing the secretariat for environmental enforcement matters pursuant to Article 18.8 of the Panama TPA entered into force. The secretariat mechanism is housed in Panama and is intended to promote public participation in the identification and resolution of issues regarding each party's enforcement of its environmental laws. The United States and Panama continued to make progress to fully stand up the secretariat throughout 2017 and 2018, including by hiring an Executive Director in 2017.

United States–Peru Trade Promotion Agreement

The United States-Peru Trade Promotion Agreement (PTPA) entered into force on 1 February 2009. The PTPA eliminates tariffs and removes barriers to U.S.

services, provides a secure, predictable legal framework for investors, and strengthens protection for intellectual property, workers, and the environment. The United States' two-way goods trade with Peru was an estimated US$18.5 billion in 2016, with U.S. goods exports to Peru totalling US$8.7 billion.

The PTPA also established the United States-Peru Forest Sector Subcommittee, the Environmental Affairs Council (EAC), and the Environmental Cooperation Commission. The Subcommittee serves as a forum for the Parties to exchange views and share information on any matter arising under the PTPA's Annex on Forest Sector Governance (Forest Annex). Through the EAC, the United States and Peru have had robust engagement concerning the implementation of the environmental obligations under the PTPA Environment Chapter and the Forest Annex. For additional information concerning U.S. engagement with Peru on these issues, please refer to the section on Trade and the Environment.

United States–Singapore Free Trade Agreement

The United States-Singapore FTA, the United States' first in Asia, has been in effect since 2004. Since 2003, the year before the FTA entered into force, two-way goods trade has increased 55%. Singapore is the 18th largest goods trading partner of the United States and reached US$49.2 billion in total goods trade and US$25.9 billion in total services trade in 2017 (latest data available). The stock of U.S. foreign direct investment in Singapore reached US$274 billion in 2017 (latest data available). Singapore is the second-largest source of foreign investment from the Asia-Pacific in the United States, while the Singapore is the top destination for outbound U.S. foreign direct investment in Asia. The United States consults regularly with Singapore to monitor implementation of the FTA, address bilateral issues, and further build and expand the bilateral relationship.

OTHER NEGOTIATING INITIATIVES

Asia-Pacific Economic Cooperation Forum

Since it was founded in 1989, the Asia-Pacific Economic Cooperation (APEC) forum has been instrumental in promoting regional and global trade and investment. It is central to U.S. efforts to achieve a seamless economy in the Asia-Pacific region that will expand opportunities for U.S. exporters, services providers, and workers, providing greater economic growth across the region.

The United States is a significant trader with APEC economies. U.S. goods and services trade with APEC economies totalled US$2.8 trillion in 2016. Exports totalled US$1.2 trillion, with goods exports to APEC economies in 2017 totalling US$972.5 billion, accounting for 62.9% of overall U.S. exports in 2017. The United States had a US$2.6 trillion in total (two-ways) goods trade with APEC economies during 2017.

In 2017, during Vietnam's APEC host year, the United States worked with APEC to build on the commitments of previous years, as well as to launch work on other issues of priority to the United States and other APEC economies that will help promote economic growth and support jobs for American workers and businesses. The United States joined with other APEC economies to advance capacity-building actions to help developing APEC economies improve at-the-border procedures, including steps that reduce the time, cost, and uncertainty of shipments. These projects match closely with the provisions of the WTO Agreement on Trade Facilitation. APEC's work in this area will make it significantly cheaper, easier, and faster for businesses to trade in the AsiaPacific region. APEC is working closely with public and private sector experts in the region to advance these goals.

APEC also advanced work on promoting services trade through the implementation of elements of the APEC Services Competitiveness Roadmap, adopted in 2016. APEC is developing a region-wide index on trade restrictiveness in services based on existing indices. APEC continued to focus attention in 2017 and 2018 on the growing importance of digital trade to economic growth and innovation. The United States is leading the effort to adopt building blocks to facilitate digital trade, including principles related to enabling cross-border data flows and preventing forced localization of data. APEC also showed leadership by continuing efforts to strengthen the implementation of good regulatory practices.

Japan

In 2017, total U.S.-Japan trade was US$283 billion, and Japan was the 4th-largest goods trading partner of the United States (latest data available). The U.S. goods trade deficit with Japan was about US$69 billion in 2017, virtually unchanged from the previous year.

From April 2017, engagement with Japan on bilateral trade issues took place under the U.S.-Japan Economic Dialogue, through which progress with Japan was made across issues such as automotive standards and the removal of restrictions on agricultural products. In April 2018, new bilateral trade and investment consultations were announced, led by U.S. Trade Representative Lighthizer and Japan Economic Revitalization Minister Motegi, in order to intensify engagement on trade to strengthen the U.S.-Japan economic relationship. Meetings took place in August 2018 and September 2018, culminating in the announcement in September 2018 that the United States and Japan would enter into negotiations for a U.S.-Japan Trade Agreement to cover trade in goods as well as other key issues including services, to be followed by further negotiations on additional trade and investment issues.

The trade ministers of the United States, Japan, and the EU announced new trilateral cooperation in December 2017 to undertake measures to combat

the non-market-oriented policies of third countries. Following Ministerial meetings in March and May 2018, the ministers confirmed their shared objective to address non-market-oriented policies and practices, their shared view that no country should require or pressure technology transfer from foreign companies to domestic companies, and the need to deepen and accelerate discussions regarding possible new rules on industrial subsidies and state-owned entities. The Ministers further agreed to deepen cooperation and exchange of information, including with other like-minded partners, to find effective means to address trade-distorting policies of third countries.

The U.S.-ASEAN Trade and Investment Framework Arrangement

The United States is pursuing several initiatives to expand and deepen economic engagement with the 10 member countries of the Association of South East Asian Nations (ASEAN). ASEAN collectively represents both the United States' fourth largest goods export market and largest trading partner. Under the Trade and Investment Framework Arrangement signed in 2006, the United States is working with ASEAN countries to enhance and deepen the U.S.-ASEAN economic relationship and support ASEAN regional integration. In 2017-2018, the United States supported the launch of the ASEAN Single Window under the U.S. Agency for International Development's US-ASEAN Connectivity through Trade and Investment (US-ACTI) program. For 2018-2019, the United States and ASEAN have decided to work together on agriculture biotechnology regulatory cooperation and continue discussions on proposals regarding electronic payment services and automotive standards.

Engagement with the Middle East and North Africa

The revolutions and other changes that swept through the Middle East and North Africa (MENA) beginning in 2011 prompted a comprehensive revaluation of U.S. trade and investment policies toward this critical part of the world. In response to these events, USTR coordinated with other Federal agencies, outside experts, and stakeholders in both the United States and MENA partner countries to develop trade and investment initiatives to support jobs and enhance regional trade. To date, the United States has focused on a number of areas, including trade facilitation, investment promotion, the information and communications technology (ICT) sector, and agricultural trade, as key priorities in developing longer-term trade and investment ties to trading partners in the region.

Although ongoing political and in some cases military turmoil in the MENA region has hampered, to varying degrees, U.S. efforts to engage MENA partner governments, the U.S. Government has sought to maintain dialogue with as many partners as possible. During the 2017-18 period, the United States continued to monitor, implement, and enforce U.S. FTAs in the region (Bahrain, Israel, Jordan, Morocco, and Oman) and held consultations under Trade and Investment Framework Agreements with Algeria, Saudi Arabia, Tunisia, and Egypt. In these discussions, the United States and partner governments have explored possible new ways to address trade and investment issues seen as important to fostering bilateral trade and investment, including with respect to customs, intellectual property, control procedures for food imports, standards development, legal harmonization, and WTO initiatives.

U.S.–EU Trade

The U.S. trade and investment relationship with the EU is the largest and most complex economic relationship in the world, with transatlantic trade flows (goods and services trade plus earnings and payments on investment) averaging over US$5.3 billion each day during 2017. The total stock of transatlantic direct investment was worth US$5.6 trillion in 2016. These enormous trade and investment flows are a key pillar of prosperity both in the United States and Europe, and countries around the world benefit from access to the markets, capital, and innovations of the transatlantic economy.

The United States interacts extensively with counterparts in the major EU governing institutions (the European Commission, the European Parliament, and the European Council) and EU member State governments on key issues for U.S. workers, farmers, and businesses, such as long-standing, systemic non-tariff barriers in the EU that impede U.S. exports of industrial and agricultural products, the protection of intellectual property rights, and joint efforts on shared concerns in third country markets.

On July 25, 2018, President Trump and European Commission President Juncker issued a joint statement in Washington announcing the formation of a bilateral Executive Working Group that would seek to reduce barriers to transatlantic trade. Ambassador Lighthizer and Commissioner Malmstrom and their teams have discussed the scope and content of the initiative several times since the end of July, and the two sides are developing priorities both for short-term and longer-term outcomes.

As noted above, the United States has been working closely with the EU and Japan at the ministerial level to address shared concerns on several issues.

Following the United Kingdom's decision in 2016 to leave the EU, the UK and the United States established the U.S.-UK Trade and Investment Working Group in July 2017 and have convened five meetings since then. The Working Group is focusing on providing commercial continuity for UK and U.S. businesses, workers, and consumers as the UK leaves the EU and exploring ways to strengthen trade and investment ties. The Working Group is also laying the groundwork for a potential, future free trade agreement once the UK has left the

EU in March 2019, and exploring areas in which the two countries can collaborate to promote open markets and free and fair trade around the world.

China

Since China's accession to the WTO, the United States has repeatedly attempted to work with China in a cooperative and constructive manner. Using intensive, high-level bilateral dialogues, the United States has sought to resolve significant trade irritants and also to encourage China to pursue market-oriented policies and become a more responsible Member of the WTO. These bilateral efforts have been largely unsuccessful – not because of failures by U.S. policymakers, but because Chinese policymakers were not interested in moving toward a true market economy.

The United States established its first high-level trade dialogue with China in 2003, with the elevation of the existing U.S.-China Joint Commission on Commerce and Trade (JCCT), as the U.S. Trade Representative joined the Secretary of Commerce as a U.S. chair and a Vice Premier began leading the Chinese side. Another high-level dialogue, the U.S.-China Strategic Economic Dialogue (SED), was added in 2006 with a broad focus on economic matters, including some trade and investment issues. The SED was expanded and replaced by the U.S.-China Strategic and Economic Dialogue (S&ED) in 2009. Finally, in 2017, the United States and China created the U.S.-China Comprehensive Economic Dialogue (CED), which supplanted the JCCT and the S&ED. Nevertheless, despite this constant high-level engagement over the years, these dialogues failed to generate needed shifts in the direction of Chinese policies and practices. China has shown a willingness to take modest steps to address isolated issues, and will sometimes make broad commitments when pressed at very high levels, but it has not been prepared to follow through on significant commitments or to make fundamental changes to its trade and investment regime. Instead, China has displayed a determination to maintain the state's leading role in the economy and to continue to pursue industrial policies that promote, guide and support domestic industries while simultaneously and actively seeking to impede, disadvantage and harm their foreign counterparts, even though this approach is incompatible with the market-based approach expressly envisioned by WTO members and contrary to the fundamental principles running throughout the many WTO agreements.

In November 2017, when President Trump met with President Xi in Beijing, the U.S. side explained that it had no interest in engaging in the types of bilateral discussions pursued in the CED and in past dialogues like the JCCT, the SED and the S&ED. Instead, the United States made clear that it is seeking fundamental changes to China's trade regime, including to the problematic industrial policies that have continued to dominate China's state-led economy. Through several subsequent high-level meetings in 2018, the United States reiterated its concerns, but to date China has not taken action to address those concerns.

Going forward, the United States will continue to hold China strictly accountable for adherence to its WTO obligations. Like other WTO Members, the United States will continue to use the WTO dispute settlement mechanism as an enforcement tool and also raise concerns during meetings of WTO committees and councils in order to highlight problematic Chinese policies and practices. In addition, the United States will continue to participate in other multilateral fora, such as the Global Forum on Steel Excess Capacity. At the same time, the United States will continue to rigorously enforce U.S. trade remedy laws, in accordance with WTO rules, when U.S. interests are being harmed by unfairly traded or surging imports from China. The United States also will take all other steps necessary to rein in harmful state-led, non-market policies and practices pursued by China, even when they do not fall squarely within WTO disciplines, as evidenced by USTR's investigation of Chinese technology transfer policies and practices pursuant to Section 301 of the Trade Act of 1974, as amended.

African Growth and Opportunity Act

AGOA has been the cornerstone of U.S. African engagement on trade and investment since it was enacted in 2000. By providing duty-free entry into the United States for approximately 6,500 tariff lines of products of beneficiary countries, AGOA has helped to expand and diversify two-way trade between the United States and sub-Saharan Africa, and helped to foster an improved business environment in many sub-Saharan African countries. AGOA was extended to 2025 by the Trade Preferences Extension Act of 2015. The renewed AGOA provides additional tools to support compliance with the AGOA eligibility criteria, including by providing greater flexibility to withdraw, suspend, or limit benefits under the program if it is determined that such action would be more effective than termination of AGOA eligibility. The renewed AGOA was also enhanced to promote greater regional integration by expanding rules of origin and by encouraging beneficiary countries to develop AGOA utilization strategies. In 2017, U.S. total two-way (exports plus imports) goods trade with sub-Saharan Africa was US$39 billion. U.S. total imports under AGOA, including its Generalized System of Preferences provisions, was US$13.8 billion and U.S. imports of non-oil goods under AGOA totalled US$4.3 billion, a more than threefold increase since AGOA entered into force.

AGOA requires the President to monitor, review, and report to Congress bi-annually on the progress of sub Saharan African countries in meeting the AGOA eligibility criteria set out in the legislation – including, among other things, making continual progress in establishing a market based economy, rule of law, and protection of internationally recognized workers' rights.

The U.S. Trade Representative makes recommendations to the President regarding which countries should be eligible for benefits based on an annual country eligibility review that takes into account information drawn from U.S. Government agencies, the private sector, non-governmental organizations, and prospective beneficiary governments. In 2018, 40 countries were eligible for AGOA benefits.

The United States-Sub-Saharan Africa Trade and Economic Cooperation Forum, informally known as the "AGOA Forum," is an annual ministerial-level meeting with AGOA-eligible countries. In July 2018, the U.S. Trade Representative led the USG delegation to the AGOA Forum held in Washington, DC. The U.S. Trade Representative and other U.S. participants met with numerous African senior officials, including trade ministers, leaders of African regional economic organizations, and representatives of the African and American private sectors and civil society to discuss issues and strategies for advancing trade, investment, and economic development in Africa. The discussion topics included how to foster greater trade and investment between the United States and Africa, and how to expand that relationship beyond AGOA in the future.

In 2018, USTR published the "2018 Biennial Report on the Implementation of the African Growth and Opportunity Act."[3] The report provides a description of the status of trade and investment between the United States and sub-Saharan Africa, changes in country eligibility for AGOA benefits, an analysis of country compliance with the AGOA eligibility criteria, an overview of regional integration efforts in sub-Saharan Africa, and a summary of U.S. trade capacity-building efforts.

East African Community Trade and Investment Partnership

The United States and East Africa Community (EAC) established a Trade and Investment Partnership in 2012 to support economic integration of the EAC and enhance the U.S.-EAC trade and investment relationship. In 2013, the United States established Trade Africa as a partnership between the United States and sub-Saharan Africa to increase intra-Africa trade and investment and to expand trade and economic ties between Africa, the United States, and other global markets. From the outset, Trade Africa focused on the member states of the EAC – Burundi, Kenya, Rwanda, Tanzania, and Uganda. Subsequently, South Sudan became a member of the EAC in 2016. Trade Africa activities included helping EAC countries implement their WTO obligations under the Agreement on Trade Facilitation, the Agreement on the Application of SPS Measures, and the Agreement on TBT. Projects also included supporting these governments' development of export and AGOA strategies; strengthening the institutional capacity of trade support institutions, such as local export-import banks, investment promotion agencies, and standards bureaus; and working with port authorities and customs agencies to reduce fees, streamline customs procedures, and improve port and border management. In 2015, the United States and EAC signed the U.S.-EAC Cooperation Agreement on Trade Facilitation, SPS, and TBT to help support implementation of these WTO agreements. In 2017, the United States had a US$1.6 billion in total (two ways) goods trade with EAC countries. U.S. goods exports to the EAC totalled US$795 million while goods imports from the EAC totalled US$828 million.

Nepal Trade Preference Program

The Trade Facilitation and Trade Enforcement Act of 2015 (TFTEA) entered into force on February 24, 2016 and directed the President to establish a country-specific preference program to grant Nepal duty-free treatment for a set of textile, apparel, and headgear products covered by 66 8-digit tariff lines in the Harmonized Tariff Schedule (HTS) with a view to assisting Nepal recover from the April 2015 earthquake and subsequent aftershocks. Due to changes in the U.S. Harmonized Tariff Schedule, the number of tariff lines for which Nepal is exempt from customs duties increased in July 2016 to 77 8-digit tariff lines. Following the determination that Nepal met certain eligibility requirements, the NTPP program was implemented by Presidential Proclamation on December 15, 2016. It is effective through December 31, 2025. In addition to the tariff preferences, the TFTEA directs the President to provide trade-related technical assistance to help Nepal implement the WTO Agreement on Trade Facilitation.

In 2017, U.S.-Nepal two-way trade totalled US$167.8 million. U.S. imports from Nepal under the NTPP were US$2.4 million in 2017 and accounted for 3% of total U.S. imports from Nepal. The U.S. government has made efforts to promote the utilization of the NTPP, including through the U.S.–Nepal Trade and Investment Framework Agreement (TIFA) Council meetings in April 2017 and during outreach events on the margins of the TIFA to explain and promote the NTPP to Nepali industry and government officials.

The Caribbean Basin Initiative

The programs known collectively as the Caribbean Basin Initiative (CBI) are a vital element in U.S. economic relations with its neighbours in the Caribbean. Initially launched in 1983 by the Caribbean Basin Economic Recovery Act (CBERA) and substantially expanded in 2000 with the U.S.-Caribbean Basin Trade Partnership Act (CBTPA), the CBI was further expanded in the Trade Act of 2002. In addition, the United States provides substantial benefits to Haiti through the Haitian Hemispheric Opportunity through Partnership Encouragement Act of 2006 ("HOPE Act"), the Haitian Hemispheric Opportunity through Partnership Encouragement Act of 2008 ("HOPE II"), and the Haiti Economic Lift Program Act of 2010 ("HELP Act").

In 2015, Congress extended this program of unilateral support for Haiti through 2025.

Since its inception, the CBERA has helped beneficiaries diversify their exports. In conjunction with economic reform and trade liberalization by beneficiary countries, the trade benefits of the program have contributed to their economic growth. In December 2017, USTR submitted its twelfth biannual report to Congress on the operation of the CBERA. The report can be found on the USTR website.[4] A list of current beneficiary countries can be found in the December 2017 report. On an annual basis, USTR is required to submit a report to Congress regarding the implementation of HOPE II. The latest HOPE II Report can also be found on the USTR website.[5]

OTHER TRADE ACTIVITIES

Protecting Intellectual Property

Given the importance of innovation to U.S. economic growth, employment and exports, the United States places a high value on the protection and enforcement of intellectual property (IP), in both domestic and foreign markets. Domestically, Congress continues to update and improve the U.S. IP legal regime, while the Administration stresses the importance of American leadership in the innovative and creative sectors. In foreign markets, a top trade priority for the Administration is to use all possible sources of leverage to encourage other countries to open their markets to U.S. exports of goods and services, and provide adequate and effective protection and enforcement of U.S. IP rights. Toward this end, a key objective of the Administration's trade policy is ensuring that U.S. owners of IP have a full and fair opportunity to use and profit from their IP around the globe. Through engagement with trading partners, the Administration advocates for strong IP protection and enforcement in other countries for, among other things, works, phonograms, performances, brands, designs, trade secrets and inventions by U.S. creators, inventors, artists, and businesses.

Top challenges for U.S. right holders abroad include copyright piracy, which threatens U.S. exports in media and other creative content. U.S. innovators, including pharmaceutical manufacturers, also face unbalanced patent systems and other unfair market access barriers. Another leading concern is counterfeit products, which undermine U.S. trademark rights and can also pose serious threats to consumer health and safety. Additionally, inappropriate protection of geographical indications, including the lack of transparency and due process in some systems, limit the scope of trademarks and other IP rights held by U.S. producers and imposes barriers on market access for U.S.-made goods and services that rely on the use of common names, such as "feta" cheese. Another longstanding concern is the theft of trade secrets, which are often among a company's core business assets and key to a company's competitiveness. Such theft hurts American businesses, including SMEs. In addition, the reach of trade secret theft into critical commercial and defense technologies poses threats to U.S. national security interests.

The United States seeks to address these concerns through multiple avenues. One major effort is negotiating binding commitments with trading partners for the strong protection and enforcement for IP rights, including through trade agreements, as well as through WTO and OECD accession negotiations. In addition, the United States engages in other ways, by pursuing commitments and implementation of commitments through Trade and Investment Framework Agreements, Memoranda of Understanding, and Intellectual Property Protection and Enforcement work plans.

The United States actively monitors and enforces trade commitments, work that is critical to the success of negotiated outcomes. In one example, the United States requested consultations with China in March of 2018 under the WTO Dispute Resolution Understanding in DS542: *China – Certain Measures Concerning the Protection of Intellectual Property Rights*. The United States also actively uses relevant enforcement provisions in its domestic law, including section 301 of the Trade Act of 1974, border enforcement measures (including in cooperation with foreign customs authorities), and criminal statutes as they may apply, including as to the misappropriation of trade secrets. The United States promotes the protection and enforcement of IP rights through multilateral vehicles including the WTO Council on Trade-Related Intellectual Property Rights, the Asia Pacific Economic Cooperation, G7, G20, and other fora. (p. 133 above provides additional information on U.S. enforcement efforts, including the investigation into China's Acts, Policies, and Practices Related to Technology Transfer, Intellectual Property, and Innovation Under Section 301 of the Trade Act of 1974.)

An important additional avenue for bilateral engagement is USTR's annual Special 301 Report and the related Out-of-Cycle Review of Notorious Markets. Pursuant to statute, USTR must identify those countries that deny adequate and effective protection for IP rights or deny fair and equitable market access for persons that rely on IP protection, which may lead to designation as a "Priority Foreign Country." In addition, USTR has created a Special 301 "Priority Watch List" (PWL) and "Watch List" (WL), placement on which indicates that particular problems exist in the listed country with respect to IP protection, enforcement, or market access for persons relying on IP. Countries placed on the PWL receive increased attention in bilateral discussions with the United States concerning the identified problem areas. USTR develops an action plan for each foreign country identified on the PWL for at least one year. USTR also conducts an annual Out-of-Cycle Review of Notorious Markets focused on online and physical marketplaces that are reportedly engaged in piracy and counterfeiting and have been the subject of enforcement action or that may merit further investigation for possible IP infringements.

Also critical to U.S. trade policy in the arena of IP protection and enforcement is technical assistance and capacity building. The U.S. Government collaborates with various trading partners on IP-related training and capacity building around the world. Domestically and abroad, bilaterally, and in regional groupings, the U.S. Government remains engaged in building stronger and more effective systems for the protection and enforcement of IP. Various U.S. government agencies provide sustained and valuable contributions, including but not limited to the Department of Commerce's Commercial Law Development Program; the U.S. Patent and Trademark Office, through its Office of Policy and International Affairs, which includes the Global Intellectual Property Academy; the U.S. Department of State's International Visitors Leadership Program and its Global Intellectual Property Law Enforcement Coordinator program; as well as trainings provided by the Department of Justice's Intellectual Property Law Enforcement Coordinator, U.S. Immigration and Customs Enforcement Homeland Security Investigations and the United States Copyright Office. Through these combined efforts, the United States is committed to ensuring that U.S. owners of IP have a full and fair opportunity to use and profit from their IP around the world.

Promoting Digital Trade

The United States places great importance on electronic commerce (or "digital trade"), which plays a crucial role in strengthening and supporting firms in every sector of the economy. Since the last U.S. Trade Policy Review, the United States has advanced engagement on digital trade issues across a range of fora, and worked to combat a rising tide of barriers to digital trade around the world.

At the WTO's 11th Ministerial Conference in December 2017, the United States joined 70 other Members in announcing a commitment to initiate exploratory work on negotiations on electronic commerce. Since then, the United States has been actively engaged in this initiative, and worked to ensure that it is a productive forum to advance a liberal global environment for digital trade. The United States also joined a consensus among WTO Members to maintain a moratorium on duties on electronic transmissions and to continue the longstanding Work Program on Electronic Commerce.

On 30 September 2018, the United States, Mexico, and Canada completed a comprehensive renegotiation of the NAFTA. The new United States-Mexico-Canada Agreement (USMCA) contains the most advanced digital trade rules that will make this agreement a model moving forward. The United States regularly raises digital trade issues bilaterally, including in consultations with FTA partners, in Trade and Investment Framework Agreement meetings, and other engagements. The United States also engages in conversation on digital trade issues in international fora such as the G20, APEC, and the OECD, using these platforms to bring attention to harmful barriers to digital trade.

Trade-related capacity building initiatives

Trade policy and development assistance are key tools that together can help alleviate poverty and improve opportunities. Through "Aid for Trade," the United States focuses on helping developing countries integrate into the global trading community. Support to countries, in the form of training and technical assistance, can help them make decisions about the benefits of trade arrangements and reforms, implement their international and regional obligations to bring certainty to their trade regimes, and enhance these countries' ability to take advantage of the opportunities of the multilateral trading system to compete in the global economy. Accordingly, U.S. assistance addresses a broad range of issues so that communities, rural areas, and small businesses, including female entrepreneurs, benefit from trade rules negotiated in the WTO and in other trade fora. The United States promotes trade and economic growth in developing countries through a wide range of trade capacity-building (TCB) activities.

An important element of this TCB work involves coordinating U.S. Government technical assistance activities with those of the international institutions in order to identify and take advantage of donor synergies in programming and to avoid duplication. These institutions include the WTO, the World Bank, the IMF, the regional development banks, and the United Nations. The United States, led by USTR at the WTO, by the Treasury Department at various international financial bodies, and by the State Department at the United Nations, works in partnership with these institutions and other donors to ensure that, where appropriate, trade-related assistance is an integral component of development programs tailored to the circumstances within each developing country.

The efforts of the United States, both through bilateral assistance and through multilateral institutions, build on a longstanding commitment to help partner countries benefit from the opportunities provided by the global trading system. U.S. bilateral assistance includes programs such as targeted assistance for developing countries participating in U.S. preference programs and coordination of assistance through Trade and Investment Framework Agreements. The United States also provides bilateral assistance to developing countries to enable them to work with the private sector and nongovernmental organizations to transition to a more open economy, to prepare for WTO negotiations, and to abide by their trade obligations.

WTO-RELATED U.S. TRADE-RELATED ASSISTANCE

International trade can play a major role in the promotion of economic growth and the alleviation of poverty, and the United States recognizes that TCB can facilitate more effective integration of developing countries into the international trading system and enable them to benefit further from global trade. The United States has and will continue to directly support the WTO's trade-related technical assistance efforts. As a major bilateral provider of TCB assistance, the United States has remained an active partner in the WTO's Aid for Trade discussion.

The United States supports the trade-related assistance activities of the WTO Secretariat through voluntary contributions to the Doha Development Agenda Global Trust Fund. In September 2017, the United States pledged an additional US$600,000 to the trust fund. Taking into account this contribution, total U.S. contributions to the WTO have amounted to more than US$17 million since 2001.

The United States provides technical support to countries that are in the process of acceding to the WTO and for post-accession implementation. Among current accession applicants, Algeria, Azerbaijan, Belarus, Bosnia and Herzegovina, Ethiopia, Iraq, Lebanon, Serbia, and Uzbekistan received U.S. technical assistance in their accession processes. In addition, Afghanistan, Georgia, Kazakhstan, the Kyrgyz Republic, Tajikistan, and Ukraine continue to receive assistance with implementing their membership commitments.

THE ENHANCED INTEGRATED FRAMEWORK

The Enhanced Integrated Framework (EIF) is a multi-organization, multi-donor program that operates as a coordination mechanism for trade-related assistance to least-developed countries (LDCs) with the overall objective of integrating trade into national development plans. The United States supports the EIF through complementary bilateral assistance to EIF participating countries. U.S. Agency for International Development (USAID) bilateral assistance to LDC participants supports initiatives both to integrate trade into national economic and development strategies and to address high priority capacity building needs designed to accelerate integration into the global trading system.

TRADE CAPACITY-BUILDING INITIATIVES FOR AFRICA

As discussed earlier, in July 2013, the United States launched "Trade Africa" with the five members of the East African Community (EAC). The United States subsequently expanded the Trade Africa initiative to Cote d'Ivoire, Ghana, Mozambique, Senegal, and Zambia, and it committed to provide technical support on trade matters to the Economic Community of West African States (ECOWAS). Cooperation between the United States and its Trade Africa partners – including through technical and capacity building assistance – could help the latter meet their WTO obligations under the Agreement on the Application of Sanitary and Phytosanitary (SPS) Measures, the Agreement on

Technical Barriers to Trade (TBT), and the Agreement on Trade Facilitation, foster an improved business climate, and address capacity issues that constrain trade.

The United States has boosted TCB assistance through Trade and Investment Hubs on the continent, which are expected to facilitate over US$200 million in new investments and foster the creation of 37,000 jobs by 2020. Under this initiative, USAID expanded its flagship Trade Hubs into Trade and Investment Hubs (Hubs). These Hubs, located in Accra, Ghana; Pretoria, South Africa; and Nairobi, Kenya, implement new and innovative initiatives to reduce bottlenecks along major trade corridors, as well as boost exports through the formation of sustainable business associations with international membership. The Hubs are responsible for creating Source Africa, the continent's largest apparel trade show. Moreover, the Hubs support implementation of the Feed the Future initiative to help improve food security by integrating regional markets and reducing the time and cost to move goods from areas of surplus to those of deficit. Supporting such investment allows key value chains to scale up, reaching tens of thousands of smallholder farmers, and create stable, long-term employment opportunities.

The U.S. Department of Agriculture's Foreign Agricultural Service (FAS) administers a number of agricultural technical assistance, training, and research programs in sub-Saharan Africa. USDA's capacity-building program objectives are to increase agricultural trade both regionally and with the United States, help develop trade policies based on sound science, support agricultural sector growth in partner countries, and promote regional food security. To this end, FAS administers programs to support SPS regulatory and policy development and improvements that will help decrease international trade constraints. This capacity building creates regional frameworks for countries to develop equivalent SPS systems that govern regional trade, including transboundary animal disease and plant pest monitoring, control, and emergency response. In addition, FAS capacity building is helping to develop food monitoring systems that will both ensure exported foods meet international requirements and that will safeguard domestic food supplies from chemical and microbiological contamination. USDA also provides support to these countries through its Food for Progress program, which encourages development of the agriculture sector and market development. USDA further supports the West African cotton sector through its research and exchange programs, specifically the Borlaug and Cochran Programs.

The Millennium Challenge Corporation (MCC) works in partnership with well-governed developing countries to tackle the most critical obstacles to private investment and economic growth to fulfil the agency's core mission: to reduce poverty through economic growth. While MCC's program with each country is different, many partner countries place a high priority on increasing their competitiveness and facilitating domestic commerce as well as regional and international trade. Since MCC was created in 2004, the agency has invested more than US$7 billion in trade-related assistance to developing countries, and more than half of that has gone to 14 subSaharan African countries through 16 MCC compact grant programs. This assistance focuses on trade-related infrastructure such as roads and electricity, improving the productivity of small and medium-sized businesses and export-oriented industries, and leveraging policy and regulatory reforms. Such support allows countries to expand their export-oriented sectors and better utilize AGOA. Major projects have included expansions to the principal sea ports of Benin and Cape Verde, upgrades to Mali's international airport, electricity sector investments in Benin, Ghana, Liberia, Malawi, and Tanzania, and roads for commerce in Burkina Faso, Cote d'Ivoire, Ghana, Liberia, Mozambique, Senegal, and Tanzania. Congress recently passed legislation giving MCC the authority to make regional investments through concurrent compact grant programs designed to address cross-border constraints to trade and economic growth.

The U.S. Trade and Development Agency (USTDA), the U.S. Government's project preparation agency, works to reduce barriers to financing infrastructure. In support of Trade Africa goals, USTDA increased its portfolio in Africa by two-thirds to stimulate the infrastructure development Africa requires to trade globally. This early-stage investment across 30 projects, including ports, airports, electricity, and telecom, and has the potential to mobilize more than US$2 billion in private and public financing during implementation. USTDA also facilitated eight reverse trade missions, in which 120 public and private sector delegates from 19 countries in subSaharan Africa participated, increasing their capacity to make informed investment decisions in their infrastructure investments.

Since 2005, the United States has mobilized its development agencies to help the West African countries of Benin, Burkina Faso, Chad, Mali, and Senegal address obstacles they face in the cotton sector. MCC, USAID, and USDA continue to work with these nations as they seek to develop a coherent long-term development strategy to improve prospects in the cotton sector. Elements of such a strategy address key challenges such as improved productivity and domestic reforms. The United States will continue to coordinate with the WTO, World Bank, the African Development Bank, and others as part of the multilateral effort to address the development aspects of cotton. This includes the active participation of the United States in the WTO Secretariat's periodic meetings with donors and recipient countries to discuss the trade, development, and reform aspects of cotton.

STANDARDS ALLIANCE

In November 2012, the United States launched a U.S.-sponsored assistance facility called the "Standards Alliance" with the goal of building capacity among developing countries to implement the WTO Agreement on TBT. The Standards Alliance provides resources and

expertise to enable developing countries to effectively implement the Agreement on TBT. The focus of these efforts in developing countries includes efforts: to improve practices related to notification of technical regulations and conformity assessment procedures to the WTO; to strengthen domestic practices related to adopting relevant international standards; and to clarify and streamline regulatory processes for products.

In May 2013, USAID and the American National Standards Institute (ANSI) entered into a public-private partnership that coordinates private-sector subject matter experts from ANSI member organizations in the delivery of training and other technical exchange with interested Standards Alliance countries on international standards and best practices. During the period under review, the first phase of the Standards Alliance, which included activities in up to 10 markets representing a variety of geographical regions and levels of economic development, ended. A second phase, which covers five countries in sub-Saharan Africa (Cote d'Ivoire, Ghana, Mozambique, Senegal, and Zambia) began. In consultation with TPSC member agencies and private sector experts, ANSI reviewed the applications received based on consideration of bilateral trade opportunities, available private sector expertise that may be leveraged, demonstrated commitment and readiness for assistance, and potential development impact.

Between 2016 and 2018, the Standards Alliance completed over 20 TBT-related trainings, workshops, and delegation visits for participants from 50 countries. These capacity-building activities have bolstered Standards Alliance countries' understanding and application of TBT-related mechanisms. Highlights from the last two-year period of Standards Alliance implementation include a series of programs on conformity assessment for the African Organisation for Standardization (ARSO), several conferences and workshops on good regulatory practices, as well as work on regulatory impact assessment.

Trade and the environment

Since the last U.S. Trade Policy Review, the United States made significant progress on a range of trade and environment matters in multiple fora, including through multilateral, regional and bilateral trade initiatives.

In August 2017, the United States, Mexico, and Canada formally launched the renegotiation of the NAFTA. On 30 September 2018, the United States, Mexico, and Canada completed a comprehensive renegotiation of the NAFTA, including the most comprehensive set of enforceable environmental obligations of any previous U.S. trade agreement. These include commitments relating to harmful fisheries subsidies; wildlife trafficking; illegal, unreported, and unregulated (IUU) fishing; the protection of marine species; marine litter; sustainable forest management; air quality; and public participation and environmental cooperation.

The United States has also continued to prioritize implementation of the FTAs currently in force. For example, the United States used a unique monitoring tool under our bilateral trade agreement with Peru in 2016 to verify that a particular timber shipment exported from Peru to the United States complied with all Peruvian laws and regulations. Following issuance of this verification report, which revealed significant levels of illegally harvested timber in that shipment, Peru agreed to undertake various reforms to address ongoing challenges of illegal logging. In 2017, the United States determined that Peru had made insufficient progress in implementing these agreed upon and necessary reforms, and on October 10, 2017, USTR took unprecedented action by instructing the U.S. Customs and Border Protection (CBP) to deny entry of future timber shipments from the Peruvian exporter subject to the 2016 verification request. In February 2018, the United States requested that Peru conduct a second timber verification, this time of three separate timber shipments exported from Peru to the United States. Peru's investigation could not establish that one of the shipments was compliant with Peru's laws, regulations, and other measures on the harvest and trade of timber products. The United States will continue to engage with Peru to address remaining challenges to combating illegal logging highlighted by the verification.

Since the last TPR, the United States kept up substantial engagement with other FTA partners. In particular, the United States had senior-level meetings with officials from Bahrain, Central America and the Dominican Republic, Chile, Colombia, Oman, Panama, and Singapore to discuss implementation of and monitor progress under the environment chapters of our FTAs with those partners. These engagements were also opportunities to review, and in some cases, update, the environmental cooperation work programs that help to support implementation of the environment chapters of U.S. FTAs. The United States also engaged with Trade and Investment Framework Agreement partners, notably Indonesia, Malaysia, the Philippines, and Vietnam, and consulted on a wide range of issues related to trade and investment, including trade-related environmental issues such as wildlife trafficking and IUU fishing.

In APEC, the United States worked with other Asia-Pacific economies through the Experts Group on Illegal Logging and Associated Trade to improve the capacity of APEC customs officials to combat illegal logging and associated trade, including by hosting a customs officials workshop held in Ho Chi Minh City, Vietnam on August 18-19, 2017. The United States also led the development of a Customs Best Practices Resource Tool designed to assist APEC customs officials in identifying illegal timber shipments and taking appropriate action. As part of this work, the United States strengthened partnerships with international and nongovernmental organizations, such as Interpol and The Nature Conservancy, who play an important role in combating illegal logging and associated trade

globally. The United States also concluded an initiative to facilitate trade and investment in sustainable materials management solutions under APEC's Regulatory Cooperation Advancement Mechanism in 2017.

The United States is also committed to combating wildlife trafficking and IUU fishing through a variety of means, including by using existing and future U.S. FTAs, environmental cooperation mechanisms, and other trade-related initiatives. For example, the United States has consistently raised these areas for discussion and collaboration in meetings under the Environment Chapters of our FTAs and included them in recent environmental programs. In October 2016, the Eliminate, Neutralize, and Disrupt (END) Wildlife Trafficking Act of 2016 became law, with the objectives of supporting anti-poaching efforts on a global scale, strengthening the capacity of partner countries to combat wildlife trafficking, and designating major wildlife trafficking countries for further strategic collaboration with the United States.[6] The President issued an Executive Order on February 9, 2017 that called for strengthened enforcement, including with respect to the "the illegal smuggling and trafficking of humans, drugs or other substances, wildlife, and weapons…."[7] Multiple U.S. government agencies participate in implementing the President's Executive Order and the END Wildlife Trafficking Act.

In regards to IUU fishing, the National Oceanic and Atmospheric Administration (NOAA) published a final rule in December 2016 establishing a Seafood Import Monitoring Program (SIMP) to combat IUU fishing and seafood fraud.[8] The SIMP establishes reporting and recordkeeping requirements for imports of 13 at-risk species needed to prevent IUU-caught or misrepresented seafood from entering U.S. commerce. The U.S. importer of record is required to report and retain key data from the point of harvest to the point of entry into U.S. commerce. The rule's requirements took effect for 11 of the species on January 1, 2018: tunas (Albacore, Bigeye, Skipjack, Yellowfin, and Bluefin), swordfish, sharks, Atlantic and Pacific cod, grouper, red snapper, and sea cucumber. The requirements for the remaining two species, shrimp and abalone, will take effect on December 31, 2018. U.S. government agencies are actively engaged in outreach to trading partners to assist with implementation efforts.

Trade and labor

Ensuring respect for workers' rights is a core value, and the trade policy agenda of the United States includes a strong commitment to ensuring that American workers and their families as well as workers around the world benefit from trade. On 30 September 2018, the United States, Mexico, and Canada completed a comprehensive renegotiation of the NAFTA, including the strongest labor provisions of any U.S. trade agreement. The new United States-Mexico-Canada Agreement includes a Labor Chapter with enforceable rules that protect the rights of freedom of association and collective bargaining;

prohibit trade in goods produced by forced labor, including forced child labor; address violence against workers exercising their rights; ensure that migrant workers are protected under labor laws; and establish mechanisms to monitor and address labor concerns.

The United States has continued its efforts to enhance U.S. Government engagement with trade partners through formal trade agreement mechanisms to improve respect for internationally recognized labor rights and to increase monitoring and enforcement of trade agreement labor provisions. Since the last TPR, the United States held senior-level meetings with officials from Bahrain, Central America and the Dominican Republic, Colombia, Mexico, Peru, and the Republic of Korea to discuss implementation of and monitor progress under the labor chapters of our FTAs with those partners. These meetings also provided opportunities to discuss labor cooperation initiatives that support implementation of the labor chapters of U.S. FTAs. The United States also continues to enhance its engagement with trade partners on labor rights through trade preference programs, and other means. In 2017 and 2018, the United States discussed labor rights issues with several countries as part of meetings held under Trade and Investment Framework Agreements, including with Algeria, Indonesia, Vietnam, Malaysia, Cambodia, and the Philippines.

As an important component of the Administration's trade agenda, the Trade Adjustment Assistance (TAA) programs assist U.S. workers adversely affected by global competition. The TAA Program was renewed by the Trade Adjustment Assistance Reauthorization Act of 2015 (TAARA), and ensures that workers harmed by foreign trade have the best opportunity to acquire skills and credentials for sustainable reemployment. The TAA Program currently offers the following services to eligible workers: training, out of area job search and relocation allowances, weekly income support (Trade Readjustment Allowances (TRA)), wage supplements for older workers (RTAA), and a health coverage tax credit to eligible TAA recipients. In FY2017, US$716,364,000 was available to carry out the program.

Small and medium-sized business trade

USTR has implemented a Small Business Initiative to increase export opportunities for U.S. small and medium-sized enterprises (SMEs) and expand efforts to address the specific export challenges and priorities of SMEs and their workers in our trade policy and enforcement activities. In 2017, USTR continued to engage with U.S. government interagency partners and foreign trading partners to develop and implement new and continuing initiatives that support small business exports.

U.S. small businesses are key engines for U.S. economic growth, jobs, and innovation. USTR is focused on making trade work to the benefit of SMEs by

helping them increase their sales to customers abroad, access and participate in global supply chains, and support jobs in local communities. USTR is working to better integrate specific SME issues and priorities into trade policy development, increase outreach to SMEs around the country, and expand collaboration and coordination on an interagency basis. USTR works closely with the U.S. Department of Commerce, U.S. Small Business Administration (SBA), U.S. Department of Agriculture, and other agencies to help provide U.S. SMEs information, assistance, and counselling on specific export opportunities. In 2017, USTR undertook significant actions in support of our SME objectives.

Tariff barriers, burdensome customs procedures, discriminatory or arbitrary standards, lack of transparency relating to relevant regulations, and insufficient IPR protection in foreign markets present particular challenges for U.S. SMEs in selling abroad. Under the SME Initiative, USTR's small business office, regional offices, and functional offices are pursuing initiatives and advancing efforts to address these issues. U.S. trade agreements, as well as other trade dialogues and fora, provide a critical opportunity to address specific concerns of U.S. SMEs and facilitate their participation in export markets.

Since the last TPR, the United States has worked to increase opportunities for SME exports. For example, for the negotiations of the United States–Mexico–Canada Agreement, one of the U.S. objectives included priorities identified by SME stakeholders, such as increased de minimis shipment value and the elimination of burdensome non-tariff barriers. The Agreement includes a small and medium enterprise chapter, to help ensure that the Agreement benefits SMEs.

The United States and the United Kingdom launched the United States-UK Trade and Investment Working Group in 2017 to explore ways to strengthen trade and investment ties between the U.S. and U.K. and to provide commercial continuity for both countries' businesses, workers, and consumers. Given the significance of small businesses to both economies, the U.S. and UK launched an ongoing U.S.-UK Small and Medium-sized Enterprise Dialogue in 2018 to promote closer collaboration and the sharing of best practices on policies and programs that support SME businesses and export opportunities in each country.

The United States and EU continue to collaborate on small business issues in the Transatlantic Economic Council (TEC). In October 2017, the United States hosted the eighth United States-EU Small and Medium Enterprise Workshop in Wichita, Kansas - the first time the United States has hosted the US-EU SME workshop outside of Washington, DC. The SME Workshop was convened by USTR, the U.S. Department of Commerce, the SBA and the EU's Directorate General for Trade and Directorate General for Internal Market, Industry, Entrepreneurship and SMEs (DG-GROW) and was hosted with the Chair of the Industry Trade Advisory Committee for Small and

Minority Business (ITAC-9). Over 100 SME stakeholders on both sides of the Atlantic attended, with discussions focusing on manufacturing SMEs in transatlantic trade; SME startups, innovation and competitiveness; best practices in apprenticeships and vocational training; and SME export promotion resources.

In 2017, USTR participated with ASEAN SME ministry and trade officials in the United States-ASEAN Third Country Training Program to discuss potential barriers to digital trade that can burden SMEs. Such trade barriers are out of step with established best practices and impede the ability of SMEs to participate in digital trade and e-commerce. Best practices include tariff-free digital trade; promoting the free flow of information; preventing costly computer infrastructure requirements; electronic signatures and online payment methods; electronic customs forms and faster customs procedures; high customs de minimis to facilitate SME trade; and protection of intellectual property rights.

In the WTO context, USTR is exploring the development of further work with other WTO Members on issues of interest to SME stakeholders, such as electronic commerce, transparency of regulatory processes, and implementation of trade facilitation measures.

Endnotes

1   See: http://www.regulations.gov.

2   For the text of the USMCA, see: https://ustr.gov/trade-agreements/free-trade-agreements/united-states-mexico-canada-agreement/united-states-mexico.

3   See: https://ustr.gov/sites/default/files/2018%20AGOA%20Implementation.pdf.

4   See: https://ustr.gov/about-us/policy-offices/press-office/reports-and-publications/2017/report-congress-operation.

5   See: https://ustr.gov/about-us/policy-offices/press-office/reports-and-publications/2017/hope-ii-2017-annual-report.

6   Eliminate, Neutralize, and Disrupt (END) Wildlife Trafficking Act of 2016, https://www.congress.gov/bill/114th-congress/house-bill/2494/text (signed into law on October 9, 2016).

7   Presidential Executive Order on Enforcing Federal Law with Respect to Transnational Criminal Organizations and Preventing International Trafficking, https://www.whitehouse.gov/presidential-actions/presidential-executive-order-enforcing-federal-law-respect-transnational-criminal-organizations-preventing-international-trafficking/ (February 9, 2017).

8   Magnuson Stevens Fishery Conservation and Management Act: Seafood Import Monitoring Program, 81 FR 88975 (December 9, 2016).